THE AGE OF WARS
OF RELIGION,
1000-1650

THE AGE OF WARS OF RELIGION, 1000-1650

AN ENCYCLOPEDIA OF GLOBAL WARFARE AND CIVILIZATION

Volume 1, A–K

Cathal J. Nolan

Greenwood Encyclopedias of
Modern World Wars

GREENWOOD PRESS
Westport, Connecticut • London

Library of Congress Cataloging-in-Publication Data

Nolan, Cathal J.
    The age of wars of religion, 1000–1650 : an encyclopedia of global warfare and civilization / Cathal J. Nolan.
        p.   cm.—(Greenwood encyclopedias of modern world wars)
    Includes bibliographical references and index.
    ISBN 0–313–33045–X (set)—ISBN 0–313–33733–0 (vol. 1)—
ISBN 0–313–33734–9 (vol. 2)
    1. Middle Ages—History—Encyclopedias.   2. History, Modern—17th century—
Encyclopedias.   3. Military history, Medieval—Encyclopedias.   4. Military history,
Modern—17th century—Encyclopedias.   5. Biography—Middle Ages, 500–1500—
Encyclopedias.   6. Biography—17th century—Encyclopedias.   I. Title.
    D114.N66   2006
    909.0703—dc22   2005031626

British Library Cataloguing in Publication Data is available.

Library of Congress Catalog Card Number: 2005031626

ISBN: 0–313–33045–X (set)
        0–313–33733–0 (vol. I)
        0–313–33734–9 (vol. II)

First published in 2006

Greenwood Press, 88 Post Road West, Westport, CT 06881
An imprint of Greenwood Publishing Group, Inc.
www.greenwood.com

Printed in the United States of America

The paper used in this book complies with the
Permanent Paper Standard issued by the National
Information Standards Organization (Z39.48–1984).

10 9 8 7 6 5 4 3 2 1

Covenants without swords are but words.

—Thomas Hobbes, *Leviathan* (1651)

You are engaged in God's service and in mine—which is the same thing.

—Philip II, of Spain

[The terms are] null and void, invalid, iniquitous, unjust, condemned, rejected, frivolous, without force or effect, and no one is to observe them, even when they be ratified by oath.

—Pope Innocent X,
On the articles of religious toleration in the *Peace of Westphalia* (1648)

Who brings famine? The army.
Who brings the plague? The army.
Who the sword? The army.
Who hinders trade? The army.
Who confounds all? The army.

—Hugh Peter,
A Word for the Army and Two Words to the Kingdome (1647)

CONTENTS

LIST OF ENTRIES

List of Entries

List of Entries

List of Entries

List of Entries

List of Entries

List of Entries

List of Entries

List of Entries

PREFACE: WARS OF RELIGION IN HISTORY

The states and empires of early modern Europe were not unique in waging "wars of religion." Wars between rival faiths, whether in the name of the gods or competing views of the place of the sacred in daily human affairs, have an ancient pedigree. Religious motivation to combat has been located by historians in most eras and among virtually all the world's diverse peoples and cultures, and usually on both sides in any given war. The hoary cry that "the gods are on our side" was among the earliest and most potent of incitements to battle, ranking alongside collective theft and rapine as perennial motivations for which men made war. The city-states that arose in the Fertile Crescent fought to impose their civic gods on one another, believing that success in war demonstrated who possessed the more powerful deities, a claim the defeated also accepted. Great riverine empires such as Sumer and Egypt developed complex civilizations that clashed with neighbors over such material reasons as a need for "living space" or to secure trade routes and frontiers. But they also had a theocratic purpose for making war, claiming that they fought at the behest of their gods to establish divine primacy over the lesser gods of enemies. Later casting of monotheism in the fires of ancient civilizations of the Nile and Mediterranean did little to break the mold of wars waged in the name of God. The ancient Israelites escaped Pharaoh into Sinai in search of religious and personal liberty, searching for new kingdoms in lands promised by Yahweh. Their kingdoms were made not by mere wandering and discovery, however, but by stealthy wars of conquest and expulsion of the beaten and the heathen. The ancient Greeks were among the most warlike of Mediterranean peoples. They sanctified incessant hoplite battles with ritual sacrifice and devotions even before Alexander became convinced of his own godhead and led a war of conquest that nearly reached the Ganges. As did the Romans, that most martial of ancient peoples. Once they achieved full military mastery over their world they closed the circle by proclaiming dead emperor-conquerors to be divine and built great temples in which to worship them.

Early Christians living in pagan Rome carefully distinguished between what belonged to God and what was owed to Caesar, but they fundamentally rethought this discomforting notion once the Caesars became Christian. From the 5th century, the Latin Church upheld a doctrine that "Two Swords" had been given to Man by God, one secular and one religious, one for the emperor and the other for the pope in Rome. For the next 1,000 years Latin Christians could not conceive of war being waged outside the just purposes of God and his anointed Church on Earth. Like pagans before them, they still believed that divine judgment was evident in the outcome of martial contests fought between knights, as between nations. Christian Orthodox in the east merged the role of warlord and high priest in the doctrine of "Caesaropapism," which effectively lodged even military policy in the Holy of Holies, in the tabernacle of the doctrines of the faith. The first Muslims spliced war and faith to form a hybrid, the "jihad" (or "holy war") waged in the name of Allah and for plunder. The first jihad, against the pagans of Mecca and the Arabian peninsula, was led by the Prophet Muhammad himself. Within a few generations, Muslim warriors swept aside older empires and opened parts of three continents to conversion and exploitation. A powerful religious impulse to war carried Bedouin warriors and their new Islamic faith far from the deserts of Arabia. In the west they conquered Christian Egypt and North Africa, crossed over to Spain, and raided even into the south of France. To the north of Arabia they overran old Christian and Jewish communities in Palestine, Syria, and parts of Anatolia, to arrive at the front porch of the Byzantine Empire. Eastward they rode over Zoroastrian Iran, pushed into Afghanistan, and conquered northern India. Jihadis also rode across Central Asia to reach as far as the western borders of China. The Latin counterattack to recover the formerly Christian lands of the eastern Mediterranean, the Crusades, began in the 11th century and persisted over several centuries of intermittent war. While religious fervor and greed for land alike ultimately expired in defeat in the Middle East, the crusader spirit more successfully waged war and forced conversion against the Moors of Spain and Christian "heretics" in the south of France. And with great gore and slaughter, the Teutonic Knights and other crusading orders brought fire and the terror of the cross into pagan Slav lands of the Baltic, Poland, and what is today western Russia. Subsequently, the impetus to "jihad" inspired a rising Ottoman tide that swept into Europe, to ultimately capture Constantinople, bring new conquests in the Balkans, and invasions of Austria that twice washed Muslim armies against the walls of Vienna. All the while, orthodox Muslims fought Muslim "heretics," as the shi'ia Safavid Empire in Iran challenged sunni empires of the Uzbeks and Ottomans.

Nor was religious warfare confined to the civilizations born of the Mediterranean world, where millennia of spiritual ferment troubled and reordered the region's history, and still does. In faraway lands which knew little of Christian and Muslim quarrels, religious justification for war was nonetheless ubiquitous. The island realm of Japan was said by its people to be ruled by the "Son of Heaven," a divine emperor to whom total loyalty was owed, even unto death. While in practice more that a few emperors were little more than prisoners of some powerful daimyo or the later shoguns, kept under effective palace arrest and compelled to carry out mind-numbing daily rituals, this cultural and religious myth had enormous power to motivate men to combat. To some degree, it continued to do so during Japan's half-century of serial wars of aggression from 1895 to 1945. The Japanese warrior ethic culminated in a cult of death from 1943 to 1945, best but not solely expressed in the extraordinary self-sacrifice of isolated island garrisons and by the "kamikaze." In Chinese history, Buddhist monasteries had become military powers where warrior monks and their armed retainers engaged in protracted fighting with local warlords and bandits. In India, the Rajputs and Marathas, and later the Sikhs, organized huge armies around religious communities. They made holy war to throw off the "Muslim yoke" of the Mughal Empire, and fought also against Christian invaders from Europe. As for the Americas, ideas of divine kingship sustained by powerful priesthoods and religious warfare also developed there historically. Along the great spine of the Andes rose the extraordinary theocracy of Inca Peru, ruled by a Sapa Inca said by his priests, and thought by his subjects, to reign as a god among men. Terrible were the bloody rites carried out by warriors, priests, and emperors of the Aztecs in the Central Valley of Mexico. For the Aztecs, war's central purpose was not just to conquer, but to capture prisoners for later human sacrifice needed to appease ferocious Aztec gods. War and faith formed a seamless, sanguinary whole: conquest of neighboring tribes and cities permitted ritual sacrifice of captives, leading to further expansion and sacrifice, all to uphold a core religious purpose according to a calendar written in the heavens by the gods. Virtually all major societies, in short, no matter how distant or diverse, have waged war for the usual reasons material and political, but also to match their religious beliefs and meet spiritual needs.

Nevertheless, in intensity of belief, ferocity of the zealotry displayed, global scope, and their lasting impact on world economic, legal, political, and military affairs, the wars of religion fought by Europeans from the 15th through 17th centuries deservedly garner special attention in world military history. These wars really began, though this is not always recognized, with the Hundred Years' War (1337–1453), which dovetailed with the later Crusades. Its effects were greatly disintegrative of the old notion of Latin unity within "res publica Christiana." It gave rise to the first nation-states, starting with England and France. Then it spilled into Italy and Spain, and to a lesser extent into Germany and even eastern Europe, as rootless and ruthless soldiers went in search of fresh vineyards and women to despoil. That prolonged conflict furthered a fundamental shift in the conception of the political order in western Europe. The change was long in the making, materially and intellectually, as Europe began to recover economically and demographically from 600 years of hunkered down, castilian defense against barbarian invaders (Goths, Vandals, Arabs, Vikings, and Mongols). The Hundred Years' War was decisive in pushing the governing classes away from the old belief in a single Christian people, whose empire and far-off crusades were seen as the finger of God writing the history of the world. This shift was greatly re-inforced by the "Great Schism" (1378–1417), which shook the old Church to its core. Replacing the Medieval worldview among the educated laity, and some clergy, was a more modern worldview which held that history should be understood in terms of human endeavor, unaided and undiluted by divine purpose or intervention. This profound awareness of the primacy of human agency as the motive force of history changed the basic conception and practice of European statecraft: denying the historical necessity of Christian unity necessarily favored the secular interests of princes, that is, of raw ma-terial power. The revolutionary change in outlook that proceeded from this fact informed the spirit of the Italian Renaissance and found high expression in the thought and writings of Niccolò Machiavelli. In turn, this resulted in a great irony and paradox of the wars of religion fought from the early 16th century: Europe's Christians slaughtered one another over doctrinal differ-ences even as their civilization was adopting a more secular focus by leaving behind a view of history which said that restoration of a single Christian empire was the will of God, the only sure path to peace, and a prerequisite to the "Second Coming of the Redeemer."

Meanwhile, during the first half of the 15th century the shell of the By-zantine Empire, that once-proud bastion of Orthodox Christianity, staggered to a tortuous end to its long conflict with the Ottoman Empire, the Great Power of the Muslim world. The Ottomans, in turn, were still engaged in an equally ancient intra-Muslim war, between sunnis and shi'ites, with the latter in control of Iran (or Persia, as this Muslim empire was ineptly known in the West). The Ottoman capture of Constantinople in 1453, the same year that saw an end to the Hundred Years' War in France, was a geopolitical earth-quake that sent a tsunami of fear and unrest across the Mediterranean, with tremors and aftershocks felt even in the faraway capitals of the rising Atlantic states of western Europe. At this exquisite historical moment, when old powers and voices like the popes invoked old ways of thinking by calling for Christian unity in support of yet another crusade against the hated Muslim foe, the Latin world was soon riven by fundamental religious and political divisions. The West thus did not answer the call—which popes and the de-vout nevertheless still made with the old fervor and insistence. But the papacy was already politically and spiritually impotent, with the Papal States themselves militarily weak even within Italy, where throughout the 15th century they struggled against other wolf-like city-states. This weakness was a long-term consequence of the "Avignon Captivity" of the papacy during the 14th century and the grave shock to the faithful caused by prolonged clerical scandal and confusion during the Great Schism. That divide had seen three popes arrayed against each other, quarreling as well over power and legiti-macy with general Church Councils. In addition, a militant "heresy" thrived in Bohemia, that of the Hussites, which 200 years before would have been crushed by the Inquisition, the power of the popes, and the ideal of Christian unity. Jan Hus was burned at the stake by the Church and Empire, but mi-gratory armies of his Hussite followers were eventually pushed out of

Germany only with great violence. Other forces of rebellion were present throughout Europe, needing only a moment of opportunity born of Catholic division to awake from political dormancy. Such a moment was pending: serial financial and priestly scandals in the Medieval Church had in fact caused fatal damage to Latin Christian unity, not least by leading local princes to become accustomed to the idea of themselves as sovereign—though they did not yet know or use that word in the early modern sense. What was needed to ignite the fires of princely ambition was a match to fall onto the broad tinder of popular religious unrest. The hand that struck the light was Martin Luther's. The conflagration he started as an argument among priests and monks would end by burning out much of Europe during vicious wars of religion that lasted nearly 150 years. Neither the old Medieval vision of a single people called "Christians" united in an empire called "Christendom," nor the threat of rising Muslim power, could overcome doctrinal hatreds and the new national and confessional geography that divided Catholic from Protestant in Europe.

Nor was the rest of the world unaffected. The European wars of the 16th and 17th centuries spread over the oceans to be fought out on several continents. The conflicts reshaped world commerce and marked the beginning of the modern, integrated world economy. Crucially, confessional-cum-national wars were fought with new weapons and tactics born of the "gunpowder revolution," the major feature of which was the eclipse of cavalry and the expansion of infantry on the battlefield. Alongside the expansion of infantry armies came the evolution of intense drill, standardized equipment, disciplined tactics and maneuver, and greater military discipline and princely control of armed forces. Above all, there was a vast expansion in the size of armies and a trend toward standing (permanent or year-round) military forces. The vast sums this required meant that the emerging nation-states of Europe undertook a wholesale reorganization of their societies, including of taxation, royal finances, state promotion of economic activity, and overseas trade. These changes were so far-reaching in their impact on the character of war, the nature of the state, and the balance of power in Europe and the world, that most military historians agree that the period is best conceived as having experienced a "military revolution." In logistics and in strategy, on the other hand, the wars of religion ended much as they had begun, as wars between armies organized as not much more than marauding hordes. It was not until the further development of the mature state structures and magazine system in the late 17th and early 18th centuries that wars were waged between true standing armies. In sum, what emerged after the fires of confessional conflict finally burned out in the orgy of destruction of the Thirty Years' War and the Eighty Years' War was a new type of warfare. In the century and a half that followed the Peace of Westphalia, until the next military revolution was revealed during the great fights occasioned by the French Revolution, wars would be fought for dynastic and other secular causes by small, professional standing armies backed by the financial and bureaucratic resources of centralized states principally organized to make war.

But all that lay in the future. To get there, Europeans first passed through generations of religious conflict and carnage in which they cleaved, smashed, stabbed, burned, and shot and bombarded each other on an unprecedented scale, without ever proving on whose side God really stood, if any.

The wars of religion which broke out at the start of the Protestant Reformation in the early 16th century were, like the Hundred Years' War of the 14th and 15th centuries, also wars of nation-building and raw princely ambition. This is crucial to note if one is to understand why it was that at the end of the period what triumphed in Europe was not one confessional Christian sect over another, but a secular states system ratified and upheld by all the powers. Nor was the essential result of these wars defeat of Muslims by Christians or Christians by Muslims (at least, not in any meaningful sense beyond the extinction of the Byzantine Empire, which had long been a shadow of its former powerful and imperial self in any case). Instead, what emerged from the era of the wars of religion was a new type of polity: the nation-state, in which absolute ideas about the will of God were displaced by ideas of absolutism and the will and sovereignty of princes. Over time, these novel secular constructions spread across the globe, displacing most other religious polities as well in favor of the modern state. This process was intimately connected to the era of the wars of religion, which closed with overseas expansion and competition that led to European global commercial and military dominance and vast seaborne empires. In short, the great doctrinal and military schism within Latin Christendom ended not with the triumph of orthodox Catholic or reformist Protestant sectarians, but in a military stalemate and stable balance of power within Europe. The era of the wars of religion was thus closed at Westphalia in 1648 not by agreement on doctrine, but by acceptance that disagreement over doctrine need not affect the affairs of princes. The vexing religious questions were buried beneath a shroud formed of the legal equality of secular sovereigns. Raw material power, not asserted spiritual authority, was the foundation stone of a new, modern international order. To the surprise and dismay of confessional fanatics, it was thus kings who emerged supreme in temporal matters. Neither popes nor preachers mattered for much after Westphalia in the councils of the great and powerful. Popes were openly flouted even by Catholic monarchs who were as jealously protective of their sovereign prerogatives as any proud Protestant prince. So angry did this make Pope Innocent X he condemned the religious toleration clauses of the Westphalian settlement as "null and void, invalid, iniquitous, unjust, condemned, rejected, frivolous, without force or effect, and no one is to observe them, even when they be ratified by oath."

Rail and rage as the pontiff might, the Reformation and the Counter-Reformation alike had failed to achieve doctrinal, political, or military supremacy. And so, the fierce passions they aroused began to fade for all but the most zealous. Finished also was any loyalty to quasi-feudal military obligations on the part of princes, or any pretension to universal authority on the part of Holy Roman Emperors. In place of old religious divisions and imperial causes, an age of mostly secular conflict among sovereign states began. With it came a new pattern of international politics and therefore also of war, in which Great Powers deployed their wealth in the form of standing armies, and battered down the small and weak. In this brave new world, amoral principles of statecraft such as *raison d'etat* and the idea of the balance of power swept away older concerns about the truth or untruth of transubstantiation, who filled the ranks of predestined salvation, or whether it was proper for clerics to sell indulgences. Not until the bracing ruthlessness of the French Revolution tempted France to seek dominion over the entire continent would Europeans again embark on protracted war to decide whose ideas were the most true.

Yet, the religious impulse to make war did not wholly depart from international politics with the passing of the wars of religion. True, diplomats who drafted the various treaties that codified the Peace of Westphalia sincerely tried to remove confessionalism from diplomacy and war by elevating the secular state to the supreme position it has enjoyed in theory and law ever since. Long afterward, however, European states and rulers continued to enunciate and pursue overtly religious goals in their foreign policies and wars. Tsarist Russia prosecuted what amounted to a sustained Orthodox crusade against the "infidel Turk" (who returned the religious insult, and the hostility) from the 17th through the 19th centuries, even as "Old Believers" at home accused more than one despotic tsar of being a usurper, or even the "Antichrist." Robespierre and more radical French Revolutionaries waged war on established religion within France, and the mature Revolution declared and made war on the legitimacy of all the monarchies of the ancien regime from 1793 onward. Some monarchs, such as Alexander I of Russia, fought France to defend the Faith as well as noble privilege, though more cynical kings and foreign ministers only said that they did, so as not to frighten pious neighbors. Napoleon, who was wholly cynical about religious affairs, was thought by some Orthodox facing his onslaught in 1812 to be the "Antichrist," even though he had secured domestic legitimacy in the eyes of Catholic subjects by snatching his crown directly from the hands of a pope. Even so late a conflict as the Crimean War, fought after the mid-point of the 19th century, was said by key participants to have started in part over a religious *casus belli*, the question of control of the keys to the Church of the Holy Sepulcher and other "Holy Places" in Jerusalem. One may be skeptical about that claim, but one cannot understand the two bloodiest conflicts fought between 1815 and 1914, the Taiping Rebellion and the American Civil War, without appreciating that they had deep religious meaning for many involved. The Taiping Rebellion, which consumed millions of lives, began as a revolt by a Christian cult led by a messianic visionary who claimed he was the brother of Jesus of Nazareth. Marked by fierce religious, class, and ethnic hatred, the Taiping Rebellion ended in massacre and death on a genocidal scale. And many who fought in the American Civil War, perhaps toward the end even including Abraham Lincoln, believed they served the will of Providence to eradicate the sin of slavery from the new promised land of North America.

It did not stop there. Through all the blood, mud, fire, murder, lethal ideology, and bombast that made up World War I, the inscription on the belt buckles of German soldiers read "Gott mit uns" ("God is with us"). That concise expression voiced a spiritual arrogance common to all armies of the Great War: Russians boasted that they fought for "God and the Tsar," until millions of them voted with their feet against both in 1917; the British stiffly proclaimed that they were making war for "God, King and Country," along with the "rights of small nations." Similar sentiments about siding with the deity were expressed by Catholic Italians and Austrians, Orthodox Serbs and Greeks, and Muslim Arabs and Turks, even as they fought co-religionists on the other side. Most French believed the same, even if many were also convinced anti-clericals and republicans. Many Americans, most notably Woodrow Wilson, felt called by Providence to redress the imbalance of the Old World with the redemptive sacrifice of boys and men from the New World. After the war, among those who had experienced four years of bloody murder and mayhem such pious cant was angrily rejected. Surviving soldiers had learned to despise civilian and religious leaders who called for yet more men to march, and to kill and maim, in the name of God.

Elsewhere, however, religious motivations continued to play a major role in interstate relations and in motivations to war. The collapse of the Ottoman Empire opened the Middle East to sectarian conflict between Muslim and Jew in Palestine; to Christian, Druse, and Muslim infighting in Lebanon; and to sunni versus shi'ia conflicts in Iraq, Iran, and Yemen. Religious conflict mixed with land hunger and ethnic hatred scarred the politics of partition in India, and thereafter contributed to three major wars between predominantly Hindu India and self-consciously Muslim Pakistan. The founding of Israel as a Jewish homeland in the old land of Palestine, and its rejection on religious and ethnic grounds by most neighboring Arabs and Muslims, led to a series of armed conflicts in the second half of the 20th century that some military historians have called the "Fifty Years' War." The Soviet invasion of Afghanistan in 1979 provoked a widespread call for "jihad" against the Soviet Union, a call answered by thousands of "mujahadeen" from across the Muslim world. Muslim conflict with the Orthodox world flared again in the 1990s with a murderous war by Russian forces in Chechnya. In the Balkans, that poor and backward corner of Europe where old hatreds were only held in abeyance between generations by outside influence, religious and ethnic hatred flared again into war as Orthodox, Catholic, and Muslim resumed in arms their ancient, sterile arguments. The terrorist attack on the United States of September 11, 2001, then revealed to a secular political world that the abiding ferocity of religious hatred was not yet confined to history. After all the posing, both pious and impious, it was made clear that war in the name of the gods had been only partially and temporarily tamed at Westphalia in 1648.

AUTHOR'S NOTE

Specialization is properly prized and admired in historians and is the fundamental basis of all advances in historical knowledge. But excessive specialization can lead to distortion in which one century's political or cultural or military evolution is misunderstood by a different set of specialists as revolution, because change is always more exciting and impressive than underlying continuities. Historical tribes comprised of period specialists are nearly as territorial as actual tribes. General studies and encyclopedias have their weaknesses as well, but at the end of the day a broad understanding of history is the goal of all who study it, or should be. For this work I have delved into sources ranging from remarkable in-depth studies of the chemistry of gunpowder combustion, the forging of tempered swords and the ballistics of trebuchets, to sweeping general interpretations of Chinese and Islamic civilization, the Crusades, the Hundred Years' War, and the Protestant Reformation. It has been a thrilling intellectual ride and a scholarly experience that revived and deepened my original enthusiasm for historical studies, even as the ubiquity of death and war came close to crushing my optimism about the human condition. For any study such as this must lead to the baleful conclusion that war has been the singular engine of change shaping human societies and cultures beyond any other intellectual, economic, or social force. Wars have built and broken empires ancient and modern, made and unmade dynasties and tyrants, shaped, reformed, or mercilessly exterminated whole nations and peoples.

War is endlessly confusing. What does it really mean that this or that border was crossed by an army, that fleets were sunk, castle walls toppled, or great cities sacked? In studying war there is a natural temptation to focus on the spectacular, to recount the great battle upon which history seemed to turn and tell tales of great commanders who supposedly turned it. But war is a far deeper phenomenon than battle, with much more elusive causes and effects. Its meaning is entwined in symbiotic relation to changes in religion, culture, politics, and economics. In and of itself, war is usually morally agnostic: it has upheld governing elites whether they were just or despotic, or overthrown them in favor of some other set of masters who had advantages in weapons or tactics but not better manners or morals. Yet war has moral significance even if it is often unclear as to moral meaning. Somehow, we know that it matters whether civilians are massacred or protected, whether prisoners of war have their throats cut or are ransomed or paroled. It is important that some men and women of conscience over the centuries have tried to limit or end war, even as others with refined consciences supported some wars as necessary (if nonetheless evil) means to longer-term or wider moral goods. It is significant that some artists and poets have celebrated war while others have lamented it, but that mothers only ever fear it.

War undresses humanity. Soldiers know better than anyone the murky moral arena in which they live and work. The Duke of Wellington, walking the field of his great victory at Waterloo, mumbled to an aide: "Nothing except a battle lost can be half so melancholy as a battle won." Half a century later and a continent away, Confederate General Robert E. Lee spoke a different truth, one far less acceptable in polite modern company but an abiding fact of war nonetheless: it has its own aesthetic, powerful and alluring. On the spectacle and lure of war he said, after repelling a Union charge at Fredericksburg: "It is well that war is so terrible, else we should grow too fond of it." On the other side of the lines William T. Sherman recalled the carnage of the American Civil War this way: "War is at best barbarism. . . . Its glory is all moonshine. It is only those who have neither fired a shot nor heard the shrieks and groans of the wounded who cry aloud for blood, more vengeance, more destruction. War is hell." It is also the most expensive, technically complex, physically, emotionally, and morally demanding enterprise which humans undertake. No art, no music, no cathedral or mosque, no great city, no space program or research into the cure for AIDS or cancer has ever received a fraction of the money, time, and effort that people and societies have regularly put into preparing for and waging war. Those hard truths have shaped my approach to this work and the tone in which it is written.

In discussing so vast a range of issues and events I have relied heavily on hundreds of specialist works by historians of enormously impressive erudition and deep regional historical knowledge. I am immensely grateful to these specialists upon whose books and articles I have relied in such measure. I have not hesitated to add interpretations of my own in areas I know well, or where it seemed to me that larger patterns in history were readily apparent and broad lessons might be fairly drawn. Yet, writing a work of history such as this is primarily an exercise in synthesis. It is simply not possible for one author to master all the primary sources which are the raw ore from which the purer metals of historical truth are smelted. My challenge has been to gain sufficient command of the specialty literature in order to provide enough detailed narrative that past events become comprehensible, while also communicating the differing interpretations to which those events may be subject. In that I cleave to the wisdom of G. M. Trevelyan that in assessing historical actors and events "the really indispensable qualities [are] accuracy and good faith." Reconstructions of past events and motivations are as accurate as I have been able to make them. I ask readers to accept that I have presented what I believe to be the facts of history and drawn conclusions about the meaning of those facts in scholarly good faith, without conscious bias or preference for the claims of any one faith over another. I have, in sum, tried to the limits of my ability as a scholar to present war in the medieval and early modern era as it really was: naked and brutal and raw, as well as complex in motivation and effects. I am content to leave it to readers and critics to determine how well I performed that task.

Concerning the comparative length of one entry as against another, it is generally true that the more distantly great events recede from the present the more the history of those events, and the historians who write about them, compress their description. Ideally, that is done because more of the original dross which always conceals the meaning of human affairs has been burned away, and the right conclusions have been drawn about what place in the larger human story a given historical event or person holds. In reality, it probably more closely reflects a common tendency and need to fix all stars in relation to one's own time and point of view. I have made what effort I can to correct for this baleful habit, but I am sure that I am as guilty of it as most. As to the length of the overall work, I may only plead in the spirit of Blaise Pascal that I would have written far less, but I did not have the time.

Logic of the Work

I have addressed the complexity of war in this period by including entries that span questions of military technology, royal finance, social and class relations, major confessional groups (including those seen as "heretics" by orthodox communities), and elite mores and conceits about combat and chivalry. I have summarized theological disputations that may seem arcane and obscure to modern readers, but which clearly animated confessional groups to do great violence to one another during the period. Also included are key military, political, and intellectual biographies. Of course, as befits a work of military history, most entries are concerned with narrative recounting of major wars and descriptions of key battles and sieges. This includes explanations of their significance to the wars in which they occurred, and discussion of tactics and weapons employed. Longer battle entries concern fights that revealed an important changing of the guard among disputing powers, or were a turning point in a given war. Some longer battle entries, however, concern fights from minor wars or that were not in themselves decisive, but which nonetheless warranted extended treatment because they exposed some key change in military technology or use of bold new tactics. Yet, other entries illustrate opposite but arguably even more important truths, that battles were seldom decisive in this period and that changes in military technology were not usually "revolutions in military affairs" because they were not always or quickly adapted to, or adopted. Why? Because fiscal or cultural or class restraints led to entrenched resistance to change.

In this work there are entries that explain minutely technical matters such as the velocity and effect of drag on a spherical shot or a musket ball, the evolution of drill, the peculiar nature of wounds caused by period weapons, battlefield manifestation of class and warrior psychology in heraldic devices and early uniforms, and the display and use of various flags from the Aztec Empire to Medieval Europe to Japan, and also the banner system of the Qing Army in Manchuria. There are entries that translate and/or define period terminology, others which describe weapons and features of fortification, and still more that explain naval construction techniques and describe the period conduct of war at sea. There is extensive discussion of the burden of logistics that so often determined the composition of opposing forces and decided the strategies pursued, from Ming failure to penetrate the deserts of Mongolia to wars of endless maneuver without battles of encounter by armies of *condottieri* in Italy, or campaigns of maneuver by locust-like armies in Germany during the Thirty Years' War. Closely related to logistics were problems of pay, so there are also entries on contributions, mutiny, military discipline, and systems of war finance. There are entries that discuss the rise and fall in the size of armies from the Ottoman Empire to early modern France, to the vast Ming and Manchu armies of Asia, to the near-guerrilla forces of rural Ireland or the Balkan *Militargrenze*. Other main entries deal with the effects of technology and disease, including on campaigns of conquest and on class structure and the social make-up of armies. On religious aspects of the period there are broad entries on all the major faiths, along with their peculiar heresies and internal controversies. There is solid coverage of outbreaks of toleration and persistent and terrible theological persecution alike, and on disputes territorial between emperors and popes, kings and barons, and the barony and rising urban classes. There are several entries on peasant uprisings and other involvement of the "lower orders" in medieval and early modern warfare, from the *ashigaru* of Japan to the great *Jacquerie* in 14th-century France, to the German Peasant War of the early 16th century.

The contemporary "clash of civilizations" thesis, which is popular among journalists and social scientists, ostensibly explains the grand historical pattern of the post–Cold War period by reference to earlier eras. It rests heavily on an ahistorical view that in pre-modern times wars were engaged across "civilizational lines." It is then suggested that these lines remain more salient today than the political borders established by modern nations and states. Yet, many of the sharpest and most unforgiving wars of religion were in fact fought among communities of a single faith, usually to destroy some sect identified as heretical. In most wars of the era of "wars of religion" the majority of Muslims who were killed in battle were thus slain by other Muslims, the majority of Christian dead were butchered or burned by other Christians, and so on. This was true even during the Crusades and the later Ottoman advance into southern Europe, both of which saw Christians and Muslims ally against clusters of coreligionists on the other side. Religious-military lines were perhaps sharper in India, though even there dynastic wars and Mughal civil wars were often more destructive than wars between Muslim conquerors on one side and Hindu Marathas or Rajputs resisting on the other. Truly protracted wars over religious differences were waged in the 16th–17th centuries within Western Christianity, as they were also between the sunni Ottoman and Uzbek empires and shi'ia Safavid Ian. The title "Wars of Religion" therefore should not be taken as implying that all conflicts of the period were rooted in theological or sectarian quarrels, that the "*ghazi*" or "crusader" spirit was always paramount. It is sufficient to note that religious justifications, sincere or merely propagandistic, were present at some level in nearly every war.

Analytically, this study starts from the straightforward observation that large states, empires, and civilizations have dominated world affairs for most of recorded history. Even so, smaller states and marginal societies sometimes have been quite influential in the larger course of world history, even if mainly as objects of aggression or imperial competition. Such societies can be interesting and important in their own right, in addition to being of regional significance. Thus, some smaller kingdoms such as Scotland in Europe or isolated Songhay and Mali in Africa are covered, at varying length, in addition to all major kingdoms and empires. Each is treated in an entry which at the least summarizes the main features of its military position and development, and which tries to situate it in the larger contexts of time and region. It remains true, however, that it was the most powerful kingdoms and empires, the major civilizations from which they arose, and the wars in which they were involved that were the prime movers of world history in this period. Even small changes within certain key societies had a more important long-term impact on world affairs than signal events within or among smaller countries. Comprehensive coverage is thus given to the policies and interactions of the most powerful kingdoms and empires, and to the dynamics which drove them, including economic, intellectual, political, and social innovation or decay. This includes some contenders for power which fell short and disappeared from modern maps, such as Burgundy.

Likewise, it is true that lesser—whether in character or talent—individuals in charge of the affairs of major states had a broad influence on world history. Often, their influence was weightier than that of a moral or intellectual titan, if the latter was confined by chance or birth to a Lilliputian land. Therefore, individuals who might be reasonably judged as of little personal consequence are sometimes given their day in this work, owing to the indisputable public consequences of their choices, actions, or omissions while in command of the public affairs of some major power. More than one otherwise insignificant pope or prince, or king or emperor, or some effete aristocratic general or admiral, has slipped into significant history via this back door, held ajar for them by the pervasive importance of raw power as a motive and moving force in the affairs of the world. Great and small alike pursued grand plans and strategic interests within an international system which reflected wider economic, political, and military realities, and upheld—or at least, claimed to uphold—legal, cultural, moral, and diplomatic norms. A full understanding of medieval and early modern affairs would be incomplete without awareness of the historical evolution and nature of the early modern "international system" (or better said, "international society"), its key terms, ideas, successes, and failures. There are, therefore, entries in this work on various treaties, legal doctrines and traditions, and evolving ideas about a rudimentary "international law" rooted in the just war tradition and cultural norms about the treatment of civilians swept up or aside by war, later supplemented by the works of key jurists and legal thinkers such as Alberico Gentili and Hugo Grotius, and codified in 1648 in the great settlement known as the Peace of Westphalia.

War as a general phenomenon—and great wars among major players in particular—receives direct attention in this work. War is more costly, and requires more preparation, effort, sacrifice, ingenuity, and suffering than any other collective human endeavor. There is no greater engine of social, economic, political, or technological change than war, and the ever-present threat of war even in times of peace. An effort was made to capture something of this reality in wide-ranging entries such as *battle*, *castles*, *horses*, and *recruitment*, among others. Moreover, war and the early modern state, and the emerging international states system, evolved together from c.1450, each greatly influencing the other. Large and protracted wars—wars which involved many powers in determined conflict—greatly compounded these manifold effects. Hence, major wars of the late medieval and early modern periods are covered in detail, including the *Hundred Years' War* (1337–1453), the *Italian Wars* (1494–1559), the *Thirty Years' War* (1618–1648), and the *Eighty Years' War* (1568–1648). Dozens of lesser wars, civil wars, and rebellions are also recounted, of course, as they constituted a good part of the local, regional, and international history of the period.

In the interest of universality, a serious effort was made to cover regions of the wider world which, objectively speaking, formed only tributary streams of the riverine flow of world history during the period. Along with something of the flavor of their local histories, it is recounted how such areas were affected by larger historical trends that brushed against them, even in their deep desert or distant continental isolation. Detailed knowledge of historical events of even better-known societies is far greater after c.1300 than before that date. As a result, there are more—and more detailed—entries for the second half of the period covered in this work than there are for the first half. Fortuitously, this division roughly corresponds with the advent of gunpowder weapons in sieges and on the battlefield, from Asia to India, the Middle East, and Europe. Special attention is paid to the evolution of gunpowder weapons, along with the great and grave social, political, and fiscal changes they wrought over several centuries. Also discussed is whether these changes occasioned a "revolution in military affairs." The technological and social changes effected by gunpowder weapons are referenced throughout the work, while recounted most directly and plainly in such general entries as *infantry*, *cavalry*, *artillery*, *siege warfare*, and *gunpowder weapons*. Major intellectual revolutions with global historical significance are also discussed, most notably the *Italian Renaissance*, the *Protestant Reformation*, and the Catholic *Counter-Reformation*. While these tumultuous upheavals were originally and primarily

European phenomena, they ultimately had profound effects on societies as far afield as Asia, Africa, and the Americas. Paradoxically, they also contributed to the spread and acceptance in Europe of secularism and the ascendancy of the early modern state.

Structure of the Work

This work is organized alphabetically. Single-word entries are easy and straightforward to locate. It is not always obvious, however, where a compound term should be listed. For ease of use by readers, compound entries are listed as they are employed in normal speech and writing; that is, in the form in which they are most likely to be first encountered by the average reader. For example, *Edict of Nantes* and *Union of Kalmar* appear under "E" and "U," respectively, with blind entries serving as guideposts to the proper location placed under "N" and "K." If readers are unable to find an entry they seek under one part of a compound term, they should have little difficulty finding it under another component of the term or phrase. Additionally, the book is heavily cross-referenced (all words in *italics*, thus), with some licence taken when cross-referencing adjectives or adverbs to entries which are actually listed as nouns, such as *feudal*, which directs the reader to a main entry head that is actually *feudalism*. Readers are advised to make use of this feature since cross-references almost always provide additional information or insight not contained in the original entry. Rather than clutter the text unduly with italics, however, common references such as "battle" or specific weapons, as well as all country names, have been left in normal font. In select instances, even terms such as "knight" or "men-at-arms" or "longbow" have been left in normal font since a cross-reference at that given point would not especially illuminate the main entry being read. Yet, all such commonly used military terms and all countries are discussed in discrete entries. In very rare cases, some common terms have been highlighted to indicate that they contain additional information that is highly relevant to the entry being perused. To avoid confusion or sending the reader on a fruitless cross-reference search, foreign words and phrases have not been italicized in the main entries (they have, however, been italicized in the entry heads). With only one exception—rare in-text references to book titles, which are clear from the context in which they appear—all in-text terms or phrases rendered in italics in a main entry indicate an active cross-reference.

Some technical points: (1) All dates are provided in the non-sectarian "Common Era" (C.E.) unless stated otherwise, in which case the designation B.C.E. ("Before the Common Era") is used. In cases where ambiguity exists, C.E. has been added to ensure clarity. For other matters pertaining to calendar issues, see the "Note on Dates" elsewhere in the frontmatter of this work. (2) I have for the most part followed the practice of modern specialists in using the Pinyin system for romanizing Chinese personal and place names. In cases where place names remain more familiar to Western readers under their Wade-Giles form, this alternate form has been provided in parentheses. (3) In areas where place names of battles or sieges differ significantly in spelling in several regional languages, I have provided each alternative place name and its language of origin at the start of the main entry. In many cases, blind entries were also added directing readers to the main entry. This is especially the case concerning Hungarian, Turkish, Greek, and other competing place names in the Balkans. (4) To avoid confusion as to which Emperor Charles or King John is being referred to, I have left German, Polish, Portuguese, Spanish, Swedish, and most Balkan names in their original languages, with blind cross-references provided elsewhere if it is likely English-language readers might look there in the first instance. Thus, Charles IX of Sweden is rendered as Karl IX in this work; Frederick V is given instead as Friedrich V, and so forth. There are rare exceptions to this: Charles V, King of Spain and Holy Roman Emperor, is so important a ruler, and so well known by that name to English-language readers, that I have listed his entry under its English spelling rather than in German. For the same reason, familiarity to English-language students of history, I have listed French monarchs by their common English names (hence, Francis II, not François II). Similarly, Ottoman emperors are listed under generally accepted English spellings of Arab or Turkish personal names.

NOTE ON DATES

In 1582 parts of Europe shifted to a new calendar issued by Pope Gregory XIII. The old Julian calendar was 14 days out of sync with the solar year. Gregory made a 10-day correction by using the Vernal Equinox as the base marker. Thus, the day after October 4, 1582, was not October 5 but October 15. He also decreed that each new year would start on January 1 and that only centuries evenly divisible by 400 would contain "leap years." The Gregorian calendar promised greater accuracy for several millennia. Even so, no self-respecting Protestant would take orders from the pope concerning the correct measure of time, a matter that rightfully belonged solely to eternity and to God. Only Catholic countries shifted to "New Style" (NS): Austria and Catholic states in Germany, France, Portugal, and Spain. Protestants cleaved to "Old Style" (OS), which left them 10 days behind Gregorian dates until 1700 and 11 days behind after that.

Once the fires of religious conflict burned out, most Protestants were prepared to accept the logic and greater accuracy of the Gregorian system. Saxony shifted to New Style in 1697. Other German states followed suit two years later. Great Britain and its overseas empire only changed to New Style in 1752. Sweden used New Style from 1700 but reverted to Old Style in 1712, which meant the same events might be recorded on three different dates. For instance, the Battle of Poltava in 1709 for many Protestants took place on June 27 (OS) but on June 28 for Swedes and July 8 (NS) for Catholics, some Protestants, and most later historians. In 1753, Sweden decided that Gregory had been right after all and reconverted to New Style. European empires imposed New Style on various conquered peoples of other continents over the course of the 18th and 19th centuries. Orthodox Russia declined to concede that the Latin West knew best how to keep God's time and remained staunchly committed to the inaccurate Julian calendar to the end of the Tsarist era. The Bolsheviks—rough reformers of everything they could conceive or lay hands to—forced Russians to shift to New Style in

1918. Other Orthodox countries resisted the change until 1923. As part of the imitative modernization of the Meiji Restoration, Japan adopted New Style in 1873. Chinese bureaucrats kept to the ancient Confucian calendar as they clung to most things traditional and non-Western. The successors to China's scholar-bureaucrats were impatient, modernizing republicans who looked to the West for models of national development. They imposed New Style on China in 1912.

Muslim societies continued to follow the Islamic calendar proclaimed in 639 by Caliph Umar I, dating "Year One" to the *Hegira* (flight of the Prophet) in 622 and marking the new year in mid-July. Western scholars designated this system the *"Anno Hegirae"* ("In the year of the *Hegira*"). The Muslim year is lunar and thus just 354 days long, an 11-day difference from all solar calendars. The A.H. calendar was divided into 12 lunar cycles of equal length beginning with each crescent moon. It did not need to add leap days or years, but the price for temporal evenness was that it took 34 solar years for a given lunar month to repeat exactly in the same place and season of the solar year. The Ottoman Empire introduced an Islamicized solar calendar but it ran 13 days behind the West. As part of a radical postwar modernization after World War I, Turkey shifted to New Style along with Latin script. Stricter Islamic societies refused the change but most Muslims eventually adopted NS for its sheer convenience, making it a common international calendar. A.H. notation remains in use to chart days of special Muslim religious obligation and observance.

Unless otherwise indicated, most Julian, Hegira, Orthodox, and Ottoman dates have been converted here to New Style, except where standard OS usage is so accepted that any change would cause undue confusion. Finally, rather than use the Christian "Anno Domini" ("In the Year of Our Lord"), all dates are given in modern, nonsectarian "Common Era" (C.E.).

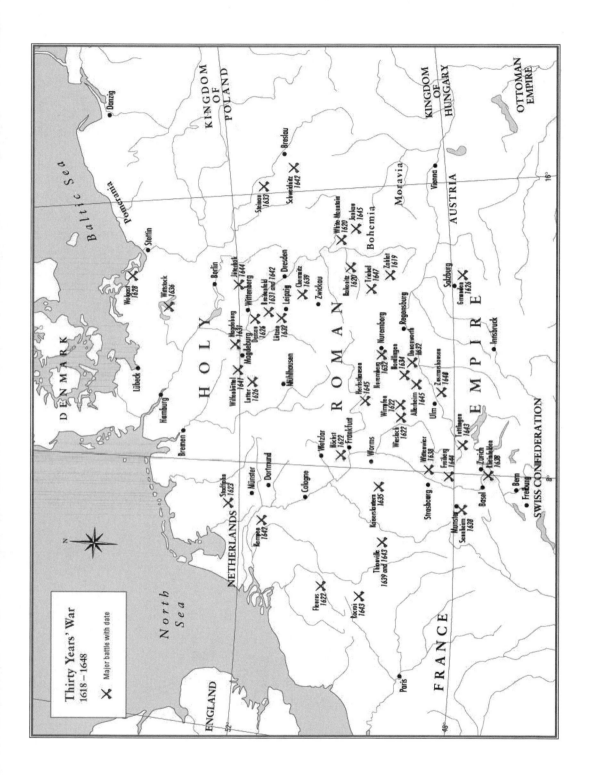

Thirty Years' War
1618 – 1648

✗ Major battle with date

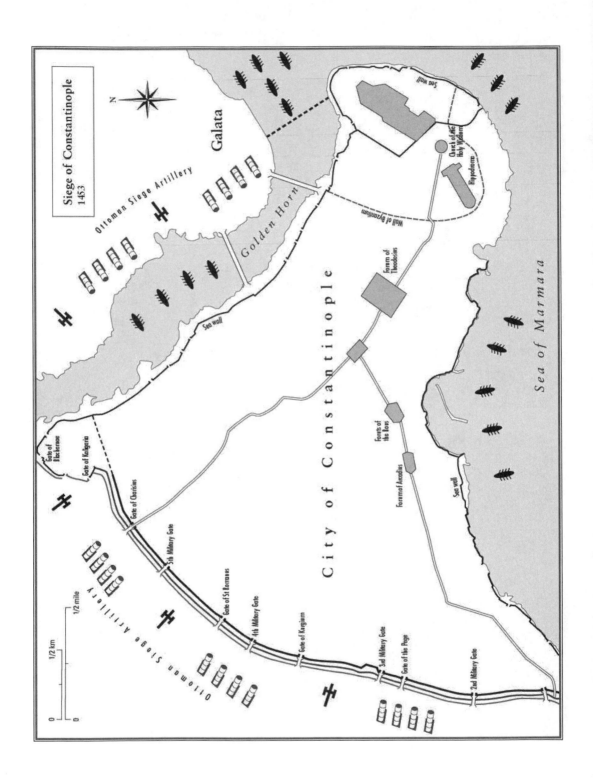

Siege of Constantinople
1453

N

Galata

Ottoman Siege Artillery

Golden Horn

Sea wall

Wall of Byzantium

Church of the Holy Wisdom

Hippodrome

Forum of Theodosius

City of Constantinople

Forets of the Boos

Forum of Arcadius

Sea wall

Sea of Marmara

Gate of Blachernae

Gate of Kaligaria

Gate of Charisius

5th Military Gate

Gate of St Romans

4th Military Gate

Gate of Kurgium

3rd Military Gate

Gate of the Page

2nd Military Gate

Ottoman Siege Artillery

1/2 mile

1/2 km

0

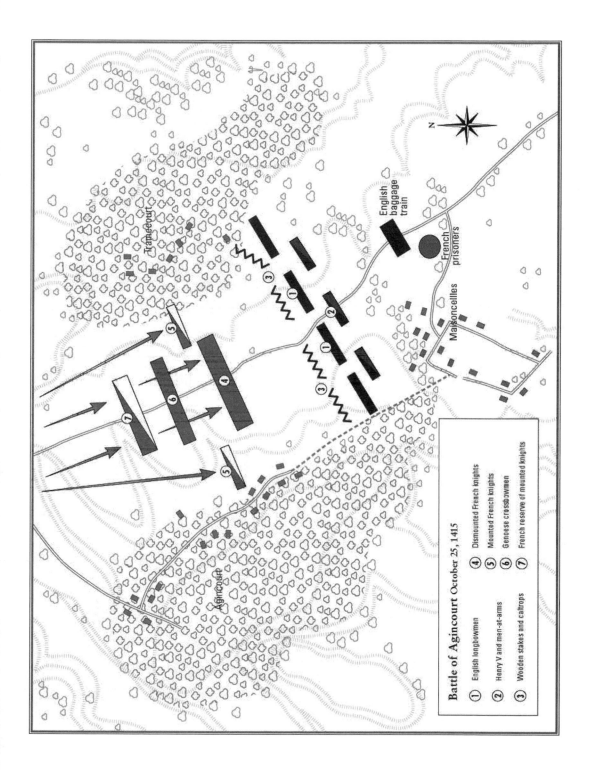

Battle of Agincourt October 25, 1415

1. English longbowmen
2. Henry V and men-at-arms
3. Wooden stakes and caltrops
4. Dismounted French knights
5. Mounted French knights
6. Genoese crossbowmen
7. French reserve of mounted knights

Tramecourt

Agincourt

English baggage train

French prisoners

Maisoncelles

N

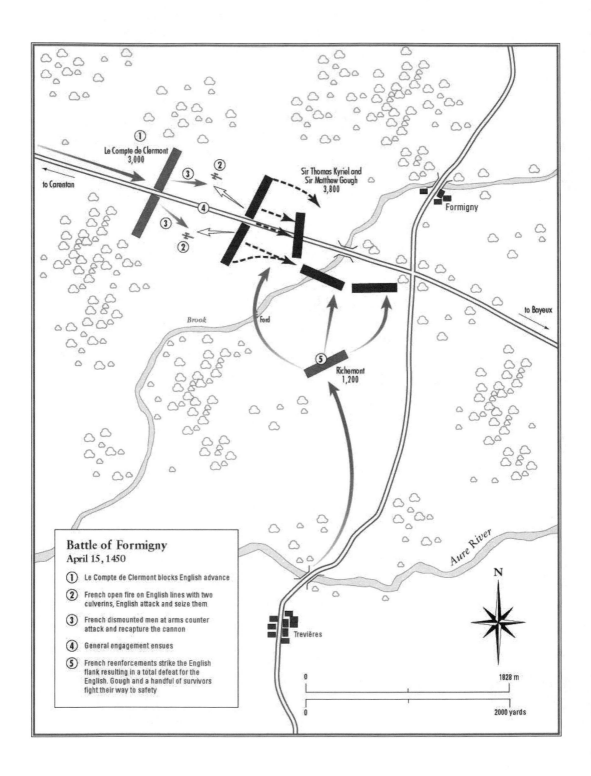

Battle of Formigny
April 15, 1450

① Le Compte de Clermont blocks English advance

② French open fire on English lines with two culverins, English attack and seize them

③ French dismounted men at arms counter attack and recapture the cannon

④ General engagement ensues

⑤ French reenforcements strike the English flank resulting in a total defeat for the English. Gough and a handful of survivors fight their way to safety

① Le Compte de Clermont
3,000

to Carentan

② ③ ④ ③ ②

Sir Thomas Kyriel and
Sir Matthew Gough
3,800

Formigny

to Bayeux

Brook

Ford

⑤ Richemont
1,200

Aure River

Trevières

N

0   1828 m

0   2000 yards

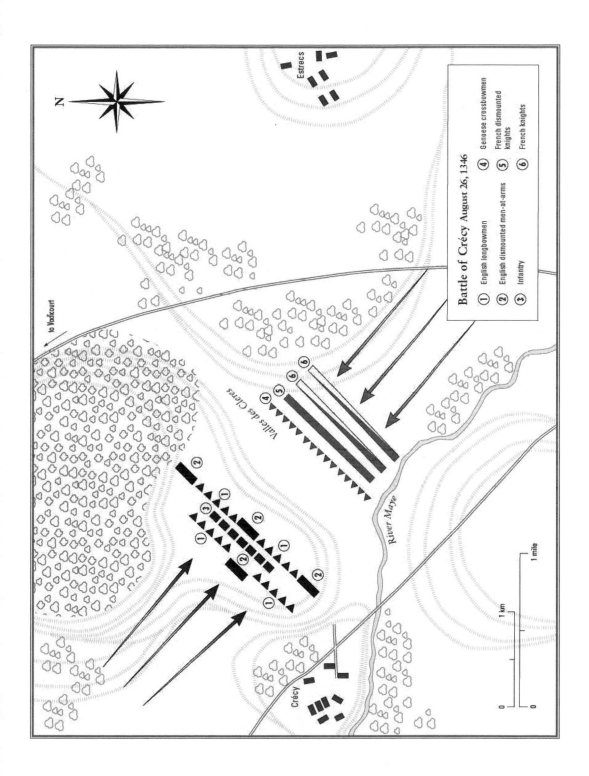

Battle of Crécy August 26, 1346

① English longbowmen
② English dismounted men-at-arms
③ Infantry
④ Genoese crossbowmen
⑤ French dismounted knights
⑥ French knights

Estrées

to Vadicourt

Vallés des Cleres

River Maye

Crécy

N

0   1 km

0   1 mile

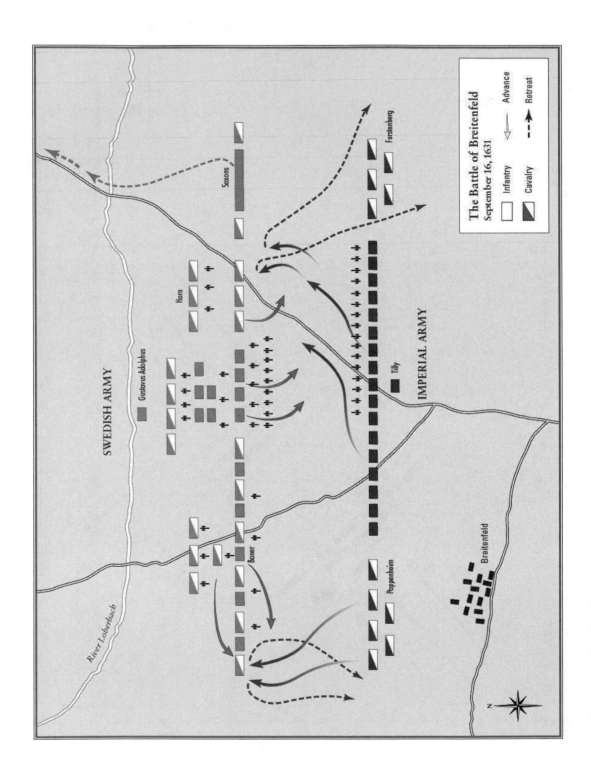

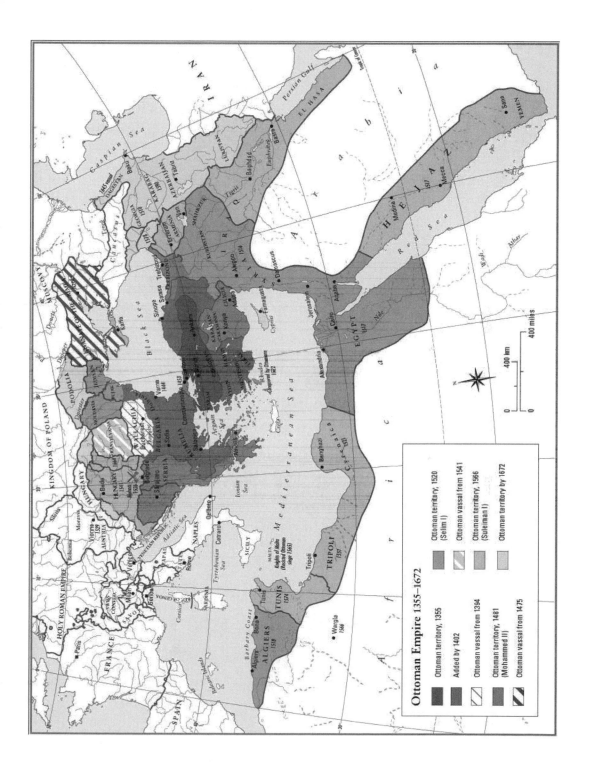

Ottoman Empire 1355–1672

Legend:
- Ottoman territory, 1355
- Added by 1402
- Ottoman vassal from 1394
- Ottoman territory, 1481 (Mohammed II)
- Ottoman vassal from 1475
- Ottoman territory, 1520 (Selim I)
- Ottoman vassal from 1541
- Ottoman territory, 1566 (Suleiman I)
- Ottoman territory by 1672

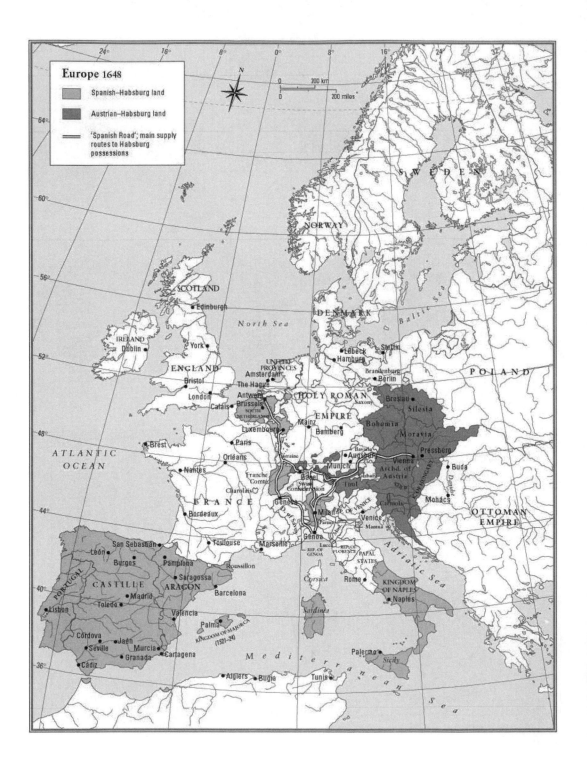

Europe 1648

Spanish–Habsburg land

Austrian–Habsburg land

'Spanish Road'; main supply routes to Habsburg possessions

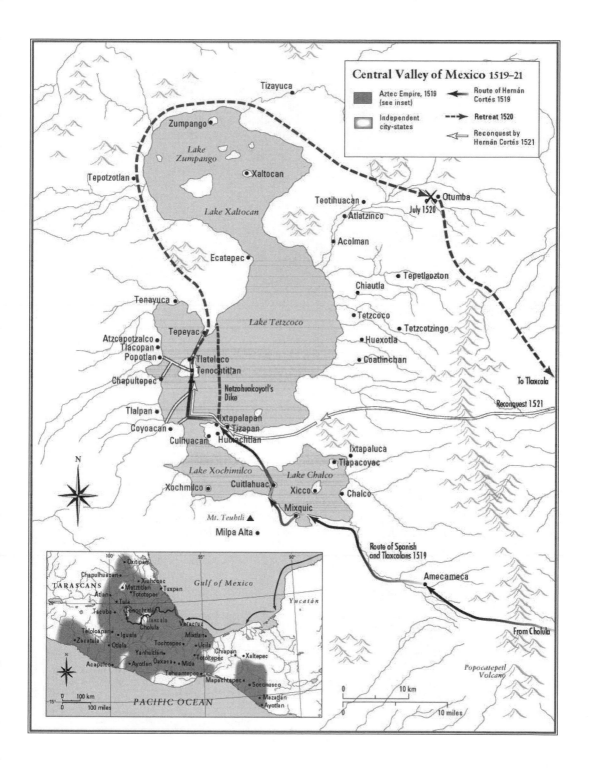

Central Valley of Mexico 1519–21

Aztec Empire, 1519 (see inset)	Route of Hernán Cortés 1519
Independent city-states	Retreat 1520
	Reconquest by Hernán Cortés 1521

Tizayuca

Zumpango

Lake Zumpango

Xaltocan

Tepotzotlan

Lake Xaltocan

Teotihuacan

Otumba

July 1520

Atlatzinco

Acolman

Ecatepec

Tepetlaozton

Chiautla

Tenayuca

Tetzcoco

Tepeyac

Lake Tetzcoco

Tetzcotzingo

Atzcapotzalco

Tlacopan

Huexotla

Popotlan

Tlatelolco

Tenochtitlan

Coatlinchan

Chapultepec

Netzahualcoyotl's Dike

To Tlaxcala

Tlalpan

Ixtapalapan

Reconquest 1521

Coyoacan

Tizapan

Culhuacan

Huitzachtlan

Ixtapaluca

Tlapacoyac

Lake Xochimilco

Lake Chalco

Xochimilco

Cuitlahuac

Xicco

Chalco

Mt. Teuhtli

Mixquic

Milpa Alta

Route of Spanish and Tlaxcalans 1519

Amecameca

Popocatepetl Volcano

From Cholula

N

0   10 km
0   10 miles

Inset map:

Oxitipan

Chapulhuacan

TÁRASCANS

Xauhcac

Gulf of Mexico

Metztitlan

Tototepec

Tuxpan

Atlan

Yucatán

Tula

Tacuba

Tenochtitlan

Veracruz

Telolapan

Cholula

Tlaxcala

Mixtlan

Zacatula

Iguala

Ucila

Otlala

Tochtepec

Chiapan

Xaltepec

Acapulco

Ayotlan

Yanhuitlan

Oaxaca

Mitla

Tototepec

Tehuantepec

Mapachtepec

Soconusco

Mazatlan

Ayotlan

PACIFIC OCEAN

0   100 km
0   100 miles

lxix

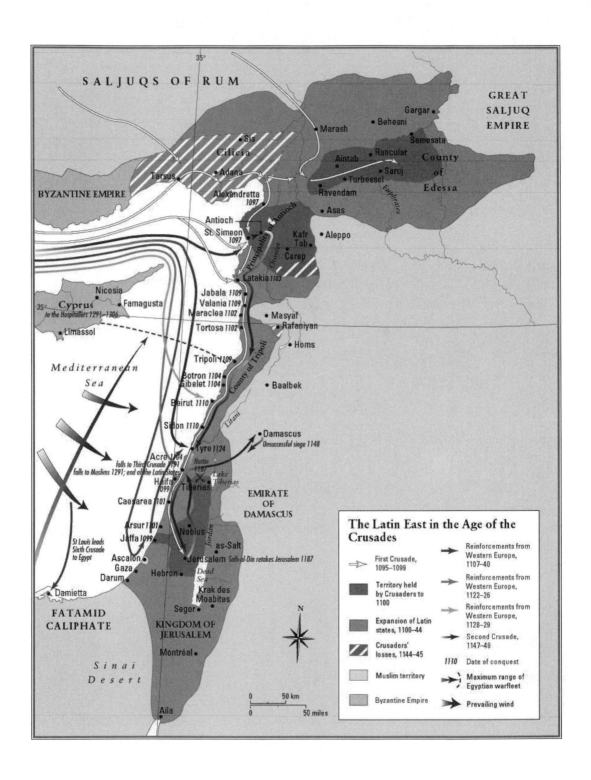

The Latin East in the Age of the Crusades

SALJUQS OF RUM

GREAT SALJUQ EMPIRE

Gargar • Behesni

Marash •

Semosata

Aintah • Rancular • County

Turbessel • Saruj • of

Ravendam • Edessa

BYZANTINE EMPIRE

Sis

Cilicia

Tarsus •

Adana •

Alexandretta 1097

Antioch

St. Simeon 1097

Asas •

Aleppo •

Kafr Tab

Cerep

Latakia 1103

Nicosia

Cyprus • Famagusta

to the Hospitallers 1291–1306

Limassol •

Jabala 1109

Valania 1109

Maraclea 1102

Tortosa 1102

Masyaf •

Rafaniyan •

Homs •

Mediterranean Sea

Tripoli 1109

Botron 1104

Gibelet 1104

County of Tripoli

Baalbek •

Beirut 1110

Sidon 1110

Tyre 1124

Acre 1104

falls to Third Crusade 1191

falls to Muslims 1291; end of the Latin States

Haifa 1099

Caesarea 1101

Arsur 1101

Jaffa 1099

St Louis leads Sixth Crusade to Egypt

Ascalon

Gaza

Darum •

Hebron •

Damietta •

FATAMID CALIPHATE

Damascus

Unsuccessful siege 1148

Hattin 1187

Lake Tiberias

Tiberias •

Nablus •

as-Salt •

Jerusalem Salh-al-Din retakes Jerusalem 1187

Dead Sea

Krak des Moabites

Segor •

Montréal •

EMIRATE OF DAMASCUS

KINGDOM OF JERUSALEM

Sinai Desert

Aila •

N

0   50 km

0   50 miles

The Latin East in the Age of the Crusades

First Crusade, 1095–1099

Territory held by Crusaders to 1100

Expansion of Latin states, 1100–44

Crusaders' losses, 1144–45

Muslim territory

Byzantine Empire

Reinforcements from Western Europe, 1107–40

Reinforcements from Western Europe, 1122–26

Reinforcements from Western Europe, 1128–29

Second Crusade, 1147–49

1110   Date of conquest

Maximum range of Egyptian warfleet

Prevailing wind

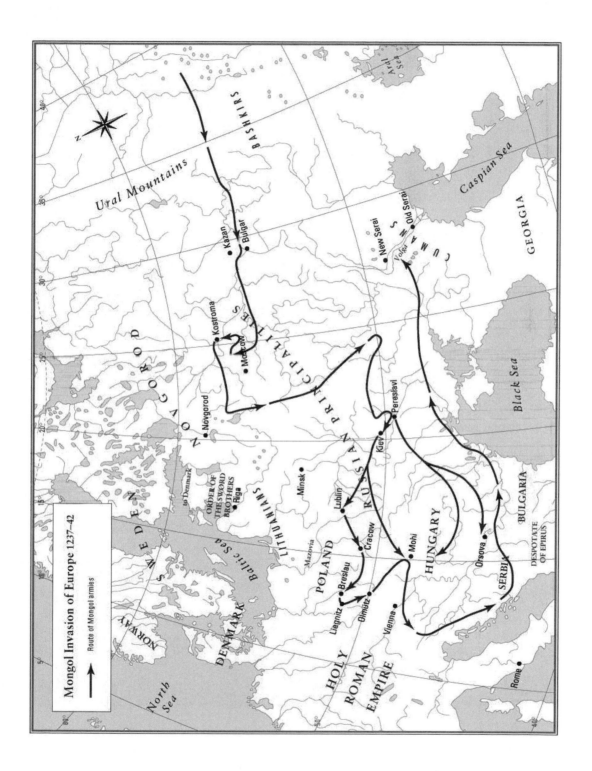

Mongol Invasion of Europe 1237–42

Route of Mongol armies

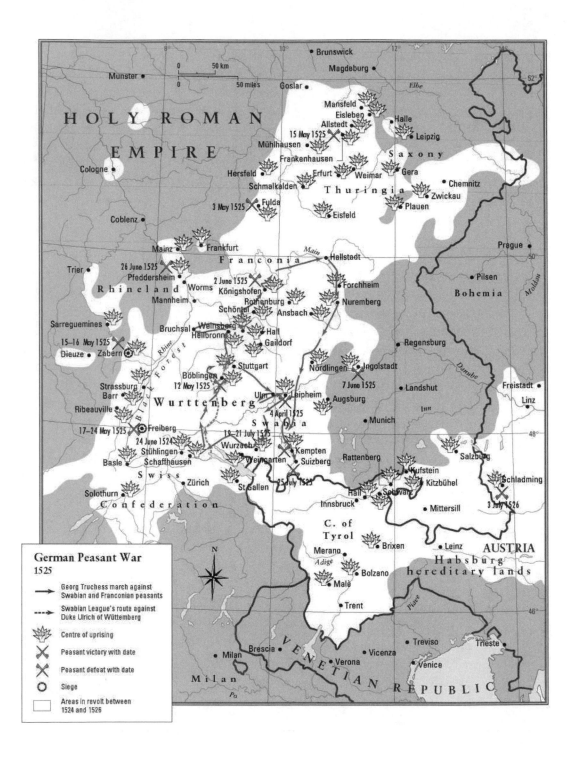

German Peasant War 1525

Legend:
- Georg Truchess march against Swabian and Franconian peasants
- Swabian League's route against Duke Ulrich of Württemberg
- Centre of uprising
- Peasant victory with date
- Peasant defeat with date
- Siege
- Areas in revolt between 1524 and 1526

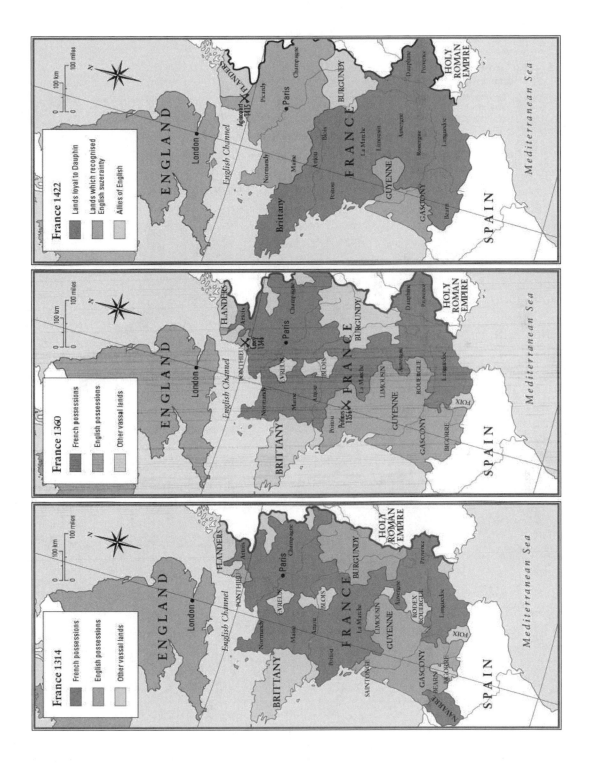

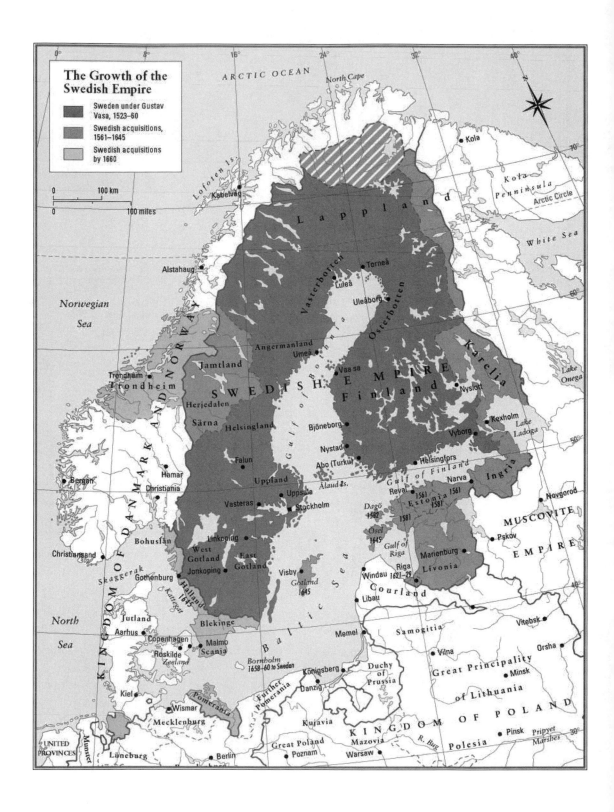

The Growth of the
Swedish Empire

- Sweden under Gustav Vasa, 1523–60
- Swedish acquisitions, 1561–1645
- Swedish acquisitions by 1660

0   100 km
0   100 miles

ARCTIC OCEAN

North Cape

Kola

Kola
Penninsula

Arctic Circle

White Sea

Lofoten Is.

Kabelvåg

Norwegian
Sea

Alstahaug

L a p p l a n d

Torneå

Luleå

Uleåborg

Vasterbotten

Gulf of Bothnia

Osterbotten

Karelia

Lake
Onega

Trondheim

Trondheim

Jamtland

Angermanland
Umeå

S W E D I S H   E M P I R E

Vaasa

Finland

Nyslott

Herjedalen

Helsingland

Björeborg

Vyborg

Kexholm

Lake
Ladoga

Särna

Falun

Nystad

Åbo (Turku)

Helsingfors

Gulf of Finland

Bergen

Hamar

Christiania

Uppland

Uppsala

Åland Is.

Reval

Narva

Ingria

Novgorod

Vasteras

Stockholm

Dagö
1582

Estonia 1561
1581

1581

MUSCOVITE

Linkoping

Osel
1645

Gulf of
Riga

Pskov

E M P I R E

Christiansand

Bohuslän

West
Gotland

East
Gotland

Visby

Gotland
1645

Marienburg

Livonia

Riga

Windau 1621–29

Courland

Jonkoping

Skaggerak

Gothenburg

Kattegat

Halland
1645

Libau

Vitebsk

North
Sea

Jutland

Blekinge

Baltic Sea

Memel

Samogitia

Aarhus

Copenhagen

Malmo

Scania

Vilna

Orsha

Roskilde
Zeeland

Bornholm
1658–60 to Sweden

Duchy
of
Prussia

Great Principality

Minsk

Kiel

Königsberg

of Lithuania

Wismar

Pomerania

Further
Pomerania

Danzig

Mecklenburg

Kujavia

K I N G D O M   O F   P O L A N D

UNITED
PROVINCES

Lüneburg

Berlin

Great Poland

Poznam

Mazovia

Warsaw

R. Bug

Polesia

Pinsk

Pripyet
Marshes

K I N G D O M   O F   D A N M A R K   A N D   N O R W A Y

Reformation in Europe 1520–1600

Mostly Roman Catholic	Mostly Anglican
Mostly Calvinist	Orthodox with Muslim minorities
Mostly Lutheran	Seigneurial lands of the King of Navarre in France
Mixed Catholic and Protestant areas	✳ Saint Bartholomew's Day massacres, 1572
Areas of waivering adherence	○ 1559 Events of special importance

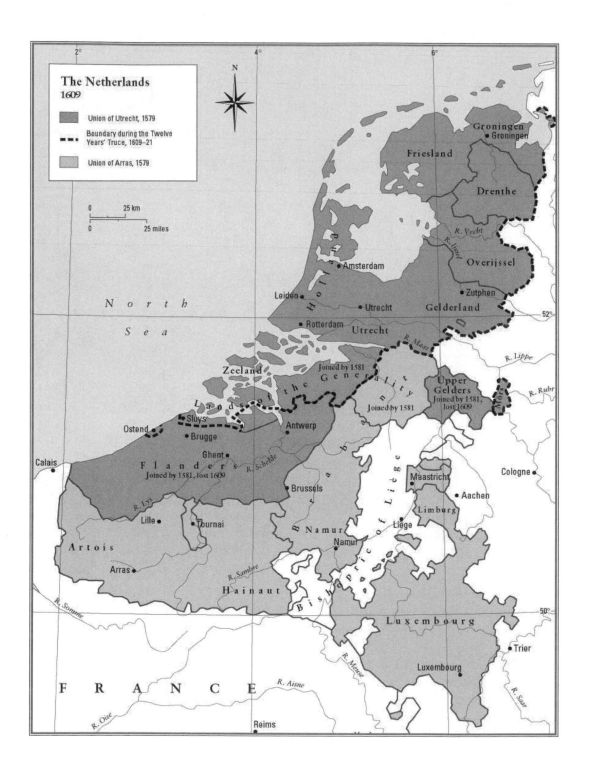

The Netherlands 1609

- Union of Utrecht, 1579
- Boundary during the Twelve Years' Truce, 1609–21
- Union of Arras, 1579

0   25 km

0   25 miles

N

North

Sea

Groningen
• Groningen

Friesland

Drenthe

R. Vecht

R. IJssel

Overijssel

• Amsterdam

Leiden •

• Zutphen

• Utrecht

Gelderland

52°

• Rotterdam

Utrecht

R. Maas

R. Lippe

Joined by 1581

the Generality

Upper
Gelders
Joined by 1581,
lost 1609

R. Ruhr

Zeeland

Joined by 1581

L a n d s

Sluys •

Ostend •

• Brugge

Antwerp

Ghent •

• Maastricht

Cologne •

Calais •

F l a n d e r s
Joined by 1581, lost 1609

R. Schelde

Brussels •

Limburg

• Aachen

Liège •

R. Lys

Lille •

• Tournai

B i s h o p r i c   o f   L i è g e

• Namur

Namur •

A r t o i s

Arras •

R. Sambre

H a i n a u t

50°

R. Somme

L u x e m b o u r g

F R A N C E

R. Aisne

R. Meuse

• Trier

Luxembourg •

R. Saar

R. Oise

Reims •

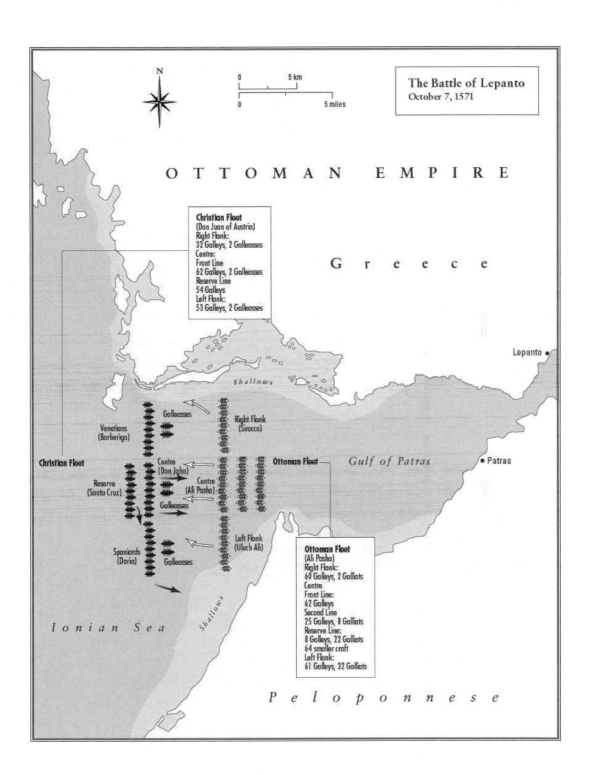

The Battle of Lepanto
October 7, 1571

OTTOMAN EMPIRE

Greece

Christian Fleet
(Don Juan of Austria)
Right Flank:
32 Galleys, 2 Galleasses
Centre:
Front Line
62 Galleys, 2 Galleasses
Reserve Line
54 Galleys
Left Flank:
53 Galleys, 2 Galleasses

Lepanto

Shallows

Galleasses

Venetians
(Barberigo)

Right Flank
(Sirocco)

Christian Fleet

Centre
(Don John)

Centre
(Ali Pasha)

Ottoman Fleet

Gulf of Patras

Patras

Reserve
(Santa Cruz)

Galleasses

Spaniards
(Doria)

Galleasses

Left Flank
(Uluch Ali)

Ottoman Fleet
(Ali Pasha)
Right Flank:
60 Galleys, 2 Galliots
Centre
Front Line:
62 Galleys
Second Line:
25 Galleys, 8 Galliots
Reserve Line:
8 Galleys, 22 Galliots
64 smaller craft
Left Flank:
61 Galleys, 32 Galliots

Ionian Sea

Shallows

Peloponnese

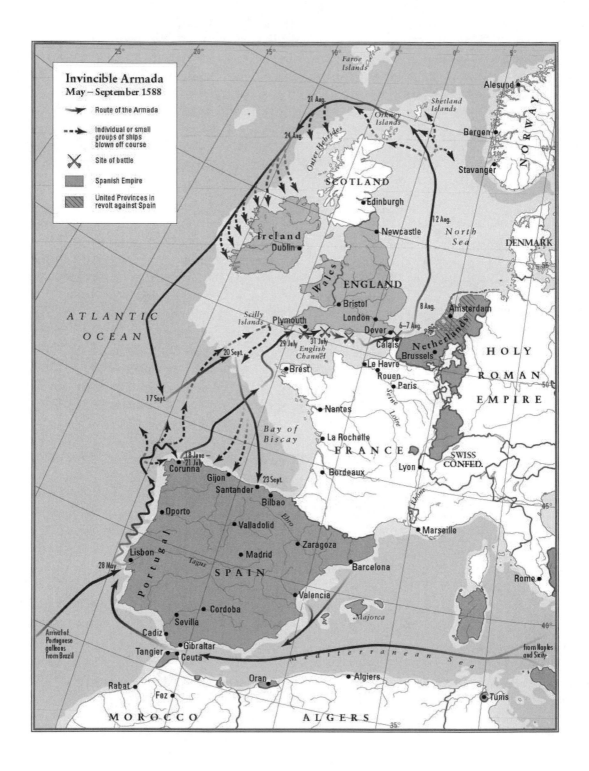

Invincible Armada
May – September 1588

Route of the Armada

Individual or small
groups of ships
blown off course

Site of battle

Spanish Empire

United Provinces in
revolt against Spain

Faroe
Islands

Alesund

NORWAY

21 Aug.

Shetland
Islands

Bergen

24 Aug.

Orkney
Islands

Outer Hebrides

Stavanger

SCOTLAND

Edinburgh

12 Aug.

North
Sea

DENMARK

Newcastle

Ireland

Dublin

Wales

ENGLAND

Bristol

8 Aug.

Amsterdam

Scilly
Islands

Plymouth

London

Dover

6–7 Aug.

Netherlands

HOLY

ATLANTIC

OCEAN

29 July

31 July
English
Channel

Calais

Brussels

ROMAN

Le Havre

Rouen

EMPIRE

Brest

Paris

20 Sept.

Seine

17 Sept.

Bay of
Biscay

Nantes

Loire

SWISS
CONFED.

La Rochelle

FRANCE

18 June –
21 July

Corunna

Gijon

Santander

23 Sept.

Bordeaux

Lyon

Bilbao

Oporto

Ebro

Valladolid

Marseille

Rhône

Madrid

Zaragoza

Rome

Lisbon

Tagus

SPAIN

Barcelona

28 May

Portugal

Valencia

Majorca

Cordoba

Sevilla

Cadiz

Arrival of
Portuguese
galleons
from Brazil

Gibraltar

Tangier

Ceuta

Mediterranean Sea

from Naples
and Sicily

Oran

Algiers

Tunis

Rabat

Fez

MOROCCO

ALGERS

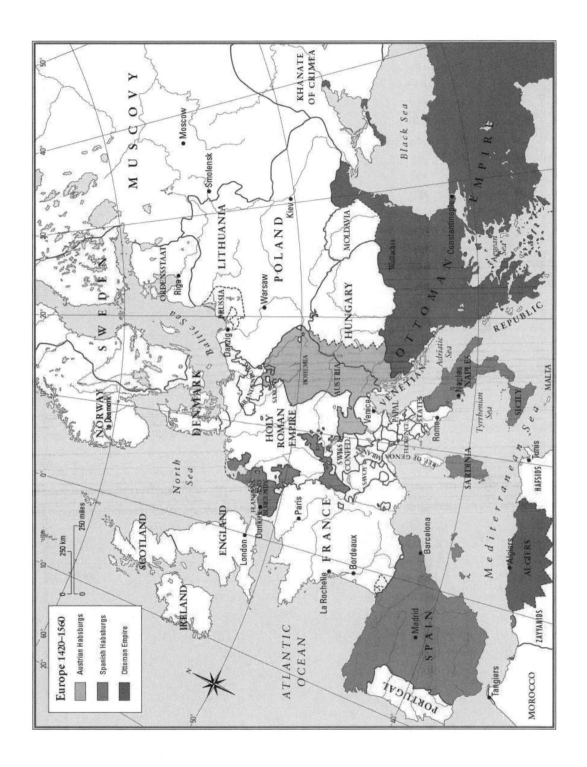

Europe 1420–1560

Austrian Habsburgs
Spanish Habsburgs
Ottoman Empire

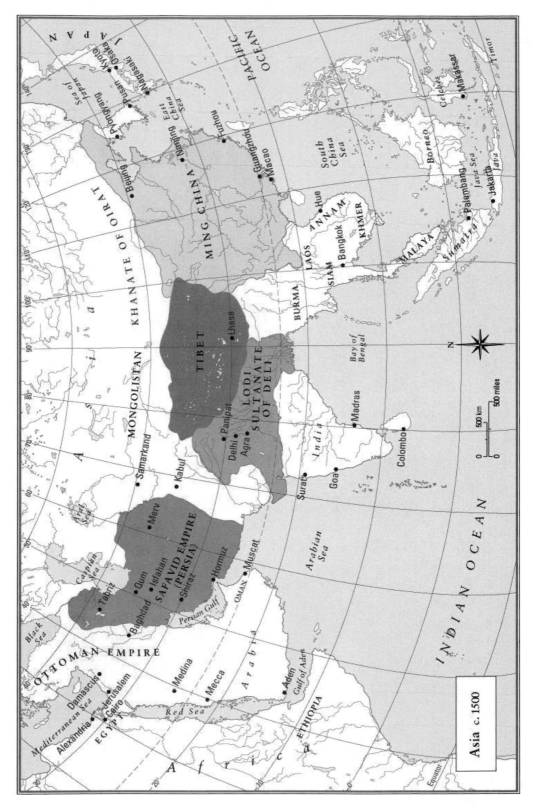

Asia c. 1500

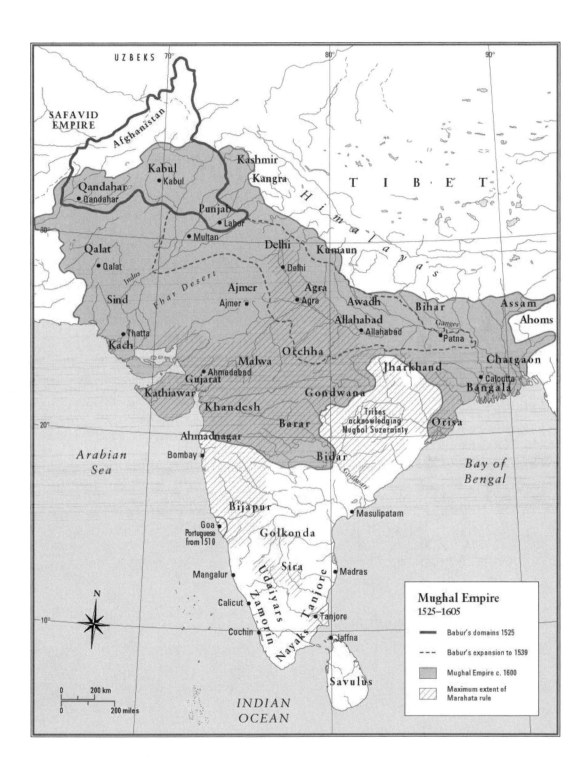

UZBEKS 70° 80° 90°

SAFAVID
EMPIRE

Afghanistan

T I B E T

Kabul
• Kabul

Kashmir

Kangra

Qandahar
• Qandahar

Punjab
• Lahor

H
i
m
a
l
a
y
a
s

30°

Qalat
• Qalat

• Multan

Delhi

Kumaun

Sind

Indus

Thar Desert

Ajmer
Ajmer •

• Delhi

Agra
• Agra

Awadh

Bihar

Ganges

Assam

Ahoms

• Thatta

Allahabad
• Allahabad

• Patna

Kach

Orchha

Jharkhand

Chatgaon

Malwa

Gondwana

• Calcutta

Kathiawar

• Ahmadabad

Gujarat

Bangala

Khandesh

Tribes
acknowledging
Mughol Suzerainty

Orisa

20°

Barar

Ahmadnagar

Arabian
Sea

Bidar

• Bombay

Godavari

Bay of
Bengal

Bijapur

Goa •
Portuguese
from 1510

Golkonda

• Masulipatam

Sira

Mangalur •

Udaiyars

Zamorin

Tanjore

• Madras

Calicut •

Nayaks

• Tanjore

Cochin •

• Jaffna

N

10°

Savulus

0   200 km

0   200 miles

INDIAN
OCEAN

Mughal Empire
1525–1605

———— Babur's domains 1525

------- Babur's expansion to 1539

▓▓▓ Mughal Empire c. 1600

▨▨▨ Maximum extent of
        Marahata rule

lxxxi

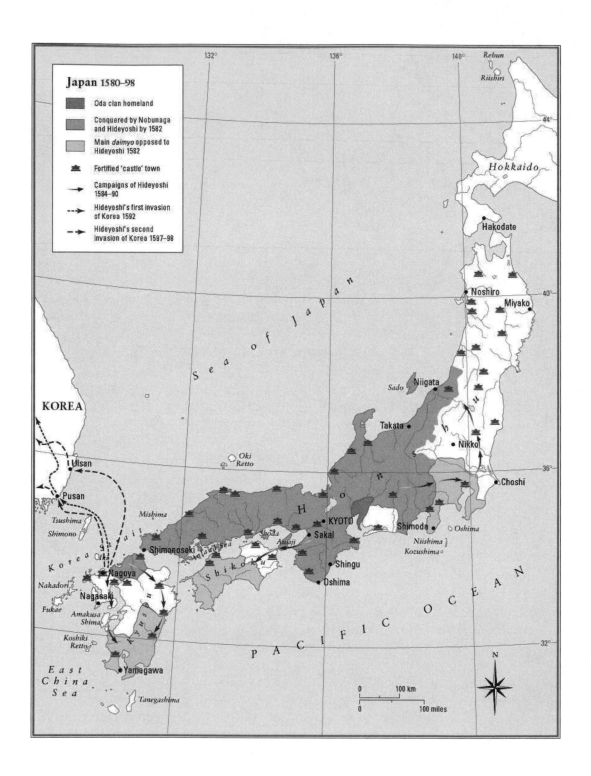

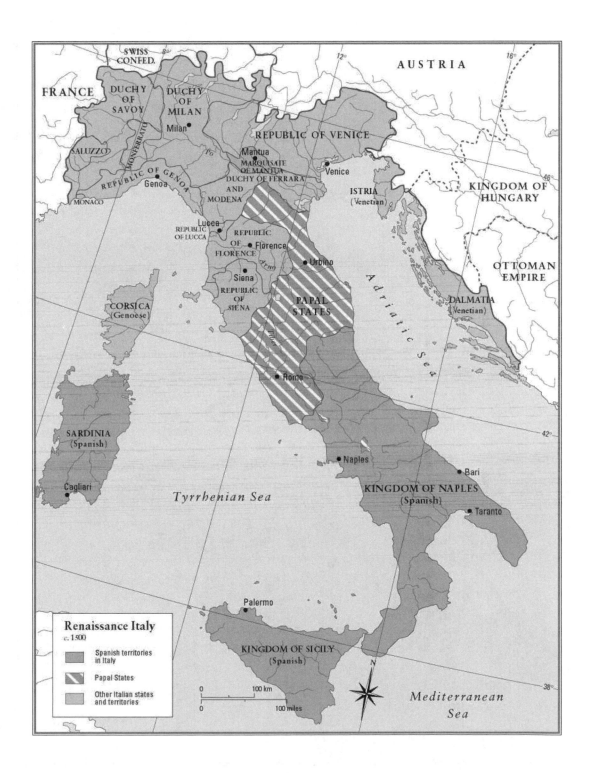

Renaissance Italy
c. 1500

- Spanish territories in Italy
- Papal States
- Other Italian states and territories

0   100 km
0   100 miles

SWISS CONFED.

FRANCE

DUCHY OF SAVOY

DUCHY OF MILAN

Milan

SALUZZO

MONFERRATO

REPUBLIC OF GENOA

Genoa

MONACO

Mantua

MARQUISATE OF MANTUA

DUCHY OF FERRARA AND MODENA

REPUBLIC OF VENICE

Venice

AUSTRIA

ISTRIA (Venetian)

KINGDOM OF HUNGARY

OTTOMAN EMPIRE

Lucca

REPUBLIC OF LUCCA

REPUBLIC OF FLORENCE

Florence

Siena

REPUBLIC OF SIENA

Urbino

PAPAL STATES

DALMATIA (Venetian)

Adriatic Sea

CORSICA (Genoese)

Rome

SARDINIA (Spanish)

Cagliari

Tyrrhenian Sea

Naples

KINGDOM OF NAPLES (Spanish)

Bari

Taranto

Palermo

KINGDOM OF SICILY (Spanish)

N

Mediterranean Sea

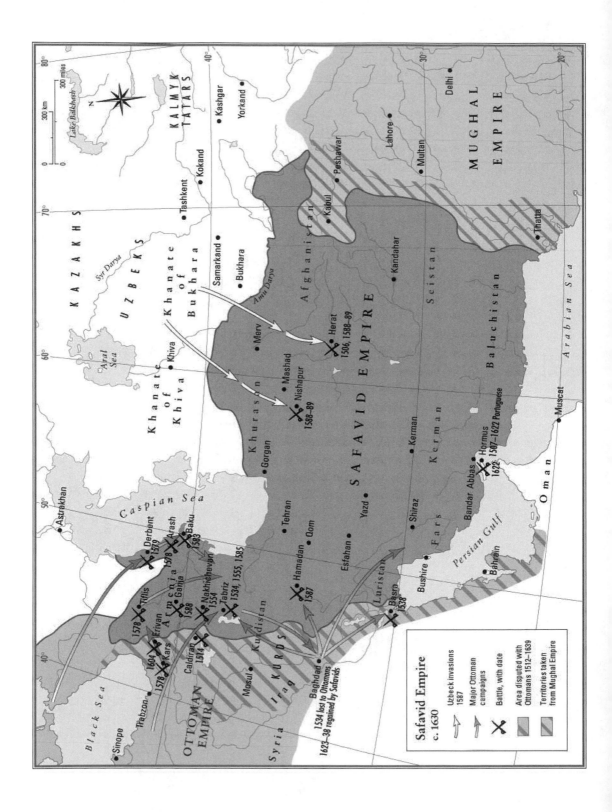

Safavid Empire
c. 1630

Uzbeck invasions
1587

Major Ottoman
campaigns

Battle, with date

Area disputed with
Ottomans 1512–1639

Territories taken
from Mughal Empire

KALMYK TATARS

Lake Balkhash

300 miles

300 km

N

KAZAKHS

Kashgar

Yorkand

Delhi

MUGHAL EMPIRE

Syr Darya

UZBEKS

Tashkent

Kokand

Lahore

Multan

Khanate of Bukhara

Samarkand

Bukhara

Peshawar

Kabul

Thatta

Aral Sea

Khiva

Amu Darya

Afghanistan

Kandahar

Khanate of Khiva

Merv

Herat
1506, 1588–89

Seistan

Baluchistan

Khurasan

Mashad

Nishapur
1588–89

SAFAVID EMPIRE

Astrakhan

Gorgan

Kerman

Hormus
1507–1622 Portuguese

Bandar Abbas
1622

Muscat

Caspian Sea

Tehran

Qom

Esfahan

Yazd

Kerman

Shiraz

Fars

Arabian Sea

Oman

Derbent
1579

Arash

Baku
1583

Hamadan
1587

Luristan

Persian Gulf

Bushire

Bahrain

Tiflis
1578

Ganja
1588

Erivan
1604

Armenia

Nakhichevan
1554

Tabriz
1534, 1555, 1585

Kars
1578

Caldiran
1514

Kurdistan

Basra
1538

Trabzon

Mosul

Iraq

Baghdad
1534 lost to Ottomans
1623–38 regained by Safavids

Sinope

Black Sea

OTTOMAN EMPIRE

Syria

lxxxiv

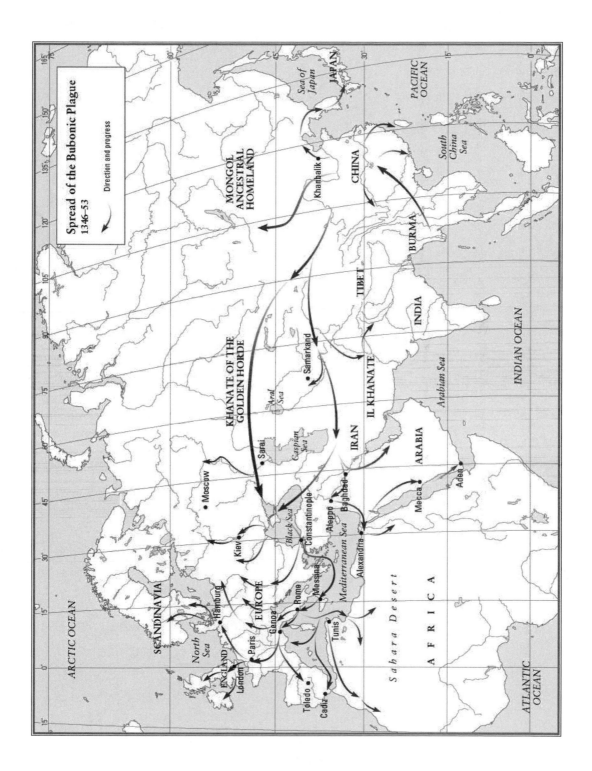

Spread of the Bubonic Plague
1346–53

Direction and progress

MONGOL
ANCESTRAL
HOMELAND

JAPAN

Sea of Japan

PACIFIC
OCEAN

Khanbalik

CHINA

South China Sea

BURMA

TIBET

INDIA

KHANATE OF THE
GOLDEN HORDE

Samarkand

Aral Sea

IL KHANATE

Arabian Sea

INDIAN OCEAN

Sarai

Caspian Sea

IRAN

ARABIA

Moscow

Mecca

Aden

Kiev

Constantinople

Baghdad

Aleppo

Black Sea

Alexandria

Hamburg

Rome

Messina

Mediterranean Sea

Sahara   Desert

EUROPE

Genoa

A F R I C A

Paris

Tunis

SCANDINAVIA

North Sea

ENGLAND

London

Toledo

Cadiz

ARCTIC OCEAN

ATLANTIC
OCEAN

abatis. An ancient field obstacle, dating at least to the wars of Rome. It was made from a felled tree laid lengthwise with sharpened branches left facing the enemy. Iron spikes were also used. Abatis protected miners and sappers working on a siege, and archers, musketeers, and cannon in the field.

Abbas I (1571–1629). "Abbas the Great." *Safavid* Shah of Iran (1587–1629). Abbas was a civilizer by inclination and a builder, not least of a grand capital at Isfahan starting in 1597. That move to central Iran was dictated by the military vulnerability of the then Safavid capital Qazwin, and the yet more vulnerable location of the original capital at Tabrīs. Mounting the throne at age 17, Abbas suffered early military defeat and was compelled to surrender large swaths of important territory to the Ottomans to the west—Christian Georgia and Azerbaijan, as well as Tabrīs—in order to concentrate on fighting the Uzbeks, who had captured several towns in northeastern Iran, including Herat (1588). This costly peace bought time to consolidate power over the fractious Iranian tribes by displacing them from their traditional place in the army. This proved to be Abbas' singular accomplishment: creation of a professional *standing army*. This was a radical change in a society where infantry played a minor role and feudal cavalry was the dominant arm. Moreover, Safavid cavalry was recruited by tribe and retained local rather than "national" or dynastic loyalties. The new system significantly reduced the number of horse soldiers available. These were replaced by infantry armed with muskets, units Abbas modeled on the *Janissaries*. This was intended to stop Ottoman gunpowder troops, who had so often beaten Iran's armies in the long century of war between these rival *sunni* and *shīa* empires that began at *Chaldiran* (1514). Abbas also drew directly from Western expertise: he built Iran's first artillery corps utilizing European *renegades*, notably *Robert Shirley* (whose brother, *Anthony Shirley*, Abbas made ambassador to the crowns of Europe). The shah also changed the ethnic mix of the army. Gone were the core Iranian tribes, replaced by Georgian, Armenian, and Circassian converts to Islam, descendants of Christian prisoners from earlier wars. These military slaves, or *"ghulams* of the shah,"* were prized and trusted because of their unique dependence on Abbas. This, too, imitated the close Janissary ties to the sultan.

As elsewhere, creation of a standing army soon led to a financial crisis. Where tribal cavalry was paid for by *servitor* warlords, the new troops were paid from central revenues. This meant, as it did with reforming monarchs in Europe, that Abbas had to modernize Iran's tax system and bureaucracy and reduce the grip of the old religious elite, in his case the *Qizilbash*. Once the reformed army was ready Abbas used it in a spectacular expansionist drive which carried almost to Iran's pre-Islamic borders, from the Indus at Kandahar to Baghdad in Iraq. In the first of a series of campaigns against the Ottomans, he retook Tabrīs in 1603. Through sieges of Erivan, Shirvan, and Mosul, he captured most of Iraq. Each side employed scorched earth tactics along the frontier to deny resources to the enemy, but in 1606 Abbas destroyed an Ottoman army at *Sis*. To the east, he retook Kandahar in 1621, a city seized by the *Mughals* under *Akbar* during his boyhood. Southward, in alliance with the *East India Company* (EIC) he captured Hormuz from the Portuguese in 1622. Shrewdly, in the rest of his empire he granted trading privileges to the EIC's main rival, the Dutch *Vereenigde Oostindische Compaagnie* (VOC). In 1623 he took Baghdad when its Ottoman garrison defected. While he was sometimes ruthless and cruel in court politics, in matters religious or commercial he was open to foreign ideas and practices. By the standards of the age he was a moderate, modernizing, and tolerant ruler.

Suggested Reading: Yves Bomati and Houchang Nahavandi, *Shah Abbas, Empereur de Perse, 1587–1629* (1998); Eskandar Beg Monshi, *History of Shah Abbas the Great*, Roger Savory, trans. (1978).

Aceh. An independent Muslim sultanate on Sumatra. In the 1530s, facing pressure from the Portuguese, it accepted military aid from the Ottoman Empire, including 300 musketeers for which it paid with four shiploads of black pepper. It contested Portuguese and Spanish control of Malacca for the next century. In 1588 *Philip II* rejected a call from his governor in India to attack Aceh, because Spain was already overcommitted to the *Invincible Armada.* In 1629, Sultan Iskandar Muda made a supreme, final effort to take Malacca. He lost the bulk of Aceh's fleet and army in the attempt: 250 ships and 20,000 men.

Acemi Oğlan. Training units of the *Janissary Corps.* They occupied two training centers in the capital where they carried out military education of boy recruits.

Acre, fall of (1291). See *Crusades*; *Knights Templar*.

adarga. A heart-shaped shield that originated among the Moors of North Africa, migrated from there to Iberia, and was subsequently adopted by Spanish *conquistadores*.

Aden. A key port in the Indian Ocean trade, located at the mouth of the Red Sea. It maintained an independent trade with Kilwa on the Sofala coast of East Africa during the 13th–15th centuries. In 1538 it was attacked by the Ottomans and captured in a classic galley action: an amphibious operation.

admiral. The term was imported to Europe from Arabic, where it meant an officer in command of a squadron (at the minimum) or fleet of ships. In most maritime communities during the Middle Ages, and well into the early modern period for some, admirals were often also land-based generals of note and authority. In several states admirals were responsible for recruiting men and outfitting ships, not necessarily for command at sea. In England, the Lord High Admiral was at times wholly land-based. He oversaw the Admiralty and naval administration. In several 16th–17th century Atlantic nations an admiral was the first rank in command of a fleet, ahead of a *vice admiral* and any *rear admiral*. See also *Laws of Olèron*.

admiralty. "Fleet." In this period, a geographical region of command, usually an expanse of coastal area for which an *admiral* (who was also often a general) was responsible. It was a practical administrative division with little significance for command rank.

Admiralty. See *Royal Navy*.

Adwalton Moor, Battle of (1643). See *English Civil Wars*; *Fairfax, Thomas*.

Affair of the Placards (October 18, 1534). French exiles had broadsheets printed in Switzerland, then pasted along routes passed by Catholics heading to Mass in Paris and other French cities. The placards were "sacramentarian" propaganda: they attacked Catholic belief in transubstantiation in vitriolic language that mocked the sacramental nature of the eucharist, and implicitly attacked its social and political purposes of communal union. The "Affair" caused deep anger among Catholics. *Francis I* responded with repression of French Protestants, increasingly seen as rebels as well as heretics. All religious printing was banned by decree. Francis turned the 1535 *Corpus Christi* procession into a heresy hunt, adding six executions by fire to the traditional feasting and prayers. Among others, the rector of the University of Paris and *Jean Calvin* fled to Geneva in the wake of the "Affair." Henceforth, distinctions between Catholic orthodoxy and Protestant "heresy" were more clear, with reform identified increasingly with rebellion as well as doctrinal error. See also *Edict of Saint-Germain*.

Afghanistan. See *Akbar*; *Babur*; *Mongols*; *Mughal Empire*; *Timur*.

aftercastle. A fighting platform or tower built over the stern of a warship from where archers or arqbusiers would shoot down onto an enemy's deck. Other fighting men would throw *caltrops*, hurl blinding lime with the wind, pour oil or resin to be lighted by fire arrows, and otherwise pelt the lower enemy deck with harmful inconveniences. Aftercastles were a common feature of 13th–14th-century ships.

Agincourt, Battle of (October 25, 1415). Fought on "St. Crispin's Day," late in the *Hundred Years' War* (1337–1453). *Henry V* crossed the Channel with 8,000 foot and 2,000 men-at-arms and embarked on an extended *chevauchée* into France. After a month's siege and losing one-third of his army, he captured Harfleur on September 22. On October 8 he headed for Calais, 120 miles away by direct march. The destruction he caused along the route and the smallness of his army provoked the French to block his crossing the Somme with a large force of men-at-arms serving as cavalry and heavy infantry. However, after six days of searching and hot pursuit Henry found a ford and slipped crossed (October 19). Outnumbered three to one, the English were forced to fight when the French pulled ahead of their line of march and blocked the way forward (October 24). Henry chose the ground: a narrow valley near the village of Agincourt, about 30 miles from Arras. His front was 1,200 yards wide, anchored at either end in small copses. He placed men-at-arms in three *battle*s at the center, each supported by longbowmen on the flanks. The archers were organized "en herse" (in farrows), adding to the line's crenelated look. Henry's small cavalry reserve was at the rear. To the front the field was sloppy with mud, after a week of rain. This careful position countered French numerical superiority, including a contingent of *Armagnacs*, which could not be exploited on such narrow frontage. Having faced longbows at *Crécy* (1346) and *Poitiers* (1356), most French knights and men-at-arms, about 8,000, dismounted to fight on foot. They deployed in two thick lines lightly salted with crossbowmen, with about 500 cavalry apiece on either flank. A large cavalry reserve formed a third, distant line.

When the French failed to advance, Henry moved his archers into range, at about 250 yards. His longbowmen planted *Spanish riders*, stuck clusters of arrows into the ground, and opened fire, sending an "arrow storm" arcing forward to kill and wound French knights where they stood. This provoked the first French line to advance through the mud, until it staggered into the English men-at-arms. As the heavily armored French slogged forward the archers leveled aim and shot them down at point-blank ranges, while men-at-arms cut them to pieces as they sank under the weight of armor, weapons, and sheer physical exhaustion. Once the archers exhausted arrow stocks they dropped bows and rushed forward to finish off the knights with dirks and short swords, or weapons dropped by dead or dying French. The second line of French men-at-arms also advanced, pushing into the backs of their panicking and dying comrades, and dying in turn as the fighting became a close and bloody mêlée. The mounted knights of the French reserve did nothing but watch and worry.

Many French were taken prisoner and shifted to the rear. When a scuffle broke out in the baggage train (armed French peasants attacked and looted it), Henry may have feared the prisoner knights might escape and attack his rear, so he ordered them killed. His men-at-arms refused, not from mercy but from concern for ransoms they might lose. Lower-class archers happily obeyed the order, however, impaling prisoners on swords, cutting throats, and burning some alive inside a thatch peasant cottage. The murders were halted when it became clear that no threat existed. In the interim 1,000 unarmed prisoners were butchered. The French reserve and survivors now balked at any suggestion of a final charge into the gore before them, and withdrew in great disorder. English dead numbered about 1,500, but as many as 8,000 French may have died at Agincourt. That was a spectacular rise in the sanguinary price of war brought about by the shift from cavalry to infantry as the principal arm of battle, and perhaps also a corresponding decline in the restraints and mores of *chivalry*. See also *Verneuil, Battle of*.

> *English dead numbered about 1,500, but as many as 8,000 French may have died at Agincourt.*

Suggested Reading: Alfred H. Burne, *The Agincourt War* (1956; 1999); John Keegan, *The Face of Battle* (1976).

Agnadello, Battle of (May 14, 1509). Early in the *Italian Wars* (1494–1559), a French army of 30,000 led by Louis XII stumbled into Venetian-paid *condottieri* at Agnadello, between Milan and Brescia. The French were part of the *League of Cambrai*, an anti-Venetian alliance dedicated to dismemberment and partition of the Republic. The Venetians fought off the first cavalry and pike assaults, but failed to bring up reinforcements as some mercenaries bolted to live to fight (or at least draw pay) another day. The rest were overrun. Venice lost several thousand men and its artillery train. After the battle, *Maximilian I* forced Venice to make large territorial and political concessions. See also *Holy League*.

Ahlspiess. A *halberd* with a medium-sized haft but an extra-long spike.

ailettes. Small armor plates sometimes attached to *spaudlers*. They provided little added protection and may have been merely decorative.

Ain Jalut, Battle of (1260). See *Ayn Jālut, Battle of*; *Mamlūks*; *Mongols*.

Aïr, Kingdom of. See *Tuareg*.

Akbar (1542–1605). "The Great." Mughal Emperor. In 1562 Akbar wrested control from his harem and regent and launched a new era in Indian history: he sought accommodation with old *Rajput* foes by hiring many into his army, and he married a Rajput woman. Still, he could be ruthless toward resisters, as when he reduced the Rajput city of Chitor and slaughtered 30,000 inhabitants in 1568. Overall, he extended toleration to Hindus, ended forced conversions to Islam, abolished the hated *jizya* tax on non-Muslims ("dhimmîs"), and lifted the Mughal ban on building new Hindu temples and shrines.

And he donated land in Amritsar to the Sikhs, who built the Golden Temple there. Akbar altered the administrative power structure of Mughal society, establishing new provincial emirs ("mansabdar") whom he watched with a vast intelligence network of spies and informers in every subdistrict, including runners and camel messengers who delivered secret intelligence directly to him. He distrusted the "ulema" (community of Islamic scholars), whom he had offended by toleration of, and apparent personal interest in, other Indian faiths. Muslims were also alienated by his fiscal assault on their hitherto tax-protected estates, even though his expensive state still rested mainly on hard-pressed peasants taxed at suffocating rates. In 1579 his policies contributed to a revolt by Muslim emirs in Afghanistan.

The mature Mughal military system laid great emphasis on fixed fortresses guarding strategic locations, manned by garrisons of loyal infantry. The field army consisted mostly of cavalry, with contingents of war elephants borrowed from the pre-Muslim Indian military tradition, and poor supporting infantry. Akbar expanded the infantry and added an artillery corps. Akbar was a restless warrior king—though not a notable general—overseeing an unstable but still expanding realm. His Rajput and Mughal generals conquered Gujarat in 1572 and Bengal in 1576. In 1581 they took Kabul, reversing an age-old pattern of invasion of India from Afghanistan. In 1592 Akbar conquered Orissa, and three years later added Baluchistan to the Empire. While he modernized the regime and army he never brought stability to the Empire or escaped the trap of further expansion that made it more unwieldy and prone to chronic rebellion. In his old age even his son, Salim, rebelled (1601), a common succession problem for empires rooted in Central Asian warrior cultures and governed by absolutist dynasties. Akbar died in 1605 after 47 years on the throne. He may have been poisoned by his son.

aketon. Also "haketon." A stuffed cloth or leather garment worn under a mail *hauberk*.

akincis/akinjis. Light horse, paid in booty. Recruited from villages and the countryside, they were a key element in Ottoman armies in the 14th–15th centuries, numbering perhaps 50,000 in all. They shrank to an auxiliary and scouting role over the course of the 16th century. They were only marginal by the 17th century as the Empire adopted state-paid, professional forces. Once the Tatars allied with the Ottomans they assumed the foraging and scouting role formerly performed by akincis.

Akritai. Frontier troops of the Byzantine Empire.

akutō. "Evil bands." Wild, independent bands of lower-class infantry and some *ronin*, who proliferated during the *Sengoku* period in Japan. They took refuge in high mountain forts (*jōkaku*).

Alais, Peace of (June 28, 1629). See *Edict of Alès*.

Alamut, Battle of (1234). See *Assassins*; *Mongols*.

al-Andalus. This Muslim kingdom in southern Spain sustained, along with southern Italy, a wealthy urban culture long after the decline of most other cities in Western Europe. It was host to the Umayyad Caliphate that ruled from Córdoba, but collapsed in 1008 to be replaced by dozens of *taifa* states. See also *mercenaries*; *Reconquista*.

Alarcos, Battle of (1195). See *Castile*; *Reconquista*.

Alba, Don Fernando Álvarez de Toledo, duque de (1507–1582). Castilian general and *Counter-Reformation* fanatic. At age 16 he signed up to fight the French in Italy. His noble birth conduced to the usual quick rise in rank, but in Alba's case bravery in action confirmed the justice of his ascent: his courage was noted at *Pavia*, in Hungary, and on *Charles V*'s expedition to Algiers. He made general by age 26 and was commander-in-chief of all Habsburg armies at 30. He fought against the *Schmalkaldic League* (1546–1547), crushing the German princes at *Mühlburg* (1547). His victories in Germany made him a court favorite, and Charles sent him back to Italy when the *Italian Wars* resumed. Alba defeated the French at Marciano (1553) and pushed *François de Guise* out of southern Italy by 1556. Alba next enjoyed the trust of *Philip II*, whom he encouraged to believe that every problem of the Spanish crown and empire—and these were legion—was amenable to an unpitying military solution and calculated cruelty. Alba represented Philip at the negotiations leading to the *Peace of Cateau-Cambrésis* (1559), ending the 65-year conflict with France over control of Italy. Philip sent Alba north in 1567, at age 60, with orders to crush the Dutch rebellion and prosecute his perpetual crusade against Protestantism. Alba promised to do the job with his usual ruthlessness, saying: "I have tamed men of iron. . . . I shall know how to deal with these men of butter." He began his sojourn in the Netherlands by garrisoning the most important towns with *tercio* veterans. Next, he established a trial court, the "Council of Troubles," which bitter Protestants quickly dubbed his "Council of Blood." Alba used the Council to try 8,950 people, many in absentia, condemning most for treason or heresy or both, and confiscating their property in the usual style of an Inquisition. Alba's Council executed over 1,000 people, including leading Flanders nobles (84 on January 4, 1568, alone), starting with *Egmont* and others who thought they had settled their differences with the king. Perhaps 60,000 more fled into exile, where they organized under the Princes of Nassau and plotted their return. This ensured that the rebellion grew in strength and determination and that Alba's name would be forever linked to the *"Black Legend"* of Spain. For all that, he was merely the trigger, not the cause, of the great revolt of the Netherlands.

Alba handily beat *Louis of Nassau* at *Jemmingen* (July 21, 1568), and subsequently pushed a mercenary army under *William the Silent* out of Brabant. As tens of thousands of refugees fled the Netherlands for Germany and England the circle of Protestant states and princes opposed to Philip II expanded. Alba did not understand this or care: his policy was always calculated terror, carried out by judicial murder of nobles and wholesale massacres of rebel and heretic townsfolk—it was later his proud boast that he executed 18,000 Dutch heretics. He even proposed breaking the dams and sluices to flood rebel areas, drowning all heretics within; but Philip forbade him. Still, whole populations in breached and broken rebel towns like Mechlen and Naarden were butchered, as was the garrison of *Haarlem* after it surrendered in July 1573. That same year Alba's troops mutinied for want of pay. Then he was checked in his attempt to capture *Alkmaar* (1573) and was recalled to Spain. At 73 he was entrusted to secure Portugal for Philip II, which he did upon winning his last battle at *Alcántara* in 1580. He died two years later. See also *maps*; *prisoners of war*.

Suggested Reading: W. Maltby, *Alba* (1983).

Albania. Mountainous Albania has most often been part of other people's empires: the ancient Greeks, the Romans, and the Byzantines all held some or all of Albania under their sway. From the 11th to the 13th centuries coastal Albania was contested ground between the declining power of Byzantium and rising seaborne power of the dominant warrior-people of Latin Christendom, the *Normans*. In the 14th century Albania was overrun by Serbs. In turn, Serbs and Albanians were conquered and ruled by the Ottoman Empire; in Albania's case for several centuries. It was conquered by the Ottomans in stages, partly with the help of Albanian chieftains who allied with the invader against local rivals, though the conquest was fiercely resisted by others. Albania's struggle against conquest was aided by a revolt of the *Janissary* garrison in 1443, but was completed by *Muhammad II* in 1468. The Ottomans governed lightly, leaving much of Albania's local custom intact though converting most of its people to Islam.

Albert, Archduke of Austria (1559–1621). Son of *Maximilian II*; husband of Isabella, daughter of *Philip II*. Appointed Spain's governor in Brussels along with his wife (they were known jointly as "The Archdukes"), Albert marched out to intercept *Maurits of Nassau* on the way to relieve the *Siege of Ostend*. They met in battle at *Nieuwpoort*, where Albert's *tercios* were badly beaten among the dunes. The insistence by the Archdukes on nominal acceptance by the United Provinces of their sovereignty over all the Netherlands was a stumbling block to peace prior to the *Twelve Years' Truce* (1609–1621).

Albigensian Crusade (1208–1229). The Albigenses, or "Cathars" ("Cathari"), were a 12th–13th-century Christian sect concentrated in Languedoc and elsewhere in southern France that cleaved to a radical vegan diet, a Manichean image of the nature of good and evil, pacifism, and rejection of the doctrine that Jesus of Nazareth had a corporeal and incorporeal nature. They held that the Catholic Church was evil, that the only true Christian faithful were the "parfaits" (or "perfecti," or "perfect ones"), known by the poverty and asceticism of their lives. Worldly wealth of the monastery, cathedral, or feudatory was a sure sign of sin, corruption, and faithlessness. This change was hotly condemned as heretical by the Church, which was eagerly supported by outraged northern French nobility. The Cathar revolt against the corrupt rich of clergy and nobility was the gravest challenge to the authority of the Church prior to the *Hussite Wars* and the *Protestant Reformation*. The Church responded to the recruiting success of the sect's ascetic preachers, including conversion of some southern nobles, by sending Bernard of Clairvaux and his Cistercian brethren, followed later by St. Dominic and his fanatic friars, to counter-preach in Cathar areas. The contest turned violent from 1208 when a papal legate was murdered. Pope Innocent III (r.1198–1216) retaliated by pro-claiming a crusade against the Cathar "heretics." Catholics lined up behind a regional warlord, Simon de Montfort, while Cathars looked to their noble converts and hired thousands of *routiers*. They also accepted informal alliance with Aragon, which had designs on Languedoc.

The northern nobility savagely repressed the Cathars, burning and wreaking much of Languedoc in a brutal *guerre mortelle*. They massacred by sword and burned Cathars at the stake, and killed routiers with merciless cruelty. In fact, so many routiers died that France enjoyed an unusual internal peace of several decades once the Cathar wars ended. Among the horrors of a notoriously awful war, Simon de Montfort had the population of the town of Bram blinded, except for an old man he left to guide

> *They massacred by sword and burned Cathars at the stake . . .*

them. In an unconnected act of justice, he was killed in 1218 by a stone trebuchet ball ("pomme") reportedly fired toward him by women from inside fortified Toulouse, which he was besieging.

As was usual in medieval warfare, the Cathar wars were a matter of sieges and savage *chevauchées* rather than set-piece battles. Only one large battle took place, at Muret (September 12, 1213), where de Montfort defeated a Cathar-Catalan army. In addition to the religious divide the war spoke to regional rivalry: Languedoc nobles who protected the Cathars were besieged in their great castles by armies of Catholic knights from the north. The Catholics brought with them the new counterweight trebuchet, with which they battered down thin-walled southern castles. Capetian monarchs also used the war to expand royal reach into Languedoc: Louis VIII personally led an ex-pedition south in 1226. After most fighting ended in 1229 a Dominican *Inquisition* set out to ferret out lingering "heresy." Over several decades all Cathars were hunted down and their belief eradicated. However, powerful regional resentments of northern and Catholic power lingered to play some role in the *French Civil Wars*, and even after.

Suggested Reading: Stephen O'Shea, *The Perfect Heresy* (2000); Steven Runciman, *The Medieval Manichee* (1947; 1961); Jonathon Sumption, *The Albigensian Crusade* (1978).

d'Albuquerque, Alfonso de (1453–1515). Portuguese admiral, explorer, and empire-builder. He voyaged to India in 1503 and again in 1506. In 1507 he led a failed expedition to capture *Hormuz*. He retreated to India where a rival Portuguese commander jailed him. He was released in 1509. The next year he took Goa, adding it to the growing number of coastal enclaves that constituted *Portuguese India*. He understood that a large territorial empire was beyond his country's abilities, if not to acquire, at least to hold. Instead, he captured Malacca in 1511 and finally took Hormuz in 1514, adding both territories to a growing seaborne but essentially coastal empire. He carefully fortified these and other enclaves which serviced armed traders and the navy and could be defended by shipboard artillery, gaining a foothold for Portugal in the international *spice trade* hitherto controlled by Muslim middlemen and dominated by Venice at its terminus in the Mediterranean.

alcabala. A form of early sales tax imposed in Castile and critical to Imperial Spain's system of *war finance*. In 1571 *Philip II* modeled a new Netherlands tax, the *Tenth Penny*, on the alcabala.

alcancia. "firepots." Small incendiaries that were thrown like hand grenades during ship-to-ship close fighting. They were in use in most navies into the late 16th century. Not to be confused with the earlier *pots des fer*.

Alcántara, Battle of (August 25, 1580). When the Portuguese king died in 1580 without an heir, *Philip II* claimed the throne for Spain. The *Duke of Alba* led a tough, veteran Spanish army into Portugal. Most Portuguese nobles backed the Spanish merger, but popular opinion did not. A ragtag army of peasants and townsfolk, and some knights, met the Spanish at Alcántara. The fight was one-sided, and after the Spanish routed the defenders Portugal and its entire empire were annexed to Spain.

Alcántara, Knights of. See *Knights of Alcántara*.

Alcazarquivir, Battle of (August 4, 1578). "Battle of the Three Kings." The Portuguese invaded Morocco in 1578, taking advantage of a Moroccan civil and religious war raging among several factions organized by fanatic desert *marabouts*. The Portuguese shrewdly engaged Muslim allies, followers of one candidate in the struggle for the Moroccan throne. The armies of three rivals met about 60 miles south of Tangier, at Alcazarquivir. The fighting was so ferocious it led to the deaths of "Three Kings": the Moroccan pretender allied to the Portuguese, the King of Fes, and King Sebastian of Portugal.

Alexandria, Siege of (1364). A Cypriot-Hospitaller galley fleet of 165 ships landed besiegers and took up blockade positions off Alexandria. The *mamlūks* defended their city with *naphtha* flamethrowers and incendiary bombs, traditional and gunpowder artillery, and liquid ammonia to blind assaulting troops. When the city fell its Christian attackers raped indiscriminately, and slaughtered 20,000 men, women, and children.

alferes. In the Iberian *Military Orders*, this low-ranking officer was the standard bearer.

Alfonso V (1432–1481). "The African." King of Portugal. He campaigned successfully against the Moors of North Africa, taking *Tangier* in 1471. But he failed in his more ambitious attempt to marry Isabella of Castile. He lost the war he waged to seize control of Castile and León. He abdicated in 1476, but was compelled to ascend the throne again under the shadow of Spain. He died of plague.

Alfonso XI (1312–1350). See *Algeciras, Siege of*; *Gibraltar*; *Reconquista*.

Alford, Battle of (July 2, 1645). Even as *Charles I* was losing the first *English Civil War* in England, the Royalist cause was waxing in Scotland under the *Marquis of Montrose*. A small *Covenanter* army moved north to check Montrose's advances. He feigned a retreat that led the Covenanters into a trap at Alford, where they suffered heavy casualties. A campaign of maneuver then took both armies south.

Algeciras, Siege of (1344). Following his victory at Río Salado (October 20, 1340), Alfonso XI moved to besiege Algeciras. His allied army from Castile and León was supported by the *Military Orders*. The Christians nearly destroyed the city in the process of capturing it, during heavy fighting. Two *Mestres* of the *Knights of Alcántara* died during the siege. The fall of Algeciras left only *Granada* in Muslim hands. The "gentle, parfait Knight" of Chaucer's *Canterbury Tales* was present at Algeciras, as were the English Earls of Derby and Arundel. See also *Reconquista*.

Algiers. Algiers was governed by a succession of Arab-Berber dynasties: Fatamids, Almoravids, Almohads, and Marinds. With the swing in military favor toward the Christian kingdoms in Iberia during the *Reconquista*, Muslim principalities in Africa faced a new naval threat. They built galley navies of their own and became known in Europe as the *Barbary corsairs*. Algiers supported major corsair raids on the lucrative trade of the western Mediterranean into the Italian Renaissance, and on a lesser scale for another 300 years after that. With the dominance of the Ottomans in the eastern Mediterranean, and with Spanish power ascendant in the West, Algiers proved unable to maintain its independence. The "corsairs" turned to the Ottomans for help against Spain and Venice. The price exacted was Ottoman suzerainty over Algiers, although the city retained de facto independence. From 1518 Algiers served as the main Ottoman port in the western Mediterranean. That year, its corsair leader was chased out by Spanish and Zayanid (a new dynasty) forces. His brother, Khair al-Din, returned in 1525 as Ottoman pasha. He resumed corsair ways, briefly occupying Tunis in 1534. A Christian fleet under *Andrea Doria* attacked in force in 1541, but was repulsed with heavy losses. Algiers and its hinterland was subsequently ruled by *deys*, nominally in behalf of the Ottomans.

Alhama de Granada, Battle of (1482). See *Reconquista*.

Ali Pasha. See *Lepanto, Battle of (October 7, 1571)*.

Aljubarrota, Battle of (August 14, 1385). Portugal was threatened with takeover by Castile when Ferdinand I died in 1383. His illegitimate half-brother, then head of the *Order of Aviz*, led the knights in blocking a Castilian succession to the Portuguese throne, proclaiming himself King Juan I. Another Juan I sat on Castile's throne, however, and he invaded Portugal with 18,000 cavalry and 10,000 foot to assert his claim. About 200 Aviz knights, along with 7,500 infantry, met the invaders at Aljubarrota, north of Lisbon. In the Portuguese ranks were English and Gascon mercenaries, tough veterans of the *Hundred Years' War* (1337–1453) with France. The Portuguese also adopted the tactics developed by *Edward III*: infantry and dismounted men-at-arms were positioned at the center of their line, protected by large units of archers anchored just forward of each flank and smaller groups at the flank of each infantry echelon. Their enemies fought in the old way. As was the case in France, in Portugal the new archery tactics and dismounted knights defeated massed heavy horse, the flower of the chivalry of Castile. The victory secured Portugal's independence from Castile.

Alkmaar, Siege of (August 21–October 8, 1573). Early in the *Eighty Years' War* (1568–1648), Dutch resolve and fighting capacity was tested at Alkmaar. After capturing *Haarlem*, the *Duke of Alba* moved with 16,000 ruthless *tercio* veterans to besiege Alkmaar, which was defended by just 2,000 militia. The townsfolk successfully resisted the first assault, then opened the dikes. Alba responded with a siege and by bringing up an inland fleet, but it was bested by the "*Sea Beggars*" in a sharp fight on the Zuider Zee. The victory was the first successful rebel defense of a major town, as well as the last battle fought in the north by Alba.

alla moderna. "The modern style." The Italian term for the new style of *bastion* fortification that was invented in central Italy, and hence known everywhere else as the *trace italienne*.

Allerheim, Battle of (1645). See *Mercy, Franz von*; *Nördlingen, Second Battle of*.

Almiranta. The vice-flagship of a Spanish war fleet. The Admiral sailed on the *Capitana*.

Almogavars. Mountain soldiers drawn from the shepherds of Aragon and Catalonia. They fought mainly for Aragon. They disdained all metal armor in preference for leather so that they were far more agile than any armored enemy, who were in any case forced by the mountainous terrain in which the Almogavars lived to dismount to fight them. Almogavar fleetness afoot gave them their name, which was derived from the Arabic "mugâwir" or "runner." See also *Catalan Great Company*.

Almohads. See *Algiers*; *caliph*; *Castile*; *Gibraltar*; *"holy war"*; *Ifriqiya*; *Maghreb*; *Morocco*; *Reconquista*; *taifa states*.

Almoravids. See *Algiers*; *caliph*; *Castile*; *"holy war"*; *Reconquista*; *taifa states*; *Tuareg*.

Alte Feste, Siege of (August 24–September 18, 1632). "Fürth." *Albrecht von Wallenstein* assumed a strong defensive position at the Alte Feste (Alte Veste) near Nürnberg to await the advancing Swedish army. *Gustavus Adolphus* grew impatient and attacked him, twice, but failed to carry the Catholic lines. After two days Gustavus withdrew with a loss of some 2,000 dead, *Johann Banér* wounded, and *Lennart Torstensson* captured. This rebuff, and the lure of Wallenstein's gold and reputation as a reliable paymaster, induced some mercenaries to switch from the Protestant side. Gustavus marched south to eat out Swabia and Bavaria, but Wallenstein marched into Saxony and took Leipzig, drawing Gustavus back north. The armies met again at *Lützen*.

Altmark, Truce of (September 26, 1629). This truce of exhaustion between Sweden and Poland was to last six years. In fact, it restored peace after seven decades of war in northeast Europe and was extended for another 26 years at Stuhmsdorf (1635). Altmark concluded the active phase of the Polish–Swedish struggle that had resumed following expiration of the *Truce of Tolsburg* in 1621. Mediated by Cardinal *Richelieu* and Georg Wilhelm of Brandenburg, it freed *Gustavus Adolphus* to intervene in Germany in 1630. It left part of Livonia in Swedish hands, but otherwise reflected the military stalemate reached earlier that summer. See also *Oxenstierna*.

Alton, Battle of (1643). See *Waller, William*.

Alva. See *Alba, Don Fernando Álvarez de Toledo, duque de*.

Alvarado, Pedro de (1485–1541). *Conquistadore*. He explored the coast of Yucatan in 1518, then accompanied *Cortés* to Vera Cruz and the Central Valley of Mexico in 1519. During Cortés' absence from Tenochtitlán (1520), Alvarado's torments of Aztec priests and murder of nobles in a relentless search for gold provoked the city to rise. He survived the causeway escape of the *"Noche Triste"* (June 30, 1520) to fight in the desperate action at *Otumba* (1520) and in the *Second Siege of Tenochtitlán* (1521). He was made "alcalde" (governor) of the city's smoking ruins. Reckless and ill-tempered, he argued constantly with other conquistadore commandants. In 1524 he campaigned in Central America (Guatemala), and later in northern Mexico and modern Ecuador (1534). Late in life he was made a *Knight of Santiago*, by then a hollow shell of the former *Military Order* which survived as a mere civil list.

Alwa. "Maquerra." An early medieval, sudanic, and Christian kingdom on the upper Nile (Nubia). In the 10th century it was still able to keep Muslim traders away from its borders, though it conducted trade with *Mamlūk* Egypt. Its king was captured by a mamlūk army in 1316, and replaced by a Muslim ruler. Alwa migrated farther south, but was unable to fend off nomadic Arabicized tribes also migrating southward. It fragmented into several smaller states, some of which survived into the late 15th century.

Amasya, Peace of (May 1555). This treaty ended a protracted Ottoman–Safavid war, whereupon the Safavids removed their capital to Qazwin from Tabrīs. Iran recognized Ottoman suzerainty over Iraq and eastern Anatolia, while *Suleiman I* accepted Iranian rule over parts of Azerbaijan and the Caucasus. The peace lasted until an Ottoman offensive in 1578, timed to take advantage of a period of weakness under Shah Muhammad Khudabanda (1578–1587). This territorial division of Muslim lands along sectarian lines paralleled Christian divisions in Germany codified in the *Peace of Augsburg* the same year.

Amboise, Conspiracy of (March 1560). The French court was dominated by the *Guise* brothers, who exerted great influence over their young nephew, *Francis II*. Armed Protestant nobles conspired to kidnap Francis from his summer palace at Amboise. Their intent was to free him from the influence of the radical Catholic Guise, whom they would dismiss, arrest, try, and execute. Before the plot could be carried out it was disrupted by troops sent to Amboise by the duc de Guise. In the aftermath, hundreds of Protestant nobles were tortured and executed, or drowned in the Loire. Corpses were left hanging on the palace walls at Amboise into April as a warning to all heretic-rebels. The Guise arrested *Condé*, who played no role in the conspiracy but whom they planned to execute to settle an old, personal score. But Francis died suddenly (December 5, 1560), permitting *Catherine de Medici* to proclaim herself regent for her other minor son, Charles IX. In the short run, the Guise were checked and retreated to Lorraine while Protestants seized towns, including Lyon, and raised troops. Longer term, the "conspiracy of Amboise" confirmed the fears of most Catholics that the Huguenots were seditious rebels even before they were heretics. *Jean Calvin* later wrote to *Coligny* disassociating himself from the attempt to usurp a king's rightful authority, though *John Knox* moved in a different direction.

Amboise, Peace of (1563). See *Edict of Amboise*.

Amiens, Siege of (1597). See *Franco-Spanish War*.

ammunition. See *arrows*; *artillery*; *ballot*; *bolt*; *bullets*; *cannonballs*; *case shot*; *chain shot*; *dice shot*; *grapeshot*; *gunpowder weapons*; *hail shot*; *hot shot*; *quarrel*; *shells*; *small shot*; *solid shot*.

amphibious warfare. See *Aden*; *Antwerp, Siege of*; *Aztec Empire*; *birlin*; *conquistadores*; *Cossacks*; *galley*; *Gravelines, Battle of*; *Drake, Francis*; *Hakata Bay, Battle of (1274)*; *Hakata Bay, Battle of (1281)*; *Henry V, of England*; *Hundred Years' War*; *Janissary Corps*; *lymphad*; *Nine Years' War*; *Normans*; *Sea Beggars*; *tarides*; *wakō*; *war at sea*.

amsār. An Arab military colony and administrative center. Initially, *Bedouin* warriors in conquered lands lived inside the amsār according to tribe. Over time, the markets they provided and the centers of military and political power they represented led to growth of administrative cities around the garrisons. As a result, amsār played a key role in Arabization and conversion to Islam of non-Arab and non-Muslim peoples. Not least important in this process was the assimilation into Arab armies of non-Arab converts who resented the entrenched privileges of Bedouin and demanded, and effected, reform.

Anabaptism. A fervent, minority Protestant sect that first arose in Zürich under the guidance of Conrad Grebel, who broke with *Zwingli* in the mid-1520s and was vehemently opposed by *Martin Luther*. It was especially prominent in the Netherlands after 1530. Elsewhere, it was a marginal movement. Doctrinally, Anabaptism was prone to frequent fractures; politically, it lurched toward anarchism. Emotionally and psychologically, early Anabaptists were excitable, often violent, *iconoclastic* utopians who believed in a voluntary church of true believers as opposed to uniform religious belief and practice enforced by the state. They objected, therefore, to infant baptism, arguing instead that baptism be confined to consenting adults who understood the spiritual obligations it demanded. This opposed them to mainstream cultural acceptance that infant baptism inaugurated a child into the spiritual

> *Anabaptists were burned, decapitated, or drowned for their faith, the latter a particularly vicious form of symbolic retribution.*

care of the believing congregation. Adult baptism was first performed in Zürich on January 21, 1525. It was made a capital offense on March 7, and families who declined to submit newborns for baptism were expelled from the city. *Charles V* made adult baptism a capital offense throughout the Holy Roman Empire in 1529. It has been estimated that between 1525 and 1618 from 1,500 to 5,000 Anabaptists were burned, decapitated, or drowned for their faith, the latter a particularly vicious form of symbolic retribution.

Anabaptism divided into two main factions. The first was determined to take up arms against all comers. Adherents of this group ran naked through the streets of Amsterdam in 1534, threatening the ungodly with swords and hellfire. One group later attacked a monastery with artillery. Others sacked churches and smashed altars, images, and statuary. A large group of aggressive, polygamist Anabaptists seized control of Münster, in Westphalia. They quickly set up a radical theocracy and persecuted all in the city who would not undergo adult baptism. Hundreds of armed Anabaptists joined them as

Münster was besieged for 18 months (1534–1535), before succumbing. Along with the *German Peasant War* (1525), the Anabaptist revolution in Münster was seen by Lutherans and Calvinists as the dark underside of Protestantism.

The other faction was eventually formed by the vast majority of Anabaptists who took the lessons of Münster to heart and became radical pacifists who eschewed arms and war, and religious separatists who declined to participate in any coercive acts or responsibilities of the state. They set up segregated communities that sought to remain aloof from worldly struggle and war, but were persecuted just as fiercely as their more aggressive and violent co-sectarians. By far, the majority executed in the Spanish Netherlands on charges of "heresy" were Anabaptists; they were also persecuted north of the rivers throughout the first four decades of the new Dutch Republic. Mennonites were specially targeted from 1596. After 1612 the situation improved as confessional lines settled down and each sect had less to fear from mass conversion or reconversion to the faith of its enemies. Anabaptists thus survived on the margin of Dutch society. In 1650 they formed about 5 percent of the Dutch population.

Suggested Reading: C-P. Clasen, *Anabaptism* (1972); A. Verheyden, *Anabaptism in Flanders, 1530–1650* (1961).

Anatolia. See *Ankara, Battle of*; *Byzantine Empire*; *Iran*; *Mongols*; *Ottoman Empire*; *Turks*.

ancient. A ship's flag; an ensign.

Andorra, Principality of. A political curiosity even for the Middle Ages. Holy Roman Emperor Charles II appointed the Archbishop of Urgel to control Andorra, but this was disputed by the local prince, the Comte de Foix. In 1278 a compromise was agreed whereby joint suzerainty was established. Andorra remained for centuries a feudal holding of the archbishops, while on the French side it was considered an independent princedom ruled by successive Comtes de Foix, who controlled Andorra to 1574 when their claim finally passed to the crown during the *French Civil Wars*.

Anegawa, Battle of (July 22, 1570). *Nobunaga Oda* and *Tokugawa Ieyasu* joined forces to defeat their main northern enemies, the *daimyo* Azai Nagamasa and Asakura Yoshikage. Tokugawa's men attacked the Asakura position while Nobunagu's forces held back the Azai. Once Tokugawa pushed all Asakura troops from the field he wheeled to take the Azai position in the right flank. Nobunaga then committed his reserve against the left flank, and the battle was won. See also *Unification Wars*.

Angola. See *Ngola*.

Angora, Battle of. See *Ankara, Battle of*.

d'Anjou, duc (1555–1584). Né François. Youngest son of *Henri II* and *Catherine de Medici*, brother of *Francis II*, *Charles IX*, and *Henri III*. Although he had no Protestant inclinations he was so politically ambitious he briefly allied with the Huguenots. Along with *Henri de Navarre*, d'Anjou was held prisoner at court for three years, from the first night of the *St. Bartholomew's Day Massacres* (August 24, 1572) until his escape on September 15, 1575. He took refuge among the Huguenots in the Midi, with whom he sided in the fifth of the *French Civil Wars*. He was closely associated with the *Edict of Beaulieu* ("Peace of Monsieur") in 1576. That reconciled him to the childless Henri III and to French Catholics worried about the succession. D'Anjou was touted as a match for *Elizabeth I*, but she found him physically repellant when they met in 1579 and probably never intended to marry him in any case. Instead, he was installed by *William the Silent* as "prince and lord" of the Dutch rebel provinces, which had rejected *Philip II* but were not yet ready to establish a republic. The deal was signed in September 1580 and d'Anjou arrived in January 1581. He proved an inept military commander immediately, and a treacherous leader over time. Fretting over restraints on his authority, he attempted a coup in Flanders and Brabant in January 1583, seizing Aalst and Dunkirk, but failing to take Antwerp. Tired of his plots and battlefield ineptitude, the Beggars forced him to leave the Netherlands. His unexpected death, in June 1584, left Henri de Navarre presumptive heir to the French throne.

Ankara, Battle of (July 20, 1402). Also known as "Angora." Having won decisively at *Nicopolis*, Sultan *Bayezid I* besieged Constantinople. Meanwhile, *Timur* invaded Asia Minor with a large Mongol-Tatar army, and sacked Aleppo, Damascus, and Baghdad. Bayezid broke off the siege and turned east to meet the Tatars at Ankara. Cavalry predominated on both sides, feudal levies for the Ottomans and light steppe cavalry under Timur. The *Janissaries* fought well, holding several hilltops in a defensive line. But the Ottoman *timariots* and *sipahis* deserted in droves before the highly skilled and motivated Tatar assault. Bayezid was captured and shortly after killed himself, setting off an Ottoman civil war over the succession.

annates. Fees tendered to a pope upon appointment to a "reserved" office. Such fees, amounting to a full year's income of a bishopric, or more, were key to papal financial adjustment to the new money economy. They also occasioned fierce opposition from all opposed to Ultramontane claims by the popes. See also *Council of Trent*.

Antichrist. The Apocalyptic opponent of Jesus of Nazareth ("The Christ") who was expected by the early and Medieval Church, and by all millenarians in spirit, to appear on Earth before the Final Judgment at the "End of the World." Depictions of confessional opponents as the Antichrist were both sincere and commonplace in propaganda of the wars of religion.

anti-Semitism. Anti-Semitism as a virulent, specific hatred of Jews was, until modern times, commonly found among Christians rather than Muslims, though it was known to Islam as well. In this period, anti-Semitism was state policy in Spain, Turkey, Poland, Russia, the Holy Roman Empire, and the Berber states. It usually took the form of proscriptions on the occupations Jews might enter and restrictions on where they could live. Jews were forced into ghettos as early as 1280 in Moorish-Berber North Africa. From the early 13th century anti-Jewish legislation became commonplace in Europe. In 1235 the Church Council that met in Arles, France, ordered all Jews to wear a yellow patch, four fingers wide, over their heart. In most cities in Europe Jews were confined to ghettos known as "Jewish Quarters." In 1290, England expelled its small Jewish community. In 1306 France expelled many Jews. In both countries, Jews returned and resettled in later decades. The Catholic Church stepped up persecution of Jews across Europe with founding of the Medieval *Inquisition* in 1232. In Castile, it was forbidden for anyone to convert from Islam to Judaism or from Judaism to Islam. In 1255 it was made illegal for Christians to apostatize. This new aggressiveness toward Jews (and Muslims) was paralleled by a more intolerant attitude toward Christian heretics and other religious dissenters. In southern France an all-out "holy war" against the *Albigensian* heresy aimed at eradicating the Cathars, against whom the Medieval Inquisition was originally targeted.

Throughout Christendom, but most notably in the Swiss lands and in Germany, Jews were blamed for the spread of the *Black Death*. There were ferocious outbreaks of anti-Semitism and massacres of Jews by German Christians in 1349, with thousands more killed by crowds stirred to religious frenzy by the *flagellants*. This had happened before, when Crusaders detoured into Jewish villages or ghettos to commit murder for Christ; it would happen again in Germany during the *Thirty Years' War* (1618–1648). In each case, Jews became victims of religious zeal run amok and of scapegoating by local elites eager to deflect blame for all the social, economic, and military turmoil that coursed over Germany and Europe in the mid-14th and again in the mid-17th centuries. Everywhere, Jews were blamed by superstitious, ignorant Christians—who also ferreted out supposed "witches" and "demon-worshipers" for persecution and death—during episodes of natural calamity or wartime suffering. Such Christians neglected to recall the persecution of their own founding generations, who were blamed for natural disasters or misfortune in war by distraught pagans of the Roman Empire. The culminating act of anti-Semitism in the Middle Ages was the *expulsion of the Jews* from Spain in 1492. Many who left were welcomed to settle inside the Ottoman Empire. Those Jews who formally converted to Catholicism in order to remain in Iberia after 1492 ("conversos") were the main target of the Spanish Inquisition over the next 150 years. Even longtime, loyal "converso" families were persecuted and expelled, including from Portugal after it was annexed to Spain in 1580.

Antwerp, Siege of (1584–1585). Eight years after the *Spanish Fury*, Antwerp was again attacked by the *Army of Flanders*, this time led by the *Duke of Parma*. The townsmen cut all dikes to protect the city, but Parma built a fortified, floating bridge and gun platforms across the Scheldt. That brought the city of 80,000 inhabitants under close artillery fire and cut it off from resupply via the sea during the lean winter months. *Sea Beggars* from Holland and Zeeland launched an amphibious relief operation in April 1585, but it was repelled by Parma's tough veterans. After 14 months of fighting, disease, starvation, and death, Antwerp surrendered in August. For once, the Spanish did not sack a defeated rebel town. Instead, they garrisoned it and forced the Protestant population to convert or leave. About 38,000 left for the north.

Appanage system. See *Muscovy, Grand Duchy of*; *war finance*.

appatis. "Truce payments." Contracts that set out the amount of protection money extorted from civilians to be paid to enemy (or even "friendly") troops garrisoned in the area, in exchange for soldiers abstaining from burning crops and villages or killing peasants or townsfolk. *Mercenaries* often demanded "patis" because pay from a distant employer was months in arrears. The worst excesses came from *routiers* or *Free Companies* who took over a stronghold and then systematically wasted the surrounding region. Their most common method of intimidation was to burn out peasant huts or an entire village or town if money was not paid. If a *chevauchée* or other scorched earth campaign was underway, even prompt payment might not spare property from being razed. And appatis might be demanded from the same village or town by two or more companies in a frontier war zone, or from multiple groups of routiers.

Appenzell Wars (1403–1411). Following the *Covenant of Sempach* (1393), the Canton of Appenzell sought to break free from the control of its feudal liege lord, the Abbot of St. Gallen. Appenzell won the initial fight at Speicher, or Vögelisegg (May 15, 1403), where the Swiss forces used *"Letzinen"* palisades to great effect, not by defending from behind the barricades but by leaving them undefended to lure the enemy into a trap. Once the troops of St. Gallen crossed over the earthworks, concealed Swiss closed behind them and a slaughter commenced. The Swiss employed the same tactic at Stoss (June 17, 1405), where the men of Appenzell, fighting under their *Banner* of an angry standing bear, similarly trapped and defeated an Austrian army behind Letzinen. Appenzell was defeated at Bregenz (January 13, 1408) by the Austrians, but it was saved by alliance with the Swiss Confederation (1411). Appenzell formally joined the Swiss Confederation a hundred years later (1514).

Aquitaine. See *Black Prince*; *Brétigny, Treaty of*; *castles, on land*; *Edward III*; *Hundred Years' War*; *Nájera, Battle of*; *Poitiers, Battle of*.

Arabs. Originally, a nomadic pastoralist (*Bedouin*) people from Arabia. More loosely, any of the Semitic peoples of North Africa, the Arabian peninsula, Palestine, Lebanon, Syria, Iraq, and northern Sudan—excluding Jews, who are also a Semitic people historically living in the Middle East, but with a distinct history and faith. Originally located on a strategically sited peninsula which joins the Indian Ocean to the Mediterranean, and the worlds of India and Asia to Europe and Africa, Arabs emerged as a people of world historical significance with the "explosion of *Islam*" out of the Arabian desert in the 7th century C.E. While Arab military ascendancy was brief and the tribes either retreated to the desert or were assimilated into more advanced civilizations they conquered, Arab language, politics, and the Muslim faith remained as a lasting influence on world history. The Arab caliphate lasted until defeat of the Abbasid caliphs in Baghdad by the *Mongols* in 1258. After that, Mongol and *Turkic* dynasties and empires, or *Mamlūks*, ruled the many and divers peoples converted to Islam under the Arab caliphs. For the Ottomans, Arab militia played an important military role east of the Jordan River, but other Arab troops allied with *Azaps* in local wars against the *Janissaries*.

Aragon. This north Iberian state became an independent kingdom in 1076. Along with Castile and Portugal, it engaged in a prolonged war of raids, plunder, and enforced tribute against the *taifa* states of *al-Andalus*. Aragon emerged as a real power under Alfonso I ("The Battler," d.1134) in the early 12th century. He summoned Christian knights from France in 1117, and with their help took Muslim Zaragoza from the Almoravids the next year. He later captured Malaga. James I ("The Conqueror," 1208–1276, r.1213–1276), captured the Balearic Islands (1229–1235), Majorca (1229), and Valencia (1238), laying the foundation for an Aragonese trading and martial empire with its economic core in Catalan Barcelona, and in control of the eastern seaboard of Iberia. Aragon was more tolerant of its Muslim subjects than was Castile: it left intact a large Muslim population in Valencia, which contributed to economic growth and a social, legal, and cultural sophistication that Castile lost by driving its Moors as refugees to Granada. See also *Albigensian Crusade*; *Almogavars*; *Ferdinand I, Holy Roman Emperor*; *Inquisition*; *Reconquista*; *Sardinia*; *Spain*; *War of the Sicilian Vespers*.

> *Aragon emerged as a real power under Alfonso I in the early 12th century.*

arbaleste. See *crossbow*.

arbalétriers. Mounted crossbowmen. They were also known by the Latin *balistarii equites*.

Arbedo, Battle of (1422). Several Swiss cantons wished to expand into northern Italy. The Milanese contracted the *condottieri* captain *Carmagnola* to defend them with an army of 16,000 mercenaries, including 5,000 cavalry. The Swiss fielded a force of just 2,500. Carmagnola surprised these men in camp. The Swiss quickly formed a pike square and held back repeated attacks by the enemy horse, until Carmagnola ordered *men-at-arms* to attack dismounted. Sheer weight of numbers forced the Swiss into a fighting retreat along a steep defile, in which they became trapped. When Carmagnola ordered no quarter the Swiss ranks stiffened and steadied. Swinging *halberds* wildly, the men of the Cantons cut their way right through the Italian foot and escaped the trap, although they left many hundreds of dead behind. Shortly after the battle a Diet was held in Lucerne that decided to add more pikes to the *Swiss square* to better protect halberdiers and archers. This reform led to the maturation of Swiss formations and tactics, so that they became the supreme infantry of the 15th century in Europe.

arceri. Fifteenth-century Italian archers armed with ordinary bows, not *crossbows*.

archers. See individual battles and *abatis*; *arceri*; *armor*; *arquebus*; *arrows*; *artillery*; *ashigaru*; *Azaps*; *Bedouin*; *bracer*; *cavalry*; *compagnies de l'ordonnance*; *composite bow*; *crossbow*; *dragoons*; *drill*; *Edward III*; *elephants*; *franc-archers*; *galley*; *heavy cavalry*; *hobelars*; *howdah*; *hussars*; *indentures for war*; *jack*; *Janissary Corps*; *junk*; *lance* (1); *longbow*; *Mamlūks*; *mercenaries*; *Mongols*; *morion*; *murtat*; *muskets*; *pavisare*; *pavise*; *pike*; *reflex bow*; *Scots Archers*; *shock*; *siege warfare*; *Swiss square*; *tate*; *torre del homenaje*; *Turcopoles*; *uniforms*; *warhorses*; *war wagons*; *yabusame*.

Argentina. See *Buenos Aires*.

Argyll, Marquis of (1607–1661). Né Archibald Campbell. *Covenanter* general. Presbyterianism was his bedrock belief, for which he fought hard and often, but not well: he was repeatedly bested in battle by the *Marquis of Montrose*. *David Leslie* defeated Montrose at *Philipaugh* (September 13, 1645), restoring control of Scotland to Argyll. At the start of the Second *English Civil War* Argyll supported *Charles I*, but he backed away from the Royalists when *Oliver Cromwell* won at *Preston* (August 17–20, 1648) blocking the border to reentry by beaten English Royalists. He led the *Whiggamore Rising* in 1648, then returned to cursing Montrose, the Great White Whale of his hatred and obsession, until Montrose was caught, humiliated by Argyll, and hanged in 1650. When Cromwell invaded Scotland, Argyll spun another of his many political pirouettes and made peace. He survived into the Restoration, but by then he had betrayed too many men and causes to die quietly in bed. He met death instead on the block, unpitied and unmourned.

Arianism. The original "Arian heresy" dated to the 4th century thinker Arius, whose arguments were condemned by the Council of Nicaea (325 C.E.) and banned and repressed by the Catholic Church thereafter. In the early modern period the term applied to believers in the "unitarian" nature of God, who emerged as a small but important, and largely urban, religious and social movement. As in original Arianism, 17th-century Arians rejected the claimed divinity of Jesus of Nazareth and the doctrine of the Trinity (or, as Muhammad once put it: "God does not beget, nor is he begotten"). Some Arians promoted radical economic and social reforms such as communal holding of property, equality of all regardless of birth or social station, pacifism, and rejection of moral or political allegiance to any state. Arianism had small but influential congregations as far afield as Poland and Ukraine.

aristocracy. See *armor*; *Aztec Empire*; *baggage train*; *Burgundy, Duchy of*; *caliph*; *cavalry*; *caste system*; *castles, on land*; *castles, on ships*; *chivalry*; *Confucianism*; *consorterie*; *esquire*; *feudalism*; *gunpowder weapons*; *Hundred Years' War*; *Hungary*; *Hussite Wars*; *infantry*; *Janissary Corps*; *Japan*; *jus in bello*; *knights*; *Landsknechte*; *logistics*; *Mamlūks*; *Mughals*; *new monarchies*; *Normans*; *officer*; *Order of the Garter*; *Order of the Golden Fleece*; *price revolution*; *Rajputs*; *Reconquista*; *Richelieu, Armand Jean du Plessis de*; *revolution in military affairs*; *samurai*; *servitor cavalry*; *sipahis*; *Teutonic Knights*; *Tuareg*; *war finance*.

arma. In 1591 *Songhay* was invaded by Moroccan troops equipped with firearms, who made an extraordinary trek across the desert to capture Timbuktu, where they completely outmatched Songhay's spear-bearing cavalry and bowmen. The Moroccans were reinforced for a number of years, but ties to Morocco were broken in 1618 when the material fruits of conquest failed to meet expectations in Marrakesh. The Moroccans abandoned in Songhay clung to power, and over time formed an ethnically distinct ruling class called the "arma" ("gunmen"). In the 1660s a succession crisis in Morocco led the arma to formally repudiate the old connection. Steeped in desert mysticism, the arma were disdainful of the older, alternate, and more tolerant Muslim intellectual tradition of Timbuktu. For another 200 years the arma, also known as the "Moors of Timbuktu," ruled an area centered on old Songhay, the cities of Gao, Jenne, and Timbuktu, but little else of what had once been governed by the Mali and Songhay empires.

Armada Real (de la Guarda de la Carrera de los Indias). Prior to 1570 Spain had no permanent navy. That year, it formed a flotilla of 12 small galleons to escort the *flota* to and from the Americas. Ten larger galleons were added in the 1580s; these formed the "Castilian Squadron" of the *Invincible Armada* of 1588. To this fleet were added the great galleons of Portugal, annexed to the Spanish Empire in 1580. After the catastrophe of 1588 the fleet was rebuilt remarkably fast, and in 1591 the Armada Real resumed escort of the flota.

Armagnacs. French mercenaries, leftovers from the *Free Companies* brought together by the Count of Armagnac in Languedoc. In 1407 they became embroiled in a local civil war, gaining a fearsome reputation for atrocities committed in the region of Paris. They were hired by French kings during the final decades of the *Hundred Years' War*. The Dauphin (later, Charles VII) allied with them, which helped drive Burgundy into alliance with England. The

French army which lost to *Henry V* at *Agincourt* (1415) had a large Armagnac contingent. During this nadir of French military fortunes, when most royal resistance to the English invasion collapsed, Armagnac captains and companies continued to resist English and Burgundian advances. After the Peace of Arras (1435) many Armagnacs joined companies of comparably brutal *Ecorcheurs*. See also *St. Jacob-en-Birs, Battle of*.

arme blanche. With bayonet fixed or saber drawn. *Gustavus Adolphus* abandoned the tactic of *caracole* by 1630, in favor of cavalry that charged with sabers drawn for maximum *shock* effect.

Armeé d'Allemagne. The French Army in the Rhineland and Germany during the *Thirty Years' War*.

Armenia. Armenia has existed in some form since the 9th century B.C.E. In 300 C.E. most of its population converted to Christianity—a faith preserved by Armenians despite conversion of neighboring populations to Islam from the 7th century. It was divided between the Roman and Iranian Empires in 387 C.E. Located at a major geopolitical crossroads, Armenians suffered repeated invasion: *Seljuk Turks*, 11th century; *Mongols*, 13th century; Turkmen tribes, 14th–15th centuries; then Tamerlane followed by the *Safavids*. The resulting waves of emigration and Armenian displacement constituted a prolonged diaspora. Armenia was conquered by the Ottomans in the 14th century, who occupied a devastated and underpopulated country.

armet. A late medieval (mid-15th-century) helmet of Italian origin that replaced the *bascinet* in most armies. It was formed of a large iron globe reaching to the ears, which were covered by separate pieces, with a long hollow projection covering the back of the neck. In front it sported a visor and gorget.

"Armies of the Religion on the Sea." See *Malta*.

arming cap. A quilted coif worn under a *helm* to ease discomfort and secure it to the head.

arming doublet. A thinner form of cloth padding that replaced the heavier *habergeon* in the 15th century as armor climaxed in form of the articulated full suit of plate.

Arminianism. A movement led by the Dutch theologian Jacobus Arminius (né Jacob Harmensen, 1560–1609) who sought a "via media" (middle path) between hardening Catholic and Protestant doctrines, and to moderate increasingly intemperate beliefs among Dutch Calvinist preachers. He rejected Calvinism's doctrine of absolute predestination (election), preaching instead that salvation was available to all who repented their sins and embraced "The Christ." This embroiled him in a lifetime of controversy which he only escaped in death, but which continued in a series of famous debates ("Remonstrances") after his passing. His followers were more rigid than he was, and as they also tended to support peace with Spain they were suspect on political grounds. Neither doctrine nor politics endeared Arminians to Calvinists or Dutch nationalists. The crisis neared civil war in Holland over the issue of *waardgelders* in 1617, which was resolved only by a coup d'etat carried out by *Maurits of Nassau*. Maurits purged Arminians from town councils, replacing them with members of old noble families.

In England, *Charles I* was a follower of Arminianism, of sorts. He got into trouble in 1637 over introduction of the Arminian prayer book in place of the Book of Common Prayer and his effort to Anglicize the Scottish Kirk. English Latitudinarians shared Arminian views. In fact, all who wished to emphasize the differences between the reformed English church and more radical, continental-style Protestantism were called "Arminians," whether or not they agreed with the views of Jacobus Arminius. For English *Puritans*, Arminianism represented all the subtle artifice, black arts, moral trickery, and doctrinal falsehood that they abhorred and more usually associated with the papacy and the Catholic Church, which was in their eyes the Whore of Babylon or even the Antichrist. See also *Grotius, Hugo*.

armor. Armor was a distinguishing characteristic of the medieval *knight* in Europe, as it was also of the *samurai* in Japan. Medieval soldiers in China wore armor as well, but in African warfare it was seldom worn, with exceptions in Ethiopia and in naval warfare. In Europe, chain *mail* was the standard form through the 12th century when the principal threat was blade strikes. *Plate* was adopted to better deflect or stop missiles as these improved in hitting power and penetration. This began a prolonged transition, starting in the 12th century and not reaching fruition until full, head-to-toe plate armor was adopted in the 15th century, just as armor became obsolete in the face of the "infantry revolution" of *pike* and *square* and more powerful *crossbows* and *gunpowder weapons*. By that time Milanese armor was widely sought after. It was much lighter and cheaper than German "gothic" armor that hitherto dominated the market. These styles were part fashion, but had a functional purpose, too: Italian warfare saw more cavalry-to-cavalry action with swords and lances, hence it took a more rounded form to ward off glancing blows. German and north European warfare involved many more archers, to which armorers responded with added grooves and crenelations to prevent penetration by quarrels or arrows. The new style of wearing *white armor* (uncovered by cloth) caught on, so that knights actually fought clad in "shining armor."

In China and Japan, chest plate for horses was produced as early as the 6th century. Several centuries later the *Mongols* made *lamellar* horse armor in which small plates were bound with leather to make larger flexible strips. Horse armor appeared in Europe in the late 12th century, usually in the form of mail. This was a response to the increasing number of archers on the battlefield. Equine plate was manufactured much later, in tandem with the move toward fully articulated suits of plate armor for riders. Again, the spur to defensive innovation was improvement in the power and volume of missile weapons on the battlefield in the 14th century. The Italians pioneered in horse armor as they did in armor generally, with Milan emerging as a major center of equine armor production. By the mid-15th century, equine plate protected every part of a battle horse except its legs. Thirty years later, just before armor in general fell out of use (though not out of fashion), some magnates ordered equine suits that covered their chargers from nose to fetlock. Late horse armor was made of iron or steel plate, but hardened leather and wood were still in wide use in the late Middle Ages. The lack of equine armor told heavily against the French at *Crécy* (1346) and *Poitiers* (1356), as a result of which French knights dismounted to fight on foot, as did 14th-century men-at-arms everywhere. At *Agincourt*, the French thought their equine armor sufficient to fight mounted again, but it was not. Even so, by the end of the armor age some warhorses were clad in full plate akin to that of their riders, which forced an increase in the size of chargers and a reduction in speed afoot.

Despite improvements in the punching power of missile weapons and the increasing tactical prevalence of pike-and-firearms infantry, knights continued to wear armor. They increased its body coverage and thickness and re-modeled it, adding crenelations and deflective surfaces. The full suit of body armor was thus a product of the end of the age of armor, and still in use into the 16th century. But personal plate became ineffective and obsolete with introduction of more powerful firearms capable of using *corned gunpowder*, which gave far greater penetrating power to handguns and cannon. At that point, the weight of ever-thickening plate became too great a burden: a fully articulated suit of 16th-century plate weighed 60 pounds. Though fully encased in metal, a fit warrior was capable of supple movement in suit armor. At least one case was reported of a knight able to turn and leap onto his horse unaided. Still, this was the exception rather than the rule: most armor restricted movement and interfered with

> *The new style of wearing* white armor *(uncovered by cloth) caught on, so that knights actually fought clad in "shining armor."*

sight and hearing to the point that dismounted knights would often fight in pairs, guarding each other's back. A number of older knights died of heart attacks, and younger ones died from dehydration or heat stroke after a hot summer's day spent in suffocating heat inside a full suit of plate. Discomfort was magnified by stuffing armor suits with shock-absorbent cloth, horsehair, or straw. Added to the problems of weight and discomfort was sharp limitation on sight, hearing, and a knight's defensive and offensive movements. These negatives came to outweigh suit armor's protective quality, and it was discarded along with the heavier horses needed to bear up a fully armored knight. Instead, cloth or leather garments were worn and smaller, fleeter steeds were newly desired: the fully armed knight and the destrier retired from war together, into romantic memory and imagination.

Professionals (mercenaries) were the first to abandon armor in order to regain combat mobility. By the 17th century most had discarded all armor other than a helmet and cuirass, in favor of cloth or leather and unobstructed sight and hearing. Speed was now to be the horse soldier's best defense, and freedom of movement replaced torpor, discomfort, tactical confinement, and immobility. By the mid-17th century even cavalry units, which were still predominantly aristocratic in origin, discarded most armor other than the helm and breastplate. Leg armor went first, replaced by three-quarter leather skirts. Over time, further recessions were made. By the end of the 17th century only bits and pieces of burnished metal survived here and there, and then mostly as polished ceremonial accouterments for officers-on-parade. A partial exception to the trend was princely armor, worn as a boastful but militarily anachronistic display by high aristocrats who refused to accept any social leveling in their politics or on the field of battle. Since such men seldom came within the range of enemy fire they could afford to continue to broadcast their social status through shiny metal burnished by some servant. Ceremonial and decorative armor lasted longest among *heavy cavalry*, the most aristocratic arm, but was more quickly discarded by pragmatic *hussars* and *dragoons*. Conversely, infantry armor became more common and heavy during the 16th and 17th centuries. This was partly because prices fell and armor retained utility for front ranks of pikemen whose job was to make contact with enemy lancers. Even so, most infantry preferred cheaper and more comfortable hardened leather *buff coats* and boots to confining breastplates and steel leggings.

Body armor was more useful and hence lasted much longer in Japan and China because effective personal firearms arrived there later than in Europe. Early Japanese armor left the right arm uncovered to allow mounted archers (the standard deployment of *samurai*) maximum freedom of movement. Later, splints of plate ("shino-gote") were added to the right arm. The lower body was covered by four large plates. Subsequently, the Japanese developed a unique form of lamellar, or scale, armor. Samurai protection from the 5th to 8th centuries, called "tanko," was made of discrete, overlapping iron plates. The Japanese developed this into "kieko" or hanging armor for mounted archers. In turn, kieko evolved into the great and justly famous "o-yoroi" armor. This was made of hundreds of small iron plates arranged like articulated blinds and was remarkably flexible. It was usually lacquered in black to prevent rusting and laced together with brightly colored silk cords ("odoshi ge"). The method of lacing allowed armorers to form intricate and beautiful patterns that gave Japanese armor its signature appearance. Sometimes leather was used in place of silk, but silk was preferred for its resistance to weather, the status it signified, and its sheer beauty. Japanese infantry originally wore a simpler form of rounded armor called "do-maru," or the still simpler armor body wrap called "haramaki." Later, infantry wore more elaborate armor known as "tatami," made of mail and plate sewn onto a fabric shirt and leggings. After meeting the Mongols twice at *Hakata Bay*, battles which were largely infantry affairs along a confined beach and wall defense, some samurai cavalry began to fight on foot. To do so they adopted functional elements of "do-maru" while retaining as much as possible of the more colorful "o-yoroi."

The Aztecs wore cotton armor sufficient to deflect the obsidian-tipped arrows and blades of their enemies, but which did nothing to stop penetration by bronze-tipped quarrels or sword blades forged from Toledo steel. Quilted "armor" was also worn in India by fierce Hindu warriors, the *Rajputs* and *Marathas*. This native armor was later adopted by some Muslim troops. As with Aztec cloth armor, it was primarily useful in defense against archers using standard bows. The *Mughals* introduced Iranian-style plate armor to warfare in India. This so-called "Four Mirrors" ("char-aina") armor was comprised of four large curved plates, tied together and worn girdle-style around the chest and stomach over a long mail coat. The upper arms were protected by mail, with smaller hinged plates ("dastana") worn over mail on the lower arm. Often, Iranian "Four Mirror" armor was cut and inlaid with gold, which added real beauty and dazzled the first Europeans to see it. The Mongols were light cavalry with no iron or metal industries, but they were not wholly unarmored. Chinese armor impressed them and they plundered and adopted hauberks and plate. Mongols generally preferred lamellar-style armor (small plates bound with leather to make larger, flexible armored strips), which they also used to protect their ponies. Because they remained highly dexterous mounted archers, they did not use armor below the elbow of either arm. Most of their armor was made from hardened ox-hide leather. Sharkskin was sometimes used, along with ox-hide, as waterproofing. In Africa in this period body armor was rare. Among the cavalry empires of the Sahel and sudan, quilted horse and body armor were common but plate was rarely used. Mail was common in North Africa among the Berbers and Moors. Braves of some of eastern North American Indian nations wore wooden armor that worked well enough against arrows, which they also learned to dodge from a young age. This wooden armor was quickly abandoned, along with the bows and arrows, once firearms were widely adopted in the 17th century and braves became expert marksmen. See also *ailettes*; *arming cap*; *arming doublet*; *armor*; *arrêt de cuirasse*; *aventail*; *barber*; *barbuta*; *bard*; *barded horse*; *bascinet*; *beaver*; *besegaws*; *bevor*; *bracers*; *brayette*; *brigantine (1)*; *byrnie*; *caparison*; *Cebicis*; *chanfron*; *chapel-de-fer*; *coiffe-de-maille*; *couters*; *crinet*; *crupper*; *cuir-bouilli*; *cuisses*; *destrier*; *elephants*; *espaliers*; *fauld*; *flanchard(s)*; *gadlings*; *gardebraces*; *gauntlets*; *genouillières*; *gorget*; *greaves*; *habergeon*; *haketon*; *hauberk*; *helm*; *Hunderpanzer*; *jack*; *jamber*; *jupon*; *karacena*; *kote*; *lance (1)*; *lance-rest*; *Landsknechte*; *legharnesses*; *mufflers*; *pauldrons*; *peytral*; *placard*; *poleyns*; *sabatons*; *salute*; *sarmatian armor*; *sashimono*; *schynbalds*; *secret*; *shields/shielding*; *sollerets*; *spaudlers*; *stop-rib*; *surcoat*; *tassets*; *tonlet*; *tournaments*; *vambraces*; *waist-lames*; *warhorses*; *white armor*; *zereh bagtar*.

Suggested Reading: Claude Blair, *European Armour, 1066–1700* (1958; 1979); Robert Elgood, ed., *Islamic Arms and Armour* (1979); Maurice Keen, ed., *Medieval Warfare* (1999); H. Russel, *Oriental Armour* (1967).

armories. In Europe, the first state armories date to the beginning of the 13th century when England, France, and the Italian city-states began to stockpile arms and armor in castles and fortified towns. Most emerging medieval polities maintained centralized arms manufacturing sites with foundries and villages or quarters housing skilled smiths, fletchers, bow-makers, and materials of war. Other polities likely did as well, but records are not extant for most. Early in the period crossbows and quarrels were the most important and numerous items stored. Other stockpiled equipment included basinets, padding to be worn by knights and men-at-arms beneath their armor, various mail, doublets, gorgets, plate, halberds, and pikes. Additionally, *catapults* and *trebuchets* and their hand-cut, stone ammunition were stored. Still, general stockpiling of weapons was not common practice until the 15th century, but from that point large concentrations of artillery, ammunition, and gunpowder were added to military storehouses kept by kings and the greater nobility. Armories were also maintained by most large towns in expectation of defense against a siege. The most famous was the *Arsenal of Venice*. From the early 15th century cannon and iron cannonballs were cast there for the galley fleet as well as stored in great warehouses near the docks. In England the main royal armory was the *Tower of London*; in Muscovy artillery and firearms were stored in the *Kremlin*. Austrian dukes and emperors kept an arsenal and foundry in Innsbruck, while the dukes of Saxony located their substantial arsenal in Dresden.

There were several advanced arsenal systems outside Europe in this period. In China the Palace Armory—as well as much Ming military production—was located in the Forbidden City and controlled by court *eunuchs*. The Ottomans carefully monitored weapons production and storage. They maintained numerous powder mills and stockpiles of charcoal, saltpeter, and sulphur, as well as copper, lead, iron, and tin, the latter imported from England. The Ottomans produced siege guns and other artillery at central foundries at the Imperial Arsenal ("Tophane-i Amire"), the state cannon foundry set up by *Muhammad II* at Pera. Assisted by *renegade* gunsmiths from Europe, the Ottomans produced unique styles of guns and effective recipes for gunpowder. In general, their technology kept pace with European developments in artillery almost to the end of the 17th century. This is the conclusion of newer research, which corrects an older view of the Ottomans as culturally closed to advances in military technology and already "backward" by 1600. See also *artillery train (1)*; *Burgundy, Duchy of*; *Henry VIII, of England*; *logistics*.

Army of Flanders. The Spanish army in Flanders. About half its manpower was recruited locally from among Flanders and Brabant Catholics. The other half came from Italy and Castile, or Germany, with a growing proportion of tough *tercio* troops as the Dutch rebellion and war became protracted. The Army of Flanders was resupplied and reinforced over many decades via the *Spanish Road*, along which some 100,000 troops traveled north between 1567 and 1620. After that, French military activity squeezed then cut the overland route. Since resupply by sea was problematic in the face of English and French privateers and ruthless ships and crews of the *Sea Beggars*, isolation often led to loss of food and pay and then to mutiny: between 1572 and 1607 the Army of Flanders mutinied in whole or part no fewer than 46 times. During the *Twelve Years' Truce* (1609–1621) it was reduced from 60,000 men to just 20,000. When the war resumed its ranks swelled again. In 1635 it still numbered 70,000 men, before declining in size, along with all other armies, in the 1640s. On its several commanders and many battles and sieges, see *Alba, Don Fernando Alvarez de Toledo, duque de*; *Alkmaar, Siege of*; *Antwerp, Siege of*; *Don Juan of Austria*; *Eighty Years' War*; *French Civil Wars*; *Gembloux, Battle of*; *Haarlem, Siege of*; *Invincible Armada*; *Jemmingen, Battle of*; *Leiden, Siege of*; *Maastricht, Siege of (1579)*; *Mookerheyde, Battle of*; *Oldenbaarneveldt, Johan von*; *Olivares, conde-duque de*; *Ostend, Siege of*; *Parma, duque di*; *Philip II, of Spain*; *Philip III, of Spain*; *Philip IV, of France*; *"Spanish Fury"*; *Spínola, Ambrogio di*; *tercio*; *Thirty Years' War*; *Turnhout, Battle of*; *volley fire*; *Zúñiga y Requesens, Luis*.

   Suggested Reading: Geoffrey Parker, *The Army of Flanders and the Spanish Road, 1567–1659* (1972).

Army of the Catholic League. See *Catholic League (Germany)*.

Army of the States. The Dutch army in the *Eighty Years' War*. See also *Maurits of Nassau*.

Arnay-le-Duc, Battle of (June 26, 1570). See *French Civil Wars*; *Henri IV, of France*.

Arnim, Hans Georg von (1581–1641). Mercenary field marshal. Nominally a Lutheran, he fought in Poland and Russia with *Gustavus Adolphus*, 1613–1617, then against the Swedes in behalf of Poland (1621). In Germany he fought for the Catholics under *Albrecht von Wallenstein*, but resigned his imperial commission in 1629 upon proclamation of the *Edict of Restitution* (1629). He commanded the Saxon Army, 1631–1635, but resigned with Saxony's signature of the *Peace of Prague*. He was arrested by the Swedes in 1637, but escaped. Back in the saddle in Saxony in 1638, he worked with *Johann Georg* to organize the smaller German states as a third force in Imperial politics leading to a general settlement. He died while that project was yet unfulfilled.

arquebus. Also "arkibuza," "hackbutt," "hakenbüsche," "harquebus." Any of several types of early, slow-firing, small caliber firearms ignited by a *matchlock* and firing a half-ounce ball. The arquebus was a major advance on the first "hand cannon" where a heated wire or handheld *slow match* was applied to a touch hole in the top of the breech of a metal tube, a design that made aiming by line of sight impossible. That crude instrument was replaced by moving the touch hole to the side on the arquebus and using a firing lever, or *serpentine*, fitted to the stock that applied the match to an external priming pan alongside the breech. This allowed aiming the gun, though aimed fire was not accurate or emphasized and most arquebuses were not even fitted with sights. Maximum accurate range varied from 50 to 90 meters, with the optimum range just 50–60 meters. Like all early guns the arquebus was kept small caliber due to the expense of gunpowder and the danger of rupture or even explosion of the barrel. However, 15th-century arquebuses had long barrels (up to 40 inches). This reflected the move to *corning* of gunpowder.

The development of the arquebus as a complete personal firearm, "lock, stock, and barrel," permitted recoil to be absorbed by the chest. That quickly made all older handguns obsolete. Later, a shift to shoulder firing allowed larger arquebuses with greater recoil to be deployed. This also improved aim by permitting sighting down the barrel. The arquebus slowly replaced the crossbow and the longbow during the 15th century, not least because it took less skill to use, which meant less expensive troops could be armed with arquebuses and deployed in field regiments. This met with some resistance: one *condottieri* captain used to blind and cut the hands off captured arquebusiers; other military conservatives had arquebusiers shot upon capture. An intermediate role of arquebusiers was to accompany pike squares to ward off enemy cavalry armed with shorter-range *wheel lock* pistols. Among notable battles involving arquebusiers were *Cerignola* (April 21, 1503), where Spanish arquebusiers arrayed behind a wooden palisade devastated the French, receiving credit from military historians as the first troops to win a battle with personal firearms; and *Nagashino*, where *Nobunaga Oda*'s 3,000 arquebusiers smashed a more traditional *samurai* army. The arquebus was eventually replaced by the more powerful and heavier *musket*. See also *cartridges*; *Charles V, Holy Roman Emperor*; *Gustavus II Adolphus*; *hackbutters*; *marines*; *Swiss square*; *tercio*.

arquebus à croc. An over-sized arquebus, usually mounted as a hook or rail gun on the side of a ship, or on the side of a heavy wagon. See also *Pinkie Cleugh, Battle of*.

arquebusiers. Infantry armed with *arquebuses*. See also *hackbutters*.

arquebusiers à cheval. Mounted arquebusiers or *dragoons*. These were special units in the *French Army* of the 15th–16th centuries. Their extremely slow rate of fire (as low as two shots every 20 minutes) limited their use to scouting and escorting, or raiding out of garrisons.

Arques, Battle of (1303). See *Courtrai, Battle of*.

Arques, Battle of (September 21, 1589). The assassination of *Henri III* (August 1, 1589) launched a new phase of the Eighth of the *French Civil Wars* by ending the Valois line and leaving the Huguenot prince and captain, *Henri de Navarre*, the most legitimate candidate for the crown. Abandoning his siege of Paris, Navarre took up a strong defensive position with about 5,000 men at Arques, near Dieppe in Normandy. He dug two sets of trenches that maximized local topographical advantages by forming a narrow frontage. The *duc* *de Mayenne* pursued Navarre into Normandy with an army of 24,000 *Catholic League* troops. He probed Navarre's fortifications for three days, then moved to assault through a thick fog. The terrain and defensive works channeled the Leaguers into a single front, barring flanking actions and disallowing the full weight of the larger army from being brought to bear. Mayenne's German infantry breached the first trench line but were stopped at the second by Navarre's hired Swiss. Once the fog lifted, heavy guns Navarre had earlier emplaced at Arques Castle opened fire, scything the Catholic ranks. The Huguenot infantry repelled repeated attacks with volley

> *Navarre dug two sets of trenches that maximized local topographical advantages by forming a narrow frontage.*

fire, killing or wounding perhaps 10,000 of their enemy. The position was so strong that Mayenne was forced to withdraw even though Navarre's Swiss defected in the middle of the battle for want of pay. After the fight, Navarre had the Swiss ringleaders executed in front of the assembled army. Six months later the two sides clashed again, at *Ivry-la-Bataille* (1590).

arrêt de cuirasse. A late medieval device, something like a bracket, used to anchor a heavy *lance* against the breastplate of a full suit of *plate* armor. It temporarily revived an offensive role for heavy armored cavalry in Europe.

arrière-ban. The shock of the crushing defeat of France's heavy cavalry at *Courtrai* (1302) at the hands of Flemish militia prompted Philip IV ("The Fair") to undertake major military reforms aimed at raising trained infantry for his army. He also sought to more efficiently mobilize money by asserting a royal right to summon all able-bodied men of fighting age to military service to the crown. This was an ancient right of French kings (the "ban et l'arrière-ban," or feudal levy) that had fallen into disuse and disrespect. Its reassertion by the monarch after Courtrai was a novel and important response to the new role of infantry on the field of battle, mainly because it allowed the crown to impose a tax in lieu of service. The money raised was then used to hire and equip military professionals, lessening the king's reliance on the old aristocracy. Still, it was not until 1448 that Charles VII used the system to establish a royal infantry reserve of 8,000 *franc-archers*. The dukes of Burgundy used a similar system until the reforms implemented by *Charles the Rash*, starting in 1470. By the 16th century, during the *Italian Wars* (1494–1559), French nobles served seasonally or they paid to avoid military service altogether, as the arrière-ban became a substitute military tax. Many nobles had to mortgage property or borrow against future rents at ruinous rates to avoid serving. See also *French Army*.

arrows. See *bodkin*; *bolt*; *broadhead arrow*; *crossbow*; *longbow*; *pots de fer*; *quarrel*.

Arsenal of Venice. In 1104, Venice founded its famous Arsenal, which grew to cover 30 hectares of enclosed shipyards, docks, warehouses, ships' armories, gunsmiths, foundries, and related crafts and services. In the warehouses were stored necessary items of war: trebuchet ammunition, tackle, oars, rigging, crossbows, and later, arquebuses, cannon, powder, and shot. By 1500 it reportedly had 12 powder mills worked by horsepower and drawing on huge storehouses filled with saltpeter, sulphur, and charcoal, the ingredients of black powder. This latent military capability allowed Venice to put much larger galley fleets into action than it maintained in peacetime. The Arsenal lagged in shipbuilding from the late 16th century, however, and never fully mastered the design of the new *galleons* ("galeones"), which it first built in 1608.

arsenals. See *armories*; *artillery*; *logistics*; *Tower of London*; *Urban VIII*; *Venice*.

Articles of War. In a *Landsknechte* company or regiment, the "Schultheiss" was an officer responsible for overseeing application of the "Articles of War." These were read out to new recruits (most of whom were illiterate). They included a nod in the direction of formal *laws of war* and related moral warnings against military sin promulgated by the Church, including the usual useless prohibitions against swearing, gambling, and whoring. Mostly, the Articles dealt with rates of pay and conditions of service, such as the penalties for cowardice in battle or desertion, the punishment for mutiny, and how *booty* would be divided. In "German" companies an oath to God and the Emperor was also sworn.

artillery. The term "artillery" originally covered all projectile equipment used in war, including ordinary bows and crossbows. It could even refer to any instrument of war, including swords, pikes, and armor. In ancient and medieval *siege warfare* torsion and counter-poise projectile weapons (*catapults*, *springalds*, and *trebuchets*) were termed artillery. They could be quite effective, hurling heavy stone balls with great smashing power against, or from within, walls of wood or stone. In Europe, there was wide adoption of the trebuchet from 1200 in response to thickening of military architecture in towns and encastellation of the countryside. It was not until the 15th century that normal military usage modified the original term to "artillery pieces," which distinguished gunpowder cannon from nonchemical artillery. Chemically powered or gunpowder artillery had appeared earlier than that, but it took centuries of slow development for cannon to be recognized as a special arm of war. The appearance on the late medieval battlefield of effective cannon hastened the end of individual combat in Europe and the chivalric values that supported it. (This pattern was repeated two centuries later when the *samurai* first faced gunpowder weapons in the hands of other samurai or peasants or wild *ashigaru*.) While this shift took centuries to complete, the pattern was everywhere the same: artillery in the hands of kings made possible centralized power, eroded established privileges of aristocracy, and made low-born master gunners a greatly valued military asset.

Why? Because artillery permitted literal bombardment of the old, fragmented *feudal* order into submission to the monarch. That partly reflected the great expense of artillery, which for the most part only kings (or emperors or shoguns or sultans) could sustain, and even they had difficulty. It also arose from artillery's raw destructive power: siege cannon, especially those firing cast iron cannonballs rather than cut stone (c.1380), enabled kings to batter in the castellan fortresses of rude or recalcitrant barons and reduce to rubble the walls of cities. Field armies had a new importance as the Middle Ages ended, for many reasons, including the rise of money economies and decline in respect for feudal institutions and social and religious mores. An additional reason was that armies with the latest artillery could do what only the *chevauchée* did before: cause so much destruction that the other side felt compelled to attack first, even though the advantage remained with the defense. Smaller nations such as the Flemings, Scots, and Swiss were able to use new infantry tactics and formations to fend off larger predatory neighbors, such as France, England, and Burgundy. Still, in the end it was only the wealthiest and most powerful monarchs who could afford enough of the best artillery and use it to smash internal enemies and overrun smaller neighbors. The new logic of expensive firepower thus advantaged the Great Powers over the small and middling, until independent cities, duchies, baronies, and petty kingdoms, with some exceptions in each case, fell to one greater sovereign or another. This meant even further concentration of military and political power, and sharp differentiation among the survivor sovereigns of the European states system.

However slowly, change wrought by artillery was inexorable and revolutionary, as gunpowder weapons excited the minds of warriors and improved in reliability and rate of fire. Records show Muslim armies in Spain using gunpowder cannon by 1342, and that three years later Edward III had 100 cannon stored in the Tower of London. Earlier or comparable dates exist concerning China. Similarly, rates of fire accelerated over time. In the late 14th century a cannon might be fired just five times per day, with the largest capable of only a single firing. By the mid-15th century the trend was toward mid-sized siege guns that could fire several dozen times per day, which made them vastly more effective and shortened sieges. Casting and related gunpowder technology only slowly spread to regions or economies where both sides lacked the wealth to buy or make enough guns to make a difference on the field of battle, but where the technology did catch on it was embraced with rarified enthusiasm and its use in battle and sieges became universal and dramatic.

The First Cannon

Gunpowder rockets were used in warfare in Asia from the early 11th century. There was also experimentation with bamboo-tube gunpowder weapons. By the 13th century the Chinese developed metal tubes that lay fair claim to be the first gunpowder cannon. The first references to gunpowder artillery in Europe are to *"pots de fer"* ("fire pots"). These were small, vase-like, bell-shaped pieces. That was important: the long-term lead Europe eventually took in casting artillery was partly rooted in the skills of bell-makers used to casting bronze bells to fill the huge demand from churches. Because "pots de fer" were fired from the ground rather than a stabilizing gun carriage they were wildly inaccurate. Also, illustrations suggest they shot thick arrows, wrapped in leather to better fit the mouth of the vase and seal in propellant gasses, not stone or metal balls. They were so ineffective they often did little or no damage to the enemy beyond making a frightful noise and belching fire and smoke to befuddle superstitious troops unused to such daemonic devices and artificial cacophonies. However, this effect cannot have lasted long once it was noticed that no one was actually hurt. Such primitive cannon posed more danger to their own side than to the enemy: a cracked or flawed bell would allow expanding gases to explode the casing into shrapnel, killing or wounding anyone nearby. Or a mishandled match might set off spare powder to scorch, sear, and blind the crew. As late as 1460 a defective cannon exploded at Roxburgh and killed the Scottish king, James II (1437–1460).

As barrels were made tubular, longer, and thicker, it was common practice to affix the gun to a thick board; this allowed adjustments to be made to the angle of fire (which remained line-of-sight only) by adding or decreasing the earth rampart on which the whole contraption rested. Only much later were gun carriages made. The first recognizable, tubular cannon of which there is a record appeared in Florence in 1314. Twelve years later guns capable of firing iron balls were certainly ordered for the defense of Florence, and guns may have been used in France that year. In 1327, Edward III probably brought small cannon ("crakys") north to use against the Scots, a prelude to his use of artillery against the French during the opening fights of the *Hundred Years' War* (1337–1453). While such primitive weapons were useful in sieges, it may be doubted they did more than frighten inexperienced enemy troops in open battle. The early inefficacy, general expense, and the huge difficulty of transporting cannon across difficult terrain largely untamed by law or many roads slowed the spread of gunpowder artillery. By the 1460s cast bronze, muzzle-loading cannon replaced built-up *bombards*, especially in France, though the older guns remained valued and in use. Despite the greater cost of bronze (three to four times that of comparable iron casting), it was preferred since it was less brittle than iron, did not rust, and was cast with fewer of the deadly imperfections that led some iron cannon to burst when fired. Two-wheeled, towed carriages also replaced older four-wheeled, unsprung gun carts.

Artillery in Asia

Ottoman sultans boasted a fine artillery train, purchased from Europe or cast in their own foundries with initial assistance from *renegade* gunsmiths. Ottoman commanders campaigning along or beyond the frontier often left the big guns in reserve. Instead, they hauled ore or iron slag to the siege site and cast guns in place as needed. This partly solved the problem of transporting huge siege guns. In China artillery progress paralleled changes occurring in Europe, though it remains unclear to what extent one civilization influenced trends or ideas in the other, or even if they did. At the end of the

15th century some Chinese guns were bigger than the greatest bombards then made in Europe. Chinese armies also mounted greater numbers of small cannon, many on two-wheeled gun carriages that made them mobile in the field or at least speeded their arrival at sieges. This progress reflected China's advanced knowledge of metallurgy and its vastly greater wealth. Chinese smiths even experimented with two-barreled cannon which faced in opposite directions while mounted on a rotary, a clever trick which doubled the rate of fire. The Chinese also invented a form of *grapeshot* as early as the 13th century and a form of exploding shell well before these were seen in Europe. Chinese armies also used rocket artillery as an adjunct to their cannon, which European armies did not.

Still, it was developments in Europe that ultimately spread to reshape world military practice and history. The key advances in development of artillery, in the sense of large-bore metal tubes firing high-velocity solid or explosive projectiles, along with the skilled and specialized troops and the science of ballistics that accompany such guns, took place in Europe during the 14th and 15th centuries. Until then, Europe's technology had just kept pace with China's (for instance, in both regions the *hoop-and-stave* or forged gun method of assembling large cannon was used, with casting reserved for smaller pieces). But thereafter Europe pulled ahead to stay. Moreover, cannon became central in a global military revolution as casting technology spread to other continents and civilizations from the decks of European armed merchants and warships, along with European traders, mercenaries, renegade technicians, and priests.

In 1511 the Portuguese brought their most modern cannon to China, where they were quickly recognized as superior to domestic models. The Jesuits were especially important in transferring casting technology to the Chinese and Japanese in the 16th century. The dual mode of technology transfer—slowly by land across central Eurasia, more rapidly by sea—meant that artillery might be technically decades ahead in one area compared even to a nearby region. Thus, the Moors in Spain probably used gunpowder weapons as early as the 12th century, and certainly Muhammad IV of Granada used it at Alicante in 1331 and after. But after that they did not have access to the advanced models of their Christian enemies. Various Turkic peoples acquired artillery in the 14th century, possibly directly from the Chinese. It is known that Turks introduced artillery to India at the latest by 1368 and that cannon were soon in wide use in the Deccan by Muslims and by

> *The Jesuits were especially important in transferring casting technology to the Chinese and Japanese in the 16th century.*

Hindu Vijayanagar. Turkish technology was dominant in north India into the 17th century, reflecting Muslim power and external contacts. That included a tendency to gigantism in artillery, with za few monster bombards exceeding 50 metric tons of iron. In southern India more modern European gun types were available as contact was made with Portuguese, French, Dutch, and English ships and traders along the coast. Ceylon (Sri Lanka) became a major center of European-style cannon manufacture in the Indian Ocean during the

16th–17th centuries. Similarly, in SE and North Asia most local powers sought to set up their own foundries, often hiring renegade gunsmiths to help them (Venetians in Malabar, Dutch in Japan, Portuguese, English or Dutch in SE Asia, Italian and German Jesuits in China). European powers also set up foundries in Asia to cast guns for their fortification and other local needs: the Dutch had a foundry in Hirado, Japan, then a much larger operation in Batavia; the Portuguese had a cannon foundry in Macao; the Spanish cast cannon for their Asian forts and ships in Gavite, in the Philippines.

Field Artillery

To kill men in battle outside their fortifications, field artillery was developed. Mobile guns light enough to accompany infantry and cavalry on the march and still be effective weapons took a long time to develop. Field guns were first used in Iberia in 1385, at Aljubarrota. The first recorded use in Italy was by *John Hawkwood*, at Castagnaro in 1387. But in no early example was a sufficient rate of fire achieved to effect anything resembling a bombardment, let alone a barrage. Bulky hoop-and-stave cannon in India were positioned to the front of the battle line but used only to signal the start of a day's fighting. Then they just lay on the field while cavalry and infantry attacked or defended. Lack of corned powder and primitive carriages also impeded development and deployment of true field artillery in India, as they did everywhere initially. That began to change in Europe in the late 15th century, where *ribaudequins* originally mounted on town or castle walls were moved onto four-wheeled carts to form an early, small-bore field artillery. The French astonished Italian defenders in 1494 when they used 40 such small cannon to knock down, in days or weeks, thin walls designed to stop scaling that had stood for months or years in prior sieges. Yet, these guns remained poor quality with low practical mobility and very low rates of fire. Slowly, more and bigger guns appeared on the battlefield in the 16th century. Once in place they could not be moved, and so were easily overrun in the thick of a fight. But they could outrange small arms and archers, and that was something.

As casting improved, barrels thinned and artillery lightened and improved. As it did so, the presence of big guns on the battlefield expanded the scale of war as opposing troops sought to move beyond hitherto unheard of killing ranges. At the start of the 16th century bombards could throw a large stone ball close to 2,500 meters, and an iron ball perhaps 1,800. No archer—not even a longbowman—came close to that range, while handguns were useless as aimed weapons past 50 meters. Artillery also encouraged broadening of formations by compelling defenders to stretch their squares so fewer ranks were exposed to frontal cannon fire, which could bore bloody holes many ranks deep through a densely packed human square. But this should not be overstated: the shift to fewer infantry ranks did not take hold until the start of the 17th century and had more to do with increasing the effect of massed offensive fire by infantry than trying to avoid cannon fire. As demand for cannon that might be deployed as field artillery grew, efforts were made to further reduce size and weight. Other experiments refined the recipe for black powder, or altered the weights of powder charges and projectiles. One result was that for a long time types of guns and calibers of ammunition proliferated wildly. This meant that even though cannon were at hand in an artillery train, available ammunition and pre-measured charges might not fit the tubes. *Charles V* was the first major ruler to standardize artillery. He ordered Imperial guns to conform to seven types. *Henri II* followed suit, ordering French guns to conform to six standard calibers (*cannon*, *great culverin*, *culverin-bastard*, *culverin-moyenne*, *faucon*, and *fauconneau*). By 1500, France had the best artillery in Europe, a lead it kept to the end of the 16th century.

The real breakthrough in field artillery did not occur until the turn of the 17th century, with the innovations of *Maurits of Nassau*. He reduced artillery used by the United Provinces to four standard calibers (6, 12, 24, and 48 pounders) at a time when the Spanish were still using over 50 types of guns spread over 20-odd calibers. Maurits also limited types and designs of gun carriages. Finally, he deployed a *siege train* of truly massive cannon. This was only possible because he also made innovative use of river transport, which could be done in the Netherlands but not everywhere. The largest guns in his train, known as "Karouwen," weighed up to $5\frac{1}{2}$ tons and had to be disassembled prior to transport by river or canal barge. This meant that their usefulness was limited to deployment against those garrisons and strongpoints reachable by barge, even in watery Flanders. On land, these behemoths needed 30 horses apiece to haul them into firing position. Dozens more horses pulled the heavy carts needed to bring their massive shot and tons of black powder used to hurl stone and iron death and destruction against enemy fortifications.

All that took time. And slowing the pace of moving armies not only decreased the chance of achieving tactical surprise while permitting improvements to be made to the defense faced upon arrival, it hugely increased the *logistics* problem of feeding men and beasts of burden. Once the logistical wall was reached, campaigns quickly failed. Even small field cannon ("demi" or "half-cannon") needed as many as 16 horses per gun to move. While wheeled gun carriages were pulled along main roads, albeit at an appallingly high rate of loss of horses or oxen to death-in-harness from overwork against the pull of mud and the raw strain of too much tonnage, they were not true field pieces since off-road maneuver was still extremely difficult. In battle, once positioned the guns stayed in place, allowing the enemy to evade their fire by moving or capturing them with a surprise attack.

The innovations of *Gustavus Adolphus* took Maurits' reforms and advanced them to deploy the first true field artillery. The great Swede accepted standardization and limited calibers, adding manufacture of interchangeable parts. Most important, he cast ultra-light, genuinely mobile guns which a single horse or two men might move. Gustavus' famous early experiment with *"leather guns"* failed, but he oversaw production of light iron cannon that were easily towed off-road and could be repositioned during battle. He cast bores as small as $1\frac{1}{2}$-pounders, and far more of his favorite 3-pounders. These he deployed in front of his infantry, and like his flexible infantry formations his field guns could adjust and move position as the battle unfolded. Some of his field pieces also achieved a rate of fire exceeding the rate of contemporary muskets. Finally, Gustavus reorganized his heaviest guns into batteries, to concentrate fire. That was a highly effective and still novel deployment. As Swedish-style guns were replicated and deployed by other armies, by the middle of the 17th century true field artillery arrived on the battlefield and changed the face of land combat.

Ammunition

The projectiles fired by cannon also changed over time. Where "pots de fer" fired darts with iron or wood "feathers," the first tubular cannon fired stone balls (the type of stone varied according to availability, from sandstone, to marble, alabaster, and granite). These were hand cut by masons to approximate the diameter of the barrel. The introduction of cast iron cannonballs greatly increased impact power by standardizing size and weight and more snugly fitting the barrel. In addition, iron balls were sometimes retrievable where stone balls were destroyed on impact. And yet, while iron cannonballs are referenced as early as 1341, stone balls were preferred much longer because they were cheaper and their raw material far more plentiful. It took discovery of new deposits of iron and better mining techniques that allowed for deeper delving after ore to bring down the cost of iron ammunition. A stone cannonball was also lighter, and so required less expensive black powder to heave it at the enemy. On the other hand, hand-cut stone balls inevitably varied in size and weight, and some fit a given barrel better than others. A bad fit resulted in wasted powder and reduced projectile force, as propulsive gasses escaped past the ball instead of pushing it from behind. This led to wide variation in the distance and accuracy of successive shots. In the 14th century, one cannoneer who hit the same target three times in succession was compelled to make a penitential pilgrimage, because observers could not conceive that this feat could have been accomplished without daemonic aid. In consequence, siege cannon—and these were by far the most common type of early guns—had to be hauled close to the targeted city or castle wall, because with point-blank shooting even imperfect guns did capable work of transforming the chemical energy of gunpowder to propellent force, as stone balls hurled at great speed cracked and broke opposing stone on impact.

Sieges

A main effect of the "artillery revolution" in hitting power and accuracy was to reduce the role of fixed fortifications and briefly restore battle to a primary place in war. It did this by forcing defenders to emerge from their fortifications and offer combat in the field, or lose. This effect was exaggerated by a general shortage of cannon that was not made up until discovery of new iron casting techniques in England, which made cheap cannon available even for emplacement in fortified defenses. This shifted the firepower imbalance back to the defense. Revived usefulness of fortifications in turn resuscitated siege warfare. By the time of the *Italian Wars* (1494–1559), cannon played a major role in deciding the outcome of sieges, though they were still problematic in battle because they remained largely immobile once position was taken and the first shot fired. Dragging cannon close to enemy parapets exposed guns and crew to capture or death should the defenders sortie, or a skilled archer land a flame-arrow among the powder sacks. That meant a besieging army had to deploy more troops to defend the guns, a tactic met by more men in the sortie, and so on. Early siege cannon were also slow-firing and defended by easy counter-measures such as hanging fascines of wood and wool wadding over outer walls. Even so, some did enough damage to stone defenses that were otherwise unbreachable to make worthwhile hauling big guns by barge or overland (using as many as 40 oxen per gun), handling the treacherous black powder that was their constant companion, paying master gunners to conduct the bombardment, and devoting hundreds of expensive mercenaries to protect the guns. All that was justified by the resulting broken walls, dead enemies, ceded positions, and war booty. Improved casting technology allowed guns to move back, out of range of archers or mounted sorties. By the early 15th century bombards could hurl stone balls 25 inches in diameter great distances, causing severe damage to fortifications unprotected by shock-absorbing earthworks. Experimentation led to gigantism, and huge bombards were assembled that were so impressive they were given names. With such great bombards as "Elipolos" ("City-Taker") *Muhammad II* smashed the high walls of Constantinople that had withstood a dozen prior sieges over a thousand years. That same year, the French used cannon to crush an English army at *Castillon*, the final battle of the Hundred Years' War. By then cast-iron cannonballs were in wider use, better recipes for gunpowder were crafted, and gunners were more skilled. Other innovations included primitive explosive shells, improved wheeled gun carriages from 1470, and rifling of some guns as early as 1520. Accuracy, throw weight, range, and power had all increased. The Age of Castles was over and the Age of Artillery began. Whatever *chivalry* and glory there ever was in medieval warfare was burned away by the new, and utterly morally indifferent, weapons of the gunpowder age.

Artillery at Sea

A distinct area of artillery development was warfare at sea. Ships' guns were used to bombard shore positions in support of amphibious operations, and in ship-to-ship or fleet actions to de-mast, demobilize, and sometimes sink enemy ships. French warships are known to have used guns in 1356; an Iberian ship mounted guns in 1359; and Genoese and Venetian ships used guns against each other from 1379. In the evolution of artillery at sea *pirates* and *privateers*, and the armed merchants on whom they preyed, played a greater role than the primitive state navies that marked most of this period. Big guns were brought to bear in war at sea earlier than in land warfare because ships solved the key problem of early artillery: its weight and lack of mobility. Cannon were housed and employed differently by *galleys* and ships of sail. Because of the weak hull construction of galleys and their straight-ahead, hard-charging tactics, all cannon were mounted forward, with perhaps a small *chase gun* or two at the rear. The prow was cut away to accommodate big, multi-ton culverins and demi-culverins, along with smaller anti-personnel pieces such as *swivel guns*. Arming galleys stimulated demand for naval artillery (there were 600 war galleys in all Mediterranean fleets in the late 16th century). Existing foundries had difficulty meeting the need. Once Atlantic-built armed merchants and purpose-built sailing warships armed with cast-iron cannon arrived in the Mediterranean, and with Venetian deployment of the hybrid *galleass*, the days of strict galley-to-galley warfare ended. Ships of sail progressively substituted weight of guns for sheer numbers of fighting men and developed new *broadside* tactics to match the change. In turn, reducing the size of a ship's crew reduced the amount of food and potable water carried in the hold. When that change was combined with new building techniques that greatly increased tunnage, long-distance navigation and commerce became possible and lucrative. And with that, *cruiser* warfare and long-range naval attrition of an enemy's merchant marine became feasible and perhaps even command of the sea.

> *Big guns were brought to bear in war at sea earlier than in land warfare because ships solved the key problem of early artillery: its weight and lack of mobility.*

Terminology

Before the era of standardized manufacture artillery pieces went by many names in many countries, each type with some novel characteristic or use. Phillipe Contamine noted that in the 14th century in Europe only two terms were used for artillery in France, "cannon" and "bombard," but that the next century saw a great proliferation in gun types and names. On gun types, European and otherwise, in addition to types cited above, see *bal yemez*; *basilisk*; *blunderbuss*; *bombard*; *bombardetta*; *cannon*; *cannon-royal*; *cannon-serpentine*; *cañon*; *cañon de batir*; *columbrina ad manum*; *coulverines enfustées*; *courtaux*; *crapadeaux*; *crouching tiger*; *culverin*; *demi-cannon*; *demi-culverin*; *demi-saker*; *esmeril*; *falcon*; *falconete*; *farangi*; *folangii*; *Karrenbüchsen*; *minion (2)*; *mortar*; *moyen/moyenne*; *Murbräcker*; *nariada*; *pasavolante*; *pedrero*; *perrier*; *pishchal*; *port piece*; *prangi*; *quarto-cannon*; *ribaudequin*; *robinet*; *saker*; *serpentine*; *Tarasbüchsen*; *verso*; *veuglaire*.

On other matters pertaining to artillery, see *armories*; *artillery towers*; *breach*; *breech*; *Burgundy, Duchy of*; *canister shot*; *case shot*; *casting*; *chamber*; *corning/corned gunpowder*; *Fornovo, Battle of*; *French Army*; *Fugger, House of*; *fusiliers de taille*; *gabions*; *galloper gun*; *Grandson, Battle of*; *gunner's quadrant*; *gunner's rule*; *gun port*; *Habsburgs*; *Hakata Bay, Battle of (1274)*; *Henry VIII, of England*; *Ivan III*; *linstock*; *Lützen, Battle of*; *Marignano, Battle of*; *Morat, Battle of*; *Nancy, Battle of*; *Nobunaga Oda*; *okka*; *port fire*; *powder scoop*; *printing*; *quick match*; *ramming*; *reaming*; *"red barbarian cannon"*; *sling*; *slow match*; *solid shot*; *spiking*; *sponge*; *stiletto*; *strategic metals*; *Tartaglia, Niccolò*; *teamsters*; *Thérouanne, Siege of*; *tompion*; *trunnion*; *worm*; *wounds*; *zarbzens*; *Zeugherr*.

Suggested Reading: Martin van Creveld, *Technology and War* (1989); H. W. Hime, *The Origin of Artillery* (1915); John Norris, *Artillery: A History* (2000); John Patrick, *Artillery and Warfare During the Thirteenth and Fourteenth Centuries* (1961); Hugh Rogers, *Artillery Through the Ages* (1971).

artillery fortress. A felicitous term introduced by historian John Lynn in reference to what traditionally was called the *trace italienne*.

artillery towers. These were mostly a product of the 16th century. Some were scratch-built, others were add-ons to existing fortifications. Many had winches and other hoist systems to raise powder and shot to the firing platform. Their purpose was to host larger defensive cannon to engage in counter-battery fire during a siege. Purpose-built artillery towers were squat and sited along killing-zones outside the walls. Some were much more impressive: Reval, in the Baltic, built a six-story artillery tower called "Kiek in de Kök" to support a roundel hosting the potbellied bombard "Fat Margaret." See also *bastion*; *casemate*; *cavalier (1)*.

artillery train (1). The guns; carriages and wagons, the gunners and assistants, all wagons filled with powder and shot, engineers and military laborers, and all others associated with an army's artillery when on the move. A "siege train" was a variant, moving the largest siege guns to their place of use.

artillery train (2). All artillery belonging to a king or state, whether on the move or in an artillery park. The size of the trains needed to move the artillery of even a small power was staggering. In 1472, Milan needed 334 wagons and 754 oxen and buffaloes to move eight large bombards, eight smaller cannons, and 34,000 pounds of powder and shot. In 1568 a French Royalist army took just 20 guns on campaign, along with 5,000 cannonballs and 91 "milliers" of black powder. To move this lot 1,550 horses were needed to haul the guns and hundreds of wagons filled with forges, tools, fodder, powder and shot, spare wheels, and parts. Nearly 3,000 men were required, including 2,000 *pioneers* to smooth the road and put shoulders to the gun carriages.

Art of War. At its narrowest definition, the "art of war" is the study of tactics and strategy. More broadly, it is all literary studies, military manuals, and guides to weapons, tactics, and strategy peculiar to a historical time and place. In China for most of this period the guiding text remained Sun Tzu's *Art of War*, dating to the 4th century B.C.E., along with associated commentaries by later writers. In 1571 the Ming author Qi Jiguang published a treatise on strategy and tactics called *Lianbing shiji*, in which he proposed major reforms that included mixed fighting brigades and a new emphasis on firearms, along with a special corps of war wagoneers and portable defensive walls for field armies. In Europe the most widely read and venerated medieval text was *Epitoma de re militari*, a study of the late Roman Army in the West written by Vegetius in the late 4th (or possibly, the early 5th) century. It was available initially only in Latin, but later was translated into most of the major vernacular languages. Vegetius stressed the inherent tactical superiority of defense in war, recommending fortification but also close-order infantry formations to enliven this principle. This emphasis on a "Fabian strategy" of defense and attrition was well-received in an era that found offensive war too difficult, expensive, and unrewarding: medieval commanders husbanded armies out of fear of the high stakes of battle, in preference for *siege warfare*, or to conduct *chevauchées*. Other medieval military lore and literature included rules and histories of the *Military Orders*, especially the *Templars*; tales, fables, and some serious memoirs of the *Crusades*; and contemporary chronicles, notably that by Froissart during the *Hundred Years' War* (1337–1453).

During the Italian Renaissance new attention was paid to histories and biographies of classical military leaders, primarily Alexander the Great, Julius Caesar, Quintus Fabius Maximus, Sulla, Scipio Africanus and other notable Roman generals, and Hannibal of Carthage. In the early 1490s *Leonardo da Vinci* published *Codex Madrid II*, a highly influential and reliable guide to gun types and gunpowder recipes. At the start of the 16th century *Niccolò Machiavelli* wrote his *Art of War* ("Arte della guerra") urging revival of Graeco-Roman virtues and citizen military systems, reflecting on the respective merits of militia versus mercenaries in his own day, and arguing for a strategy of annihilation of enemy armies as the path out of indecisive yet ruinous *condottieri* wars. Although Machiavelli did not transform Florentine military capabilities as he hoped and has received sharp criticism from modern military historians, his work was quite influential on developments in the Netherlands a century later where it inspired *Justus Lipsius* to write *De Militia Romana* (1596). In turn, that helped shape neoclassical military reforms introduced by *Maurits of Nassau*. The key contribution made by Machiavelli and Lipsius was renewed emphasis on *military discipline* and *drill*. In the view of Max Weber, this led to a shift in military norms that initiated the final transformation to true gunpowder armies: "gunpowder and all the war techniques associated with it became significant only with the existence of discipline."

Professionalism and social acceptance of military careers as suitable for the middle classes took hold by necessity and in advanced imaginations during the 16th–17th centuries. Printing presses and expanded lay literacy led to a proliferation of new military manuals and texts. Most had some practical utility and reflected the new cultural empiricism, even though many merely relied on reworkings of classical texts and formal ideas. *Niccolò Tartaglia* published his extraordinary study of ballistics, *Nuova Scientia*, in 1537. In France, Marin du Bellay's *Discipline Militaire* appeared in 1548, while John Smythe published *Instructions, Observations, and Orders Mylitarie* in England in 1598. On the new style and techniques (*alla moderna*) in fortification, J. Perret published *Des fortifications et artifices d'architecture et perspective* in 1594; a Dutch military engineer, Simon Stevin, published *De Sterctenbouwing* in 1594. The real impact of military literature came with illustration of the new tactics and drill methods introduced by the Dutch. In 1607, Count Johann of Nassau, brother of Maurits, published the first fully illustrated drill manual under the nom de plume "Jacob de Gheyn." His *Exercise of Arms for Calivres, Muskettes, and Pikes* (the English translation) was widely copied, amended, and reprinted in multiple languages. His sponsorship of a military academy in Siegen ("Schola Militaris"), to educate better officers in the service of Dutch

Reform in arms, led to wide dissemination of Dutch ideas and drill techniques. Its director, Johann Jacob von Wallhausen, published numerous training manuals. Lesser authors still found it necessary to pretend to a classical pedigree in order to gain wide acceptance. Thus, in 1616, John Bingham, an English officer who had served with the Dutch, published *The Tacktics of Aelien*, purporting to study classical principles of war but really reporting on the Dutch system. More self-consciously empirical and up-to-date was Robert Barret's 1598 tract *Theorike and Practike of Moderne Warres*. Other influential works included Nicholas Goldman's *La nouvelle fortification*, published in Leiden in 1630. As a result of the *English Civil Wars* (1639–1651) a host of manuals and works in English appeared, including how-to books by artillerymen and other veterans such as John Vernon's *Young Horseman, or Honest Plain-dealing Cavalier*, published in 1644. Others were solid memoirs published decades later by experienced field commanders such as *George Monk*. See also *drill*; *strategy*; *tactics*; *tournaments*.

ashigaru. "Lightfoot." New infantry that appeared in the chaos of 15th-century Japan. They began as wild successors to the rural *akutō*, but were recruited more from townsmen than surrounding peasants. They were men themselves uprooted by war or attracted to the easy prospect of booty. Some were so destitute they fought wearing only sandals and loincloths, or naked. Most were armed with *kumade*, *naginata*, or *yari*, and all used arson as a weapon. They earned an evil reputation for atrocity. Later, ashigaru evolved into a trained infantry supporting more expensive *samurai* cavalry. In *Sengoku jidai*–era battles ashigaru spearmen acted much like European pikemen, protecting archers and arquebusiers from cavalry within a "yari fusuma" (spear circle). See also *aventuriers*; *Celâli Revolts*; *Ecorcheurs*; *fire*; *Free Companies*; *guerre couverte*; *ronin*; *schiltron*; *wakō*.

askeri. The servitor military class of the Ottoman Empire, mainly the *sipahis* and *timariots*. They were exempt from taxation, unlike the "reaya" (taxpayers, mostly peasants). Jealous protection of their legal privileges led them to accept performance of military labor rather than see civilians do the work. This was very different from the attitude of comparable warrior classes elsewhere, notably in Europe. See also *Kapikulu Askerleri*.

Assassins. A secret sect of *Ismaili* fanatics known as "hashshāshin" ("hashish eaters"), or "Assassins." They were followers of a radical, messianic Ismaili cult of Islam that awaited the return of the rightful caliph, or "hidden Imam." From 1090 these *shī'a* fanatics were headquartered in a mountain redoubt at Alamut, in northern Iran. From there they spread into Syria, building fortress retreats ("eagle nests") in high mountain passes. The Grand Masters of the hashshāshin ordered campaigns of terror and political murders of orthodox (*sunni*) Muslim princes, whom they deemed illegitimate, supposedly to clear the way for the return of the hidden Imam. They also fought the Latin kingdoms of the *Crusaders* in Syria into the 13th century, in a *jihad* that promised martyrdom to *mujahadeen* high on Allah and hashish. Yet, some Assassins paid tribute to the *Templars* and *Hospitallers* in northern Syria. Their favorite weapon was a poison dagger. The Assassins were displaced from Iran in 1256 by the *Mongols*, who massacred most of the brethren they found. The last Syrian Assassins were overwhelmed by a combination of military pressure from the Mongols in the north and the *Mamlūks* of Egypt to their south.

Suggested Reading: Bernard Lewis, *The Assassins* (1967).

Assize of Arms. A traditional military obligation of all free Englishmen was to bear arms in the general defense (*fryd*). Henry II proclaimed the Assize of Arms in 1182, listing the arms, and armor nobles were expected to provide retainers according to their lands and wealth. A "knight's fee" detailed equipment for each service-bound knight, and the Assize expanded service to all "free and honourable men." It was later used to distrain men of property but ignoble birth to become *knights*. In 1230 "unfree" English were added to the rolls. The Assize was revised again in 1242. Twenty-two years later another revision assigned every village a quota of infantry to raise and equip, akin to the old "select fryd." The Assize was eventually replaced by *scutage* and other sources of revenue used to hire professional soldiers.

Astrakhan, Conquest of (1554–1556). See *Ivan IV*.

astrolabe. An instrument for calculating a ship's latitude by measuring altitude from the horizon of known stars (notably, the Pole Star) or the Sun. Despite its utility, the astrolabe was never a common item in a ship's stores. Even after the astrolabe became available, for decades most navigators clung to *dead reckoning*, the simple *cross-staff* or magnetic *compass*, and close navigation of known coastlines.

astrology. The pseudo-science of astrology was believed in by the rulers of most countries in this period, as well as mercenary generals and ordinary folk. Among the leaders who consulted astrologers and their charts when making major political and military decisions were *Christian IV, Elizabeth I, Ferdinand II, Ivan III, Ivan IV, Albrecht von Wallenstein*, a good many popes, and most every Ottoman sultan and Chinese emperor. Even such great empirical scientists as Johannes Kepler were devotees.

Atahualpa (c.1502–1533). See *Inca Empire*.

atlatl. A sling used by *Aztec* warriors to hurl their javelins. It greatly extended the range and velocity of their spears.

atrocities. See *Agincourt, Battle of; akutō; Albigensian Crusade; Armagnacs; ashigaru; Aztecs Empire; Baghdad; Black Prince; Buddhism; civilians; Coligny, Gaspard de; condottieri; confraternities; Constantinople, Siege of; Cortés, Hernán; Cromwell, Oliver;*

Crusades; Dorpat, Sack of; Drogheda, Sack of; Eighty Years' War; Fort Caroline; Frastenz, Battle of; French Civil Wars; German Peasant War; Grandson, Battle of; guerre guerroyante; guerre mortelle; Haarlem, Siege of; Hawkwood, John; Hideyoshi Toyotomi; hostage-taking; Hundred Years' War; Indian Wars; Ivan IV; Japan, Jerusalem; jus in bello; Kakure Kirishitan; Kalmar War; kerne; Knights Templar; Maastricht, Siege of (1579); Maastricht, Siege of (1632); Magdeburg, Sack of; Mongols; Naseby, Battle of; Nicopolis, Battle of; Nobunaga Oda; Oprichnina; Pequot War; Philiphaugh, Battle of; Pizarro, Francisco; prisoners of war; Rajputs; Roosebeke, Battle of; Rupert, Prince; scalping; Selim I; Sempach, Battle of; siege warfare; "skulking way of war"; St. Augustine Massacre; St. Bartholomew's Day Massacres; Tenochtitlán, First Siege of; Tenochtitlán, Second Siege of; Teutonic Knights, Order of; Timur; True Pure Land; Vassy Massacre; Wexford, Sack of.

attrition. French: "guerre d'usure." German: "Ermattungsstrategie." Wearing down an enemy by eroding his forces and morale, and destroying his resource base and supplies. In the era covered in this work, in which dense fortifications made battle a rare event, this was a major strategy of war. The central way it was accomplished was by *raiding* and burning or the grand *chevauchée*. Attrition was not accomplished by battle, as it would be in the appallingly destructive wars of the 20th century. Instead, raids exhausted the enemy's treasury, burned out his lands, and forced his armies into starvation or surrender, while the attacker's troops lived off the fat of enemy farms and towns in order to make "war pay for itself." See also *bellum se ipse alet; castles, on land; fortification; guerre guerroyante; siege warfare*.

Augsburg, Peace of (September 25, 1555). Following the *Convention of Passau (1552)*, *Ferdinand I* and *Charles V* agreed to a general settlement of the confessional and princely wars in Germany. What occasioned concession for Ferdinand was pragmatism; for Charles it was military defeat and personal melancholia, which also moved him to abdicate. Augsburg established a principle of religious truce, rather than peace, based on limited tolerance between Catholics ("the old religion") and Lutherans (those "espousing the *Augsburg Confession*"). The great principle of the Peace was: "cuius regio eius religio" ("whosoever rules the territory decides the religion"), although that famous summary phrase was not coined for many more years. The toleration afforded at Augsburg was importantly limited by the *reservatum ecclesiaticum* and freezing of the religious status quo in Imperial Cities, with only 8 out of 60 confessionally divided. Calvinists, Anabaptists, and other reformed faiths were explicitly excluded from the settlement ("all such as do not belong to the two above named religions shall not be included in the present peace but be totally excluded from it"). Nor did Augsburg toleration apply outside the confines of the Holy Roman Empire. Still, the Peace of Augsburg tempered

> *Attrition was not accomplished by battle, as it would be in the appallingly destructive wars of the 20th century.*

the religious question in Germany for 50 years, until it broke down leading into the *Thirty Years' War* (1618–1648). This was a major accomplishment in the very land that midwifed the *Protestant Reformation*, and where tri-confessional zealotry burned perhaps most fiercely. No one thought that permanent peace would result from the agreement; few even desired such an outcome, since all sides regarded the Church as indivisible. It was understood by all that religious debate would continue, just as all were convinced that the obvious truth of their own position must surely prevail. Augsburg promised only a military peace, not civil or social tranquility. A cynic might say that it only delayed the violent resolution of confessional conflict until the next century, and then at the cost of perpetuating Germany's fragmentation even as other powers around it were emerging as powerful *"new monarchies."* An idealist would say that Augsburg presaged a future where medieval civil and religious authority gave way to rational secularism in politics, leading to broad tolerance of the disparate beliefs of individuals in civil and private affairs. A realist would say that it was an expedient, short-term pause in a ferocious conflict that had temporarily exhausted both sides, and that it was probably the most that could be achieved at the intersection of limited religious imagination and the hard confessional realities of the day.

Augsburg is all the more remarkable for the contrasting solutions essayed by other rulers in other states at that time. In Spain, *Philip II* refused a request from his Burgundian subjects to permit limited tolerance of individual conscience, then launched a crusade to repress traditional liberties in the Spanish Netherlands that provoked the Dutch to rebellion and led directly to the *Eighty Years' War* (1568–1648). Philip also made war against Elizabethan England in the name of a Catholic policy while she sent *Francis Drake* to sack his ports and supported Spain's Protestant enemies in the Netherlands. While Germany remained at peace, the *French Civil Wars* (1562–1629) tore that society apart, ravaging France for 30 years as Catholics and Calvinists (*Huguenots*) killed with abandon and kept France in a chronic state of weakness, civil war, and murderous strife. Given those choices and national tragedies, the German peace achieved at Augsburg must be judged a considerable success, even if by the 1570s confessionalism became more rigid and pronounced as all sides recognized a new reality of perpetual doctrinal warfare and a divided Church in fact. The most direct parallel to Augsburg was actually in the Islamic world, where the *Treaty of Amasya*, also signed in 1555, divided the territory of Muslims between hostile *shi'ia* and *sunni* states just as Augsburg divided German Christians. While both treaties offered respite, neither ultimately kept the peace. See also *Carafa War*; *Counter-Reformation*; *Declaratio Ferdinandei*; *Edict of Nantes*; *jus emigrandi*; *Westphalia, Peace of*.

Augsburg Confession (1530). "Confessio Augustana." A great summary statement of *Martin Luther*'s theological positions. In law, from 1555 it was the only Protestant creed deemed legal within the *Holy Roman Empire*. That meant all followers of *Jean Calvin* or *Zwingli* or *Anabaptism* were excluded from toleration. In practice, from 1555 German Calvinists claimed and often received the Augsburg protections afforded Lutherans.

'**Auld Alliance.** The long military, political, and sometimes also dynastic alliance of Scotland and France, which held from the 13th to the 17th century, mainly as a result of mutual propinquity to a common enemy: England. It was shattered by the diplomatic revolution that accompanied the *Protestant Reformation*, which saw England, France, Scotland, Spain, and the Netherlands take different doctrinal paths that redefined who was a potential ally and who was seen as an eternal foe. See also *Scottish Wars*.

Auldearn, Battle of (May 9, 1645). During the first *English Civil War*, the *Marquis of Montrose* kept the Royalist cause alive in Scotland even as it was losing in England. At Auldearn, with a small force of 2,200 men, he routed a much larger *Covenanter* army, thereby protecting the Gordon lands from invasion and burning.

Auray, Battle of (1364). The final stage of fighting in the *War of the Breton Succession* (1341–1365). It secured the decision for John of Montfort, the English candidate for the ducal title.

Austria. In 1156 the dukes of Austria gained the right to abstain ("Privilegium minus") from the military expeditions of the *Holy Roman Empire* sent to territories beyond its immediate region. This was a key loosening of ties that allowed it to evolve separately from Germany, under control of the *Habsburgs* from c.1300. Habsburg Austria devolved defense of the *Militärgrenze* against the expanding Ottoman Empire to local nobles and clan lords, while Vienna was increasingly occupied with wars in southern Germany or Italy. During the 14th century Austrian knights were repeatedly bested in battle by Swiss infantry. At the start of the 15th century Austria was drawn into the *Appenzell Wars* (1403–1411) with the Swiss and the more important and protracted *Hussite Wars* (1419–1478) in Bohemia. *Maximilian I* (1459–1519) married Mary of Burgundy after her father, *Charles the Rash*, was killed at *Nancy* (1477) by the Swiss. This gained Burgundy, greatest of all French medieval feudatories, for the Austrian Habsburgs. The rest of Europe looked on in envy as once again Austria used dynastic marriage to expand without making war ("Tu, felix Austria, nube" or "You, happy Austria, marry"). Another marriage produced a son who came into a spectacular inheritance: *Charles V*, who united Austrian and Spanish empires in his person. This preeminence did not go unchallenged: Austria was deeply involved in the *Italian Wars* (1494–1559) against France through the reign of Charles V, and fought off the Ottomans who besieged Vienna itself. From 1530, Charles was concerned with *Martin Luther* and the *Protestant Reformation* in Germany, culminating in war against his own subjects in the *Schmalkaldic League*. A truce was called in Germany with the *Peace of Augsburg* (1555). Charles abdicated and retired into melancholia and an early death in Spain.

By the mid-16th century Austria's rulers were too weak to reimpose Catholicism on those of their subjects who embraced Protestantism, although *Ferdinand I* tried hard to do so. From 1568 to 1571, *Maximilian II* instead legalized Protestant parishes in Lower Austria and even approved their reformed Prayer Book. That was prudent, since by the 1570s the majority of Upper and Lower Austria's nobility was Protestant. The rights of Protestants of the lower orders and in the towns were not as secure. The Imperial Court remained staunchly Catholic, moreover, while a Catholic revival was already underway in Inner Austria by the 1560s. Protestants there, notably the citizens of Graz and three other large towns, were granted toleration because of the Ottoman threat. But these temporary freedoms were whittled away by *Jesuit* missionaries as the threat from Constantinople receded and the spirit and tactics of the *Counter-Reformation* seized the Catholic world. From 1599 to 1601, Catholic bishops in Graz and other towns, supported by Imperial and Austrian troops, suppressed reformed religion in Inner Austria. They closed reform churches, burned Lutheran and Calvinist books, and exiled or even burned Protestant clergy. The start of the 17th century saw Austria pulled reluctantly into the indecisive *Thirteen Years' War* (1593–1606) with the similarly reluctant Ottomans, and 10 years later into the *Uzkok War* (1615–1617) with Venice. A decisive turn of fortune, for the worse, came when Bohemia rejected the candidacy of then Archduke Ferdinand, later *Ferdinand II*, and carried through the *"Defenestration of Prague"* (1618). That launched Bohemia, Austria, and Europe into the *Thirty Years' War* (1618–1648). Austria emerged from that titanic contest a lesser power than before, but with more clearly defined boundaries and Catholicism more uniformly enforced and established. See also *Bergfreid*; *Catholic League (France)*; *Catholic League (Germany)*; *Don Juan of Austria*; *Fugger, House of*; *German Peasant War*; *The Grisons*; *March*; *Oñate, Treaty of*; *Reichskreis*; *Ritterstand*; *Rudolf II*; *Silesia*; *Swabian League*; *Vienna, Siege of*.

Suggested Reading: R. Kann, *History of the Habsburg Empire, 1526–1918* (1974); V. S. Matmatey, *Rise of the Habsburg Empire, 1526–1815* (1978); Robin Okey, *The Habsburg Monarchy* (2000).

Austrian Army. Throughout this period the Austrian Habsburgs did not maintain a *standing army*. Instead, they relied on the *Reichskreis* and on *contributions* and recruiting skills of mercenary captains such as *Albrecht von Wallenstein*. In 1648, Vienna finally decided to maintain a permanent force of 25,000 men, begun with leftovers from the *Thirty Years' War* (1618–1648). Some of these regiments served the Habsburgs until 1918. See also *Appenzell Wars*; *armories*; *Breitenfeld, First*; *Breitenfeld, Second*; *The Grisons*; *Italian Wars*; *Jankov, Battle of*; *Laupen, Battle of*; *Lützen, Battle of*; *Maximilian I*; *Mercy, Franz von*; *Morgarten, Battle of*; *Näfels, Battle of*; *Nemçe*; *Pappenheim, Graf zu*; *partisan (2)*; *Reichskreis*; *Sempach, Battle of*; *Thirty Years' War*; *Tilly, Count Johann Tserclaes*; *Uzkok War*; *Vienna, Siege of*; *Wallenstein, Albrecht von*; *war finance*; *Westphalia, Peace of*; *White Mountain, Battle of*; *Zusmarshausen, Battle of*.

Auszug. See *Swiss Army*.

auto de fe. "Act of faith." Public declarations of the judgments of the courts of the *Inquisition*, and execution of the court's judgments by secular authorities. Penalties ranged from fines or imprisonment to banishment and confiscation of all property, to death by cruel torments and burning at the stake. See also *Corpus Christi*; *expulsion of the Jews*; *expulsion of the Moors*.

auxiliaries. Settled civilizations which bordered the Asian steppe learned to hire nomad warriors as effective light cavalry auxiliaries. This was important to counter other, more dangerous steppe peoples who conducted raids against settled populations. Essentially, nomads were used to fight nomads. The Chinese thus employed *Mongol* auxiliaries to fight other Inner Asian peoples, including other Mongols. This not only solved the problem of not having an indigenous light cavalry capability, it answered the problem of China's lack of grass-fed horses that could pursue fleeing raiders across the steppe (most Chinese horses were grain-fed). The Russians similarly solved their *Cossack* problem by alternately conquering and co-opting Cossacks to fight other Cossacks. In Europe, comparable frontier and fringe zone peoples who were enlisted as auxiliaries in foreign armies included, at various times: the Celts (Irish, Scots, and Welsh); Croats and other Balkan populations in service to the Austrians; and *Tatars* who fought in large numbers for the Ottomans. See also *Derbençi*; *feudalism*; *Hakata Bay, Battle of (1274)*; *Hakata Bay, Battle of (1281)*; *hobelars*; *Hungary*; *Janissary Corps*; *levend/levendat*; *mercenaries*; *Militargrenze*; *Ming Army*; *Morgarten, Battle of*; *Raya*; *Sekban*; *St. Jacob-en-Birs, Battle of*; *turcopoles*; *Voynuqs*.

avariz. An Ottoman land tax initially imposed only on peasants to pay for advance purchases of grain used by the army on campaign but still marching within the borders of the empire. By the mid-17th century it ceased to be an extraordinary war tax and became a fixture of Ottoman *war finance*. It was also expanded to include townsfolk.

aventail. A *mail* curtain hung from the helm to protect the neck. See also *coiffe-de-maille*.

aventuriers. French "new bands" of the 16th century, or troops only called up during wartime. Like their medieval predecessors, the *routiers*, they were disbanded upon the making of peace and often scoured and scourged the countryside until the next war began. See also *akutō*; *ashigaru*; *Ecorcheurs*; *guerre couverte*; *ronin*; *wakō*.

"Avignon Captivity" of the papacy (1314–1362). See *Great Schism*; *Guelphs and Ghibellines*; *Holy Roman Empire*; *Italian Renaissance*; *Papal States*; *res publica Christiana*; *War of the Eight Saints*.

Aviz, Order of. In 1211, Alphonso II of Portugal gave the town of Aviz to a set of Brethren who evolved into a new *Military Order*. Although the *Hospitallers* were also important in Portugal, it was the knights of Aviz who dominated military affairs. In 1383 the bastard half-brother of Ferdinand I, *Mestre* of the Order, led the Brethren in blocking a Castilian succession to the Portuguese throne. Using the tactics of *Edward III* the Portuguese learned from the *Black Prince*, he won at *Aljubarrota*. He was crowned Juan I, first king of the Aviz dynasty that ruled until 1580 when *Philip II* of Spain seized a vacant throne. The knights played a role in *Enrique the Navigator*'s southward expansion. Along with his *Knights of Christ*, in 1437 knights of Aviz mounted a raid-in-force on Tangier. They met defeat, humiliation, and death.

axes. Small axes could be thrown, often in unison, but most medieval battle-axes were too large for that and were swung instead. The Viking, or "Danish," axe was of two types: the "skeggøx" or beard axe, and the "breidex" or more familiar broad axe. German axes had a Gothic appearance, with multiple spikes added to the main blade. By the 14th century most short battle-axes were discarded by the infantry in favor of *pole-axes*. However, as cavalry cast aside the heavy *couched lance* some took up light axes in its place, which they swung downward in battle. See also *halberd*; *lochaber axe*; *Mordax*; *tournament*.

Axtorna, Battle of (1565). See *Nordic Seven Years' War*.

ayatollah. "The sign of God." A title of senior clerics within the *shī'a* tradition of Islam. See also *caliph*; *imam*; *mahdi*; *sultan*.

Ayn Jālut, Battle of (September 3, 1260). "The Spring of Goliath." A *Mamlūk* army out of Egypt met and defeated a *Mongol* horde in Galilee, stopping its southward march of conquest. Babyars, the Mamlūk commander, was a Kipchack Turk who had been captured by the Mongols as a boy and thus knew their fighting style and tactics. The Egyptians also outnumbered the Mongols by five to one. On the other hand, the Mongols had adopted some weapons of their Middle Eastern enemies: in addition to their usual light cavalry of archers armed with composite bows they had some heavy lancers in their ranks. The Mongols attacked with their usual and predictable aggression. Babyars turned this to his advantage by feigned retreat of a small part of his army, luring the main body of over-eager Mongols deep into a narrow valley. Then he revealed the ruse by closing the trap behind them and on each flank. The Mongols fought hard but were wiped out almost to a man. The few allowed to surrender were sent to the galleys or into some other slavery. Following the victory Babyars rode north, scourging and scorching the land to deny food and fodder to any successor Mongol horde that might enter Syria seeking revenge.

Azaps. "Azabs" or "bachelors." Infantry archers, mostly volunteer Turkic or Kurdish tribesmen from Anatolia, in auxiliary service to the Ottomans. These bowmen were drawn from among the hunters of the Anatolian rural population, and were not equal to the highly trained slave archers of the *Janissary Corps*, with which Azaps maintained a fierce rivalry. During the 14th century many Azaps served as marines with *Beylik* or Ottoman fleets. Although some adapted to firearms, by the early 16th century most were employed in support roles as ammunition carriers, runners, guards, or sappers. By the end of the century, however, their combat role was revived as new volunteers from the frontiers of the Empire joined Azap units.

Azerbaijan. This Central Asian, mainly *shī'a* land was part of the *Safavid Empire* established in Iran at the start of the 16th century. It was surrendered to the Ottomans by *Abbas I* at the start of his reign, and subsequently became a province in the Ottoman Empire.

Azores. An uninhabited island group in the Atlantic which came under Portuguese control after being discovered in 1427 by ships sent out by *Enrique the Navigator*. Portuguese settlement followed from c.1439, with heavier settlement in the 1460s. Unusually, slavery did not take hold in the Azores since its climate was not conducive to plantation agriculture. The islands were conquered by Spain in 1582. See also *Canary Islands*.

Aztec Empire. The Aztecs began as four discrete Nahuatl-speaking tribes—Achlhua, Chichimecs, Mexica, and Tepanecs—who migrated from the north into the Central Valley of Mexico in the early 13th century. The Toltecs (centered on the city of Tula) and Mixtecs had preceded the Mexica (Aztecs) into the Central Valley. But their states were in decline by the 12th century. Through mercenary service to these city-states, which were engaged in chronic warfare, the Mexica evolved as a fierce warrior people, tributary servants of Mezoamerican peoples who preceded them in status, wealth, and accomplishment. When the Mexica were defeated in a war by the Tepanecs they became supplicants of Culhua, and subsequently minor allies as their status increased through success in battle. However, when Culhua sent a princess to the Mexica to fix the alliance through marriage, the Mexica misread the offering and sacrificed her instead. Enraged, Culhuacan warriors drove the Mexica away, leaving them outcast in the Valley. They settled on a barren, scrubby island inside Lake Texcoco. This proved a felix culpa, a happy fault: in 1320 they began to build their capital there, Tenochtitlán, and a sister city, Tlatelolco, strategically sited at the junction of the three main powers in the Central Valley: Culhua, Tepaneca, and Achlhua. During the 14th century the Mexica remained vassals of Tepaneca. In 1420, however, in a "reneversement des alliance" they turned on Tepaneca in concert with another city-state, Tecacoco, and a rebellious tributary of the Tepanecs, Tlacopan. The Mexica shucked off their tributary status and made war to gather tribute for themselves. After the three upstart cities overthrew

> *...when Culhua sent a princess to the Mexica to fix the alliance through marriage, the Mexica misread the offering and sacrificed her instead.*

Tepaneca and ritually sacrificed its ruler and nobility, they formed a "Triple Alliance" and divided the rich Central Valley, though Tlacopan got the lesser share. This set the mold for future Aztec expansion: conquered lands were distributed to an ever more distant aristocratic and military elite which lived for wars of conquest that marched tens of thousands of prisoners to Tenochtitlán in dreary files to feed a voracious appetite for human sacrifice, while fields were worked by an enserfed peasantry cowed by religious, military, and state terror.

The Aztec were driven by an imperial-religious ideology which demanded annual, ritual human sacrifice on a scale that expanded with each extension of Aztec rule. Every time a "tlatoani" (emperor) was crowned, religion and ritual demanded "coronation wars" be fought whose principal aim was to take prisoners to Tenochtitlán for ritual sacrifice, so that their blood would renew the Sun, Earth, and seasons. Other Mezoamerican states practiced ritual sacrifice, but after formation of the Triple Alliance and conquest of the Central Valley traditional communal checks on Aztec megalomania were shredded, as each tlatoani seemed to grow more bloodthirsty. Itzcoatl (d.1440) consolidated control of the Aztec Empire, which was a confederation of city-states dominated by the Mexica of Tenochtitlán, rather than a unitary empire. Moctezuma I (or Motecuhzoma, d.1469) greatly expanded the Aztec Empire, conquering the Mixtecs, razing their temples, and sending long, miserable lines to ritual murder in Tenochtitlán. Axaycatl (1450–1481), elected tlatoani at age 19, was a failure under whom war broke out with Tlatelolco in 1473. Axaycatl won this and several other small wars, but led the Aztecs to a crushing defeat at the hands of Tarascan to the northwest. Tarascan was the only other Mesoamerican civilization to have organized a grand confederation comparable to the Aztecs. Over 30,000 Aztec warriors may have perished in battle with the Tarascans in 1479. Ten years was spent reconquering vassal cities that rebelled in wake of that catastrophe, a pattern that marked the history of the Aztecs' unstable empire of fear. It would repeat in climactic form when the Spanish arrival triggered a massive Indian uprising against the Aztecs from 1519 to 1521. The climax, though not the end, of Aztec bloodlust came under Ahuizotl (r.1486–1502). His coronation war was no small affair. It was a sweeping campaign to suppress vassal city rebellions and instill mass terror in all tributary lands, and in Tenochtitlán itself. To rededicate the Great Temple in Tenochtitlán in 1487, Ahuizotl had hearts ripped from 20,000 captives. The slaughter lasted four days, during which the steps of the Great Temple literally ran with blood, to form black pools in the plaza below. The skulls of the dead were then assembled in a great skull-rack ("tzompantli"), so that after death they continued to terrify the living. The next year, Ahuizotl killed all the adults in two conquered cities, redistributed 40,000 captive children across the empire, and resettled 9,000 married Mexica couples in the dead zone. This was "ethnic cleansing," 15th-century-Aztec style.

The Aztecs expanded in part because their economic system required it, and because they were led by dynamic emperors chosen by the military elite for their promise as warlords, not because they were law givers or great builders (except of more bloodstained temples). The coronation act itself demanded war and human sacrifice, which meant both practices were built into the religious-political structure of the society and state. Each war of expansion was followed by another, then another. New peoples were terrorized into submission and annual tribute, and the appalling levels of annual sacrifice kept rising. In 1502, *Moctezuma II* was elected. He, too, waged a coronation war, sacrificed thousands to propitiate the gods, and expanded the Aztec Empire. By the time of his reign the Aztecs had conquered cities and territory so far outside the Central Valley that they controlled a vast and complex tributary domain stretching to northern Guatemala. In Tenochtitlán a highly privileged military-theocratic elite rode herd on a mass of peasants, artisans, and conquered and cowered Mesoamerican nations. From these ranks, sacrificial victims were taken by the thousands each year, not just to feed a religious rite but also as a deliberate policy of political terror: the sacrifices atop the Great Temple could be seen from every point in the city. Terror undergirded a ferocious theology in service to a merciless warrior-god, Huitzilopochtli. The warrior elite also engaged in ritual cannibalism as a reward for courage displayed in battle, with the choicest flesh (arms and thighs) awarded to the bravest warriors. Terror kept the military and nobility in power, but it also made the Aztec Empire brittle and unstable. Aztec social, political, and military structures were all overly hierarchical, as the problem of chronic rebellion showed. The Aztecs were so deeply hated by city-states and tribes they conquered and exploited, and from whose populations they may have taken several hundred thousand lives in war and as tribute over the course of the 15th century, that even a band of unwashed Christian savages from Spain who also slaughtered with zeal and abandon might be viewed as liberators, of a sort, for a time. Something similar happened in Ukraine in 1941.

Technologically, the Aztecs were centuries behind the *conquistadores* who invaded the Central Valley of Mexico from 1519 to 1521. Aztec weapons were primarily obsidian knives, simple bows that shot obsidian-tipped arrows, fire-hardened darts, and blunt javelins used to stun rather than pierce flesh. Simple stone-throwing slings were also common, and could be effectively lethal. The Aztecs used blunt wooden swords without thrusting tips. Instead, shards of obsidian were embedded along the edges to make a shallow cutting weapon. These swords were of minimal lethality unless multiple strikes were made: they were designed to cut, bleed, and weaken an enemy so that he could be captured and sacrificed, not to kill him outright. Aztec knights wore cotton armor that stopped such blades when wielded by similarly armed Mesoamerican enemies. However, their equipment was of little avail against European weapons, from bronze-tipped crossbow bodkins designed to penetrate armor, to swords sharpened to open gaping wounds and pointed for lethal thrusts, to iron balls and jagged projectiles fired from arquebuses, demicannon, and falconetes. Moreover, Aztec warriors did not use *shock* tactics or fight in close order. They preferred loose formations, fighting almost as individual braves, as warriors rather than soldiers, with an emphasis on capturing enemies, not killing them right away. Although they mustered and fought by region, their tactical units were led by officers (renowned warriors) who led by displays of personal courage rather than selecting tactics and ordering concerted, practiced actions. This befitted a style of combat whose main purpose was not to kill the enemy, but to stun or blind and then bind him, so he could be passed back through the ranks and taken away for later sacrifice. The greatest warriors and generals wore the most gaudy and distinctive headdresses and decorations, which made them easy to identify as key targets for Spanish lancers, swordsmen, or marksmen. Once these great knights were killed, leaderless groups of lesser Aztec warriors often dispersed.

Although the first Spanish came with barely a dozen horses—an animal then unknown in the Americas—and a few cannon, they wore plate armor and carried arquebuses, crossbows, and deadly swords made of Toledo steel. These impious Iberian cutthroats and brigands were led by a brilliant strategist and at least capable tactician, *Hernán Cortés*. In 1520 he led 550 conquistadores in a peaceful entry into the Aztec capital, Tenochtitlán. But his men plundered with a greed that astonished the Aztecs, and caused the death of Moctezuma. This caused an Aztec rising that cost the Spanish most of their gold and half their men in the bloody *First Siege of Tenochtitlán* in June 1520. After a fighting retreat and the sharp exchange at *Otumba*, Cortés regrouped. He gathered more Spanish amphibious pirates to his command, and returned—crucially aided by thousands of Indian allies—in the summer of 1521 for the *Second Siege of Tenochtitlán* and great slaughter of the city's people. In the course of the conquest of Central Mexico the Spanish and their Indian allies—or was it Indian rebels with a few Spanish allies?—threw down three Aztec emperors from life or power and destroyed the Aztec Empire.

For all the advantages afforded to Cortés by European weaponry and shock tactics, the Aztecs were not primarily the victims of technological inferiority; that is a crudely technologically deterministic thesis argued by those historians who also cling to the ahistorical view that conquistadores harkened back to a supposed 2,000-year tradition of "linear warfare" unique, and uniquely lethal, to the West. Disregarding the fact that war in the West from Greece to Spain did not share a linear history, and that Medieval warfare was closer to the style of the warriors of Tenochtitlán than the ruthless squares of Sparta or the Legions of Rome, it remains the case that the Aztecs were not overthrown by a tiny force of 2,000 (counting reinforcements) technologically advanced Spaniards with a superior military culture, but by a vast Indian rebellion that rallied tens of thousands of warriors to an alien banner because it afforded an opportunity to overthrow a loathed and brittle imperial theocracy. The second great ally of the conquistadores was pandemic disease. This not only wiped out huge numbers of Aztec warriors; it may have demoralized the Aztecs and undermined their religious and cultural supports when they needed them most. In sum, the Aztecs were not conquered by the Spanish so much as by a massive uprising of their long subject and suffering Indian tributaries that was triggered by the arrival of the Spanish. Aztec defeat was made more likely by ravages of virgin diseases and to a lesser extent, perhaps the coincidences of events with Aztec prophesy. On the other hand, the Spanish provided critical leadership and military advantages, and Cortés showed exceptional tenacity in pursuing his goal of conquest, and not just plunder, of the Aztec Empire.

The psychological-religious factor may have been critical to the conquest of Mexico: both sides believed that "God" or "The Gods" were with them, so that each victory or defeat took on a religious as well as strategic meaning. Beyond that, it is hard to say more. In the traditional version, faith in the potency of Aztec gods supposedly cracked when Moctezuma was kidnaped by Cortés, then killed. That fissure of doubt widened as thousands of warriors went down in droves in battle against strange enemies with thunderous weapons and a magical ability to kill at a distance. The worldview that upheld Aztec martial confidence then broke apart when pandemic disease devastated their warriors and people—all this suffering, death, and disease was taken as a sign that the Aztec gods were weak, or had deserted them, and that the cyclical destruction of the world they deeply believed in and had been prophesied was now at hand. For the Spanish, the same events confirmed that they were divinely favored over the pagan civilization whose blood-smeared priests, dressed in cloaks of human skin, who performed human sacrifice and rit-

> ... *"We came here to serve God and the King, and also to get rich."*

ual cannibalism, they slew in the name of their Catholic faith and emperor. Victories in arms and the mass death of enemies by disease were read as clearly affirming the justice of the conquistadore "cause." And if external events failed to inspire, priests were ready to say Mass, preach the rectitude of crusade against heathens, and console or intimidate doubters. One unusually honest conquistador, Bernal Días del Castillo, who accompanied Cortés to plunder Aztec temples, those sites of awful carnage in the midst of glorious urban vistas and sophisticated building and craftsmanship, put it succinctly: "We came here to serve God and the King, and also to get rich." On the other hand, Ross Hassig—the leading contemporary military historian of the Aztec Empire—argues forcefully and convincingly that the Aztecs "did not surrender, did not relinquish their beliefs, and were not paralyzed, but rather fought to the end—bitterly, effectively, and valiantly—with no sign of the various forms of ideological or psychological collapse to which their defeat is often attributed."

It is possible that over 1 million Mesoamericans died during the course of the Spanish conquest, 1519–1521, most from disease but several tens of thousands in battle. When pandemics also wiped out Mesoamericans like the Tlaxcalans who were allied with the conquistadores, the Spaniards were left to collect the spoils of victory won by the Indian rebellion. They quickly enslaved Aztec and Tlaxcalan alike, driving the pathetic and demoralized remnants of Indian city-states into the *encomienda system* the "conquerors" set up on the ashes of Mesoamerican civilization in Mexico. This was possible because the collapse of the Aztecs was sudden, and left the other city-states still divided by old hostilities and deeply distrustful. Over the next three years the Spanish played off one Indian power against another, conquering them severally then altogether. The original population of Mexico and Central America then underwent a catastrophic decline from exposure to a Pandora's Box of epidemic diseases of European and African origin, to which Mesoamericans had no native resistance. Within 50 years of the conquest the Indian population fell by 90 percent, from 25–30 million to just 2–3 million. By 1620 there were only 1.2 million Mesoamericans left in Mexico, at which point demographic decline stopped, to slowly reverse during the 17th century as natural resistance built. Given the horrors of the Aztec state it might be argued that the tragedy of the conquest was not their political downfall, but the unintentional killing of 95 percent of the Mesoamerican population by pandemics that would have arrived by ship from Europe and Africa even if Cortés and the conquistadores had borne gifts and good will, not swords and muskets. See also *chimalli*; *cihuacoatl*; *eagle knight*; *flower wars*; *jaguar knight*; *Xochiyaoyotl*.

Suggested Reading: Inga Clendinnen, *Aztecs* (1991); Geoffrey Conrad and Arthur Demarest, *Religion and Empire* (1984); Noble Cook, *Born to Die: Disease and New World Conquest, 1492–1650* (1998); Nigel Davies, *The Aztec Empire* (1987); Ross Hassig, *Aztec Warfare* (1988) and *Mexico and the Spanish Conquest* (1995); Richard Townsend, *The Aztecs* (1990; 2000).

B

Babur (1483–1530). Né Zahir ud-Din Muhammad. King of Kabul; founder of the *Mughal Empire*. Babur was descended from *Timur* and *Chinggis Khan* by blood, and in his predatory warlordism. However, in the Uzbeks he faced a formidable enemy he was not able to overcome: they resisted his repeated attempts to recapture Samarkand and other, formerly Timurid cities in Central Asia. This forced Babur into Afghanistan, where he took Kabul in 1504. From there he continued to battle the Uzbeks, failing again to take Samarkand in 1512. Babur next looked to India as a wealthy yet vulnerable land ripe for raiding, to enrich his dynasty. In 1519 he began raiding in force into north India. In 1526 he met and defeated a much larger Indian army at *Panipat* (1526), killed the sultan, took Agra and Delhi, and toppled the *Delhi Sultanate*. The next year, at *Khanwa*, he won a key victory over the *Rajputs*. This laid open all of northern India for invasion rather than mere raiding. His grandson, *Akbar*, completed the Mughal conquest of north India.

   Suggested Reading: Babur, *The Babur-nama in English*, Susannah Beveridge, trans. (1921); Bamber Gascoigne, *The Great Moghuls* (1971).

bacinet. See *bascinet*.

back-staff. See *cross-staff*.

Baden, Margrave George Frederick (1577–1622). See *Wiesloch, Battle of*; *Wimpfen, Battle of*.

baggage train. As European armies expanded during the 16th and 17th centuries, so too did the baggage trains which followed them in the field and into camp. These required an enormous effort in organized transportation that strained to the limits the logistical capabilities of the day. Thus, in 1602, *Maurits of Nassau* needed over 3,000 four-horse wagons to support a field army of just 24,000 men, and even this great land convoy carted only about 10 percent of the food or fodder which his troops consumed. The rest was bought or plundered from the countryside, from peasants and from villages or towns so unfortunate as to reside along the chosen route of march. Aristocratic officers used to a pampered life of personal servants and luxury goods were a particularly heavy logistical burden on armies. For instance, on his 1610 campaign, Maurits requisitioned 942 wagons of which just under 130 were devoted to hauling goods and baggage for staff officers and his own household. As to camp followers, Martin Van Creveld estimates that a typical 16th-century European army of some 30,000 troops (principally homeless mercenaries reliant on the army for their pay, food, and shelter) needed 4 horses to each 15 men, and was likely followed by a throng of servants, *sutlers*, prostitutes, and wives and children of the troops, totaling perhaps 150 percent the size of the actual army. The women of the train were wholly dependent on the men for their living, some as wives who might become prostitutes if their husband was killed, others as prostitutes who hoped to become wives. One bit of crucial military work done by the train, in particular by women and children, was to dig field works which European (though not Ottoman) professional soldiers in this period regarded as beneath their dignity. This attitude to the spade was not changed until the reforms of *Gustavus Adolphus*. See also *bombard*; *Hurenweibel*; *Provost*.

Baghdad, Siege of (1638). Baghdad had 211 defensive towers and 52 crenels fixed in 25-meter-high walls that were 15 meters thick at the base and 7 meters at the top. They were built of hard brick in the *Horasani* mode, surrounded on three sides (the Tigris protected the fourth wall) by three wide rings of dry moats, each up to 40 meters across. *Abbas I* took this impressive fortress-city in 1623 only because its garrison defected. Over the following 16 years the Ottomans devoted most of their military resources to its recapture. A seven-month siege failed in 1625–1626. A second attempt was made in 1630, with a caravan of 2,000 camels carrying bales of cotton to fill in the dry moats. However, the *Safavid* garrison counter-mined and trapped the attackers in a concealed pit, where they were slaughtered. It took a 39-day siege in 1638 to finally crack Baghdad's defenses. For the final siege the Ottomans brought 24,000 *beldar* (military laborers) and another 8,000 *lağimci* (sappers and miners), as well as specialized engineers and thousands of assault troops. Instead of cotton bales, brush and boughs to make *gabions* were carried in from lusher locales, on top of the regular kit of the laborers and soldiers, during the last leg of the march. Immediately, sapping of zigzag trenches began a mile out from the walls. Once the main guns were in place, on high ramparts on top of filled-in moats, shifts of *Janissaries* kept up a slow but constant bombardment of the inner defenses. A wide breach was made and the city was stormed after hard fighting atop the broad walls, not just with firearms but also with older weapons, including bows, sabers, hatchets, halberds, and knives.

Bagirmi. A small Central African state with its capital at Massenya. Around 1500 its governing class converted to Islam. Along with adoption of cavalry and firearms, this spurred it to violently expand. It did so mainly through slave-raiding at the expense of technologically less-advanced, pagan peoples to the south, around the Lake Chad basin. It also made war on *Bornu*.

Bahamas. A chain of hundreds of small islands of which but a handful were inhabited by Lucayas Indians. To fill out the *encomienda system*, from 1509 the Lucayas were deported by the Spanish to Hispaniola, where the local Indian population was dying in droves from disease and maltreatment. The Lucayas were subsequently made outright slaves and bought and sold in island marketplaces. Within four years there were no Lucayas left on the Bahamas. Permanent European settlement started in 1647.

bahşiş. The Ottoman pay system of cash bonuses given to members of the regular army; this was less a reward than a permanent salary increase (*terakki*). It was unrelated to payment from spoils (*"ganimet"*), the system used by the sultans to reward irregulars and auxiliaries.

bailey. A ringwork fort or enclosure made of timber, across a moat or dry ditch dug when building up a *motte*. The bailey afforded refuge inside a simple fort and allowed stockpiling of supplies. However, it was extremely susceptible to *mining* and *fire*. See also *keep-and-bailey*; *motte-and-bailey*.

bailli. A French official in charge of a "bailliage," the basic unit of government in medieval France. Traditionally, his military duty was merely honorary: he summoned the feudal levy (*arrière-ban*).

bakufu. "Tent government." The military bureaucracy, dominated by one major clan or another, which supported emperor-rule in Japan from 1185. The bakufu played a key role in mobilizing Japanese defenses against the *Mongol* invasion attempts that led to the *Battles of Hakata* (1274 and 1281). The Kamakura bakufu was displaced by the Muromachi bakufu in 1333. Under the *shoguns* the "baku-han" system (shogunal administration with local authority delegated to the *daimyo*) maintained a pretense of national government. Later, "bakufu" referred to the civil bureaucracy of the *Tokugawa shogunate* centered in Edo (Tokyo) and monitoring the Imperial Court at Kyoto and all regional daimyo. The lead bakufu council in charge of foreign policy and daimyo relations was the "Rōjū." The bakufu wrote the "Code for Military Houses" which established control over the daimyo, regulated commoners, enforced the Tokugawa ban on Christianity, and oversaw submission of the *samurai*.

balance of power. See *'Auld Alliance*; *Elizabeth I*; *Ethiopia*; *gunpowder empires*; *Habsburgs*; *Italian Renaissance*; *Italian Wars*; *Lodi, Peace of*; *Machiavelli, Niccolò di*

Bernardo; *Pavia, Battle of*; *Philip II, of Spain*; *Revolution in Military Affairs*; *slavery and war*; *Thirty Years' War*; *Venice*; *Westphalia, Peace of*.

baldric. A leather sword belt or harness, usually slung over the breast or back.

balestrieri. Italian infantry of the 15th century armed with ordinary crossbows. If they were armed with the much heavier type of crossbow that had to be transported on wheeled carts and manned by a firing crew of three or four men, they were known instead as "balestrieri ad molinellum."

balinger. During the 14th–16th centuries, a class of *clinker-built*, oared ship, with a single mast and sail. Originating in the Basque whaling industry, its design migrated to England where balingers were used in war and trade, displacing English *galleys* from local waters during the 14th century. See also *barge*.

balistae. Naval *crossbows*, whether ship-mounted or hand-fired.

balistarii equites. Mounted crossbowmen. They were known to the French as "arbalétriers."

Balkh, Battle of (1602). See *Uzbeks*.

ballista. See *springald*.

ballock. See *daggers*.

ballot. The action of, and loss of power and accuracy caused by, *solid shot* rebounding from side-to-side inside the bore as it traveled up the barrel of an artillery piece. This was unavoidable in early cannon, each of which had individualized and idiosyncratic bores. The problem was compounded by the fact that big guns fired nonstandardized stone shot. Since stonecutters only approximated the fit of shot to a specific bore, despite their great skill at cutting each cannonball was as unique in size, shape, and trajectory as the individual bores of the guns that fired them. The problem was worsened by a natural tendency to cut the ball significantly smaller than the bore to ensure a fit, which dramatically reduced propellent power of the expanding, explosive gases. The problem of balloting was lessened by later adoption of cast-iron cannonballs and standardized cast iron or bronze cannon, but it is in the nature of artillery ballistics and physics that it cannot be perfectly resolved for gravity-directed ordnance and remains a problem today.

Baltic. See *Christian IV*; *Danzig*; *Denmark*; *Dominum Maris Baltici*; *Gustavus II Adolphus*; *Hanse*; *Livonian Order*; *Muscovy, Grand Duchy of*; *Northern War, First*; *Poland*; *Sigismund III Vasa*; *Sound Tolls*; *Sweden*; *Teutonic Knights, Order of*; *Thirty Years' War*; *Wallenstein, Albrecht von*; *War of the Cities*.

bal yemez. Intermediate-size Ottoman siege guns, firing 24-okka shot (equivalent to 68-pound shot).

Banbury, Battle of (1469). See *Wars of the Roses.*

bandeiras. See *Brazil.*

bandolier. See *cartridges.*

banduq. A light matchlock firearm in use in India from the 15th century.

Banér, Johann (1596–1641). Swedish general. He served *Gustavus Adolphus* in Livonia, Poland, and Russia before moving with the king into Germany in 1630. He fought at *First Breitenfeld* (1631), where he commanded the Swedish horse on the right. He also fought at *Rain.* He was wounded at *Alte Feste,* but remained in command in the west while Gustavus marched to his death at *Lützen* in 1632. In 1634 Banér led 16,000 men into Bohemia, joined with the Saxons, and marched on Prague. He was recalled after the Swedes lost at *First Nördlingen.* He next fought and won at *Wittstock* (1636), but could not hold the territory taken. In 1637 he retreated into Pomerania. In 1639 he defeated the Saxon Army at Chemnitz, and went on to occupy parts of Bohemia. After wintering in the west, 1640–1641, Banér tried to seize Regensburg in a rare winter campaign, but fell short. He died later that spring.

> *In 1634 Banér led 16,000 men into Bohemia, joined with the Saxons, and marched on Prague.*

ban et l'arrière-ban. The feudal levy of France. See also *arrière-ban.*

banking. See *Fugger, House of; war finance.*

banner (*bannières*) (1). A small, square flag used as the ensign of a band (*banneret*) of *knights* fighting as a group under the designated commander of their *constabulary,* or unit of 10 or more knights. Such banners were celebrated and venerated under the code of *chivalry,* and were fiercely defended. They slowly evolved into sophisticated heraldic devices of the great magnate families of Europe. See also *choragiew; flags; pennant; sashimono.*

banner (*bannières*) (2). A small tactical unit, several of which made up a *battle,* which was the main medieval cavalry formation in Europe. They were often recruited on a lineage basis. Knights were supposed to cluster around the banner, which served as a rally point; but they also relied on discrete *battle cries.*

Banner (Swiss). Cantonal units each carried large flags, "Banners" displaying the unique symbol of their Canton. Around these, cantonal troops formed a

Swiss square. In battle, the Banner was carried at the center of the square by a "Venner" ("ensign"), tasked to keep close to the "oberster Feldhauptmann" (commanding officer). The Banners were capable of arousing deep devotion and sacrifice in battle, as the Swiss fought ferociously to defend standards in which they stored great pride. They were assigned honored hand-picked guards, over two dozen in some cases, who represented the guilds or towns of the Canton. If the army was confederate (an alliance of cantons), then all the major Banners were gathered around the main Swiss banner under heavy protection. The Banners provided each square with a central focus on the march, in assaults, and in defense. This enforced tight combat discipline and helped make the Swiss famously maneuverable. It also inspired confidence in commanders and in the collective endeavor. These large flags were often works of embroidered art, carefully stored and protected in peacetime by a designated officer. Most Banners were accompanied by fifers and drummers. The larger and wealthier cantonal Banners also retained *"Harsthörner"* ("Great War Horn") players, to inspire their own men and frighten the enemy. See also *carroccio*; *Fähnlein*; *Grandson, Battle of*; *mercenaries*.

banneret. From the 13th century an "officer" knight, usually a baron, in command of a small group of knights gathered to fight under a square *banner*, in place of each flying his own *pennant*. This formation was called a *constabulary*. In English armies a banneret had 10–15 knights and men-at-arms.

banner system (China/Manchuria). Chinese: "baqi," Manchu: "jakūn gūsa." A highly effective military organization established among the *Manchus* (Jürchen) by *Nurgaci*. While there is evidence of banner organization as early as 1595, it is conventionally said that Nurgaci arranged his 150,000-strong army into four banners in 1601. Each was grouped beneath a colored "plain" banner commanded by one of his kinsmen: blue, red, yellow, and white. In 1615–1616 he added four banners under "bordered" flags using the same four colors. About 300 "households" made up a company (Chinese "zuoling," Manchu "niru"), with 25 companies comprising a banner. This organization allowed coordinated and flexible tactical maneuvers; and the banners built unit solidarity and morale. Yet, they remained loyal to their generals as much as to Nurgaci or his son, Hong Taiji, until the conquest of Ming China. Late in that campaign, which lasted in the north from 1618 to 1644, Han Chinese and Mongol banners were formed within the Qing army from "ujen cooha" immigrant units which fought under a distinct black banner in the early 1600s. Chinese martial banners and Mongol units were officially added in 1642, raising the number of banners to 24 (with additional specialized companies): eight Manchu, eight Mongol, and eight Chinese. Additional banners were added later for "New Manchus" (the Sibo of Siberia) and Muslims from Turkmenistan. Many of the ethnically Han soldiers were experienced professionals, released prisoners of war who swore allegiance to the Manchus, or they were *renegades*. Unlike the Manchus, the

Chinese knew how to cast cannon and were skilled in siegecraft, which was important when facing China's fortified cities. On the other hand, Han banners did not tend herds in the winter but had to be maintained year-round, unlike Manchus and Mongols who were used to life as seasonal campaigners. This fact forced the Qing to modernize their empire and added incentive to acquire richer lands in China. After 1644 an elite guard drawn from the banners was positioned around Beijing displacing the armed *eunuchs* who previously guarded the Forbidden City. A few Russian captives also served in Qing banners. The banners survived to the end of the dynasty (1911). They were formally eliminated by the dictator Yuan Shikai in 1914.

banner system (Japan). Under the *Tokugawa*, "bannermen" ("hatamoto") served as shogunal retainers and guards of the main routes to Edo. This was of minimal military significance since the Tokugawa ended Japan's chronic civil wars, bringing a peace that lasted over 250 years.

Bannockburn (June 24, 1314). A key battle of the *Scottish Wars* fought astride the Bannock Burn, a small creek that fed into the Forth River. England's Edward II sent a relief army north to try to lift sieges of the last castles his men held in Scotland, at Berwick and Stirling. The English army comprised 2,000 knights and 12,000 *men-at-arms*, archers, and other infantry. The Scots, under Robert "The Bruce" (later Robert I) had just 8,000 men, mostly armed with pikes, along with 700 to 800 noble horse, and a few other mounted men-at-arms. Although outnumbered, the Scots knew about the dramatic lesson taught by Flemish militia to French knights at *Courtrai* (1302). Bruce chose the high ground, setting his right flank in a bend of the Burn while anchoring the left flank against a small wood. The English horse crossed the Bannock in broken formation. Bruce saw the opportunity to strike before his enemy was in position and sent four *schiltrons* of pikemen down the slope in echelon formation to close with the English knights. This lessened the impact of Edward's longbowmen, who tried to outflank the Scots but were met instead by a charge of the Scottish cavalry which scourged and scattered the archers. As the English knights turned to run the sheer weight of their own armor and horses trapped them in the fens astride the Bannock Burn, with the Scots pursuing and killing from the rear with bloody pikes and dirks. Thousands of knights and men-at-arms fell on the single bloodiest day for English *chivalry*. It was also a bloody day for the Scots, who lost half their men. Still, Stirling Castle soon surrendered, leaving only Berwick in English hands for a few years more. After Bannockburn, Scotland was assured of remaining an independent kingdom.

Suggested Reading: W. M. Mackenzie, *Battle of Bannockburn* (1913).

bannum. The feudal right of public *recruitment* and command of military service of vassals in one's immediate household or set of retainers. It was held by many noble ranks, from emperor to kings, dukes, counts, and other magnates. It was different from the obligations of military service based on the *fief*. See also *Imperial Army*.

banquette. See *parapet*.

Barbados. The Spanish never bothered to settle Barbados, concentrating on richer Caribbean islands. It was settled by England from 1627. Intended as a base from which to penetrate the monopoly of Iberian trade with New Spain and as a site to grow tobacco, it quickly became a refuge for *privateers*. When the tobacco crop failed planters turned to sugar, importing African slaves to work the fields. The success of sugar had an unintended consequence: Barbados became a market for food crops and fish that helped keep the tentative New England colonies viable. By the 1640s Barbados was dominated by a planter elite and made a small market for luxury goods in an increasingly integrated and burgeoning English empire in the Atlantic.

Barbarossa (c.1483–1546). Né Khayr ad-Din. Muslim corsair. As *dey* of Algiers he expanded the hinterland, took over the slave trade, fought off the Spanish, and imposed his will on other pirates with the help of European *renegades*. In command of an Ottoman galley fleet in the name of *Suleiman I*, in 1534 this red-bearded ("barbarossa") pirate and nominal Ottoman vassal captured Tunis. The next year he was driven off by *Andrea Doria* in command of an Imperial fleet sent by *Charles V*. Barbarossa built a Barbary battle fleet that scourged the western Mediterranean, raiding for slaves and capturing prizes on a grand scale. When not corsairing, this fleet supported the Ottoman navy. Barbarossa's skills were such that he commanded the entire Ottoman fleet at *Preveza* (1538), inflicting a sharp defeat on Andrea Doria and the Holy League. From 1541 to 1544 he raided Spanish coastal territories in Italy, in secret accord with France. Thirty years later, the corsair fleet he built up was annihilated at *Lepanto* (1571).

Barbary corsairs. While some actual *pirates* infested the North African coast, most of the so-called "Barbary corsairs" were navies of small Muslim states (*Tunis*, *Algiers*, and *Tripoli*) in the Maghreb which harassed and plundered Mediterranean commerce, especially after the end of the *Reconquista* in Spain. Regarded as pirates by Europeans, these "corsairs" were a thorn in the side of *Ferdinand* of Aragon, who fought them from 1490 to 1511, but then became their tacit protector against the Ottoman Empire as the Barbary states loosened ties with Constantinople. *Charles V* violently opposed them, and *Oliver Cromwell* sent an expedition against them in the 1650s. See also *Ifriqiya*.
  Suggested Reading: Peter Earle, *Corsairs of Malta and Barbary* (1970).

barber. A layer of iron plate worn on top of other armor for extra protection during a *tournament*.

barbican. An overhang or outer barrier emplaced to protect the gate (the weakest point of defense) of a castle or city wall. Some contained *machico-lations* through which hot oils and water could be poured on attackers, or missiles hurled or fired down at them. They were later replaced by *boulevards*.

barbuta. From the 15th century, a widely used armored helmet hammered out in the style of ancient Corinth: it fully covered the head, neck, and throat, with a T-shaped slit in front instead of a visor. It offered maximum protection while preserving visibility and was thus highly popular among soldiers.

bard. An early form of quilted blanket armor for horses, comparable to a *caparison*. Also, a generic term for horse armor. See also *chanfron*; *crinet*; *crupper*; *flanchard(s)*; *peytral*.

barded horse. A horse covered by a thick, armored blanket (*bard*) worn as light armor. See also *caparison*.

bardiche. A type of *halberd* with an elongated blade-head that curved back toward the haft. Also called a "vouge."

barge. In this period (14th–16th centuries), not a flat floating or towed craft as today, but a *clinker-built* oared ship with a single mast and sail used in trade or war. Fifteenth-century versions were larger than their cousin-in-design, the *balinger*.

bark. A class of 16th-century, small, sea-capable sailing ship. The variety of vessels covered by the term was vast. The key distinction was not size but ocean capability.

Barletta, Battle of (1502). See *Italian Wars*.

Barnet, Battle of (1471). See *Wars of the Roses*.

Barons' Wars (1215–1217 and 1264–1267). See *England*.

barony. Throughout the Middle Ages in Europe a lack of revenue and administrative skills in the lay population forced kings to rely on the most powerful magnates to help them raise armies greater than those drawn from royal lands, retinue, and vassals. Only the barons, dukes, and other great subjects had the capability to gather large numbers of followers from their extended family and vassal networks, equip them for war, and lead them into battle. The price paid by kings for lack of revenues and state structures sufficient to maintain a *standing army* was acceptance of the effective military independence of powerful magnates, who could and frequently did use private armies in rebellion, lead them away on *Crusades*, or spend them fecklessly in private wars over some local grievance with another great noble. See also *boyars (Russia)*; *boyars (Ruthenia)*; *boyars (Ukraine)*; *Burgundy, Duchy of*; *Casimir IV*; *feudalism*; *Guise family*; *Hundred Years' War*; *knights*; *Muscovy, Grand Duchy of*; *Poland*; *Polish Army*.

Bärwalde, Treaty of (January 1631). Signed by Cardinal *Richelieu*, this treaty promised a French subsidy of 400,000 taler per year in support of intervention by *Gustavus Adolphus* and the Swedish Army in the *Thirty Years' War*. It was superceded by another alliance treaty in 1635.

bascinet. A conical, visored helmet which had an *aventail* attached at the back to protect the neck. It was widely adopted in the 14th century, mainly by *knights* and *men-at-arms* but also by common soldiers who captured one in battle. They slowly evolved a high point to deflect glancing blows from swords and arrows. They came with various types of moveable visor, including a snout visor that gave the bascinet a pig-like appearance. The "great helm" was sometimes worn over the bascinet. The *armet* replaced the bascinet in the mid-15th century. See also *beaver*; *mail-tippet*.

Basel-Ferrara-Florence, Council of (1431, 1438, 1439). An *Ecumenical Council* of the Medieval Church which dealt with the Hussite rebellion in Bohemia and Hussite invasions of Austria, Hungary, and Germany. The moderate Hussites (*Utraquist*) accepted a compact that brought them back into the Catholic fold, but the offer was rejected by the more radical Taborites. See also *Hussite Wars*.

Bashi-Bazouks. *Mercenaries* in service to the Ottoman Empire. As irregulars, they fought in tribal dress rather than Ottoman uniform, and took payment in plunder rather than wages. Originally, they were mostly Afghan tribesmen. In later periods they came from marginal tribes of various ethnic backgrounds from all over the Empire. They were widely renowned for ferocity and merciless treatment of civilians.

basilard. See *daggers*.

basilisk. The term "basilisk" was most commonly used in England for 15th–16th-century big guns of the *cannon* class. The earliest were typically breech-loaded. The most famous was a huge gun, over seven meters in length, nicknamed "Queen Elizabeth's Pocket Pistol," a brass 12-pounder cast in Germany in 1544. It was presented to *Henry VIII* by *Charles V* when those monarchs allied against France. In 1643, during the *English Civil War*, it was deployed by *Charles I* and the *Cavaliers* at the siege of Hull. It was later captured by the *Roundheads* and used against the Royalists at the siege of Sheffield. By the end of the 16th century the term referred to the biggest guns (thousands of pounds deadweight) of the cannon class. These used huge amounts of black powder to hurl a 90-pound shot 750 yards with good accuracy and effectiveness. Theoretically, they could fire heavy projectiles as far as 4,000 yards.

bastard feudalism. See *feudalism*; *war finance: England*.

bastard musket. An early 17th-century English gun that weighed less than the standard "Dutch musket." It had a larger bore than a normal musket but was smaller than a *caliver*. The bastard musket fired one-ounce bullets (16 to a pound of lead). It saw limited service in a time of sustained peace in England.

bastille. A siege tower, or "counter-castle." By the 14th century they achieved final form as large towers built on earthen bases 30–40 yards wide and 2–3 yards high. A great bastille might house up to 500 men-at-arms and archers.

bastion. A shaped mound of earth surrounded with geometrically arranged walls, forming two angles and two faces in relation to the curtain wall of a castle or other fortification. It permitted defenders to fire in enfilade along the curtain wall, moat, or dry ditch. The development and spread of bastions swung the military advantage away from field armies back to defended strongpoints, mainly fortified towns and restructured castles. This forced most fighting, with important exceptions, back into prolonged sieges. J. R. Hale has convincingly demonstrated that the origins of the *trace italienne* date to a variety of sources around 1450. The complex geometrical bastion or full trace italienne was perfected in central Italy by Guilliano da Sangallo (1445–1516) between 1500 and 1515 and was widespread in its final form by 1530. See also *casement*; *chemin de ronde*; *counter-guard (1)*; *crownwork*; *demi-bastion*; *demi-lune*; *front*; *rampart*; *ravelin*.

> *The complex geometrical bastion or full trace ialienne was perfected in central Italy by Guilliano da Sangallo . . .*

Batavia. The Dutch naval base and entrepôt at Jakarta, Asian headquarters of the *Vereenigde Oostindische Compaagnie* (VOC) and the most valuable Dutch colony in the Far East. It served the *spice trade*. In Jonathon Israel's words, Batavia was "the foremost military, naval, and commercial base in Asia" in the 17th century, with "the largest concentration of Europeans anywhere in Asia," at 6,000 souls.

Báthory, Stefan (r.1575–1586). Duke of Transylvania; king of Poland. He was elected by the powerful Polish nobility, who compelled Anna *Jagiellon* to again marry a foreign prince to give him legitimacy on the throne. Báthory added Poland's military might to his own efforts to resist Ottoman pressure on Hungary and Transylvania. This required that he assert central control over the irascible and independent Polish nobility, raise taxes, and reform the bureaucracy and the army. In 1578 he reformed the infantry, units in which nobles had less interest or control. He established elite "wybraniecka" units which were attractive to peasants because military service freed them from *feudal* labor service. He had less luck with the cavalry, where the nobility predominated. His new taxes and tribunals and religious tolerance were resisted by Polish nobles across the land, and his engagement in foreign wars was deeply resented and opposed. *Danzig* refused to accept his election and in 1576 invited Denmark to intervene. Báthory blockaded Danzig by land and sea, but was unable to force the well-fortified and defended city to terms. In 1577 he agreed to effective autonomy for Danzig in exchange for nominal annual tribute. In the interim, Muscovy moved against Livonia, threatening greater Polish interests. Báthory led his new army on three expeditions into Russia during the *First Northern War* (1558–1583). See also *Polish Army*.

battalion. A basic infantry unit comprised of about 600 men. See also *brigade*; *company*; *drill*; *Ming Army*.

battery (1). "Ship's battery." The array of large cannon mounted on a single side of a ship; alternately, an array of broadside guns mounted on a single gun deck of a ship.

battery (2). "Shore battery." An array of large guns mounted along a shore-line or cliff's edge, usually protecting a harbor or placed at the mouth of a navigable river to fire upon and deny access to enemy ships.

battery (3). An array of cannon emplaced together on a battlefield to concentrate fire of the guns on a specific point in the enemy line. The usual number of guns per battery was 4, 6, or 8.

battle (1). The major division of a medieval army. A large medieval army was divided into three or four "battles," with each battle subdivided into *banners*. In cavalry armies, one or more battles might wait in reserve until the main battle had either broken against or through the enemy's line. Wings were added to protect the flanks. By the end of the Middle Ages cavalry armies usually had a main battle, a rearguard, two wings, and a small van. See also *pulk*.

battle (2). Combat at sea was for centuries mostly an affair of *piracy* and *privateering*, or amphibious actions intended to capture or relieve important coastal bases. Only occasionally did opposing fleets meet in open battle. When they did, until the 16th century the principal tactic was to close rapidly and grapple and board the enemy vessel. Combat at sea was, until the mounting of gunpowder cannon in the prows of galleys and broadside artillery on ships of sail, largely a matter of closing, ramming, grappling, boarding, and hand-to-hand and face-to-face killing and maiming. Opposing ships of sail would first maneuver for position, trying to catch the *weather gauge* and *windward* position. In a galley-to-sail action, the galleys had the upper hand initially as they were faster and more maneuverable, especially into the wind. As ships closed, if one had *castles* and the other did not, the height-advantaged troops would shower the enemy with missiles: stones, quarrels, and arrows, arquebus and swivel gun fire. If the wind was to their back they would throw lime over the enemy to blind him, unless he had anticipated this and erected protective nets. Also thrown were pots of hot pitch, resin, and oil, started aflame with fire arrows. Or soaps might be spilled, slicking the enemy's deck to impede his boarders or hamper his defense. *Greek Fire* was spat from flamethrowers by Byzantine ships. In the Atlantic *pots de fer* were launched at the enemy, or flaming tar arrows fired into his hull and deck. Weapons specialists with unique broadhead arrows that tore through sails went into action, while men with scythes cut the enemy's rigging, disabling his ship while other men fought his crew and marines. Once ships grappled, every slashing, puncturing, clubbing, thrusting, murderous hand weapon available for land warfare was used at sea as well. Close fighting seldom allowed for taking prisoners or for giving or receiving quarter.

Land combat was largely a matter of prolonged sieges and confused skirmishes. Small garrisons sallied to harass enemy lines and camps, or attacking infantry stormed broken town or fortress walls where a beech was made by artillery bombardment or a sapper's tunnel or mine. When field armies clashed the fighting was at remarkably close quarters. The carnage and savagery of a *Swiss square* was awesome, as men hacked off limbs or heads from other men and their horses, and impaled each other with "push of pike." Even when arquebusiers arrived on the battlefield fighting remained close: early hand guns were hardly accurate past 50–75 yards, and produced so much obscuring smoke that beyond the first volley or two little visual contact was had with the enemy, or even one's own formations. As a result, after discharging single-shot, muzzle-loading arquebuses or muskets, infantry advanced to engage in hand-to-hand fighting, deploying pikes, using muskets as clubs, thrusting and slashing at legs and belly with hard steel axes or swords or halberds. If winning cavalry had chased the opponent's horse from the field, it overran the baggage train or pivoted to attack into the flank of the enemy's infantry. As one side prevailed at the bloody, slogging, smoke-beclouded front, the enemy's formation disintegrated as file after file broke and ran from the rear, abandoning beaten comrades in the front files to wounding or death. From the 11th to 15th centuries it is thought that the losing side in the average battle left from 20 to 50 percent of its men dead on the field. At *Courtrai* (1302) the French lost 40 percent of their army, the same figure for French losses at *Poitiers* (1356) and *Agincourt* (1415).

This sort of encounter was, understandably, highly risky in the eyes of commanders. Not just the military outcome of a given battle, but the political stakes of the whole war were put in jeopardy by the vagaries of combat. Also, threat to life and limb of nobles was extremely high; even worse, destitution loomed possible if one was captured and had to pay a huge ransom to regain liberty. Field armies were also expensive and most of all, extremely hard to supply. Reserve armies were rare to nonexistent because it was just too expensive and inefficient to raise and billet an army and not use it. A single defeat of a king's field army might prove decisive, losing the war and with it much territory, titles, prestige, and wealth. In addition to the usual haphazards and chance outcomes of battle, field commanders could never be sure of the loyalty or fighting quality of the numerous *mercenaries* in their employ: would these men fight or run? And for whom would they fight? More than one commander rose on the morning of battle to observe that, during the night, a part of his army had gone over to the enemy and had lined up on the other side of the field, where the pay was better or the chance of survival deemed greater.

Mercenary captains made war as a game in which competitive positioning of field armies by each commander was designed to avoid more than to engage in battle, while gaining some slight advantage should battle nevertheless result. Both might then withdraw without offering combat, one giving an admiring salute to his opposite number in concession that he had been outmaneuvered and lost the advantage of topography or secure lines of supply. Given the contingency and risk of battle, wise commanders and monarchs usually preferred the controlled risks of a siege. Kingdoms could be, and were, made and unmade in battles that turned on some chance event or unpredictable act of heroism or cowardice by some underling. An old English nursery rhyme captured this reality well: "For want of a nail the shoe was lost, for want of a shoe the horse was lost; for want of a horse the battle was lost, for want of a battle the kingdom was lost." In China also, commanders often tried to avoid battles, seeing them as too risky militarily and politically. Dynasties rose and fell as a result of battles, cities were saved or sacked, thousands lived or died. That meant those who had wealth and power usually hunkered down behind solid fortifications and fought to keep it at the least possible risk, while those who sought power or plunder employed ruses and stratagems of any and every kind to force a battle that might bring the chance to rise high in the world in the course of a single hour or day. See discrete battles and *castles, on land*; *chevauchée*; *chivalry*; *condottieri*; *fortification*; *knight*; *raiding*; *siege warfare*; *war at sea*.

battle-axe. See *axes*; *poleax*.

battle cries. A common means to either pluck up collective courage, or signal rally points, or issue commands was the battle cry. The Ottomans timed pre-battle shouts to the crash of musket volleys, to frighten the enemy and raise their own spirits. Constant beating of battle drums served similar purposes. Battle cries of this period, as in all war, were extremely varied. Only a handful of illustrative samples are listed here. Among the most famous and most typical of an age that mixed God and battle in every recipe for war was the battle cry of the *Teutonic Knights*. They shouted as they charged toward some poor Wend or other pagan village on the Baltic coast, or against a more equal Lithuanian host: "Gott mit uns!" ("God is with us!"). French Crusaders fighting Muslims or heretics yelled "Dieu le veut!" ("God wills it!"). Matching deity to deity, when Muslims drew swords they shouted toward heaven: "Allah akbar!" ("God is Great!"). The yell of *Hospitallers* was "St. Jean! St. Jean." When *Hussites* fought the *Ordensstaat* in the 1450s they beat a war drum made from the skin of their dead commander, *Jan Žižka*, and sang the battle hymn: "We, warriors of God!" which ended: "slay, slay, slay, slay them every one." It was common to shout out the name of one's country alongside that of the deity. The *conquistadores* who slew with *Cortés* shouted "Castilla! Castilla!" as they charged into the Aztecs at *Otumba* (1520) and at *Tenochtitlán* (1521), while Mezoamerican allies chanted the name of their city-state: "Tlaxcala! Tlaxcala!"

Some battle cries were intended more for enemy ears than one's own. Finnish cavalry fighting for *Gustavus Adolphus* in Poland or Muscovy or Germany raised terror among their enemies when they foretold bloodthirsty deeds to come: "Hakkaa paalle!" ("Cut them down!"). In battles of the *Thirty Years' War* fought after the *sack of Magdeburg* by a Catholic army in 1631, Protestants cried: "Magdeburg Quarter!" meaning they would give none. Royalist gunners in the *English Civil Wars* (1639–1651) rather languorously exclaimed the politically sophisticated battle cry: "First shot for the devil! Second for God! Third for the King!" Conversely, some things just were not said on the battlefield. For instance, in medieval English armies it was forbidden to

> *...crying "Havoc!" was a self-issued warrant from the most savage soldiers to commence murder, burning, pillaging, and rape ...*

shout "Monte" ("to horse!"), because it tended to induce panic if mistaken as the signal to dismounted knights to remount and flee. On the other hand, crying "Havoc!" was a self-issued warrant from the most savage soldiers to commence murder, burning, pillaging, and rape, a practice recalled, though predated to ancient Rome, by Shakespeare's "Cry Havoc! And let slip the dogs of war!" (*Julius Caesar*, Act III, Scene I).

Bavaria. See *Catholic League (Germany)*; *Guelphs and Ghibellines*; *Gustavus II Adolphus*; *Holy Roman Empire*; *Maximilian I*; *Rupert, Prince*; *Swabian League*; *Swabian War*; *Thirty Years' War*; *Wallenstein, Albrecht von*.

Bayezid I (r.1389–1402). Ottoman sultan. Following the *Battle of Kosovo*, he consolidated the European holdings of the Ottoman Empire and absorbed remaining independent Turkic statelets in Anatolia. From 1390 he built a *standing army*, including a large artillery train and expanded *Janissary Corps*. His navy challenged the fleets of Venice and Genoa and pressured the coastline of the weakening Byzantine Empire. He defeated a Christian coalition army at *Nicopolis* (1396), but was himself defeated and taken prisoner by *Timur* at *Ankara* (1402). Unable to bear humiliation and torment, he committed suicide in captivity. His defeat and death set off a civil war within the Ottoman Empire that did not end until the emergence of *Murad II*.

Bayezid II (1447–1512). Ottoman sultan, 1481–1512; successor to *Muhammad II*. He continued the Ottoman advance into the Balkans, built up the

Ottoman artillery train, and expanded the *Janissary Corps*. In a naval war with Venice, 1499–1503, his fleet severely damaged the Venetians at *Lepanto* (1499), thereby securing domination of the eastern Mediterranean. He was less successful regarding the Mamlūks of Egypt, whose army he fought in Iraq. He was stymied by the zealous *Safavid* regime in Iran, partly because in his last decade he concentrated on domestic reform and personal religious study. A tolerant ruler, he accepted 200,000 Jews into the Empire after their expulsion from Spain, Portugal, and Italy, settling most near Salonika. Bayezid was deposed by his murderous son, *Selim I* ("The Grim").

Bay of Seine, Battle of (1417). See *Hundred Years' War*.

bayonet. Named for Bayonne, where it originated. Blades had long been attached to hunting weapons to finish off wounded animals without reloading or wasting shot and powder. The earliest military use of bayonets was by the French Army in 1647, at Ypres. These were plug-fitted into the barrel. That prevented firing once they were mounted, but allowed musketeers to act as their own pikemen, which gave infantry formations greater firepower. By 1650 some muskets had bayonets fixed to the gun at manufacture, hinged and foldable back along the barrel. French fusiliers adopted the plug bayonet as standard equipment in 1671; English fusiliers followed suit in 1685. The socket, or ring, bayonet did not appear until shortly after this period when it was introduced to the French Army by Sébastien le Prestre de Vauban. See also *child-mother gun*.

Béal Atha Buí, Battle of (1598). See *Nine Years' War*.

beat the drum. Recruiting parties offering pay, board, and other enticements to prospective soldiers marched through towns accompanied by a boy or young soldier beating a small drum. After a crowd gathered the recruiter made his pitch, which usually included a token up-front payment (known as "beer money" in England). This crude approach was surprisingly effective.

Beaugé, Battle of (March 21, 1421). A Franco-Scots army raided English lands in Normandy and Maine, provoking an English army into the field. The two forces met at Beaugé in Anjou. The English cavalry made a French mistake—over pursuit—and were cut off, surrounded, and slaughtered. The English infantry arrived later and fared better, pushing the French and Scots from the field, but not compensating for the loss of the English horse. This victory for France was a small premonition of the coming turn of the tide in the *Hundred Years' War* (1337–1453).

beaver. A moveable face-guard on a *bascinet*. Sometimes connected to, other times replacing, the visor.

beaver wars. Large-scale wars between the Iroquois and Huron Indians of northeastern North America in the 17th century, fought over control of the fur trade. They engaged armies with many hundreds of braves, not small war parties conducting frontier raids. See also *Indian Wars*.

bedel-i nüzul. An exceptional surtax used to provide grain to the army, increasingly relied on by the Ottoman sultans in the 17th century as military expenditures rose. It was partly offset by compulsory state buying of grain at local market prices along the lines of march, so that it proved more a boon than a bane to the peasantry. This contrasted greatly with the European system of *contributions*.

Bedouin. Nomadic tribes originally of the Arabian desert, but after the expansion of Islam found across North Africa and into southern Iraq. While the majority of early Muslim rulers and generals were townsfolk from Mecca or Medina, most warriors of the first decades of Arab expansion were tough desert tribesmen, schooled in the *razzia* tactics and caravan warfare of the Arabian desert. Their style and strategy has often been compared to war at sea, where the deep desert provided refuge from more powerful infantry armies which could not penetrate it, while also offering opportunities for lightning strikes against high-value targets around its perimeter. In this they most closely resembled the Mongols, although the camel was nowhere near the quality of war animal that the Mongol grass-fed pony was. Archery from a camel's back was even more difficult than from horseback. Also, camels could not be made into a desert equivalent of *heavy cavalry* since they would not charge the way a trained *destrier* did. Bedouin instead fought as *dragoons*, riding to battle but dismounting for combat. In defense, camels took the Bedouin deep into the desert where neither horse cavalry nor infantry from plush riverine lands in Egypt or Iraq could follow.

Bedouin caught the fire of religious zeal when they converted to Islam in the 7th century. They joined Muhammad on the first *jihad*, conquering and converting pagan Arabia. Then they burst outward in one of the most explosive and lastingly influential campaigns of conquest in world history. Wherever possible, conquering Arab-Bedouin armies preferred to set up military bases where their barren desert refuge bordered on conquered agricultural lands. Of course, where a major city such as Cairo or Damascus fell it became a new Arab capital. Garrison towns of Bedouin military colonists grew from tent encampments into administrative centers of a vast empire, then into rich and prosperous cities (*amsār*). Such was the case with Basra in northern Iraq, Qomm in Iran, and Qaurawān in Tunisia, all centers of Islamic and Arab military power that were originally Bedouin military camps. Over time, Bedouin were assimilated by the more advanced urban populations they conquered. Traditional Bedouin ways of military and cultural life persisted in Arabia and deep inside other desert fringes such as the northern border of the Sahara. There, Bedouin skills remained finely honed by a climate unforgiving of error. From there, religious revivals of a puritanical nature would sweep Bedouin mujahadeen out of the desert to assault coastal Muslims seen as grown lax in the faith. African Bedouin frequently came under the influence of desert *marabouts*, and warred with the coastal city-states of Africa. Later, they fiercely resisted European penetration of Tunisia, Tripoli, and Morocco.

beeldenstorm. See *Eighty Years' War*; *iconoclasm*.

beg. See *bey*.

Beggars (*"Gueux"*). See *Eighty Years' War*; *Margaret of Parma*; *Sea Beggars*.

Beijing, Fall of (1214). See *China*; *Mongols*.

Beijing, Fall of (1644). See *China*; *Ming Army*.

Bektashi Order. See *Bektaşi Order*.

Bektaşi **Order.** An important dervish order founded by Hacci Bektash Veli. Moderate Bektashism was broadly tolerated by Ottoman sultans, and Bektashi troops served in the army alongside orthodox sunni and Christian soldiers. See also *Janissary Corps*; *Ottoman warfare*.

belatores. "Men of war." The second class in the mature feudal worldview of three orders: clergy, nobles, and peasants. "Belatores" were great nobles and *knights*, men who lived for and from war.

beldar. Ottoman military laborers. Employed mainly in trench digging during sieges, they were civilians recruited in Anatolia (one from every 20 households) and used solely for military labor, not as fighting men. See also *lağimci*.

belfry. A moveable siege tower that could be rolled against a castle or town wall to permit storming. It was made of wood, usually with hide, lead, or copper shielding to block or impede arrows.

Belgium Nostrum. The idea of a single "fatherland" encompassing all 17 provinces of the Habsburg Netherlands. It did not survive the *Protestant Reformation* and *Eighty Years' War*.

Belgrade, Siege of (1456). See *Hunyadi, János*; *Muhammad II*.

Belgrade, Siege of (1521). See *Suleiman I*.

bellum hostile. A *just war* waged by a rightful, sovereign ruler. If proclaimed by right authority and recognized as such, no legal or moral impediment barred his doing harm to the lives and property of enemy civilians (subjects of the enemy lord against whom the "bellum hostile" was declared and fought).

bellum justum. See *just war tradition.*

bellum se ipse alet. "War should pay for itself." A widely accepted principle holding that armies should sustain themselves to the highest degree possible by plunder. In countries with semi-representative bodies, usually controlled by the nobility, there was a corresponding belief that war was largely the king's business and that he should pay for it from royal revenues rather than new or general taxes. See also *attrition*; *chevauchée*; *contributions*; *logistics*; *war finance.*

Benburb, Battle of (1646). See *English Civil Wars*; *O'Neill, Owen Roe.*

Benevento, Battle of (1266). See *Saracen.*

Benin, Kingdom of. A West African city-state centered on the walled Edo city of Benin. In the 13th century (the precise date is unknown) Benin adopted a dynasty from the prestigious and ancient *Yoruba* city of Ife, to fill the position of "Oba," and settled into a stable period. In the mid-15th century it began to expand and sell prisoners as slaves to the Portuguese, who arrived in 1486, based on São Tomé and Principe. From 1520, Benin chose a policy of isolation from European traders. It remained insulated from Europe for nearly 200 years. Within its region it maintained trade and political relations with the Yoruba city-states, toward which it steadily expanded. By the end of the 16th century Benin governed most Edo as well as some Ibo and Yoruba within the Niger delta.

Berbers. Hamitic peoples of North Africa living along the Barbary Coast, and penetrating as well into the Sahara desert. Their peak influence in world history came when, united under the Almohads ruling from Marrakesh from the 12th century, they governed all the Maghreb and most of Spain. Their military was predominantly light cavalry who wore mail armor and spiked onion-helmets. They used javelins or thrusting spears, not *lances*. Their infantry were normally black slave soldiers armed with stabbing spears, slings, and bows. Their tactics were to swarm the enemy, overwhelming with numbers. However, the Christian *Reconquista* eroded this advantage as attacks by *heavy cavalry* routinely broke up the Muslim battle-order. See also *caliph*; *Granada*; *"holy war."*

Bergen-op-Zoom, Siege of (1622). See *Eighty Years' War.*

Bergerac, Peace of (September 17, 1577). See *French Civil Wars.*

Bergfreid. A type of early castle typical of the mountainous regions of Austria, Germany, Italy, and Switzerland. It was characterized by a watchtower rather than a *motte*, built on a highpoint.

Bernardines. See *Bernhard von Sachsen-Weimar*.

Bernard of Clairvaux (1090–1153). Cistercian Abbot. See also *Albigensian Crusade*; *Crusades*; *Knights Templar*.

Bernhard von Sachsen-Weimar (1604–1639). "Saxe-Weimar." Mercenary general. A minor noble without income, he became a mercenary at an early age and saw action in many of the key battles of the *Thirty Years' War*. He served *Frederick V* of the Palatinate first, losing at *Wiesloch* and *Wimpfen* in 1622, and *Stadtlohn* in 1623. Where other captains, such as *Graf von Mansfeld*, were greedy but dilatory and incompetent, Bernhard was ruthless and avaricious but at least kept his regiments together. He hired out to *Christian IV* in 1624, and *Gustavus Adolphus* in 1630. He was courageous at *First Breitenfeld* (1631), for which he reaped the reward of the bishoprics of Würzburg and Bamberg.

> *Where other captains . . . were greedy but dilatory and incompetent, Bernhard was ruthless and avaricious, but at least kept his regiments together.*

He fought at *Lützen*, rallying the Swedes to victory after Gustavus was killed and personally capturing the Imperial artillery train. In command of the *League of Heilbronn* army, Bernhard and Horn were beaten at *First Nördlingen* (1634), losing 21,000 out of 25,000 men. The next year Bernhard allied with the French and campaigned in Alsace and northern Germany. He fought at *Rheinfelden* and took the key fortress of Breisach, in December 1638. When he died on July 18, 1639, of smallpox, his contract army (the "Bernardines" or "German brigade") was released to *Louis XIII*. Bernhard's generalship was spotty, but he was second only to *Albrecht von Wallenstein* as an entrepreneur of war. Both men enforced *contributions* on occupied territory more ruthlessly than any other field commander. See also *prisoners of war*.

besagaws. Small, round pieces of *plate armor* that protected the underarms.

besonios. Raw recruits for the *Army of Flanders* trained by the Spanish in Italian garrisons before sending them up the *Spanish Road* to glory or to gory death.

Bestallungbrief. "Letter of appointment." A document issued to a mercenary captain laying out terms of payment and the number of men he was expected to recruit, and naming him or some other officer as the *Obrist* (colonel) of the *Landsknechte* company raised.

Bethlen, Gabriel (1580–1629). Transylvanian prince. A tolerant Protestant, he allied with *Friedrich V* against the Habsburgs. After the *White Mountain* (1620), he made peace with *Ferdinand II* and retained control of parts of

Hungary. Mansfeld tried to link with Bethlen in 1626, after losing at *Dessau Bridge*. Bethlen then confirmed his understanding with Ferdinand.

bevor. An armored collar worn to protect the chin and throat.

bey. Turkish: "beg" ("lord"). The term had three related meanings. Originally, it referred to semi-independent Turkic or Kurdish begs who ruled large parts of eastern Anatolia after the collapse of the Abbasid Caliphate. From this, it was later used for any provincial governor in the Ottoman Empire ruling a territory called a *Beylik*. The "sanjak bey" governed a sanjak, the main administrative unit of the Empire. A "kahya bey" acted as the field agent of the *Grand Vezier* in military and political affairs. More generally, a "bey" was the local ruler of any independent Muslim principality. The honorific was used in this sense throughout the *Maghreb*. In Tunis and Algiers the bey was formally, though not always actually, subordinate to the *dey*.

Beyliks. In its original meaning, this referred to minor Muslim (usually, Turkic) principalities that emerged in Anatolia after the collapse of the Abbasid caliphate, the defeat of the Crusader states, and the defeat and retreat of the Mongols. The westernmost Beyliks waged a prolonged frontier war with the declining *Byzantine Empire*. Further east, the Beyliks were steadily gobbled up by the expanding Ottomans. Later the term was applied to any Ottoman province governed by an autonomous official called a *bey*. See also *Piyadeğan militia*; *Yaya infantry*.

Bhutan. A mountain kingdom ruled from Tibet in the 16th century. Under Buddhist rule, it followed a policy of strict isolationism throughout this period.

Bicocca, Battle of (1522). See *La Bicocca, Battle of*.

bill. See *brown bill*; *gisarmes*; *halberd*; *staff-weapons*.

billhook. See *brown bill*.

birlin. A small oared warship used for raids and amphibious assaults in the isolated West Highlands and outer islands of Scotland. They were still in use into the 17th century. See also *galley*.

Biscuits, Battle of (1594). See *Nine Years' War*.

Bishops' War, First (1639). This bloodless war of maneuver was provoked by the effort of *Charles I* to impose episcopacy on Scotland, along with a Scottish Book of Common Prayer. Outraged, the Scots drafted a National Covenant and stripped bishops of all authority, while *Alexander Leslie* raised a *Covenanter* army and seized Edinburgh and other Royalist outposts. The king planned a campaign to include an amphibious landing and tried to raise an Irish army, but it never mustered. Instead, about 15,000 English troops, mainly drawn from the *trained bands* moved to York under Arundel, an inept Catholic general favored by the Queen. Forward detachments of the two armies brushed near Kelso but no fight ensued there or the next day at Duns Law (June 5). Charles lost his nerve despite vastly greater numbers, and opened negotiations. This handed the Scots a strategic victory without the risk or sacrifice of battle. Meanwhile, wild Gordons routed a small Covenanter detachment at Turriff, the first bloodletting of the *English Civil Wars*.

Bishops' War, Second (1640–1641). *Charles I* again tried to raise an Irish army in 1640, to supplement pressed men from England he raised instead of the *trained bands*. However, *Alexander Leslie* recruited a *Covenanter* army of 20,000 "godly soldiers," officered by veteran Scots mercenaries. Leslie crossed the Tweed and took Newcastle hostage to the king's word before the English fully mobilized. The armies finally met at Newburn, where the English foot fled after losing several hundred men. With his army badly commanded and under-funded, Charles agreed to pay for upkeep of the Covenanter army and sought to seal the truce through elevation of Leslie and other Scots nobles to English peerages. His Irish army later entered the fray of the great Irish rebellion that began in 1641. See also *English Civil Wars*.

Suggested Reading: Mark Fissel, *The Bishops' Wars* (1994).

Black Bands. Mounted arquebusiers active in the *Italian Wars* (1494–1559).

Black Company. Bohemian mercenaries hired by King Mathias (1458–1490) of Hungary to supplement his *hussars* and artillery train.

Black Death. Repeated episodes of pandemic plague affected large areas of Eurasia over millennia. The "plague" was almost certainly a combination of bubonic plague (rat flea borne, and highly disfiguring), pneumonic plague (a more lethal variety, and because air-borne also the most infectious strain), and septicaemic plague (human flea borne, and a quick killer). Early records suggest it may first have struck in Mongolia in 46 C.E., wiping out over half the population. Other outbreaks, most probably of the "Black Death," devastated large parts of China between 312 and 468 C.E. A Mediterranean outbreak in the 4th century may have fatally undermined the western Roman Empire. In the mid-14th century these variants of plague combined to devastate much of Asia and Europe. The pandemic was not usually called the "Black Death" at the time. It was known as the "Great Plague" or the "Poor Plague" or simply as "The Plague," though in France it was called "le morte bleue." The disease most likely originated in Central Asia in the early 1330s, spreading in all directions from there. It may have arrived in China in 1331, where 9 of every 10 people in Hopei province died of some still unidentified epidemic. A plague pandemic was reported in China for 1353–1354. The dislocation caused by these waves of plague destabilized China, compounding the distress of a dramatic shift in the course of the Yellow River in 1344 that killed more millions. The social pressures these events released underwrote a calamitous civil war that saw radical Buddhists, the *Red Turbans*, topple the Yuan dynasty and allowed a peasant, Zhu Yuanzhang, to found the Ming dynasty as the *Hongwu* ("Vast Military") emperor. The plague may have halved China's population within just a few decades, dispiriting survivors and opening frontiers to deep raiding by Inner Asian nomads exquisitely organized for war.

The plague also became established in Inner Asia, doing its worst work in the towns and cities that straddled the main trade routes, notably parts of the old Silk Road. It was likely spread by itinerant merchants unknowingly carrying flea-infested rats hitching rides in grain bags, and by infected Tartar and Turkic invaders. It reached India in 1338. Even as it scourged the subcontinent it penetrated Iran. Moving directly west from Central Asia, an outbreak was reported in the Crimea in 1346, where it interrupted the Mongol siege of Caffa. From the Crimea it spread throughout the Mediterranean basin on merchant ships. It arrived in Europe by several routes, but certainly on Genoese galleys pulling from Caffa, their crews fleeing the infection and invading Tartars but in fact bringing the disease with them. Plague first broke out in Italy at Messina in October 1347. Three major centers of Mediterranean contagion then developed: Sicily, Genoa, and Venice (Milan was virtually untouched at first). The Black Death moved thence to Tunis and North Africa, on to Iberia, and up and down Italy. Everywhere, it hit coastal towns first and hardest, then migrated inland, along with the men who made their living from inland riverine commerce. It appears to have moved into Russia with infected crews arriving from the northwest via the sea, not overland from the Tartars. It came not by horse and rider, but inside fleas riding on rats aboard Baltic cogs and on plague ships from England, the Netherlands, and infected cities of the *Hanse*. It killed 200,000 in a late outbreak in Muscovy in 1570.

Mortality rates reached from 30 percent to 90 percent everywhere it appeared. Death might occur within 24 hours of the first outward signs of contagion, a speed which only heightened the terror. At least one-third of Europe's 25 million people died in the first outbreak (1347–1350). The populations of China, India, and Europe all declined intermittently but unrelentingly from fresh outbreaks during the next century. Fear gripped the healthy: suspected plague ships arriving in Genoa were driven away by clouds of flaming arrows fired by militia upon the desperate urging of terrified city-folk. Victims were viewed with almost as much revulsion as fear: as well as bringing death the plague was horribly disfiguring of beauty and dignity. Physicians offered no real aid, and survivors were usually so stunned and overwhelmed by the scale of loss and grief that charity and solace was rare. The old social custom for leprosy was revived: 40 days' quarantine on the first sign of infection, although this was difficult to enforce. Almost overnight the plague made arable land— the true coinage of the medieval economy—more plentiful, while sharply curtailing available labor and thus driving higher wages and prices. Thus, inflation contributed its own evils to a sharp economic decline already underway from other 14th-century upheavals and torments such as the *Hundred Years' War* (1337–1453) and the *Reconquista*. The plague briefly interrupted those conflicts, in the former by killing more English and French in a passing summer than had killed each other in the prior 10 years. After its first wave, field armies were much smaller than a century before. And although the plague freed land, it killed off so many peasants and landlords and so reduced demand for foodstuffs in depopulated towns that marginal agricultural areas were left fallow or allowed to return to bog or forest.

The Black Death recurred in frequent but less virulent waves for 130 years, until resistance was built up among survivors. Even then, plague could bring catastrophe at a moment's notice, as it did in 1575–1577 and 1630–1631 in Venice where outbreaks killed one-third of the population; or Naples where it killed 300,000 in 1656; or the "Great Plague of London" in 1665; or from 1648 to 1652 and again from 1677 to 1685 in northern Spain, where it advanced that country's decline as a major economic and military power. During the *English Civil Wars* (1639–1651) outbreaks of plague in 1644 and 1645 decimated armies and cities on both sides. This lingering threat of plague lent a sense of psychological precariousness to private and public affairs that surely contributed to the general breakdown of religious authority in Europe that anticipated the great religious disturbances of the 16th–17th centuries. The plague underlay abortive revolutions, peasant uprisings, civil wars, and economic, social, and millenarian-like religious unrest, as many concluded that the Black Death was the "flagellum Dei"—the "scourge of God"—sent to punish Mankind for its wickedness. But since the plague scourged godly and wicked alike its work among men raised doubts about the moral standing of the Church and even about the Christian worldview. The utter devastation of normal life that plague brought encouraged excesses of both piety and hedonism, dislocations experienced from Ireland to Byzantium, from Italy to Scandinavia, and throughout the Middle East and North Africa. In some countries peasants and townsfolk were aroused to murderous rage against scapegoat populations. In the Swiss Confederation and Germany, Christian mobs murdered thousands of Jews with a ferocity and zealous hate not seen again in Germany until the 20th century, not even during the anti-Semitic outbursts of the *Thirty Years' War* (1618–1648). Some rulers tried to stop such persecutions but lacked the means; others encouraged the pogroms. Many Christians in Germany also turned to mass flagellation to expiate the weight of sin thought to have caused this terrible punishment. Elsewhere, those called "heretics" or accused of *witchcraft* were targeted and killed. Many now openly said what previously only a few had dared to think: the Church, too, perhaps even especially, had provoked God's righteous anger with scandalous misbehavior by the clergy and endemic corruption, including selling indulgences in this life as a guarantee of reduced suffering in the afterlife. This established an important intellectual legacy of anti-clericalism that blossomed into "heresy" in Bohemia, Germany, and

England in the 14th century, and to some degree underlay the later religious upheavals and wars attending the *Protestant Reformation*.

Muslims in general took a harder attitude than Christians (or Hindus) against quarantine or other "ungodly" efforts to deny the apparent will of Allah to use plague to separate the wicked from the good. In the long run this weakened Muslim regimes, which were more urban and hence more susceptible to the spread of pandemics than Balkan Christian or Hindu or other rural populations they governed. Also, by decimating Mongol, Uzbek, Tartar, and other nomad populations of the Eurasian Steppe which had a lesser ability to recover population losses, the Black Death opened the way for the settled civilizations of Russia, Iran, and China to expand into, and finally control, the great grasslands of Eurasia. That reversed a trend of world migratory and military history several millennia old. The plague subsided in Europe partly because new construction techniques eliminated thatch roofing as a

> *...many concluded that the Black Death was the "flagellum Dei"—the "scourge of God"—sent to punish Mankind for its wickedness.*

nesting place for plague rats. It was eliminated only in the 18th century when an invasion of Europe by non-plague-bearing grey house rats helped squeeze out the last dormant bacillus clusters. In China and India, however, in times of war or famine especially, major outbreaks of plague occurred as late as the 1890s: an outbreak in Bombay in 1898 may have killed six million. In Egypt there was a significant outbreak as late as the 1940s. See also *Council of Trent*; *Crusades*; *Falkirk, Battle of*; *Gibraltar*; *Hanse*; *Hongwu emperor*; *Reconquista*; *Red Turbans*; *Teutonic Knights, Order of*.

Suggested Reading: John Kelly, *The Great Mortality* (2005); William H. McNeill, *Plagues and Peoples* (1977; 1998); Philip Ziegler, *The Black Death* (1969).

Black Guard. See *Landsknechte*.

Black Legend. Iberian and Latin American historians have long debated the character of Spanish government in Europe and the fundamental nature of Spanish colonial rule. The "Black Legend" refers to Spain's reputation among those historians, mainly classical liberals, who condemned Spanish civilization and government as especially oppressive, backward, and obscurantist, even by the standards of lingering Medievalism and early modern history and colonialism elsewhere. The principal contribution to the Black Legend was the *Inquisition*, notorious for its corruption, repression of conscience, torture and inspired terror, and burning of books and people (*auto de fe*). The Black Legend was also advanced by English Protestant historians who wrote about the great war with Spain from a nationalist and Protestant perspective. Also contributing was the widespread Protestant perception that the policies of *Charles V* and *Philip II* were driven by a core ambition to restore a single Catholic empire, by any means, including deliberately sending ruthless generals such as the *Duke of Alba* to slaughter Protestants in the Netherlands. The *Spanish Fury* in Antwerp also advanced the legend. With regard to Spain's colonies, the picture was attended by portrayal of pre-colonial Indian political and social life as pacific and idyllic, which was far from the truth concerning the *Inca* or the *Aztec*, at the least. The converse propaganda produced by Spanish and Catholic historians was a "White Legend" which stressed the benefits of the *Pax Hispanica*, and the supposed mildness of conditions of slavery in New Spain as compared to Brazil or the English slave colonies of the Caribbean and North America.

Black Prince (1330–1376). Edward, Prince of Wales. At age 16 his father, *Edward III*, put him in command of the English right flank at *Crécy* (August 26, 1346). When the young prince asked for reinforcements his father declined, supposedly saying "Let the boy earn his spurs." In 1355 the Black Prince led a bloody *chevauchée* from Bordeaux to the Mediterranean Sea, burning hundreds of towns and villages in a wide swath of destruction and round trip of 900 km in just two months. The Black Prince won a victory for England at *Poitiers* (1356), where he captured and held for ransom the French king, Jean II. He took his father's infantry tactics into Iberia, where he used them to win a victory for *Pedro the Cruel* at *Nájera* (1367). In 1370 he carried out an atrocity in Limoges, slaughtering 3,000 civilians. Late in his father's reign, the Black Prince championed the clerical faction in a growing quarrel among the English elites over the place of the Church in national life, royal revenues, and papal authority. He never ruled as Edward IV because he predeceased his father by a year. His son, Richard II, reigned from 1377 to 1399. See also *Brétigny, Treaty of; Jacquerie*.

Suggested Reading: H. Hewitt, *The Black Prince's Expedition of 1355–1357* (1958).

Black Riders (*Schwartzenreiter*). German *Reiter* cavalry who wore all black armor. They were active in the war between *Charles V* and the *Schmalkaldic League*.

Blackwater River, Battle of (1598). See *Nine Years' War*.

Blake, Robert (1599–1657). Parliamentary soldier in the *English Civil Wars*. He was a talented tactician and leader, winning several early defensive battles against superior Royalist forces. In 1649 he was appointed "General at Sea." He subsequently proved equally adept in naval warfare as he was on land, against the Royalists and later in the Republic's several wars with the Netherlands.

blockade. Sea blockades, in the modern sense, were beyond the capabilities of this era. The most that was assayed was occupation of small harbors, such as by Ottoman galleys during the *sieges of Malta*. More common were river blockades in densely populated areas like Germany and the Netherlands. On land, the small size of many castles meant that, unlike towns, they were susceptible to circumvallation and blockade. Land blockades sometimes deployed a "counter-castle" ("siege bastilles") or small fort used to intercept commercial traffic, but the main technique was starvation-induced despair. This meant burning all crops, hamlets, and villages surrounding a castle or town. See also *convoy*; *Danzig*; *Eighty Years' War*; *freedom of the seas*; *Hanse*; *Invincible Armada*; *Jeanne d'Arc*; *Leicester, Earl of*; *Macao*; *Normans*; *Olivares, conde-duque de*; *Oliwa, Battle of*; *Rhodes, Siege of (1522–1523)*; *Sea Beggars*; *siege warfare*; *spice trades*; *tribute*; *True Pure Land*; *Twelve Years' Truce*.

blockship. Any vessel, though for obvious reasons usually confined to value-less, leaky, unseaworthy ships, sunk on purpose with the intent to block a channel or obstruct traffic in a harbor. See also *scuttle*.

Blois, Treaties of (1504–1505). Louis XII (1462–1515) continued the *Italian Wars* (1494–1559) started by his predecessor, the reckless Charles VIII (1470–1498), who invaded Italy in 1494. Following breakdown of a Franco–Spanish agreement to partition Naples, fighting resumed in 1502. The French suffered serious reverses and while they held on to Milan and Genoa, by these treaties they were forced to agree that Naples should go to *Ferdinand II*, who already controlled Sicily.

Blore Heath, Battle of (1459). See *Wars of the Roses*.

blunderbuss. Dutch: "Blonder bus" ("thunder gun"). The term was used as early as 1353 in reference to a variety of early hand cannon in the Netherlands. By the mid-17th century it was reserved to short-barreled, large-bore guns with a flared muzzle—either round or oval—which permitted fast reloading. They came in musket and pistol types, either of which could fire several small balls or jagged metal fragments at once for a powerful shotgun effect at close ranges. This made the blunderbuss an ideal weapon for close defense against tightly packed infantry on land, or in boarding actions at sea where fighting was always intimate. Some armies and navies built large blunderbusses that approached artillery calibers. Smaller versions were used by couriers, customs officials, and the first mail deliverers.

boarding. Rushing aboard an enemy ship to which one's own was grappled, lashed, or bound, to engage in hand-to-hand fighting in an effort to gain control of the enemy's ship. Usually carried out by shipboard infantry (marines), this was a costly and risky tactic. On land, the same tactic of rushing a breach in a defended position was called *storming*. See also *castles, at sea*; *Invincible Armada*; *Lepanto, Battle of (October 7, 1571)*.

boatswain. Originally, a minor naval officer responsible for navigation of a ship. On later, specialized warships the boatswain was generally responsible for overseeing the ship's rigging, tackle, and sails, and the crewmen who worked them.

boatswain's mate. A petty naval officer who assisted the *boatswain* in his duties, and apprenticed for his position.

Böblingen, Battle of (1525). See *German Peasant War*.

Bocskay Rebellion (1604–1606). See *Bethlen, Gabriel*; *Hungary*; *Rudolf II*.

bodkin. An arrow fitted with a stiff, straight metal point to better penetrate *plate* armor. It was lighter and flew straighter, at a lower trajectory yet farther, than the earlier *broadhead* arrow. The old barbed broadhead was now reserved for use against cavalry, to gash and bring down horses. See also *longbow*.

Bogomil heresy. See *Bulgaria*.

Bohemia. See *Counter-Reformation*; *"Defenestration of Prague" (1419)*; *"Defenestration of Prague" (1618)*; *Ferdinand II, Holy Roman Emperor*; *Hussite Wars*; *Maximilian I, of Bavaria*; *Protestant Reformation*; *Thirty Years' War*; *Tilly, Johann*; *Wallenstein, Albrecht von*; *White Mountain, Battle of*.

Bohemian Brethren. A small reform religious community in Bohemia. Although influenced by Calvinism, it had roots in the older and native Bohemian *Taborite* movement.

Boisot, Louis (c.1530–1576). *Sea Beggar* admiral. Given command by *William of Orange*, he smashed a Spanish fleet at Sud-Beveland in early 1574, severely harming Spanish interests and military prestige. He fought his way into Leyden, across fields flooded by broken dikes, to lift the Spanish siege later that year and bring herring and white bread to the starving population. In 1576 he failed to lift the siege of Zierikzee, where he was killed.

bolt. A thick-shafted short arrow with a diamond-shaped iron or steel head fired from a *crossbow*; also called a *quarrel*. Most were made from ash or yew, as were most bows. Early bolts had wood fins; others were fitted with feathers. Very large iron bolts with large wooden fletchings were fired from *springalds* and could kill several men at once.

bomba. See *fire-lance*.

bombard. "Stone throwing engine." The term "bombard" is somewhat arbitrary, but generally referred to the largest guns of the medieval period. They were usually breech-loaders, using removable *"pots de fer"* containing powder, wadding, and a stone cannonball. Some balls thrown by these guns were gigantic, so large they were cut at the site by masons rather than transported with the bombard. Several were in use over many decades, some for centuries. Bombards were mainly used in sieges during the 14th–15th centuries. Most were made by the *hoop-and-stave* method rather than cast, although a few were cast in two pieces, barrel and breech. The biggest bombards were so powerful they could hurl stones three kilometers. This was so impressive, and really big guns so rare, that bombards were given distinctive noms de guerre and passed down from emperors and kings to successor princes in royal wills and charters. The "King's Daughter" was a famous English bombard. "Mons Meg," weighing in at 15,000 pounds of iron, was ordered by Philip the Good for Burgundy's arsenal in 1449. "Dulle Griete" ("Mad Margot") was the bombard of Ghent, while "Chriemhilde" served Nuremberg. At 40 tons, the largest stone-throwing bombard ever made, the "Tsar-Pushka," was built by Muscovy to frighten the Tatars. It was never fired.

Very large bombards were built by *renegade* gunsmiths for the Ottoman sultans. These were so heavy that 60 oxen were needed to move one on dozens of carts, before which 200–300 men leveled the roadway along which they moved. In action, they were served by gun crews of dozens and closely guarded by 200 men. The Ottomans had not only the greatest armory of big guns but the most numerous. The most extraordinary was a bombard called "Elipolos" ("City-Taker"), which could hurl a stone ball of 300 kilograms some 1.5 kilometers. In 1453 this gun, and several sister pieces, was used to reduce the walls of *Constantinople*. Bombards were also built in India. The Mughal bombard "Raja Gopal" weighed an extraordinary 40 metric tons of iron. Only by water transport on barges were such guns manageable, which greatly restricted their utility at any distance from the waterway. The lack of gun carriages carried over to the battlefield, where bombards were raised on mounds of sloped earth or piles of logs. Angle of fire was adjusted by adding or removing earth, or hammering or removing wedges under the logs. By the mid-15th century some bombards had lifting rings attached to facilitate repositioning on stepped firing blocks. By the mid-16th century bombards were outmoded, replaced by smaller but more powerful cast cannon using corned powder and firing iron shot. Yet, as late as 1807 the Ottomans fired some ancient bombards against enemy ships in the Straits. More generally, the late medieval bombard survived into the early modern period redefined as the *mortar*. See also *artillery*; *artillery towers*; *gunpowder weapons*; *invincible generalissimo*; *Muhammad II*.

> The Mughal bombard "Raja Gopal" weighed an extraordinary 40 metric tons of iron.

bombardetta. "lombarda." An older Spanish wrought-iron breech-loader, used mainly on armed merchant ships. The English term for similar guns was "port-piece."

bombardier (1). A gunner working any of the various types of artillery employing gunpowder.

bombardier (2). An early (c.1420) infantry weapons specialist who threw primitive, usually two-handed, bombs or grenades.

bonaventure. See *masts*.

Bondetal. The Swedish system of raising armies via direct peasant levies. See also *Swedish Army*.

bonfire of the vanities. See *Savonarola, Girolamo*.

Bonnets Rouges. "Red caps." A self-descriptive term by a band of a thousand armed peasants who rose in 1593 in Burgundy to prevent troops crossing their lands during the climactic period of the *French Civil Wars*. See also *club men*; *Tard-Avisés*.

boom. See *spar*.

booty. Moveable enemy property which was claimed as part of the spoils of war. Most prized were portables such as gold, coin, or jewels, but armor, weapons, and warhorses were considered nearly equally valuable. See also *Articles of War*; *ashigaru*; *chevauchée*; *contributions*; *Ecorcheurs*; *Free Companies*; *guerre couverte*; *guerre mortelle*; *logistics*; *plunder*; *ronin*; *routiers*.

Bornholm, Battle of (August 1457). *Danzig*, a major port of the *Hanse*, took a lead role in the "*War of the Cities*" (1454–1466), a revolt within Prussia to break free of the overlordship of the *Teutonic Knights*. Danzig built a war fleet on orders from its ally and suzerain, *Casimir IV* of Poland. Supplemented by hired *privateers*, these warships harassed Dutch and Danish shipping plying the Baltic trade with the Teutonic Knights. In August 1457, three Danziger ships met a Danish-Teutonic fleet off the island of Bornholm and, in a battle that lasted on-and-off for nearly two weeks, the Danziger fleet defeated at least 16 enemy warships.

Bornu. An independent West African emirate under the Saifawa dynasty, located near Lake Chad during the African middle ages. It traded with *Kanem* and the *Hausa* states, and was a terminus of the trans-Saharan trade route which led to Tripoli. It later migrated south of the lake to evade pressure from Kanem—itself collapsing and migrating to the southwest—and to conduct slave raids in southern sudan to feed the ancient trade with North Africa. Its armored knights resisted a Kanem migration in the 16th century. They repeatedly raided deep into Hausa lands to the south, and warred with the *Tuareg* to the north. After the fall of *Songhay*, Bornu was the largest state in sub-Saharan Africa. It faced pressure from Bulala, which had occupied much of old Kanem in the 15th–16th centuries, and later also from *Bagirmi*, another cavalry power of central sudan. Bornu reconquered much of old Kanem from the Bulala in the late 16th century, forcing the Bulala to accept tributary status. Bornu passed its peak during the 17th century, falling well behind the Hausa states in military capabilities.

Boroughbridge, Battle of (March 16, 1322). Fought during a baronial revolt against Edward II. The Royalists successfully deployed dismounted men-at-arms and longbowmen to unhorse and defeat the rebel noblemen and their knights and retainers. Boroughbridge was one of a string of early battles where infantry defeated *heavy cavalry*, altering the tactical balance of military power in Europe.

Bosnia. This mountainous province was ruled by Catholic Croatians in the Middle Ages (12th–15th centuries), then was briefly an independent duchy before becoming a province of the Ottoman Empire, 1463–1878.

Bostancilar. "Gardeners." The elite guard of Ottoman sultans.

Bosworth, Battle of (1485). See *Wars of the Roses*.

boulevard. A late addition to castle and town fortifications, replacing the *barbican* with an advance work that protected the gate(s). This permitted enfilade fire along external moats or dry ditches.

Boulogne, Siege of (August–September 1544). In alliance with *Charles V* against France, *Henry VIII* took an English army to besiege Boulogne, which surrendered after two months (September 14, 1544). Five days later Charles made a separate peace with France without consulting Henry. In 1550, England sold Boulogne back to the French.

Bourbon, Charles, duc de (1490–1527). Constable of France (1515). He quarreled with *Francis I* and conspired with *Charles V*. When his treason was discovered he fled to the Empire and took up arms with the Habsburgs. In 1524 he invaded France from Italy in an effort to depose Francis. He fought also at *Pavia* (1525). He was killed in the Imperial assault on Rome.

Bourbon dynasty. The branch of the Capetian dynasty which ascended the throne of France in the person of *Henri IV*, and held it until overthrown during the French Revolution (1792). Its ancient rival was the *House of Valois*. See also *French Civil Wars*.

Bouvines, Battle of (1214). See *routiers*.

bow(ing). Handling and angling a ship's gun through a gun port so that a cannon normally mounted and fired broadside could track and fire forward, in the direction of the bow.

bowlines. See *rigging*; *sails*.

bows. See *arrows*; *crossbow*; *longbow*; *reflex bow*; *Turkish bow*.

bowsprit. See *sails*.

boyars (Russia). Originally, the military retinue of princes of Muscovy. By the 15th century, a noble *servitor class* below the rank of prince. Used especially about those hereditary servitors residing in and around Moscow. They had the right to representation in the Boyar Duma. See also *strel'sty*; *"Time of Troubles."*

boyars (Ruthenia). A Lithuanian petty service class. Ruthenian boyars did not enjoy the social status, wealth, or political influence of Russian boyars.

boyars (Ukraine). See *Poland*; *Ukraine*.

boys. See *Acemi Oğlan*; *beat the drum*; *Black Prince*; *Cortés, Hernán*; *Devşirme syssirme system*; *eagle knight*; *ensign*; *esquire*; *Mamlūks*; *revolution in military affairs*; *ship's boys*; *slavery and war*; *St. Augustine massacre*; *taifa states*; *top*; *tribute*; *uniforms*.

bracer. A leather covering for the left wrist of an archer protecting against the snap of the bow string.

bracers. *Plate* armor for the arms. They were comprised of "rerebraces" covering the upper arms (originally, the back side only); "vambraces" for the lower arms; and "spaudlers" to cover the shoulders.

Braddock Down, Battle of (1643). See *English Civil Wars*; *Hopton, Ralph*.

Branxton, Battle of (1513). See *Flodden Field, Battle of*.

brayette. *Mail* underpants, worn beneath even fully articulated suit armor to protect the groin.

Brazil. Discovered for Europe by Pedro Cabral, coastal Brazil fell into the Portuguese sphere of influence under terms of the *Line of Demarcation*. At first, sparse settlements cleaved to the coastline, planted there to support escort ships protecting the Portuguese merchants returning from India around Africa. The main threat was French *privateers*, a naval contest that continued to the end of the 16th century. In 1532, Lisbon decided to encourage more settlement in order to forestall encroachment. The native population, mainly Tupí-speaking Indians, was too politically divided and heavily engaged in intertribal warfare to effectively resist. The various Tupí peoples were killed mainly by disease, though some were exterminated deliberately. All were overrun, with survivors pushed into the interior of the Amazon basin in a slow but steady process that covered some 200 years. In 1549 a local government was established by royal decree, at Salvador. In 1570 the devout

Catholic King Sebastião decreed all Indians free. Exceptions were made for cannibals or rebels, which provided the excuse needed for planters to keep most Indians in slavery despite the king and the efforts of the *Society of Jesus*. However, there were not enough Indians left alive to fill the forced labor needs of a growing colony. Therefore, white settlers started importing African slaves in larger numbers to work on plantations growing sugar, a new crop imported from the Caribbean. African slaves were first imported in 1538, when only about 2,000 settlers and traders were in Brazil. The number of African slaves thereafter grew rapidly. During Portugal's "Spanish Captivity" (1580–1640), Portuguese coastal settlements in Brazil were targeted by Dutch and English privateers. In 1624, marines of the Dutch West Indies Company (WIC) invaded Brazil, but were repulsed by the settler militia. A WIC fleet returned in force and captured Recife after a bloody battle in 1630. Dutch settlers arrived, and skirmished constantly with local Portuguese. At one point, the Dutch controlled 2,000 miles of Brazilian coastline. When Portugal reasserted its independence from Spain in 1640, Lisbon and Amsterdam became uneasy allies. This new geopolitical reality in Europe abated fighting in Brazil, but did not end it: the local Dutch were not defeated (driven into Surinam) until 1654, and then mainly by Brazilian militia rather than Portuguese soldiers. See also *Eighty Years' War*; *Hendrik, Frederik*.

breach. A gap made in a defensive wall by mining or artillery.

Breda, Siege of (1625). See *Eighty Years' War*; *Maurits of Nassau*; *Spínola, Ambrogio di*.

breech. The rear end of the bore of a gun that held the charge and *shot*. In *muzzle-loaders* the breech was the inner chamber at the rear of the gun. Early breech-loaders had detachable chambers, roughly cylindrical in shape, which were pre-loaded with powder and shot then wedged into place for firing. However, the seal was never airtight and this reduced reliability and range. Some breech-loaders were screwed into place, but heat from ignition of the prior shot often expanded the thread so that the gun could not be reloaded until the metal cooled, which might take several hours. Breech-loaders were slowly phased out in favor of muzzle-loaders as the *hoop-and-stave* method of building cannon was displaced by improved technology that permitted casting of guns in single pieces. This occurred along with invention of *corned gunpowder* which raised firing pressures beyond what hoop-and-stave guns could handle. Muskets were actually welded shut at the breech to prevent explosive gases erupting into the eyes and searing the face of the musketeer.

breeching. Ropes attaching a naval gun to the side of the ship to control its recoil and movement.

breech-loader. See *breech*.

Bregenz, Battle of (1408). See *Appenzell Wars*.

breidex. A Viking-style broad axe. See *axes*.

Breitenfeld, First (September 17, 1631). A major victory for the Swedish Army under *Gustavus Adolphus* over the Imperial Army and the army of the *Catholic League* commanded by *Johann Tilly*. It was the largest battle of the *Thirty Years' War* (1618–1648). Gustavus was looking for a fight. He needed to shore up shaky German alliances by proving to cautious Protestant princes that his army could hold its own in battle against the immense forces of the Habsburgs of Austria and Spain and the Catholic states of southern Germany. He got his wish at Breitenfeld, northwest of Leipzig. His artillery train of 70 small but highly mobile and rapid-firing field guns was under the able command of *Lennart Torstensson*. The Swedish army of 24,000 was supported by 18,000 coerced Saxons and troops of the *Leipziger Bund*. These were on the Swedish left flank, commanded by the timid Elector *Johann Georg*. Gustavus faced 35,000 Spanish on loan to *Ferdinand II*. Tilly's *tercios* were supported by Bavarians, Croats, and others from the Catholic League. He had 30 big but immobile guns: the Catholic guns were large 24-pounders, not true field artillery. They required teams of 24 horses each to tow and an additional dozen or more draught animals to pull carts burdened with ammunition and casks of black powder. Once emplaced, it was almost impossible to shift these behemoths even if the battle drifted out of range. Torstensson placed his highly mobile 3-pounders in batteries in front of his infantry. These true field pieces were served by crews of two men, and could be swung around or moved with speed and ease by a pair of horses. Gustavus had also integrated gunners into his army: he did not depend on civilian specialists for hire as did the Catholic army. Highly trained, the Swedish gunners supported equally well-drilled musketeers and achieved a rate of fire that may have exceeded that of their enemies by three-to-one. Gustavus also set blocks of infantry between his cavalry, so that each arm supported and steadied the other two. Tilly positioned his army in standard formation: solid blocks of infantry at the center, with two cavalry wings. His artillery was at his center-right in front of his infantry.

Torstensson opened the fight, peppering the Imperial cavalry with accurate fire from his forward field guns. This seems to have provoked *Graf zu Pappenheim* to charge with one wing of Imperial cavalry, but Swedish musketeers cut down the Imperial horse. Swedish light cavalry counterattacked and drove Pappenheim's cuirassiers from the field. On Gustavus' left Imperial cavalry under Count Fürstenberg had attacked upon seeing Pappenheim move. Unlike the Swedes on the right, after just a few salvoes the Saxons wavered, then ran, leaving their artillery to be overrun. Johann Georg also galloped off in fright, tending to neither the exposed flank of his ally nor to his own men. The suddenly exposed Swedes held fast, articulating their flexible infantry line to meet the onrushing Imperial horse, and blasted away at the surprised cavalrymen—who had expected to roll up an exposed flank—with heavy musket fire supported by their light field cannon, which had also repositioned and now blasted away with grapeshot at intimate ranges. The Imperials fell back under withering fire while taking heavy casualties. The Swedes rushed forward and recovered the Saxon cannon which Fürstenberg's cavalry had overrun but was forced to leave behind. As the Imperials also neglected to spike the guns, the Swedes turned them around and fired into what was now the enemy's exposed flank. Then the Swedes again articulated their line, moving with a tactical speed the clumsy tercios simply could not match. Thus, they enfiladed the Spaniards (and Walloons and Croats) and poured musket fire into exposed ranks and files from both front and side. Meanwhile, some Swedish cavalry maneuvered to the rear of the tercios, cutting at their back ranks with sabers or stabbing with lances. The fighting went on for seven hours, with the Swedes tearing up the Imperial tercios with musket and artillery fire.

> *Casualty estimates vary, but as many as 12,000 Habsburg–Catholic League troops were left dead or dying . . .*

Gustavus personally led his Finnish cavalry reserve (about 1,000 horse) in a fierce charge against the Spanish, already bled white by his artillery and badly exposed by the earlier flight of their cavalry. Many were crushed or trampled to death by comrades as panic set in and the tercio ranks finally broke. Tilly was wounded thrice, in the neck, chest, and arm, and taken by his bodyguards from the field.

Casualty estimates vary, but as many as 12,000 Habsburg–Catholic League troops were left dead or dying on the field, to just 2,000 lost by Gustavus (and two-thirds of those were allied troops, not Swedish). Another 6,000 Imperials were taken prisoner, along with all the heavy Imperial artillery and 120 regimental and company standards. That represented two-thirds losses for an Imperial Army previously undefeated in battle with Protestant forces. The victory, the first major success by the Protestant side in 12 years of fighting, opened the way for Gustavus to move west or south. This was critical, as he had eaten out his original base and resupply areas in Pomerania and Brandenburg. First Breitenfeld scattered the surviving Habsburg and Catholic troops. Gustavus failed to pursue them, but that was largely due to the more pressing need he had of bringing his own army into fat new lands from which it could feed. After the battle, the Catholic position in north Germany, the Rhineland, and parts of southern Germany, utterly collapsed. The next year, Gustavus invaded Bavaria, occupied Munich, and threatened Vienna. The more general consequence of Breitenfeld was discrediting of the old tactics of "push of pike" by infantry squares in favor of more mobility and greater firepower, a lesson read and applied all over Europe.

Suggested Reading: Fletcher Pratt, *Battles that Changed History* (1956).

Breitenfeld, Second (November 2, 1642). Swedish Field Marshal *Lennart Torstensson* besieged Leipzig with 20,000 men, intent on pushing Saxony out of the *Thirty Years' War* (1618–1648). Arrival of a larger Imperial force, under

Archduke Leopold Wilhelm, brother of *Ferdinand III*, and *Piccolomini*, lifted the siege. Leopold then vigorously pursued Torstensson as he withdrew six miles to Breitenfeld. The battle began with an Imperial artillery bombardment intended to cover a cavalry charge on the left. But the Swedish cavalry did not wait to be killed by whirling chain or solid shot: it charged, catching the Imperial horse in the flank. As Leopold's cavalry fled in broken disorder, Torstensson wheeled left to attack enemy infantry pressing hard on the Swedish infantry at the center. These Imperials also wilted, leaving only cavalry on Leopold's right and that, too, was soon engulfed by the Swedes. Those Imperial troops who did not die or fall wounded, or spur their horses to flight, soon surrendered. About 5,000 Imperials were killed and an equal number taken prisoner. Swedish losses were light. Imperial fortunes never recovered from this defeat, the military nadir for the Habsburg cause in the Thirty Years' War.

Brentford, Battle of (1642). See *English Civil Wars*.

Brest, Union of. See *Union of Brest*.

bretasche. A wooden screen used to protect skirmishers, archers, and others engaged in *siege warfare*.

Brétigny, Treaty of (1360). This treaty ended the first phase of the *Hundred Years' War* (1337–1453) in France, though fighting continued in Brittany to 1364 and broke out in Castile in 1365. It was forced on the French by the capture of Jean II ("The Good," 1319–1364) by the *Black Prince* at *Poitiers* (1356). Also contributing was a sorrowful *chevauchée* in 1359–1360, in which an English army cut a swath of destruction many miles wide from Calais to Reims, through the heart of Burgundy, and on to the suburbs of Paris. Finally, the French monarchy was faced with internal fears and challenges born of the *Jacquerie* of 1358 and, more important, virtual secession of several provinces under powerful barons. France had had enough of war for the moment, and agreed to a huge ransom for Jean II (three million "livres tournais"), gave most of the Aquitaine as an independent fief to the Black Prince, and surrendered nearly a third of France to English sovereignty in a new "Gascony" that was vastly enlarged by territory taken from neighboring provinces. The treaty brought formal peace with England but not real peace within France: disbandment by both armies of common troops and thousands of mercenaries led to formation of over 100 *Free Companies*, some of mixed French and English troops, who moved through the land taking or burning whatever they wished. More fighting took place in Brittany and Normandy and along the border of English Languedoc. The larger war between England and France broke out again in 1369. See also *routiers*; *War of the Breton Succession*.

Breton Succession, War of (1341–1365). A war for control of Brittany fought within the larger context of the *Hundred Years' War* (1337–1453). It was sparked when the duke of Brittany died without a clear heir. England's *Edward III* backed one candidate, John de Montfort, while France supported the claim of Charles of Blois. The first phase left England in control of Brest, which it held from 1346 to 1362 and from 1372 to 1397, securing lines of supply and trade with Gascony. The fighting in Brittany was intermittent, with only a single set-piece battle at Auray (1364). During that clash Charles of Blois was killed. The fate of Brittany was settled the next year when France recognized Montfort's claim in the Treaty of Guérande.

brevet. A royal decree bestowing some privilege. Brevets conceding limited military rights to the Huguenots were key to the short-term success of the *Edict of Nantes*.

Brielle, Battle of (April 1, 1572). See *Brill, Battle of.*

brig (1). A military prison, especially if on a ship.

brig (2). See *brigantine* (2).

brigade. A basic infantry formation of the 15th and 16th centuries, of varying size. In the 17th century standardized brigades were formed modeled on the Dutch system of *Maurits of Nassau,* in which four battalions or regiments formed a single brigade. This cut Dutch battlefield deployment time in half, or even to a quarter that of other armies: Hans Delbrück suggested that the Dutch could deploy 2,000 men in under half an hour, where opponents could deploy 1,000 in no less than an hour. *Gustavus Adolphus* also adopted a brigade system, which allowed Swedish armies to articulate their lines to cover open flanks or otherwise adjust to battle conditions. His brigades had four squadrons each, with three forming an arrow-head formation and the fourth in reserve. Each brigade was supported by nine regimental field pieces. See also *First Breitenfeld.*

brigandine. See *brigantine* (2).

brigantine (1). Also "brigandine." A type of armored jacket or "coat of plates" made from overlapping plates of armor sewn onto a leather or canvas vest. Commonly worn in land battles and sea actions.

brigantine (2). A small 16th-century oared warship, two-masted and square-rigged on the foremast. *Hernán Cortés* built 14 brigantines which his men launched from the shore of Lake Texcoco. See also *Tenochtitlán, Second Siege of.*

Brill (Brielle), Battle of (April 1, 1572). In early 1572 the *Sea Beggars* were denied use of English harbors where they had been based since 1568. In search of a safe harbor, a fleet of 28 Beggar ships (*galleys, vlieboots,* and *cromsters*) carrying 600 "Gueux" entered the Scheldt estuary and anchored off Brill on Walcheren Island. Beggar marines took the town—the garrison was absent, guarding the border with France—then scoured and burned all Catholic churches. The Spanish counterattacked with small boats, but these were broadsided out of the water with much loss of life. Five days later the Sea Beggars were invited into Flushing, on the Scheldt. Major risings followed in the towns of Zeeland and Holland, with Spanish garrisons killed or expelled. The Sea Beggars secured most of Walcheren by the end of April, establishing a secure haven for supporters of *William the Silent* and the rebellion. This marked a definitive shift from small-scale rebellion to the full-scale warfare of the "Great Revolt," or *Eighty Years' War.*

British Army. Strictly speaking, there was no "British Army" prior to the Act of Union of 1707, though a certain "Britishness" existed from the union of the crowns under *James I/VI* in 1604 and proclamation of the title "Great Britain." The main outlines of the English military system are covered here under *English armies.* See also *Edward III; English Civil Wars; Hundred Years' War; Ireland; New Model Army; Scottish Wars; Wars of the Roses.*

broadhead arrow. An arrow tipped with wide (broad) and angled head that ripped gaping wounds in flesh. After invention of the *bodkin* they were used mainly to bring down horses in a cavalry charge, so that their riders might be killed as they turtled on the ground.

broadside. This term had several meanings. At its simplest, it referred to the broad side of a ship, as opposed to the prow or stern. From this, it was used in reference to an array of guns along the broad side of a ship. Lastly, it meant firing all the guns along the broad side of a ship at the same time. Ships in this period would sometimes steer in a figure-eight pattern so that guns along one side could be reloaded while firing from the other broadside. Some historians consider the development of broadside artillery and tactics to constitute a *revolution in military affairs* at sea, though that was not fully evident or evolved until the late 17th century.

Brömsebro, Peace of (August 1645). Having lost *Torstensson's War* (1643–1645), Denmark was forced to cede Gotland, Jämtland, Ösel, and Härjedal to Sweden, and to cede Halland for 30 years.

brown bill. Precursor to the *pike*, but closer in idea to the *halberd*, this English polearm was fitted with a flat iron blade. The blade always rusted, leaving a browned surface that gave the weapon its name.

Bruce, Robert (1274–1329). See *'Auld alliance'; Bannockburn; Falkirk, Battle of; Scottish Wars; Wallace, William.*

Brunkeberg, Battle of (1471). See *Denmark; Union of Kalmar.*

Brustem, Battle of (October 28, 1467). Fought outside Liège as a result of Burgundy's efforts to expand at the expense of neighboring free cities and other minor territories. The squares of Liège militia entrenched at the edge of the village of Brustem, with prepared positions for their *culverins* and *cannons*. The Burgundian van was made up mostly of mounted archers and pikemen, supported by artillery. An exchange of artillery began the battle. After that, artillery played little further role. The Burgundians prevailed, forcing the Liège militia to abandon guns and positions.

buccaneers. "Boucaniers." French *pirates*. Initially, they raided Spanish and Portuguese shipping in the Caribbean and partway down the Atlantic coast of South America from bases nestled in caves and coves of Central America. Raids by "boucaniers" (or "buccaneers," as they were known to English seamen who faced them) caused the Spanish to evacuate all settlements on the north coast of Hispaniola in 1603.

Buckingham, 1st Duke of (1592–1628). Né George Villiers. A relative unknown, he emerged as a fey court favorite of *James I* at age 22 and soon was recipient of so many titles, lands, and royal favors that intense jealousy followed him everywhere. In 1623 he traveled in secret to Madrid with *Charles I*, only to be rebuffed in his effort to arrange a royal match. This was partly due to Buckingham's arrogance and pretension, but more because a Protestant match had no appeal for Spain. This soured James and Charles on Spain, contributing to their foolhardy decision to declare war. Buckingham soon arranged for Charles to marry a French Catholic princess, Henrietta. He remained favored at court after Charles succeeded James in 1625. Bringing a Catholic queen to England did not win him many favors with the country, however. Buckingham led an ill-planned raid on Cadiz in November 1625, in which he lost 30 ships and accomplished nothing. In 1627 he led another badly executed expedition to relieve the Huguenots at *La Rochelle*. They refused to admit him to the harbor, so he landed on Île de Ré, where his men fought and died to no end. While in Portsmouth to organize a third expedition he was assassinated by a subaltern. The fleet sailed to La Rochelle without him. It did no better, but perhaps less badly, for his absence.

buckler. An early medieval *shield*, small and round with a metal boss in the center and a bar or straps at the back by which it was held or secured to the arm.

Bucquoy, Count de (1571–1621). Né Charles de Longueval. Catholic general. During the opening rounds of the *Thirty Years' War* he caught *Graf von Manstein* strung out on the march and bested him at *Sablat* (1619). He commanded the Austrian wing of the Imperial Army in support of the army of the *Catholic League* under *Johann Tilly*. In that role he helped smash the Protestant army of *Anhalt*, *Mansfeld*, and *Thurn* at the *White Mountain* (November 8, 1620).

Buddhism. A world historical faith founded by the Nepalese aristocrat Prince Siddhartha ("The Buddha," or "Enlightened One," 563?–480? B.C.E.). Buddhism was distinctively Indian in origin, though in later times it is hardly to be found in India. That shift was brought about by disruptive invasions, by the co-option of the Buddha in north India into a revived *Hinduism* (as an Avatar in the cult of Vishnu-worship), and in part by violent repression by a new devotional cult of Shiva-worshipers (bhakti), who slaughtered so many Jains they wiped out that faith in south India. The Asoka emperor (269–232 B.C.E.) was more kindly disposed, and sent out Buddhist missionaries to Sri Lanka and west Asia. Buddhism spread from north India to Bhutan, Burma, China, Indochina, Japan, Sri Lanka, Thailand, and Tibet. It reached Southeast Asia in the 1st century C.E. Buddhism was introduced to China in the Han dynasty and enjoyed a "golden age" there from the 5th to the 9th centuries, until it was harshly repressed by the Tang from 845 C.E. In defense, Buddhist monasteries were rebuilt as mountaintop fortresses and housed thousands of well-trained and armed monks. A "White Lotus" sect of Buddhism evolved a military offshoot known as the *Red Turbans*, who were so adept at the martial arts they helped overthrow the Mongol (Yuan dynasty) in 1368.

> *These great souls could intercede for the salvation of the still earth-bound and unenlightened.*

Classical Buddhism was rooted in the mystical traditions of ancient Indian belief, but was founded also as a reaction against Aryan ritual and rigidity. The Buddha rejected Brahman claims to simply inherit piety. Instead, he posited that suffering could be eliminated only through self-perfection and through prajna, or "enlightenment," in which an end to Earthly woes came from the extinction of desire via the "eightfold path" (right conduct, effort, meditation, memory, occupation, resolve, speech, and views) of right living on the "middle way" between extremes of radical asceticism and hedonism. Classical Buddhism thus stressed a tolerant, moderate, personal discipline and self-correction leading via a cycle of reincarnations to nirvana (in the Mahayana tradition, a condition of holiness, purity, and release from all desires and travails of earthly life—an end to suffering rather than a mystical paradise). One may halt the cycle of births and deaths only with full enlightenment and merger with the Buddha, the first being to achieve nirvana. This later led to development of the doctrine of "Bodhisattvas," or enlightened souls, of whom the Buddha (Siddhartha) was the first. These great souls could intercede for the salvation of the still earth-bound and unenlightened. Along with elevation of Buddha to godhead came development of a monastic movement dedicated to preservation of the original doctrine—in short, Buddhism became more anthropomorphic as well as rigidly doctrinaire over time. As also happened in medieval Christianity, its monastic movement shifted from purist contemplation to great material wealth, lurched into radical reformism, then repeated the cycle in some variant form. A highly meditative version of Buddhism developed in China known as "Chan" (in Japan, "Zen").

Socially, Buddhism tended to promote fatalistic resignation by the masses, but encouraged charity and good works that gave rise to its hugely influential and widespread monastic movement. Buddhist monasteries played an important role in the accumulation of wealth and dissemination of learning and culture in Asia, directly comparable to the great Cistercian and other monastic movements in European history. Politically, Buddhism was associated with traditional kingship systems. In Japan, Buddhism thrived for many centuries before its monasteries and sectarian armies were crushed in the 16th century by *Nobunaga Oda* and *Hideyoshi Toyotomi*. Under the *Tokugawa shoguns*, Buddhism was co-opted to serve the *bakufu* state, though in Satsuma prefecture a break-away sect emerged that was heavily persecuted. See also *Nichiren Shoni*; *True Pure Land*.

Suggested Reading: William T. de Bary, ed., *The Buddhist Tradition in India, China, and Japan* (1972); N. McMullen, *Buddhism and the State in 16th Century Japan* (1984); R. Robinson, *The Buddhist Religion* (1982).

Buenos Aires. A colony established by Spain in 1515 at Río de la Plata to block southward expansion by Portugal. In fact, the Portuguese were barely ensconced along coastal Brazil and in no position to expand further. Buenos Aires was so distant from other Spanish colonies it was beyond the effective reach of Madrid's rule for many decades. As such, it became a haven for Dutch, English, and French smugglers (that is, free traders). *Privateers* found in the port a refuge and market for pirated goods. This distorted development arose because Madrid forbade Buenos Aires to trade even with other Spanish colonies, including Peru and New Spain. This was done to staunch untaxed, illegal silver moving overland to Buenos Aires from the silver mines of Mexico and Peru, and thence to Europe.

buff coats. Thick leather coats that replaced most armor on the continent during the *Thirty Years' War* (1618–1648), and in Britain during the *English Civil Wars* (1639–1651). *Oliver Cromwell* dressed his *Ironsides* cavalry in buff coats and high leather boots. These were not cheap garments: although some infantry wore them, they were mostly restricted to more affluent cavalry troopers. What made them different was that during manufacture the leather was washed in lime and heavily oiled. This made it more resistant to wear, hardening, and rot, the main hazards facing cavalrymen. Buff coats provided protection against slashing swords and bills, but not *musket* or *caliver* balls. *Gustavus Adolphus* was wearing a buff coat when he was pierced by several musket balls at *Lützen* (1632). The result would have been the same had he worn armor, and that would have militated against his new cavalry doctrine and tactical innovations, which is why he wore buff instead.

Bukhara, Battle of (1220). See *Mongols*.

Bulgaria. In the 9th century the population of Bulgaria was converted to Orthodox Christianity and made a rough peace with the Byzantines. This truce was upset by the "Bogomil heresy," a dualist belief which split its intense adherents from communion with the larger body of Orthodox believers. The new doctrine began in Bulgaria and was most deeply rooted there, though it spread to other areas of the Balkans. Heavily persecuted, Bogomil belief nonetheless lasted for several centuries in remoter areas. Intra-Christian quarrels ceased to mean much once Bulgaria was conquered by the Ottomans in 1396. It remained under Ottoman rule for nearly 500 years.

bullets. Standardized, centrally produced, and issued ammunition was not in general use before the end of the 17th century. Instead, soldiers were issued lumps or bricks of lead, with each expected to cast his own bullets from a mold he carried in his kit. A soldier issued a *bastard musket* would cast 16 one-ounce bullets from a pound of lead; one with a *caliver* cut a smaller ball at 20 to the pound; a full musket took a ball cut 12 to the pound, or $1\frac{1}{2}$ ounces per bullet.

bullionism. A crude, mercantilist practice in which sovereigns desperate to maintain the full *war chests* thought necessary to military strength restricted exports of monetary metals. The practice arose from the quite literal need for bullion and coin to finance a nation's wars, and from a basic misunderstanding of the nature of the underlying value of monetary metals. See also *war finance*.

burden ("burthen"). The internal volume of a ship's hull; the carrying capacity of a ship. See also *tonnage*.

Bureau, Jean (1390–1463) and Gaspard (d.1470). These brother engineers were the driving force behind France's acquisition of the best artillery train anywhere during the final days of the *Hundred Years' War*. The Bureau brothers brought powerful cannon to bear in over 60 separate sieges of English fortified positions and in several field battles. As suppliers and advisors to the French Army they gave *Charles VII* a superior siege train as he set out to retake Normandy from the English in 1449–1450. They helped take Rouen on October 19, 1449, then directed successful assaults on Harfleur (December 1449) and Honfleur (January 1450). They were also instrumental in the campaign in Guyenne in 1451–1453. They likely convinced the king to switch to cast-iron cannonballs, greatly increasing the hitting power of his artillery and taking full advantage of *corned gunpowder*. The Bureau brothers perfected the siege artillery technique of seeking to hit the same spot in a wall several times with smaller ordnance rather than the medieval method of seeking a single crushing hit. See also *Castillon, Battle of*; *Formigny, Battle of*.

Burgundian-French War (1474–1477). In 1428 and 1443 forays were made into the French-Imperial borderlands by Philip the Good of Burgundy, who also expanded toward the Low Countries. This westward thrust was consummated by a reckless invasion of Alsace and Lorraine by *Charles the*

Rash in 1474. Charles lacked his father's tact and diplomatic skills. Rather than make up for these deficiencies in superior generalship, he was inadequate in that area also. Instead of maximizing alliances with local German princes who wanted to see France humbled and reduced, Charles alienated potential friends by striking in too many directions at once. He provoked René of Lorraine into an alliance with the Swiss, alienated powerful cities such as Strasbourg, lost the favor of the Medici bank, and provoked the hostility of Louis XI (1461–1483). The predictable end was defeat.

Burgundian-Swiss War (1474–1477). Burgundy's conflict with the Swiss Confederation resulted principally from the effort by *Charles the Rash* to expand his domain and elevate his Duchy to the rank of kingdom and even one of the Great Powers of Europe. To connect his core holdings in the north with rich Italian lands to the south, he sought to carve a path of conquest and annexation through the Swiss Confederation. The inevitable clash came at *Héricourt* in 1474, where mature *Swiss square* tactics allowed the men of the Cantons to catch in a pincer maneuver a mercenary relief column, mostly comprised of armored cavalry, and destroy it. The next major encounter came at *Grandson* (1476), where the Swiss captured the Burgundian artillery train of over 400 very fine cannon and many more ammunition and support wagons. However, the Swiss pursuit floundered when it reached Charles' hastily abandoned camp and a frantic and ill-disciplined scramble for booty began. The Cantons thereby missed a main chance to destroy the Burgundian army. The two forces met again at *Morat* (1476), where some 12,000 Burgundians and allied mercenaries in *lance* formation fell to Swiss 'push of pike' and the spears and pistols of allied cavalry from Lorraine. At Morat, a further 200 Burgundian cannon were lost to the Swiss, giving them one of the finest trains in Europe. This string of defeats unhinged what might have become a Burgundian empire. Along with mutinies and treachery by mercenary garrisons, Charles' power and territorial holdings were alike eroded. The final act came at *Nancy* (1477), where Charles lost another battle through stilted tactics to a superior and more disciplined enemy, saw the Burgundian army built up over a century destroyed, and surrendered his life. The defeat ensured that Burgundy would not emerge as one of the Great Powers of the early modern age but would instead see its territory eaten by more powerful and militarily successful neighbors, especially Austria and France.

Burgundy, Duchy of. During the *Hundred Years' War* (1337–1453) the Valois dukes of this largest and greatest of all French medieval feudatories moved into the enemy's camp, allying with England (to which its duke handed over *Jeanne d'Arc*) and establishing themselves as a rising power. Burgundy switched back to the French side, restoring occupied Paris to France in 1435, once it was clear France would win the Hundred Years' War. Like Austria, Burgundy often expanded by making love rather than war: the dynastic marriage of Philip the Bold to the daughter of the Count of Flanders and

Artois in 1369 was the first of many such bloodless advances. When Louis de Malle died in 1384, Margaret inherited Flanders, which was joined to Burgundy. Brabant and Limburg were added in 1404–1406, Namur was annexed in 1421, followed by Hainault in 1428, Holland and Zeeland in 1425–1428, Luxembourg in 1451, with Utrecht taken by force in 1455 and Gelderland invaded in 1473. The dukes were also students of the art of war. They were the first to add gunpowder artillery units to a regular army, and the first to appoint salaried nobles as artillery officers (most nobles preferred to serve in the cavalry, the traditional arm of aristocracy). They were also the first to concentrate cannon in batteries, rather than disperse them evenly across a battle front. In a series of military reforms from 1468 to 1473, the Burgundian army was remade, partly on the French model but also making use of a unique four-man *lance* as its core unit. Subsequently, Burgundy fought with France (1474–1477), then with the Swiss (1474–1477), in the hope of becoming a full kingdom and one of the emerging Great Powers of Europe, stretching from Lorraine to Milan. Instead, the Swiss destroyed the Burgundian army and killed *Charles the Rash*. Control of Burgundy was then contested by claimants from the Houses of Habsburg and Valois, and later also by the Bourbons. Charles' daughter, Mary, married Emperor *Maximilian I*, which gave most Burgundian possessions to the Habsburgs. The original duchy, however, was annexed to France by *Louis XI*. See also *Brustem, Battle of*; *Grandson, Battle of*; *Landsknechte*; *Morat, Battle of*; *Nancy, Battle of*.

> *Like Austria, Burgundy often expanded by making love rather than war....*

Suggested Reading: R. Vaughan, *Valois Burgundy* (1975).

Burma. The site of several ancient kingdoms, it was also ruled at times as a Chinese province. In the 11th century C.E., a long Burman struggle entered a new phase with conquest of an ancient rival state, the Mons, a Buddhist kingdom to the south. The enlarged Burman empire survived until overrun by the *Mongols* (under Kublai Khan) in 1287. When the Mongols departed, control of Burma was contested between Burman and Mons dynasties. In the 16th century the Toungoo dynasty (Burman) was ascendant.

Burnt Candlemas (1356). A harrying expedition, or small *chevauchée*, conducted by *Edward III* into Scotland. This was a poor substitute for invasion and occupation and in fact a sign of military weakness, or at least preoccupation with the *Hundred Years' War* with France. See also *Scottish Wars*.

Bursa, Siege of (1317–1326). The Ottomans crossed into Europe after securing control of Asia Minor (Anatolia). Although the siege of Bursa lasted nine years, little detail is known. Still, it is clear from duration alone that the Ottomans did not have adequate siege artillery (theirs was primarily a cavalry army) and that Byzantine morale and resolve was high. *Osman I* died just before the walls were breached and the victory won. His son, Orkhan, made Bursa the Ottoman capital from 1326 to 1366.

busby. See *hussar*.

bushidō. "Way of the Warrior." The feudal martial code of honor of the Japanese warrior elite, the *samurai*. It was rooted in vassal obedience to the *daimyo* and supported by Confucian and Buddhist teaching about self-sacrifice and mastery of physical pain. It was not adhered to by lower-class Japanese infantry or *ashigaru*.

Byland, Battle of (1322). See *Scottish Wars*.

byrnie. A long *cuirass* or coat of *mail*, whether made from *cuir-bouilli* or metal rings.

Byzantine Empire. From the 9th to 11th centuries the Byzantine Empire enjoyed a succession of strong emperors as well as a respite from imminent danger of being overrun by fragmenting Islamic foes. However, it faced a new enemy in the form of seaborne attacks by the *Normans*, who rounded Iberia by longship from their Atlantic strongholds to loosen much of southern Italy from Constantinople's grasp, and rip Sicily away from the Muslims. They also raided and plundered along the Adriatic coast. The Byzantines held on to territory in Italy for some time in the face of this threat, but never again went on the offensive in the West or otherwise tried to restore "the glory that had been Rome." Byzantium's final doctrinal break with the *res publica Christiana* in the West came in 1054, with formal confirmation of a schism brewing for centuries in a cauldron of disputes in earlier Ecumenical Councils and conflicting bulls, spiced with conflicting episcopal and conciliar decrees. The argument produced false histories issued by the Patriarchate in Constantinople and the Papacy in Rome, each supporting narrow claims. Meanwhile, Venice emerged as commercial competitor for the eastern Mediterranean carriage trade, though also as a partner carrying Byzantine goods to the West. This relationship was eventually cemented by granting a monopoly on trade to Venetian ships. As always, when the Empire enjoyed relative peace its depths of talent in law, art, philosophy, architecture, and high culture enjoyed a renaissance befitting one of the world's great civilizations. In military affairs, too, the Byzantines were far advanced in comparison to the fragmented states of Europe. Byzantium was a major territorial empire, with a sophisticated and effective tax system and bureaucracy. It had a powerful *standing army* and *permanent navy*, both capable of long-distance and sustained campaigns and wars. However, over the course of the 11th century, central control by the emperors was weakened by provincial lords whose semi-feudal authority gave them great political and military independence.

Even leaving aside such internal troubles, the Byzantines could never rest secure for long: some new and grave external threat always arose. The next danger came from the East in the form of the *Seljuk Turks*, a nomadic warrior people from Central Asia then engaged in constructing an empire of their own in the greater Middle East in place of the old Arabicized caliphates. Pressure from the Seljuks, who first broke through Byzantine defenses in Anatolia in 1058–1059, prevented reinforcement or even proper defense of provinces in the West, even as the Normans moved out from their fortified bases to attack Byzantine Apulia and Calabria. The Seljuks captured Asia Minor upon defeating a Byzantine army at the crucial and decisive Battle of Manzikert (1071), where Emperor Diogenes was unhorsed and captured. In grave and imminent danger, and despite the bitter schism with the West, the Byzantines turned for help to their co-religionists in the Latin states and to the popes. The result was the fanatically exuberant Latin military response known as the *Crusades*. The next 200 years saw extensive and direct intervention by Latin Christendom in the affairs, external and domestic, and the wars of Byzantium and the eastern Mediterranean basin. This gained immediate relief for the Byzantine Empire during the 12th century, but led to disaster in 1204 when cruder knights and retainers of the Fourth Crusade sacked Constantinople instead of attacking Muslim armies in the Holy Land. They displaced the ancient Greek empire from its capital, and established in its place the "Latin Empire of Constantinople."

All this occurred just as another scourge from Inner Asia arrived in the Middle East and Levant: the *Mongols*. Remarkably, the Byzantine Empire was not entirely finished: its Hellenic peoples persisted and resisted, preserving essential institutions and the line of Byzantine succession intact in Nicaean and other exile, until they were able to expel the faux-emperors of the "Latin Empire" and restore Byzantine emperors to their palace in Constantinople in 1261. The Byzantines then plotted the *War of the Sicilian Vespers* (1282–1302) in order to forestall an Angevin invasion from the West. But they had lost control of their outer provinces to other invaders: Bulgars, Serbs, and Slavs. They next faced a renewed assault from a new and rising Muslim power: the *Ottoman Empire*. The Ottomans pressed home a sustained invasion of Byzantium, taking *Bursa* in 1326 and progressively cutting off Constantinople from its Balkan hinterland, one province after another. Other vultures circled as well: corsairs from North Africa, armed merchant ships from Venice and Genoa, and Slavs and Bulgars in the northern mountains. The Empire was reduced to the confines of its capital and a tiny hinterland by the middle of the 15th century. Under *Muhammad II* the Ottomans crossed the Straits with a huge army that battered down the famous walls of Constantinople with great bombards, even as his navy hammered them from the fabled harbor of the Golden Horn. In 1453 the *Siege of Constantinople* finally ended in defeat and massacre, including inside the great, 1,000-year-old cathedral of Hagia Sophia ("Church of the Holy Wisdom," subsequently converted into a grand mosque). Thereafter, the cities and lands of what had been Byzantium were made over in the image of its Muslim conquerors. The fall of Constantinople was an event of world historical importance, despite the fact that the Byzantine Empire was a fraction if its former self. Its violent end sent psychological shock waves through Europe and the Middle East. Explorers, adventurers, misfits, and conquerors of the *Age of Exploration* would ride these waves around the entire world in the century to come.

Bitterness over the great betrayal by fellow Christians in the sack of Constantinople in 1204 remained deeply felt among the Greeks who lived thereafter under Ottoman rule. Byzantium's success as a civilization and its longevity at the crossroads of world-shaking military conquests and civilizations must impress. It stood for a millennium under constant military threat from warlike peoples from Arabia and North Africa, fierce nomadic invaders from Central Asia, and crude Franks and Normans from Western Europe. To survive all that, to recover at all after the betrayal of the Fourth Crusade, was a remarkable achievement attributable to flexible Byzantine diplomacy, determination, and an advanced culture and skilled people. "Byzantine" later became a synonym in the West for excessive adornment and "oriental bureaucracy," corruption, and license. In fact, it describes an advanced, powerful, centralized state akin in its sophisticated political and military culture to that of Imperial China, and centuries ahead of later states and empires in the Muslim world or the Latin West.

Suggested Reading: Michael Angold, *The Byzantine Empire, 1025–1204* (1997); Humfrey Bartusis, *The Late Byzantine Army, 1204–1453* (1992); Robert Browning, *The Byzantine Empire* (1992); Edward Gibbon, *Decline and Fall of the Roman Empire* (1960); John Haldon, *Byzantium* (2000); D. Oblonsky, *The Byzantine Commonwealth* (1971).

C

cabasset. Also "cabacet." A 16th–17th-century Spanish helmet in the basic style of a *morion* but with a narrow brim and overall almond shape, and pointed at the rear.

Cadiz, Raid on (1587). See *Drake, Francis*; *Invincible Armada.*

Cadiz, Raid on (1596). See *Raleigh, Walter.*

Cadiz, Raid on (1625). See *Buckingham, 1st Duke of*; *Charles I, of England.*

Cairo, Sack of (1517). See *Selim I.*

Calais. Early in the *Hundred Years' War* (1337–1453) this crucial port was besieged (September 4, 1346–August 4, 1347) by *Edward III*, during which siege artillery may have been used for the first time in Europe. The townsfolk of Calais resisted vigorously for 11 months. A French relief army arrived at the start of August 1347, but withdrew in face of the strength of Edward's forces. Shorn of hope, the town surrendered. Edward expelled the population and resettled Calais with English, making it the forward base for a planned conquest of France. In this, the capture of Calais accomplished far more for English policy than the celebrated battlefield victory won the year before at *Crécy* (1346). At the end of the Hundred Years' War England was forced to reduce its holdings in France to the port of Calais, which it held for another 100 years. It lost Calais when *Philip II* married *Mary Tudor* in 1558. That drew England into Philip's war with France, so the French attacked. The Calais garrison surrendered to the *duc de Guise* after a five-day siege (January 1–6, 1558). Thirty years later the *Invincible Armada* hove to at Calais (August 6, 1588) on its way to disruption and defeat in the Channel.

Calatrava, Knights of. See *Knights of Calatrava.*

Calicut, Battle of (March 18, 1506). A Portuguese naval squadron of just nine ships of sail, but mounting broadside artillery, met and bested a large galley fleet of the "Zamorin of Calicut" said by some to have numbered over 200 small galleys. The victory was a milestone in Portuguese and sailing ship dominance of the Indian Ocean. A similar episode had occurred at the *Siege of Constantinople* in 1453, where more than 120 Ottoman galleys failed to stop a dash for the Golden Horn made by just four Genoese galleasses defended by broadside cannon and missile troops in high castles.

caliph. A spiritual and temporal leader claiming succession from the Prophet Muhammad (570–632 C.E.) in his guidance and political functions, and thus the right to rule all Muslims. The title "caliph" ("Khalīfa") meant "Successor of the Prophet of God," or more ambiguously but also more importantly, "Deputy of God." Claimants thus asserted the ambitious claim to supreme religious and temporal authority over the entire "Community of the Faithful" ("Umma"). The main division in *Islam*, between the majority *sunni* and minority *shī'a* traditions, is rooted in a dispute over the proper succession to the early caliphate. The first four caliphs were all related to Muhammad and chosen by the "Companions" of the Prophet, and on their legitimacy there was such general agreement that they are known as the "Rāshidan" or "Rightly-Guided Ones." Alternately known as the "Orthodox Caliphs," they ruled in succession from 632 to 661 C.E.

Abu Bakr was the first (573–634, r.632–634), the direct successor to Muhammad by virtue of election by the "Companions of the Prophet." He was succeeded by Umar (c.581–644, r.634–644), with majority though not unanimous support among the Companions. Umar was the first to claim the title "Commander of the Faithful." He was assassinated by a Christian slave. Uthman (or Usman, c.574–656, r.644–656) was the third caliph, and the first from one of the aristocratic families of Mecca. During his reign most of Syria, Iraq, Iran, and Egypt were conquered by the Arabs. He was murdered by fellow Muslims, Egyptian converts but mutineers, a fact which severely troubled the intensely devout Umma. Uthman was succeeded by Ali (c.598–661, r.656–661), made caliph by the mutineers who killed the third caliph. Ali was acceptable because he was cousin to Muhammad and son-in-law by virtue of his marriage to Fatima, the Prophet's daughter. Thus was set in play a deep and lasting division between those who accepted an elective caliphate (sunnis), and those who insisted that only members directly descended from the Prophet's family could rule Muslims (shī'a). Ali, too, was assassinated (661) by Muslim Arab rebels against his claimed authority. His successor was Mu'awiya, head of the Meccan clan of Umayya, who founded the Umayyad Caliphate (661–750). He and his clan successors were accepted by sunnis as legitimate, but were rejected by the shī'a minority who viewed only familial descendants or relatives of Ali as rightful successors to the Prophet. Shī'a claimants thus became known as "Alid" candidates, for their insistence on sole descent through Ali. They cleaved to this view despite Ali's own son, Hassan, renouncing his familial claim and recognizing the legitimacy of Mu'awiya and the Umayyads.

The Umayyads ruled most of the Islamic world from Damascus. Their conservative reign saw the consolidation of the early Arab conquests despite internal upheavals and civil wars with Kharijites and the shī'a. Some of these events are commemorated still in bloody annual rituals of self-flagellation in shī'a communities, 1,300 years after they took place. At first, Umayyad policies of discrimination against non-Arabs and half-Arabs worked. Over time, however, non-Arab Muslims called for a return to the original message of a single Umma, all equal before God irrespective of tribe or race. The Umayyads were overthrown and succeeded by a shī'a dynasty, the Abbasids, which asserted descent from Muhammad's uncle. The Abbasids moved the caliphate to Baghdad and reigned—more in the imperial Iranian than the tribal Arab style—over the "Abbasid Caliphate" (750–1258). In response to the majority faith of the populations they ruled, the Abbasids slowly became less overtly shī'a and leaned more toward the orthodox sunni Islam of their subjects. Drawing on pre-Islamic Iranian example, the Abbasids also established the first *standing army* in the Islamic world, thereby lessening their reliance on Arab tribal levies and opening the military to promotion of the numerous non-Arabs who had converted to Islam. The Abbasids were not recognized in Spain, however, where a branch of the Umayyads survived and ruled from 756 to 800, while a successor and even more localized "caliphate" governed *al-Andalus* from Córdoba to 1008. Nor after a time were the Abbasids accepted in Egypt (868) or in the *Maghreb*, where a rival shī'a dynasty rooted in a Berber resurrection, the Fatamids, claimed the caliphate based on direct ("alid") descent from Fatima. The Berber Fatamids thereby partly reversed the Arab conquest of North Africa, in ethnic and religious if not in cultural or linguistic terms. The Fatamids ruled in Egypt, 909–1171, and sometimes controlled Syria, too. This allowed the desert Bedouin between them to raid the frontiers of the rival caliphates. Long before the Fatamids lost control in Egypt in 1171, to *Salāh-al-Dīn* and his Ayyubid successors, they had already lost most of the Maghreb to rival Berber dynasts: the Almohad Caliphate, based in Marrakesh. And they lost Jerusalem (1099) and most of Palestine and Syria to the Crusaders.

A separate shī'a dynasty in Iran, the Būyids (932–1055), attacked the Abbasid caliphs from the east. In 946 they took Baghdad and captured the caliph, whom they kept a prisoner in his palace. This marked an Iranian interval between the collapse of Arab power and the rise of Turkic peoples to overlordship in the Muslim Middle East, culminating in the *Seljuk Turks* occupation of Baghdad and rule as "Great Sultans" while leaving the Abbasid caliphs in place as useful puppets. The main line of Abbasids was overthrown by the Mongols when Baghdad fell to them in 1258. The last Abbasid caliph to reside in Baghdad was brutally murdered. The remnant of the Abbasids retreated to Egypt at the behest of the *Mamlūk* general, Baybārs, who had overthrown and murdered the Ayyubid sultan, Turan Shah, in Cairo. Following the Seljuk example, he supported the Abbasids as a convenient front for his own rule (Egypt had long since seen the end of the Fatamid caliphs). These so-called "Cairo caliphs" had no effective authority, as real power was held by successive slave-soldier (Mamlūk) sultans. Meanwhile, Berber warriors established the Almoravid caliphate in the far western reaches of North Africa. Still fresh with founder's zeal, they intervened in Iberia in the 12th century. They overran extant Muslim *taifa* states, which they saw as impure, and much Christian territory. These radical *jihadis* ruled their Iberian-North African empire from Córdoba. In the main Arab lands the title "caliph" was allowed to lapse by the Ottomans upon *Selim I*'s conquest of Egypt in 1517. Later claims made by Ottoman sultans were more political than theological, as Ottoman rulers used the title to reinforce the legitimacy of their imperium over Arabs and other subject Muslims. Partly because they did not claim the title early, and partly because of the Alid issues, Ottoman emperors did not earn acceptance as caliphs by all Muslims within their own empire, let alone the millions of Muslims in far-off Africa, India, Indonesia, and Inner Asia who entirely rejected Ottoman pretensions to a right to govern all Muslims. Regional potentates and "heretics" (false claimants) sometimes adopted the title "caliph," though without asserting the Alid claim that they stood in direct line to the Prophet and without claiming the right to rule Muslims beyond those they actually did. See also *ayatollah*; *imam*; *mahdi*; *mullah*; *sultan*.

Suggested Reading: Marshall Hodgson, *The Classical Age of Islam* (1974) and *The Expansion of Islam* (1974); Hugh Kennedy, *The Prophet and the Age of the Caliphates* (1986).

caliphate. The jurisdiction of a *caliph*. Theoretically, this extended to all Muslims. Historically, after the split between *sunni* and *shi'a* Islam and the later rise of non-Arab, Muslim empires, the authority of caliphs was often disputed or ignored in more distant provinces or by rival empires.

caliver. An English corruption of "calibre" used about early types of handguns more widely known as *arquebuses*. Most 16th-century calivers were heavier and had a larger bore than the average arquebus, but were still lighter than the heavy *musket*. They fired a small ball cut 20 to a pound of lead, where a musket fired a ball cut 12 to the pound. See also *bastard musket*.

Calixtines. From the Latin for "chalice." Those who accepted service of the sacrament in *sub utraque specie* ("in both kinds"), as both bread and wine. This was an issue of ferocious, even murderous, disputation in the 14th–16th centuries. See also *Hussite Wars*; *Utraquists*; *Zwingli, Huldryeh*.

caltrop. A simple devise in which metal spikes were arranged around a core in such a way that, like a child's "jumping jack," no matter how the caltrop landed one spike would point upwards. They were scattered by the hundreds in front of infantry or artillery positions to hobble the horses of advancing enemy cavalry. They were used effectively by the English to protect longbowmen at *Crécy* (1346) and *Agincourt* (1415), among many other battles. They were also used in war at sea, before the general shift from boarding to broadside tactics in the mid-17th century. Just before boarding, attackers would throw caltrops onto the opposing deck in front of the enemy defenders as an anti-personnel weapon of considerable—but potentially double—effect.

Calven, Battle of (May 22, 1499). This was the second large battle of the *Swabian War* (1499), a frontier conflict between the Holy Roman Empire and the Swiss Confederation. The Germans held a strong position and out-numbered the approaching Swiss. Neither advantage availed: the terrible *Swiss squares* tore into the German ranks without hesitation, scattering many who would not stand and fight, butchering those who did. The victory secured independence for *The Grisons* but did not end the Swabian War.

Calvin, Jean (1509–1564). See *Calvinism*.

Calvinism. The stern, reformed confession founded by a French exile, Jean Calvin (1509–1564). Trained as a lawyer and theologian in Paris, and deeply read in Christian humanist scholarship, Calvin fled France for Basel in 1535 to escape persecution following the *Affair of the Placards*. In Switzerland he was influenced by several leading reformers already preaching there. In 1536 he published the first of many editions of his *Institutes of the Christian Religion*, which was outlawed and burned in France from 1542. Nevertheless, it became the key reformist text in shaping French Protestantism in particular, as well as defining a community of believers more generally. His adherents were soon called "Calvinists," distinguishing them from followers of the German reforms of *Martin Luther*. Calvin moved to Geneva in 1536 and immediately tried to institute his reforms in the city's law and practice. This proved too much for a population who only recently had disposed of a Catholic bishop and was in no mood to accept a new dogmatist: Calvin was dismissed in April 1538. He resided in Strasbourg from 1538 to 1541, refining and revising his views. Then he returned to Geneva, where he moved more cautiously to put "godly rule" into practice. In the interim he published *Ordonnances ecclésiastiques* (1541). Once firmly established, he ruled with a hard hand against all he deemed "heretics." His political and religious enemies were burned or beheaded, infamously including, in 1553, the phy-sician Michael Servetus, an incident Reformation historians depict as the Calvinist equivalent of the Catholic inquisition trial and ultimate silencing of Galileo Galilei.

> *His adherents were soon called "Calvinists," distinguishing them from followers of . . .* Martin Luther.

Calvin accepted many of Luther's published positions: justification by faith alone (though with greater emphasis on the "Fall from Grace"); the literal truth of the Christian Bible and corresponding primacy of scripture over papal and episcopal authority; the associated doctrine of a "priesthood of all believers"; the sanctifying role of grace; and the doctrine of predestination ("eternal election, by which God has predestined some to salvation, others to destruction"), in which faith is the fruit of a predestined salvation and "divine grace" offers no consolation for the damned. Also with Luther, Calvin rejected Catholic ideas about Purgatory, praying for the dead, the cult of saints, and intercession through prayer. Calvin's lasting impact thus did not lie in developing much new theology but instead in providing an expanded, more legally informed and clearly reasoned, and above all more easily communicated set of explanations of reformed beliefs.

Calvin also dwelled on the dark, corrupt attributes of human nature, seeing the "ways of the flesh" as perversely opposed to a disciplined will beloved of God. This gave his views a distinct sexual puritanism that he combined with an overbearing personal paternalism. On the other hand, Calvin freed many laity from the Catholic cult of celibacy, which he dismissed as "this ornament of chastity." Approving clerical marriage, one of the truly successful reforms of the Reformation, arose partly from Calvin's own lusty appetites but also because celibacy was observed mainly in the breach by a corrupt Catholic clergy that openly practiced concubinage then forgave each other's sexual sins in the confessional. In other ways Calvin opposed the severe asceticism espoused by more radical Protestant reformers. But his paternalistic instincts as well as the tenor of the Age drove him to favor strict obedience to secular authorities as God's lieutenants on Earth. This was the defining characteristic of early Calvinists: their insistence that true faith transformed not just the inner life of individuals but the pubic sphere as well.

Calvin's refusal to sanction the *Huguenot* revolt in France did not prevent a good many rulers, Lutheran and Catholic, from suppressing Calvinism there or elsewhere. Still, Calvinism spread across Germany where the ground was prepared by Lutheranism; throughout the Swiss Confederation, where by mid-century Calvinists and Zwinglians joined in confessional and military alliance against Swiss Catholics; and into southern France. Calvin's teachings crossed the Channel to Scotland and England, carried there by refugees returning from Geneva, most notably *John Knox*. Calvinist political thought after the death of the founder in 1564 often tended to political radicalism which threatened or alienated temporal rulers. What offended Catholic and Lutheran monarchs especially were the social implications of the way Calvinist communities were organized and Calvinist doctrine enforced—this was crucial, as all three confessions saw Christianity more as a body of believers than a body of beliefs, and all thought the 16th-century state duty-bound to intervene in spiritual affairs. In Calvinist communities social and spiritual discipline was upheld by a council of elders (consistory), that merged church and state into one body with powers of punishment in both the mortal and immortal realms: death and excommunication. These twin threats, and much social coercion, were used to restrain natural human passions, condemn backsliding and perceived spiritual weakness, and govern and guide the laity in the way of the flesh and the ways of the Lord. If Catholic and Lutheran communities used the church to legitimate and uphold temporal power, in Calvinist communities the reverse was true.

Luther died in 1546, leaving Calvin the preeminent reformer by default and by virtue of his extraordinary writings. In 1555 he drove his last enemies off the council in Geneva, even as Calvinists were excluded from the *Peace of Augsburg* in Germany. Also that year, he launched his mission to France to recruit leading nobles to protect the vibrant Huguenot communities of artisans and professionals concentrated in the towns of the Midi. These conversions of nobles proved crucial when the *French Civil Wars* broke out in 1562. The only reform confession barely tolerated by Catholics was Lutheran, as defined in the *Augsburg Confession* (1530). In 1557–1578, Lutherans, too, drew up a rigidly anti-Calvinist declaration called the *Formula of Concord*. This increased isolation of Calvinists within Germany but pushed them into foreign alliances with reform communities in England, France, and the Netherlands. The militancy of the Huguenots in France and the fanatic reaction against them of the *Guise* and the *Catholic League* contributed much to prolonging the French Civil Wars. Dutch Calvinists could also be severe, to the point that Flemish Catholics who shared Dutch political grievances were driven back under the protection of Spain during the *Eighty Years' War*. And in 1595, Lutheranism was banned by the Calvinist regents of Amsterdam, while an outbreak of plague in that city in 1602 was blamed on secret Lutheran services. Later in the 17th century accommodations were made in some Dutch and German cities between Lutherans and Calvinists, including Amsterdam.

At the mid-16th-century mark few reform territorial princes had accepted Calvinism over Lutheranism. In Saxony the brief reign of the crypto-Calvinist Christian I (1586–1591) was followed by Lutheran revenge taken against Calvinist theologians, preachers, and laity. Some progress was achieved in the first half of the 17th century, so that by the onset of the *Thirty Years' War* several key princes, among them two Imperial Electors, had converted to Calvinism. Of these, the most important were the Landgrave of Hesse-Kassel, the Elector Palatine, and the pro-Dutch Johann Sigismund of Brandenburg. But Calvinism only gained legal standing within Germany in the *Corpus Evangelicorum* at Westphalia, in 1648. In Bohemia, many erstwhile *Utraquists* also moved into the Calvinist camp but they were either killed, driven into exile, or forcibly recatholicized after 1620. Calvinists played leading roles into the mid-17th century in the expansion of Dutch commercial and military power. They were prominent as well in the *English Civil Wars* and engaged in rebellion and national and dynastic conflict in England and Scotland even longer than in Germany or the Netherlands. See also *Amboise, conspiracy of*; *National Covenant*; *New Model Army*; *Protestant Reformation*; *Puritans*.

Suggested Reading: William Bouwsma, *John Calvin* (1988); John McNeill, *History and Character of Calvinism* (1957); Meena Prestwich, ed., *International Calvinism* (1985).

Cambrai, League of (1508–1510). An alliance of Pope Julius II (r.1503–1513), Louis XII (1462–1515) of France, Emperor *Maximilian I*, and *Ferdinand II* of Spain, as well as several Italian states. In name it was a treaty that aimed at punishing the Ottomans. In fact, it was an aggressive alliance that aimed to dismember Venice and divide the carcass of that watery empire. A French army defeated the Venetians at *Agnadello* in 1509.

The alliance quickly collapsed, however, as a result of too many competing ambitions and interests among the allies. Spain withdrew into neutrality and the Papal States switched sides upon receiving some concessions from Venice, and in order to forestall further French advances in Italy. See also *Italian Wars*.

Cambrai, Treaty of (1529). "The Ladies' Peace." See also *Italian Wars*.

camels. See *Bedouin*; *logistics*; *magazines*; *Mamlūks*; *martial music*; *Mughal Army*.

camino francés. "French Road." A pilgrim road leading to Santiago, in Spain. It was, as the name suggested, frequented mainly by French pilgrims. It was sometimes protected by French knights.

camp followers. Civilians, mainly women and children, but also *sutlers* and craftsmen, following an army to beg, steal, or sell goods or themselves (as prostitutes). They supplied services from laundry to cooking to nursing to sex. In Europe, women and children also dug entrenchments and gun pits because soldiers viewed military labor as beneath them. This was not the case in the *Ottoman Army*. See also *baggage train*; *casting*; *gabions*; *logistics*; *mulkgiri*; *Naseby, Battle of*; *wounded*.

Canada. See *Champlain, Samuel de*; *Haudenosaunee*; *Indian Wars*.

Canary Islands. Located in the Atlantic off West Africa, they were discovered around 1350 by Castilian and Portuguese explorers. In 1393 a Castilian expedition took the first slaves from the native population (Guanches). Portugal also claimed the islands, but settlement was delayed by strong native resistance. A Castilian invasion captured several small islands in the chain in 1402. Portugal invaded Grand Canary in 1425 and the Guanches were overcome by this twin assault. The Canaries were granted to Castile by a treaty confirmed by the pope in 1479, in exchange for which the Portuguese gained title to the Azores, Madeira, and the Cape Verde Islands. This proved a forerunner of the later, more sweeping *Line of Demarcation* (1493) and Treaty of Tordesillas (1494) that purported to divide the world beyond Europe between the Iberian powers.

canister shot. Unlike the more sophisticated *grapeshot*, canister was simply a can or sack full of nails or other bits of jagged metal. It burst when fired to scatter shrapnel at close ranges, with the spray effect of a shotgun but on a cannon-scale. There are records of canister shot dating to 1410.

cannibalism. See *Aztec Empire*; *Brazil*; *Cortés, Hernán*; *Indian Wars*; *rations*; *"skulking way of war"*; *Tenochtitlan, First Siege of*; *Tenochtitlan, Second Siege of*; *Thirty Years' War*.

cannon. The term "cannon" (from the Greek "kanun," and the Latin "canna") meant "tube weapon." It was originally used about any tubular weapon that fired heavy-caliber ordnance, such as stone or cast-iron balls, but using gunpowder as propellant. "Cannon" was later confined to mean a specific class of gun that fired heavy shot over relatively short distances. These second-generation weapons normally had cast barrels, rather than barrels assembled by the *hoop-and-stave* method used in crafting early *bombards*. By the 16th century basic cannon were relatively standardized. They could hurl 50-pound *solid shot* to an effective hitting range of 600 yards, and a maximum (though largely ineffective) throwing range of 3,500 yards. At sea, cannon remained inaccurate dueling pieces when used at long range. This fact midwifed the phrase "long shot," in reference to the high risk of firing at a distance without real effect, which allowed one's enemy to close before a cannon could be reloaded. Cannon proved to be adept ship-killers at close ranges. On land, they were powerful siege weapons, though unwieldy even when mounted, without much mobility, and hence of little use in battle. Firing 1,000 rounds from a battery of full cannon consumed 32,000 pounds of iron shot and 20,000 pounds of powder. This presented a massive logistics problem to any early modern army seeking to move its guns. Other large caliber guns classed as "cannon" (as opposed to long-barreled *culverins* or stubby *mortar* types) included: *basilisk*, *cannon-royal*, *cannon-serpentine*, *demi-cannon*, and *quarto-cannon*. See also *artillery*; *siege warfare*.

cannonballs. See *artillery*; *ballot*; *casting*; *chain shot*; *fortification*; *gunpowder weapons*; *hot shot*; *solid shot*.

cannon-royal. A big gun of the *cannon* type, that could fire 60-pound solid shot to an effective range of 750 yards and a maximum range of 4,000 yards. The only larger class was the *basilisk*.

cannon-serpentine. A big gun, in service by the end of the 16th century, that threw 42-pound solid shot to an effective range of 500 yards and a maximum range of 3,000 yards. While smaller than the *cannon-royal* or *basilisk*, it was more powerful than several *cannon* or *culverin* types.

cañon. A Spanish *demi-cannon*.

cañon de batir. A full-sized Spanish cannon with a bore of 7–8 inches and a length of 10–12 feet. English equivalents were called "double cannon."

caparison. Early horse armor comprised of a heavy quilt or leather "blanket." See also *armor*.

Capitana. In a Spanish armada, this was the flagship that bore the commander.

capitulations. Contracts drawn up with mercenary companies, especially Swiss or *Landsknechte*.

capo de squadra. See *corporal.*

caprison. See *caparison.*

capsquare. See *trunnion.*

captain. At sea, this rank was used in the Mediterranean to mean a commodore or commander of a squadron of ships. An officer in charge of a single galley was called *patron*. On land, a captain was the leader of a sizeable body of troops, usually a *company*.

capture. The legal right whereby a state took ownership of enemy property seized at sea during a war. See also *prize court.*

Capuciati. "White Hoods." See also *routiers.*

caracole. Once *wheel lock* pistols and carbines made it possible for cavalry to fire while mounted, European troopers—especially *Reiters*—adopted the tactic of "caracole." This was first used in battle at *Dreux* (1562). It involved lines of horsemen riding one-by-one or two-by-two up to the pike hedge of an infantry square, discharging their pistols (each rider carried a brace), then whirling away to reload at a safe distance before returning to fire weapons a second or third time. However, since 16th-century pistols had an effective range barely past six feet and the average pike was 18 to 24 feet long, and the reach of musket balls much farther than that, human nature encouraged riders in the caracole to fire from outside effective pistol range. The caracole thus presented great danger to the cavalry while offering little offensive punch against infantry. Danger was heightened when facing aggressive infantry with hooked spears or halberds, or where pikemen protected arquebusiers or musketeers behind them.

The caracole thus presented great danger to the cavalry while offering little offensive punch against infantry.

So why try the caracole? Because cavalry had been forced out of its historic *shock* role and was still searching for a replacement on the battlefield. At least the caracole engaged large bodies of infantry so that cavalry could do more than scout ahead or chase down stragglers. More importantly, the caracole was actually an effective tactic when engaging other cavalry, especially lancers. The problem concerning infantry was partly solved by *Gustavus Adolphus*, who replaced his cavalry's wheel lock pistols with lances and a return to slashing sabers. This discarded the caracole cantor in favor of a return to attack at the gallop, albeit on lighter horses and dressed in leather and cloth rather than encased in armor. In short, Gustavus ordered a return to full-speed charges by lancers, a throwback to shock as the staple tactic of horse soldiers. On the Catholic side, *Pappenheim* also disdained the caracole in favor of shock. Yet, even in Sweden, Gustavus' reforms took decades to implement: recent research has shown that Swedish cavalry squadrons did not wholly abandon the caracole prior to the 1680s. Other nations effected changes at varying rates, so that mixed tactics were often in play. In Poland, *Pancerna cavalry* employed the pure caracole to the end of the 17th century.

Carafa War (1556–1557). The Archbishop of Naples, Giovanni Carafa was elected Pope Paul IV in 1555. A confessional fanatic of the first order, and a warrior pope, he sharply opposed the *Peace of Augsburg* in Germany. When *Charles V* abdicated Carafa allied with France and moved to seize Naples from the Habsburgs. *Philip II* sent the *Duke of Alba* to Italy where he quickly won the war and occupied the Papal States to punish the pope. See also *Cateau-Cambrésis, Peace of*.

caravel. "carvel." Originally, this was a two- or three-masted, all-lateen sail ship, *skeleton-built* by Spanish and Portuguese shipwrights in the 15th and 16th centuries. First laid down at less than 70 tons displacement, these shallow-draft vessels were sleek and handy. Fast and versatile, it was used for trade, small raids, and in *piracy*. The caravel migrated northward, where it grew in Dutch shipyards to about 200 tons displacement. By the mid-15th century it was rigged with three or four masts that lofted square mainsails and lateen foresails. In this form it moved back into the Mediterranean, captained by Iberian, Catalan, and Sicilian merchants. Juan II (r.1481–1495) of Portugal shifted cannon mounted on caravels to near their waterline, to fire through gunports cut in their sturdy hulls. This lowered the center of gravity and allowed caravels to carry many more guns, on two decks. Some carried as many as 40 cannon or culverins; most carried 15–20. Caravels made ocean-crossing voyages possible and played a key role in exploration. Christopher Columbus took two, the Niña and Pinta, on his first voyage west in 1492–1493.

Carberry Hill, Battle of (1567). See *Mary Stuart, Queen of Scots*.

Carbiesdale, Battle of (April 27, 1650). After five years in exile, the *Marquis of Montrose* returned to Scotland with 1,500 men, including 500 Swedish mercenaries, hoping to raise a larger Royalist force and take the war to *Oliver Cromwell*. Some Scots rallied to him, but most did not. Montrose was taken by surprise at Carbiesdale by Puritan cavalry that quickly routed his infantry. He was later betrayed out of his hiding place, and hanged at Edinburgh (May 21, 1650) by *Argyll*.

carbine. Ottoman: "karabina." A shortened *musket*, cut down to make it light enough to be used on horseback. It had a short-range and lacked punching power but was better than a *wheel lock* arquebus or pistol.

carbiniers. Irregular French horse soldiers who accompanied war tax collectors ("intendants").

Cardinal of Lorraine. See *Guise, Charles, Cardinal de Lorraine.*

Carmagnola, Francesco Bussone (1390–1432). Italian *condottieri.* Named for his place of birth near Turin, he entered military service at age 12 with a company of condottieri hired by Milan. When he was just 30 he took command of an army of mercenaries and led them to quick success in a Milanese civil war over the ducal succession. In 1422 he commanded a large Milanese and mercenary army against the Swiss at *Arbedo*, where his order to deny any quarter so stiffened Swiss resistance that a much smaller force hacked its way through his men and escaped. Fear of his ability and ambition on the part of his Milanese employer led to an offer of a strictly civilian post in 1525, as governor of Genoa. More interested in the lucrative life of a mercenary playing all sides against the middle, Carmagnola offered his services to Venice, which he then persuaded to attack Milan. He was appointed Captain-General of St. Mark (1526) and led Venetian forces in a costly, but inconclusive, war with Milan which he did much to deliberately prolong. All the time, he secretly negotiated a possible return to Milanese service. The *Council of Ten* learned of this treachery and brought him to trial. Upon conviction, he was beheaded.

carpenter. A skilled naval craftsman who, by the 17th century, served under the *master carpenter.* The carpenter's job was to keep the ship weatherly and ready for action, and to effect repairs during and following combat, such as by hammering wooden plugs into holes punched in the hull by enemy cannonballs and repairing masts and spars. See also *impressment*; *ship's boys.*

carrack. An ocean-capable ship which could be fitted out for trade or war. Originating in Bayonne, it was dominant in northern waters during the 15th–16th centuries. It was a hybrid design, combining the *clinker-built* hull of the *cog* with sleeker *skeleton-built* lines of ships of the Mediterranean, where carracks were known as *cocha.* Its distinguishing feature was a set of high *castles* at the bow and stern, full *rigging*, and a *sternpost rudder.* The 100-ton Santa Maria, flagship of Christopher Columbus on his 1492–1493 voyage, was a carrack (or *nao*, as carracks were known in Spain). As they moved north to trade, Atlantic seaboard and Baltic shipwrights admired and imitated them. They built a hybrid version with a clinker hull. This produced the first great warships of the "Age of Fighting Sail" of the 16th–18th centuries. *Henry V* added to his oared fleet of 15 *balingers* and *barges* several great carracks, including the 500-ton *Trinity Royal* (1416), the 1,000-ton *Jesus* (1416), the 700-ton *Holy Ghost of the Tower* (1416), and the massive 2,750-ton *Grace Dieu* (1418), a warship as big as an 18th-century man-of-war which may have only cruised once, in 1420, and was accidentally burned in the River Hamble in 1439. A general slump in shipping ended the carrack line. As N.A.M. Rogers put it: "They continued to be valued as 'capital ships' well into the sixteenth century, but in the long run they represented a 'dead end' in warship design." See also *junk*; *kurofune*; *man-of-war*.

   Suggested Reading: N.A.M. Rogers, *Safeguard of the Sea: A Naval History of Britain*, vol. I (1997).

carreaux. Any of several types of early, almost wholly ineffective gunpowder weapons that hurled large iron and wood *quarrels* rather than stone or iron balls. A synonym was "garrots."

carroccio. A war wagon of the Italian communes in the 13th–14th centuries. It was not a fighting vehicle like the Hussite *Wagenburg*, but an oxcart filled with talismans, religious relics, and the town's holy banners. It was heavily guarded and its loss in battle was a cause of common shame. For instance, in 1237 the Milanese carroccio was captured and, to add to Milan's humiliation, it was hauled through the streets of its enemy by an elephant to be jeered at by the crowd. See also *banner (1)*.

cartridges. Paper cartridges that held a fixed amount of black powder and protected it from dampness or rain were in use by 1560. This significantly improved the performance of muskets, arquebuses, and cannon. A further advance came in 1590, when fixed cartridges that included the ball as well as the powder were invented. For much of the 17th century the preferred ammunition of musketeers was a pre-measured cartridge charge in a wooden or metal container, affixed to a bandolier worn as a belt or over the shoulder.

carvel. See *caravel*.

casemate. A chamber built into the earth or stone wall of a rampart, with loopholes or gunports through which defenders could fire. Large casemates doubled as barracks.

casement. A bomb-proof vault built into the curtain wall or *bastion* of a stone fortification, or under the rampart, and used to house guns and defenders. Probably a corrupt usage of *casemate*.

case shot. Invented about 1410, there were two forms of this short-range artillery ammunition: *canister shot* and *grapeshot*. All case shot were short-range projectiles made of nails or metal fragments, or encased iron balls, fired from a cannon. It could mow down an assaulting force of infantry or cavalry. Its antonym was "*solid shot*."

Casimir III (1310–1370). See *Poland*; *Ukraine*.

Casimir IV (1427–1492). Grand duke of Lithuania (1440–1492); king of Poland (1447–1492). The major accomplishment of his kingship was to decisively defeat the *Teutonic Knights* in the *War of the Cities* (1454–1466). The conflict started badly for Casimir, who barely escaped alive from the disaster of *Chojnice* in 1454. He forced the Brethren to cede "Royal Prussia" to Poland in the *Second Peace of Torun* 12 years later. Through dynastic marriage of his son to a *Habsburg* princess, Casimir secured Poland's southern borders. Other marriages secured the hold of the *Jagiellon dynasty* over the thrones of Bohemia and Hungary. On the other hand, the decline of the authority of the Knights set in motion a struggle for power and territory in the eastern Baltic that pulled Poland into endemic warfare which lasted for over a century, during which its powerful nobility and constitutional decentralization ultimately fatally handicapped its chances. Casimir contributed to this outcome by confirming, in 1467, the traditional privileges of the feudal nobility. This was contrary to the general trend in Western Europe, where monarchs were increasingly consolidating and centralizing power at the expense of the feudal barons.

Cassel, Battle of (August 1328). Following the catastrophic defeat of the French nobility at *Courtrai* (1302), the revolt of Flanders gained nearly three decades of independence for the Flemish towns. However, *Philip VI* ascended to the French throne in 1328 determined to reverse the verdict of Courtrai. His army was comprised of *heavy cavalry* but included a mass of infantry and archers. At Cassel, French heavy horse slammed into the Flemings, overwhelming the militia and killing many thousands. After the battle Philip restored his vassal as Count of Flanders, which returned to French control for half a century.

Castagnaro, Battle of (1387). See *ribaudequin.*

Castelnaudary, Battle of (September 1, 1632). With the fall of *La Rochelle* the *Huguenot* threat to the policies of *Richelieu* and *Louis XIII* was finally ended, but internal instability continued. Next came a rebellion of noble families led by the Marshall of France, duc Henri de Montmorency, and the king's bitter brother, the duc d'Orléans. A royal army handily defeated the rebels at Castelnaudary, ending their revolt. Montmorency was executed, but not Orléans.

Castile. Castile began as a rough province where war-hardened colonists sprinkled the land with rude castles to seize and hold it from others just as hardened. It was recognized as a kingdom in 1035. In the 11th and 12th centuries, Castilian armies went on the offensive, raiding and burning the lands of small Muslim states, the *taifa* of *al-Andalus.* During the 11th century Fernando I (1035–1065) used the threat of raids to exact tribute ("parias") from *Granada* and the taifa states. A turning point came in 1092 when "El Cid" (Ruy Díaz de Vivar) captured Valencia for Castile. The Christians of Castile benefitted greatly from the division of Muslim power among the petty taifa states. However, a more powerful Muslim foe, the Almoravids, intervened in Iberia's wars. These puritanical Berbers from North Africa crushed Castile's army at Badajoz, forcing Castile back on the defensive before a new, united, and militant Muslim power. A set of still more fervent *jihadis*, the Almohads, overthrew the Almoravids and invaded Iberia in 1146. By 1172 they were in full control of all Muslim lands in Morocco and Spain and began to move against Christian territory. In 1195 the full forces of the African-Spanish empire of the Almohads met and destroyed Castile's army at Alarcos (July 18, 1195). A Christian victory at Las Navas de Tolosa (July 16, 1212) stanched the Almohad advance. That was followed in 1230 by unification of Castile and León. The central plain of Iberia then came under Castilian control over the second half of the 13th century, elevating Castile to the front rank of Iberian powers and the sword's edge of the so-called *Reconquista*.

Because Castile's method of conquest was to strip Muslims of land and forcibly remove them from surrendered cities, its southward expansion drove tens of thousands of refugees before it. That impoverished the agricultural lands it overran, much of which reverted from rich farming to poorer ranching, mainly of sheep for their wool. The loss of population also despoiled urban economies. By the end of the 13th century Castile crossed the "olive line." It conquered Toledo, and forced Seville into tributary status. The only substantial Muslim power left in the peninsula was mountainous Granada, toward which the frontiers of Castile stretched out converted ranch lands ("latifundia") and an engorged medieval barony. After the death of Alfonso XI in 1349 a 20-year civil war broke out between his son, Pedro the Cruel (r.1350–1369), and the eventual successor, Enrique of Trastamara (r.1369–1379). Until the early 15th century (1412), Castile's southward crusade paused and it fought mostly with neighboring Christian kingdoms, especially Portugal and Aragon. The Trastamaran capture of the crown of Aragon subdued the conflict with Castile and smoothed the way for a union of the crowns of Castile and Aragon under *Ferdinand and Isabella* in the second half of the century. After recovering from another civil war provoked by a succession crisis, which once more witnessed intervention by Portugal, Castile retook the lead in renewal of the campaign to expel Moorish power from Iberia. This final campaign culminated in the fall of Granada in 1492. From that point, Castile was the core territory of the new state and empire of "Spain," shaping its imperial and crusading spirit more than any other component part—Castile became to Spain what England later was to Great Britain. Living out Castile's crusading spirit, but also to escape from its stifling orthodoxy, nearly one million Castilians left their homeland for the New World in the 200 years after Columbus claimed it for Spain. See also *conquistadores*; *Cortés, Hernán*; *Inquisition*; *Philip II, of Spain*; *Philip III, of Spain*; *Philip IV, of France*; *Spain*.

Castillon, Battle of (July 17, 1453). Also known as "Chastillon." The final battle of the *Hundred Years' War* (1337–1453). It stemmed from an English occupation of Guyenne, which had risen against the French and allied with England. *John Talbot*, then in his seventies, led 3,000 English troops into Bordeaux. He was reinforced by his son with 3,000 more men. The French dispatched several armies to the region and set up a siege camp ("parcq en champ") around the town of Castillon, which was held by some 5,000–6,000

English infantry and 1,000 horse. This maneuver induced Talbot to sally forth to relieve the garrison at Castillon. With about 6,000 English and 3,000 Gascons, he made a 30-mile forced march to the French camp, then immediately attacked with his cavalry before his infantry could join him. This rash decision brought on the battle. The French were mostly armed with bows, swords, axes, lances, and other nongunpowder weapons. Although an engineer rather than a noble, *Jean Bureau* took effective, though not official, command. Also present was Giraud de Samian, a famous and experienced cannoneer, and Jean's brother, Gaspard. The Bureau brothers had pioneered the royal French artillery, and may have brought as many as 300 guns to the battle. Their exact types are not known. These guns are ofttimes reported as being all "cannon," but 300 cannon would have been a fantastic number for the period and simply beyond credibility. It is likely that the largest number were handguns of various types (though these may have been large caliber muskets, resting on tripods and served by two or three men each). Some larger cannon were also certainly present.

In any case, the French had more gunpowder weapons and field guns at Castillon than any battle fought to that time in Europe, and they used these to inflict enormous, flesh-tearing losses on the English. Talbot and his forward cavalry detachments were lured onto a preset firing line of big guns by a feigned withdrawal of the French wagons and baggage. Following blocks of English horse were thus caught in enfilading fire even as they were torn apart by point-blank cannonades from the big guns to the front. Arrows storms also rained down on the English, while French *arquebusiers* peppered their ranks. The English infantry arrived late, piece-meal, and exhausted, adding their numbers to the carnage without increasing the fighting power or position of Talbot's force as a whole. The cumbersome English artillery train never even made it to the battle. Talbot's horse was killed beneath him by a cannonball, and the old man was finished off while on the ground by an axe swung by a French archer. At *Formigny*, just three years earlier, two French cannon had played an important role in the victory but the French infantry and cavalry did most of the killing. Castillon was the first battle where gunpowder weapons, and specifically artillery, unquestionably decided the outcome against a less-modern and more poorly armed force. The casualty toll confirmed the one-sided outcome: compared to about 100 French dead the English lost nearly 4,000 men, almost all who made it to the battlefield. If red revenge was still wanted by the French for their misery and losses at *Crécy* (1346) and *Agincourt* (1415), it was had in full measure at Castillon. Bordeaux surrendered on October 19 and the last English troops in France (other than at Calais) were allowed to sail home from La Rochelle.

> *...the French had more gunpowder weapons and field guns at Castillon...*

casting. While barrels for small *artillery* pieces were easily cast as early as the 13th century, most larger cannon and the great *bombards* were constructed by the *hoop-and-stave* method. It was not until improved casting techniques and mature foundries were developed that large barrels could be made as single pieces of cast metal, first in iron and bronze, and later still in brass. By c.1550 cast barrels of muzzle-loaders were cooled as a single, solid piece, after which the bore was *reamed* and a touch-hole drilled. Iron cannonballs were also being cast from greased, clay molds. Women from among the *camp followers* were frequently employed as laborers to dig the pit in which the mold was cast, gather faggots for the casting fire, dig out the gun after the metal cooled, and drag it to its siege site or for emplacement on the walls of a nearby castle or fort. During the 17th century *Jesuit* priests taught Chinese gunsmiths and generals up-to-date Western casting methods. English gunsmiths worked with local forges in India, and Dutch traders and governors brought the new technology to the Spice Islands, where guns of varying caliber were cast in local forges for use in Dutch fortifications and ships. Late medieval and early modern artillery varied greatly in size, caliber, and utility, but over time certain locales gained reputations as centers of quality gun manufacture. Permanent, large-scale foundries were set up and an international trade in cannon, it must be said, boomed. Northern Italy, Flanders, and Nuremberg were known for casting the best bronze guns. England and Sweden grew famous for casting cheap iron cannon in very large numbers that were nonetheless of excellent quality.

As cannon grew in importance in land and sea warfare in the mid-16th century the Spanish crown set up arsenals and foundries at Medina del Campo, Malaga, and Barcelona, and another at Seville in 1611. However, Spain lacked the skilled labor to meet its foundry needs—partly because its economy stagnated after expelling the Jews and Moors—and so remained dependent on additional purchases from the cannon markets of Flanders, Italy, and Germany. This lack of foresight and strategic planning cost Spain dearly as the *Eighty Years' War* (1568–1648) led to an acute crisis in armaments that was compounded by war with Elizabethan England and later also with France. This lack of cannon hamstrung Spanish armies and fleets. Due to shortage of skilled labor, Spain's foundry at Seville barely produced three dozen average caliber guns per year during the first half of the 17th century. In contrast, England, the Netherlands, and Sweden each had multiple foundries that cast 100–200 cannon per year. Spain was cut off from these northern markets by its wars with England and the Dutch rebels, although merchants in England sometimes sold to Spain in evasion of royal bans on exporting cannon outside the realm. Portugal also failed to develop a serious cannon production capability. Its chronic shortage of cannon for ships and fortified bases overseas was a significant factor in the loss of empire in Asia to the better armed Dutch and English in the 16th–17th centuries.

During the 15th and 16th centuries German foundries cast guns for use in Italy, by Spanish armies, and in the Netherlands. The *Thirty Years' War* (1618–1648) created a huge domestic demand for cannon, but so disrupted the metals trade and skilled labor markets that German production declined. English, Dutch, and Swedish guns were imported and dominated that war.

German cannon foundries recovered quickly after 1648, however, and soon challenged England and Sweden in international gun exports.

Netherlands foundries supplied the Dutch army's growing need for artillery, which was driven by its prolonged war with Spain, its ultimately very large blue water as well as coastal navy, and the huge requirements of fortifying border towns as well as a growing overseas empire. The Netherlands also became a major exporter of first-rate artillery pieces of all calibers. This was not the case at first. The Dutch rebellion cut off the northern provinces from the industries of southern Flanders and the important metals market of Antwerp, which the Spanish still occupied. Over much of the last four decades of the 16th century, until foundries were built north of the rivers and skilled labor imported or trained, the Dutch imported cast iron cannon from England that were happily supplied by *Elizabeth I* to a Protestant ally against Spain. By 1600, Dutch foundries were so efficient they met domestic needs and began exporting ordnance to other European markets. Eventually, the Dutch set up a system whereby bronze ordnance was cast at home while iron cannon were cast in Dutch-owned foundries in Germany and at overseas bases. In Asia, the Dutch cast bronze cannon in Batavia for local use using "red copper" from Japan, but cast iron cannon wherein sufficient ore was available and nearby forests provided charcoal fuel.

Sweden and Russia were late starters in the foundry business. Both had great natural advantages—large deposits of iron, copper, and tin, and rich and abundant forests to produce charcoal for the blast furnaces of their great foundries—but only Sweden took full advantage in the 16th and 17th centuries to catch up to the rest of Europe, once social and military-cultural inhibitions to the adoption of gunpowder weapons were overcome. In Sweden the crown played a central role in encouraging casting of guns. Wrought-iron cannon were made from the 1530s; casting of bronze ordnance began in the 1560s; cast iron foundries overtook the older method of making iron cannon after 1580. By the time of *Gustavus Adolphus*, Swedish foundries were among the world's best. Using both local labor and imported "Walloons" (gunsmiths from the Low Countries), Sweden emerged as a leading maker and exporter of cast guns in the 17th century. Tolerance of imported Catholic master gunsmiths in Sweden contrasted sharply with Spain, where Protestant gunsmiths eventually refused to work because they were not exempted from torments and execution by the *Inquisition*. The Dutch brought iron casting techniques to Russia, establishing a foundry at Tula in the 1630s. As skilled labor did not exist in Russia at that time, gunsmiths were imported from the Low Countries and Sweden, while unskilled peasants hewed the forests and worked the charcoal pits. Despite foreign aid, Russia remained a minor power in terms of both gun casting and artillery deployment until the great military reforms of Peter the Great around the turn of the 18th century.

English gun casting declined in the 17th century as the countryside was badly stripped of forests to feed the blast furnaces of the foundries and the shipbuilding industry. England's long continental peace also sapped innovation and profit from its military industries. France similarly went into decline after an early lead in gun design and manufacture. The great French siege trains of the early *Italian Wars* (1494–1559) were no longer seen in the 17th century, as royal armies declined and skilled workers left for better-paying markets or to escape religious persecution of the *French Civil Wars* (1562–1629), during which Frenchmen killed each other mainly with imported cannon. This situation was not reversed until *Richelieu* reestablished the French cannon industry to meet the demands of the Thirty Years' War on land, and of a vastly expanded French navy. See also *armories*; *corning/corned gunpowder*; *strategic metals*.

Suggested Reading: Carlo Cipolla, *Guns, Sails, and Empires* (1965).

castles, on land. In inspiration, castles were instruments of raw military power. They also reflected political independence of local magnates and aristocratic warlords who exacted taxation from the surrounding population and economy. In return, they dispensed primitive justice, or injustice, with or without formal legal right. Every noble's castle was his home ground and fortress, and every castellan was a miniature king ruling his own "civilization of stone." This was true despite a *feudal* legal distinction between "jurable" castles (those held in behalf of the king by an oath) and "rendable" castles (which had to be handed over to the king or lord in times of danger). Many castles were also centers of economic activity, not just places of refuge when locals faced an enemy raiding party. They provided a market for manufactured arms and armor, for grain, meat, horses, sheep, cattle, pots, and cloth. These local markets attracted merchants and craftsmen, who in turn drew in more buyers and sellers. All this activity created portable wealth and that, along with the even more valuable land on which a castle stood and protected, brought armed men from afar determined to steal it. Thus, defense and occupation of surrounding lands remained the first order of business of any castle, however humble.

In Europe

During the early Middle Ages simple stone roundtowers enabled and encouraged chronic "small wars" among petty nobles and hundreds of greater castellans whose private fortresses—some 500 in France alone by the 13th century—ran up and down mountainsides, controlled great rivers and valleys, and dominated open country. Local lords of all they surveyed, but not much more, showed little regard for "national" claims of a distant king, let alone the universalist pretensions of pope or emperor. Greater authority in law was defied by force majeure in fact, by armed and armored men hunkered with their private armies inside nearly unbreachable stone perimeters. Control of castles and the lands they dominated was thus the principal issue at stake in most local quarrels and in the great "national" wars of the Middle Ages. For instance, many Austrian, German, Italian, and Swiss castles date to the 11th-century Wars of Investiture with the papacy, which saw local uprisings against an excommunicated emperor that produced outright anarchy in Saxony and areas of southern Germany. The reality of fragmented polities and private military power together made the Middle Ages an era of chronic if low-level warfare in which a scourge of warlords defined politics by the crudest forms of force majeure. This near-anarchy of the Medieval countryside separated that period from the era of universal law and empire that ended with the fall of Rome, and from the era of political and military consolidation that followed with the rise of powerful monarchies and then the nation-state.

A wave of castle-building began around 1000 C.E., representing political fragmentation as well as physical fortification of the countryside. Castles could be as simple as an earth and wood *motte-and-bailey* fort or a round tower like those of coastal Ireland. Or they might rise above already grand natural heights as some extraordinary multi-towered and bastioned edifice, as in Normandy and the Aquitaine, Castile and Catalonia, or Syria and Palestine. In the 12th and 13th centuries stone fortifications remained nearly unbreachable by torsion artillery, although a patient and well-organized attacker might be able to sap under thick walls, or batter down thin ones with a *catapult* or *trebuchet*. Alternately, a surrender might be forced through surprise attack at night or at dawn, or intimidation by slow torture or execution of prisoners in view of the defenders. If the attacker could afford the money and the men, assault from a siege tower might bring a mighty castle down. This was rarely tried, however, as loss of life in a storming—from a siege tower or through a breach in the wall—was usually prohibitive. Also, the solution to such direct assaults was simple and obvious: build stone walls higher at the top and thicker at the base. That proved an effective response by military architects at least until the advent of truly effective gunpowder artillery forced defensive walls to shorten and demanded their reinforcement and insulation with external earthworks.

> *Castles could be as simple as an earth and wood motte-and-bailey fort or a round tower . . .*

Castles rose to dominate the countryside in region after region. The most heavily encastellated region of Europe was Italy, because it was the richest and most worth the expense of erecting stone defenses. Castle-building was extensive even in modestly urbanized areas, such as Castile, southern England, Normandy, Saxony, and Thuringia. Castles were built along important overland trade routes to better sweep in taxes and monitor suspicious travelers, or as centers for local administration, or to display private overlordship, power, wealth, and privilege. Given the option of simply out-waiting an enemy, defenders became ever more reluctant to fight a numerically superior, equal, or even slightly inferior army on the battlefield. Encastellation thus led to a characteristic form of medieval warfare wherein battles took place almost exclusively between besieging and relieving armies. Otherwise, commanders stayed behind high stone walls to try to outlast enemy besiegers, perhaps occasionally sending out a sortie to disrupt and kill sappers or overturn and burn a *siege engine*. If caught in the open, defenders tried to regain the castle or sometimes just ran away. The most effective way to entice defenders out to give battle was to assault their economic base by burning crops and killing livestock. In short, by ravaging the land around the castle with a *blockade* or *chevauchée*.

Castle innovation moved in step with improvements in siegecraft, after some earlier design was proven faulty by being overcome. Earth and timber also gave way to stone with rising wealth. Then came improved central design around a *keep* (or *donjon*). Walls grew higher and thinner to deny assault from various siege engines, while gate design grew more complicated and deceptive in order to protect what was the weakest point of any fortification. Moats, dry ditches, and earth banks were added to slow and expose attackers to defensive fire. As artillery improved, square façades became too vulnerable and were displaced by rounded keeps and towers to deflect rather than absorb high velocity stone or iron shot. Walls also dropped in height as bombardment rather than storming emerged as the main danger to defenders. Castles grew in scale with the expansion of economic activity and enclosure of additional buildings within the outer walls. Multiple towers were now located along extended curtain walls, linked by wall-walks and sited within crossbow shot of one another. The larger enclosed areas could accommodate expanded garrisons; some later castles had more than one large *enceinte*. Architecturally attractive, but principally functional defensive features proliferated: *merlons* and *crenels* atop the curtain wall, *machicolations* and *barbicans* above the gates. These modifications were fitted into a grand redesign of the whole fortification on a geometric pattern such as a quadrangle. Some late castles were built as complex octagons with their many sides supported by *boulevards* and *bastions*, features also added to older structures to extend their useful life. At the end of the castle-building era, around 1450 in Europe (170 years later in Japan), stone walls were fitted with *slings* and *swivel guns*. Larger defensive cannon were placed inside or atop specially built *artillery towers*, while squat gun platforms were built behind preexisting curtain walls with gun ports cut close to ground level.

In Asia

Hideyoshi limited all *daimyo* to a single castle and razed all smaller forts. As a result, the daimyo put all their efforts into the one edifice permitted to them so that Japanese castles built in the late-15th and early 16th centuries rose on the most secure and solid foundations and to spectacular heights. Around them grew up *jōkamachi* ("castle towns"). This does not mean that 16th-century Japanese castles would have remained impregnable, as one historian suggested, until aerial bombardment became possible in the 20th century. That most late Japanese castles did in fact survive into the 20th century is testimony to the long peace under the Tokugawa shoguns, during which no castle was tested by modern weaponry, not to their intrinsic qualities as fortifications. During the Tokugawa shogunate an increasingly useless and parasitic *samurai* warrior class was organized around the jōkamachi built during the *Sengoku jidai*, and sustained by a bonded peasantry. China did not build castles per se (with exceptions). Instead, Chinese emperors and warlords walled in entire cities and put enormous effort, especially during the Ming dynasty, to defend the Inner Asian frontier with the *Great Wall* and many lesser defensive walls. Similarly, Indian fortifications tended to be super-massive city defenses rather than "castles" in the countryside. Some of these were so substantial they later withstood bombardment by 19th-century artillery. See also *Albigensian Crusade*; *artillery*; *bastille*; *bastion*; *Bergfreid*; *feudalism*; *keep-and-bailey*; *Livonia*; *murder holes*; *Normans*; *portcullis*; *shell-keep*; *siege warfare*; *tower-keep*.

Suggested Reading: W. Anderson, *Castles of the Middle Ages* (1970); Motoo Hinago, *Japanese Castles* (1986); Maurice Keen, ed., *Medieval Warfare* (1999); D. Pringle, *The Red Tower* (1986).

castles, on ships. Hoisting rounded tubs of missile troops to the masthead of galleys was a long-standing practice of the *Byzantine Empire*. From there, the practice of missile platforms on ships spread to Venice and around the Mediterranean. Ships' castles may have been separately invented in England. Once stable hulls became available, permanent platforms were built to replace the first ad hoc arrangements. Their elevated, crenelated look and use as missile perches caused them to be termed "castles." From the 12th to 15th centuries, "forecastle" referred to a fighting platform or tower built in the fore of a ship in the style and appearance of a tower on land. Its essential purpose was to gain a height advantage over would-be boarders, to better shower them with lime, stones, crossbow bolts, arquebus shot, or other missiles. From the 16th to 18th centuries, "forecastle" referred to an upper deck built over top of the fore end of the main deck. From the 13th to 16th centuries, a "top castle" was a fighting platform secured to a top mast. See also *close-fights*; *cog*; *gun port*; *junk*; *line ahead*; *ship-smashers*.

castle towns. See *jōkamachi*.

Castra Dei. "God's Camp." The northern terminus of the *Spanish Road*. See also *Eighty Years' War*.

casualties. See individual battles, armies, sieges, and wars.

cat (*"chatte"*). One of many names given to various smaller siege engines, usually erected on carts or rollers so that they could be moved right against the walls of a castle or fortified town. They were constructed of wood with some metal and leather shielding to retard fire.

Catalan Great Company. "Universitas Catalanorum." An early and highly unusual example of a *Free Company* or band of *condottieri*. It was formed in Sicily in the 13th century by Aragonese and other veterans of the early *Reconquista*. After the *War of the Sicilian Vespers* (1282–1302) ended fighting in Sicily in 1302, some 6,000 men of the Catalan Great Company (about 4,000 of them *Almogavars*) moved east to operate in the outer provinces of the *Byzantine Empire*, and later fought for the Latin state erected in Greece after the Fourth Crusade expelled the Byzantines from Constantinople. The Catalans learned much from the victory of the Flemish infantry at *Courtrai* (1302), and adapted Flemish tactics in their own fight at *Kephissos* in 1311.

That year, they took control of the principality of the "Duke of Athens" and used this as their base until the dissolution of the Company in 1388. See also *prisoners of war*.

Catalonia, Revolt of (1640). From 1635 billeting of Castilian and Italian troops in Catalonia under terms of the "Union of Arms" proclaimed by *Olivares* added to the heavy tax burden he imposed to pay for the protracted wars of Imperial Spain. There was also a growing sense in Catalonia that the Empire was failing, and a corresponding rise of local patriotism which took a sharply devotional form among peasants. In May 1640, agrarian workers known as "segadors" ("reapers") attacked tax collectors and soldiers in the towns. The mobs congealed into a peasant army whose leaders proclaimed a holy war against the corrupt and oppressive Spanish state (a change from earlier peasant disturbances that the clergy aimed at Jews, Moors, "heretics" or "Turks"). On the feast of *Corpus Christi* (June 7, 1640), a mob from the peasant "Christian Army" entered Barcelona where they cornered *Philip IV*'s viceroy and beat him to death in the street. The urban elite of Catalonia shared many of the peasants' grievances, but they feared to rebel and were frightened by this display of lower-class violence. In December an Imperial army entered Catalonia from Castile. Popular agitation demanded a fight as rebel leaders proclaimed a Catalan republic. This complicated their appeal to *Louis XIII* of France to take them under his protection in exchange for their acceptance of his title as "Count of Barcelona." This appeal to a foreign monarch and historic enemy of the Habsburgs made the Catalan rebels unforgivable traitors in the eyes of Madrid. For the next 11 years Catalonia was fought over by France and Spain, and by pro-French and pro-Spanish Catalans, in what was called locally the "guerra dels segadors." In October 1652, resistance finally crumbled and Barcelona surrendered to the armies of Philip IV.

catapult. An ancient as well as medieval siege engine that threw projectiles (stones, carcasses, fireballs) great distances with reasonable accuracy. The projectile force came from torsion built up by twisting strong fiber (often, human hair), then releasing the arm. Catapults worked best in dry climates: moisture affected both the wooden frame and fiber properties. The *trebuchet* was a major advance over the catapult since it threw greater weight of stone shot, and weight was more important than range in siege warfare. See also *armories*; *artillery*; *castles, on land*; *fortification*; *Osaka Castle, Siege of*.

Cateau-Cambrésis, Peace of (April 2–3, 1559). Two treaties were agreed that finally ended the *Italian Wars* (1494–1559) between Habsburg and Valois waged on-and-off for 65 years. The settlement was prompted by French defeats at *Saint-Quentin* (1557) and *Gravelines* (1558), and the rising need of *Henri II* to deal with militant Protestantism in France. On April 2, 1559, representatives of France and England signed a treaty whereby *Elizabeth I* agreed to withdraw from military commitments in France. The next day, representatives of Henri II and *Philip II* of Spain signed the more important agreement wherein Henri conceded the key point at issue in the war: Habsburg claims to primacy in north Italy. Specifically, France returned control of Piedmont and Savoy to the Duke of Savoy while recovering Charolais. Paris retained control of more important and defensible territories, notably Saluzzo, Calais, and the key fortresses and bishoprics of Metz, Toul, and Verdun. Spain acquired Franche-Comté. The treaty was cemented with dynastic marriages between the royal houses of Savoy and France, and France and Spain. Cateau-Cambrésis codified de facto Spanish supremacy in Italy, granting legal rights which Madrid defended for the next 150 years. It gravely weakened the Valois since most Frenchmen regarded it as a national humiliation. In sum, a temporary accommodation was reached between the greatest powers in Europe. As France fell into civil war, Philip II was freed to resume twin crusades against Islam and Protestantism. See also *Vervins, Peace of*.

Cathars. See *Albigensian Crusade*.

Catherine de Medici. See *Medici, Catherine de*.

Catholic Church. The Medieval Catholic Church upheld belief in the apostolic succession of bishops, including the primacy of the pope (bishop of Rome) on matters of faith and doctrine; at least it did so other than in periods such as the 14th–15th-century *Great Schism*, which ended when the Council of Constance decreed ("Sacrosancta") that Church Councils were superior to popes, deposed three contending popes, and elected a new one. The Medieval Church maintained a vast scheme of moral and theological doctrine, much of it actively debated and challenged from within by clerical dissidents and other reformers. On matters of abstract doctrine the hierarchy was often ferocious, as during the *Albigensian Crusade* and *Hussite Wars*. The Medieval Church also evolved formal moral teaching that essentially upheld saintly lives and clerical piety and celibacy as idealized models for the laity. However, in practice the Church tolerated corruption in the sale of benefices and *indulgences*, open fornication and clerical concubinage, pilgrimages and reliquaries that scammed the credulous faithful, pagan folk beliefs and superstitions among the laity that even found representation (for instance, gargoyles) in the great cathedrals, and other daily vices and outlets for spiritual emotion that made life worth living for the majority of plain folk. The Catholic Church did not move to harden and enforce its doctrinal and moral positions until forced to do so by the severe challenge of the *Protestant Reformation*, which was marked from the outset by disobedience by the clergy and radical innovation in doctrine by theologians.

During the late Middle Ages the papacy weakened not from doctrinal challenge but due to decentralization of the Church, and from the corrosive absenteeism of hundreds of bishops who preferred to live in Rome rather than supervise conformity with Catholic teachings in their sees. That allowed regional churches to take on a territorial and even proto-national character. Popes were unable to counteract this trend away from the old ideal of a single *res publica Christiana* due to: damage done to their reputation by the *Wars of Investiture* and their general involvement in temporal politics; preoccupation of warrior popes with such conflicts as the *War of the Eight Saints* (1375–1378); the scarring scandals of the *"Avignon Captivity"* of the papacy (1314–1362) and Great Schism; and strong resistance to papal authority by territorial princes and "national churches," notably the *Gallican* Church in France. Meanwhile, conciliar reforms floundered on revived papal resistance anchored to the need of warrior popes of the *Italian Renaissance* to collect *annates* from new bishops to finance their wars. Papal influence also waned as once cosmopolitan and "vertical" religious loyalties became more territorial and "national," as educated lay administrators replaced literate clergy in the royal bureaucracies of powerful *new monarchies*. This process was greatly advanced in England and France during the *Hundred Years' War* (1337–1453), in Spain and southern Italy under *Ferdinand and Isabella*, and in the rest of Italy, though only regionally, during the chronic city-state wars of the Renaissance before and after the *Peace of Lodi* (1454). German princes were made supreme by the Golden Bull of 1356 and secured in that independence by the fractured condition of the *Holy Roman Empire* into the 17th century. Even within the Church, enhanced state control was defended during the 16th century by Catholic "Erastians" in general and Gallicans in particular.

The building challenge to corrupt Church practices, then quickly also doctrine, spiraled out of control during the opening years of the Reformation, from 1517 to 1530. The Catholic response was unsystematic repression for several decades, then a calculated hardening and counterattack at the mid-century mark that mirrored early generations of Protestants in its spirit of doctrinal intolerance and spiritual coercion. The *Council of Trent* became the centerpiece of this *Counter-Reformation*, and the *Jesuits* its commandos. Even so, before the mid-16th century, Catholic observance and commitment among the general population was weak across much of Europe, especially in England, Germany, and the Netherlands. Similarly, Protestant conversions remained confined mainly to towns. Among the vast rural population awareness of the fierce doctrinal and reform disputes underway was sketchy or nonexistent. Folk belief, including growing belief in the prevalence of witches, daemons,

> *Folk belief, including growing belief in the prevalence of witches, daemons, and dark magic, was predominant.*

and dark magic, was predominant. This nonconfessionalism of the masses changed around the turn of the 17th century, when Catholic and Protestant elites alike seized on religious education of the laity as the route to confessional expansion, as well as to military power and political privilege. In deepening confessionalism, raw coercion—mandatory church attendance, spies, informers, courts of the *Inquisition*—played a large role on both sides of the doctrinal divide.

On controversies and conflicts involving the Catholic Church that were formative in medieval and early modern history see *anti-Semitism*; *Arianism*; *Arminianism*; *Calvinism*; *Catholic League (France)*; *Catholic League (Germany)*;

Charles V, Holy Roman Emperor; *Crusades*; *Ecumenical Councils*; *Edict of Restitution*; *Eighty Years' War*; *English Civil Wars*; *Erastianism*; *feudalism*; *flagellants*; *French Civil Wars*; *Guelphs and Ghibellines*; *gunpowder empires*; *Henry VIII, of England*; *heresy*; *Holy Roman Empire*; *iconoclasm*; *Index Liborum Prohibitorum*; *Italian Wars*; *Jeanne d'Arc*; *just war tradition*; *Kakure Kirishitan*; *Lollards*; *Luther, Martin*; *Orthodox Churches*; *Papal States*; *Pax Dei*; *Philip II, of Spain*; *prohibited weapons*; *real patronato*; *requerimiento*; *serpentine*; *Thirty Years' War*; *Treuga Dei*; *two swords, doctrine of*; *Union of Brest*; *witchcraft*; *Zwingli, Huldrych*.

Suggested Reading: Owen Chadwick, *The Popes and European Revolution* (1981); John O'Malley, ed., *Catholicism in Early Modern Europe* (1988); Steven Ozment, *The Age of Reform, 1250–1550* (1980).

Catholic League (France). "Holy Union." When the *duc d'Anjou* died unexpectedly in June 1584, *Henri de Navarre* became presumptive heir to the French throne, then occupied by *Henri III*. The *Guise* grew in power as Henri III weakened, and Catholic militants rose in ferocious opposition to the idea of a Protestant succession. This was the essential, perhaps the only, common goal of the Catholic League: spiritual predecessors of the 17th-century *dévots/dévotes* joined with Guise schemers and Catholic Royalists to block the ascension of a Protestant king to a throne they regarded as uniquely Catholic and sacral, a common purpose made clear in a manifesto of 1585. *Philip II* of Spain lent support to these "guerriers de Dieu" ("warriors of God") in the *Treaty of Joinville* (December 1584). The Guise and other aristocrats provided the officer corps of the League's military wing. The higher bourgeoisie, led by lawyers and magistrates, formed the main body within the towns and cities. All members swore an oath to take up arms to defend Catholic control of the throne. Heavily armed fanatics partook of violent self-abnegation, marching in *flagellant* processions, beating themselves bloody to accompaniment of martial music. As the movement grew, not all League cells were controlled by the Guise. Most importantly, in Paris the "Sixteen" (named for "committees of public safety" set up in the 16 quarters of the city) was controlled by some 255 upper bourgeoisie. This key cell had wide public support inside Paris. It was politically independent and more radical than the Guise.

The League forced the *Treaty of Nemours* (July 1585) on the king, who capitulated to demands for revocation of all prior concessions to the Huguenots. This launched the eighth of the *French Civil Wars* ("War of the Three Henries"), in which Leaguers promised to "exterminate the heretics by blood and fire." In this project they were opposed by the king and more moderate Catholic *politiques*. In April 1588, Henri III ordered Henri Guise to stay out of Paris, but the king lost control of the city on May 12, the *Day of the Barricades*, when the Sixteen and the Catholic League rose against him. He was driven from the city in favor of Henri Guise. For the next five years the Sixteen and Leaguers ruled Paris and several other Catholic cities. Their grip was made tighter by Henri III's disastrous decision to murder the duc and the Cardinal of Guise in December 1588, which deed was followed by a League rebellion and inspired assassination of the king (August 1, 1589). League dictatorships were set up in most Catholic towns, no longer under the Guise but run by local bourgeoisie. Afterward, ascetic radicals in the League became near-hysterical in their millenarianism and hatred for the Huguenots and their prince, Henri de Navarre. The League refused to accept this heretic and excommunicate on the sacral throne. Instead, Leaguers seized the major cities and launched a terror purge of Protestants and Catholic compromisers. However, the League lost on the field of battle to newly combined armies of Huguenots and royalist Catholics. In September 1589, *Mayenne* lost 10,000 League troops in battle with Henri IV at *Arques*. Six months later, Henri pushed aside the last Leaguer army at *Ivry-la-Bataille*, and besieged Paris. In desperation, the League turned once more to Philip II, who ordered *Parma* to relieve Paris with a Spanish army from the Netherlands. Die-hard Leaguers looked to seat a foreign Catholic on the throne after 1590, but most French Catholics balked at such an assault on the grand tradition of the Gallican Church. When Henri abjured Calvinism and reconverted to Catholicism on July 25, 1593, the political fight was over. During the next two years League military bitter-enders were run down by royalist troops.

Suggested Reading: Frederic Baumgartner, *Radical Reactionaries* (1975).

Catholic League (Germany). "Liga." An alliance of German Catholic princes formed under the Treaty of Munich signed on July 10, 1609, which gave *Maximilian I* of Bavaria control over the *Kriegskasse* of the *Reichskreis* and command of all troops raised. It was formed in response to the founding of the *Protestant Union*, and stayed together thereafter to promote "the one, all-embracing, true church." It ultimately included 15 bishops, 5 abbots, the city of Aachen, and Bavaria. In addition to *confessionalism*, the League promoted autonomy of its members and Bavarian influence in the Empire. However, an Imperial attempt to co-opt the League by forcing the admission of Austria resulted in break-up of the original League in 1617. Two years later Bavaria reformed a confessional alliance with neighboring bishoprics, again explicitly excluding Austria. Spain's intervention in Bohemia in May 1619, lessened concern over Austrian predominance and the Liga was accordingly reconstituted under Bavarian leadership. The "Army of the Catholic League" gave as much or more aid to *Ferdinand II* as did Spain during the Bohemian revolt. It scored a signal victory at the *White Mountain* (November 8, 1620), where it destroyed a patchwork Protestant coalition army led by *Anhalt, Mansfeld*, and *Thurn*. That secured Bohemia permanently for the Habsburgs and allowed them to forcibly recatholicize it.

The Liga signed a treaty of neutrality with the Protestant Union at Ulm in 1620 in a joint effort to prevent the war from spreading to Germany; but it could not restrain Ferdinand from pursuing *Friedrich V* into the Palatinate and thereby widening and prolonging what became the *Thirty Years' War* (1618–1648). From 1621 to 1623 the Liga Army repeatedly outfought its opponents, largely because its commander was *Johann Tilly* and not the divers incompetents who commanded the Protestant armies. The Liga benefitted in early battles from fighting alongside tough Spanish veterans of the Imperial *tercios* and against divided enemies and mostly feckless, confessionally indifferent mercenaries. It did not do as well against the fervently Lutheran Swedes when they entered the war in 1630, under *Gustavus Adolphus*. The reputation of the Liga Army was darkened by participation in the *sack of Magdeburg* in 1631. The next year, it joined Wallenstein outside Nürnberg, before *Alte Feste*. On average, the Liga Army fielded 30,000–40,000 troops before 1635, when it was dissolved under terms of the *Peace of Prague*. See also *Jülich-Kleve, Crisis over*; *Maximilian I, of Bavaria*.

Catholic Reformation. See *Counter-Reformation*.

cavalgada. A fast, vicious cavalry raid. These were the most common feature on both sides of Iberian warfare during the *Reconquista*. See also *chevauchée*; *raiding*; *razzia*.

cavalier (1). A small tower, 10–12 feet high at most, made of earth and stones and used either as an observation post or as a platform to mount small guns.

cavalier (2). A generic term for a trooper in any cavalry unit.

Cavaliers. Originally used as a term of contempt for gentlemen adventurers supporting *Charles I* in the *English Civil Wars*, who played at war the way they hunted, followed fashion, and pursued fast women—for sport. It was later used in reference to Royalist cavalry, and to the more serious nobles and retainers who fought not so much for Charles, who played a feckless *Machiavelli* to his own interests, but to preserve traditional religion, class structure, and the English constitution. Many were English Catholics (up to 40 percent of all loyalist officers) who stood to gain nothing and to lose much from a Parliamentary or Puritan victory.

cavalry. Soldiers who fought from horseback, not *dragoons* who rode to battle but dismounted and fought on foot. There were several great cavalry empires in antiquity, notably the Parthians and Persians. The late Roman Empire saw a transition away from the infantry legions which had built it toward cavalry, necessary to defend it against the horse soldiers of invading barbarian tribes. During the second millennium C.E., the *Fulbe* of West Africa built an empire from horseback, as did the feudal knights of *Songhay*. In fact, cavalry empires dominated West Africa until they met their match in the infantry of the *Ashante* and other coastal and forest peoples, newly armed with European firearms. The *Bedouin* empire was won by Arabian cavalry, while the *Mongols* conquered the greatest land empire in history from the backs of fleet war ponies, and with composite bows and incomparable ruthlessness. The *Mamlūks* of Egypt were a cavalry dynasty that held the reins of overlordship in much of the eastern Mediterranean for nearly 800 years. They survived in truncated form nearly to the 19th century, until crushed by Napoleon at the

"Battle of the Pyramids" in 1798. Ottoman armies were dominated by *akinci* freelance cavalry, heavy mailed *sipahis*, light cavalry *timariots*, and allied *Tatar* scouts and skirmishers. Even at the peak of *Janissary* enlistment Ottoman armies never exceeded one infantryman for every two horse soldiers. The armies of the *Safavids* of Iran were almost exclusively cavalry until the time of *Abbas I*. Then the Safavids shifted from cavalry as their principal arm, not least because they lost too often and badly to Ottoman gun-bearing infantry and mobile artillery. Horse cavalry did not dominate Indian warfare primarily because the humid Indian climate was inimical to most breeds. Instead, Indian armies relied on *elephants* as cavalry, military transports, and in construction of fortifications.

Whatever the breed of *warhorse*, and despite sharp limitations imposed on horse archers by *siege warfare*, only cavalry could effectively patrol borders, provide swift reinforcement of threatened areas, and hound and pursue a defeated enemy. Medieval Europe was constructed socially as well as militarily around the mounted warrior, as much or more than it was based on the Church. In England, medieval cavalrymen were divided into *bannerets*, *knights*, and *men-at-arms*. In France the key distinction was between those knights who were "dubbed," and those who were not (*sergeants* or *squires*) Knights became progressively more heavily armored in response to the penetrating power of the crossbow and of early *gunpowder weapons*. They were the core of all *Crusader* armies and frequently won against staggeringly greater numbers of Muslim infantry and light horse. Their dominance of the battlefield in Europe began to erode from the late 13th century when England's heavy cavalry was surprised and defeated by *William Wallace*'s army of fierce Scots at *Stirling Bridge* (1297). More influentially, Flemish militia decimated the French mounted nobility at *Courtrai* (1302). Learning from this, Robert I ("The Bruce") defeated the English again at *Bannockburn* (1314). In all these fights, heavily armored men on big horses, of the type that dominated Norman and European warfare for 200 years, were met and bested by common infantry. To even greater educational and psychological effect, Swiss infantry formed into *pike* squares began to inflict ever greater defeats on Austrian knighthood, at *Morgarten* (1315), *Laupen* (1339), *Sempach* (1386), and *Näfels* (1388). Once they had fully incorporated the pike into their tactics, after a close battle at *Arbedo* (1422), they destroyed the Burgundian heavy horse at *Grandson* (1476), *Morat* (1476), and *Nancy* (1477).

> ...*the* Mongols *conquered the greatest land empire in history from the backs of fleet war ponies* ...

Within Europe, the distinction of cavalry from infantry was military and social: the French "chevalier" ("horse warrior") or Italian warrior from one of the *consorterie* came from the aristocracy. He was distinguished from a peasant or town militiaman by his warhorse, armor, and weapons, especially the *couched lance* and *sword*. Such a heavy cavalryman was recruited from between 2 and 4 percent of the population, at most. Only in France, therefore, did large population and national wealth mean that armies were made up principally of aristocrats. Elsewhere, infantry from the lower orders necessarily supplemented small feudal levies. In *chivalric* warfare most horse actions involved a line of armored horsemen (1,500 to 2,000 three or four ranks deep formed a line one mile wide) charging en masse to achieve maximum *shock* effect. Opposing infantry either opened alleys before the great, panting and pounding *destriers*, or broke apart and scattered. In either case, armored nobles happily slaughtered with lance and sword the unarmored peasants or town militia as they ran in terror. However, infantry tactics evolved around various forms of the pike that effectively countered cavalry shock. When first faced with disciplined arrays of infantry with long spears, and still brimming with an arrogant sense of class and martial superiority, noble cavalry rode on in the same old way to meet disaster at Courtrai, Bannockburn, and elsewhere. Of course, adaptation came with time. The first, simple expedient was a new role assigned to specialized infantry. As enemy archers did their best to interrupt one's heavy cavalry charge with harassing fire into the assembling mass of lumbering horsemen, it became the crucial job of friendly pike infantry to protect friendly archers deployed to pin down the enemy archers interfering with the charge. A sort of light artillery duel ensued, with archers fighting archers. While this occurred, the heavy cavalry could form and move, accelerating into a full charge against the enemy line of infantry or horse at the critical moment (from about 50 to 100 meters out). Where such counter-archery preliminary to the charge was not employed, where the cavalry instead charged first and unsupported by infantry archers as the French did at Courtrai, the result was massive defeat and heavy casualties among the noble horse.

Cavalry slowly learned to avoid the head-on charge in favor of sweeping wide to encircle the infantry's flanks, or to maneuver to the rear to attack the *baggage train*. However, the main shift in horse soldier tactics—starting in England in the early 1330s—was for cavalry to dismount so that men-at-arms could fight on foot, using their lances as pikes before turning to the sword and mace for close-in fighting. Such tactics still permitted dismounted men to resume a cavalry role for pursuit of a fleeing enemy once close fighting and archery had broken his line. In this the English nobility had learned much from their earlier defeats by pikemen in the *Scottish Wars*, when they were led by Edward I and his son, Edward II. Under the grandson, *Edward III*, radical new tactics were used to defeat a far larger Scots army at *Halidon Hill* (1333). The new English tactics called for longbowmen protected by shaved stakes or stands of pikemen to stand forward of the flanks of the main body of English men-at-arms, who dismounted to hold the center of the English line. Or, longbow formations were placed at the flanks of each of two or three smaller ranks of dismounted knights. The archers then shot out arrow storms at long range, breaking up the enemy formations or provoking them to premature attack, which was met well by the dismounted men-at-arms. In this way, Edward destroyed the Scots national host. These new tactics were taken to France by Edward III and his son, the *Black Prince*, and by their successors during the *Hundred Years' War* (1337–1453). The heavy cavalry of the French nobility first ran into them at *Crécy* (1346). The scale of that defeat taught the

French nobility to also dismount so that they, too, fought on foot at *Poitiers* (1356) and later. Lessons learned are often forgotten, however, so that decades later *Henry V* again used Edward III's formations and tactics to kill and capture thousands of mounted French knights at *Agincourt* (1415).

The gunpowder revolution greatly increased infantry firepower at the expense of cavalry, while siege warfare hampered cavalry's effectiveness. The advent of effective firearms in time unhorsed the knight by rendering his own armor and that of his mount equally useless. In Western Europe, 14th- and 15th-century cavalry tried to counter with their own firearms by adopting the pistol and developing the *caracole*. But this proved of little effect against pike squares and musketeers, who drove cavalry to the margins of the battlefield. During the early years of the *Thirty Years' War*, cavalry made up about 20–25 percent of most armies. Heavy cavalry was often supplemented with "dragoons," musket-bearing mounted infantry, who provided mobile firepower. *Light cavalry* provided reconnaissance and skirmishers to the large infantry armies that dominated the early 17th century. The great innovator was *Gustavus Adolphus*, who modeled his cavalry reforms on the Polish style, reducing armor in favor of leather (*buff coats*) or plain uniforms, and replacing the ineffective pistol and caracole cantor with the slashing saber and full-speed charge. This change was captured in the fierce and merciless battle cry of his feared Finnish horse: "hakkaa paalle!" ("cut them down"). Sweden's success provoked imitators throughout Germany and as far afield as England, where at mid-century *Cromwell* and the cavalry of the *New Model Army* adopted the proven Swedish tactics and training and drove the individually more skilled horsemen of the *Cavaliers* from the field. On the continent, the ratio of cavalry to infantry increased dramatically after 1635, to 50 percent or more. This was largely due to logistical problems: horsemen could forage more widely, which was necessary in lands burned and eaten out over several decades of war.

In Eastern Europe, things were very different. Light cavalry *hussars* and medium cavalry of the *Polish Army* dominated, fighting against vast horse armies of *Tatars* and *Cossacks*, as well as against Swedish horse and Russian *servitor cavalry*. The most probable explanation of this significant difference was topography rather than "inferior" or "backward" military culture, as too many Western European histories have suggested. The need for infantry in chronic warfare with mounted nomads, other than in garrisons armed with firearms, was minimal. Instead, eastern armies properly recognized that foot soldiers, other than dragoons, could not yet make up in firepower on the vast eastern plains what they lacked in mobility, even when protected by pikes. And since infantry was mostly ineffective in Eastern Europe and on the Ukrainian and Russian steppes, cavalry remained the principal arm. Likewise, light cavalry could not operate as well as infantry in the densely populated, heavily forested, and riverine geography of Western Europe (or the mountains of Japan), so that infantry over time became the preferred arm in those areas, with archers and gunmen protected by pikemen or *ashigaru*. See also *arbalétriers*; *arquebusiers à cheval*; *castles, on land*; *chivalry*; *close order*; *conrois*;

demi-lancers; *doubling the ranks*; *drill*; *fortification*; *hobelars*; *Ironsides*; *jinetes*; *Lisowczyks*; *motte-and-bailey*; *open order*; *Pancerna cavalry*; *Parthian shot*; *Reiters*; *scourers*; *secret*; *slavery and war*; *stradiots*; *tournaments*; *turcopoles*.

Suggested Reading: Andrew Ayton, *Knights and Warhorses* (1994); Patricia Crone, *Slaves on Horses* (1980); R. Law, *The Horse in West African History* (1980); John Ellis, *Cavalry: The History of Mounted Warfare* (2002).

Cebelu. An armed cavalry retainer in service to a *timariot* or *sipahi*.

Cebici başi. An Ottoman officer in charge of an arsenal.

Cebicis (cebicilar). "Armorers." A specialized unit of support within the *Janissary Corps* responsible for making and repairing armor and weapons. They also formed a small, separate fighting unit. In the mid-16th century they numbered fewer than 1,000 men and were attached to the artillery. In the 17th century their number was expanded many times, and they worked inside large garrisons.

Cecil, William (1520–1598). "Lord Burghley." English statesman. Chief minister to *Elizabeth I*. Under *Mary Tudor* he outwardly conformed to Catholicism. In 1558, Elizabeth appointed him secretary of state, a position from which he guided her and England's policy with unparalleled shrewdness for 40 years. His main interest was to secure Elizabeth on the throne, which made him a lifelong enemy of *Mary Stuart*. Cecil viewed her as twice damned, as a Catholic enemy of England and as a harlot queen and traitor. His extensive network of spies finally gathered the evidence he needed to persuade the reluctant Elizabeth to execute Mary for treason. Cecil was instrumental in most of the successes of Elizabethan government.

Cecora (Ţuţora), Battle of (November 20, 1620). Outraged by the second burning of Constantinople harbor by the *Cossacks* inside five years, a huge Ottoman army of 160,000 invaded Poland-Lithuania (Moldavia). At Cecora, 40,000 Tatars and Ottomans met just 9,000 Poles and Cossacks, who suffered a crushing defeat. That opened Galicia to pillage.

Celâli **Revolts.** A series of mutinies in segments of the Ottoman military probably caused by the loss of income due to confiscation of the "timars" of some 30,000 *timariots* for failure to report for military duty during the *Thirteen Years' War* (1593–1606). Adding to the turmoil was the demobilization without pay of thousands of *sekban*. The main revolt was suppressed by 1603, but rootless troops continued organized robbery and violence in the country to mid-century, behaving rather like *Free Companies* or *Ecorcheurs* in Europe or the *ashigaru* of Japan.

celata. An early Italian *barbuta* helmet. See also *sallet*.

Les Cent-Suisses. "The Hundred Swiss." See also *palace guards*.

Ceresole, Battle of (1544). See *Italian Wars*.

Cerignola, Battle of (April 21, 1503). Spain's "Gran Capitan" *Gonzalo di Córdoba* had been beaten by a Franco-Swiss army at *Seminara* in 1495. To counter Swiss tactics, at Cerignola he dug a ditch in front of his line. This broke up the cadence of the Swiss pikers, exposing them to murderous Spanish arquebus fire. Once the enemy lines grew ragged Córdoba sent his *tercios* forward. These were newly reformed units with added pikes and more arquebusiers, which gave the Swiss a taste of their own famous "push of pike." The Spanish infantry drove the Franco-Swiss troops backward and downslope, while Spanish cavalry pursued and cut down individual soldiers as they ran. The French artillery train was captured. Naples fell to Córdoba on May 13. While the pike remained an integral part of the Spanish tercio, it was the arquebus and musket that gave the formation its power at Cerignola. The battle was the beginning of the end for Swiss infantry dominance. See also *Marignano, Battle of*.

Český-Brod, Battle of (May 30, 1434). "Lipany." The major battle of the second civil war among the *Hussites*, in which the radical *Taborites* fought the more moderate *Utraquists* 20 miles east of Prague. The Taborite general and former priest, *Procopius the Great*, led an army of Bohemian peasants and townsmen against a force dominated by Utraquist nobility, who had reconciled and allied with Bohemian Catholics at the *Council of Basel*. The clash on the field of battle was unusually sanguinary, reflecting the vicious hatreds of a full-fledged religious civil war. Perhaps 18,000 Czechs died that day on both sides, all killed by fellow Czechs and Hussites. This toll severely weakened the Hussites for when they next faced external enemies. In 1436 they were temporarily subdued by *Sigismund*.

Ceuta. This coastal enclave was occupied by Portugal in 1415 as part of an effort to bypass North African middlemen and gain direct access to the gold of Guinea. Prince *Enrique "the Navigator"* was present at the capture. Afterward, he launched new coastal explorations from Ceuta. See also *Melilla*; *Morocco*.

chaiky. A shallow *galley* some 40–80 feet long, used from the 16th century by *Cossacks* to raid *Tatar* settlements in the Crimea and Ottoman towns along the Black Sea coastline.

chain shot. A form of cannon *shot* used in war at sea. It was comprised of a hollowed cannonball inside which rested a chain affixed to two loops linking the half-spheres of the shell. When fired the shell separated to the length of the chain, creating a whirling bola that tore through an enemy ship's rigging and any sailor or marine unlucky enough to stand in the way.

Chaldiran, Battle of (August 23, 1514). The *Janissaries* of the Ottoman Empire, fighting for *Selim I*, smashed the army of the *Safavids* of Iran in this first major battle between the two Muslim empires. The wholly lopsided outcome resulted from the more modern gunpowder weapons and advanced infantry tactics of the Janissaries, but also because the Iranian army was almost exclusively cavalry archers recruited from tribal levies and lacked modern firepower. The Ottomans deployed serried ranks of Janissary musketeers behind wagon-forts. They had also hauled as many as 200 heavy cannon to the battle. The musketeers and cannon exacted a great toll of Iranian horse archers, many thousands of whom fell. Most military historians agree that Ottoman artillery was decisive in the battle, though the Janissary infantry also played a key role in stopping Iran's cavalry which had scattered the Ottoman *timariot* cavalry, before falling in droves before the guns. There is some evidence that the Iranians had access to artillery but foreswore it as unmanly and unworthy of *holy war*. Chaldiran did much to disabuse them of that prejudice while resetting the frontier between the Ottoman and Safavid empires and securing Azerbaijan and Kurdistan to the Ottoman Empire. After Chaldiran the Safavids removed their capital from vulnerable Tabrīs to more distant Qazwin.

Chalgrove Field, Battle of (1643). See *English Civil Wars*.

chamber. In breech-loading guns, a detachable chamber pre-loaded with shot and powder. In muzzle-loaders, the rear part of the bore which narrowed to accommodate a smaller powder charge, and to provide "shoulders" on which the wadding and cannonball rested.

chambre ardente. "Burning Chamber." Instituted by *Henri II* in October 1547 immediately upon his ascension, this was a court of royal inquisition into "heresy" set up in the Parlement of Paris. Its punishments ranged from torments and fines to death by hanging (for repentant heretics), to execution by burning (for unrepentant heretics). Extant records show that the chambre ardente was principally concerned with the spread of heresy among the clergy, which was the class most directly responsible for the early direction of the *Protestant Reformation*.

Champlain, Samuel de (1567–1635). French explorer and soldier who set the early pattern of French colonization in North America, which emphasized trade over settlement. His first voyage to the New World was actually in service to Spain, to the Caribbean in 1599–1601. He sailed to Canada on a fur trading expedition in 1603, during which he explored the outer St. Lawrence River valley. He returned to chart the coasts of Nova Scotia and New England, 1604–1607. In 1608 he founded Québec city as a military outpost and trading center. In alliance with the Huron, he led several French-Indian expeditions against the empire of the powerful Iroquois League, traditional enemies of the Huron, from 1608 to 1609. In 1611 the French pushed further up the St. Lawrence and established another fortified out-post at Montréal. He went to Paris in 1612 to obtain royal approval of his monopoly over the lucrative fur trade, then returned to New France as its governor. In 1615 he led another expedition against the Iroquois. He was active in the Anglo-French War of 1626–1630, and was forced to surrender Québec to English troops in 1629. When the town was restored as part of a general settlement in 1632 he resumed his governorship of the colony. As governor, he continued to promote French exploration and expansion into the interior of North America. His close alliance with the Huron set the stage for a century of French-Indian wars with the British and their North American colonists. See also *Indian Wars*.

chanfron. Equine *plate* armor that protected the head of a medieval *warhorse*. See also *peytral*.

chapel-de-fer. A light, iron *kettle-hat* type of infantry helmet, bowl-shaped to cover most of the head with a wide brim. It was similar in appearance to World War I British helmets and was the most common infantry helmet in Europe for several centuries.

char-aina. See *armor*.

Charles I, of England (1600–1649). A sickly youth, he did not speak until age five or walk until age seven, and retained a stammer all his life. A competent scholar and amateur theologian, but arrogant and aloof, his first foreign misadventure came in 1623 when he traveled to Madrid with *Buckingham* to negotiate a dynastic marriage, and was rebuffed. That contributed to his decision to fight Spain in behalf of his exiled brother-in-law, *Friedrich V*. Buckingham arranged his marriage to a French Catholic princess, Henrietta Maria (1609–1669), sister of *Louis XIII*. The match was viewed with suspicion in England for its pro-Catholic clauses. Charles succeeded as king on March 27, 1625, and the next month received Henrietta at Dover. Within a year he grew tired of her two dozen priests and 400 attendants and sent them all back to France. Thereafter,

> *Thus began in foreign misadventure the long and fatal crisis of his reign.*

Henrietta was a cardinal influence in his life and policy. Charles intervened in Europe militarily, and foolhardily, from 1625 to 1630. His war aims were wholly beyond his means: a vague defense of Protestantism everywhere; restoration of Friedrich V to the Palatinate; even toppling of Spanish hegemony. In pursuit of these chimeras he joined the *Hague Alliance*. When Parliament refused to fund his promises of aid, he dissolved it and tried to force a war loan. Thus began in foreign misadventure the long and fatal crisis of his reign.

The war against Spain was going badly when Charles also went to war with France, sending Buckingham to relieve the Huguenots at *La Rochelle*. Two expeditions were so ineptly planned and executed they were an international humiliation for England, and did nothing to prevent the Huguenot surrender to *Richelieu* and Louis XIII. After Buckingham's assassination Charles ended the foolhardy war, signing the Peace of Susa (April 14, 1629). He ended his other useless conflict, the long-distance naval war with Spain, the next year. It was too late: his foolish and expensive wars, his Catholic marriage, and his dismissal of Parliament reopened fissures of confessional and constitutional politics in England which would only widen in the deceptive years of peace that remained before the start of the *English Civil Wars*.

In 1634, Charles imposed collection of *ship money* from the coastal towns. In 1637 he extended this arbitrary tax to inland counties. That year, he also tried to impose the *Arminian* prayer book on the Scottish Kirk. In 1639 he provoked the *First Bishops' War* (1639) by seeking to impose episcopacy on Scotland. Without Parliament to pay for England's defenses, Charles looked to raise an Irish army to fight the *Covenanters*, but was forced to back down. The *Second Bishops' War* (1640–1641) started when Charles broke his word on imposition of episcopacy. Again, he was compelled to retreat after failing to raise an Irish army. Charles was finally forced to recall Parliament. When the Commons met its members were hostile and defiant and refused to vote the king war monies until long-standing grievances were addressed. Charles dissolved this "Short Parliament" (April 13–May 5, 1640) and tried once more to govern by fiat. On November 3 he was compelled to recall Parliament as the Scots invaded northern England. This "Long Parliament" sat well after Charles lost his crown and the head that carried it, until dismissed by *Oliver Cromwell* in 1653 (formally, to March 16, 1660).

Over the king's meek objections Parliament, led by John Pym (1584–1643), impeached his key advisers, the Earl of Strafford and Archbishop Laud, executing the former. Charles cast the iron dice of war on January 4, 1642, when he sent troops into the Commons to arrest five members, all of whom took flight. Charles declared war on Parliament from his camp at Nottingham on August 22, 1642. During the four years of civil war that followed he proved as cautious and competent a general as he was rash and incompetent a king. He was in command at *Edgehill* (1642) and *First Newbury* (1643), and defeated a small Roundhead army at Cropedy Bridge (1644). He led the Royalist to a decisive defeat at *Naseby* (1645), however, despite displaying real personal courage in a lost cause.

Leaving his headquarters in Oxford, Charles surrendered to *David Leslie* at Newark on May 5, 1646. The next January the Scots sold him to Parliament. He was closely guarded near Northampton for four months, and three more at Hampton Court. He spent more time on the Isle of Wight. He was seized by the Army on June 2, 1647. In December 1648 he was brought to Westminster on the insistence of Oliver Cromwell and the *New Model Army* to be tried by Parliament as a "tyrant, traitor, and murderer." It was, perhaps, the king's finest hour: he refused to plea, rejected the competence of any English court to try a sovereign, and conducted himself with great personal dignity as he was convicted and condemned to death. On the scaffold before

Whitehall he proclaimed anew his view of sacred monarchy: "A subject and a sovereign are clean, different things." His final declamation before the executioner's axe fell on January 30, 1649, was: "Remember!" See also *exact militia*; *Fifth Monarchists*.

Suggested Reading: L. Reeve, *Charles I and the Road to Personal Rule* (1989); Kevin Sharpe, *The Personal Rule of Charles I* (1992).

Charles II, of England (1630–1685). See *Cromwell, Oliver*; *Dunbar, Battle of*; *English Civil Wars*; *Worcester, Battle of (1651)*.

Charles V, Holy Roman Emperor (1500–1558). Habsburg emperor of the Holy Roman Empire; king of Spain; duke of Burgundy. During the *Italian Wars* (1494–1559), his grandfather *Ferdinand I* (of Aragon) acquired extensive holdings in Italy, giving Charles titles and domains in Naples and Sicily as well as Spain. He was duke of Burgundy by inheritance of his mother, Mary of Burgundy, daughter of *Charles the Rash*. On January 12, 1519, *Maximilian I* died. After paying handsomely to secure election, Charles was elevated to "king of the Romans" on June 28, 1519. At age 19, he already possessed more power, lands, wealth, and legal authority than any king since Charlemagne, in whose capital, Aachen, he was crowned Holy Roman Emperor on October 23, 1520. Europe was impressed, as was Charles, with the idea that the old universal empire (*res publica Christiana*) might be revived in his person. Charles was also titular master of the immense new world empire claimed by Spain in the Americas. In the same year he came into his German inheritance, *Hernán Cortés* began the conquest of the *Aztec Empire*; within two years this immensely rich land was added to Charles' dominion. Before he was 40, the gold rich *Inca Empire* and most of the remainder of Central and South America also came under his sway. And Charles would add the crowns of Hungary, Bohemia, and Lombardy to his many lesser titles. All that came at a price: throughout his reign he had hostile fronts on many frontiers, not least in the *Militargrenze* against an expanding Ottoman Empire.

Charles I's European holdings encircled France on three sides. Although this was the product of serial accidents of birth, death, and inheritance rather than intention, France was implicitly threatened. And Charles inherited the ongoing Italian Wars with young *Francis I* determined to secure Milan. To fight him, Charles relied on the Spanish way of war and military system of heavy infantry squares, or *tercios*. The apex came early, when Charles personally won a great victory at *Pavia* (1525), capturing Francis I and holding him in Spain until he agreed to a peace, which he immediately renounced upon his release. Charles thus remained committed in Italy against France continuously, with brief respites in 1526, 1529, 1538, and 1544. In 1527, angry with Pope Clement VII's involvement in the *League of Cognac*, Charles sent an army to occupy Rome. While there, unpaid mercenaries mutinied and sacked the city, raping nuns and murdering civilians. They also took Clement prisoner. The pious Charles was shocked (some historians date his later, paralyzing melancholia to this incident). He restored Clement both from

141

principle and in order to obtain his assistance dealing with the religious revolt then in full-throated roar in Germany.

When *Martin Luther* made his resounding protest against Church abuses in 1517 young Charles was faced with a crisis that would bedevil his efforts to either crush or compromise with religious dissent in the Empire. The theological thunderstorm and wars of the *Protestant Reformation* that followed would long outlast him. But he was there at the beginning. In March 1521 he called the Diet of Worms to consider Luther's writings. It condemned them and ordered Luther's books and pamphlets burned. The next year, Charles extended the Inquisition to his Burgundian holdings, shocking the tolerant Netherlands. Yet, it was Charles' preoccupation with his wars with France and the Ottomans that probably saved the Reformation: before 1530 Charles never even ventured into the Empire, and by the time he did Lutheranism had taken permanent root in many of its provinces. The next year, German Protestant princes formed the *Schmalkaldic League* to oppose him and any recatholicization. Thus religious and secular revolt blended. For the rest of his life Charles remained determined to hold the empire together and to defend the Catholic faith, as he understood it. He would fail, but also pass his urgent sense of Habsburg religious mission down to his son, *Philip II*.

Financed with loans from the *Fuggers*, in 1535 Charles defeated the Ottomans and captured *Tunis*. Then it was back to Germany to fight rebellious princes and make a final effort to heal the religious breach. He convened another Imperial Diet, in Regensburg (1641). However, Charles was again pulled into war with the Ottomans and France, who allied against him and all conventional religious allegiance. In 1542 a combined Franco-Ottoman fleet raided Habsburg territory. Charles won a major victory over the Protestant princes at *Mühlberg* (1547), but badly overreached in restoring imperial authority, thereby alienating even Catholic princes. By 1552 Charles was losing to rebels and the French in Germany, and to foreign armies on several other fronts. In deep despair, he agreed to the *Convention of Passau* in 1552, then the great compromise of the *Peace of Augsburg* (1555) which granted legal protections to his Lutheran subjects. Considering that the Habsburg domains were too diverse and scattered to be ruled from one place, but also afraid of the crypto-Protestant sympathies of his brother, *Maximilian II*, Charles divided his inheritance. He abdicated in two installments: first, he stepped down as Holy Roman Emperor (1555) in favor of another brother, *Ferdinand I*. In 1556 he abdicated in Spain in favor of his son, Philip II. Then he retired to a monastery in Estramadura, where he died in a profound melancholy in 1558.

Habsburg power peaked with Charles, though for a time it looked as though Philip II might succeed where Charles had failed. Because of the division of his inheritance the Habsburg territories evolved as separate Spanish and Austrian empires, allied yet increasingly discrete and apart. Charles also left Philip a "political testament" which called for defense of the Catholic faith even above empire. Charles cautioned Philip to permit more rights to the conquered

Indians of the New World, but to crush the effort of the Dutch to break free of Habsburg control. He feared this would lead to disintegration of the entire Habsburg edifice. In fact, the empire was already too large when he inherited it, with too many distant borders and far-flung enemies; and he had expanded it since then. What he assayed had been too grand, his empire too unwieldy to be defended with the military technology and fiscal and transportation systems of his day. Mostly, however, Charles failed because he sought to preserve two ideas which over the course of his life and reign were increasingly anachronistic and out of favor with the Age: a sole, unifying Catholic faith for all Christendom, and a single empire to rule the same. Tragically, his son and grandson would continue to tilt at these imperial and confessional windmills from their base in Spain, over another half-century of bloody but ultimately useless religious warfare. See also *Alcántara, Battle of*; *Anabaptism*; *artillery*; *Counter-Reformation*; *Cortés, Hernán*; *encomienda*; *Imperial Diet*; *Knights of Calatrava*; *Malta*; *Moctezuma II*; *Passau*; *Preveza, Convention of*; *Rhodes, Siege of (1522–1523)*; *Santiago, Matamoros*; *Tenochtitlán, First Siege of*; *Tenochtitlán, Second Siege of.*

  Suggested Reading: Martyn Rady, *Emperor Charles V* (1988; 1995); James Tracy, *Emperor Charles V, Impresario of War* (2002); Royall Tyler, *Emperor Charles the Fifth* (1956).

Charles VII, of France (1403–1461, r.1429–1461). See *Armagnacs*; *Bureau, Jean and Gaspard*; *compagnies de l'ordonnance*; *Ecorcheurs*; *franc-archers*; *French Army*; *Hundred Years' War*; *Jeanne d'Arc.*

Charles VIII, of France (1470–1498, r.1483–1498). See *Fornovo, Battle of*; *franc-archers*; *Italian Wars*; *Seminara, Battle of.*

Charles IX, of France (1550–1574). See *French Civil Wars*; *Medici, Catherine de*; *St. Bartholomew's Day Massacres.*

Charles IX, of Sweden. See *Karl IX.*

Charles de Lorraine (1524–1574). See *Guise, Charles, Cardinal de Lorraine.*

Charles the Rash (1433–1477). "Charles the Bold." Compte de Charolais; duc de Burgundy, 1467–1477. Son of "Philip the Good," he clashed early with *Louis XI* of France, whom he briefly imprisoned in 1468. That same year he secured an English alliance by marriage to Margaret, sister of King Edward IV. A military perfectionist who believed in the ideal of rational organization of soldiery, and that ideal formations and battle plans could be formulated in advance, he planned elaborate schemes of deployment, carefully accumulated an enviable artillery train, and generally was in the lead of most innovations in the military arts. The core element of the Burgundian army he set up was a force of 1,250 *lances*, which he subdivided into 100 lance units. In a famous ordinance in 1473, Charles set up *"compagnies de l'ordonnance"* of four uniformed squads, each comprised of five lances of nobility of the sword. But he was not blind to the new role of infantry on the European field of battle. He raised infantry regiments from traditional town militia and incorporated these into his army, and added regular infantry to his compagnies de l'ordonnance, which were comprised of a core of *men-at-arms* but also mounted archers, infantry crossbowmen, and a large number of "couleuveriniers" (hand-gunners). Ultimately, Charles' compagnies de l'ordonnance were built on redesigned lances that counted nine infantrymen for every man-at-arms (three archers, three pikemen, and three couleuveriniers).

On the other hand, as a battlefield commander Charles left much to be desired by his men and duchy. His life's ambition was to elevate Burgundy to a full kingdom and himself from duke to king. He hoped, in addition, to make Burgundy one of the emerging Great Powers, stretching from Flanders to northern Italy and rivaling France and the Holy Roman Empire in wealth and lands. That meant he needed to conquer and annex Alsace and Lorraine and cut a swath through part of the *Swiss Confederation*. His assault on Lorraine brought him into direct conflict with the allied Swiss, whose pike squares destroyed his Burgundian and mercenary armies at *Grandson* (1476) and *Morat* (1476). In his last battle with the Swiss, at *Nancy* (1477), Charles lost his army, then his mount and his life: he was hooked from his horse by Swiss

> *...he planned elaborate schemes of deployment, carefully accumulated an enviable artillery train...*

halberdiers, who then hacked him to death on the ground. The historical chance for Burgundy to emerge as an independent state, perhaps even as a Great Power, died with him: shortly after his demise Burgundy was claimed and partitioned between Austria and France. See also *Burgundian-French War*; *Burgundian-Swiss War*; *Charles V, Holy Roman Emperor*; *condottieri*; *drill*; *Héricourt, Battle of*; *League of Public Weal*; *Maximilian I*.

Suggested Reading: R. Vaughan, *Charles the Rash* (1973).

charter colony. A colonial settlement founded by grant of a Royal charter or license, such as Virginia. This loose legal connection allowed exploration and exploitation of new colonies by private interests within a framework that formally recognized the authority and indirect rule of a distant sovereign.

charter company. Private commercial enterprises that were granted governing powers over colonial territories by distant governments which did not wish to take on the commitment or expense of direct rule. The most spectacular examples were the *East India Company* (EIC) and the Dutch *Vereenigde Oostindische Compaagnie* (VOC). Other charter companies were founded by various European countries to explore and monopolize trade with the Caribbean, China, Muscovy, Africa, and the Americas. (Spain was an exception, governing its overseas colonies through vice royalties, the *real patronato*, and the

Council of the Indies.) Joint-stock companies allied the interests of monarchs and commercial classes in bellicose overseas adventures that promised high profits and gave both an interest in naval affairs. In England and the Netherlands, this helped form an incipient sense of "nationhood" around support for permanent navies.

chase gun(s). Originally, a main gun mounted to the fore of a *galley* to permit firing when chasing enemy ships. This tactic was also imitated in sailing ships. Later, "chase gun" referred to cannon mounted in the rear of sailing vessels, used to fire upon pursuers or to give a "parting shot" as the ship turned to reload its broadside guns out of range. See also *frigate*; *weather gauge*.

Chastillon, Battle of (1453). See *Castillon, Battle of*.

Châteauneuf-de-Randon, Fall of (1380). See *Hundred Years' War*.

Châtillon. See *French Civil Wars*; *Montmorency, Anne, duc de*.

Chaul, Siege of (1571). The sultan of Ahmednagar sent an army of 150,000 to besiege this Portuguese *artillery fortress* defended by a garrison of just 1,100 men. With its back to the sea, from whence it was resupplied by Portuguese ships, the bastioned fort held off the sultan's host for six months, after which the Indian troops withdrew.

chausses. Leggings made of *mail*. They were widely adopted by European knights and men-at-arms from the 12th century. Comparable armored leggings were worn by Ottoman soldiers and by warriors in India, Iran, and China.

chauve-souris. "Bald mouse" (that is, a bat). A French *halberd* marked by a long central spike flanked by double side blades resembling a bat's ears.

chemin de ronde. A path for either infantry or cavalry atop a wide *rampart*, used to quickly reinforce weak or threatened parts of a fortification under attack. See also *terre-plein*.

Chemnitz, Battle of (April 14, 1638). Following the *Treaty of Hamburg*, which provided Sweden with badly needed French subsidies, a Swedish army under *Johann Banér* defeated the Saxon Army at Chemnitz and went on to occupy parts of Bohemia.

Cherasco, Peace of (1631). See *Richelieu, Armand Jean du Plessis de*; *War of the Mantuan Succession*.

Cheriton, Battle of (1644). See *English Civil Wars*; *Hopton, Ralph*; *Waller, William*.

chertva **lines.** See *servitor classes*.

chevalier. See *cavalry*; *knight*.

chevauchée. Its original meaning was "riding services," one of the three forms of military obligation of *knights* under the *servitium debitum*. Its later and more general and lasting meaning was a major cavalry raid, in the Angevin and later English tradition and style. In a major chevauchée arable land outside town or castle walls was devastated in order to provoke the owners to sally out to defend it in battle. A chevauchée also garnered plunder, and hence helped war pay for itself (*bellum se ipse alet*). Foragers and plunderers from a chevauchée moving through open country typically devastated land five to seven miles broad ("havoc radius") on either side of the line of march of an advancing army, and sometimes well beyond that range—in 1356 the *Black Prince* wasted lands as far as 40 miles on either side of his army's path. England's *Edward III* was a master of the large-scale, strategic chevauchée. He led one into Scotland in 1333 that provoked the Scots to meet him in battle at *Halidon Hill*, where he crushed their army and relaunched the *Scottish Wars*. He led a chevauchée through northern France in 1339 in an effort to provoke the French king and nobility to fight. He began by besieging Cambrai, but tired of the effort after just 19 days. When that attempt at provocation failed he moved into the countryside, where he burned and plundered some 200 French villages and towns. *Philip VI*, who was the stronger party militarily, did not take the bait. Instead, he responded with a Fabian strategy and scorched earth policy of his own to deny Edward's army the food and fodder it needed to continue the raid.

Edward led or ordered a dozen major chevauchées against his Scottish or French enemies: 1339 to Cambrésis, the first English campaign of the *Hundred Years' War*; one in each of 1340, 1342, and 1345; two in 1346, when the English burned out Barfleur, Cherbourg, most of the Carentan peninsula, and provoked the French to fight at *Crécy* in 1346, and a second in Scotland which led to the Battle of *Neville's Cross*; 1349 to Toulousain; three in 1355, one in Ireland, a second in Scotland, and the third in Languedoc; two in 1356, one of which provoked the French to fight at *Poitiers*; and a climactic great chevauchée in 1359–1360 from Calais to Burgundy and Paris, which forced France to accede to the *Treaty of Brétigny*. In the 1355 chevauchée in France, Languedoc was torched by the Black Prince who rode from central France to the Mediterranean and back, scorching some of the richest agricultural provinces in Europe. In its course the English burned over 500 castles, large villages and towns (if hamlets and small villages are counted, the number was over 1,000), and two large cities: Toulouse and Narbonne. In the 1355 riding the Black Prince devastated four times the area his father destroyed in 1339. Not to be outdone, the next year Edward III led a chevauchée into Scotland, the *"Burnt Candlemas"* raid. As usual, he savaged, burned, plundered, and killed, laying further waste to an already poor and thinly populated land. Additional major chevauchées took place in France in 1369, 1370,

1373, and 1380. Other raids, comparable in the ferocity with which they brought death and destruction, though carried out on a smaller scale, took place from similar enmities between smaller entities; for instance, Liège campaigned against Namur in 1430.

After the exhausting defeat and huge loss of territory in 1360, the French devised a two-part counter to the chevauchée. First, they upgraded the fortification of major urban centers. Next, they developed a strategic response: shadowing a raiding English or Burgundian army with a large field army. The French still did not offer battle, but the effect of keeping a battle-capable army near the raiding force at all times was to compel the English to concentrate. This narrowed the path of destruction they could cut through the French countryside, which lessened the political and economic effect of their raiding while limiting the plunder and supply available to the raiders. If the English Army was intent on conquest, this counter-strategy forced it to resort to time-consuming and expensive sieges, which were then absorbed by the improved fortifications. If the English interest was merely plunder, they were limited in what they could damage or carry away. Even so, shame and dishonor, along with aristocratic overconfidence, occasionally prompted the French into a foolhardy decision to accept or offer battle. The most famous example of this was the incursion into France made by *Henry V* in 1415, an extended chevauchée that provoked the French to move a large army of *heavy cavalry* and Genoese mercenaries to block his path back to Calais, which in turn led to a crushing French defeat by Henry's hand at *Agincourt* (1415). After that, Henry returned to a slow campaign of sieges and successfully conquered Normandy.

The effects of a chevauchée were complex. The first effect was physical devastation: people were scattered or killed, or returned to burnt-out homes, shops, and farms that could no longer provide shelter or sustain livelihoods; barns, windmills, water mills, and other capital investments were special targets and usually burned down; stores of grain and wine were plundered; herds of livestock (pigs, sheep, cattle) were herded away, or slaughtered. The amount of physical destruction of whole towns and villages was staggering, and extended also to monasteries, convents, abbeys, village churches, and alms houses, amounting to many hundreds of thousands of hours of labor reduced to cinders in just hours or days. Second, repeated chevauchées drove up the cost of defense as towns that had been open throughout the early Middle Ages now fortified against wrack and ruin. This included enforced garrison and guard tower duty for the inhabitants, on a rotating but most burdensome basis. And it meant destroying existing buildings that came too close to the new walls, either to create interior boulevards for quick defense and "interior lines," or to deny the enemy use of outer buildings for shelter or a base for his siege. A chevauchée also stripped most capital from the economy, as soldiers extorted vast sums in protection money (*appatis*) from nobles, towns, villages, or hamlets in the path of men of war. A particularly unfortunate village might have to pay off both sides, or even four, five, or more independent bands or *Free Companies* hovering in the region. This impoverished the locals and also the king, who lost tax revenues, which was a goal of all the destruction in the first place. Fourth, long-distance trade fell off to nothing as the safety and upkeep of roads could not be guaranteed. Fifth, local nobles were freed to also extort and exploit the misery of towns and peasants. This led to rural uprisings such as the great and brutal *Jacquerie* of 1358, which was followed by noble reprisals far more savage than even the "Jacques Bonhommes" committed.

The motives behind undertaking a chevauchée were also mixed. In part, they arose from the principle of "bellum se ipse alet" by which kings deferred the wages of war to plunder by soldiers. A more important reason was strategic: to wage a war of economic attrition against the enemy so as to weaken his legitimacy in the eyes of his people, lessen his capacity to wage war, and intimidate the population into demanding from its king or lord peace on any terms. For this reason troops did not just burn buildings: they cut down fruit trees and destroyed vines, stopped to burn down mills that otherwise gained the attacker nothing, spoiled wells and polluted creeks, and slaughtered livestock they could not themselves herd away or eat even though this made it more difficult for the attackers to live off the land themselves in future campaigns. All this served a strategic purpose: to provoke an enemy to battle, as happened at Crécy, Poitiers, and Agincourt.

The suffering induced by the great chevauchées was great and the men who caused it were pitiless, but the kings and states that commissioned such raids were too strong to be defeated quickly so that wars and suffering became protracted. Yet, the chevauchée was used to deliberately target civilians because in the end it worked: major raids caused political, economic, strategic, and military damage to the enemy, usually at far greater levels than either risky battles or costly sieges. See also *cavalgada*; *civilians*; *cog*; *Nordic Seven Years' War*; *Otterburn, Battle of*; *raiding*; *razzia*; *routiers*; *war finance*.

Suggested Reading: Philippe Contamine, *War in the Middle Ages*, Michael Jones, trans. (1984; 1990); Clifford Rogers, "By Fire and Sword: *bellum hostile* and Civilians in the Hundred Years' War," in Clifford Rogers and Mark Grimsley, eds., *Civilians in the Path of War* (2002).

chevaux de frise. French: "Frisian (or Friesland) horses," Dutch: "Vriesse ruyters" or "Frisian horsemen," German: "spanische Reiter" or "Spanish horsemen." A field obstacle that may have originated with the Dutch for use in the siege of Groningen during the *Eighty Years' War* (1568–1648). Chevaux de frise were made from a log or timber axle about 10 feet long, driven through in three directions with long iron spikes (lances). This made a six-point hedgehog that stood on its own while opposing a row of lethal stakes to the enemy. They were employed chiefly to check cavalry assaults, acting as an inanimate substitute for pikemen so that the Dutch could increase the number of musketeers firing into the Spanish ranks. Alternately, they were set across a breach in a town wall to block the men of the *Army of Flanders* from storming the defenses. In addition to field or siege defense, they were used to block roads or serve as primitive field works where there was no time to make permanent structures or where the ground was frozen or too soft or hard to erect a palisade. They might be made in advance and transported to a battlefield or held ready inside a town to fit any breach. Alternately, iron spikes were hauled by cart to the battlefield and chevaux de frise easily made on the spot from logs culled from felled trees. While highly effective against cavalry, they seldom held up infantry and were highly vulnerable to artillery fire. On occasion, large chevaux de frise would be sunk in a shallow river or harbor, to block passage by enemy ships by ripping out the bottom of their hull. See also *abatis*; *swine feathers*.

chevaux-légers. "Light horse." Discrete companies of 100 French cavalry each made up of nobles who served outside the gendarmerie.

Chiksan, Battle of (1597). See *Toyotomi Hideyoshi*; *Korea*.

child-mother gun. A Chinese adaptation of the European *musket*, utilizing features of the *swivel gun* as well. It was essentially a musket (the "mother") with a removable breech (the "child"). The Chinese also developed a plug bayonet to fit the muzzle. See also *ten-eyed gun*.

Chile. See *Inca Empire*.

chimalli. A small, oval shield used by an *Aztec* warrior. It was usually brilliantly painted and decorated with colorful plumage.

China. In 1211 northern China was first invaded by the *Mongols*. Beijing fell in 1214, and the whole north was overrun between 1217 and 1223. The Southern Song were crushed later, in 1279, after a five-year siege of the fortress at Hsiang-Yang (1268–1273). The end for the Song came with a final naval battle off Guangzhou (Canton) in April 1279. Their thirst for conquest unslaked, the Mongol khans looked to invade Japan utilizing the Chinese and Korean navies. Two invasion attempts were blocked more by inclement weather than by *samurai*, at *Hakata Bay* in 1274 and 1281. The Mongols ruled China for a century but never gained acceptance. The widespread belief that the Yuan dynasty lacked the "mandate of heaven" seemed confirmed when the *Black Death* struck in the 1330s and 1340s, and when the Yellow

> *The Mongol grip on China was so shaken ... the door was opened to a violent change of dynasty.*

River shifted its course to the south in 1344, causing massive destruction and loss of life and provoking a prolonged period of banditry, religious (mainly Buddhist) rebellion, and peasant uprisings. The Mongol grip on China was so shaken by these catastrophes the door was opened to a violent change of dynasty. Zhu Yuanzhang, a former leader of the "*Red Turban Rebellion*," captured Nanjing in 1356. He then won the key naval battle of *Lake Boyang* (1363), which opened the path for his Ming army to defeat the rival rebel territory of Han (centered on Wuhan). Next, he crushed Wu, the third major rebel area to have broken with the Yuan dynasty. The Wu capital of Suzhou fell to the Ming in 1367. The Ming dynasty was then proclaimed in 1368, although it took more fighting to subdue several smaller rebel provinces in the south. Zhu broke with the Red Turbans (a White Lotus Buddhist sect) to claim descent from the former Song dynasty, a move necessary to acquire greater legitimacy than mere conquest. He was proclaimed emperor under the reign name *Hongwu* (r.1368–1398). He governed from Nanjing, with ever greater cruelty rooted in deepening paranoia. In military affairs he harkened to pre-Mongol traditions while in fact retaining several key Mongol military innovations.

During the 15th century Ming China experienced a surge in economic growth and launched an impressive overseas exploration, but then turned inward to defense of the northwest frontier and radical isolationism. Following a brief war of succession Hongwu was followed to the throne by the third Ming emperor, *Yongle* (r.1402–1424). He moved the capital north to Beijing, from where he could more easily rule a vast empire that he regarded as including both China proper and Mongolia. It was the Yongle emperor who commissioned the first six of seven spectacular transoceanic voyages made by *Zheng He* from 1405 to 1433. During these decades, China experienced a surge in population growth to 130 million. Ming blue-water ships, merchants, ambassadors, and admirals spread into Asia and as far afield as eastern Africa, opening markets and establishing direct trade relations nearly 100 years before Columbus sailed west in far flimsier and much smaller vessels. These contacts influenced local histories, but faded from memory and significance in China after 1433, when the Xuande emperor dry-docked the fleet, forbade overseas trade, and banned all construction of ocean-capable ships. In 1436 he imposed radical isolation on China, abandoning its huge lead in naval power and turning its face from the seas to the Inner Asian frontier. Within 150 years European galleons, not Chinese war junks, took command of the world's oceans. Meanwhile, *wakō* ravaged long stretches of China's coast. Worse, the Ming emperors penalized differential economic growth in the coastal regions, since they believed that wealth garnered from overseas trade threatened central control and imperial unity. This policy stifled possibilities for early capitalism in China by redirecting mercantile wealth and investment into land rather than manufactures. It helped set the table for the "great divergence" from the West after 1500.

In the late 15th century China was still a world leader in many areas of technology, having enjoyed advanced economic development for many centuries before the West. However, it began to suffer from worsening ossification of the central government and scholar-elite into endemic corruption and a rigid interpretation of *Confucianism* which ultimately was unable to adapt the rural economy to the expanding population. Late Ming China slowly withered under a baleful climate of stifling bureaucracy and self-imposed insulation from the emerging centers of world trade and technological innovation, which were shifting from China to Europe. For instance, the tendency to concentrate firearms production and casting artillery in centralized locations may have inhibited innovation in design. Political crisis also interfered with military reform and adaptation. At least on land the Xuande emperor had been a committed war leader. His son, Zhu Qizhen (Zhengtong Emperor), was not. Goaded to invade Mongolia, he was captured and lost an army of 500,000 to the Mongols at *Tumu* in 1449, after which the Mongols advanced on Beijing. After that, the terrified Ming rebuilt old frontier fortifications and added 700 new miles of *Great Wall* to huddle behind in fear of Mongol raids—in short, they surrendered the old claim to rule Mongolia and shifted to a purely defensive strategy. From 1474 wall-building intensified and the number of firearms troops multiplied, with most in garrisons along the walls. Since their major enemies lacked fortifications, Chinese field tactics emphasized the use of guns mainly in defense. It was only in civil wars that Chinese gunners faced the tactical problem of overwhelming fortifications.

The Portuguese first reached China in 1514, but a seven-year effort to establish formal relations floundered over an earlier Portuguese attack on Malacca, which was a Ming tributary. The Ming were impressed with the advanced firearms the Portuguese brought to Asia, recognizing them as superior to extant Chinese and Ottoman makes. In 1521 the Ming experienced firsthand the power of these Portuguese cannon when a trade dispute led to a fight in a southern harbor. The Portuguese did much damage but were too few in number to remain. The next year the Portuguese returned to try to force a trade deal on China, but one of their ships was destroyed and another boarded by the Chinese. Within three years Chinese gunsmiths cast copies of recovered or captured Portuguese cannon, at which point the Portuguese made a virtue out of reality by selling their weapons expertise to Chinese smiths. China also acquired and copied European muskets from the Portuguese before the mid-16th century. These were important advances in military technology but they did not constitute a military revolution and did not stop the Mongols from raiding deep into China in force in 1541, 1545, and 1547–1549. These raids-in-force were an attempt to compel a resumption of trade which the Ming had cut off in the north as punishment for earlier Mongol raids. In 1550 a Mongol army attacked Beijing but could not breach the city's improved walls. Annual Mongol raids continued to 1566.

Over the 277 years of Ming rule there were more than 600 rebellions or incidents of banditry on a scale sufficient to be noteworthy. The prolonged crisis of Ming regime and military paralysis was personified and aggravated by the steady isolation of, and then gross abdication of governing responsibility by, the *Wanli* Emperor (r.1572–1620). As he withdrew from imperial responsibilities daily governance in China was left to a corrupt and tyrannical cadre of court *eunuchs*. This exposed the country to new external threats, such as *Hideyoshi*'s two invasions of Korea in the 1590s with large Japanese armies. The Ming opposed those invasions with hastily dispatched armies sent into Korea. The wars against Japan over Korea were extremely costly in Ming lives and treasure and further destabilized China, but they disrupted Hideyoshi's scheme to overthrow the Ming and replace them with the Japanese emperor

151

in a great, new Japanese empire in Asia. Internally, matters continued to deteriorate. In a system where all power flowed from the top, the Wanli Emperor's withdrawal resulted in administrative paralysis, the rise of provincial warlordism, and increasingly violent factionalism in the imperial court. Tax revenues fell, army mutinies and desertions increased, and a hugely damaging inflation set it with the arrival of large amounts of monetary metals associated with European seaborne trade.

Then, to the north at the start of the 17th century, *Nurgaci* began to build the *Manchu* empire. In 1618 he invaded China proper. His Mongol *banners* inflicted a crushing defeat on the Ming at *Sarhu* (1619), forcing them to ask the Portuguese in Macau for aid. They received several late model European bronze and cast iron cannon ("*red barbarian cannon*"), recovered from a sunken English or Dutch ship. Ming gunsmiths copied the guns with help from several *Jesuit* master smiths. And they bought more powerful cannon cast in a Portuguese foundry set up in the south in 1623. With these new cannon and firearms they held back the Manchus in 1626. But the Ming now faced active threats on too many fronts. In the south and west, by 1630, Li Zicheng and Zhang Xianzhong emerged as powerful warlords in full rebellion. They each commanded huge armies and controlled large parts of China. The country was additionally ravaged and destabilized by outbreaks of epidemic disease and famine. Continuing internal political divisions—especially between the scholar-elite and out-of-control imperial eunuchs—and desertions to various enemies by several key Ming generals, contributed to more political fragmentation and a fatal decline in military effectiveness.

After the death of Nurgaci the Qing ("Pure") army mobilized under his son, Hung Taiji, and readied to finish the conquest of China. This involved dozens of campaigns and hundreds of battles over 30 years. As more and more Han prisoners joined the Qing they brought knowledge of firearms, cannon, and siegecraft to the Manchu generals. This closed the technological gap with Chinese armies and fortified cities, as the Qing learned to decide fights with guns. In 1631 the Qing had 40 Portuguese-cast and quality cannon manned by a special all-Han gunnery unit. The Ming also faced a massive rebellion by the regional warlord Li Zicheng. On April 24, 1644, Li took Beijing. The last Ming emperor, Chongzhen, hanged himself the next day, from a tree on Coal Hill outside the Forbidden City. Li Zicheng proclaimed himself emperor and prepared to crush the last Ming armies in the north. In desperation, a Ming "traitor," General Wu Sangui, now caught between the Qing and the rebels, allied with the Qing. Into the chaos of rebellion and civil war rode the huge Qing army, a massive force born of a frontier horse culture bred and organized for nothing but war, now supplemented with skilled Chinese banner troops who knew how to take down a city. General Wu marched on Beijing to capture it for the Qing, drove off Li Zicheng, buried the Chongzhen emperor, then bent to serve a new set of foreign masters. For the Qing claimed the "mandate of heaven" fell to them, and smashed all rebel and Ming resistance in the north. Qing armies then rode south in ethnically cohesive units of Manchu, Mongol, and Han banners. Fighting continued in southern China against "Ming Princes" (pretenders and die-hards) for another 17 years, from 1644 to 1661. The last Ming prince fled to Burma. His retainers were slaughtered on arrival and he and his family were made prisoners by the Burmese king. Handed over to Wu Sangui, who invaded Burma for the Qing in 1661, they were all strangled to death. See also *gunpowder weapons*; *Ming Army*; *mutiny*; *war wagons*.

Suggested Reading: Charles Hucker, *China's Imperial Past* (1975); J. Langlois, ed., *China under Mongol Rule* (1981); Ann Paludan, *Chronicle of the Chinese Emperors* (1998); Jonathan Spence and John Wills, *From Ming to Ch'ing* (1979).

Chinese armies. China had a highly sophisticated recruitment system well before any in Europe, Under *Hongwu* the Ming maintained parts of the older Mongol military system which involved registration of all households according to types of service owed to the state, including military service. Beyond commoners, hereditary military households were most numerous. These were exempted from taxes but were expected to maintain themselves in colonies located on lands granted by the regime and scattered across the country. The major Qing military innovation was the *banner system*. On other aspects of Chinese arms and armies, see *fortification*; *Great Wall*; *gunpowder weapons*; *logistics*; *Manchus*; *Ming Army*; *Mongols*; *Nurgaci*; *Red Turbans*; *Sarhu, Campaign of*; *Tumu, Battle of*.

Chinggisid Empire. See *Mongols*.

Chinggis Khan (1162–1227). "Jenghiz Khan" and "Ghengis Khan." See also *Mongols*.

chivalry. Chivalry was a medieval institution and tradition that had military, social, and religious manifestations. The military aspect of chivalry revolved around the *knight*. Specifically, it was an aristocratic code of conduct closely associated with equestrian "shock" combat. A noble's social function was given religious sanction, and his military function granted sanctification, in the oath-taking and dubbing ceremony ("Benedictio novi militis"). In this ceremony a knight swore solemn vows of religious obligation, then a sword blessed by the Church was used to confer his new social and military status. This reconciled the formally proclaimed peaceful ideals of Christianity and the ethical code of the *just war*

> *In this ceremony a knight swore solemn vows of religious obligation . . .*

with the reality of a thoroughly militarized society in which the "Fathers of the Church" were a major power, and the many orders of clergy numbered among the principal beneficiaries of a steeply hierarchical social system. During the *Crusades* the normal ideals of chivalry were set aside in fighting pagans in the Baltic and eastern Europe, and Muslims in the Middle East, Spain, and the Balkans. During the *Hundred Years' War* (1337–1453) the high ideal of chivalry was proclaimed by nearly all, although dishonorable conduct, theft, murder, savage punishment, and rapine abounded among the knightly classes of England and France. Chivalry thus might be understood as a pragmatic and quasi-legal response to the near complete absence of strong states, wherein the clergy sought to secure social order by direct communication with the armed classes. A powerful and just monarch remained the political ideal, but if strong kings could not be found or crowned at least knights might be dubbed and sworn to justice by the Church. In this way, the just war tradition and the ideal of chivalry were kin, a relation embodied in the widespread cult of martial saints such as St. George and St. Denis, and seen also in the ecstatic reception given by the French to the advent of *Jeanne d'Arc*, the Maid who won for France where so many knights had failed.

The decline of *heavy cavalry* as the principal arm in European warfare hastened the end of martial chivalry. At *Courtrai* (1302), Flemish militia stood and slaughtered the flower of French chivalry. That disaster was repeated at English hands at *Crécy* (1346), *Poitiers* (1356), and *Agincourt* (1415), where French knights were killed in their thousands by English archers. Austrian knights were similarly done in by Swiss peasants and guildsmen at *Morgarten* (1315), *Laupen* (1339), *Sempach* (1386), and *Näfels* (1388). Burgundy lost its duke, its army, and its independence as a result of defeat by Swiss infantry at *Grandson* (1476), *Morat* (1476), and *Nancy* (1477). After the Crusades ended and the military importance of *Military Orders* faded, forms of chivalry assumed a more secular tone and ideal. Personal honor and courtly love displaced Christian zeal and love of God and the Church as the central ambition of the knight, who was now more likely to be a harmless courtier than a heavily armed and dangerously aggressive warrior. In its final and most decadent form, chivalry was tamed and turned by the great monarchs of Europe, who usefully twisted its lingering fantasies into velvet chains to bind the remnant of hereditary knighthood to court service. That was the essential purpose of such feckless associations as the *Order of the Garter* and the *Order of the Golden Fleece*.

It should also be remembered that most of the population lived outside the circle of chivalric grace, beyond the mercy that the brotherhood in arms extended to itself and to women of the noble class. Despite the efforts of some in the Church to expand the ideals of chivalry, peasants were not considered protected by its rules. Instead, they could be robbed, burned out, even killed with relative impunity from the laws of Man or God. It was, for instance, a fairly common practice to hold peasant women until they paid a "ransom" in sexual favors. Such routine rape was not usually the fate of upper class women, unless they were so unlucky as to be in a town or city that fell by storm, in which case they, too, were subject to the accepted right of sack and rapine. Chivalry, in sum, protected its practitioners from legal, moral, and heavenly consequences; it did not protect the common people from depredations by the chivalrous. See also *civilians*; *esquire*; *page*; *prisoners of war*; *siege warfare*; *tournaments*; *two swords, doctrine of*.

Suggested Reading: R. Barber, *The Knight and Chivalry* (1970); G. Duby, *The Chivalrous Society* (1978); M. Strickland, *War and Chivalry* (1996); D. Trim, ed., *The*

Chivalric Ethos and the Development of Military Professionalism (2003); Malcolm Vale, *War and Chivalry* (1981); Juliet Vale, *Edward III and Chivalry* (1983).

Chocim, Battle of (1621). See *Khotyn, Battle of*.

Chodkiewicz, Jan Karol (1561–1621). Polish general. Despite fighting for a rash and vacillating king, *Sigismund III*, he led Polish cavalry armies to a series of battlefield victories over armies of Cossacks, Ottomans, Russians, and Swedes. He was also adept at *guerre guerroyante* along the Cossack and Russian–Swedish frontiers. He took Riga and Dorpat in 1601. In 1605, at *Kirkholm*, he defeated a much larger army led by *Karl IX*. He won again over the Swedes in 1609. His march into Russia in relief of the Polish garrison occupying Moscow failed when his troops mutinied. He was killed in the midst of a victory over the Ottomans and Tatars at *Khotyn* (Chocim) in 1621. Chodkiewicz's success with cavalry against larger infantry armies, feats which place him in the front rank of horse soldiers, so impressed *Gustavus Adolphus* that he reformed the Swedish cavalry along Polish lines.

Chojnice, Battle of (September 18, 1454). Conitz or Konitz. The first major battle of the "*War of the Cities*" (1454–1466), fought between Poland-Lithuania and the *Teutonic Knights*. The Poles, led personally by *Casimir IV*, anticipated support from Prussian peasants then in rebellion against the warrior monks, their hard overlords. The Polish army of 16,000 men was itself mostly drawn from feudal peasant levies, badly officered by quarrelsome nobles. Chojnice was a critical entrepôt and a main base of the remaining economic power of the Teutonic Knights, which a small force of Saxons occupied in their behalf. The city had been under ineffective siege by a Prussian peasant army, and some mercenaries, since April. But a combination of inept Polish officering and a shortfall of Prussian monies to pay the mercenaries left the city in Teuton-Saxon hands. Casimir now ordered his main army to Chojnice. Since the great strength of the Poles was noble cavalry, and since fortified towns rarely if ever succumbed to horse soldiers who disdained sapping or trench work, the city stood firm. In early September a large band of German mercenaries (9,000 horse and 6,000 foot) arrived in answer to a summons from the Teutonic Knights. These professionals gave the advantage to the Knights who, along with levies of peasant conscripts, smashed the Polish army and nearly captured Casimir. The Teutons went on to recapture numerous Prussian towns. Unfortunately for the Knights, however, they did not have the money to pay such a large mercenary force. The Grand Master of the Order was therefore forced to promise Prussian cities as collateral to the Germans in the event he could not meet the payroll due in February 1455. This deal cost the Teutonic Knights the war in the end as they lost mercenary support and the greater strength and manpower of Poland told against them. But for awhile longer the victory at Chojnice and the infusion of German mercenaries meant the war continued.

choragiew. "Troop," "company," or "*banner.*" In the *Polish Army*, the choragiew was the smallest tactical unit. It was led by a *rotmistrz*, who recruited the men, contracted for their pay (and for *dead-pays*), and appointed junior officers ("*porucznik*"). There was, as a result, no uniform size to these units, which could number as few as 60 men or exceed 150. Multiple choragiews were grouped into a larger tactical unit, the *pulk.*

Christendom. See *res publica Christiana.*

Christian Brotherhood. See *German Peasant War.*

Christian humanism. See *Francis I*; *Italian Renaissance*; *Luther, Martin*; *Protestant Reformation.*

Christianity. See *Albigensian Crusade*; *anti-Semitism*; *Arianism*; *Arminianism*; *Byzantine Empire*; *Calvinism*; *Castile*; *Catholic Church*; *Catholic League (France)*; *Catholic League (Germany)*; *Charles I, of England*; *Charles V, Holy Roman Emperor*; *chivalry*; *Confederation of Kilkenny*; *Coptic Church*; *Counter-Reformation*; *Cromwell, Oliver*; *Crusades*; *Ecumenical Councils*; *Edict of Restitution*; *Eighty Years' War*; *English Civil Wars*; *Erastianism*; *feudalism*; *Fifth Monarchists*; *flagellants*; *French Civil Wars*; *Great Schism*; *Guelphs and Ghibellines*; *gunpowder empires*; *Henry VIII, of England*; *heresy*; *Holy Roman Empire*; *Hospitallers*; *Hussite Wars*; *iconoclasm*; *Index Librorum Prohibitorum*; *Inquisition*; *Ireland*; *Italian Wars*; *Japan*; *Jeanne d'Arc*; *Jesuits*; *just war tradition*; *Kakure Kirishitan*; *knights*; *Knox, John*; *Livonian Order*; *Lollards*; *Luther, Martin*; *Military Orders*; *Orthodox Churches*; *Papal States*; *Pax Dei*; *Philip II, of Spain*; *prohibited weapons*; *Protestant Reformation*; *Puritans*; *real patronato*; *Reconquista*; *Renaissance*; *requerimiento*; *res publica Christiana*; *Spain*; *Teutonic Knights, Order of*; *Third Rome*; *Thirty Years' War*; *Treuga Dei*; *two swords, doctrine of*; *Union of Brest*; *War of Cologne*; *War of the Eight Saints*; *witchcraft*; *Zwingli, Huldrych.*

Christian IV (1588–1648). Duke of Holstein; king of Denmark. He also controlled the fortified bishoprics of Bremen, Halberstadt, and Verden, but later lost them to *Ferdinand II*, then Sweden. Christian longed to be well-regarded for his military virtues and prowess, though he had few of the first and none of the second. He posed as a devout champion of Protestantism, but in private was a womanizer and heavy drinker who spent as much or more time consulting astrology charts as the Bible. His major policies were promotion of the interests of the mercantile classes (he chartered a Danish East India company in 1614 and sought to control the Baltic trade), and expensive military adventurism that cost Denmark its preeminent position in the Baltic, starting with a loss to Sweden in the *Kalmar War* (1611–1613) and ending with his disastrous intervention in the *Thirty Years' War* (1618–1648). In 1625, Christian was elected commander (*Kreisoberst*) of the Lower Saxon Circle (*Reichskreis*). He gathered the *Hague Alliance* around a plan to intervene in Germany and plunged into war against vastly superior enemies, personally leading 20,000 mercenaries across the Elbe. What drew him in was dynastic interest, a desire to block intervention by his old enemy Sweden (*Richelieu* was already courting *Gustavus Adolphus*), and perhaps also the Protestant cause.

The Danish *Estates* refused to pay for his German war: two aggressions inside 15 years was too much for the Council. That forced Christian to fight as the Duke of Holstein, using revenue from his demesne lands, the *Sound Tolls*, and subsidies from France, the Netherlands, and England (which paid less than one-third of what it promised). Retreating from early defeats in Germany, Christian was pursued and routed in 1626 by *Johann Tilly* at *Lutter-am-Barenberg*. He fled the battlefield, leaving half his army dead or captured on it. The next year he was driven into Holstein by an Imperial army led by *Albrecht von Wallenstein*. Christian's anti-Habsburg alliance now melted: Brandenburg returned to neutrality; England was untrustworthy; in 1627 France allied with Spain against England; and Sweden was still fighting Poland over Royal Prussia instead of entering the German war. Denmark lay open to invasion. In 1628, Christian reinvaded Germany in an attempt at preemption, but was again soundly beaten, at *Wolgast*. Wallenstein then occupied Jutland. On July 7, 1629, Christian came to terms with Ferdinand in the *Peace of Lübeck*, in which he surrendered all claims within the Holy Roman Empire, with Bremen, Halberstadt, and Verden ceded outright to the Emperor. Twenty years later he was tempted to re-enter the German war, but all his machinations earned him was another defeat at the hands of Sweden, in *Torstensson's War* (1643–1645). For all his defeats, Christian IV left Denmark with a national *standing army* officered by Danish professionals, despite his famous prejudice in favor of foreign mercenaries.

Suggested Reading: P. D. Lockhart, *Denmark in the Thirty Years' War, 1618–1648* (1996).

Christian of Anhalt-Bernburg (1568–1630). Protestant general in the *Thirty Years' War*. Before 1618 it was his grand ambition to form and lead a grand military coalition against the Habsburgs and the *Counter-Reformation*. He tried to do this with the *Protestant Union*, but opposition from the cities that provided most military finance blocked his ambition. He encouraged the Bohemian *Estates* to depose *Ferdinand II*, and thereafter was commissioned by *Friedrich V*, whom he served as regent in Amberg, to raise an army to defend Friedrich's claim to the Bohemian throne and make war on Austria. Anhalt joined his force with a mercenary army commanded by *Mathias Thurn*. This allied army was smashed by *Tilly* and *Bucquoy* at the *White Mountain* (November 8, 1620).

Christian of Brunswick (1598–1626). Administrator of Halberstadt and reckless military adventurer. This brash German prince earned a reputation for courageous impetuosity in battle, but not much else. His failure to link with *Graf von Manstein* before *Wimpfen* (May 6, 1622) cost the Protestants the battle. He fought a brilliant, because desperate, holding action at *Höchst* (June 20, 1622). He was dismissed by Friedrich on July 13, 1622. Two months later he and Mansfeld joined and beat Tilly at *Fleurus*. That victory pushed the Imperials out of the Netherlands, even though Christian lost most of his infantry and one of his arms in the fight. At *Stadtlohn* (August 6, 1623), Christian lost badly to Tilly and the army of the *Catholic League* and was finished as a field general. He commanded indifferently in several minor campaigns before his death in 1626.

El Cid. Né Ruy Díaz de Vivar. See *Castile*; *mercenaries*; *Reconquista*; *siege warfare*.

cihuacoatl. An Aztec senior commander, roughly equivalent to a general. They wore large and colorful headdresses made of animal skins and/or feathers which made them easily identifiable in battle. This worked well enough when facing other Mesoamericans, but it allowed *Hernán Cortés* and his men to single out Aztec commanders, kill them quickly with arquebus, lance, or sword, and thus paralyze and defeat much larger Aztec armies. See also *Otumba, Battle of*.

cimarónes. Or "cimarrones," or "maroons." Runaway black slaves from Spanish colonies who established independent enclaves in the Caribbean, notably along the Mosquito Coast. These free black and mulatto communities lived by their wits and by waylaying passing ships. They traded fruit and produce with English, French, and Dutch *privateers*, and sometimes allied with them to prey on Spanish ports and shipping. See also *Drake, Francis*.

Cinque Ports. Five strategically located English ports first listed in a Royal Charter in 1155: Dover, Hastings, Hythe, New Romney, and Sandwich. Rye and Winchelsea were added a few decades later, and seven more towns were associated with the Cinque Ports in the 15th century. In theory, these ports were obliged to provide 57 ships and supporting crew for a fortnight's service upon notice from the crown, in exchange for special privileges amounting almost to self-governance. This was the only compulsory naval service in England before the introduction of *demurrage* and *impressment*. From time to time the Cinque Ports gave service to the crown when a war was in their own interest, notably in the 13th century. Thus, the majority of ships used to transport and supply Edward I in his conquest of Wales, 1277–1283, came from the Cinque Ports: 25 in 1277 and another 40 in 1282–1283. During the *Hundred Years' War* (1337–1453), ships from the Cinque Ports accompanied numerous English expeditions, but so did ships from other coastal towns. The *Black Death* ravaged the Cinque Ports, as did major raids and burnings by the French and their allies. The move to a *permanent navy* in the 16th century eliminated any rationale for special privileges, in addition to which some of the harbors of the Cinque Ports silted badly.

Circles (of the Holy Roman Empire). See *Reichskreis*.

circumvallation. See *lines of circumvallation*.

citadel. More than a *donjon*, tower, or stronghold inside a *castle* or fort, a citadel was an entire fort occupied by a garrison positioned well inside a city. They were most common in the Muslim Middle East, where many cities had strong inner forts but only thin outer walls. This reflected the fact that in Arab states the main military danger was often from within, in form of rebellious troops or a palace coup. Citadels also played a role in repressing popular discontent where some unpopular ruler (say, from a *shi'ia* dynasty ruling over a *sunni* populace, or vice versa) was unsure of the ultimate loyalty of the city. The same phenomenon sometimes occurred in Europe where occupying armies could not be certain of the loyalty of the common people. See also *jōkamachi*.

çit palankasi. Simple reed-palisade forts constructed by the Ottomans in areas where stone forts (*kale*) were not needed or were too expensive to build. Often, they were also poorly garrisoned and hence easily overpowered or forced to surrender.

city-states. See *Aztec Empire*; *Hanse*; *Italian Renaissance*; *Machiavelli, Niccolò di Bernardo*.

civilians. In the Middle Ages it was mostly taken for granted that brutal treatment of civilians ("inermis" or "unarmed persons") was part of war. This was because of the nature of *raiding* and the *razzia* for slaves, or the *chevauchée* in which destruction of property, foodstuffs, and livelihoods was an essential part of strategy. Contributing to indiscriminate killing was the general absence of uniforms comparable to those which had clearly demarcated soldiers in Roman times. Lastly, ferocious religious zealotry led to atrocity against civilians of other faiths, as in the *Crusades*, or against *heretics*. Despite the mores of *chivalry*, making life miserable for the population of enemy territories was a main tool of medieval warfare, as it was also in early modern times. There was, in fact, no prohibition in the chivalric code in Europe against attacking civilians. There was a prohibition in the *jus in bello* and the *Pax Dei*

> *There was, in fact, no prohibition in the chivalric code in Europe against attacking civilians.*

against violence directed at clergy, women, children, Jews (generally considered noncombatants, though some in Spain were forced to serve in garrisons), hermits, merchants, shepherds, farmers, and the unfree. This effort to restrain war remained mostly a distant ideal, as it was practically unenforceable. Throughout this period, in Europe and Africa, Asia and the Americas, the effects of war on civilian populations was roughly comparable. Some died in rank atrocities, others from sacks of towns and razing of villages. Most died from disease or starvation. Ancillary effects of the dislocations and privations of wartime included higher infant mortality rates and low fertility rates among malnourished adults. Family life always suffered: marriages broke down, older children were kidnaped into armies or ran away, old people died off in droves from disease or abandonment. The cost of foodstuffs always rose in war, as grain grew scarce or not at all in fallow fields. Abandoned children usually became beggars; abandoned women turned to prostitution, trailing armies as *camp followers*. In general, if a war was underway it was far safer to be a soldier. See also *Alba, Don Fernando Álvarez de Toledo, duque de*; *Albigensian Crusade*; *Anabaptism*; *anti-Semitism*; *appatis*; *askeri*; *baggage train*; *Bashi-Bazouks*; *beldar*; *bellum hostile*; *Black Prince*; *booty*; *camp followers*; *chivalry*; *club men*; *Constantinople, Siege of*; *contributions*; *Cromwell, Oliver*; *Crusades*; *Derbençi*; *disease*; *Dorpat, Sack of*; *Drogheda, Sack of*; *expulsion of the Jews*; *expulsion of the Moors*; *French Civil Wars*; *Grotius, Hugo*; *guerre couverte*; *guerre mortelle*; *heresy*; *hors de combat*; *Inquisition*; *Ireton, Henry*; *Jews*; *jus in bello*; *just war tradition*; *logistics*; *Maastricht, Siege of (1579)*; *Magdeburg, Sack of*; *military discipline*; *Parma, duque di*; *Raya*; *Reconquista*; *requisition*; *routiers*; *Rupert, Prince*; *scorched earth*; *Sempach, Covenant of*; *siege warfare*; *"Spanish Fury"*; *St. Bartholomew's Day Massacres*; *teamsters*; *Thirty Years' War*; *Tilly, Johann*; *Treuga Dei*; *Wexford, Sack of*; *witchcraft*; *women*.

Civitate, Battle of (1053). See *cavalry*; *heavy cavalry*; *Normans*.

claymore. A two-edged (not two-handed) broadsword original to the Scottish Highlands. Later, the term was also used in reference to a short broadsword, sometimes single-edged with a classic basket-hilt. This type of claymore was more commonly used by the Scots from the 16th century.

Clermont, Battle of (1358). See *Jacquerie*.

clinker-built. An expensive, northern shipbuilding technique that constructed a roundship's hull by overlapping planking, starting at the keel and working out and up, not inward from a skeleton as was the practice in the Mediterranean. This used a lot of iron riveting but produced sturdy, walnut-shaped hulls that would be very large (over 1,000 tons displacement) by medieval European standards, though still small compared to contemporary Chinese vessels. See also *balinger*; *barge*; *cocha*; *cog*; *galleon*; *skeleton-built*.

Clontibret, Battle of (1595). See *Nine Years' War*.

close-fights. Bulkheads built at the fore and aft end of a warship, under the *castles*, as a final defense against boarders. They worked by giving cover to defenders and by compartmentalizing the ship to prevent it being overrun all at once. They were made of heavy wooden slats and fitted with loop-holes for firing guns and bayonet work. From this came the synonym and additional meaning of fighting an enemy hand-to-hand and face-to-face, or at "close quarters."

close-haul. See *haul close*.

close order. In the cavalry: the spacing between horses side-by-side in a troop; generally three feet, but sometimes as close as 1½ feet. This was the mode in which *heavy cavalry* charged in order to maximize *shock*. In the infantry: *Maurits of Nassau* enforced a model of close-order *drill* that was ultimately emulated by all modern armies. See also *open order*.

close-quarters. See *close-fights*.

club men. Gentry and others who supported neither side in the *English Civil Wars*, but instead raised local forces to interfere with recruiting by the king and impressment by Parliament. They objected to unpaid quartering to troops and the common abuses of soldiers against civilians. After *Naseby*, they seriously impeded cross-country movement by *Fairfax* and *Cromwell*, who dealt violently with several thousand at Hambledon Hill on August 5, 1645. See also *free quarter*; *Tard-Avisés*.

coaster. Small, coast-hugging transport ships of various types. They played a prominent role in the *Crusades* and in later trade and military supply in Mediterranean warfare.

"coat-and-conduct" money. In the English system of military recruitment, this was money raised and paid at the county level to new recruits to buy a proper coat and travel to a designated muster point. It was paid following complaints by the army and navy about the utterly destitute condition of too many recruits, who were clearly the dregs of society sent up to fill the county quota and to spare its more favored sons. The coats provided varied greatly and did not constitute a uniform.

coat of plates. See *brigandine*.

cocha. In the 14th–15th centuries, a mid-sized ship representing a redesign of the *cog*. It could be fitted for trade, war, or both (as an armed merchantman). It was first laid in the Mediterranean, where the *skeleton-built* system of the south blended with the *clinker-built* designs of the north to produce this hybrid. In northern waters it was called a *carrack*.

cog. In the 12th–15th centuries, a flat-bottomed single-masted ship that probably first employed the true *sternpost rudder*. It was developed and most widely used in the Baltic and Atlantic. Built primarily for trade—it could sit on a mud flat at low tide to load or unload—it was also well-armed for defense against predatory *galleys* and *longships*. It had a high freeboard that made boarding from lower-lying oared ships difficult while permitting defenders to throw stones or shoot quarrels into the attacking ship. Later versions sported high *castles* to maximize this effect, taking additional advantage of the cog's unusual stability. The Danes and *Teutonic Knights* used primitive cogs to crush Wend oared seapower in the Baltic from 1210, and to attack pagan Prussia and Lithuania in the 13th and 14th centuries. England relied on the cog to transport thousands of *warhorses* and carts and baggage horses used in *chevauchées* to France during the *Hundred Years' War* (1337–1453). See also *clinker-built*; *tarides*.

Cognac, League of (1527). An alliance among Pope Clement VII, *Henry VIII* of England, the Republic of Venice, and Florence, against *Charles V*. It was formed in the wake of the defeat and capture of *Francis I* by forces led personally to victory by Charles V at *Pavia* (February 25, 1525). It was an ineffective alliance, however, whose main accomplishment was to provoke Charles V to send an army to Rome to punish the pope for his disloyalty. While there, it ran amok, sacked the city, and took the pope captive, all of which appalled Charles. After a few summers of desultory fighting the first phase of the *Italian Wars* ended with the *Peace of Cambrai* (1529).

coiffe-de-maille. A *mail* head piece worn under a helmet. It incorporated an *aventail*, but also protected the chin and cheeks from slashing wounds.

Colchester, Battle of (1648). See *English Civil Wars*.

Coligny, Gaspard de (1549–1572). Admiral of France. He gained his position by virtue of vast land holdings in Normandy and the prominence at Court of his powerful uncle, *Anne de Montmorency*. Coligny was taken prisoner by the Spanish, along with Montmorency, at *St. Quentin* (1557). He was held captive for three years. A moderate Protestant, he condemned the *"conspiracy of Amboise"* but joined the *Huguenot* army at the onset of the *French Civil Wars* (1562–1629). Along with *Condé*, he fought Montmorency at *Saint-Denis* (1567). After Condé's murder at *Jarnac* in March 1569, Coligny became military leader of the Huguenots. Later that year he took revenge for Jarnac by ordering a slaughter of Catholic prisoners and peasants, for which a price of 50,000 gold écus was placed on his head. After the *Edict of Saint-Germaine-en-Laye* restored peace, Coligny returned to Court at Blois where he urgently argued for war with Spain, both to advance his own fortunes and heal the religious divide by turning outward against a common and hated enemy. Welcomed by Charles IX to Court, he was distrusted by *Catherine de Medici*. It was thought by many Parisians (probably falsely, but intensely nonetheless) that Coligny had undue influence over the young king and that he had persuaded Charles to back Protestant Dutch rebels against Spain. An attempt to assassinate Coligny in Paris failed on August 22, 1572. The attempt was certainly a *Guise* plot. Wounded, but determined to uncover the assassins, Coligny remained in Paris. That was a fateful and fatal decision: he was among the first to die—killed personally by the duc de Guise—during the first hours of the *St. Bartholomew's Day Massacres* two nights later. His head was cut off and embalmed to be sent as a trophy to the pope. The rest of his corpse was hurled to the street where it was given a mock trial then dismembered and dragged over the cobblestones of Paris by a Catholic mob. For good measure, and in punishment for "heresy," his various body parts were burned and thrown into the Seine.

Suggested Reading: J. Shimizu, *Conflict of Loyalties* (1970).

colonel. Originally, the rank of officers in the Spanish army of *Ferdinand and Isabella* in command of a "coronelia," a unit of 12 companies of 500 men each. The title spread, along with the fame of Spanish infantry. In 1507 the *Diet of Worms* laid out that a colonel had a right to a personal staff of 22 attendants. In practice, size and quality of a staff varied with the wealth of the colonel. By the mid-17th century, evolving from the original Dutch model, regiments of 1,000 to 1,200 men in most armies were commanded by colonels. The equivalent title in the French Army prior to 1661 was *mestres de camp*. See also *Fähnlein*; *Landsknechte*; *Trabanten*.

colonialism. See *England*; *Elizabeth I*; *Netherlands*; *Ottoman Empire*; *Philip II, of Spain*; *Portugal*; *Spain*.

columbrina ad manum. A mid-15th-century French gun falling between a "hand cannon" and a small artillery piece. It was a portable, shoulder-fired weapon.

combat. See *battle (2)*.

commandery. The basic organizational unit of knights of the *Military Orders*. The *Teutonic Knights* set the minimum at 12 brother-knights, plus sergeants, per commandery. *Santiago* set the maximum at 13. In both cases the idea was imitation of "The Christ," or rather the apostles of Jesus of Nazareth. Spanish commanderies tended to be fortified towns while Military Orders in Palestine and Syria built hilltop forts along with some extraordinary mountaintop castles. As professional troops displaced Military Orders in the affections and employment of kings, the number of knights per commandery fell to as few as four in the early 14th century and just one at century's end. See also *encomienda*; *torre alberrano*; *torre del homenaje*.

Committee of Both Kingdoms. A unified English-Scots command formed in 1644 to coordinate military operations by the Scots army in England allied to Parliament's forces fighting *Charles I*.

Commonwealth of the Two Nations. *Poland-Lithuania* after the *Union of Lublin* in 1569.

communis exercitus. See *Scotland*.

compagnies de l'ordonnance (du roi). Mid-15th-century military reforms carried through by Charles VII set up mixed units of infantry archers and heavy cavalry (nobility of the sword), supported by smaller groups of specialist troops. All told, they comprised 1,800 men-at-arms, 3,600 archers, and 1,800 auxiliaries. They were organized at the tactical level into *lances*. These "compagnies" comprised a rudimentary corps in peacetime, not a full *standing army*. Still, this was a rare permanent force in early modern Europe. Also, it provided a military option for that important minority of French nobles who were determined to display their nobility the old way, in feats of arms. As captains, they filled the compagnies with relatives and "clients" who wore their family livery and carried their pennants into battle. The French compagnies served in the final campaigns in Normandy (1449–1450) and Guyenne (1451–1453) that closed out the *Hundred Years' War* (1337–1453). They were the mainstay of Royalist armies deep into the *French Civil Wars* (1562–1629), surviving until France adopted reforms on the Dutch model pioneered by *Maurits of Nassau*. Comparable reforms and units, utilizing the same terminology, were made in Burgundy by *Charles the Rash*. See also *Ecorcheurs*; *French Army*.

company. The main body of recruitment and tactical maneuver in armies of the early modern period, which had not yet developed the regimental system of the late 16th–early 17th centuries. Companies varied in size by their place of origin and the army served, averaging anywhere from small units of 100 men to very large companies of 500 or more. In the French Army of the mid-16th century companies were made up of *lances* and ranged from 40 to 100 men. Their captains were all nobles. The term was of continental European origin. In the early 17th century English military professionals adopted it in preference to the older term for civic militia, "trained bands." A shift to regiments as the main tactical unit in European armies started in the Netherlands in the 1590s with the reforms of *Maurits of Nassau*. The Dutch retained companies as sub-regimental units, averaging between 200 and 300 men. Mid-17th-century English armies kept small companies of 100 to 120 men within regiments formed by 10–12 companies. See also *Catalan Great Company*; *colonel*; *dead-pays*; *Fähnlein*; *Free Companies*; *regiments*; *Rotte*.

> *In the French Army of the mid-16th century companies were made up of* lances *and ranged from 40 to 100 men.*

compass. As a serious aid to naval and commercial navigation the magnetic compass was useful long before it became widely adopted in Europe during the 13th century (probably via contacts with Muslims, who got it from the Chinese). Prior to its adoption, and for decades afterward, even experienced navigators preferred to steer by *dead reckoning* and stayed close to known coastlines so that they could use direct sighting from point to point. See also *astrolabe*; *cross-staff*.

composite bow. A powerful bow composed of three or more layers of materials of different strength: wood, bone, and sinew. They were harder to make than plain bows but their complex forms and reinforcing tensile qualities imparted much greater force and range to arrows than either the *crossbow* or *longbow*. See also *Mongols*; *reflex bow*; *Turkish bow*.

Comyn Wars (1297–1304). See *Falkirk, Battle of*; *Scottish Wars*; *Stirling Bridge, Battle of*; *Wallace, William*.

Condé, Henri I, de Bourbon (1552–1588). Son of *Condé* (Louis de Bourbon), father of *Condé* (Henri II, de Bourbon). He took up his father's Protestant cause with passion, but spent most of his foreshortened life in the political and military shadows cast by more talented men. He served under *Coligny* and saw action at *Moncontour* (October 3, 1569), where his face was slashed by a saber. Upon Coligny's murder in the *St. Bartholomew's Day Massacres*, the young Condé dwelled in the shade cast by *Henri de Navarre* from the first night of the massacres, when they were both forced to abjure Calvinism. In 1574, Condé was elected commander of the republican defensive alliance formed by surviving *Huguenot* towns in the Midi. He fought alongside Henri de Navarre in the sixth, seventh, and eighth of the *French Civil Wars* (1562–1629).

Condé, Henri II, de Bourbon (1588–1646). He was born several months after the death of his father, Henri I, *Condé*. Henri II eventually abandoned the Protestantism of his famous rebel family and converted to Catholicism. He then fought against the *Huguenots* in behalf of *Louis XIII*, becoming one of their fiercest persecutors. Toward the end of the *Thirty Years' War* Henri conspired with the king's enemies, foreign and domestic, and took up arms in revolt against him.

Condé, Louis de Bourbon (1530–1569). Military leader of the *Huguenots* in the early *French Civil Wars*. In 1555 he visited Geneva on his way home to Navarre from campaigning for France in the *Italian Wars*, and converted to Calvinism. The *Guise* arrested him as part of their anti-Huguenot campaign that included execution of hundreds of Protestant nobles who partook of the "*conspiracy of Amboise*" to kidnap *Francis II*. Condé had not participated in the plot but would have been executed anyway had not the young king suddenly died. Instead, *Catherine de Medici* moved quickly against the Guise, declared herself regent for her minor son, Charles IX, and freed Condé in an effort to heal the confessional rift within France. But the Guise rejected Catherine's call for religious toleration set out in the *Edict of Saint-Germain* (1562) and instead attacked Huguenot worshipers at *Vassy*. A Protestant synod formed in the wake of Vassy called upon Condé to raise and head an army of protection for the Huguenots. Along with *Coligny*, Condé led the Huguenot army during the first three Civil Wars that marked out the early struggle of French Protestants for royal recognition. He was felled at *Jarnac* (March 13, 1569) while leading a charge into a superior Catholic force. As he lay prisoner on the ground, having broken his leg in the charge, a Royalist officer murdered him with a pistol shot. See also *Saint-Denis, Battle of*.

Condé, Louis II, de Bourbon (1621–1686). "Great Condé," duc d'Enghien. At age 22 he won a spectacular victory at *Rocroi* (May 19, 1643). He won again at *Freiburg* (August 5, 1644), and at *Lens* (August 29, 1648). His major military successes and failures came after this period, in behalf of Louis XIV.

condottieri. "Contract captains." From the Italian "condotte" or military contracts. Condottieri refers to great mercenary captains who hired highly trained mercenaries and formed them into large companies ("masnada" or "conestabularia"), in whose behalf the captains negotiated terms. But it is also used about the companies and men they hired and led. The condottieri were cavalry-heavy units which dominated warfare in Italy before the *Italian Renaissance*. The prominence of the condottieri was made possible (and necessary) by the expansion of the money economy and endless warfare among the city-states of Italy. Initially, they were hired for just a few weeks or months—for a summer's campaigning. They were generally asked to provide their own armor and weapons, though crossbow bolts were supplied by the cities that hired them. Like the *Free Companies* of France, to which some condottieri owed their origin, seasonal warfare left them unpaid and unemployed over the winter months, with predictable results of unauthorized marauding, rape, and pillage. At their height, they held entire cities to ransom and stole vast amounts of wealth. Many of their men were Germans, including as many as 10,000 men-at-arms drawn to Italy for its riches, climate, and chronic but relatively bloodless warfare. Hungarians, English, French, Iberians, and many Italians also joined.

Various "Great Companies" were formed, usually named for their commanders. A German Free Company formed in 1334, called "Knights of the Dove," rampaged over central Italy for years. In 1339 another German outfit, the "Company of St. George," fought in the wars of Lodrizio Visconti. In 1342 a Great Company was assembled by Werner von Urslingen, one of some 700 German cavalry leaders identified by historians. His personal motto, engraved on his breastplate, captured the ferocity of all early condottieri: "Enemy of God, Enemy of Piety, Enemy of Pity." When the *Treaty of Brétigny* (1360) paused fighting in France, mixed Free Companies of unemployed French and English infantry drifted into Italy. The most powerful company of this type was the "*White Company*," initially commanded by *John Hawkwood*. Despite overseeing a massacre of 5,000 Italian innocents, he finished his days in peaceful opulence thanks to a Florentine salary and ill-gotten titles and estates from the condottieri wars. Other famous condottieri captains were Montreal d'Albarno ("Fra Moriale," an ex-*Hospitaller* executed in Rome in 1354); *Francesco Carmagnola* (beheaded by Venice in 1432); Prospero Colonna; Conrad von Landau (partner of Fra Moriale); Michele ("Micheletto") degli Attendoli, who was prominent from 1425 to 1429 in the service of nearly all the Italian states; his cousin Francesco; Paolo Vitelli; and Giovanni Gonzaga (1466–1519), whose condottieri army was devastated by the French at *Fornovo* (July 6, 1495), marking the beginning of the end of the condottieri way of war. Those captains who were not executed for disloyalty often acquired large fiefs, titles, and fabulous wealth. In the late 15th century the pattern of military migration reversed as condottieri fought for pay outside Italy, notably for *Charles the Rash*.

The primary interest of the condottieri was to survive to eat, drink, whore, and collect payment another day. They fought almost as artisans, with a minimum of violence. As a result, battles among condottieri armies were few and far between, and those few that were fought were often desultory affairs wherein hired men on both sides of the field of battle shied away from taking risks or life, and refused to expose themselves to mortal dangers. Instead, they applied their skills (which were real enough) to unhorse or slightly wound some ransomable opponent. The most prized command skill was the art of maneuver, which was engaged in by officers as often, or more often, to avoid a potential battlefield as to secure a superior position on it. Taking prisoners for ransom was almost always the first objective. *Machiavelli* reported on several condottieri "battles" in which as few as a handful of skilled men-at-arms were killed, but tens or hundreds of prisoners surrendered themselves. These either joined the company of their captors or were ransomed back to the city-state so unfortunate as to have hired them in the first place. Charles Oman, writing in 1921, summed up condottieri warfare as "a mere tactical exercise or a game of chess, the aim being to manoeuvre the enemy into an impossible situation, and then capture him, rather than to exhaust him by a series of costly battles. It was even suspected that condottieri, like dishonest pugilists, sometimes settled beforehand that they would draw the game. Battles when they did occur were often very bloodless affairs."

As the Italian city-states gained greater control over condottieri the latter's fortunes declined, and inconstant captains and soldiers were more often executed or banished. This was mainly a result of the Italian city-states developing sizeable town militia that freed them from condottieri extortion: captains died off or entered long-term salaried service as "Captain-General" of one of the city-states; their leaderless soldiers of fortune were then absorbed into emerging *standing armies*. Machiavelli held the condottieri in unique contempt, devoting a lengthy part of his thinking, writing, and organizational energy to training citizen militia to replace them. He hoped his militia would shoo untrustworthy and militarily useless professionals from the field. He even thought that Florence, and perhaps Italy as a whole, might rid itself of feckless and troublesome mercenaries if it inculcated civic and martial virtue in its young men, and trained and armed them in permanent and motivated republican militia on the model of the ancient Roman Republic. In this he was out of tune with his time, though perhaps also ahead of it by about 200 years. It should also be recalled that for all the savagery that characterized condottieri warfare and the mayhem caused, the mercenary wars in Italy were almost civilized compared to the horrors witnessed in Germany and France during the religious wars of the 16th and 17th centuries. See also *Agnadello, Battle of*; *Catalan Great Company*; *Fornovo, Battle of*; *Lodi, Peace of*.

Suggested Reading: M. E. Mallett, *Mercenaries and Their Masters* (1974); G. Trease, *The Condottieri, Soldiers of Fortune* (1970).

conestabularia. A company of *condottieri.*

Confederate Army. The forces that gathered to defend the view of Irish nationhood set out in the *Confederation of Kilkenny*. At its core were thousands of Irish veterans returned from the *Army of Flanders*, joined later by more veterans of tough Spanish or French armies. These organized and officered poorer clan militia raised by the Gaelic lords of the Irish countryside, with the addition of a few *redshanks* from Scotland. The Confederates led the Irish rebellion of 1641–1653 that in turned triggered civil war in England in 1642 and blended with the Scottish civil war to form the "War of the Three Kingdoms," a fight rich in religious and ethnic hatreds and ferocity. The Confederate Army armed itself with guns taken from town armories and cannon lifted from shipwrecks or enemy prizes. They received munitions, money, and still more guns and cannon via Irish ports, shipped in by foreign Catholic powers. The Confederate Army was divided into four commands that corresponded to each of the Irish provinces: Ulster, Leinster, Munster, and Connaught. The Confederates also put to sea an impressive *privateer* navy of a dozen or so "Dunkirk frigates" and over 30 foreign warships. See also *English Civil Wars*; *O'Neill, Owen Roe.*

Confederation of Kilkenny (May 10, 1641). A document laying out the principles of the Catholic leaders of the Irish rebellion. Unlike the *National Covenant* of the Scots, it rejected rebellion against *Charles I*. Royalist on the surface, it was cognizant of divisions among *Old English*, *Old Irish*, and *New English*, all of whom were seen as "Irish." It thus was a patriotic document that defined the kingdom in Ireland along legal and confessional (Catholic), rather than ethnic lines. It did not, however, necessarily speak for the Gaelic peasantry, who resorted to more spontaneous and less abstractly motivated violence against their hated English or Scots landlords, especially in Ulster.

Confessio Augustana **(1530).** See *Augsburg Confession*.

confessionalism. Generally, the distinct religious convictions of discrete communities organized around some confession of faith or theological system. More narrowly, in German historiography confessionalism ("Konfessionalisierung") is identified as a process of more pervasive influence of strict religious belief in all walks of life in the latter 16th and early 17th centuries, a hardening of dogma and sharper separation among well-defined communities of faith, and a greater role of secular power in enforcing uniformity of belief. During the *Protestant Reformation* in Germany confessionalism took the form of Lutheran princes (the "temporal sword") forming close alliances with "godly" (reform) preachers. These preachers warned the faithful to submit to the prince's authority in return for princes defending reform preachers and flocks against Catholic efforts to advance the *Counter-Reformation*, as well as encroachment by more radical Calvinists. This idea appealed to territorial princes more than to anointed kings because it did not recognize the sacral nature claimed by early modern kings, and indeed threatened efforts by powerful monarchs to impose religious peace (meaning, uniformity) within their kingdoms. Calvinist princes did likewise, but there were fewer of them and the strongest were outside Germany. Catholic territorial princes also formed secular-clerical alliances, though they did so more uneasily than Calvinists or Lutherans since the Empire and Church were so much more powerful than they.

Despite strenuous efforts by priests and preachers, the majority of English, Dutch, French, Germans, and other Europeans as late as 1600 were not clearly Catholic or Protestant but only vaguely "Christian." This was especially true outside the large towns where the rural population stayed wedded to peasant folklore and superstitions, for which they were ferociously condemned by "men of God" (soi-dissant) on all sides. The intensity of confessionalization programs in the late 16th century had much to do with the fact that most people did not yet reside in the Castra Dei ("God's Camp") of any of the major sects. And it should be recalled that neither Catholicism nor the variants of Protestantism were voluntary or "democratic" faiths then as they are today: most adherents were forced into confessional identification and compliance by coercive institutions of church and state, and by social and moral pressure from fanatic adherents. Why did this matter? Because it was the political danger posed by the chance that some other faith might convert the weak-willed or un-committed first that elevated fears and led to interconfessional violence and atrocity. By the mid-17th century, however, confessional communities had solidified so that few further gains could be made by any of the major re-

> *And it should be recalled that neither Catholicism nor the variants of Protestantism were voluntary ...*

ligious camps. It is not a coincidence that around the same time the fires of the "wars of religion" burned out, leaving only the odd smoldering ember here or there to warm bitter memories of past wrongs. See also *Anabaptism*; *Antichrist*; *Augsburg, Peace of*; *Calvinism*; *Catholic Church*; *Catholic League (France)*; *Catholic League (Germany)*; *Charles I, of England*; *Confederation of Kilkenny*; *Corpus Catholicorum*; *Corpus Evangelicorum*; *corpus mysticum*; *Cossacks*; *Council of Trent*; *Edict of Nantes*; *Eighty Years' War*; *English Civil Wars*; *Estates*; *Ferdinand II, Holy Roman Emperor*; *Formula of Concord*; *French Civil Wars*; *Henri III, of France*; *Holy Roman Empire*; *Huguenots*; *Imperial Diet*; *Jülich-Kleve, Crisis over*; *Leipziger Bund*; *Luther, Martin*; *Malcontents* (1); *Maximilian II*; *Missio Hollandica*; *politiques (France)*; *politiques (Netherlands)*; *printing*; *Protestant Union*; *reservatum ecclesiaticum*; *Richelieu, Armand Jean du Plessis de*; *Rudolf II*; *sacre* (2); *Thirty Years' War*; *War of Cologne*; *Westphalia, Peace of*; *Zsitva Torok, Treaty of*.

confraternities. Originally, French Catholic devotional societies which grew up in the towns as defense associations first in 1562, again in 1568, and most importantly after the *Edict of Beaulieu* in 1576. They represented popular frustration with the failure of the Crown to extirpate "heretic" Protestantism from French soil, so that a holy mission of Catholic piety to purify and cleanse the body social and the body politic alike could be fulfilled. The confraternities took on something of the fanatic spirit and habits of mind of earlier crusades as piety and religious zeal led to murder and massacre. They were run out of towns in the south where the Huguenots were strong, but elsewhere they proved a real bulwark against the spread of Protestantism and a vehicle of violent religious "cleansing" of the population. They also served as a conduit of men and arms to Catholic armies fighting against the Huguenots in the protracted *French Civil Wars* (1562–1629).

confratres. See *confrère knights*.

confrère **knights.** An honorary "knight brother" of one of the *Military Orders*. They served only for short periods, donating half their property for the opportunity. Unlike full brethren, they were permitted to marry. The *Hospitallers* and the *Templars*, among other Orders, allowed confrères.

Confucianism. A philosophical system founded by Confucius (Kongfuzi, or K'ung Fu-tse; 551–479 B.C.E.), and amended by his major disciple Mencius (372–289 B.C.E.). It was crucially important in shaping the histories of China, Japan, Korea, and Vietnam. Some scholars view Confucianism as an ethical system existing in the absence of formal religion since, in spite of historical association with religious rites in various countries and eras, classical Confucianism did not insist upon piety or adoration of a deity or produce a priesthood per se. Others see it as a broad, but essentially still religious worldview. Its main texts are comprised of Confucius' known writings and compendiums of his teachings arranged by disciples into two compilations. First is the "Four Books," or *Analects* of Confucius (dialogues with rulers and students) and the *Mencius*; along with parts of the *Book of Rites* or *Great Learning* (which most think was written by Confucius), and the *Doctrine of the Mean*. The second set is the "Five Classics," or *Book of Changes* ("I-ching"), *Book of Documents*, *Book of Songs*, *Book of Rites*, and a collection of antiquarian writings usually ascribed to the Shang and Zhou periods. These nine works were the core curriculum of the famous Chinese examination system. For 2,500 years Chinese civilization to a remarkable degree aspired to implement the ethical constructs of Confucius. During the Song dynasty renaissance, official "neo-Confucian" ideas added a sternly hierarchical thrust through an emphasis on virtue rooted in contributing to harmonious family, social, and political relations, or the "Three Bonds" of minister to prince, children to parents, and wives to husbands. Confucian family and political ideas were thus broadly similar and mutually reinforcing, amounting to a call for familial and social unity under a single authority.

Classical Confucians believed in moral perfectibility through education, a tradition which marked Chinese culture and government for two millennia. From 136 B.C.E. to 1911 C.E., China's imperial system upheld blended versions of "Imperial Confucianism" ("Legalism," or "Neo-Confucianism") as a state philosophy, and most dynasties based crucial scholar-elite (roughly, civil service) exams on its main texts. However, Confucian scholars tended to denigrate the callings of merchants and warriors, while state Confucianism repeatedly ossified into rigid conservatism. In the view of some scholars, this tendency held China outside the scientific and mercantile progress made in the West after 1500. Some Chinese blamed the whole tradition for the fall of the Ming dynasty. In contrast, a school of Confucian scholars returned to a purified canon, convinced that corruption of classic texts, rather than obedience to them, caused China's relative decline and martial weakness. They carried out close textual analysis of records dating to the Han dynasty, exposing numerous forgeries in the canon. Some looked to later periods, elevating the Song at the expense of the Ming. And a few smuggled Western and more recent Chinese ideas into gaps in the classical canon opened by the criticisms of the "New Text Movement." See also *bushidō*; *mandate of heaven*; *tribute*.

Suggested Reading: William T. de Bary, *The Trouble with Confucianism* (1991); Irene Eber, *Confucianism* (1986).

Congo. See *Kongo*.

Congregatio de Propaganda Fidei. "Congregation for the Propagation of the Faith." A Catholic committee established by Pope Gregory XV (1554–1623) to supervise foreign missions and proselytize among native populations, and most of all, to recatholicize those parts of the Empire overrun by *Ferdinand II* and his allies. It was centrally involved in the success of the *Counter-Reformation* in Germany, despite its main colleges being located in Italy.

Conitz. See *Chojnice, Battle of*.

conquistadores. Principally, a term used for the Spanish adventurer-soldiers who conquered the Americas. Secondarily, it is used about similar Portuguese slavers and raiders who operated in the African interior from coastal bases. These were truly ruthless warriors, literally soldiers of fortune who disdained literacy, manual labor and commerce, in favor of moving in mercenary companies—like flocks of raptors—whose members shared in the spoils of war and conquest. In their lifestyle they resembled the many nomad warrior tribes which invaded Western Europe after the 5th century. Their methods were learned, and their hearts steeled to cruelty, in generations of *"holy war"* against Muslim states during the Iberian *Reconquista*. In the New World, they first conquered the Caribbean islands. From there, *Hernán Cortés* led an expedition to conquer the *Aztec Empire* in the Central Valley of Mexico (1519–1521). Inspired by the vast wealth Cortés and his men obtained, *Pizarro* led an even smaller group of conquistadores on a remarkably similar conquest of the even larger *Inca Empire*. From these two fallen centers of Mesoamerican power and wealth smaller conquistadore expeditions fanned out in all directions to overrun southern Mexico and Central America in the 1520s and 1530s, though they did not complete the conquest of the inland peoples of northern Mexico until c.1600. From Cuzco in Peru, in the 1530s and 1540s conquistadores moved north into Panama, south to the Río de la Plata, and thence north again into what is today Paraguay. Other expeditions penetrated the Amazon Basin, with equal ruthlessness and torment of the local Indians but far less luck in finding the mythical city of gold ("El Dorado") or escaping with their lives. There was little honor among these cutthroats, thieves, and amphibious pirates. Within a generation of the conquest of the New World, with no sizeable empires or even concentrations of Indians left to conquer, many of the conquistadores in Peru rebelled violently against Spain's attempt to assert imperial authority over their claimed lands. Other conquistadores made war on each other. A wise few, foremost among them Cortés, returned to Iberia engorged with gold and silver to buy landed estates and noble titles. See also *Alvarado, Pedro de*; *encomienda*; *Otumba, Battle of*; *Peru*; *requerimiento*; *Tenochtitlán, First Siege of*; *Tenochtitlán, Second Siege of*.

Suggested Reading: Michael Wood, *Conquistadors* (2001).

conrois. A squadron of medieval European cavalry numbering anywhere from a handful of *knights* to several hundred. It practiced tactics of feint, false retreat and flank attack as well as the heavy charge. See also *tournaments*.

conscription. See *English armies*; *English Civil Wars*; *French Army*; *fryd*; *Ottoman Army*; *Polish Army*; *recruitment*; *sekban*; *Spanish Army*; *Swedish Army*; *Swiss Army*.

consorterie. The aristocratic clans of the Italian communes and city-states. They were tasked with raising cavalry for civic armies. They were largely displaced by the *condottieri*.

Conspiracy of Amboise. See *Amboise, Conspiracy of*.

constable. In late Medieval England a constable was a junior military "officer" assigned to lead a unit of about 100 foot soldiers raised by quota from country villages. He might sometimes serve, with his men, as a constable of marines under a ship's *master*. See also *English armies*.

Constable of France. The highest military office in France, above even maréshal, and carrying political as well as military responsibilities as commander-in-chief in the absence of the king. See also *Montmorency, Anne, duc de*.

constabulary. In the European Middle Ages, a battle group of at least 10 *knights* gathered under the *banner* of a great magnate (a duke or baron).

Constance, Council of (1414–1418). A general council of the Catholic Church held at the close of the *Great Schism*, to which it helped put an end.

Constance reaffirmed earlier condemnations of the teachings of *John Wycliffe* and ordered the trial for "heresy" of *Jan Hus*, arrested and burned at the stake in violation of an Imperial safe conduct. This betrayal provoked confessional violence in Bohemia and launched the *Hussite Wars*. See also *Ecumenical Councils*.

Constantinople, Sack of (1204). See *Byzantine Empire*; *Crusades*; *Orthodox Churches*; *Venice*.

Constantinople, Siege of (April 5–May 29, 1453). From its founding in 660 B.C.E., the ancient Greek city Byzantium commanded the strategic Dardanelles. In the early 4th century C.E. it was officially renamed "Constantinoupolis Nea Roma" or "Constantinople the New Rome" by Constantine the Great (274–337 C.E.). More simply, it was called "Constantinople" ("City of Constantine"), or by the Greeks, just "The City." It was the most famous and important city in the Western Hemisphere, and occupied the most strategic ground: it guarded the Bosphorus, the straits that linked the Mediterranean with the Black Sea and divided Europe from Asia. Slavs called it "Tsarigrad" ("City of the Emperors"), and many converted to the *Orthodox* faith it championed and defended. The Christians of Armenia knew it as "Gosdant-nubolis." Even the distant Norse heard of it: they called it "Mikligaard" ("The Big City"). After the sacks of Rome (410 and 455 C.E.) and the end of the Western Empire (476 C.E.), Constantinople remained for a thousand years capital of the *Byzantine Empire* (except for an interlude of Latin occupation and Nicaean exile for the emperors following the Fourth *Crusade*). For all that time it was the epicenter of politics, religion, and culture for the whole Hellenistic and Orthodox world. By the mid-15th century, however, the Byzantine Empire was reduced to an enclave, stripped of Balkan provinces by rebellion or conquest and encircled by the burgeoning Ottoman Empire. As the Ottomans gathered for the final battle following their defeat of the Hungarians at *Kosovo Polje* (1448), the Byzantines once more called on fellow Christians in the West for military aid. But the spirit of the Latin Crusades was nearly spent: few replied, and fewer still came. It was principally for geopolitical rather than religious reasons that Genoa, Venice, and the Papal States sent minor aid: detachments of 200, 400, and 700 men to a city forlorn of hope that all knew must soon fall.

In April 1452, *Muhammad II* tasked 1,000 masons to construct a stone artillery fort on the Bosphorus across the Straits from the city as a prelude to his planned crossing and siege of Constantinople the next year. This fort was called "Cutter of Throats" ("Boghaz-kesen"), but later renamed "Rumeli Hisar." It was complemented by an older fort built by *Bayezid I* some six miles south of Constantinople, "Anadolu Hisar." These artillery positions gave the Sultan command of the Bosphorus and platforms from which to pound Constantinople into submission with his great *bombards*. What faced Muhammad was a metropolis that withstood nearly two dozen sieges before him, and which never fell to assault—its capture by Latin knights in 1204 was achieved by treachery from within. The city was protected by three great, concentric walls on its landward side. The outermost wall had eight gates, each flanked by guard towers, and continued along the south shore of the "Golden Horn," the main harbor with its great iron boom to block enemy galleys. The second wall, the "Wall of Constantine," was half the size of the outer perimeter. The innermost or "Byzantine" wall formed a sea wall where it abutted the Straits. More importantly, it enclosed the central hub of the city and the Hagia Sophia, the "Church of the Holy Wisdom" built by Emperor Justinian from 532–537 C.E. and host of the Patriarchate for over 1,000 years. All told, there were four miles of land walls and nine miles of sea walls, paralleled by a deep ditch. The defenses also boasted 100 watch and guard towers. However, to defend these long walls Emperor Constantine XI Paleologus (r.1449–1453) had only 6,000 soldiers, supplemented by 3,000 foreigners from various Italian city-states or just mercenaries. Another 700 Genoese arrived in January. Their leader, a tough captain called Giovanni Giustiniani, was given command of the city's defenses.

Starting early in the new year the Sultan amassed 120,000–150,000 men across from the city. At the core of his army were thousands of elite *Janissaries* and tens of thousands of *Bashi-Bazouks*, irregular tribal mercenaries of ferocious reputation. Muhammad began with fire from his cannons and culverins immediately, while still positioning the bombards. These had to be dragged overland on a purpose-built road. The greatest, "Elipolos" or "City-Taker," could hurl a 600-pound stone ball three-quarters of a mile, with devastating impact and reasonable accuracy. The Sultan protected his big guns with an earth palisade built with dirt removed from a protective ditch he ordered prepared in front of his lines. His men were all in place by April 5. A fleet of 200 galleys arrived on April 12, with supplies and more assault troops. A minor breach was made in the outer wall and a probing assault was launched on April 18, but it was easily repulsed. Two days later four Genoese *galleasses* broke into the harbor. They raced across at flank speed to escape fire from Ottoman shore batteries while repelling boarders from Ottoman galleys by firing down from high *castles* into the lower Muslim warships. Muhammad reacted to this seaborne relief with real imagination: he had 30 galleys rolled overland on logs to bypass a secondary sea wall on the north shore of the harbor, at Galata. The ships moved along another purpose-built special road constructed by his superb corp of military engineers. Thus, the Ottoman ships slipped past the great chain by land and quickly took strategic control of the Golden Horn.

With Ottoman galleys inside the main harbor all hope of relief failed. The next three weeks inside the city were grim as multiple saps were dug toward the walls, covered by a continuous bombardment. On May 6 a second breach of the outer wall was made near the Fifth Gate, the "Military Gate of St. Romanus." Muhammad's early morning attack was stopped only because the defenders built a secondary wall behind the breach during the night, then held it with fierce resolve, pikes, and muskets. Ottoman siege towers were burned and blocked as troops pulled them toward the wall, and further sapping and mining was defeated by brilliantly effective Byzantine countermining. All the while, the outer walls were pounded by the distant bombards and by cannon and culverins, while powerful mortars hurled ordnance and incendiaries into the city to smash and burn buildings and demoralize civilians. Muhammad's artillery hammered at the defenses for 55 days, the first mass bombardment of a major city in military history. More breaches were made on May 28, and several all-out assaults were made by Bashi-Bazouks and Janissaries, starting just after midnight of the following day. But these attacks did not take the city. It fell by accident, or perhaps from treachery: a small gate was left open through which Muslim troops rushed, seized a guard tower, and struck into the flank of the last defenders at the gate. Emperor Constantine fell with his men, defending his broken city to the last.

Emperor Constantine fell with his men, defending his broken city to the last.

There followed a bloodbath that lasted several days and took the lives of nearly all the defenders and tens of thousands among the civilian population. Most were slaughtered in their homes and shops or in the streets. Churches and nunneries offered no protection. Those who did not die were taken away to be sold as slaves. Muhammad ordered an end to the killing, but not even he could easily damp down the bloodlust of an army fresh inside after two months of hard siege. When the massacre was over Muhammad had the blood washed from the floors of Hagia Sophia, pulled down its icons, and converted the church into one of the main mosques of the Islamic world. Then he took up residence in what became the Ottoman capital, strategically situated at the center of an expanding empire and symbolically located between the original Asian capital of his ancestors at Brusa and their first European capital at Adrianople. From Constantinople, Muhammad and his descendants gazed west and north toward future conquests in Europe, east toward their core Anatolian possessions and beyond to *shi'ia* foes in Iran, and south across the eastern Mediterranean, now an Ottoman lake, to their empire in Africa.

The fall and sack of Constantinople sent cultural, political, and military shock waves around the Christian and Islamic worlds. For Muslims the city was a prize sought for centuries and its capture confirmed that Islam was still advancing as Allah willed. For the Orthodox nothing could salve the tragedy. For Latin Christians the realization suddenly struck that a new and powerful enemy was moving in the east. Ottomans, too, understood that a new Great Power had arrived on the world stage, one animated by military success and freshly confident of its religious and imperial mission. Commercially, the fall of Constantinople blocked Italian city-states and merchants from their traditional markets in the eastern Mediterranean, and beyond to China. That gave them and Iberian and other competitors a huge incentive to find alternate routes to the sources of the *spice trade* in India and Cathay, sending the

Portuguese ever further around the edges of Africa and a Genoese captain across the Atlantic in 1492. Finally, to all military men the city's fall seemed to announce like a clarion that the best medieval defenses could not stand against the new gunpowder artillery. The Middle Ages were over.

Suggested Reading: Michael Antonucci, "Siege Without Reprieve," *Military History* 9/1 (April 1992); J.F.C. Fuller, *Military History of the Western World*, Vol. I (1954; 1955); Edward Gibbon, "End of the Roman Empire," in *Decline and Fall of the Roman Empire* (1783); Steven Runciman, *The Fall of Constantinople* (1903; 1968).

continuous bullet gun. A remarkable Chinese invention of a multi-shot gun. It used paper cartridges that were pre-loaded in sequence with lighted fuses, while bullets dropped into place from an attached holder before each charge exploded. It was, in effect, a primitive machine gun.

contravallation. See *lines of contravallation*.

contributions. With the dramatic expansion in the size of 17th-century armies and navies, and their establishment on a more permanent basis, the problem of military finance overwhelmed the primitive bureaucratic structures and tax systems of early modern states. A notable exception was the Netherlands, whose advanced economy enabled the Dutch to actually pay their troops on time and in full. This gave them a huge advantage in the long run over the Spanish, whose troops in Flanders were usually owed many months' back pay and who mutinied dozens of times. To solve this problem the Habsburgs turned to the "contribution system" first imposed by *Ambrogio Spínola* on the Palatinate in 1620, which reached maturity under the mercenary entrepreneur *Albrecht von Wallenstein* a few years thereafter. The old system of supply was simply seizure or requisition of foodstuffs and fodder by troops from towns and villages along the line of march, or surrounding a garrison, in exchange for promissory notes on the Habsburg treasury that most often went unpaid. This encouraged peasants and sutlers to hide grain and goods rather than supply the army, and eroded support for the Habsburg war effort in Catholic provinces. Spínola and Wallenstein substituted a system of cash taxes ("contributions") paid directly into their *war chest*. Then the commanders distributed the cash as payment to mercenaries and to buy foodstuffs, fodder, and equipment. This ensured that professional soldiers were paid regularly and was acceptable to peasants and merchants because the money or tax taken flowed back into the local economy. Most importantly, contributions relieved soldiers of the need to forage widely in search of plunder in lieu of pay, or just to keep body and soul together.

Contributions were a ruthless but efficient method of extortion at pike and musket point, in which pay displaced plunder as the principal form of compensation for fighting men. It was also a much more effective system of supply, freeing armies to move more quickly and making commanders virtually self-sufficient—a crucial feature in an era dominated by mercenary generals on all sides. The system was eventually adopted by nearly all armies in the *Thirty Years' War*. Contributions, along with sales of confiscated Protestant estates and some revenue from the Habsburg hereditary lands, kept the Imperial Army in the field and damped down mutiny. However, it attached primary loyalty to the army's commander, especially Wallenstein. This became clear when he was dismissed for the first time in 1630. His refusal to provide collected contributions to his successor, *Johann Tilly*, paralyzed the Imperial Army. The fact that Imperial troops were primarily loyal to their paymaster and commander was a major concern to *Ferdinand II* and other Catholic princes. Ultimately, it posed such a threat to the Emperor he secretly dismissed Wallenstein a second time in 1634, then sent assassins to kill him. From 1635 Imperial garrisons were no longer principally supported by forced contributions. Instead, taxes were agreed to by the princes and *Estates* under terms of the *Peace of Prague*, extended to the end of the war by the *Imperial Diet* in 1641. In effect for decades, the practice of collecting cash contribution, and the war taxes that replaced this system within the Empire, permanently raised levels of taxation. After 1648 high taxes dating to the war were kept in place by princes and monarchs all over Europe to support their new *standing armies*. See also *bedel-i nüzul*; *Engagements*; *free quarter*; *logistics*; *mutiny*; *Propositions*.

conversos. After the pogroms of 1391 in Iberia, Jews converted to Christianity, either sincerely or to protect themselves from persecution at the hands of Christians, were called "conversos." See also *expulsion of the Jews*; *galley slaves*; *Inquisition*; *moriscos*; *war finance*.

convoy. For centuries, Venetian merchants traveled the Mediterranean in convoy as protection against pirates and predatory rivals. Corporate bodies of merchants, such as the "Bayonne Shipowner's Society," also organized convoys for mutual protection. English kings arranged convoys of merchants to Gascony from the 12th century (Henry II). In the 13th century they extended this system to traders plying the Irish Sea and to ships headed for Calais. Warship escorts were added in the 14th century, a late date reflecting the paucity and impermanence of English naval power prior to the late 15th century. The most famous convoys of the period were the great treasure fleets that sailed from the New World to Spain. In 1562 the city of Seville, confirmed by royal decree issued by *Philip II* two years later, forced merchants sailing to the Spanish Main into two convoys—the "flota" and "galeones," each of which sailed annually from Seville. The flota sailed in April for Veracruz, New Spain, while the galeones sailed in August for Panama. After wintering and taking on cargos of treasure and other New World goods, all ships rendezvoused in Havana in order to return as a single fleet numbering some 80–100 vessels. From 1568 the treasure fleets were escorted by a squadron of warships; by 1584, this squadron comprised eight large ships and six *galleons*. Other Spanish warships patrolled the Atlantic and Caribbean coasts, but not in convoy. The annual treasure fleet made port in Spain every autumn, at Seville until 1717.

The convoy system mostly worked: from 1588 to 1603, when Spain's shipping was hunted by English, Dutch, and French privateers, more gold and silver reached the Spanish treasury than in any other period of comparable length. During the *Eighty Years' War* the Dutch captured the treasure fleet just once, and not for want of trying: Piet Hein of the Dutch West Indies Company pounced on it off the Cuban coast in September 1628. The loss of the treasure fleet led immediately to a major fiscal crisis for Spain, where American silver was crucial to sustain Spain's already debased currency; to pay its mercenary troops fighting in Germany, Italy, and the Netherlands; and to pay off *Fugger* and Genoese loans and notes. Spanish convoys were harder to organize in the Indian Ocean and across the vast Pacific, and hence more rare. This was due to the far greater distances involved and a lack of ships and men on either side of the fight, hunted and hunter.

An additional purpose of the treasure fleets was less obvious: to concentrate royal control over trade and the importation of monetary metals. In this, the convoy system was less successful than in fending off privateers: there was much conniving at smuggling silver when loading and unloading the treasure fleet, and more smuggling by single ships slipping into some port other than Seville—in all, perhaps as much as one-quarter of all the silver entering Europe was smuggled. Alternately, silver smugglers might take the long, dangerous Pacific route to Manila, and thence to the markets of China where goods were bought with illegal or stolen silver to be sold in Europe the next year—a sort of 16th-century international money-laundering scheme. Also, not all merchants sought the protection of the king's ships since the king took a share of all cargoes as tax for his troubles. Many preferred to take their chances alone on the high seas in armed merchantmen that fought even as they ran from English or Dutch pirates or privateers. The fact was that profit margins were so high if a ship made it back to Europe with a New World or Chinese or Indian cargo, that it was cost-effective to chance losing the ship and all its cargo by running the gauntlet of pirates, privateers, enemy commerce raiders, and the occasional formal but ineffective naval blockade.

In contrast to Spain, most English and Dutch merchant ships plying the Atlantic trade in the 16th century were private. But they still used convoys: only a few captains risked pirates and privateers by sailing alone to the sugar isles of the West Indies, though some did it for the same profit motive that moved Spanish sailors to cross the wild and storm-tossed Pacific (a most ill-named ocean). Most English captains preferred to sail together, to afford mutual protection from bad weather and accident as much as from enemy action. Ships headed for the rich fisheries off Newfoundland (nearly 200 per year) or Cape Cod, or plying the Chesapeake trade, most often traveled together but without the protection of the king's (or queen's) warships. Later in the 17th century English merchants formed armed convoys of up to 100 ships to the Caribbean. These sailed at regular times of the year to avoid winter weather and to arrive in time to collect highly perishable tropical crops. They were seldom molested. See also *Flanders*; *Gibraltar*.

Suggested Reading: Timothy Walton, *The Spanish Treasure Fleets* (1994).

Coptic Church. The Christian church and community in Egypt dating to the 3rd century C.E. It maintained links to Christians in Ethiopia for over 1,000 years. After conversion of most Egyptians to Islam in the 8th century, Egyptian Copts clung to a minority but tolerated position. Their distinctive rite was old Monophysite, dating to association with the Orthodox patriarchate in Constantinople. The Copts were first distanced from Christian traditions in the Latin West and the Orthodox world by the decision taken against the extreme Monophysite view of the nature of "The Christ" (a singular divine nature, not divided by a subordinate human nature). That position

> *Their distinctive rite was old Monophysite, dating to association with the Orthodox patriarchate . . .*

was condemned by the *Ecumenical Council* of Chalcedon in 451, which left the Copts in schism. Copts were additionally distanced by their discrete and distinct hierarchy. The Coptic Church in Egypt upheld a paternal relationship with the Coptic Church in Ethiopia, to which it sent bishops and other high clerics into the late 20th century.

Çorbasi. "Soup maker." An officer in the *Janissary Corps* in command of an *Orta* (company) of 100 men and roughly comparable to *colonel*. The title derived from his original role as the man who fed the sultan's slave soldiers. He was assisted by other officers with titles similarly derived from kitchen functions, which in later years bore no relation whatever to their military roles: the "master cook," "cook," "head scullion," and "scullion." This culinary motif of the Janissaries was best represented by the *Kazan*—the prized cooking pot that was the center of Janissary camp life and part of every battle order.

Córdoba, Battle of (1236). See *Reconquista*.

Córdoba, Caliphate of. See *caliph*; *itqa*; *Reconquista*.

Córdoba, Gonzalo di (1453–1515). "el Gran Capitan." Castilian general who reformed the *tercios*, reducing reliance on polearms and bringing more guns to reinforced pike formations that could operate independently because of their increased firepower. He fought in Castile's civil war that attended the ascension of Isabel to the throne. Next, he fought in the long war to conquer *Granada*, and again against Portugal. He was sent to Naples from 1495 to 1498 to stop the French conquest. He lost to Swiss mercenary infantry at *Seminara*, but adjusted his strategy and slowly pushed the French out of southern Italy. He used the same tactics in Italy that worked in Granada: progressive erosion of the enemy's hold over outposts and the countryside, blockading garrisons, and avoiding pitched battles where he could. He fought the Swiss again, and won, at *Cerignola* (1503), handing them their first battle loss in 200 years. He beat them again that year at their encampment on the *Garigliano River*. Between fighting the French and Swiss he fought rebellious Moriscos in Granada and against the Ottomans in behalf of Spain and in alliance with Venice. He retired in 1506, well-regarded as a great general of pike and arquebus warfare.

corned gunpowder. See *corning/corned gunpowder*.

cornet (1). A junior officer in an English cavalry troop, charged with protection of the standard of the troop (also called a cornet).

cornet (2). A troop of cavalry.

cornette **(1).** A French cavalry standard or pennant.

cornette **(2).** The standard bearer ("le cornette").

corning/corned gunpowder. A process (and its product) for refining gunpowder developed in France c.1429. Mealing gunpowder ingredients—charcoal, saltpeter, and sulphur—in a dry container only led to later reseparation by weight of each component: saltpeter sank to the bottom since it was heavier than sulphur, which in turn outweighed charcoal. This separation happened through ordinary transport by horseback, backpack, or from rough jogging in an unsprung cart. An interim solution was to delay mixing until the gunpowder was actually needed, but this only posed different dangers. Moreover, mealed or "serpentine" black powder was too fine to combust efficiently. Coarser grains were needed to provide a lower surface-to-volume ratio to aid fast combustion. In corning the three ingredients were mixed with water or, more often with vinegar, wine, brandy, or urine from hard drinkers. The thick paste thus formed was forced through a perforated plate or animal hide to even the grains. Then it was shaped into cakes (in German, *Knollen*, in French, *petite mottes*) and dried under the sun or in a powder room. The Knollen were later milled and the resulting granules sorted by degree of coarseness. This method not only produced more sure and powerful combustion, it solved the problem of spoilage of black powder in storage.

Corning permitted standardized powder to be prepared, eventually leading to a triple division of corned powder grades. The finest grains were reserved as "musket-grade," while coarser sorts were used in cannon, mines, and for making fuses or *quick match*. This method solved the separation problem while making gunpowder quicker burning and more explosive, but also more expensive to manufacture. The additional power of the new powder provided a great incentive to also improve *casting* techniques as it was now much more likely that refined powder would explode older guns made with the *hoop-and-stave* method. Larger forges capable of bigger castings resulted and that meant a progressive move from *breech-loaders* to *muzzle-loaders* as single-cast guns were better able to contain the expanding gases and explosive force of corned powder. At the same time, corning stimulated development of hand guns, notably the long-barreled *arquebus*. By the middle of the 16th century corned powder had compelled a basic redesign of all guns from cannon to muskets and pistols, including the length of the barrel, the shape and diameter of the bore, the form of the breech, and the weight of the shot. The Japanese and Chinese acquired corned powder from Europe in the mid-16th century, the same time they first obtained European muskets. It appears that Indian gunpowder was not corned until very late. That was just as well since most Indian cannon were still hoop-and-stave and could not handle corned powder, which is of course precisely why intelligent Indian gunners did not use it. See also *Bureau brothers*.

Suggested Reading: Bert Hall, *Weapons and Warfare in Renaissance Europe* (1997).

coronal. A blunted spearpoint attached to a practice lance for use in a fight "à plaisance" (for pleasure or for fun) in a medieval *tournament*. It stopped the lance from punching through the opponent's armor and causing grave injury.

coronation wars. See *Aztec Empire*; *Moctezuma II*.

coronelia. See *colonel*; *Spanish Army*.

corporal. From the 16th century, a junior or noncommissioned officer who acted as assistant to a *lieutenant*. In the Spanish army, from which the English and most other armies copied the rank, the "capo de squadra" was the man in command of a company subunit, a *squadron* of 20–25 men. A variation on this was introduced by the Dutch in the great military reforms of the 1590s.

Corpus Catholicorum. The collective body of Catholic *Estates* of the Holy Roman Empire, numbering 72 members large and small, that gathered to negotiate the *Peace of Westphalia* from 1644 to 1648. At Westphalia it was agreed that future confessional disputes would be settled not by the *Imperial Diet* but by negotiations with its counterpart, the *Corpus Evangelicorum*, representing Protestant interests and including for the first time Calvinists as well as Lutherans. While most members supported the Emperor at Westphalia, two subgroups did not: an anti-Imperial faction that was prepared to use concessions to France and Protestant Germans to counterbalance the Habsburgs, and a militant Catholic faction ("Triumvirs") backed by Spain and—even after 120 years of stalemated religious wars in Europe—still opposed to religious toleration.

Corpus Christi. The Catholic feast of the "Body of Christ," a central ritual of the faith for the medieval and early modern Church. Princes and kings, even Emperor *Ferdinand II*, marched at the head of Corpus Christi processions. These had a quasi-martial character that exuded the spirit of the *Crusades* long after those military misadventures ended. *Francis I* used the 1535 feast to reinforce and advertise his persecution of Protestants in the wake of the *Affair of the Placards*. The *Inquisition* sometimes added *autos de fe* to the festivities. In 1640, Corpus Christi rites triggered riots that quickly became the *revolt of Catalonia*.

Corpus Evangelicorum. The collective body of Protestant *Estates* of the Holy Roman Empire, numbering 73 members, including for the first time both Lutherans and Calvinists, gathered from 1644 to 1648 to negotiate terms leading to the *Peace of Westphalia*. It was divided into a small state and more Calvinist faction that wanted total revocation of the *Edict of Restitution* and full toleration for all Protestants everywhere in the Empire, and larger principalities, mainly Lutheran, who wanted real peace more than some abstract argument on toleration. Eventually, the Corpus Evangelicorum proved more united than its counterpart, the *Corpus Catholicorum*, representing Catholic interests. At Westphalia, on March 14, 1648, it was agreed that all future confessional disputes within the Empire would be settled not by the Imperial Diet but by negotiations with the Corpus Catholicorum, and on the basis of a *Normaljahr* of 1624.

corpus mysticum. "Mystical body." The idea that royal sanctity (and sovereignty) resided not in the physical body of the monarch but in his or her "corpus mysticum." This competed directly with claims to unique personal holiness made by the clergy, a contest which played out in the great struggle between popes and Holy Roman Emperors and their surrogates among *Guelphs and Ghibellines*. From this claim to special sanctity the idea of the "Royal Touch" developed in France and England, by which monarchs claimed the power of miraculous healing of scrofula by laying on hands. The problem of mortality was resolved around 1500 with promotion of the idea of the monarch's "dignitas," which survived death of the sovereign's earthly body. In practice, European monarchs soon approached ancient Egyptian, Alexandrine, or Roman claims to semi-divinity, while maintaining the theological assertion that the king remained human even if he ruled "by the grace of God." This was especially true in France, where kings took the title *Rex christianissimus* and asserted a quasi-divine status. To maintain this elaborate fiction religious rituals continued even after the physical death of a sovereign. Thus, *Henri III*'s deceased body was "fed" twice daily for several weeks before its interment.

With the *Protestant Reformation* and Catholic *Counter-Reformation*, thinkers on both sides of the religious divide reexamined kingly claims to a sacred, incorporeal body. Although the full movement to secular political theory did not occur in this period, in one sense it began with a shift in theology that moved the corpus mysticum away from the king to reside instead in the people as a whole. Why? Because the long search to secure the "corpus mysticum" of the old Christian commonwealth, to build the ideal Christian polity, failed in country after country: in Spain, the Crusader spirit led to national calamity; in England, there was religious civil war and the grave moral disappointment of the Puritan republic; in France and Germany confessionalism ushered in decades of civil war and breathtaking atrocities by one body of Christian believers against another. By the mid-17th century many devout Catholics and Protestants believed with equal fervor that Babylon, not Jerusalem, was ascendent in affairs of the world. Given absolute sovereign power as conceived in Thomas Hobbes' *Leviathan*, which began to displace the old idea of the *res publica Christiana* formally and in fact from the *Peace of Westphalia* in 1648, such devouts seemed proven right just as the fires of the "wars of religion" finally burned out, leaving only embers of emnity glowing in the darker fringes of the continent.

corsair. "To chase." Arab and Berber merchant clans who governed Algiers. Contrary to popular belief, their war galleys were usually rowed by free Muslim soldiers, not by Christian slaves. The latter were used in corsair coastal transport and trading galleys. Slaves took up too many places that were needed for fighters to be used in a fighting ship. Corsairs, or *Barbary pirates*, engaged in trade, raids, and outright *piracy* in the Western Mediterranean for centuries. See also *Algiers*; *Barbarossa*; *dey*; *Tunis*.

Cortes. See *Estates*.

Cortés, Hernán (1485–1547). *Conquistador* and conqueror of the *Aztec Empire*. Born in Estramadura, Cortés studied at a fairly high level at Salamanca but, at age 19, he left for the Caribbean to try his hand as a plantation farmer in Hispaniola. He first fought in the New World with a conquistadore army that brutally occupied Cuba in 1511. There, he witnessed a mindless slaughter of Indians. A decade later he said he was determined to avoid repeating this error when he invaded Mexico. It was not moral sensibility that drove him to that conclusion: his preference was to instead exploit Indian labor within the *encomienda* system. He left Cuba on February 18, 1519, under orders from the governor of Cuba, Diego Velásquez, to conquer Mexico. He had just 11 ships carrying 550 men, 16 horses, some war dogs (mastiffs), and 10 brass cannon. They landed on the Tabasco coast where they allied with the Totonac people, a coastal tribe that was nominally a vassal of the Aztec. They supplied 20 young girls and women slaves to Cortés, who took "*La Malinche*" as his interpreter and mistress. Cortés moved up shore, then paused for four months to reconnoiter the Aztec position. Bypassing his superiors in Cuba, he sent a ship laden with gold and a secret letter written directly to *Charles V*, asking for the concession of the conquest of Mexico. Meanwhile, he mishandled two Aztec tax collectors, the first representatives of that empire he met. Puzzled, Emperor *Moctezuma* (Motechuzoma) II sent an embassy bearing gifts of gold, religious costumes, and food. Cortés thereafter received orders from Diego Velásquez, who had learned of his insubordinate correspondence with Charles V, to return to Cuba. Cortés disregarded the command and instead made his base camp at a site he named Vera Cruz ("The True Cross"). From there he gathered more intelligence from the Totonac and other tribes. He learned that many tribes and cities were fiercely opposed to the Aztecs and hated their submission to a tribute system that exploited them economically and took people from their communities for ritual sacrifice in the Great Temple in Tenochtitlán. Indian warriors willing to fight alongside Cortés were thus legion. In the Spanish telling, Cortés added thousands of Mesoamerican slingers and javelin throwers to his tiny army. From the vantage point of the Totonac and other Indians, they added small but unique Spanish military capabilities to an armed rebellion they were preparing to rid themselves of the Aztecs.

Before moving inland Cortés sank his remaining ships to show there was no going back and to leave his reluctant men no choice but to follow. On August 16, 1519, he started for Tenochtitlán 150 miles inland, across a range of volcanoes. Over the mountains, he arrived at Tlaxcalan, an independent city-state 70 miles from Tenochtitlán which the Aztecs had never been able to conquer. An army came out to crush the strangers and their Indian allies. In a sharp battle, Spanish discipline and firepower won the day: arquebuses and muskets broke up loose Tlaxcalan lines before their warriors could approach to hurl stones and javelins. The 16 Spanish lancers then further deformed the Indian ranks and picked off their leaders. Then the Spanish foot charged, shoulder-to-shoulder with swords and pikes, slashing and stabbing hundreds of warriors to death before they could swing heavy obsidian clubs in reply. Armor and steel, but even more discipline and ferocity, won over the Mesoamerican style of warfare that emphasized individual heroism in loose, lightly armed formations, and taking an enemy alive so he could be sacrificed later.

> *. . . Cortés sank his remaining ships to show there was no going back and to leave his reluctant men no choice but to follow.*

This victory at Tlaxcalan was a key moment in the conquest because the Tlaxcalans immediately allied with Cortés. They, too, thought his unusual military skills could be used against the hated Aztecs. Tlaxcalan henceforth provided tens of thousands of dedicated, veteran Indian warriors. And it became the key forward base and logistical center for the Spanish for the next two years. Reinforced with 3,000 more Mesoamerican allies, Cortés reached the Aztec tributary city of Cholollan (modern Cholula). Moctezuma tried a stratagem: the Spanish were invited into the city where a trap was laid of missile troops hidden on the rooftops, with ditches filled with sharp stakes to impale riders and horses. But the trick was betrayed so that Cortés struck first, killing Cholollan troops and commanders without mercy.

Moctezuma was unable to muster his full army because it was harvest season. Instead, he made a fatal—and fateful—decision: he invited Cortés, the conquistadores, and 3,000 Tlaxcalan warriors into Tenochtitlán, which the expedition reached on November 8. Possibly, Moctezuma hoped to arrange a second, larger Cholollan-style trap, using urban confinement to neutralize the demonstrated superiority of the Spanish in the field. Far less likely is the widely popular legend that he lost confidence due to belief in an old prophesy that Cortés appeared to fulfill, which foretold of a feared, pale Aztec deity (Quetzalcoatl), who would return from the east to reclaim his Aztec kingdom.

The allied intruders were quartered in an older palace, off the ritual square at the city center. After two weeks, Cortés feared such a trap and decided to spring his own first. He asked for an audience with Moctezuma, whom he seized and kept prisoner for six months, effectively decapitating the regime and paralyzing its response. The Aztec nobility obeyed Moctezuma's initial command to bring the city's gold to the conquistadores, to whom they also brought food and women. Doubt about the superiority, let alone quasi-divinity, of their guests grew as they watched the Spaniards eat, rut, and defecate as did other men, and exhibit an extraordinary lust for gold. A crisis for Cortés came when he led most of his men back to the coast to fend off a rival force of 900 conquistadores from Cuba. This group knew of the planned conquest, had orders to arrest Cortés, and intended to take their share of gold. Cortés attacked by surprise, killing a few and capturing their leader (Pánfilo de Narváez). With oratory laced with Crusader ecstacy and promised plunder, he persuaded the survivors to join his little army and together they returned to Tenochtitlán. However, so cruel was the occupation of the man he left in charge in the city, *Pedro de Alvarado*, so insatiable was the Spanish lust for gold, and so numerous the murders of priests and Aztec nobles they committed (probably on the orders of Cortés), the Aztecs at last rebelled. But first they shrewdly let Cortés re-enter the city, which he did against the advice of his Mesoamerican allies.

On June 24, 1520, the Aztecs cut the causeways that led to the city, trapping 1,200 Spanish and about 2,000 Tlaxcalans, along with mounds of hoarded gold in the temple and palace complex. The *First Siege of Tenochtitlán* lasted a week. After several sorties failed, on the night of June 30, Cortés led an effort to sneak out of the city which ended in a desperate flight that left half his men dead or trapped in the temple complex, surrounded by tens of thousands of enraged Aztecs. As Cortés pulled out from Tenochtitlán he left it burning and Moctezuma dead (whether from errant Aztec missiles or Spanish strangulation is unclear). Streams of Spanish and Tlaxcalan blood literally flowed down the temple steps as men left behind or cut off were captured and ritually sacrificed for all to see. The remnant fled with Cortés down the causeway, fighting off thousands of pursing Aztec warriors en route to a dramatic stand at *Otumba*. The Aztecs were by now in full roar: they had killed enough Spaniards, in battle or by ritually cutting out their hearts, to know they faced not demi-gods but mere men who bled, screamed, died, or ran in fear like other men. Their horses, too, were demystified by death and dismemberment.

Cortés lost 70 percent of his horses and 65 percent of his men. The Tlaxcalans suffered as heavily, and in far greater numbers. In the Spanish accounts, it was now that Cortés proved himself an exceptional leader with qualities of strategic foresight, tactical brilliance, and above all, thorough ruthlessness and pitiless single-mindedness of purpose. He spent the rest of 1520 gathering a new anti-Aztec alliance from surrounding cities, and awaiting the successive arrival at Vera Cruz of seven squadrons of ships bringing new cannons, arquebuses, crossbows, powder, and shot. With the weapons came more conquistadores, some intent on revenge for dead brothers or fathers, others keen to crusade against the rumored pagan "empire of cannibals." The smallpox that came with the Spanish now decimated Aztec ranks, killing Cuitláhuac as well. This reduced the numbers of warriors the Spanish faced and may have undermined Aztec morale, but it also ravaged the Tlaxcalans and other tribes allied with the Spanish. Cortés busied some men with raids against Aztec tributaries, cutting off supplies to Tenochtitlán. Others he set to building 14 *brigantines*, using timber and struts from the wreaks at Vera Cruz. He then had these small ships dismantled and hauled to the shores of Lake Texcoco by thousands of Mesoamerican porters. The 500 Spaniards Cortés had left after Otumba were reinforced by 400–500 fresh arrivals at Vera Cruz, who brought much-needed fresh horses and more arquebuses and cannon. This still left him mainly reliant on Tlaxcalan warriors who were determined to overthrow the Aztecs. Some Indians adapted their weapons to make them more lethal, for instance, switching to copper-tipped arrows with metal obtained from the Spanish. The second expedition—was it a Spanish assault with Indian allies or the reverse?—arrived at the foot of the causeways across Lake Texcoco on April 28, 1521. The aqueducts were quickly broken, cutting off Tenochtitlán from its supply of food and fresh water. The brigantines went into the lake to destroy the Aztec war canoes. This was quickly accomplished. The *Second Siege of Tenochtitlán* now began. It lasted three months. On August 13, 1521, the third and last Aztec leader to face the Spanish assault and Indian vassal rebellion, the boy-emperor Cuauhtémoc, surrendered the city.

Cortés subsequently became governor of the conquered Aztec lands and one of the richest men of the Age. He ruled cruelly, in accordance with his nature: he was an unimaginative, brutal kleptocrat with no regard for the welfare of the Indian population, except an instrumental concern with Indian welfare such that the encomienda system was sustainable. Tenochtitlán was razed so that a Christian citadel of the Spanish Empire in America, Mexico City, might be built atop its ruins. Cortés called in Franciscan priests and other religious radicals to destroy the last temples and indoctrinate Mesoamericans with the usual Catholic pieties. Those Indians who survived were weakened morally as well as physically by pandemic diseases, and were also politically weak and divided. They were effectively enslaved by Spanish settlers who hurried to Mexico following the conquest, many of whom demonstrated even less conscience than did Cortés. The native economy was destroyed, its riches plundered and exported to buy estates or pay royal taxes in Spain. Central Mexico would take centuries to recover from the decimation.

Cortés led several more expeditions to expand "Spanish America," including to Central America in 1524 (during which he had Cuauhtémoc murdered), and later to Baja California. In 1528 he returned to Spain to regain his Mexican governorship, which had been taken from him by a royal appointee. He was unsuccessful, but received a captaincy, a noble title, and a huge land grant in Mexico along with tens of thousands of encomienda forced laborers. Ever the conquistador, he did not rest content in landed wealth. He later fought in Africa, joining the Habsburg attack on Algiers in 1541. He died of dysentery, amidst his riches, in Spain.

Suggested Reading: Ross Hassig, *Mexico and the Spanish Conquest* (1995); Hugh Thomas, *Conquest* (1994).

Cossacks. Turkish: "kazak" or "outlaw." A blended people comprised of masterless Turkic and Slavic horsemen from southern Russia, Poland, and Ukraine, occupying the grassland frontiers between Christian and Muslim, and Orthodox and Catholic. Cossacks were at first little more than self-defense bands ("vatahy") living off the steppe. These grew and founded fortified camps (*sich*), as Cossackdom evolved from seasonal hunting and grazing on the wild grassland into a year-round livelihood. From the 1480s Slavic Cossacks appeared, mostly runaway slaves or serfs but also down-and-out burghers, penurious nobles, and defrocked priests. Others descended from nomadic invaders who had passed through in earlier centuries, and local tribes beyond the reach of the tsars of Muscovy or the khans of Central Asia. During the 15th and 16th centuries there was an explosion in Cossack numbers as military burdens increased in surrounding societies, making private warfare, and hunting and farming far more attractive than staying at home to be enserfed or conscripted. Cossacks enjoyed broad autonomy for several reasons: they were too ferocious to conquer without great cost; their land was not deemed valuable enough to warrant full-scale invasion and conquest; and their scattered grassland fortresses and superb natural cavalry set up effective and useful buffer zones between Poland and Muscovy on one side and the Ottoman Empire and its *Tatar* allies to the south.

In 1553–1554 the Zaporozhian Cossacks built a sich south of Kiev on the island of Mala Khortytsia, "below the rapids" ("za porohamy") on the Dnieper. The "Zaporozhian Sich" then became the center of Ukrainian Cossackdom. Indifferent to confessionalism but reserving a violent hatred of Jews, they accepted any Christian male who applied (women and children were barred). This rough, democratic, propertyless military brotherhood was led by an "otaman" or "hetman," aided by "osavuly" (lieutenants). The "chern" (ordinary Cossacks) lived in wooden barracks ("kurin") and elected their officer corps ("starshnya").

Cossacks were divided by wealth and ethnicity, by town and rural living, and by which contending power they faced at their nearest grassy frontier. The majority in the Dnieper basin were Ukrainian, while Russians settled farther south along the Don. Without any uniform religious leaning during this period Cossacks, especially the "Little Russian Cossack Host," were hard pressed to determine if their interest lined up best with expanding Orthodox Muscovy, contracting Catholic Poland, or the sprawling Muslim empire of the Ottomans. As a result, they raided deep into all three states at one time or another. In addition, from 1572 Poland registered "town Cossacks," recognizing them as a distinct social class and employing them as salaried frontier guards and a buffer against unregistered, rural Cossacks. By 1589 there were 3,000 registered Cossacks compared to 50,000 unregistered, both distinct from the Zaporozhians. In the early 17th century they conducted deep amphibious raids against the Ottomans along the Crimean and Black Sea coasts.

In 1615 they slipped into Constantinople harbor and burned it. The next year they broke the pens of the slave market in Kaffa, freeing thousands. They burned Constantinople harbor again in 1620, then joined the Poles to fend off an Ottoman-Tatar invasion, 1620–1621. In the 1630s the Zaporozhians fought the Polish-Lithuanian Commonwealth, joined by many peasants. Cossacks were deeply involved in the savage upheaval in Ukraine and Poland known as the Khmelnitsky Uprising (1648–1654). In the Treaty of Pereiaslav (1654), some accepted protection and pay from Muscovy. See also *Cecora, Battle of*; *chaiky*; *Eternal Peace*; *Khotyn, Battle of*; *Pancerna cavalry*; *Polish Army*.

Suggested Reading: G. Gajecky and A. Baran, *Cossacks in the Thirty Years' War*, 2 vols. (1969).

couched lance. A long equestrian spear (not a javelin) made of sound wood that tapered to a lethal point, tipped with metal. Its use required adoption of the stirrup and a heavy saddle that hugged the horse and had a cantle (perpendicular board) to brace the rider's back and keep him in the saddle when his lance met opposing armor or flesh. This combination of saddle and stirrup made it possible for a mounted warrior to brace his feet and back while leveling and "couching" the lance under his arm in the charge. The technique channeled the weight of rider and horse into the lance point as the blow was delivered, penetrating armor and shielding and impaling the man inside or behind it. When this effect was multiplied by *heavy cavalry*, or lines of armored men riding great *destriers*, new "*shock*" tactics came to dominate the medieval battlefield for over 200 years. See also *chivalry*; *knight*; *lancers*; *plate armor*; *shields/shielding*; *warhorses*.

coudières. See *couters*.

couleuveriniers. French hand-gunners of the 15th century. "Coulverine" was then still used as a generic for almost any kind of gun, from *arquebus* to *culverin*.

coulverin à main. A French term for early handguns: "hand culverins."

coulverine. See *culverin*.

coulverines enfustées. A mid-15th-century French gun falling between a "hand cannon" and a small artillery piece. It was a portable, shoulder-fired weapon.

Council of Blood. See *Alba, Don Fernando Álvarez de Toledo, duque de*; *Eighty Years' War*; *French Civil Wars*.

Council of Ten. The governing body of the Republic of *Venice*. See also *Carmagnola, Francesco Bussone*; *Machiavelli, Niccolò di Bernardo*; *Lepanto, Battle of (October 7, 1571)*.

Council of the Indies. Set up in 1524, this council of the king and his advisers administered and made law for Spain's possessions in the Americas. In theory, it commanded Spanish viceroys and captains-general, regulated trade, conducted Spain's overseas wars, and was the final court of appeal of any decision taken in the audiencia (local courts) of Spain's discrete colonies. In fact, local officials had a great deal of autonomy from Spain.

Council of Trent (1545–1563). A general council of the Catholic Church that met to consider and condemn "errors" of Protestantism, which it opposed on every major point of doctrine. Its proclamations revised Church doctrine, revived Catholic confidence, and encouraged a new militancy in the politics and military activity of Catholic princes. It doctrinal achievement is generally known as the "Tridentine Reform" (from the Latin "Tridentum" or Trent). The Council was called in 1534 by Pope Paul III, who was known to favor reform and wished to end the religious wars in Germany. It opened in 1545 after a decade of delay by those opposed to real Church reform, but also with solid preparation by those supporting change. Trent's deliberations were interrupted by plague several times, so that it met only from 1545 to 1547 (under Paul III), 1551 to 1552 (under the still more pro-Habsburg Julius III), and 1562 to 1563 (under Pius IV). The *Jesuits* were especially influential in its intermediate session, under Julius.

The Council denied Protestant insistence on the sole authority of scripture, upholding tradition (papal and conciliar rulings) as an additional authoritative source of religious truth. The Council addressed clerical abuse of simony (selling indulgences or relics), imposed new restrictions on clergy intended to end the problem of absentee bishops, and addressed common lay practices such as "secret marriages." Its sessions on doctrine led to rebuttal of the Protestant thesis on "justification by faith," for which Trent substituted the traditional medieval position of the need for good works inspired by "caritas" (love). It affirmed that transubstantiation took place during the Mass and spoke directly against the *Hussite* and *Utraquist* position by admonishing lay reception of the eucharist in the form of bread alone. Trent defined the

> *The reforms that followed on the ground were the most effective and important in Catholic history.*

nature and set the number of Catholic sacraments at seven, reaffirming such controversial sacraments as penance. It forbade clerical marriage while imposing harsh punishment for clerical concubinage; confirmed the existence of Purgatory and the propriety of indulgences; and reaffirmed veneration of saints and relics. Its deliberations culminated in issuance of a definitive statement of Catholic belief: the "Catechism of the Council of Trent" or "Roman Catechism." This both answered and competed with Jean Calvin's *Institutions* in the growing campaign to confessionalize the peasantry and broad masses.

The reforms that followed on the ground were the most effective and important in Catholic history. They significantly reshaped and restated

Catholicism and informed and hardened the *Counter-Reformation*. However, they thereby widened the divide with Protestant communities that were by then also settling into final molds. Even some Catholic monarchs, notably those of France, resented Trent's conciliar and papal infringement on the traditional liberties of national churches. In addition, *Francis I* and his son, *Henri II*, had no interest in advancing the cause of religious peace in Germany, where even heresy might be welcome if it worked to weaken their political enemies, just as alliance with the Ottoman sultan was an established fact of French policy. Henri II ordered French bishops not to attend Trent and cut off the traditional payment to Rome of a bishopric's income for a full year upon a new bishop's appointment (*annates*). Later, *Charles Guise, Cardinal de Lorraine*, represented France at sessions of the Council of Trent, upholding the *Gallican* position despite his reputation at home for Catholic fanaticism. See also *Ecumenical Councils*; *Joinville, Treaty of*.

Suggested Reading: H. Jedin, *History of the Council of Trent* (1957; 1961).

Council of Troubles. "Council of Blood." See also *Alba, Don Fernando Álvarez de Toledo, duque de*; *Eighty Years' War*.

counter-castle. See *bastille*; *blockade*.

counter-guard (1). A small, supplemental defense work—often a narrow, detached rampart—emplaced before a more important fortification to protect against its being breached.

counter-guard (2). Part of the hilt of a sword. It protected against an enemy blade sliding down to injure the hand.

counter-march. See *caracole*; *drill*; *La Bicocca, Battle of*; *Maurits of Nassau*; *volley fire*.

counter-mining. See *mining*.

Counter-Reformation. The term "Catholic Reformation" is preferred by Catholic historians to refer to efforts at self-reform by the Catholic Church that actually began in the late medieval period, well before the *Protestant Reformation*. Many reject "Counter-Reformation" entirely as a "reactionary" term. Even most non-Catholic historians now regard the Counter-Reformation as more a continuation of medieval reform than a wholly new effort made in reaction to the Reformation. In the early 15th century the Catholic Church was divided over differences between lay and clerical piety and practices and the scandal of the *Great Schism*. The Council of Constance ended the schism by asserting conciliar authority over the popes. This left unresolved demands for moral and administrative reform, whose need was made clear by the *Hussite Wars* and widespread lay disgust at ongoing Church corruption.

During the 15th century efforts at reform were stymied by papal opposition to the conciliar movement and the increase in cardinals and bishops who resided in Rome while drawing income from absentee benefices. In 1460 a papal decree reasserted the primacy of the Renaissance popes and thus placed the reform program back in the hands of anti-reformers. The last effort at internal reform came just before the Reformation broke out in Germany. The Fifth Lateran Council (1512–1517) was convened by Pope Julius II in opposition to a renegade council called by Louis XII, with whom the Papal States were then at war. As it drew to a close, Fifth Lateran had no effective response to the Protestant broadsides that emanated from Geneva, Zürich, and Wittenberg. The papal monarchy and Church had failed to reform itself in time or in depth before the advent of full-throated Protestant rejection of Catholic doctrine and papal authority. In the first flush of conflict with radical clergy who would no longer wait for reform, men soon to be known as "Protestants," Counter-Reformation popes would attack as well all internal conciliar and episcopal efforts at reform, denouncing them as crypto-Protestantism.

By 1540 Catholic and Protestant alike were horrified by the prospect that they might split Latin Christendom permanently (they had long become used to hostile division from Orthodox and Copts). A final effort was made to heal the breach when *Charles V* convened the *Imperial Diet* at Regensburg in January, 1541. It failed. Thereafter, the Catholic position hardened at the *Council of Trent* (1545–1563) while Charles went to war with the German Protestant princes and free cities of the *Schmalkaldic League*. Even when German Catholics and Lutherans agreed to a religious truce in the *Peace of Augsburg* (1555), popes and some bishops elsewhere continued a powerful counterattack against the Reformation, with the new order of *Jesuits* the "sword and shield" of doctrinal and missionary warfare. In this period the Counter-Reformation surely was reactionary, as revival of the *Index* and *Inquisition* demonstrate. Its character was marked by a new militancy and sharp reaction against the "sins of Luther," which were clerical disobedience and doctrinal invention. Certainly, Catholics of the day agreed that repression of Protestants and suppression of heresy were proper complements to any internal reform. The return to parochial conformity of doctrine and practice was aided by Tridentine reform of the episcopacy, which relocated bishops from Rome back to their sees. As the competition for conversions outside the towns intensified in the 1570s, more rigid confessionalism was evident among elites on all sides. In Germany, there was sharp movement away from respect for the terms of the Augsburg peace by Protestant princes in the north and by Catholic emperors and princes in the south. *Maximilian II* had some sympathy for toleration of Protestantism, but he gave way to firmer Counter-Reformation views under *Rudolf II*, succeeded seven years later by open fanaticism under *Ferdinand II*.

It is less clear what role the Catholic laity played, though recent research has uncovered important insights into this neglected area of confessional history. It is clear that Catholic missionaries within the "Indies of Europe" kept what they told the laity deliberately simple, as compared to the clergy's improved religious education and instruction in the formalism of Tridentine doctrine. Insistence on priestly interposition between believer and God contrasted with Protestant printers and preachers bringing scripture directly even to children. But Catholics made an easier peace with traditional folk religion and superstitions than doctrinally more utopian (and more rigid) Protestants. Bishops issued instructions to clergy to steer Catholic flock away from complex doctrinal questions, which were considered answered by rote recital of the Roman Catechism, with belief additionally garnished with certain "mysteries of the faith." Given this lower standard for conversion and observance, and a good deal of coercion, whole principalities earlier converted to Lutheranism or Calvinism were reconverted to Catholicism by the Counter-Reformation. In the Habsburg hereditary lands of Bohemia and Inner Austria this reconversion was harsh, effective, and nearly complete. In southern Germany (Silesia was an exception), the frontier of Protestantism was rolled back by Tridentine reform and *Catholic League* and Imperial troops and state support of the Church. In Poland and Lithuania, entire populations reconverted. But the Counter-Reformation was not successful in Prussia, Courland or Livonia, nowhere in Scandinavia, and only marginally in England and Scotland.

Counter-Reformation teaching was deeply contemptuous of the material and political world. It inserted a new puritanism into Catholic life by radical rejection of the "ways of the flesh." It endorsed moral and physical self-denial, including medieval mortifications of the body from sado-masochistic devotional practices like flagellation, to hair shirts, excessive kneeling at prayer, and extreme fasting. More generally, it turned away from the celebration of family and lay sexuality within marriage promoted by Protestant, especially Calvinist, churches. Instead, even nonclerical lust was to be curtailed by strict regulation and monitoring by a (putatively) celibate clergy. This movement for renewed piety and clerical authority received support from several, though not all, Habsburg monarchs. Catholic extremism clashed directly with comparably militant—and in the case of Calvinism, even more militant—Protestantism. Together, confessional fanatics combined to wage protracted, highly destructive sectarian wars. These climaxed internationally in the *Eighty Years' War* and the *Thirty Years' War*, while ripping apart France internally during the *French Civil Wars* and convulsing the three island kingdoms of England, Ireland, and Scotland in the *English Civil Wars*. Of course, underlying those conflicts and infusing papal and conciliar policy on one side and princely and sectarian responses on the other, were princely egos, divers reasons of state, and class and ethnic bigotry that had little to do with religion. The deepest political legacy of the Counter-Reformation was probably etched in Spain, always the most ideological and committed of the Catholic nations. When the wars of religion ended Spain was left cocooned within rigid dogma and religious and racial reaction, dethroned from its former hegemony and thus culturally brittle.

Suggested Reading: C. H. Carter, ed., *From the Renaissance to the Counter-Reformation* (1965); N. S. Davidson, *The Counter-Reformation* (1987); Steven Ozment, *The Age of Reform, 1250–1550* (1981); A. Wright, *The Counter-Reformation* (1982).

counterscarp. The exterior sloping wall of a defensive ditch surrounding a fortified position, usually supporting a *covered way* and sometimes also the *glacis*.

counter-sinking. See *fortification*; *trace italienne*.

coureurs. "Runners." Men assigned by an army on the move to serve as outriders, to scout out and forage for food and fodder, and to raid, kill, burn, and pillage enemy subjects and provinces. See also *chevauchée*.

courser. A breed of *warhorse* less expensive, smaller, and fleeter than the *destrier* or *rouncey*. It was the preferred mount for cavalry raiding and *chevauchée*.

courtaux. A medium-size medieval French canon.

Courtrai (Kortrijk), Battle of (July 11, 1302). "Battle of the Spurs." On a soggy field south of Ghent, Flemish militia infantry met the *heavy cavalry* of France in battle, and annihilated it. The trigger was a Flemish siege of Courtrai Castle. At the order of Philip IV ("The Fair"), against whom the revolt aimed, a French relief army set out. It was comprised of 2,500 *knights* and *men-at-arms*, led by Robert of Artois, along with 8,000 German and Genoese mercenary infantry. The Flemings chose the ground well, taking up defensive positions in three echelons of eight ranks each with a fourth in reserve facing toward the French garrison in the Castle to the rear. In front was a marshy flat, crisscrossed with small streams and muddy ditches: a natural cavalry trap. The critical error was Robert's, but it reflected a wider contempt for the Flemings on the part of all his knights. Before Genoese archers could thin and demoralize the ranks of Flemish militia armed with *goedendags* (a short, stabbing pike), clubs, and flails, Robert ordered a charge of his heavy horse. As mounts floundered in the marsh and muck they were gashed open or had forelegs hacked off. French knights by the hundred were pulled from the saddle with hooked polearms; well-disciplined militiamen methodically slaughtered these turtled noblemen, without mercy. A counterattack was assayed by Robert's hired foreign infantry, but it failed. All knights who could, turned and fled, followed by panicking Germans and Genoese. The Flemings could not pursue mounted knights on foot, so they concentrated on finishing off wounded and stragglers.

Courtrai is usually cited as marking the end of dominance of the battlefield by heavy cavalry, although historian Norman Housley adds the wise caution

> *The critical error was Robert's, but it reflected a wider contempt for the Flemings on the part of all his knights.*

that it was "a triumph over stupidity as much as a revelation of what infantry could achieve." Through recklessness and stupidity then, but also raw Flemish courage and tenacity, the French lost perhaps half their strength, including several dozen top nobility and as many as 1,000 men-at-arms. Spurs taken from 500 dead French knights were hung as trophies in St. Mary's Church in Courtrai, where they remained until retrieved by the French 80 years later, after *Roosebeke*. The next year, at Arques, the French were again defeated by town militia, though more ambiguously. The shock of these defeats persuaded Philip IV to undertake a major military reform, the *arrière-ban*, which aimed at raising better infantry for his army. His reformed army had better success against the Flemings at *Mons-en-Pévèle* (1304). Even so, the lessons of Courtrai were widely touted. Sometimes they were even applied, as by the *Catalan Great Company* at *Kephissos* (1311) and the Scots at *Bannockburn* (1314). It is possible that Swiss tactics at *Morgarten* (1315) were also inspired by Courtrai, though the difference in terrain militates against that conclusion. It is clear, on the other hand, that at *Laupen* (1339) the Swiss applied lessons learned from Courtrai. See also *cavalry*; *England*; *French Army*; *Scottish Wars*.

couseque. A French *halberd* type marked by a long central spike flanked by double side blades.

couters (*coudières*). Armored elbow-caps.

coutillers. In medieval French armies, foot soldiers armed with short swords.

Coutras, Battle of (October 20, 1587). *Henri de Navarre* led a ragged but veteran *Huguenot* army, 6,300 men in all, out to meet a young and inexperienced Catholic force of 5,000 foot and 1,800 horse under the duc de Joyeuse. Although Navarre had seen combat before, this was the first real test of his field generalship. He interspersed groups of musketeers between units of cavalry, with his line spanning a narrow valley between two wooded hills. The Catholic cavalry, mostly young nobles dressed in silks and plumage, were cocky and overconfident. In contrast, the Huguenots were dour veterans, praying and singing Protestant psalms before the battle. Expecting an easy victory, the Catholic cavalry charged Henri's lines, only to be cut down by volleys of accurate gunfire. The remnants were overridden by a counterattack of Huguenot horse. Within two hours Joyeuse and 3,500 of his troopers were dead. The Protestants lost fewer than 200 men. Henri then squandered these fine results by tending to his mistress at Béarn rather than to his army, which broke up while he played fecklessly at fornication.

Covenanters. Adherents to the principles of the "National Covenant," the central document of the Scottish patriotic and religious revolt of 1637. It declared that the "true Christian faith and religion" found expression in the Kirk of Scotland, and that all true Scots "abhor and detest all contrary religion and doctrine." This was radical patriotism united to, and defined by,

Calvinist (Presbyterian) *confessionalism*. The great commanders of the Covenanters were the *Earl of Leven* (Alexander Leslie) and *David Leslie*, while the main political leader was the *Marquis of Argyll*. The latter's bête noire was a former Covenanter turned Royalist, the *Marquis of Montrose*. Montrose won at *Tippermuir* (September 1, 1644), and three times in the summer of 1645, at *Auldearn* (May 9), *Alford* (July 2), and *Kilsyth* (August 15). But he came to a bad end at the hands of Argyll after *Carbiesdale* (1650). Internationally, the Scots found a ready ally in Sweden for whom Scottish mercenaries had fought for decades. In 1638 the Swedes released Scots officers to return to their homeland, where they trained the new levies that opposed the king in the *Bishops' Wars*. See also *Charles I, of England*; *Confederation of Kilkenny*; *Cromwell, Oliver*; *English Civil Wars*; *Kilsyth, Battle of*; *Knox, John*; *Philiphaugh*; *Preston, Campaign of*; *"Root and Branch" petition*.

covered way. Also "covert way." In field fortification, any wide path sheltered from enemy view and fire by a sunken road or trench, usually atop the *counterscarp* but shielded ("covered") by the *parapet* and crest of the *glacis*. In permanent fortifications the covered or covert way ran astride the counterscarp as an outwork sunk below the glacis. Troops used it to defend the glacis against an enemy lodgement and as an assembly or rally point. See also *lodgement*.

"Cowardice Peace" (1328). See *Edward III*; *Scottish Wars*.

coxswain. A minor (petty) officer put in charge of the crew of a ship's boat.

Cracow, Battle of (1241). See *Mongols*.

Cracow, Peace of (1525). See *Livonia*; *Prussia*; *Teutonic Knights, Order of*.

cranequin. A mechanical device for drawing a powerful *crossbow* that could not be spanned by muscle alone. It involved a tiller that turned a cogwheel, which engaged a "tooth" that bumped along a ratchet bar until the cord was taut. The quarrel or bolt could then be loaded and fired. Its pull was much greater than with a *graffle* or *windlass*, but its reloading speed meant that the weapon could fire no faster than twice a minute.

crapadeaux. A medium-size medieval French cannon.

Crécy, Battle of (August 26, 1346). A key battle in the opening phase of the *Hundred Years' War* (1337–1453). England's *Edward III* (1312–1377) led an army on an extended *chevauchée* into northern France with the intention of provoking *Philip VI* to give battle. The tactic nearly backfired when the French burned several bridges in an effort to trap the English against the Somme: Edward was fortunate to ford under cover of his skilled archers. Two days later the armies met near the village of Crécy, in Normandy, where they formed opposing battle lines 2,000 yards long. The English were well-rested and fed. Though outnumbered 2:1 they took position atop a low ridge with their left flank abutting a stream, the Maie, and their right flank touching Crécy Wood. At the center were three blocks of men-at-arms with protecting pikemen. Two sets of archers with *longbows* were on the flanks, each in a "V" formation. Each archer had ready about 100 *broad arrows*, their lethal metal tips pushed into the ground to permit rapid reloading. Hundreds of *caltrops* were scattered atop the sod and mud to their front, to hobble oncoming *warhorses* or infantry. Tens of thousands more arrows were packed in wood and leather quivers stacked in carts to the rear. This large supply was key to the English victory. The initial rate of fire of a good longbowman was from six to ten arrows per minute, falling thereafter as muscle fatigue set in. Several hundred thousand arrows thus were likely fired toward the French that day, most from beyond the range of effective retaliation by the gay, pennant-decked lances of the French knights, looking splendid in burnished armor, colorful livery, and plumed helms, but utterly exposed to plunging arrow storms. Nor could Edward's archers be reached by Genoese mercenaries on the French side firing stubby quarrels from crossbows, a deadly and feared weapon of their chosen profession that was wholly outmatched in range by the longbow on this bloody day.

Neither French cavalry nor Genoese infantry nor the Czech mercenaries of "Blind King John," an allied prince, had ever faced the longbow. In ignorance and battle lust, they arrived piecemeal on the field of battle in the late afternoon, hungry and tired but straining to attack the English line. Heavy rain had soaked the field, turning it into sticky mud. The sun also favored the English, as it shone into the faces of the French. When the French heavy cavalry arrayed for the attack it formed in the old manner: a mass of armored horse supported by crossbow fire on the flanks and to the front. It is thought that Edward fired several small cannon at the Genoese to break up their formations. If true, these guns would have been so primitive they likely produced more a psychological than a physical effect. What mattered was that the Genoese were slowed by the Normandy mud and then slaughtered by flights of English arrows, not cannon, well before they got into crossbow range. Worse, in the rush to battle most had left their *pervase* with the baggage wagons. Nor could their slow-loading crossbows do comparable damage to the rapid-firing Welsh and English archers, thus rendering the Genoese attack ineffective and leaving the English lines unbroken and unharried before the French horse arrived. As casualties mounted among the Genoese they broke, turned, and ran, mud sucking at their boots and adding to the agony of panic as they exposed their backs to deadly enemy archers, firing aimed shots at the level.

The French knights, filled with Gallic disdain for everything on foot, spurred callously through the retreating Genoese, slashing at hired infantry in utter contempt, some with cries of "kill this rabble!" A large earthen bank channeled the French cavalry into a narrow front. Edward's archers, positioned nearly perfectly, now turned their bows against the plodding, funneled cavalry and cut it down, too. Ill-formed, repeated French charges, with horsemen at the rear pushing hard against the forward ranks, were repulsed time and again by the longbowmen. Most were broken apart before they began, with staggering losses among the brave but reckless fathers and sons of the nobility of France. Edward's archers kept up an extraordinary rate of fire, impaling knights and horse alike and hundreds of men-at-arms. No cowards the French, despite the carnage they charged, again and again. It is thought they made as many as 16 charges that day, utterly bewildered at their inability to beat or even reach an inferior enemy. For two centuries heavy cavalry had dominated battlefields from Europe to the Holy Land. But at Crécy there were no tattered squares of scrambling peasants to skewer on great lances, no clumps of overmatched men-at-arms to chase down with mace or run through on one's sword. Instead, the chivalry of France met flocks of missiles that felled knight and mount alike at unheard of killing distances. Eye-witnesses reported French awe at the flapping, vital sounds of thousands of feathers on long-shafted arrows arcing in high swarms from an unreachable ridge, to plunge into men, horses, or both. Baleful accounts survive telling how arrows ripped through shields and helmets, pierced face-plates and cuirasses, and arms, legs, and groins, or pinned some best friend to his mount.

Much of this occurred at incredible distances, as unaimed plunging fire reached the French from as far away as 250–300 yards. Longbow accuracy only improved at closer ranges, as bows were leveled and each shot singly aimed at the lumbering steel and flesh targets the French cavalry presented. In prior battles cavalry had been safe at 200 yards or more, the usual distance where riders massed before trotting forward to about 60–100 yards, the distance at which they began the charge. Now death and piercing wounds fell from the sky at double the normal range, slicing through shields and armor to stab deep into chest or thigh, or horse. The French could make no reply to this long-distance death with their lances and swords: knights died in droves that day without ever making contact with their enemies. Armor was pierced and limbs, backs, and necks broken as falling knights entangled in bloody clots of swords and snapped lances, and kicking and screaming dying men and horses. So they charged: anything was better than standing beneath such lethal rain. The nearly 8,000 longbowmen at Crécy probably fired 75,000–90,000 arrows in the 40–60 seconds it took the French to close the range, each arrow speeding near 140 miles per hour, each archer keeping two and some three in the air at once. Those knights who reached the English lines piled up before them, pierced with multiple arrows and forming an armor-and-flesh barrier in front of the English men-at-arms that impeded fresh assaults. With French chivalry broken and its survivors staggering in the mud, the English infantry and Edward's dismounted knights closed in to kill off the lower orders and take nobles prisoner, to be held for later ransom. Then the English stood in place through the night, holding in case of a renewed attack in the morning which never came.

Most casualties at Crécy were inflicted by the longbow and thus losses were hugely lopsided: between 5,000 and 8,000 French and Genoese were killed, including as many as 1,500 knights, compared to about 100 of Edward's men. This was a huge number for a 14th-century battle, and left nearly every castle and chateau in France in mourning. The defeat of its warrior elite shattered France's military capabilities and shook its confidence for a generation. This one-sided battle further eroded the old illusion that heavy cavalry was invincible against common infantry, and elevated recognition of the importance of archers across Europe. A parallel effect was that for the next 50 years French knights, too, preferred to dismount to fight, a practice they followed until better horse armor was made that enticed them back into the saddle at *Agincourt*. See also *artillery*; *Black Prince*; *Calais*; *gunpowder weapons*.

Suggested Reading: Andrew Ayton and Philip Preston, *The Battle of Crécy, 1346* (2005); Alfred H. Burne, *The Crécy War* (1955; 1999); G. C. Macauly, ed., *The Chronicles of Jean Froissart* (1904); Henri de Wailly, *Crécy, 1346: Anatomy of a Battle* (1987).

crenel. An open space between two *merlons* on a castle or town wall through which defenders could fire on besiegers below or in an opposing *bastille* or *belfry*.

Crete. During this period Crete, the largest island in the eastern Mediterranean, was the object of near constant naval warfare (blockades, sieges, piracy, privateering, raids, and so on) between Venice and the Ottoman Empire. It was not finally taken from the Venetians, after a long Ottoman siege, until 1669.

crinet. Articulated, laminated or mail equine armor that sat below the *chanfron* and protected the neck of a *warhorse*. This replaced the original mail curtain that had protected the throat from slashing weapons but was insufficient to stop powerful missile weapons like crossbows or arquebuses. More generally, "crinet" referred to armor that filled the spaces between larger, single pieces such as the *crupper* and *peytral*.

Croatia. See *Austria*; *Hungary*; *Militargrenze*; *Ottoman Empire*.

cromster. A Dutch merchant ship developed as a coastal warship by the *Sea Beggars*. A shallow-draughted, wide-beamed cargo vessel, it was designed to carry trade in the shallow waters of the Netherlands coast and river estuaries. In wartime its sturdy hull accepted a heavy brace of guns. Cromsters also were popular with English allies of the Dutch.

Cromwell, Oliver (1599–1658). Puritan general and revolutionary. He converted to *Puritanism* after his marriage in 1620, and like many converts embraced his new faith with unbridled zeal. First elected to Parliament in

1628, he rose to prominence during the "Long Parliament" as both statesman and military leader. At the start of the *English Civil Wars* he served as colonel of a cavalry regiment in the *Eastern Association Army*. Having spent the winter in training, he led 400 of his new *Ironsides* troopers in a small but sharp action against 800 *Cavalier* cavalry at Grantham (May 13, 1643), in Lincolnshire. He served under *Thomas Fairfax* at *Winceby* (October 11, 1643), and afterward helped secure the eastern counties. On July 27, 1643, Cromwell led 1,800 Ironsides in scattering 2,000 Cavaliers at Gainsborough. Under *Manchester* and Fairfax, he led his Ironsides and dragoons well at *Marston Moor* (1644). He broke with Manchester after *Second Newbury* (1644), bringing charges that forced him to resign. He strongly supported Fairfax's creation of the *New Model Army*. On June 10, 1645, he was appointed Lieutenant General of Horse with *Ireton*, his future son-in-law, his subordinate. At *Naseby* (1645) Cromwell began the fight in command of the right wing but dramatically rallied the left and played a crucial role in the overall

> *...Cromwell led the Puritan faction in insisting on taming the king...*

victory. After *Charles I* surrendered and was handed over to Parliament by the Scots, Cromwell led the Puritan faction in insisting on taming the king, whom he fundamentally distrusted, and with good reason. Charles conspired endlessly from his seat of exile on the Isle of Wight, then from Holdenby House, encouraging the Scots to rise and intriguing with Catholic ambassadors to bring about foreign intervention, all the while dragging out negotiations with Parliament. At this, Cromwell lost all patience. On June 2, 1647, he had the king seized and brought under the Army's control and "protection" at Newmarket.

When Parliament voted to disband part of the New Model Army and send the rest to Ireland, raised *trained bands* and brought *reformadoes* and deserters into regiments loyal to itself, Cromwell and Fairfax chose the Army over Parliament. They occupied London on August 6, 1647, and chased their opponents from Westminster. After putting down a mutiny by *Levellers*, Cromwell pacified Wales (May–July 1648). Then he moved north and won a brilliant victory over the Scots at *Preston* (August 17–20, 1648). Determined to settle with the king he pressured Charles to come to terms with the results of the civil wars but could not convince him to do so. Cromwell moved the Rump Parliament to charge Charles with treason. The king was tried in December 1648, and executed on January 30, 1649, "a cruel necessity" in Cromwell's words. Cromwell next led a punitive expedition to Ireland, 1649–1650, a campaign remembered to the present day in Ireland for its reputed special savagery, including massacres of the captured garrison towns *Drogheda* and *Wexford*. Fighting continued against his sub-commanders as the Irish reverted to guerrilla warfare until 1653. That year, Cromwell dismissed the Long Parliament and erected a military dictatorship. He ruled for the next five years as "Lord Protector" of the Commonwealth. See also *Dunbar, Battle of*; *Fifth Monarchists*; *Navigation Acts*.

Suggested Reading: Frank Kitson, *Old Ironsides* (2004); John Morrill, *Oliver Cromwell and the English Revolution* (1990); James Wheeler, *Cromwell in Ireland* (1999).

Cromwell, Thomas (c.1485–1540). "Malleus monachorum" ("hammer of the monks"). He served as a mercenary in the *Italian Wars* from 1504 to 1512. He worked for Cardinal Wolsey by 1514 and was elected to Parliament in 1523. Fawning his way into the king's good graces, he counseled *Henry VIII* to cower the nobility and break the independence of the Church. He advised Henry to resolve the "great matter" of his divorce by splitting from Rome, a policy carried through in the Act of Supremacy (1534). He suggested resolution of the king's fiscal problem by dissolution of the monasteries, which he implemented from 1536 to 1539. He was central to the religious terror that cost Thomas More and other men of conscience their titles, property, and lives. His advocacy of Anne of Cleves as wife to Henry, and the general hatred and contempt in which he was held by so many, led to his arrest and beheading on Tower Hill. See also *printing*.

Cropedy Bridge, Battle of (1644). See *Charles I, of England*; *English Civil Wars*; *Waller, William*.

***Croquants*.** "Country Bumpkins." See *Tard-Avisés*.

crossbow. The crossbow was invented in China during its wars of unification, sometime prior to 221 B.C.E. Early crossbows were made from horn, wood, and some small metal parts, with the horn lashed to a wooden stock with cords or animal sinew. Later composite crossbows were heavier and sturdier, with the bow attached to the stock through a mortise and tenon, and held by metal bands in place of cords. The key to all crossbow fighting was that it took both hands (and usually, also both feet) to draw even a simple crossbow, which was done while sitting or standing stooped over the bow. More advanced models could be drawn only with a mechanical aid. Christian Europe at first viewed the weapon as morally ambiguous. A widely perceived diabolical nature was illustrated by placing crossbows in daemons' hands in illuminated manuscripts. At Toulouse cathedral daemon gargoyles were sculpted as having trouble drawing crossbows, which at least got part of the tale right. This early sense that the crossbow was inherently evil led to its condemnation in 1096 by Pope Urban II. The ban was reiterated by the Second Lateran Council (1139). As with most measures of moral condemnation of highly useful and richly rewarding things, these grand proscriptions had no effect: by the end of the 12th century the crossbow was in wide use as both an offensive and defensive weapon, especially in sieges: Richard I ("Coeur de Lion") was mortally wounded by a crossbowmen while conducting a siege in Limousin. In light of the weapon's popularity the ban was subsequently eased to permit use against Muslims and heretics and in all wars deemed "just" by the Church.

Early Muslim crossbows encountered by the Crusaders were shorter, composite types held together with hammered sinew from the neck of oxen, and glue made from boiled fish bladders. The "Frankish crossbow" used by the Crusaders was more powerful and greatly impressed Muslims who encountered it in battle. As crossbows became more powerful a "goat's foot lever" or rack-and-pinion device was used to draw them. Starting in the late 14th century crossbows were made from tempered steel that made them more powerful as well as lighter. Steel also gave the crossbow a draw weight of over 1,000 pounds, which compelled adoption of a *windlass* to arm the weapon which in turn slowed down the rate of fire from perhaps four shots per minute to just two. Modern experiments have shown that steel crossbows could penetrate heavy plate armor from as far away as 350 yards, though at such extreme ranges accuracy was problematic. By the 15th century there were two major types of crossbow in use. The "arbaleste" was mainly deployed in Western Europe. It used either a claw ("graffle") to draw the bow, or a pulley system, with more powerful models using a windlass. A different type was found mainly in Central Europe and among the Swiss, who employed a windlass called a *"cranequin"* to draw the string. For all types, both hands were needed to span the bow and load the quarrel or bolt. Modern experiments have achieved quite rapid rates of fire, up to six bolts per minute where two to four was earlier thought by historians to be the maximum. Such a high rate of fire would have been utterly exhausting in battle, however, and would not have permitted proper aiming.

Crossbows were also widely used in war on the water, particularly in *galley* fighting in the Mediterranean. One highly specialized naval crossbow fired a crescent-headed bolt designed to tear up the rigging and sails of ships. Some Italians became so adept with the weapon they were prized as specialized mercenaries and hired out to armies all over Europe. Many Genoese and Pisans, especially, made their fortunes fighting for the kings of France. They were used to break up enemy ranks prior to the traditional charge of French heavy horse. In all-Italian wars crossbowmen were shielded by *pavisare* while they reloaded, a practice made necessary by the weapon's slow rate of fire and the need to use both hands to draw the string or wind the windlass. The later *Swiss square* incorporated crossbowmen behind the front ranks of pikers, and at times deployed mounted archers as scouts and skirmishers. They would dismount to fight in front of the *Vorhut* (van) before melting into it for protection as it closed with the enemy. Hungarian and Provençal forces also mounted some crossbowmen.

It is probable that the penetrating power of the crossbow is what forced a shift from mail to plate armor during the 13th–14th centuries. A great advantage of the crossbow was the fact it did not require men to be born to arms: the ease with which commoners were trained to use crossbows made it superior even to the longbow, which was harder both to make and master. Also, heavy defensive crossbows could shoot large quarrels with far heavier heads than the longbow could manage, especially once crossbows were made from steel instead of bone and wood. The steel crossbow dominated battlefield and siege archery in continental armies even after the proven success of the longbow during the *Hundred Years' War* (1337–1453), and was not finally displaced until the advent of truly effective muskets, departing most battlefields by about 1550. Some later crossbows were built to shoot bullets instead of quarrels, but outside of the German *Schnepper* and some sporting weapons, this idea did not find its way to the battlefield. See also *arbalétriers*; *arceri*; *armories*; *balistarii equites*; *crossbow à croc*; *crossbow à jalet*; *equites*; *goat's foot lever*; *graffle*.

Suggested Reading: Jim Bradbury, *The Medieval Archer* (1985).

crossbow à croc. A crossbow mounted on a wooden rest or support to aid in aiming and firing.

crossbow à jalet. An adaptation of the traditional crossbow that permitted it to fire stones or small lead balls.

cross-staff. Also called "Jacob's staff." A portable astronomical instrument used in maritime navigation. It was probably invented in the early 14th century by a Jewish scholar from Provence, Levi ben Gershon (1288–1344). The cross-staff assessed distance via trigonometry by measuring angles formed by lines drawn to two distant points that diverged along the central line-of-sight of the instrument. Latitude was estimated by measuring the elevation of the noon sun above the horizon, adjusted in accordance with navigational tables that related the varying inclination of the Earth's axis by time of year. The "back-staff" was a later model cross-staff that measured from a target, which allowed the user to avoid looking directly into the sun. The cross-staff was used at sea until it was surpassed as a distance-estimator by invention of the telescope.

crouching tiger. A compact, short-range Chinese cannon, no more than two feet long. It had no carriage. Instead, it could be carried on horseback or even by a man (it weighed under 50 pounds). It was fired from the ground, to which it was staked with iron pegs and hoops. It mostly fired *grapeshot*, a favorite Chinese anti-personnel ammunition.

crownwork. In fortification, an outwork made with two full *bastions* connected to each other by a curtain, and to the main *enceinte* by parallel joining walls. It secured advantageous ground that lay outside the enceinte.

cruising. Warship patrols in the modern sense were not possible during most of this period, mainly due to deficiencies in ship design that required large crews on small ships (this was especially true of *galleys*), which placed absolute logistical limits on long-distance "cruising." Most navigation hugged the coasts in the medieval period and even into early modern times. That meant galleys were the principal ship type used in coastal patrols in closed or nearly closed seas, such as the Mediterranean and Caribbean. Long-range oceanic cruising, whether as *convoy* escort or *privateer*, became feasible only with development of the *galleon* in the 16th century. At first cruising was sharply limited by shipboard diseases born of prolonged exposure to bad food and water in confined conditions, and vitamin deficiency (scurvy) whose effects were felt after much time was spent at sea, which had not been a problem before. Fast *frigates* improved on galleons and cut back on disease by shortening journeys; and a preventive for scurvy, lime juice, was eventually discovered.

crupper. Large plate armor that protected the rear half of a *warhorse*; introduced in Europe in the mid-15th century.

Crusades. The motivations behind the Crusades, which occupied over 200 years of Latin interaction with the Islamic world of the Middle East, were deep and complex. They included economic pressures born of a growing European population and renewed prosperity, regional competition arising from a revival of long dormant trade within the Mediterranean, and the alternately politically shrewd and spiritually sincere movement behind the *Treuga Dei*. The Crusades also represented a historic reversal of 600 years of invasions of Europe by Asiatic, Arab, and Viking non-Christian peoples. The shift to offense was at first led by Medieval Christendom's leading warrior-culture, the *Normans*. Later, German knights and the new *Military Orders* played key roles. The Crusades got underway as Western European societies as a whole were moving from hunkered castellan defense against invasion to aggressive territorial expansion in the name of the Christian faith. Crusading also offered alternate careers to members of the warrior classes no longer needed for domestic defense against pagan or Muslim invaders, but whom Europe still strained to maintain through *feudal* social and economic structures. The Crusades thus may have provided a martial and economic release for societies increasingly wealthy and urban, whose populations were rapidly expanding and desirous of internal peace. It would have been shrewd to send away on *"holy war"* the superfluous and dangerous armed men the countryside continued to produce but who were no longer needed for the homeland defense of Christendom. Yet, it would be an error to overemphasize such material motivations, for the Crusades also bespoke an apocalyptic religious tradition, genuine and deep piety, and a mass penitence movement seeking climactic expiation of sin. Thus, scholars note that it is difficult to tell Crusader from Christian pilgrim until about 1200, so mixed were the populations who moved east and so complex were their material, martial, and spiritual motives. This admixture of godly and godawful impulses helped sustain the crusading spirit for 200 years, sending vast amounts of silver east in the form of donations, legacies, and support for individual knights, along with a thinner and inconstant stream of armed monks and other reinforcements.

Crusading was enormously expensive: to outfit and maintain a knight and his mounts, along with his attendants and armed retainers, might take four years' income of a reasonable sized estate. It was crucial, therefore, that crusading was made hugely spiritually attractive by the Church, not least so that it might be self-financing. Several popes, and even more the body of the Church and the Latin Christian people as a whole (*res publica Christiana*), embraced crusading. The pious were granted "remission of sins" as crusading was licensed by the clergy as a form of penance. Indulgences thus went to holy warriors, while the more brutal among them also enjoyed the fact that the *just war* restrictions of the Church were waived for those fighting "infidels." Reinforcing this sense of religious mission and strategically underlying the Crusades was an even older geopolitical antagonism to Muslim power and interruption of Mediterranean trade, a related hatred for corsairs and "pirates" operating from the Muslim emirates of North Africa, and a new antagonism to Islamic revival in Egypt and Anatolia and the consequent military pressure that had brought to bear on fellow Christians, albeit Orthodox, in the *Byzantine Empire*.

The First Crusade was called at the Council of Clermont on November 27, 1095, by Pope Urban II (the "Clermont Appeal"). Its proclaimed aim was to retake Jerusalem from the Muslims, who had held it since their original imperial surge out of Arabia took it away from older communities of Christians (Armenians, Syrians, Nestorians, and others) in 638. It was a fortuitous year to launch a crusade to the Middle East, for the Islamic world was deeply divided politically and in great religious turmoil at the end of the 11th century: Muslim Syria was under prolonged assault by *Seljuk Turks* and the Fatamid Caliphate in Cairo was collapsing into its terminal stage. Medieval Europe, in contrast, was bursting with martial energy, ascendant societies, confident warriors, and aggressive kings. These facts prompted René Grousset to conclude that the First Crusade should be seen as a victory of "French monarchy over Moslem anarchy."

> *It was a fortuitous year to launch a crusade to the Middle East ...*

Or at least, Muslim divisions. Whether or not Grousset overstates the case, the fact was that in 1099 the First Crusade took, then sacked, Jerusalem, where Crusaders mercilessly put to the sword thousands of Muslims, Jews, and even eastern rite Christians, whom they did not recognize as co-religionists or whom they disdained. That atrocity is remembered still in the Middle East, a region with more than its share of recalled horrors. Yet, news of the fall of Jerusalem and the "Holy Land" to the First Crusade was received in the West as an obvious blessing by God of the effort to recover Christian lands lost to "infidel" Islam during that other warrior faith's first *jihad*.

In other words, at the strategic level the Crusades were seen as a counterattack by Christians to recover for Christendom lands lost to the Muslim jihad (just as today many Muslims see attacks on Israel or even Spain as a strategic counterattack against usurpers of part of the historic *Dar al-Islam*). A string of Latin (mainly Norman) principalities was established along the coast, linking Antioch, Edessa, and Tripoli to Jerusalem. Initially, the Muslim response was tepid, as the Islamic world was divided among quarrelsome emirates, rival caliphates, and sectarian factions. In the longer run, however, the greater population and military resource advantages lay with the Muslims. Once the "Franks" (as Crusaders were called by Muslims, who did not distinguish Norman from German or English knights) raided and attacked the heart of Islam in the *Hejaz*, the Muslim world was roused to an outraged military response. On the other hand, the Seljuk state was rising at this time in the north to straddle Iraq and Syria, from Mosul to Damascus. This new power warred with the Latin states over access to Egypt, where the Fatamids were collapsing. These Seljuk wars absorbed most northern Muslim energies in fratricidal conflict.

The Second Crusade (1147–1149) was preached by Bernard of Clairvaux, and called by Pope Eugene III in response to the fall of Edessa to the Muslim warlord Nur al-Din in 1144. A mostly German army was led by Emperor Conrad III, while a discrete French army set out under Louis VII. Each army passed overland through the Byzantine Empire, eating out much of the countryside and pillaging the Christian populations. The Byzantines therefore eagerly agreed to provided ships to take the Crusaders to Asia Minor (and thereby, out of their Empire). Once in the Holy Land the Germans were met in battle by a Turkic force against which they fared badly. This induced them to join with the French. This joint army assaulted Damascus in July 1148, but could not take it, in part because of treason by jealous knights resident in the Holy Land. The two kings left for home having accomplished nothing of lasting significance except uniting Muslim Syria against the Latins and irreparably harming Frankish military prestige. Nur al-Din seized effective control of "Fatamid Egypt" in 1168. Jerusalem remained in Frankish hands, as the "Latin Kingdom of Jerusalem," until 1187. That year the great *Salāh-al-Dīn*, successor to Nur al-Din (who died in 1174) and Sultan of all Egypt and Syria, destroyed a Latin army at Hattin (July 4, 1187) in Galilee and recaptured Jerusalem for Islam (October 2, 1187). A Third Crusade (1188–1192) was proclaimed and three Western armies set out to retake the "Holy City," led by three great kings: Richard I (Coeur de Lion) of England; Philip II (Augustus) of France; and Friedrich I (Barbarossa) of Germany. The Germans never arrived, Emperor Friedrich having drowned en route in Asia Minor. The Anglo-French armies arrived separately and never fully joined forces. Still, they recaptured Acre in 1191 after Richard's fleet defeated a Muslim navy. (The only other major naval battle of the Crusades was in 1123, when a Venetian fleet defeated the Fatamid navy off Ascalon.) Salāh-al-Dīn asked that Muslim civilians be spared, but Richard massacred men, women, and children. The Crusaders were unable to capture Jerusalem in two attempts, one of which fell short by just 12 miles. Philip returned to France later in 1191 and made war on Richard's possessions. Richard left for home the next year after agreeing to a treaty with Salāh-al-Dīn and selling Cyprus to the Templars.

Several small Crusader kingdoms survived for awhile in the Levant, while others took root on Malta, Rhodes, and Cyprus under the Military Orders.

But the Latin states had lost their defensible borders and stood now as isolated, vulnerable outposts surrounded by larger hostile populations. Reinforcements declined in wake of the failure of the Third Crusade to recover Jerusalem. The Fourth Crusade (1204) never even made it to the Holy Land, instead diverting to Constantinople where it overthrew the Orthodox emperors and sacked the city. A Latin kingdom was set up in Constantinople that lasted from 1204 to 1261. The Fifth Crusade (1217–1221) was recruited heavily among French knights, but it too failed to achieve lasting results. Emperor Friedrich II crusaded in 1228 and secured Christian access to Jerusalem to 1244, when it fell to a Khorasmian assault. Louis IX ("St. Louis") led the Sixth Crusade in 1248–1250, to Egypt. He fared badly, was captured and held, literally, for a "king's ransom." He returned at the head of the Seventh Crusade (1267–1270), this time attacking Tunis. Again he failed, and this time also died. Two years earlier the Latin Kingdom of Antioch surrendered to the Muslims. In 1289, Tripoli reverted to Berber control and in 1291 Acre fell, ending the era of Crusader states in the Holy Land.

Muslim counterattacks had worn down outlying Crusader states and finally drove the Military Orders to island refuges in the eastern Mediterranean. Conflicts in Europe kept potential Crusaders at home to contest for power in the fractured West. As reinforcements thinned, women donned armor and fought in Crusader garrison defense and field battles. Chronic shortages of men also forced the Crusader states to hunker down inside massive fortifications and pursue a strictly defensive strategy. Few pitched battles were fought toward the end of this long religious war, as for Muslim and Christian alike raiding became both the dominant and preferred mode of warfare. Moreover, both sides faced a new, common threat: the *Mongols*. Mongol invasions of Syria and Palestine did not unite local Muslims and Christians, however. Instead, they were mutually distracted and weakened. The Crusader states thus barely held on after the Third Crusade. Ultimately, their isolation, lack of reinforcements, and greater Muslim population and superior resources led to their demise. The era of crusades to the Middle East ended in military failure in the Holy Land and with secular depression of Europe's population and economy during the 14th century, partly as a result of the *Black Death*. Their principal legacy was not territorial conquest or new military skills learned from distant enemies. It was development of capabilities of military bureaucracy in their home states in the West, where an enormous effort was made to organize, transport, feed and supply over huge distances, large expeditions and campaigns that lasted more than two centuries. It would not be the last time Europe displayed unique, though not necessarily admirable, martial qualities: the Crusades provided an early logistical training ground for later expansion of European empires and global military dominance after 1500.

Christian offensives against Muslims outside the core Holy Lands were more successful than the campaigns in the Middle East. Castilian Crusaders overran the Muslim *taifa* states of Iberia in a *"Reconquista"* that was part crusade and part migration that lasted from the 8th century to the fall of Granada in 1492. The zealous religious impulses and material greed that underlay the Reconquista influenced Spanish policy for another 150 years, sustaining fanatic military opposition to the *Protestant Reformation* and driving conquest and conversion of the Americas and parts of Asia. Southern Russia and Ukraine, where Orthodox Kievan Rus had flourished before falling to Mongol and Tatar armies, was also "recovered" from Islam by a martial spirit of crusade that animated Muscovy. The language of "holy war" still coursed in Russian foreign policy and propaganda toward Central Asian emirates in the 19th century, and about the Ottoman Empire into the early 20th century. The *Teutonic Knights* and *Livonian Order* forcibly converted or exterminated and expropriated the lands of pagan tribes residing in Prussia and around the Baltic coast. (Centuries later, Crusader talk recurred among German invaders of the Soviet Union in a perverse Nazified-Christian form in 1941, recalling in tones of fascist romanticism prior eastern crusades that were also genocidal invasions of Slavic lands.) The *Albigensian Crusade* in France was fought simultaneously with the Fifth Crusade to the Holy Land, to suppress heresy. Smaller "crusades" were proclaimed by popes to punish personal and excommunicate enemies in Italy. On the other side of the ledger, in 1453 the Ottomans captured Constantinople and in general brought a muted form of Muslim "holy war," the jihad, into eastern and southern Europe.

A lasting irony attending the Crusades is that the war with the Latin states in the Holy Land was ultimately won by the Muslims, many of whom never forgot or forgave the "infidel" Christian intrusion into the Dar al-Islam. Yet, the Crusades were largely ignored or forgotten in the West even while still underway, as Europeans turned to fight each other with greater intensity culminating in fratricidal wars of religion over fractures in their once common faith in the 16th–17th centuries. See also *Assassins*; *cruzada*; *Cyprus*; *Hospitallers*; *Hussite Wars*; *Inquisition*; *jihad*; *just war tradition*; *Knights Templar*; *Lithuania, Grand Duchy of*; *Livonian Order*; *Mamlūks*; *Nicopolis, Battle of*; *Northern War, First*; *Rhodes, Siege of (1444)*; *Rhodes, Siege of (1479–1480)*; *Rhodes, Siege of (1522–1523)*; *turcopoles*; *Varna, Battle of*.

Suggested Reading: E. Christiansen, *The Northern Crusades* (1980); J. France, *Western Warfare in the Age of the Crusades* (1999); Carole Hillenbrand, *Crusades: Islamic Perspectives* (2000); P. M. Holt, *Age of the Crusades* (1986); T. Madden, *Concise History of the Crusades* (1999); Hans Mayer, *The Crusades* (trans. and rev. ed., 1988); Jonathon Riley-Smith, *The Crusades* (1990) and *A History of the Crusades* (2000); Jonathon Riley-Smith, ed., *Oxford History of the Crusades* (1999).

cruzada. A special tax on Spanish clergy and laity permitted by the pope to finance the *Reconquista* against the Moors of Granada. After 1492 it remained in place, providing the Spanish monarchy as much revenue as it gleaned from the silvermining of its American empire.

cuartel general. An agreement on exchanges of *prisoners of war* first signed by Spain and the Dutch rebels in 1599 and reissued periodically after that. It stipulated that ransom of all prisoners should occur within 25 days of capture. Prisoners were exchanged by rank, with higher officers also requiring cash ransoms. In 1637 its terms were published in English. Two years later it was also adopted between Spain and France.

cuirass. An armored breastplate with or without matching back piece. It was originally made of *cuir-bouilli*, later of iron and early steel. The breastplate alone was sometimes called a "half-cuirass." See also *byrnie*.

cuirassier. A term for the new type of *"heavy cavalry"* that appeared in Europe during the *Thirty Years' War* (1618–1648). They were lightly armored, often wearing just a helmet and cuirass, but rode a larger mount. They were distinguished from fully armored mounted *knights* and *lancers* or *dragoons*. The latter were even more lightly armored, often wearing just a helmet, and they rode small ponies or nags, rarely a true *warhorse*.

cuir-bouilli. A form of early *plate armor* in the 13th century, made not from metal but of leather hardened by cooking in wax or oil, shaped to fit, then dried.

cuisses (*cuissart*). Plate armor for the thighs.

cuius regio eius religio. "Whosoever controls the territory decides the religion." See also *Augsburg, Peace of*; *Prague, Peace of*; *reservatum ecclesiaticum*; *Westphalia, Peace of*.

culebrina. See *culverin*.

cultellus. A large, dagger-like infantry weapon whose principal use was to kill unhorsed cavalry.

culverin. French "coulverine," Spanish "culebrina." The types of gunpowder weapons covered by this term varied greatly. The main usage referred to cannon, but a secondary meaning was small firearms that evolved into the first handguns (coulverines à main). These fired lead rather than stone or iron shot. Even concerning *artillery* alone, the term was used for guns of greatly varying and imprecise sizes, including light guns less than three feet long with bores as small as one inch (*esmeril*, *demi-saker*, *falcon*, *falconet*, *minion*, *pasavolante*, and *serpentine*). Some early types were small, firing 1/3-pound shot 200 yards or less. Others were medium-sized guns that could throw 6- to 9-pound shot several thousand yards, though just one-tenth that distance with any accuracy or power. The largest were capable of hurling 32-pound stone or iron balls several thousand yards with moderate accuracy. In time, "culverin" came to mean fairly large and long, thick-barreled guns designed to throw shot accurately at extended ranges. The French carted two "coulverines" to *Formigny*, one of the last battles of the *Hundred Years' War* (1337–1453).

Culverins were useful in sieges to hammer walls and provide covering fire for engineers, sappers, and military laborers engaged in digging or infantry guarding approaches and mines. A hundred years later culverins were the main gun used in war at sea, as long-range chase weapons or ship-smashers that could cripple a ship if fired broadside at close range. In the early 16th century one type of naval culverin was standardized at a caliber of 140mm. It fired *solid shot* or specialized ordnance up to 8 kilogram in weight. By the start of the 17th century "culverin" described a gun 11–12 feet long, that could shoot 18-pound shot to an effective range of 1,700 yards and a maximum range of 6,500. A "culverin-bastard" was a 9-foot gun that fired 12-pound shot an effective range of 600 yards and a maximum range of 4,000. A "demi-culverin" ("media culebrina" or "*culverin-moyenne*") was also nearly 9 feet long, but fired 10-pound shot to a greater effective range, 850 yards, and a maximum range of 5,000 yards. The "culverin-royal" was the monster of the class at many tons deadweight and 16 feet in length. It could hurl 32-pound shot with reasonable accuracy and great effect to 2,000 yards, and had an impressive maximum range of 7,000 yards. Never before had killing been possible at such distances. See also *artillery*; *gunpowder weapons*; *hackbut*; *Invincible Armada*.

culverin-bastard. See *culverin*.

culverin-moyenne. See *culverin*.

culverin-royal. See *culverin*.

curtain wall. In permanent fortified defenses, the straight outer wall formed by the *rampart*. In early works the curtain wall might be uninterrupted except for the town or castle gate. In later times, it was divided into sections by *bastions* and towers. See also *casement*; *castles, on land*; *fortification*.

Cyprus. A *Crusader* kingdom was set up on Cyprus by the *Hospitallers* after the island fell to Richard I of England. They were later joined by the *Templars*, until their Order was persecuted to extinction. In 1364, Cyprus and Rhodes mounted an expedition that sacked and butchered the population of *Alexandria*. The *Mamlūks* struck back in 1426, razing Nicosia and forcing the Cypriots into vassalage. In 1440 the Hospitallers agreed to neutrality in the religious wars of the eastern Mediterranean, leaving Rhodes as the last Crusader outpost. Cyprus became a forward commercial and naval base for Venice in 1489. In July 1570, an Ottoman fleet landed 50,000 invaders who overran the island and besieged an isolated garrison (7,000 men) at Famagusta. Christians in Europe made Crusader-like noises, but sent no relief. Famagusta surrendered on August 3, 1571, whereupon its governor and a few others were murdered by the victors. See also *Lepanto, Battle of (October 7, 1571)*.

Czasniki, Battle of (1564). See *Ivan IV*; *Northern War, First*.

D

dag. English slang for a stubby, short-range pistol commonly wielded by light cavalry.

daggers. Early medieval daggers were little more than iron spikes on handles of wood or bone. Their principal use was to punch through armor in close quarter fighting among knights. Or they were plunged into gaps between armor plates and mail protections, usually at the neck, armpit, or groin. Daggers went by names such as ballock, basilard, and rondel, none of which were uniform in design. See also *Assassins*; *cultellus*; *gomeres*; *main-gauche*; *misericord*; *Schweizerdolch*; *stiletto*.

daimyo. "great names." The *feudal* lords of Japan, the great barons who controlled the countryside; not emasculated court nobles ("kuge"). Late medieval daimyo ("shugo") were displaced by regional warlords ("Sengoku daimyo") during the *Sengoku jidai* era. These men exercised enormous power over peasants and household *samurai*, and were effectively independent of emperors and shoguns alike. Among the most important were the Hōjō, Usegi, and Takeda in central Japan; the Ouicha and Mori of western Japan; the Otomo and Ryuzoji on Kyushu; the powerful Shimazu of the south, and the Arima of the Shimabara peninsula. All these and many more were destroyed or coerced into submission by the end of the *Unification Wars*, leaving *Oda Nobunaga*, *Toyotomi Hideyoshi*, and *Tokugawa Ieyasu* as Japan's military hegemons. Subsequently, the daimyo were tamed and remained subservient for over 250 years under the *bakufu* and Tokugawa shoguns.

Danubian principalities. Moldavia and Wallachia, which stood astride the strategic mouth of the Danube River. In the 13th century they were overrun by the Ottoman Empire.

Danzig. This great Pomeranian city (population 50,000 by 1600) was a key entrepôt in the Baltic grain and other trades, and a leading member of the *Hanse.* During the *"War of the Cities"* (1454–1466) it appealed to Poland, with which it had ancient ties predating the Teuton conquest, for help in throwing off the economic yoke of the *Teutonic Knights.* Its small but powerful navy defeated a combined Danish-Teutonic war fleet at *Bornholm* (1457). Danzig then accepted a Polish alliance and garrison. From inside its walls Polish troops and Danziger militia sortied to defeat the Teutonic Knights at *Swiecino* (1462). Danzig was annexed to Poland, becoming its major Baltic outlet under terms of the *Second Peace of Torun* (October 19, 1466). In 1576 Danzig rejected the election of *Stefan Báthory* as king of Poland and invited Denmark to support its rebellion. Bathory blockaded Danzig without much success. The city hired mercenaries who helped it push Báthory's army away from its walls. The next year, agreement was reached on autonomy for Danzig in exchange for payment of annual tribute to Poland.

Dar al-Harb. "Realm of War" or, literally, "Realm of the Sword." In *Islam*, all territory not occupied or ruled by Muslims. For militant Muslims the term implied that, in the fullness of time, it would be. The idea dated to the original era of Islamic expansion in the first century after the death of the Prophet Muhammad. Over time, its more aggressive implications faded. It is doubtful, for instance, that later Ottoman armies were inspired by fierce religious zeal more than they were by common material desires and interests.

Dar al-Islam. "Realm of the Faithful" (Submission), or "Abode of Islam." All territory occupied or ruled by Muslims that must be defended against reversion to pagan or non-Muslim control. The Christian *Crusades*, seen in the West as a strategic counterattack to recover the birthplace of the Christian faith overrun by Muslim invaders in the 7th–8th centuries, were thus viewed by Muslims as an invasion of a region divinely ordained for Muslim rule, as evidenced by the fact that they ruled it.

dastana. See *armor.*

Day of the Barricades (May 12, 1588). In the midst of the eighth of the *French Civil Wars* (1562–1629), the long-simmering dispute between *Henri III*'s Royalists and the *Catholic League* came to a head. Angry over Henri's move of 4,000 Swiss guards to Paris, for his own protection, and bestowal of titles and riches on court favorites ("mignons"), the Committee of *The Sixteen* set in motion a long-planned coup d'état. Paris rallied to this revolt against a despised king, spurred on by rising food prices and recent battlefield misfortunes and losses. Fearing a royal massacre akin to the *St. Bartholomew's Day Massacres* of 1572, only this time of Catholics, the population of Paris erected barricades and took up arms. This caused Henri to waver as he waited pensively in the Louvre. By the time he decided to act it was too late: Paris had gone over to the League. The king fled the city in haste and disguise, leaving Paris under the control of the radical, even revolutionary, bourgeois Committee of The Sixteen. Paris greeted *Henri Guise*, who did not fully embrace the radical agenda of The Sixteen, with wild acclaim. The low point of the monarchy was reached and the Catholic side in the civil wars fatally divided. Next came Henri III's murder of Guise, followed by his own assassination shortly thereafter.

deadmen's eyes. See *rigging*.

dead-pays. Imaginary private soldiers credited to the roster of a company or regiment so that the captain could collect their wages, sometimes for company use but most often for himself. While this was one way of compensating officers, it meant that few units ever mustered at their paper strength. As many as five or six dead-pays per 100 men was not uncommon. The dead-pay "system" was normal for most armies in early modern Europe, from England to Poland. Similarly, in the Ottoman Army dead *Janissaries* were kept on the roll by comrades in order for Corp members to collect their much-valued *esame* (pay tickets). See also *choragiew*; *dziesietniks*; *Haiduks*; *rotmistrz*.

dead reckoning. Estimating the position of a ship without benefit of instruments or astronomical observations by calculating how far the ship had drifted or sailed, on what course, from the known port of departure. See also *astrolabe*; *compass*; *cross-staff*.

Declaratio Ferdinandei. A commitment made by Catholic negotiators prior to final agreement on the *Peace of Augsburg* (1555) permitting Lutheran cities or knights to continue in the reformed faith if they had practiced it for some time. See also *reservatum ecclesiaticum*.

"Defenestration of Prague" (1419). Radical Czech priests, furious over the betrayal and judicial murder of *Jan Hus*, led an angry mob to the center of Prague where they threw seven despised members of the Town Council out a high window to fall to their deaths on paving stones below, or onto the pikes of the town militia. This proved to be the opening act in the *Hussite Wars* between Bohemia and the Holy Roman Empire and Catholic Church.

"Defenestration of Prague" (May 23, 1618). Imperial regents representing Austrian Archduke and future Holy Roman Emperor Ferdinand of Styria (later, *Ferdinand II*), a known Catholic fanatic, met with Bohemian Protestant leaders at Hradein (Hradshin) Castle in Prague. The Protestants, led by Count *Matthias Thurn*, engaged in heated argument with the regents, accusing them of abusing the rights of the Bohemian *Estates*. The confrontation in fact had been planned months in advance, to set up murders of the seven regents. Their deaths would shut the door on compromise with Ferdinand, who had in 1617 shut the leading Protestants out in a stage-managed coronation as king-designate of Bohemia. In turn, that would give him the Imperial crown upon the death of Emperor Matthias. Thurn denounced two of the bluntest regents, William Slavata and Jaroslav Martinic, as traitors and had them and their secretary thrown out a high window, or "defenestrated," whence they landed in a pile of dung and debris that filled Hradein's dry moat. A Protestant mob waiting to complete the murders instead collapsed in applause and laughter. That allowed the regents to escape with their lives, albeit with their Imperial dignity badly stained. Catholic propagandists portrayed their survival as a miracle, circulating prints showing them borne up by angels or the Virgin Mary. Protestant propagandists replied with prints that showed the regents arriving at the dung heap, which grew in malodorous size which each retelling and printing. With this quasi-comic incident Bohemia and Austria started Europe down the road to a general war that ended laughter on all sides. For also left in the dung was any chance for agreement that Ferdinand should be named king of Bohemia. And that was a title he was determined to have, since Bohemia held the decisive vote among the seven *Kurfürsten* in the Imperial Diet who selected the emperor.

> *A Protestant mob waiting to complete the murders instead collapsed in applause and laughter.*

The "Defenestration of Prague" thus signaled the revolt of Bohemia, a kingdom with a tradition of bitter dissent against Catholic orthodoxy and Imperial rule dating to the *Hussite Wars*. Thurn and the rebels offered the crown to any prince of Protestantism prepared to defend Bohemia against the Habsburgs. Most demurred, unwilling to face the military might of Austria and Spain. The challenge was finally accepted by 22-year-old *Friedrich V*, Elector Palatine. He raised a small Protestant army, engaged several minor allies, and marched to Bohemia to accept the crown. After a brief flurry of Bohemian offensive action toward Vienna, Spain and Austria were joined by Bavaria and other south German Catholic estates in marching a large coalition army into Bohemia. The decisive clash came at the *White Mountain* (November 8, 1620), where the rebels were crushed. Friedrich was cast out of Bohemia and into history as the "Winter King," whose reign had lasted but a year, to melt with the spring thaw. The great German war which followed was so devastating it is recalled still for unusual barbarity, ideological ferocity, and physical destruction: the flames of rebellion and religious war overleaped all diplomatic fire lines, to roar up the Rhine and burn out Friedrich's Palatinate. From there it fanned out, to lick the walls of fortified Protestant cities in Denmark, the United Provinces, and Germany. In the end, all the Great Powers of Europe were engulfed. Thus from a constitutional ember grew the conflagration of three decades of general war in Europe. See also *Thirty Years' War*; *Uzkok War*.

defilade. In *fortification*, any position or works providing protection against flank or enfilading fire.

Delhi, Sack of (1398). See *Delhi Sultanate*; *Panipat, Battle of (December 17, 1398)*; *Timur*.

Delhi Sultanate (c.1200–1526). The original Muslim sultanate in India. The universal claim of its title notwithstanding, it was but one of several Muslim Indian kingdoms. It was ruled by the Khalji dynasty, then the Saiyids, and finally the Lodi dynasty. It was attacked by *Timur*, but survived a massive defeat at *Panipat* (1398) and the sack of Delhi. It was finally overthrown by *Babur*, who founded the *Mughal Empire* on its ruins. See also *Gujarat*; *Panipat, Battle of (April 21, 1526)*.

demi-bastion. An outwork, a half-bastion with only one face and flank. See also *hornwork*.

demi-cannon. A 16th-century gun weighing about 4,000 pounds that fired 32-pound shot to an effective range of 450 yards and a maximum range of 2,500. See also *cannon*; *cañon*.

demi-culverin. Spanish: "media culebrina." From the later 16th century, a type of cannon that could hurl 10-pound shot to an effective range of 850 yards and a maximum range of 5,000 yards. See also *culverin*.

demi-lancers. French: "launciers." A type of English light-to-medium cavalry, sporting more armor and weapons and riding bigger horses than true *light cavalry*, but not as slow or cumbersome as older *heavy cavalry*. An innovation of the 16th century and forerunner to *Roundhead* cavalry of the 17th, they discarded leg armor in favor of leather boots, dispensed with lower back armor in favor of a cuirass, and discarded *helms* in preference for soft hats. Many favored *wheel lock* pistols as a supplement to their primary weapon, the "demi-lance" or short-staffed lance.

demi-lune. In *fortification*, an outwork (detached) *bastion* in shape of a crescent—hence the name—protecting a section of the *curtain wall*.

demi-saker. *Minion.* A medium caliber gun that fired 6-pound shot to an effective range of 450 yards and a maximum lobbing range of 3,500 yards. See also *saker*.

demurrage. Payment made (or only promised) to ship owners when a ship was detained beyond an agreed date upon being *impressed* into the service of the king. See also *Cinque Ports*.

Denmark. Denmark tried to force Sweden into a more unitary monarchy than was envisioned in the *Union of Kalmar*, but lost badly at Brunkeberg (1471). Sweden formally broke away in 1523, under *Gustavus I*. Denmark remained hostile to Sweden's independence. It had a great advantage since it controlled both sides of the *Baltic Sound* and all toll revenue on passing ships—including *Hanse*, Dutch, and English vessels—plying the rich trade between the Baltic and the Atlantic and Mediterranean ports of Europe. Denmark rose in prominence and became a significant naval power when the Oldenburg dynasty built a large fleet of warships. It overreached, however, in laying specious claim to a *Dominum Maris Baltici*. The Danes also failed to enforce tolls on the Archangel route, which they based on claims to the Faroes and Iceland. During the 16th century the Danish elite converted to *Lutheranism*. Denmark stayed out of the war between *Charles V* and the *Schmalkaldic League* (1546–1547), but fought the *Nordic Seven Years' War* (1563–1570) with Sweden. As a result of the *First Northern War* (1558–1587), under Frederick II (1559–1596), Denmark retained supremacy in the Baltic and even gained some island territories.

Danish soldiers were assigned to farms in an "allotment system" ("Tidelning"). They lived on and worked these farms as tenants in peacetime. If Denmark was attacked its kings could exercise their right of "Opbud" to call up emergency levies. This was the constitutional right of the kings of Denmark to raise militia levies (one man in every five) to defend the realm when it came under attack. However, this right did not extend to any of the king's wars fought for aggressive ends beyond the recognized borders of the kingdom, which is why *Christian IV* was forced to wage his aggressive wars, and pay for them, not as the Danish king but in his capacity as Duke of Holstein. The Danish infantry conscription system was known as "Udskrivning" ("Registration"). For cavalry, Denmark relied on the *Rostjeneste*.

Denmark enjoyed sustained maritime hegemony in part due to Sweden's protracted dynastic struggle with Poland-Lithuania, lasting into the 17th century. Denmark was permanently knocked from its perch of great power pretension by the foolhardy decision of Christian IV to intervene in the *Thirty Years' War*. From 1625 to 1629, the so-called "Danish Phase" of that conflict, Danish and Protestant arms suffered a series of unmitigated defeats, even though by 1629 Christian was able to raise 22,000 troops from Denmark, 6,000 in Norway, and 19,000 from Schleswig. No effective Protestant coalition formed around Christian, and after four years of fighting which devastated north Germany and lower Denmark, the Danes were beaten into submission. When war threatened again in 1637–1641, Denmark raised its first ever peacetime army: 16,500 Danes, 6,500 Norwegians, and 11,000 Holstein mercenaries. Altogether with the Rostjeneste, this represented a standing army of 40,000 men in 1642. The Danes were quiet during the climax of the confessional wars in Europe, only venturing into another brief and disastrous conflict in *Torstensson's War*.

Suggested Reading: Paul Lockhart, *Denmark in the Thirty Years' War, 1618–1648* (1996); S. Oakley, *War and Peace in the Baltic, 1560–1790* (1992).

Derbençi. "Pass guards." Ottoman auxiliaries specializing in mountain warfare. They were first recruited in the 15th century among subject Greek, Kurdish, and Tatar populations. They were basically civilians given a semi-military, specialized function. As guns became available the central government tried to stop the Derbençi from acquiring them, fearing rebellion. This policy did not survive the acquisition of firearms by mountain bandits, against whom the Ottomans opposed the Derbençi at minimal cost.

desertion. Desertion was a chronic problem for all armies in this period. Although especially pronounced among infantry serving under compulsion, feudal nobility was also prone to "desert" once their obligation under the *servitium debitum* ran out. Or they might just run, if battle loomed or turned out badly, as when a third of the French cavalry at *Poitiers* (1356) rode from the field without engaging the enemy. English armies suffered high desertion rates in wars in Wales and Scotland, where walking or riding home was relatively easy. There were fewer desertions during the *Hundred Years' War* due to the difficulty of transport back to England, but more because that was at first a popular and profitable war. Garrisons were prone to desertion from want of pay, hunger, or bribery, so that control of whole frontiers might change without combat. English troops in the Netherlands during the *Eighty Years' War* were especially guilty of this. Numerous battles turned partly on the number of troops who deserted in advance. The usual cause of desertion was lack of pay and food. Outside the Dutch and Ottoman armies where pay was plentiful and regular, most troops in this period could expect pay to be several months, and sometimes even several years, in arrears. Withholding pay was sometimes used as an incentive to keep contract armies in the field, but this risked mass desertion or mutiny. See also *Agnadello, Battle of*; *Ankara, Battle of*; *Arques, Battle of*; *Articles of War*; *Dunbar, Battle of*; *fitna*; *Edgehill, Battle of*; *English Civil Wars*; *French Army*; *French Civil Wars*; *impressment*; *Kildare Rebellion*; *La Rochelle*; *Laupen, Battle of*; *Mansfeld, Count Ernst Graf von*; *Mary Stuart, Queen of Scots*; *military discipline*; *Ming Army*; *Mookerheyde, Battle of*; *Nancy, Battle of*; *Nine Years' War*; *Nördlingen, First Battle of*; *Panipat, Battle of (April 21, 1526)*; *Polish Army*; *Prévôt des maréchaux*; *Provost*; *reformadoes*; *Rhodes, Siege of (1479–1480)*; *Rhodes, Siege of (1522–1523)*; *Teutonic Knights, Order of*; *Thirty Years' War*; *uniforms*; *Wars of the Roses*.

Deshima. This small (600' × 200') artificial island in Nagasaki harbor was reserved to foreigners, in order to limit their contact with Japanese. It was prepared for the Portuguese in 1636 but given to the Dutch *Vereenigde Oostindische Compaagnie* (VOC), which was ordered to move there from Hirudo in 1641. Until the late *Tokugawa* era the Dutch were the only Europeans allowed in Japan. Only the VOC factor could leave Deshima and then solely to perform a required annual ceremonial visit to the Imperial Court at Edo. For the Tokugawa, trade with the Dutch was relatively unimportant. Deshima was more valued for its window of key intelligence on the outside world and the access it permitted to European military technology. Nearby was the much larger "Chinese Quarter" of Nagasaki where *Qing* merchants and traders resided and conducted the far more valuable Japanese trade with China and Korea.

Dessau Bridge, Battle of (April 25, 1626). *Graf von Mansfeld* moved south with an army of 12,000 mercenaries intent on finding and defeating *Albrecht von Wallenstein*, the great mercenary general in overall command of Catholic and Imperial forces. Wallenstein knew of Mansfeld's plan and moved faster. With 20,000 men he crossed the Elbe and set up a blocking position before the bridge at Dessau, forcing Mansfeld to attack him. The old man fell into the tactical trap set by Wallenstein, who hid the greater part of his force. When the fight was over nearly one-third of Mansfeld's men were dead. He was driven back to Silesia and died soon afterward, whereupon his contract army dissolved.

destrier. The "magnus equus" or "great horse" of the Middle Ages in Europe that helped give *heavy cavalry* its battlefield preeminence. The name derived from the Anglo-Norman "destrer," which in turn came from the rough Latin "dexterius," or "dexterarius," meaning "right-handed." This large breed was best known across Europe by the French "destrier." First bred in the 12th century, it became the main battle horse of every full-fledged, wealthier *knight*. It was always a stallion, highly spirited, and trained to charge straight toward the enemy. It was led to the fight by hand rather than ridden, being mounted only in training, perhaps in *tournaments*, or for real battle. It was never used for mere transport. The great destriers of the 14th century were huge horses by the standard of the day; probably 16 hands and 1,300 pounds, not the 18 hands sometimes cited, but still 3–4 hands bigger than the average medieval horse. At first these great horses were clad in padded cloth and gaily decorated with personal coats-of-arms. As missile power increased they were given mail trappers. Later, they wore plate armor on their head (chanfron) and chest (peytral). A knight in full armor needed assistance of his attendants to mount a great warhorse (leading to the expression that well-captured a common knightly smugness and assumed superiority, "mount one's high horse"). These large chargers were hugely expensive, costing from 5 to 35 times the price of a hackney, a horse type used solely for transport of men or goods. This meant they were ridden almost exclusively by the great nobles and wealthier knights, but not by the average man-at-arms. They were taken to the Levant on the *Crusades*, where they sometimes succeeded in "shock" defeats of Arab and Turkic armies. But they could be easily blown under heat, which exposed them to Muslim tactics of closing after a failed Crusader charge to fight at close quarters with bows, lance, or sword from fleeter and more maneuverable Arabian mounts. See also *couched lance*; *courser*; *hauberk*; *rouncey*; *warhorses*.

Deulino, Truce of (January 1619). It established a 14-year truce between Poland-Lithuania and Muscovy. Muscovy ceded Smolensk, Seversk, and Chernihiv to Poland.

Deutschorden. "German Order." See *Teutonic Knights, Order of.*

Deutschritter. "German knight." See *knights.*

Deventer, Siege of (1591). See *Maurits of Nassau*.

dévotes/dévots. Devout Catholics who belonged to, or just supported, the *Catholic League* during the protracted *French Civil Wars* (1562–1629), especially after the *Edict of Beaulieu* (1576). Most were petty nobles or bourgeoisie, or monks, nuns, and fanatic laity. Women played a key role in their political and devotional activities. Military and political defeat of the League in 1593–1594 turned dévots away from politics to a renewed concentration on personal piety. Many despised Cardinal *Armand Richelieu* as insufficiently devout, and feared that his anti-Habsburg policy would divide the Catholic world (which was in fact already badly divided) and aid the survival of Protestantism (which it did, but only outside France). Their main foreign sympathies lay with Spain as champion of Catholic causes. They also supported the Habsburgs in Germany, since success for Catholic arms there would help undo the *Edict of Nantes* at home, which was a key goal. However, by the time Richelieu took France into the *Thirty Years' War* on the side of Sweden and against Catholic Spain and the Catholic emperor, the dévots were too internally divided over the acceptability of *Jansenism* to actively oppose the king's war policy. They enjoyed a brief revival of influence at court during the regency of Louis XIV. See also *politiques (France)*.

Devşirme **system.** "Recruitment of Tribute Children." The recruitment system of accepting levies of boy slaves, ages 8 to 20, taken from the Christian villages of the Ottoman Empire starting in the 1390s. The boys were raised as Muslims and either inducted into the *Janissary Corps* or the state bureaucracy. The system may have had origins in a prior Byzantine system which took one-in-five male Slav children as military slaves. In any case, it sustained the Janissaries for two centuries, though it was stopped for several decades after the incursions of *Timur* at the start of the 15th century. *Murad II* revived it in 1438 and it lasted until 1648 (with one last attempt at a European draft in 1703). The formula was one child every five years taken from a set of 40 Christian households with two or more sons, totaling 5,000–8,000 boys per year. In practice, the numbers taken were often smaller, as the state placed a premium on fiscal prudence and worked to keep the Janissary Corps small, with retired or dead Janissaries replaced with caution and care. Devşirme drafts rotated through the rural areas of the Balkans and Christian villages in Anatolia. Most towns and cities were exempt, as what was wanted was healthy, country youths with the stamina for military training and war. The Greek islands were exempt by the treaty terms under which they entered the Empire. Jews were excluded, as were miners needed to dig the metals and minerals required by early modern war. Also exempt were Christian households which performed garrison duty along strategic roads. Christian villages forced to surrender their children initially seethed over this form of

> *The formula was one child every five years taken from a set of 40 Christian households with two or more sons . . .*

tribute. Later, some volunteered children to what was from any peasant's perspective an affluent and desirable future as an elite soldier in the capital. Some Islamic scholars objected to the Devşirme system as a violation of the Koranic proscription against enslavement of the sultan's own subjects, rather than permitted slavery of non-Muslim enemies or prisoners of war. Proponents argued for the spiritual advantage to boys raised as Muslims rather than in a "false faith." In that claim, they used terms strikingly similar to arguments made by Christians who forced conversion of Iberian Muslims (and Jews) after 1492. The system was abolished in the early 18th century.

dey. The title of Ottoman military commanders in Algiers and Tunis. It was an electoral rather than hereditary office, chosen initially from among the local *corsairs*. See also *Barbarossa*; *bey*.

dhal. A Persian-Mughal style of small, round shield. It was made of beaten and polished steel with a small boss in the center, outlined by four or five smaller bosses. Carried in the left hand or on the arm, it was principally used by swordsmen and javelin troops.

dhow. A generic European term for Arab and Iranian sailing vessels, lateen-rigged, which dominated trade and war in the waters between Africa, Arabia, and the Indian subcontinent until the 15th century. They were largely displaced during the 16th century by the arrival of *caravels* and *galleons*.

dice shot. Anti-personnel ammunition comprised of many small, jagged pieces of iron. It was fired from point-blank range from a ship's rail or swivel guns down onto the crew of an enemy ship.

Diet of Worms (1495). See *Maximilian I*.

Diet of Worms (1507). It set out rules governing ranks, rates of pay, and general organization of the Imperial Army and defined the personal staff permitted to a *colonel*.

Diet of Worms (1521). See *Charles V, Holy Roman Emperor*; *Luther, Martin*.

dirlik yememiş. Ottoman troops paid a regular salary from general revenues. If they performed well in battle they might be promoted to payment from *timar* revenue or, in exceptional cases, from a *ziamet*.

Dirshau, Battle of (October 17–18, 1627). The "new model" Swedish army under *Gustavus Adolphus* met the Polish-Lithuanians in another battle for control of Royal Prussia. Gustavus deployed skirmishers to try to lure the Polish cavalry onto his well dug-in musketeers, but the Poles did not budge from their lines. Outnumbered 7,800 to 10,200, the Poles were withdrawing when Gustavus sent in his cavalry in a surprise assault. A hussar counterattack saved the Polish infantry from being pushed into a bog. Depicted by Swedish historians as the first time the new model Swedish cavalry bested Polish hussars at their own game, it is probably more accurate to say that Swedish infantry firepower again proved master of the cavalry charge, which is why the Poles did not attempt one except to counterattack when facing death and defeat in the bog. Gustavus Adolphus was lightly wounded in the neck during the fighting.

discipline. See *military discipline*.

disease. As in all wars prior to the 20th century, death from disease was far more common among soldiers in the medieval and early modern eras than violent death at the hand of enemies in some now-forgotten siege or vaguely remembered battle. In military camps and among itinerant camp followers, pestilence of all kinds bred and spread. Bad food, worse water, lack of simple hygiene, rotten teeth, common respiratory infections, cold weather, damp clothes, and moldy straw beds, all conduced to febrile suffering, infection, and death. And there was plague, of all kinds. The *Black Death* of the mid-14th century carried away so many lives that death appeared as the Grim Reaper, the great harvester of souls who scythed down humans by the bushel without regard for their age, moral quality, or worldly goods and status. Could anything have more unsettled rigid hierarchical societies and old faiths? The suddenness with which epidemic or pandemic disease wiped out sizeable populations could, and often did, have a devastating impact on military operations. In 1524, for instance, 12,000 Swiss heading home from the *Italian Wars* lost no fewer than two-thirds of their complement to an uncertain plague. Three years later, a Habsburg army that had just raped and butchered its way through Rome was nearly wiped out by "camp disease," a generic for any killing fever. The conquest of the Mezoamerican empires of the *Aztec* and *Inca* cannot be understood in the absence of the work of pandemic disease, which was far more devastating to their defenses than any Toledo steel blade or Castilian arquebus or lance wielded by the unwashed conquistadore who unknowingly infected them. Similarly, the English and French conquest of eastern North America was accomplished more by disease than battle, in which the local Indians were usually markedly superior. The fantastic reduction of the Indian population by disease in the 15th century, while immigration swelled the settler population, meant that the *Indian Wars* of the 16th–18th centuries were hugely lopsided and determined more by demographics than combat. On the other hand, while disease in the Americas preempted effective military opposition to European conquest and domination, African diseases blocked Europeans from settlement beyond a handful of coastal enclaves. As one forlorn Portuguese sailor wrote in the late 15th century: "God, in all the entrances of this Ethiopia [Africa] we navigate...has placed a striking angel with a flaming sword who prevents us from penetrating into the interior...whence proceed these rivers of gold."

Matters were, if anything, worse at sea. Dysentery, known to sailors as the "bloody flux," was so commonplace as to be taken for granted as a normal hazard of a sailor's occupation. Not so with scurvy, a much feared disease of longer voyages and then unknown cause, called by sailors "plague of the sea." It was encountered once new ship designs made long-distance sailing possible, thereby extending time spent at sea beyond the reach of fresh fruits and vegetables. Other illness came from food that rotted during months of storage in the bottom of a ship's hold, or from small beer or wine or water gone bad and scummy in green wooden casks. Waves of sickness swept over whole battle fleets, including the *Invincible Armada* of 1588 on its tragic return voyage, wiping out crews and *military discipline* in tandem. The general lack of potable water at sea, the need to relieve bodily functions below decks during storms or heavy swells, unhealthy companionship of livestock and animal offal in a ship's hold, and ignorance of basic hygiene killed the better part of many a crew on privateers, armed merchants, and warships. When new ship designs permitted long-range voyages to the coasts of West Africa, Brazil, or the Caribbean, a tropical stew of strange new diseases was introduced that further ravaged crews without any natural immunity. See also *Indian Wars*; *mourning war*; *Nine Years' War*; *siege warfare*; *Tenochtitlán, Second Siege of*.

Dithmarscher. A medieval levy available to German rulers who wished to raise peasant infantry. A Dithmarscher call up was made as late as 1500 for a war with Denmark.

Diu. See *Portuguese India*.

Diu, Battle of (February 2, 1509). A small fleet of Portuguese ships under Francisco de Almeida used highboard deck cannon to blow a much larger (at least 15,000 men) but low-lying Arab and Indian fleet out of the water. Victory over the combined *Mamlūk* and *Gujarati* galley fleets off Diu enabled the Portuguese to break the Arab-Venetian monopoly on the East Asian *spice trade*. Within a few years Gujarat was eliminated as an Indian Ocean sea power, replaced by Portugal. The victory was so decisive it secured Portuguese control of Indian Ocean trade routes and coastal markets for decades.

divanî hizmet. See *Kapikulu Askerleri*; *sipahis*.

divine fire-arrow. An early, primitive firearm developed in Ming China, though probably dating to the pre-Ming 13th century, made of bronze and firing an arrow over two feet long. See also *Yongle Emperor*.

dolman. See *hussars*.

do-maru. See *armor*.

Dominum Maris Baltici. "Dominion over the Baltic Sea." This was the claimed right and status of the Danish monarchy, which demanded tolls of all shipping passing through the Baltic Sound. The Netherlands and England were content to pay for access to the rich Baltic trade with Sweden, Muscovy, and the cities of the *Hanse*. As Sweden developed a serious navy it moved to challenge Danish hegemony over the Sound. Denmark and Sweden fought two major wars over this issue, from 1563 to 1570 and 1611 to 1613. The defeat of *Christian IV* in 1629 and the intervention in Germany by *Gustavus Adolphus* the next year secured dominion of the Baltic for Sweden. See also *Northern War, First*; *Sound Tolls*.

Donauwörth. The most westerly Bavarian fortress. It was the site of numerous sieges in the wars of the 14th–17th centuries. *Gustavus Adolphus* took it on April 10, 1632, five days before the fight at *Rain*.

Donauwörth Incident (1607). See *Holy Roman Empire*; *Protestant Union*; *Reichskreis*.

donjon. The inner keep, tower, or stronghold of a castle. During the 12th century the donjon replaced the *motte* in most European castles, as siege techniques improved to the point that earth-and-timber forts were too easily and regularly breached and overwhelmed. During the 13th century donjons were rounded to account for the greater hitting power of the *trebuchet*. Square donjons were only built in outlying and more militarily backward areas after that, such as Ireland.

Don Juan of Austria (1547–1578). Bastard son of *Charles V*; half-brother of *Philip II*. He held commands on land and at sea. In 1568 he led a squadron of Spanish galleys against the corsairs of Algiers. Over he next two years he led a brutal, systematic, and successful suppression of a Morisco revolt in occupied Granada. In 1571 he led the Christian fleet to a spectacular victory at *Lepanto*. The next year he captured Tunis, briefly restoring the Hafsid dynasty. He was sent to the Netherlands in 1576 to subdue the Dutch Revolt. Initially, he lacked troops and money and was forced to acquiesce in the *Pacification of Ghent* as he tried to rebuild royal authority from the ruble that *Alba* left behind. But after a few months Don Juan returned to arms to repress the rebellion. Together with his cousin, the *Duke of Parma*, he routed a Beggar army at *Gembloux* (January 31, 1578). He died of fever in October 1578.

Doppelgänger. "Counterpart" or "dead ringer." In a *Landsknechte* company or regiment, recruits passed through a symbolic portal erected in the camp. As they passed, the muster officer called out their name, rate of pay, and the military equipment they were required to possess. Other officers watched to ensure that no "Doppelgänger" passed through the portal to collect double pay, and to prevent recruits wearing armor or carrying weapons borrowed solely for the purpose of the walk-through but whose actual absence would leave the company underarmed for battle. This was important to ensure a company's head count was correct and that all men carried the arms called for in the mercenary contract. See also *Doppelsöldner*.

Doppelhacken. A German wall or hook gun in common use in town defense in the 15th–16th centuries. See also *hackbut*.

Doppelsöldner. "Double pay." An experienced mercenary in a *Landsknechte* company who earned double pay (*Sold*) for standing in the front ranks in battle. In an army of Landsknechte a *Doppelgänger*, in the sense of "dead ringer," was always engaged in scamming the company whereas a Doppelsöldner received honest double pay for assuming extra combat risk. See also *Gevierthaufen*.

Doria, Andrea (1468–1560). Genoese naval *condottieri*. He built a private pirate fleet to capture Barbary and Ottoman ships and raid Muslim ports. In 1528 he retook Genoa from the French. Made an Imperial admiral by *Charles V*, he pushed the Ottomans from the Morea, which provoked *Barbarossa* to counterattack and take the fight to coastal Italy. Doria led the great Imperial assault on *Tunis* in 1534. In 1537 he lifted the Muslim siege of Corfu. He finally forced Barbarossa to fight at *Preveza* (1538), only to lose to the Algerian corsair and dey. Andrea Doria opposed, but led, a disastrous expedition to *Algiers* in 1541. He retired in 1555, handing command to his nephew, *Gian Andrea Doria*.

Doria, Gian Andrea (1539–1606). Nephew of *Andrea Doria*. He inherited command of the Genoese and allied galley fleet from his uncle. His conduct on the Christian flank at *Lepanto* (1571), was less than stellar. His failure to engage the enemy led to speculation that he made a secret deal with the sultan.

Dornach, Battle of (July 22, 1499). This was the third major clash of the *Swabian War* (1499) between *Maximilian I* and the *Swiss Confederation*. The Swiss had already beaten Swabian troops twice that year, at *Frastenz* and *Calven*. On the field of Dornach, south of Basel, the *Swiss square* first met its great imitator, the *Landsknechte*. Marching through the night, the Swiss caught the careless Germans wholly unprepared for battle, startling them awake in poorly protected field works. The fight was short-lived but the slaughter immense, as the Swiss pitilessly ran down and butchered fleeing Landsknechte. The victory at Dornach confirmed the independence of the Swiss Confederation for once and all. Within 15 years Basle, Schaffhausen, and Appenzell all agreed to join, raising the number of unified Cantons to 13. The Swiss were thereafter free of invasions of their homeland for over 200 years.

Dorpat, Battle of (1501). See *Livonian Order*; *Muscovy, Grand Duchy of*.

Dorpat, Sack of (January 1558). *Ivan IV* denounced the *Livonian Order* as criminal heathens who did not follow the true religion and sent a large army to slay its way through Estonia. At Dorpat the Muscovites slew at least 10,000 civilians as an example to inspire terror elsewhere. The tactic worked: they moved on to capture Narva and 20 other cowed and terrified towns.

double cannon. See *cañon de batir*.

double volley. See *volley fire*.

doubling the ranks. Infantry and cavalry were usually aligned in ranks of even number (12, 8, or 6, the latter being the preferred Swedish number introduced by *Gustavus Adolphus*). That meant the frontage of guns they opposed to the enemy could be easily doubled by ordering back ranks forward, each man filling a gap between two men in a front rank. Such a maneuver was called "doubling the ranks." See also *drill*.

Dover, Battle of (August 24, 1217). A large French squadron sailed for England from Calais under Eustace the Monk. The English, under Hubert de Burgh, gained the *weather gauge*, bore up to the French and attacked. The English broke apart the French formation and proceeded to defeat their ships in detail. This was a highly unusual, because mobile, medieval sea battle. It secured England from assayed French invasion for many generations.

The Downs, Battle of (October 11/21, 1639). *Olivares* sent 20,000 Spanish reinforcements north in a grand convoy of 40 Spanish (and a few English) transports and 60 warship escorts, a fleet he built up for years to wrest strategic initiative from the Dutch. The convoy was met by a much smaller Dutch fleet under Admiral *Marten van Tromp*. The fleets engaged briefly on September 16 and again on September 18. While the Spanish regrouped and made for neutral English shores, the Dutch reinforced. Off the mouth of the River Thomas in "The Downs," a small English squadron tried to prevent the fight. Tromp attacked the Spanish fleet after brushing aside the English ships. The highly proficient Dutch navy systematically raked and bombarded the desperate Spanish, sinking, burning, or taking as prizes fully 70 Spanish ships. The defeat was far more thorough and decisive than that of the *Invincible Armada* of 1588, and helped push Spain to the peace table at *Westphalia*. See also *Eighty Years' War*; *Spanish Road*.

> *...bombarded the desperate Spanish, sinking, burning, or taking as prizes fully 70 Spanish ships.*

dragoons. Soldiers who rode to battle but dismounted to fight on foot, as opposed to *cavalry*, or soldiers who rode to battle and fought from horseback. Firearms encouraged development of dragoons because it was difficult to fire a gun with any accuracy, and impossible to reload, from horseback. Firearms dragoons appeared in China by 1429. Within 100 years, light cavalry units that dismounted to fight were to be found all over Asia, the Middle East, and Europe. These troops specialized in scouting, raiding, foraging, devastation of the countryside, and convoying supply trains. In terms of accuracy and firepower, they remained a poor match for horse archers until cartridge-using, breech-loading carbines made firing and reloading from horseback feasible. See also *arquebusiers à cheval*; *Bedouin*; *equites*; *ghulams*; *hobelars*; *petronels*; *pishchal'niki*; *stradiots*; *strel'sty*; *Tüfeçis, turcopoles*.

drake. A 16th–17th century naval gun of varying caliber.

Drake, Francis (1540–1596). "El Drache." English *privateer*. Born to the Devonshire gentry, he was mentored by *John Hawkyns*, accompanying him on his third voyage in 1569 which ended in disaster and defeat at San Juan de Ulúa. Only Drake and Hawkyns escaped, with their ships badly damaged and with bloodied and depleted crews. From 1570 to 1573, Drake preyed on the Spanish, seeking not just profit but also revenge, and cooperating toward those ends with French corsairs. He raided treasure ships of the Spanish *flota*, securing a great fortune while winning lasting fame in England and infamy in Spain. His constant aggressions against the shipping and ports of the New World ensured that Spain enjoyed "no peace beyond the line" (of demarcation) set by the pope between Spain and Portugal in the 1494 *Treaty of Tordesillas*. In 1572 he seized Nombre de Dios after a brief skirmish with the town militia in which he was wounded. This forced him to withdraw, leaving the town and its full treasure house to be retaken by Spanish reinforcements. Drake allied with *cimarónes* the next year to carry out a failed ambush of a mule train carting silver overland to Nombre de Dios. He joined *Huguenot* pirates in a second try a few months later, and seized so much treasure his men could not carry it. Already a court favorite and perhaps also a royal lover to *Elizabeth I*, Drake sailed for Peru in December 1577, in the race-built galleon the "Golden Hind," with four smaller ships in tow. He sacked Valparaiso, captured a treasure ship, and decided to return to England via the Pacific. That meant traveling from Peru to Java, but then to Sierra Leone, the last leg covering 8,500 miles without benefit of friendly ports. He arrived back in Plymouth on September 26, 1580, having circumnavigated the globe and proven that ocean-going trade and war were now feasible. In 1585–1586, Drake undertook still wider and more damaging raids against Spanish interests, carrying 12 companies of soldiers armed with firearms to be put ashore by his fleet on amphibious raids. One of the captains in this small fleet was *Martin Frobisher*. On November 17, Drake landed his infantry east of Santiago in Cape Verde. They stormed the city while he bombarded it from the harbor. On January 1, 1586, he used the same drill to capture Santo Domingo. A subsequent attack on well-defended Cartagena was met by stronger resistance and return fire from several harbor galleys, but he carried that town also.

On April 11, 1587, Drake sailed for Cadiz, where he burned a half dozen Spanish warships, desecrated Catholic churches, and generally "singed the beard of the King of Spain." In 1588 he was one of four captains who led the English fleet during running battles in the Channel with the *Invincible Armada*. The next year Drake commanded an English fleet that was supposed to destroy the remnants of the Spanish Armada at Santander. Instead, he sailed to Lisbon, where his marines were repulsed with casualties. Ever the pirate, he took 60 neutral *Hanse* ships as prizes off the Tagus. After sacking Vigo, Drake sailed for the Azores in hope of intercepting the annual treasure fleet en route to Seville, but missed it. With hundreds of men dying onboard ship, he returned profitless to England. This failure kept Drake out of favor with the Queen for the next five years. In 1595, Drake and Hawkyns sailed to plunder the Caribbean with 26 ships and 2,500 men. The two "sea dog" captains had a falling out over strategy which was only resolved by Hawkyns' death from fever on November 22, 1595. Drake went ahead with his preferred attack on Puerto Rico, which was repulsed as Hawkyns had warned. Drake took Nombre de Dios (January 6, 1596) landing 600 men in hope of again intercepting the silver mule train from Panama. But he came down with fever and died aboard ship on February 7, 1596.

Suggested Reading: Kenneth Andrews, *Drake's Voyages* (1968; 1970); Harry Kelsey, *Sir Francis Drake: The Queen's Pirate* (1998); John Sugden, *Sir Francis Drake* (1992).

Drang nach Osten. "Drive to the East." See *Teutonic Knights, Order of*.

drekkar/drekki. "Dragon ship(s)." A generic term for any very large warship, but notably a *longship*.

Dreux, Battle of (December 19, 1562). The first set-piece battle of the *French Civil Wars* (1562–1629). A *Huguenot* army of 11,000 men was led by *Condé* and *Coligny*. They faced a Catholic-Guise army numbering 19,000 under *Anne de Montmorency*, Constable of France. The Catholics crossed the Eure and formed a battle line between two villages south of Dreux. After two hours of hesitation over whether to spill the blood of fellow nobles and Frenchmen, at last some Protestants charged the Catholic line. They were beaten off in part because their hired *Reiters* used the ineffective tactic of *caracole* and fell back in disorder after first contact with enemy artillery. After reforming, the Huguenot cavalry penetrated the Swiss pike ranks on the Catholic left, then routed the Royalist cavalry and captured Montmorency. While the Swiss stood fast, the rest of the left wing of the Catholic line turned and ran. The Huguenot cavalry overpursued, overrunning even the baggage train. As they returned they again engaged the Swiss, who were attacked simultaneously by companies of *Landsknechte* in Huguenot pay. The Swiss repulsed their hated German enemies, then attacked the Huguenot guns. As they fell back from that failing effort German Reiters charged them, thinking the victory secure and hoping to plunder royalist baggage and pick over Swiss corpses. The Huguenot cavalry was by now badly dispersed. That permitted a counterattack by the right wing of the Catholic army, which had stood fast all through the heavy action on the left. The Catholics now attacked into the exposed Huguenot infantry, bereft of any cavalry screen or flank protection. Great damage was done and Condé was captured. Coligny rallied 1,000 Huguenot horse and sallied from the woods. This prevented a rout of the Protestant infantry, which withdrew protected by Coligny's cavalry. The whole fight had taken just two hours. Each side was badly mauled and neither was sure it had won or lost. At least 6,000–8,000 lay dead, many among them Swiss and German mercenaries. The Swiss had proven their mettle in battle yet again and remained in Royal service, but French monarchs never again hired Landsknechte companies. Among the dead were nearly 1,000 French nobles, a fact that stunned France when it was later learned and hardened hearts against compromise. Catholics claimed victory in the end, but they had paid a huge price: several of their top leaders were dead or taken prisoner, the crown was near bankruptcy, and the rebellion continued.

drill.

In the Infantry

As foot soldiers displaced *heavy cavalry* from the battlefield, men raised to war were replaced with commoners recruited for a season or two of campaigning. Drill became the key to victory in battle for these new armies, as a means of turning inexperienced townsmen or peasants into soldiers. New infantry tactics were developed by Flemings, English, Scots, and Swiss during the 14th century, and mimicked deliberately by everyone after that. These required keeping tight formation above all else, with pikes supporting halberdiers, arquebusiers, and archers. If a square became disordered enemy cavalry could break into it, opening alleys of confusion, panic, searing wounds, and death. On the other hand, if a formation was too tight men could not swing slashing polearms or load guns or shoot bows or crossbows. Drill was developed to teach the new infantry to keep in formation while on the move, and to shift from march order to battle order, and into different tactical deployments. It was crucial to move with alacrity from line or column into pike squares (or later, battle lines), whether on the attack or in defense. Defensive drills were the most important as defense in this era, as in all, was inherently more potent and rugged than offense. Drills were devised to practice fighting from inside or behind palisades or other fortifications, as well as on an unobstructed field of battle. Drill became so important several European rulers tried to outlaw popular games and replace them with military exercises and martial arts. During the *Hundred Years' War* (1337–1453), France and England both passed laws or issued edicts banning games such as bowls and dice, and ordered plain folk to instead practice archery on Saturdays. *Charles the Rash* of Burgundy, as in all matters related to the theory if not the actual practice of war, took the lead in enforcing rigorous drill. Constant practice in uniform procedures produced unforeseen positive side effects, notably greater unit cohesion: men who drilled together tended to stay together in battle, to obey unit orders, and to develop an early form of esprit de corps.

The breakthrough to modern firearms drill came with reforms inaugurated by *Maurits of Nassau* in the 1590s. The "Dutch system" became the standard for all European and modern armies during the 17th century. It involved a number of discrete areas of infantry training. First was small arms drill, wherein men practiced how to load and fire their muskets in files (small units). Next came practice of maneuvering to the beat of a drum, with the main emphasis on learning drum signals. Some armies used brass trumpets instead, or voice calls, but the low reverberations of drums—like an elephant's trumpeting—carried farthest in battle and was therefore the most widely adopted means of signaling. The next major drill was movement of larger units (*squadrons* and *companies*). This included "distance marching," or practicing various regular spacings between ranks and files. *Open order* drill with wider spaces was permitted for marching to battle, but *close order* drill was required for action during battle. Other large unit drills included "*doubling the ranks*," where ranks in echelon merged by back ranks stepping forward. This was especially important for pikemen. Separation of doubled ranks was also practiced, as was facing left, right, and about on command. Also drilled was double-time marching and counter-marching, the latter a complex maneuver wherein ranks in echelon practiced moving through or around one another in both forward and reverse directions. Wheeling involved movement either at right angles to one end of the line or anchored at the center. Once squad and company drill was mastered, battalion (battle group) drill was practiced. On rare occasions, rehearsed maneuverings of an entire army were carried out.

In the Cavalry

Older medieval weapons training and horsemanship skills learned in *tournaments* gave way during the late 15th century to a variety of new battlefield maneuvers that emphasized not the blunt charge, but quicker wheeling formations designed to bring missile weapons to bear (such as the *wheel lock* pistol), not to try to break through the ranks of a deadly pike-and-arquebus square by force majeure. Such drill was as much about training the horses as training their riders. It was essential to practice deployment from columnar march formation into a battle frontage. Fighting drill usually concerned halving cavalry ranks from eight to four, or later, from six to three, and "facing about" to right or left to widen the frontage presented an enemy. Redoubling ranks would produce additional frontage. While this created highly vulnerable flanks of one's own, if properly executed these maneuvers offered the chance of catching a less well-trained enemy cavalry troop in the flank. Against infantry, cavalry practiced the *caracole* until some returned to shock tactics under reforms introduced by *Gustavus Adolphus*. See also *Feldweibel*.

Drogheda, Sack of (September 11, 1649). *Oliver Cromwell* moved against Drogheda, in Ireland, with 10,000 hardened Puritan veterans of the *English*

Civil Wars. Awaiting them were just 3,000 Irish and English Catholics under *Ormonde*. Cromwell blew down the town's thin walls with his artillery and his men stormed and sacked the city. All Catholic clergy were butchered, along with many civilians, in a massacre that embittered Anglo-Irish relations for many decades. See also *Wexford, Sack of*.

dromon. A large *galley* peculiar to the Byzantine navy. It sported two banks of 25 oars each.

drums. See *drill*.

Druse. A small Middle Eastern sect in schism from mainstream *Islam* since the 11th century, and highly secretive and socially closed as a result. The Druse fought the Christian invaders during the *Crusades*, but in later centuries they were mostly left alone in their mountain isolation by the Egyptian *Mamlūks*, and by the Ottomans. See *Ismaili*.

druzhyna. The armed retinue of the princes of Kievan Rus.

Dunbar, Battle of (April 27, 1296). See *Scottish Wars*.

Dunbar, Battle of (September 3, 1650). To put down Scottish support for the exiled Charles II, *Oliver Cromwell* moved north with 16,000 veterans of the English and Irish wars, assisted by *George Monk* and *John Lambert*. The Puritans were met by a Scottish army of 25,000 under *David Leslie*. The Scottish general cleverly maneuvered Cromwell against the coast, even as the English army was reduced by some 5,000 men through harassing attacks, disease, and desertion. Under pressure from Presbyterian fanatics and clerics to crush the English, Leslie gave up his advantage in the heights above Cromwell and moved downslope to attack. It was a mistake: Cromwell smashed Leslie's right flank, then charged across the field to dismantle his center. Cromwell lost few men, but Scottish losses were staggering: 3,000 dead and 10,000 prisoners, most of whom were forcibly deported to the West Indies as indentured laborers.

> *It was a mistake: Cromwell smashed Leslie's right flank, then charged across the field to dismantle his center.*

Dungan's Hill, Battle of (1647). See *English Civil Wars*.

Dupplin Moor, Battle of (1332). See *Edward III*; *Scottish Wars*.

Dutch Army. At the start to the *Eighty Years' War* (1568–1648) the Dutch relied on their superb urban militia, the *schutterijen*, supplemented by German and other mercenaries. In the 1590s, *Maurits of Nassau* was commissioned to undertake a major modernization and reform of the army. In addition to the qualitative changes he made in its training, tactics, transport, and weapons, it grew from 20,000 men in 1588 to 32,000 by 1595. By 1607 it was second only to the Spanish in size, at 51,000 men, and first in the world in technical proficiency and advanced tactics and training. During the *Twelve Years' Truce* (1609–1621) it was cut back to 47,000 men, then to a low of 29,000. When the war resumed in 1621 the numbers rose again, to 48,000 in the garrisons alone. At its greatest enlistment, during the late 1620s, the Dutch Army mustered 130,000 (including garrisons). About 70,000 of these were raised directly from the population by the government of the United Provinces, the rest were foreign mercenaries. All troops were paid through a sophisticated tax and war finance system unique in Europe (only the Ottomans were more advanced during this period). In training, equipment, and professionalism, the Dutch Army was the most modern and effective in Europe, unbeatable by the also tough and talented, but badly overstretched and underfinanced Spanish. Note: The figures here do not include the sizeable and powerful Dutch navy, originally run by the *Sea Beggars* and later by the state.

Dutch exercises. See *counter-march*; *drill*; *Maurits of Nassau*.

Dutch musket. See *Gustavus II Adolphus*; *Maurits of Nassau*; *muskets*.

Dutch Revolt. See *Eighty Years' War*.

dziesietniks. "Tenth-men." A low-rank, closer to a modern NCO than a modern officer, in charge of a file of 10 Polish infantrymen inside a *rota* of pikers, shield-bearers, arquebusiers, and musketeers. Given the extent of *dead-pays*, each rota was probably only eight or fewer men. See also *Haiduks*.

E

eagle knight. A class of elite soldier of the *Aztec Empire*. They wore an elaborate eagle mask and headdress decorated with eagle feathers and presenting a projecting beak and feral appearance. On ritual occasions the best warriors were given the thigh or arm of a captured and sacrificed enemy to eat. Eagle knights took in boys for military apprenticeship, training them in the "Eagle House" ("cuauhcalli"). The other class of elite Aztec warrior was the *jaguar knight*.

Eastern Army. See *Ōnin War*; *Sekigahara, Battle of*.

Eastern Association Army. The most famous of the regional armies that fought the *English Civil Wars*, because it hosted *Oliver Cromwell*'s regiment of *Ironsides* cavalry and operated in the critical theater around London. It comprised forces from Cambridge, Hertford, Norfolk, and Sussex. It was dissolved in 1645, its veterans joining the *New Model Army*.

Eastern Route Army. See *Hakata Bay, Battle of (1281)*.

East India Company (EIC). "John Company." Ultimately the most successful of several East India Companies, it received a monopoly charter from *Elizabeth I* on December 31, 1600. Dutch, French, and Danish East India companies were founded in 1602, 1604, and 1614, respectively. The EIC was not much active before 1604, when peace with Spain ended profits made close to home (in the Channel) from *privateering*. London's merchants then became more interested in joint stock monopolies to exploit more distant opportunities. The EIC was not an imperial exercise: Asian trade, unlike that with America, was not associated with settlements via crown or charter colonies, but with entrepôts and pure trade unsaddled by settlements. The first EIC expedition to India threaded through the Portuguese-controlled Indian Ocean in 1608.

Its first factory was established at Surat in 1612. In 1622 the EIC allied with *Abbas I* of Iran, ferrying his troops to engage the Portuguese on *Hormuz*. With the Portuguese gone Abbas gave control of trade with western Iran to the EIC. Cleverly, Abbas granted monopoly access to the rest of his empire to the Dutch *Vereenigde Oostindische Compaagnie* (VOC). Thereafter, the EIC employed a factory system of fortified trading posts in competition with the VOC over the *spice trade*, and with the French to penetrate the Indian interior and control nawab allies and armies. It broke relations with the VOC in 1623 after 10 EIC officers were murdered in Amboina. In 1640 it built a fort and factory in southwest India that later grew into the metropolis of Madras. Its glory days lay ahead of this period, in the 17th–18th centuries.

Suggested Reading: Philip Lawson, *The East India Company* (1993).

East Prussia. "Ducal Prussia." The historic base of the Order of the *Teutonic Knights*. It was incorporated into Brandenburg-Prussia during the late Middle Ages. See also *Elbing, Battle of*; *Prussia*; *War of the Cities*.

East Stoke, Battle of (1487). See *Wars of the Roses*.

Ecorcheurs. "Skinners" Successors to the *routiers* and *Free Companies*, these murderous, pillaging bands ran amok in France and western parts of Germany in the later part of the *Hundred Years' War* (1337–1453). Many were former *Armagnacs*. Charles VII turned some of these dangerous men into frontier garrison troops, taming their wilder and more desperate natures with a constant salary. He placed others in his *compagnies de l'ordonnance*. See also *akutō*; *ashigaru*; *aventuriers*; *Celâli Revolts*; *guerre couverte*; *ronin*; *wakō*.

Ecumenical Councils. General church councils called to consider matters of faith and doctrine and to determine what was orthodox belief and what might be condemned as *heresy*. For the Catholic Church they provided guidance on doctrine in addition to scripture, at least wherever popes decreed conciliar findings to be canon law (or councils so decreed, as during the 15th century). The first seven councils were accepted by the Orthodox Church as authoritative, but from the eighth onward Catholics and Orthodox divided over conciliar authority in a schism which only hardened over the centuries. The main issue in the divide was papal assertion of superior doctrinal and governing authority. Most Protestants accepted the first four councils as "ecumenical," but following the advice of *Martin Luther* they did not consider canon law to be binding in preference to revelations of scripture or even individual conscience. The most important ecumenical councils of the period of concern here, were: First Lateran (1123), which spoke to new issues arising from the *Crusades*; Third Lateran (1179), which condemned the Waldensian and *Albigensian* "heresies" and led to savage military suppression of heretics in southern France; it also founded the Medieval *Inquisition*; Fourth Lateran (1215), which marked the peak power of the Medieval Church in Western

Europe; Lyons (1245), which excommunicated Holy Roman Emperor Friedrich II and preached a Crusade that was led by the Louis IX ("St. Louis," 1215–1270); Vienne (1311–1313), held during the "Avignon Captivity" of the papacy, which repressed the *Knights Templars* and other accused "heretics"; *Constance* (1414–1418), which ended the *Great Schism* and condemned and executed *Jan Hus*, triggering the *Hussite Wars* in Bohemia; *Basel-Ferrara-Florence* (1431, 1438, 1439), which again dealt with the Hussite rebellion and invasions of Austria, Hungary, and Germany; Fifth Lateran (1512–1517), whose planning for a crusade by the *Holy League* against the Ottomans was interrupted by the initial public protest of Martin Luther and the start of the *Protestant Reformation* in Germany; and *Trent* (1545–1563), which condemned the "errors" of Protestantism and set the stage for hard confessional confrontation and the *Counter-Reformation*. See also *Coptic Church*.

Edgecote Moor, Battle of (1470). See *Wars of the Roses*.

edged weapons. See *axes*; *daggers*; *halberd*; *lance (1)*; *mace*; *pike*; *poleax*; *swords*.

Edgehill, Battle of (October 23, 1642). The first major battle of the *English Civil Wars*. Parliament sent an army of 15,000 poor foot and 5,000 horse, under the *3rd Earl of Essex*, to defend London against a *Cavalier* army of about 13,500 led by *Charles I* that was strong in cavalry but weak in infantry. The *Roundheads* deployed in two lines of eight ranks each, Dutch style. The Royalists lined up Swedish style: five blocks with cannon to the front and cavalry on the wings. One troop of Roundheads advanced, fired into the ground and changed sides. The fight really began with a Cavalier charge led by *Prince Rupert*, and another on the far wing that routed both wings of Roundhead horse. But the impetuous Rupert overpursued (a bad habit of English cavalry as late as Waterloo). That left the Royalist infantry exposed. Essex attacked with his infantry and captured the Royalist artillery train. Rupert returned, horses spent, but in time to prevent disaster. About 2,000 were killed or wounded in total, but no decision was reached. Still, Charles went on to occupy Banbury and Oxford and remained in control of Wales and the west of England.

Edict of Alès (June 28, 1629). "Édit de Grace Alès." This royal edict issued by *Louis XIII* established peace between the confessional communities in France following the surrender of *La Rochelle* in 1628. It confirmed the loss by the *Huguenots* of all fortress towns and military rights guaranteed in the royal brevets of the *Edict of Nantes* (1598). While disbanding corporate and military structures, it affirmed the Huguenots as a distinct religious community within the French nation, but one now clearly defined as an island of heresy within a broad Catholic sea, never again a continent apart or a state-within-a-state.

Edict of Amboise (March 19, 1563). First of the "edicts of pacification," this compromise by *Catherine de Medici* and *Condé* formally ended the first of the *French Civil Wars*. It amended the terms of the *Edict of Saint-Germain* to permit *Huguenots* to worship in the suburbs of one town in each bailliage of France. Protestant nobles were additionally allowed to worship in the new fashion within their homes and on their estates. This grant spoke to the prominent military role of Protestant nobles but left the main locus of religious strife, non-noble Protestant communities in the towns, outside the limits of official toleration. Notably, it was sent directly to provincial governors instead of the parlements. In Orléans, Protestants burned churches rather than hand them back to Catholics. While Protestants were disappointed, Catholics were enraged. Most wanted war to drive "heresy" from the sacred kingdom and repress rebellion. Paris was especially vigilant in ferreting out and murdering Protestants and preventing the return of pardoned heretics. The effort at Amboise to bypass confessional opposition by imposing peace on nonreligious lines thus failed.

Edict of Beaulieu (May 6, 1576). "Peace of Monsieur." *Henri III* ended the fifth of the *French Civil Wars* with this edict, forced upon him by bankruptcy that denied him an army sufficient to meet the *Huguenot* army and German mercenaries massed in the south. His brother, Francois, also aligned against him. Beaulieu represented an unexpected about turn for Huguenot fortunes following the catastrophe of the *St. Bartholomew's Day Massacres* (1572). It called on Protestants to restore Catholic worship inside towns, forbade Protestant services in Paris, and provocatively referred to the Huguenot faith as the "religion prétendue réformée." Nevertheless, Beaulieu was an affirmation of Huguenot military and political rejuvenation and Henri III's weakness. For the first time since the persecutions of *Francis I*, Protestants were granted freedom of conscience and religion everywhere except within the walls of Paris. The massacres were formally declared a crime and the number of fortified "surety towns" (*place de sûreté*) permitted the Huguenots was raised from four to eight. A set of "secret articles" not published with the main text granted extensive lands and pensions to leading Protestant princes and Catholic *Malcontents* as a hoped-for guarantee of future quietude. Many of its articles were revived in whole or part by *Henri IV* in the *Edict of Nantes*. See also *devotes/dévots*; *politiques (France)*.

Edict of Châteaubriant (1551). See *Henri II, of France*.

Edict of January (1562). See *Edict of Saint-Germain*.

Edict of Longjumeau (March 1568). "The Little Peace." The peace that ended the second *French Civil War* as mass desertions and shortage of funds and supplies struck both armies. It restored the terms of the *Edict of Amboise*: Protestantism was recognized by the crown and allowed in one suburb of one town in each bailliage, and on the estates of *Huguenot* nobles. Since it was the failure of Amboise that sparked the Second Civil War, its revived terms in Longjumeau only suffered loathing and opposition from the *Guise* and from most Catholics, inside and outside France. The *Cardinal de Lorraine* secured revocation of the edict in August. Some historians posit that Longjumeau was never intended to keep the peace but was a trap set for the Huguenots, since they partly disarmed but the Catholics did not. Within just six months the third of the *French Civil Wars* broke out.

Edict of Nantes (April 13, 1598). A royal edict issued in four separate documents by *Henri IV*, including a number of secret articles that exempted specific towns and individuals from its terms. It extended legal toleration to the *Huguenots* and established temporary religious coexistence within France. The traditional view was that the Edict of Nantes was intended by Henri to establish religious toleration of *Calvinism* and thereby settle forever the deep confessional division that led to the *French Civil Wars* (1562–1629). Recent scholarship stresses instead that the edict was never intended to, and did not, establish a permanent religious settlement. Nor was it a direct anticipation of the 18th-century idea of religious toleration achieved along secular lines, as older histories often argued. What it did was more limited in ambition and effect: call a halt to confessional warfare and active persecution in order to give the nation time to heal in an atmosphere of cold war between hostile confessions. Intriguingly, the edict did not refer to the doctrinal issues that divided the Christian world into warring camps, largely because the religious divide was as much social as doctrinal and the edict wisely aimed to bridge the first by ignoring the second. In its 92 general articles and 56 secret articles,

> *The Edict of Nantes was not universally well-received, but was especially opposed by the majority Catholics.*

and two royal brevets, the Edict of Nantes drew heavily from the *Edict of Beaulieu* (1576). Its articles allowed freedom of conscience and worship in Huguenot towns and the homes of Protestant nobles, and made provision for Protestant instruction; other articles exempted specific Catholic towns from having to suffer Protestant services. Huguenots were granted full civil rights in education, public offices, and matters of inheritance, but not to levy taxes or raise armies, erect fortifications, or otherwise act as if they were a sovereign republic within France. On the other side, the sacral and Catholic nature of the French crown was affirmed and Catholic worship was to be permitted everywhere, including Protestant areas where it had been banished during the civil wars. Moreover, Huguenots were obliged to keep and respect all Catholic feast days, to marry under the Catholic rite, and to pay tithes to the Catholic Church. This was not a treaty between equals: it was a peace based on a guarantee of limited minority rights for Protestants within a kingdom clearly defined as permanently and fundamentally Catholic.

The royal brevets were key. They proved effective since they did not have to be registered with provincial parlements (courts), which were still dominated by Catholic militants and which had earlier rejected all royal attempts to extend limited legal rights to Calvinists. By that same token, the brevets could be (and would be) revoked by Henri's successors. The first granted Protestants a subsidy for the salaries of their pastors, somewhat assuaging the requirement to tithe to Catholic bishops. The second brevet guaranteed limited military rights, including to armed Huguenot garrisons in some 200 fortified towns, with the Protestant militia paid by the crown. This military brevet was to expire in eight years, confirming that Henri expected the Huguenots to abjure and return to the Gallican church, and that even he would not forever tolerate Huguenot demands that they be left as a state-within-a-state. In 1606 he would be forced by circumstance to renew the second brevet for another eight years, but he managed to cut the subsidy in half. His successor would revoke the military brevet entirely, but for the moment it helped secure the Huguenots in their core holdings and hence kept the peace.

The Edict of Nantes was not universally well-received, but was especially opposed by the majority Catholics. What forced acceptance was the understanding that rejection meant resumption of the bloody civil wars, against which even the peasants were now rebelling. Even so, the edict was not formally registered by the Parlement of Paris until February 25, 1599, while radical Rouen did not ratify it until 1609. Still, the edict achieved broad if begrudging support from moderate Catholics, Protestants, and Royalists. The peasants probably did not understand it, but they welcomed anything that ended fighting in the countryside. The edict's main purpose and effect was to bring a 10-year halt to protracted civil wars that had weakened France internationally and led to repeated armed foreign intervention over a period of 30 years. France regained a measure of internal stability that enabled Henri to rescue it from bankruptcy and begin to repair a shattered political and economic order, even as he hoped that in time abjuration by all Huguenots might restore social peace as well. If the military articles of the edict rankled against Henri's assertion of indivisible royal authority and sovereignty, they upset his successor more, and they enraged the *dévots*, spiritual successors to the Catholic League. After a brief Huguenot revolt following Henri's assassination in 1610, with small fighting lasting to 1614, the young *Louis XIII* renewed the amended brevets of the edict. Its main military provisions remained in effect until Richelieu finally crushed the Huguenots militarily and took La Rochelle in 1628. That led to the *Edict of Alès* in 1629 which left the Edict of Nantes' religious terms intact but ended all Protestant military rights. The religious terms were observed until Louis XIV formally revoked them in 1685, 87 years after their promulgation.

Suggested Reading: Janine Garrison, *L'Edit de Nantes et sa révocation* (1985); Mack Holt, *French Wars of Religion, 1562–1629* (1995).

Edict of Restitution (June 1617). See *French Civil Wars*; *Louis XIII*.

Edict of Restitution (March 28, 1629). An imperial edict by *Ferdinand II* ratified on March 6 and published on March 28, 1629, dealing with the religious question in the Holy Roman Empire. Its assumption of Imperial victory, and tone of Catholic triumphalism, marked the summit of Habsburg power and of *Counter-Reformation* influence over the course of the *Thirty Years' War*, and the beginning of the end for both. It reaffirmed that Calvinist worship remained illegal within the empire and promised in effect to reduce Lutherans to a weak minority, despite the support Ferdinand had received in the war from several important Lutheran princes. It called for restoration to Catholics of ecclesiastical rights, offices, and properties secularized since the *Convention of Passau* (1552). In the view of Catholics this perfected the "Religionsfriede" (religious peace) agreed at *Augsburg* in 1555, but for Protestants that peace was illegally invalidated by the new edict. If implemented as written, the edict promised to settle the religious question in the whole empire the way it had been settled in Bohemia after 1621: by stripping Protestants of titles and lands, returning numerous monasteries and bishoprics to control of the Catholic Church, revoking religious toleration that had taken deep root over the preceding 75 years, and driving many Protestants into exile. Moreover, Ferdinand planned to put family members into several of the restored bishoprics, extending Habsburg power into parts of Germany it had never before reached. All this was, in the words of Ronald Asch, "a political miscalculation of gigantic proportions. If a chance for a concerted religious crusade against Protestantism all over Europe ever existed, it was already gone by spring 1629." The reaction came at a meeting of Ferdinand and the Electors at Regensburg in August 1630. Ferdinand was refused election of his son as King of Rome, he was not voted funds for his army in Italy, and the resignation of *Albrecht von Wallenstein* was insisted upon. Seldom has a would-be autocrat fallen so far, so fast. By promoting a Catholic policy above reasons of state, the authors of the edict—Ferdinand, and his lawyers and priests—failed to realize that much of Catholic Europe was already past any willingness to support a "Catholic" war. For its own "raisons d'etat," Catholic France was at that moment readying to wage war, if need be, against Catholic Spain and Catholic Austria, in open alliance with Protestant princes and kings and tacitly also with the Sultan of the Ottoman Empire. See also *Arnim, Hans Georg von*; *Edict of Alès*; *Ferdinand III, Holy Roman Emperor*; *Magdeburg, Sack of*; *Prague, Peace of*; *Westphalia, Peace of*.

Suggested Reading: Ronald Asch, *The Thirty Years' War* (1997).

Edict of Saint-Germain (January 17, 1562). "Edict of Toleration" or "Edict of January." Issued by *Catherine de Medici*, this edict granted limited but legally recognized toleration of the *Huguenots*. It denied them rights of worship within town walls and forbade them nighttime assembly or the right to bear arms. It permitted peaceful and open preaching of the new faith only in the countryside and in daytime. Nevertheless, it was the first act of formal toleration by the crown since *Francis I* began persecution of French Protestants after the *Affair of the Placards* in 1534. It represented the Queen Mother's effort to avoid civil war by uniting all within the Gallican Church, but it had the opposite effect: it unhinged the *Guise* and unsettled even more moderate Catholics. The Parlement of Paris initially refused to register it, warning that "every kingdom divided against itself goes to ruin." It quickly proved unenforceable, as Catholics led by the Guise responded to its call for toleration with a massacre of Protestant worshipers at *Vassy*. The shots fired there were the first in the protracted agony known as the *French Civil Wars* (1562–1629).

Edict of Saint-Germain-en-Laye (August 8, 1570). This compromise "peace" is normally viewed as a genuine effort by *Catherine de Medici* and the crown to end the *French Civil Wars* (1562–1629). Reflecting revived *Huguenot* military fortunes, it reinforced religious privileges previously granted to Protestant nobles and extended the right of public worship more generally inside two towns in each of the 12 "gouvernements" of France. While toleration was not extended to Paris or the Court, the edict was the first to grant civil and judicial protections to Protestants on equality of taxation, restoration of seized property, admission to schools and universities, and holding public offices. It left Catholics bitterly opposed, as the Huguenots secured control of four key fortified towns, *place de sûreté* (La Rochelle, La Charité, Cognac, and Montauban). Therein, they continued to arm and train. On the other hand, Protestants were delivered paper rights that often proved unenforceable in face of Catholic majority opposition. Each confessional community was thus left deeply anxious that the war would resume on terms adverse to its own position. Within two years the Peace failed, as the Queen Mother's effort to bridge the religious divide by marrying her daughter to *Henri de Navarre* instead occasioned the *St. Bartholomew's Day Massacres* (1572).

Edict of Toleration (1562). See *Edict of Saint-Germain*.

Edict of Union (July 1588). Forced on *Henri III* by the *Catholic League* after his flight from Paris on the *Day of the Barricades*, it reaffirmed the harsh terms of the *Treaty of Nemours* and admonished the king to uphold his sacred coronation oath and thus never make peace with heretic *Huguenots*. It also compelled him to call into session the Estates General to raise funds for a final war to exterminate the Huguenots. The Edict of Union recognized Cardinal de Bourbon as the rightful heir in place of *Henri de Navarre*, acknowledged government by The Sixteen in Paris, and placed *Henri Guise* in command of all Royalist and Catholic forces. See also *Estates*; *French Civil Wars*.

Edward I (1239–1307). "Longshanks." See *England*; *Falkirk, Battle of*; *longbow*; *Scottish Wars*; *Stirling Bridge, Battle of*; *uniforms*; *Wallace, William*.

Edward II (1284–1327). See *Bannockburn*; *longbow*; *Scottish Wars*.

Edward III (1312–1377). King of England, 1327–1377. His father, Edward II, was deposed in 1327. Edward III began his reign with an effective coup three years later, in which he arrested and executed his mother's consort, Roger de Mortimer, and sent his mother back to her homeland, France. He moved quickly to reverse a settlement arranged by the regency in 1328, whereby he had renounced the Scottish throne first claimed by his grandfather, Edward I, in 1296. Edward III's revived hegemonic ambitions for the island of Great Britain were aided by an ongoing civil war in Scotland. His intervention revived the *Scottish Wars*. Aware of the success of Flemish militia against knights at *Courtrai* (1302), and of the Scots against his father at *Bannockburn* (1314), Edward experimented with bold new tactics designed to substitute armored infantry defense for mounted armored attack. His most notable move was to dismount his *men-at-arms* and deploy them as armored infantry in three close formations at the center of his line where they used their lances like pikes. The archers were positioned somewhat forward on each flank, thereby flanking any enemy who chose to attack the men-at-arms in the middle. Edward kept a small cavalry unit in reserve in a wagon park for exploitation and pursuit of the defeated enemy. Or he placed them in a nearby wood, in ambush. The archers shaped the enemy attack and drove it onto the men-at-arms at the center. These tactical innovations were wrapped in a strategic overview in which Edward never offered battle except on ground of his own choosing, which he compelled his enemies to accept by a policy of scorched earth that challenged their legitimacy as sovereigns through deliberate and widespread terrorism against their subjects.

Edward III altered the English way of war and contributed to a general shift in European warfare away from heavy cavalry toward heavy infantry supported by light infantry archers. The new system enabled Edward to win repeatedly against the Scots, including at *Halidon Hill* (1333), a battle that set the mold for his later successes in France during the opening phase of the *Hundred Years' War* (1337–1453). In 1339 he led a major *chevauchée*—along with besieging an important town, this was the principal instrument of English terrorism used to provoke enemies to battle—in France, besieging Cambrai and burning out hundreds of towns. The next year he commanded at the naval *Battle of Sluys* (June 23, 1340). He won a substantial and famous victory at *Crécy* (1346), and led a 1346–1347 siege of Calais. His son, the *Black*

> *...Edward experimented with bold new tactics designed to substitute armored infantry defense for mounted armored attack.*

Prince, used the same infantry tactics to achieve victory at *Poitiers* (1356). Edward was preoccupied to his final days with the Scottish and French wars, which were partly linked by the *'Auld Alliance*. He also had to contend with the ravages of the *Black Death*, which reached England during his reign. Edward's later years were marked by personal and political decline, and a growing quarrel within his faction-ridden court over royal revenues that might be extracted from the Church, and over the degree of papal authority to be exercised over the national church in England. The Black Prince died two years before Edward, but the king's tactical innovations remained the standard for English armies into the mid-15th century. See also *Aljubarrota, Battle of*; *chevauchée*; *chivalry*; *Free Companies*; *Jacquerie*; *Nájera, Battle of*; *routiers*; *war-horses*.

Suggested Reading: H. Hewitt, *Organization of War under Edward III, 1338–1362* (1966); Clifford Rogers, *War Cruel and Sharp: English Strategy under Edward III, 1327–1360* (2000).

Edward IV (1442–1483). See *Wars of the Roses*.

Edward VI (1537–1553). See *Elizabeth I*; *Henri II, of France*; *Henry VIII, of England*; *Mary Tudor*.

Effingham, Admiral Lord Howard of (1536–1624). See *Howard, Charles*.

Egmont, Lamoral Graaf van (1522–1568). Flemish general. At the head of a Spanish army he defeated the French at *Saint-Quentin* (1557) and, with English naval aid, again at *Gravelines* (1558). Although a Catholic partisan, he preached toleration for Protestants and worked against the persecutions of Cardinal Granvelle, *Philip II*'s much-hated representative in Flanders. A defender of the traditional liberties of the Dutch *Estates*, Egmont was arrested by the *Duke of Alba* in 1567, illegally detained and tried on trumped up charges of treason, then executed in 1568. That hard act helped spark the great Flanders revolt that became the *Eighty Years' War*.

Egypt. Following the fall of the ancient empire of the Pharaohs, Egypt was repeatedly conquered by external powers: first came the ancient Persians and Greeks (under Alexander the Great, who moved Egypt's capital from the Nile to a new city he founded on the Mediterranean coast, at Alexandria); next it was the Romans, followed by their eastern successors the Byzantines. Each of these foreign empires left behind settlers and distinctive cultural contributions which mixed with the culture and populations already there. Additionally, the Greeks and Romans fundamentally changed Egyptian history by reorienting it toward an expansive Mediterranean trading civilization, and away from Egypt's earliest roots in Nilotic Africa. In the 7th century C.E., Arabs (*Bedouin*) rode out of the desert to conquer and convert Egypt to a new world faith: *Islam*. Over time, most but not all of Egypt's *Coptic* population (which had converted to Christianity during the heyday of the Roman Empire under and after Constantine I), was converted to Islam. Along with the Arabs, who settled in large numbers from the 8th century, came a new institution: the *caliphate*. Egypt was thus governed from outside for several centuries, first by the Umayyad caliphs, then by the Abbasids based in Baghdad. A schismatic and rival *shi'a* caliphate, that of the Berber Fatamids, seized control and ruled in Egypt from 909 until 1171. The Fatamids came to rely increasingly on the slave soldiery of the *mamlūks*. Egypt was spared devastation by the Mongols at *'Ayn Jālut* ("The Spring of Goliath") in Galilee in 1260, when a mamlūk army out of Egypt defeated a Mongol advance party, stopping their southward invasion. The mamlūks subsequently blocked multiple Mongol attempts to conquer Syria, and themselves absorbed Syria as a protected province. During the *Crusades*, Egypt was the base from which the Islamic counterattack was organized. As the Fatamids declined, Egypt's Grand Vizier and effective ruler, *Salāh-al-Dīn*, used its great wealth to gather Muslim armies with which he recaptured *Jerusalem* and confined the Latins to a strip of coastal kingdoms in northern Palestine and Syria. These, too, were eventually overwhelmed and the Crusaders forced to take refuge on various eastern Mediterranean islands (Cyprus, Malta, Rhodes). In 1250 the Ayyubid dynasty that had been founded by Salāh al-Dīn lost control to the Mamlūk general Baybārs. There followed a long contest between the Mamlūks in Egypt and the *Il-Khans* of Iran. A peace was agreed between these rival centers of Muslim power in 1323. Meanwhile, Egypt was ruled by a Circassian-Turk military dynasty, the Bahri (River) Mamlūks, 1250–1382, and then by the Burji (Citadel) Mamlūks, 1382–1517. Thus was established a pattern in which Egypt's great wealth and population enabled ostensibly provincial governors owing allegiance to more expansive empires to nod in the direction of the empire, but rule autonomously in fact. Similarly, after *Selim I* sacked Cairo in 1517 the Ottomans governed Egypt only nominally, through appointed Mamlūk generals.

Eighty Years' War (1568–1648). "Revolt of the Low Countries." The long struggle of the United Provinces for independence from Spain. Confessional warfare broke out in Flanders 13 years after the great religious peace was achieved in Germany, where the *Peace of Augsburg* was agreed to in 1555 by Emperor Maximilian. *Philip II*, an austere Catholic zealot, continued *Charles V*'s campaign against noble liberties and the spread of Protestantism. To meet the first goal he needed to make a "revolution from above" that rationalized administration and taxation of the Netherlands. This would save his larger empire from financial collapse. However, his reforms threatened local freedoms with war taxes and new restrictions on commerce, the source of Dutch prosperity. As for religion, Phillip's sense of personal godly and Spanish imperial mission, support for the *Counter-Reformation*, and stern refusal to reign in the northern *Inquisition*, all gave great offense. The crisis arrived in 1559 with the end of the *Italian Wars*. The Netherlands' already-strained finances were taxed again to pay the old war debts of Philip II from the French war and finance a new whole war with the Ottomans. This bad news arrived even as Philip tightened the thumbscrews of the Inquisition in his northern possessions. When the *French Civil Wars* began in 1562, Philip saw the *Huguenot* revolt as a baleful example of what might happen to his own cosmopolitan empire if he did not establish religious conformity and crush any and all signs of heresy and rebellion, which were incestuously linked in his mind. The Eighty Years' War began as an effort led by Netherlands nobles to preserve their traditional liberties from reforms imposed at the top, as well as by the old city-states to return to the golden days of their autonomy from any kings, and not as a radical or nationalist revolution. Nevertheless, due to Philip's hard religious policies and fiscal needs, it soon became radicalized along confessional lines that also divided Flanders regionally.

Repression and Revolt

Catholics and Calvinists alike saw Philip's reforms as an unprecedented extension of royal power that impinged on local liberties. On April 5, 1566, some 200 nobles took "The Petition of Compromise" to Brussels demanding an end to the Inquisition, but not yet to the monarchy or the dominant role of the Catholic Church. They were dubbed "Beggars" ("Gueux") by *Margaret of Parma*, who nevertheless sought real compromise. A delegation she sent to Spain was rudely dismissed, however, by the hard men around Philip II and by the king himself. Rejection of reasonable grievances turned noble petitioners into leaders of a burgeoning national resistance, just as follow-on harsh treatment of bread rioters turned bourgeoisie and urban protesters into armed rebels. Stirred by "hedge-row" Calvinist preachers, a wave of violent *iconoclasm* ("beeldenstorm") broke out in August: Calvinists in Flanders smashed Catholic statues and paintings and stole Church gold and silver plate, even breaking into convents to do so. In Brussels, they were cheered on by excited mobs crying "Vivent les Gueux!" ("Long Live the Beggars!"). The "beeldenstorm" spread north of the rivers in late August, becoming more systematic as it was organized by local nobles. In Catholic cities, retaliation broke up Protestant services and forced Catholic baptisms on the cowed and unwilling. Wherever local *schutterijen* (militia) did not oppose the mobs, whole towns were protestantized or recatholicized by force. Alarmed, Margaret called in royal troops to suppress Walloon Protestants, but that only provoked nobles north of the rivers to arm and organize. The country was fast dividing on confessional and regional lines.

With royal authority disintegrating in 1567, and against Margaret's advice, Philip sent the *Duke of Alba* north with 10,000 men to reimpose order with fire, blood, and steel. In fact, before he arrived the rebellion had already abated, with some cowed Calvinists reconverting to Catholicism and others fleeing north or to London or into Germany. Rebellion broke out again, in earnest, in 1568 once Alba executed *Egmont* and hundreds of other nobles on trumped-up charges accepted by a toady "Council of Troubles," which Protestants dubbed the "Council of Blood." It did not help that Alba also raised taxes, built citadels, and garrisoned German troops across the Netherlands. The princes of Nassau and Orange led the renewed armed revolt. *Louis of Nassau* beat a small Spanish army at Heiligerlee (May 23, 1568), an early but lonely rebel victory. Two months later, Alba handily beat Louis at *Jemmingen* (July 21, 1568). Louis' brother, *William the Silent* ("Orange"), invaded Brabant with an army recruited in Germany but Alba defeated Orange, too. He followed up with construction of citadels and punitive billeting of troops on disloyal towns, and introduction of the *Tenth Penny* tax by decree on July 31, 1571. Following their Stadholder, and provoked by the new punitive measures, Holland and Zeeland took up arms. Even Catholic Flanders was restless under Alba's hard rule.

With the rebellion stymied on land, initiative passed to the *Sea Beggars*, based in England from 1568 to 1572. Denied ports in England from early 1572, Beggar ships and marines took *Brill* on Walcheren Island on April 1, 1572, then Flushing, on the Scheldt, five days later. The northern Netherlands now rose in full-throated revolt. Spanish garrisons were killed or expelled. Louis of Nassau invaded Hainault with a mercenary army and took Mons. However, the *St. Bartholomew's Day Massacres* in France interrupted plans to send a large *Huguenot* army north to the aid of Calvinist brethren. A second rebel force took Zutphen, as Gelderland and Overijssel also rebelled. A third army invaded Brabant out of Germany in August, and dozens of towns declared for Orange. William tried to keep to the moderate road, but was unable to contain a new wave of iconoclastic, anti-Catholic "beeldenstorm" that arrived in his wake, driving Catholic refugees south to loyalist towns. Alba took Mons back in September, then countered the rebellion with wholesale, calculated terror and frontal assaults on rebel cities, including sacks and massacres of Mechlen and Zutphen, towns which had rebelled but not resisted the return of Alba's men. Alba ordered the massacre of the entire population of Naarden, down to the last child (December 2, 1572). The next summer, his troops butchered the rebel garrison of *Haarlem* after a brutal eight-month siege in July 1573. Alba was stopped from carrying out more atrocities only by a lack of money to pay his executioners. That summer, the first of many mutinies began which hamstrung Spain's war effort: between 1572 and 1607 the *Army of Flanders* mutinied no fewer than 46 times. Frustrated, Alba proposed to break the Dutch dams and sluices and flood the rebel areas, but Philip forbade this on moral grounds. Alba was checked by Sea Beggar ships and a handful of schutterijen at *Alkmaar* early in 1573, and again the Zuider Zee (October 11, 1573), where his fleet and royalist ships from Amsterdam lost to the Sea Beggars. Alba was recalled in November, and replaced by *Luis Requesens y Zúñiga*. He fared little better. In 1574, Zúñiga failed in an attempt to crush the Sea Beggars in a naval battle off Walcheren (January 29, 1574). On land, Zúñiga won a sharp fight at *Mookerheide* in April 1574, killing many Flanders nobles, including Louis and Henry of Nassau. However, he failed to complete the critical *Siege of Leiden* (May 26–October 3, 1574) after Orange daringly broke the dikes on the Maas and floated in a Sea Beggar fleet in relief.

A New State Emerges

By 1575 the northern Netherlands was beyond the physical control of Spain. Yet, Philip would not be reconciled to a negotiated peace that permitted Protestant services and rights. A regional revolt led by nobles in defense of traditional privileges had become a civil war within the Netherlands, and a war of religious ideology between Spain and the Calvinist, northern half of its colony. In late 1575 the fiscal crisis that underlay all Philip's troubles resulted in one of his periodic bankruptcies, leaving the Army of Flanders, 70,000–90,000 troops who cost 30,000 ducats a day to maintain, without pay through July 1576. The troops mutinied, starting just hours after rebel

Zierikzee surrendered to them: they sacked the town, then sacked Aalst three weeks later. The worst was yet to come, at Antwerp. On November 4–5, 1576, in acts of murder and mayhem remembered still in the Low Countries as the "*Spanish Fury*," much of the city was destroyed and 8,000 civilians were butchered. It was a decisive moment in the war: all 17 Dutch provinces, with a population of some three million, united around the goal of removal of Spanish troops and restoration of the medieval freedoms of the old city-states, as codified in the *Pacification of Ghent*. Yet, beneath the surface alliance Catholic–Protestant fissures existed that would ultimately prove unbridgeable, as fresh outbreaks of iconoclasm and religious rioting confirmed. More importantly, deeper and far older cultural differences existed between the regions north and south of the rivers.

And so the provinces divided. The southernmost, Walloon provinces—the major ones were Artois, Drouet, Flanders, Hainault, Liege, Limburg, Luxemburg, and Namur—combined to defend Catholicism in the Union of Arras ("Unie van Atrecht") on January 6, 1579. In reaction, Holland, Zeeland, and Utrecht formed the Union of Utrecht on January 23, 1579. The Union of Utrecht gained the early endorsement of Orange, who was forced to accept its intolerant Calvinism because the populace rejected his idea of "Religious Peace" in the north, while Spanish military success in Flanders and Brabant denied him those rich and populous southern areas as a base for the rebellion. Organized around the growing hegemony of Holland over the north, as well as an explicit Calvinist identity, by 1580 the Union of Utrecht added Friesland, Gelderland, and Overijssel, plus Drenthe (deemed too poor and under-populated to warrant a vote) and other small territories. In 1594, after the fall of Groningen to Maurits and a purge of the local Raad and all Catholic clergy, it added that city to the surrounding Ommelands as a seventh voting province. This consolidated the core of the "United Provinces of the Netherlands." In theory a loose sovereign confederation, during the 17th century the United Provinces emerged as a strong federal state dominated by Holland and a rising military and economic power. Meanwhile, under pressures of Spanish occupation but also out of mutual attractions of shared language, history, and religion, the Union of Arras declared for Catholicism, and eventually also for Spain. This fateful partition was reinforced by "ethnic cleansing" of religious minorities on both sides of the rivers in the early 1580s, and mirrored intolerance of alternate forms of worship.

In the end, Protestants could not accept a king or fellow countrymen who would not tolerate their faith, while Philip would not concede toleration to any part of his empire lest confessional divisions tear apart the whole. As the war proceeded, the Army of Flanders routinely hung Calvinist ministers and church elders, while Beggars butchered Catholic priests, nuns, and prisoners. On land, fighting henceforth was mostly a matter of breached canals and dikes, fortification and slow sieges, long waits in winter quarters, and very occasional battles. Denied the ocean lanes by the Sea Beggars, Spanish supplies and reinforcements had to make the slow crawl up the drawn-out, difficult "*Spanish Road*." Decade after decade, reinforcements from Italy or

Castile wended up this dangerous road through Lombardy, *The Grisons*, and the Rhineland, to spill into the "Castra Dei" ("God's Camp") in the Spanish Netherlands. Often, they detoured to engage in other Habsburg wars in Italy or in the great German war after 1618. Then they resumed the northward trek to lay in sieges and fight an occasional summer battle in the heavily fortified, close-confined, and densely populated Netherlands.

In 1576, Philip sent *Don Juan* of Austria north, the third commander dispatched to quell the "Revolt of the Netherlands." After a year of forced compromises Don Juan and his cousin, the *Duke of Parma*, returned to a policy of military confrontation that would reconquer the south for Philip by 1585. They began by routing a rebel army at *Gembloux* (January 31, 1578), a near-bloodless Spanish victory but a crushing defeat for the rebellion in the south. Parma succeeded Don Juan as governor when the latter died in October, and set out to appease Catholics while reducing all Protestant outposts by force. His troops sacked *Maastricht* in 1579, murdering over 10,000 civilians and thereby ensuring the rebellion continued. Orange proposed the *duc d'Anjou* as sovereign of the Netherlands, and a baleful experiment with this unstable and untrustworthy prince began in January 1581. In July, Philip II was formally renounced in an Act of Abjuration passed by the States General and sworn to by oath. With the north–south split now clearly irreducible and Parma on the march, Orange returned to Holland and the States General transferred from Antwerp to The Hague. With 45,000 local troops at his disposal in 1580 and 61,000 tough *tercio* veterans by 1582 (released by the end of Philip's war with the Ottomans), Parma reduced rebel towns in a systematic campaign. He took Tournai and Breda in 1581, advanced through Gelderland in 1582, and reduced Ieper, Bruges, Ghent, and Ypres in 1584. With the main outposts taken he conducted a successful, 14-month *Siege of Antwerp* (1584–1585). In desperation, a Dutch mission offered sovereignty to *Henri III* of France in February 1585, but he declined out of fear of

> *His troops sacked* Maastricht *in 1579, murdering over 10,000 civilians . . . ensuring the rebellion continued.*

the fanatics of the *Catholic League* and of the reaction in Spain. Other Frenchmen, in the Catholic League or among the Huguenots, intervened in the Netherlands on occasion, though more often Spanish armies from Flanders intervened in France. Meanwhile, in Delft in May 1584, Orange was assassinated by a Catholic fanatic. In the deed's aftermath Parma rolled up more rebel towns in Flanders and Brabant, leaving only Holland among the major provinces unoccupied. Parma then moved directly north across multiple river barriers and past fortified garrisons, while a second Spanish army attacked from the east toward Utrecht, Holland, and Zeeland. This threat of a Dutch military collapse brought *Elizabeth I* and England openly into the fray. She, too, declined an offer of sovereignty over the Dutch but lent substantial aid in return for real military rights and powers, as agreed in the *Treaty of Nonsuch*. This moved England and Spain from undeclared naval warfare closer to direct military confrontation. Much fighting thereafter took place at sea, inaugurating the world's first global maritime war as English privateers and Sea Beggar ships preyed on Iberian and neutral shipping. Philip retaliated with an embargo against trade with the United Provinces from 1585 to 1590, reimposed by *Philip III* in 1598. These embargoes did more damage to the stagnant and overstretched Spanish economy than to the more modern and diverse Dutch economy: Netherlands manufacturing and trade expanded in the 1590s, on the way to becoming the preeminent commercial system in the world in the 17th century.

An "English Interregnum" under the *Earl of Leicester*, Elizabeth's chosen commander and court favorite, lasted in the Netherlands from 1585 to 1587. It was marked by tensions between Leicester and the regents of Holland, and between extremist Calvinists and more moderate "politiques." Finally, there were hard frictions between Dutch towns with memories of the *English Fury* of 1580, and unpaid and hungry English troops. The crisis arrived in January 1587, when English garrisons in Deventer and near Zutphen, two key defense points, defected to Parma. The populace reacted with anger and violence against other English garrisons, so that more went over to the Spanish. Leicester attempted a coup in September 1587, entering The Hague with troops, but his plot fizzled and he returned to England, leaving Anglo-Dutch relations in tatters on the eve of the *Invincible Armada*. Parma wanted to continue his steady conquest but Philip was absorbed by the looming invasion and ordered Parma to muster the Army of Flanders for rendevous with the Invincible Armada, a Channel crossing, and a triumphal march on London. When the Armada was instead lost to storms and English fireships and captains, Spain's prestige was seriously damaged and its military reach shortened. The next year Philip again diverted a reluctant Parma, ordering him to intervene in behalf of Catholics in the French Civil Wars. After a brief campaign in France, Parma again advanced in the south and east Netherlands in 1589. The English garrison at Geertruidenberg betrayed itself to him and Dutch troops were pushed back across the IJssel. And yet, everything was about to change in favor of the Dutch Republic, as a military and diplomatic revolution took place with the end of the French Civil Wars that led to new alliances and conflicts that shaped the early 17th century.

Philip's attention was on France from 1590, where the Huguenot *Henri de Navarre* stood to ascend the throne as Henri IV. When the fighting finally stopped in France in the mid-1590s, Henri IV threw military resources behind the Dutch revolt as a counter to Spain. With *Oldenbaarneveldt* skillfully negotiating a fresh alliance with England, and shifting effective political power from the Raad to the Holland regents, the United Provinces enjoyed newfound security. *Maurits of Nassau* now rose to prominence upon his elevation to Stadholder, then through command and reform of the Dutch army. A driving force behind his successful military reforms was the fact that the United Provinces were unable to "make war pay for itself" (*bellum se ipse alet*) by billeting troops abroad or forcing *contributions* from a foreign population. Reliance solely on customs and direct taxes was a great incentive to make the most of military resources. In addition to meeting strategic interests, there was a civil and moral concern arising from Calvinist sexual mores to site the army in garrisons along the frontiers, far away from the main towns. Over time, the reforms undertaken told the tale on land against the Spanish tercios the way Sea Beggar ships already did on the water. In 1590, with his *New Model Army*, Maurits surprised the Spanish and retook Breda. The next year he liberated Zutphen, Deventer, Hulst, and Nijmegen in a series of brilliant sieges. He used the IJssel to move his heavy artillery by barge and paid bonuses to soldiers to dig siege trenches, a rare use at that time of soldiers as military labor in European warfare. In 1592, Maurits took Steenwijk and Coevorden, and he retook Geertruidenberg after a celebrated four-month siege in 1593. These victories opened the IJssel, Rhine, and Waal to Dutch river trade with Germany, further strengthening the economy of the United Provinces. Maurits cleared the Spanish from Groningen in 1594. In a second major offensive that made use of riparian transport to move siege guns, in 1597 Maurits advanced along the Rhine to capture the key fortress of Rheinberg. He then took the garrison towns of Oldenzaal, Enschede, and Grol, before crossing into Germany to capture Lingen and Moers. Maurits then stunned the Spanish in the field at *Turnhout* (September 22, 1597). The end of the Franco-Spanish war, codified in the *Treaty of Vervins* in 1598, freed more enemy troops for the Netherlands. But the same year witnessed the death of Philip II and passing of the Spanish Netherlands to his daughter Isabella and her Austrian husband, Albert, together known as "The Archdukes." In 1599, a year after the death of Philip II, the Army of Flanders mutinied yet again. All these events forced *Philip III* to reconsider Spain's strategy.

Stalemate and Truce (1609–1621)

The flow of military events continued to favor the Dutch as the new century turned: Maurits defeated a Spanish army on the dunes outside the privateer port of *Nieuwpoort* (1600), though no great strategic gain resulted. He took Sluis in 1603, then IJzendijk and Aardenburg. And although he supplied the army from the sea as it fought to relieve the three-year *Siege of Ostend*, the city finally fell to *Ambrogio di Spínola* in 1604. After Ostend and Nieuwpoort, Spínola partly revived Spanish military fortunes by daringly outrunning Maurits into Brabant, taking Oldenzal without a fight. In early 1606, Spínola crossed north of the Rhine. Taking and garrisoning key fortresses as he passed, he moved to the IJssel to threaten Zutphen and Deventer and sow panic in the United Provinces before withdrawing. Maurits counterattacked in the fall but did not reverse all Spínola's gains. A prolonged stalemate ensued in which each side built advanced fortified defenses while the diplomats talked. Philip III had made peace with France at Vervins in 1598 and with England in 1604, following Elizabeth I's death. In 1607 he offered to recognize the Dutch Republic in return for dismantlement of the *Vereenigde Oostindische Compaagnie* (VOC) and return of Iberian outposts in the Indies. But the Dutch balked and instead inflicted great damage to Spanish pride and a Spanish fleet at *Gibraltar* (1607). That forced Philip away from a lasting peace. In 1609 he instead accepted terms of the *Twelve Years' Truce* with the United Provinces, granting them de facto but not de jure recognition. In effect, Spain finally decided to let the Dutch "heretics" go to hell after their own theological fashion. The war would resume later because Madrid's war aims shifted from religious crusade to more limited secular, but still unachievable, goals: sustaining hegemony in the European states system rather than imposing a religious *monarchia universalis* upon a permanently fractured Christendom. And it resumed because the Dutch were consumed by commercial greed and would not stop aggressing against Iberian interests in Asia.

During the Twelve Years' Truce the Dutch economy continued its remarkable expansion and the VOC continued to predate in the Indies, while other Dutch fleets muscled into the rich Baltic and Russian trades. Meanwhile, Dutch international status soared as the Netherlands became known as the little Protestant country that fought mighty Catholic Spain to a standstill. Even Muslim powers (Algiers, Morocco, the Ottoman Empire) recognized the Dutch republic as sovereign. Prudently, the Dutch did not pose as the champion of Protestantism within Europe—that role would be played in the 1620s–1630s, without much success and at great cost, by the Palatinate, Denmark, and then Sweden. As the end of the truce neared pro-war parties took power in each belligerent. In Spain, the accommodating *Duke of Lerma* was dismissed while the secret *Treaty of Oñate* (1617) cleared the way for an aggressive alliance with *Ferdinand II* of Austria, who was bent on suppressing Protestantism and rebellion in the Holy Roman Empire. In the Netherlands, the United Provinces succumbed to bitter factionalism over matters of religion, trade, and the virtues of resuming the Spanish war. Civil war loomed by 1617 as Holland and Utrecht raised discrete *waardgelder* units which swore municipal, not national allegiance. This provoked Maurits to launch a coup d'état in August 1618, and later to execute Oldenbaarneveldt. The new supremacy of Calvinist "Counter-Remonstrants" under Maurits turned the United Provinces into the champion of confrontational Protestantism, even as Habsburg and Catholic power was resurgent. Then a revolt in distant Bohemia began the *Thirty Years' War*. That general conflagration drew in Spain and the Netherlands because of deep confessional loyalties and hatreds, but also out of old dynastic interests and new reasons of state.

Conflagration (1621–1648)

Once the Twelve Years' Truce expired in April 1621, the Netherlands war and the German war merged. Hoping to detour Spain into Germany, Maurits was deeply complicit in encouraging the brash *Friedrich V* to accept the Bohemian crown, sending subsidies and 5,000 Dutch troops (or Dutch hires) to fight at the *White Mountain* (November 8, 1620), and at Pilsen. The Dutch also paid for 4,000 English troops who set up in the Palatinate. With religious casus belli of diminished importance, economic warfare was the new order of the day. The embargos and river and port blockades resumed in April 1621, ending Dutch trade with Iberia and the Levant and Spanish trade with Flanders. Privateers reemerged from Dunkirk and Ostend, and Spanish warships attacked Dutch merchants off Brazil and in the Caribbean. The powerful Sea Beggar navy replied in kind. On land, the Army of Flanders expanded threefold from 20,000 men during the truce to 60,000 in 1621. The Dutch army leaped from 30,000 to 48,000 well-trained professionals, almost all deployed in a hard ring of fortresses around the frontier and none paid with foreign subsidies, all of which had stopped in 1609. By 1622, Maurits changed his mind and tried to back out of the war, but now *Philip IV* and *Olivares* took a hard line. Spínola took Jülich early that year, but was forced to abandon his siege of Bergen-op-Zoom after taking sharp losses. Dutch policy in Germany looked defeated after *Stadtlohn* (August 6, 1623), but Spínola failed to take strategic advantage while Maurits played for time by pretending negotiations. Spínola besieged Breda from 1624 to 1625, even as another Spanish army attacked from the east. Plague and butter tax riots broke out across Holland. As Maurits grew ill and died in April 1625, a noticeable malaise spread among the Dutch. Maurits was replaced in command by *Frederik Hendrik*, his half-brother. At first he could not stem the Spanish advance in Brabant or Germany. Fortunately for the Dutch, Spain could not sustain war on several fronts. In May 1625, Madrid cut funds by one-sixth and went strictly on the defensive in the Netherlands, in order to concentrate on its wars in Italy and Germany. England also entered the fight, briefly, in 1625. This pause in offensive action in the Netherlands shifted the military balance of power in favor of the Dutch, who wisely used it to rebuild and rearm as Spain cut back the Army of Flanders from 80,000 to 50,000 men.

In 1628 the fleet of the Dutch West Indies Company (WIC) captured the Spanish treasure fleet off Cuba. This deprived Philip IV of finances for his wars even as it allowed the Dutch to fund a large army of 128,000 men, including thousands from the WIC preparing to invade Brazil. For the first time, the Dutch fielded an army superior in numbers as well as quality to the Army of Flanders. Frederik Hendrik used the army in a sustained offensive that captured Wesel by storm and 's-Hertogenbosch by siege, forcing abandonment of Amersfoort by its Spanish garrison and a pullback across the IJssel from Utrecht and Gelderland. This was the greatest blow to Spanish arms and prestige since the failure of the Invincible Armada in 1588. Over the next two years, with Spain distracted by the *War of the Mantuan Succession*, Hendrik forced out nearly all Spanish garrisons in northwest Germany. The Spanish reached a point of near total military collapse: their river blockade failed and *Johann Tilly* was given control of all remaining forts. However, Tilly was killed at *Rain* in April 1632. The Dutch next moved to drive Spain from southern Flanders. In June, they took Venlo, Roermond, Straelen, and Sittard in rapid succession, then besieged Maastricht, which fell on August 23. The Republic was now secure. Henceforth, it waged war not just to survive but to gain rich overseas markets, and because of intrigue at home.

In early 1635 the United Provinces and France agreed to invade the Spanish Netherlands, granting sovereignty should the southern provinces rise against

Spain but partitioning and annexing them if they did not. Spanish garrisons fought hard against a French invasion in the south while trying to carry the war home to the United Provinces with a counterattack in the north. Spanish arms enjoyed a partial reversal of military fortune in the Maas valley and along the Dutch frontier. This reflected a new aggressiveness following *First Nördlingen* (1634) in Germany. Indeed, Jonathan Israel argues that Madrid made its most massive military effort "in terms of outlay and manpower of the entire Spanish-Dutch war" from 1635 to 1640. Even so, final victory eluded Philip IV. From 1635 the Spanish Road was blocked by the French, who also occupied Alsace, Lorraine, and Trier. And in 1636—the year of the tulip craze—Frederik Hendrik retook the key forts lost to Spain the prior summer. But Frederik was rebuffed with much loss at Kallo in 1638. Despite the victory, Spain remained stymied on land. Olivares therefore tried to resupply the Army of Flanders and to win the war by a concerted effort at sea. That meant facing the French and Dutch navies in the Channel and North Sea. In late 1639, Olivares sent 20,000 reinforcements north in a convoy of 40 transports and 60 escorts, only to have nearly the entire fleet destroyed at *The Downs* (October 21, 1639) by Admiral *Marten van Tromp*. After that, reinforcements reached Flanders only in single ships that ran the gauntlet of French and Dutch naval power as best each could. The loss at sea ended Spain's last hope of imposing hard terms on the Dutch. The *Revolt of Catalonia* began in May 1640, followed by a coup and full-scale rebellion in Portugal in December. Uprisings against Spanish rule also broke out in Naples and Andalusia. Seizing the moment, the Dutch moved to reduce the territory of the Spanish Netherlands, taking Gravelines (1644), Hulst (1645), and Dunkirk (1646).

> *The loss at sea ended Spain's last hope of imposing hard terms on the Dutch.*

Overseas, the WIC lengthened the strip of coastal Brazil it controlled (1638). Expeditions to Africa captured Pernambuco and Elmina (1637), and Luanda (1641). The VOC set up a fortified settlement on the Cape of Good Hope to service ships plying the waters of what was already a transoceanic Dutch empire that rivaled Spain's and overshadowed Portugal's. This had enormous consequences for African and world history. Mostly, it meant that Africa was to be drawn into a dynamic world trading system—mainly via the slave trade, which was soon mostly taken over by merchants and ships from the United Provinces. This rising sea power had far greater capabilities to penetrate the African interior than poor Portugal had ever exerted. Meanwhile, the VOC occupied Ceylon (1638–1641) and Malacca (1641). The Dutch first sent a flotilla around the Horn to raid the west coast of South America in 1624; they did so again, with impunity as well as impudence, in 1643. Authorities in distant Japan correctly read the shifting tide and transferred the Portuguese monopoly at *Deshima* to the Dutch. Meanwhile, Portuguese possessions in East Africa, other than Luanda, and most of India were bypassed. Dutch ships sailed farther south and east, then turned north to the Spice Islands. As a result, Omani military power and slaving revived in the western Indian Ocean.

The Dutch finally won the Eighty Years' War because of superior finance, their more modern economy and army, their rich overseas commercial empire, an exceptional national political effort, skilled leadership, and highly defensible and heavily fortified terrain where canals and river barriers formed successive lines of natural defense that were easily reinforced with artificial structures and barriers. More important even than the Dutch effort, however, were the problems faced by Spain. The Spanish had to supply and maintain a large army without access to the sea lanes and with the Scheldt estuary and the Flemish ports usually denied to them. That left only the vulnerable Spanish Road, and not even that reliably after France joined the German war in 1635. Despite this enormous difficulty in conducting large-scale military operations in the Netherlands, the Spanish made an extraordinary military effort over eight full decades. But with the rebel cause favored by topography and supported by the key classes in the local population, reconquest of the Netherlands proved impossible. When peace was finally agreed with the Dutch in the *Treaty of Münster* (1648) Spain was beaten, bitter, exhausted, bankrupt, inward-looking, and in terminal decline as a major power. And it was still at war with France, until 1659. In contrast, the Netherlands was self-confident, modernist in outlook, advanced economically and technologically, and enriched by its long war of overseas expansion and empire-building, even if it was abridged in size by the loss of southern Flanders and already peaking in its brief historical moment as a world power. See also *Fleurus, Battle of*; *Jülich-Kleve, Crisis over*; *Portuguese India*; *Taiwan*.

Suggested Reading: Paul C. Allen, *Phillip III and the Pax Hispanica, 1598–1621* (2000); A. Duke, *Reformation and Revolt in the Low Countries* (1990); Jonathon Israel, *Conflicts of Empires* (1997) and *Dutch Republic* (1995); Geoffrey Parker, *The Dutch Revolt* (1977; 1985); Marco Van der Hoevan, ed., *Exercise of Arms* (1997).

einschildig Ritter. "Single-shielded knight." See *Heerschildordnung*.

Elbing, Battle of (September 15, 1463). This naval battle was fought for control of access to the Vistula, whose mouth was guarded by the ancient *Teutonic Knight* fortress at Elbing. Twenty-five Polish warships engaged 44 ships of the Teutonic Knights. Overcoming the adverse odds, the Poles defeated the water-borne Brethren. Elbing, which had been a castle town of the Order since 1237, then fell to Polish land forces. It was followed in due course by most of the other Teutonic towns of Prussia.

El Dorado. The fabled "Kingdom of Gold" of the mythical tribe of "Amazonians." Unfortunately, too many *conquistadores* believed the myth, so thousands of Indians were tortured to death in the belief they were withholding information about its whereabouts. *Walter Raleigh* also looked for it in 1595.

elephants. Elephants as war animals were in common use in ancient Persia and North Africa. Most famously, Hannibal of Carthage crossed the Alps with several war elephants in 218 B.C.E. to descend with them into the north Italian plain on the road to Rome. In this period they were used extensively in warfare in India. Indian war elephants carried "howdahs," or high platforms for as many as a dozen archers or javelin throwers. Swords were sometimes attached to their tusks: as the war elephant swayed his great head from side to side in rage and confusion, these opened terrible slashing wounds in infantry or cut down the horses of opposing cavalry. However, the main use of war elephants was as living rams to smash through enemy formations. The disadvantages of elephants over conventional cavalry were twofold. First, elephants were overlarge and inviting targets for missile weapons. This was an exaggerated form of the same trait—the vulnerable bulk of the great medieval warhorse, or *destrier*—that drove English, and later French, knights to abandon their mounts and fight on foot. Second, elephants were more easily frightened and stampeded than were horses by the noise and smoke of gunpowder weapons. If wounded, they often went berserk with pain and panic, to trample and crush nearby friendly troops as much or more than the enemy. To try to preserve these great beasts in battle, elephant armor was introduced. The main piece was made of plate sewn into a large blanket and hanging to the knees. Other pieces covered the throat (to prevent slashing from beneath by a swordsman), the face and trunk, but not the ears, which though left exposed to injury were not vital. However, plate armor thick enough to stop musket balls proved too heavy even for an elephant to bear, as well as too expensive even for a maharaja or Mughal emperor to provide to his elephant corp. War elephants were also used in southern China and across southeast Asia. In the final campaigns of the *Hongwu* emperor, a Ming army used its superior firearms and cannon to panic or kill a number of war elephants employed by southern rebels. Similarly, a Ming army sent by the *Yongle* emperor into Dai Viet in 1424 used firearms to frighten and stampede enemy troops mounted on the backs of elephants. Elephants were not normally used in fighting in northern China. See also *Akbar*; *carroccio*; *Khanwa, Battle of*; *Panipat, Battle of (April 21, 1526)*; *Panipat, Battle of (November 5, 1556)*.

Suggested Reading: Simon Digby, *Warhorse and Elephant in the Delhi Sultanate* (1971).

Elizabeth I (1533–1603). Queen of England, 1558–1603. Daughter of *Henry VIII* and Anne Boleyn (1504–1536). Given the complexities of the succession and her parentage (her father had her mother judicially murdered), Elizabeth barely survived childhood. Fairly or not, she was suspected of complicity in the plot known as *Wyatt's Rebellion* (1554), which aimed to depose her half-sister and Catholic fanatic, *Mary Tudor*. Elizabeth was for a time imprisoned in the Tower of London, in jeopardy of execution for treason. Instead, in 1558 the childless Mary died and Elizabeth succeeded to the throne. Mary's widower, *Philip II* of Spain, offered to marry Elizabeth in order to keep his title as King of England. She demurred and played him well—she needed his help against the French—leaving him the first but by no means the last prince and suitor spurned by the "Virgin Queen."

Elizabeth ascended the throne outwardly a faint Catholic. Inwardly, most suspected she was already a Protestant. Her ascension at the age of 25 was therefore greeted anxiously by Catholics but with relief by her mostly Protestant subjects, as whatever her ceremonial trappings she ended the persecutions of Protestants carried out by Mary and was more tolerant of religious difference. Elizabeth generally tacked with winds favorable to Protestantism, recognizing that England was part of an increasingly Protestant northern Europe. In 1559, now more secure in her hold on power, she decreed that overt Protestant rites should displace Catholic ritual in national church services. For that and for establishing Protestantism over the next decade, in 1570 she was excommunicated by Pope Paul IV, who held her succession to be illegitimate in any case.

Excommunication of the monarch ensured that henceforth the cause of Protestantism merged with that of English patriotism and that Elizabeth was seen as champion of both. For centuries, England had allied with Castile against France and Scotland (the *"Auld Alliance"*), a balance of power whose last gasp was the dynastic marriage of Philip to Mary Tudor. Elizabeth's slow revelation of her Protestant sympathies forced a diplomatic revolution of the first order, aligning Protestant England with Dutch rebels waging the *Eighty Years' War* (1568–1648) against Spain. Serious and responsible as a ruler, almost to a fault, before plunging into Europe's confessional warfare Elizabeth spent a quarter century consolidating her grip on power in face of repeated disloyalty and assassination plots by members of the nobility and a former Queen of France, *Mary Stuart*, also Queen of Scots. Mary was a Catholic with a fair claim to the English throne and enjoyed support from the Habsburgs, France, and the pope. Such plots—over her reign Elizabeth survived more than 20 assassination plots—arose from the confessional wars coursing through Europe. (It should be noted that Elizabeth used assassins as well, to be rid of some of the Gaelic lords of Ireland, for instance.) They also centered on the succession problem, which grew more urgent as Elizabeth aged unmarried and barren of a direct heir; Elizabeth was destined to be last of the Tudor monarchs. Having kept Mary Stuart a prisoner for 20 years, with great public reluctance and much sincere private distress, Elizabeth ordered her fellow monarch's execution. It was carried out on February 8, 1587.

As queen, Elizabeth rationalized England's troubled finances as best a monarch could in an age of limited financial structures or knowledge of economics. She improved the administration of justice, fortified national defenses, and encouraged commerce. She reformed the Church of England, completing the process of making it subordinate to the state in return for establishment by the state. She had the foresight to charter the *East India Company*, and reigned over a tolerant cultural renaissance that witnessed and welcomed the likes of Francis Bacon, Edmund Spenser, and William

Shakespeare, when writers and thinkers elsewhere were harried, hounded, and burned by the *Inquisition* or Protestant confessional fanatics. Still, "Elizabethan England" remained a minor power, distinctly disadvantaged vis-à-vis the true Great Powers by its small population and the weakness of its army. Elizabeth compensated for weak territorial defenses by building a first-class navy and commissioning *privateer* ships and captains. She used this naval power to deflect French plans to invade Scotland in support of the Catholic party there (1558, 1560, and 1600). She instructed her privateers in a long though unofficial war at sea with Spain, from which she profited handsomely. With the help of *William Cecil*, she was brilliantly effective at diplomacy. She kept the pot boiling between an ancient foe, France, and a new archenemy, Spain, to keep both distracted and from her shores. She declined a desperate offer of sovereignty over the Netherlands in May 1585, but materially supported the Dutch "Beggars" as they stumbled toward near-defeat, exacting hard terms for her aid in the *Treaty of Nonsuch*. She dispatched privateers to the Caribbean to troll for treasure ships and to Newfoundland to harry the Iberian fishing fleets off the Grand Banks. When Philip replied with an embargo on English trade she sent *Francis Drake* to raided the Spanish coast in 1587, "singeing the beard" of the king by burning his ships and warehouses. Drake's insouciant desecration of Catholic churches and smashing of shrines in Spain, along with Elizabeth's execution of the Catholic Queen, Mary Stuart, provoked Philip to finally declare war on the "harlot usurper" in London.

Added to Elizabeth's mounting blows against Spain's economic interests and her alliance with the Dutch rebels was Philip's belief that it was God's plan that he should annex England to his empire to return it to the Catholic fold. Direct conflict no longer could be avoided. In 1588 the Navy Royale, along with bad weather in the Channel, defeated—or rather, deflected northward—the *"Invincible Armada"* sent by Philip to collect an army from Flanders and convoy it to England. That victory, or more accurately that avoidance of defeat, appeared so miraculous that many of Elizabeth's subjects came to see in England the New Israel, defended by God himself and his favorable "Protestant Wind." Her generals pressed the war hard against Catholic rebels in Scotland and Ireland who had accepted Spanish backing. Inflows of troops extended the Elizabethan conquest of Ireland, that dangerous Catholic neighbor and potential strategic backdoor to England, during the *Nine Years' War* (1594–1603). Upon Elizabeth's death in 1603, she left a kingdom more secure and united and more stable and prosperous than she had found it. And she left a realm that was ready to set out on a path of overseas colonization that would culminate in a world-spanning empire. Though her wars left the country financially crippled, that was not a situation of her choosing or a result she might have avoided. It was the common fate of royal finances in an age of chronic confessional warfare and ever expanding armies and navies. Among her

> *. . . Elizabeth survived more than 20 assassination plots . . .*

greatest achievements was recognition that it was in England's interest to oppose any large power that might dominate the Continent, be it Spain or France. She never carried confessionalism in foreign policy to the point of foolish promotion of the unattainable goal of destruction of either Catholic power. Reduction or distraction of the threat they posed to her small kingdom was enough. Besides, it was better that they balance against each other while she prepared the way for England's maritime expansion and later military greatness. To her anguished regret, Elizabeth died a childless spinster, last of the Tudors. She was succeeded by *James I*, son of her archrival Mary Stuart. See also *Essex, 2nd Earl of*; *French Civil Wars*; *Hanse*; *"King's Two Bodies"*; *Knox, John*; *Walsingham, Sir Francis*.

Suggested Reading: Paul Hammer, *Elizabeth's Wars* (2003); A. L. Rowse, *Expansion of Elizabethan England* (1955); R. Wernham, *The Making of Elizabethan Foreign Policy, 1588–1603* (1980) and *The Return of the Armadas* (1994).

embargo. See *Eighty Years' War*; *Philip II, of Spain*; *Philip III, of Spain*; *Twelve Years' Truce*.

emir. A Muslim chieftain or prince.

enarmes. Leather straps securing a *buckler*, or other *shield*, to the arm.

enceinte. A fortified enclosure. This was often a simple *keep* or *donjon* in early fortifications, but grew to become the main defensive perimeter—excluding all *outwork*—in later defensive complexes. See also *hornwork*.

encomienda. "Entrust system." This was the Castilian equivalent of the *commanderies* run elsewhere in Europe by the *Hospitallers* and *Teutonic Knights*. It was basically a military organization of economic life during the *Reconquista*, designed to sustain expansion and control of conquered territory in Iberia. It was subsequently introduced to the New World by Columbus. On Hispaniola it developed into a system of Indian forced labor, in which form in later years and decades it spread throughout the West Indies and much of Spanish America. In this system Spanish settlers obtained rights to compulsory Indian labor for their plantations or mines. This service was formally distinguished from slavery only by a legal veneer which instructed the Spanish "employer" to hold the physical and spiritual welfare (defined as conversion to Christianity) of their Indian laborers "in trust." *Charles V* issued a suppression edict in 1520 but this came too late for the *Aztecs* and other soon-to-be conquered Indian nations of the Central Valley of Mexico: *Hernán Cortés* impressed Mexico's surviving Indians into the encomienda system after 1521, while banning Indian forced labor in mines, work for which he thought Indians were ill-suited. The Dominicans and *Jesuits* opposed Indian enslavement, and won a legal—though in some ways hollow—victory against these practices in "New Laws" promulgated in 1542 following reports to the Court by the Dominican Bartolomé de Las Casas (1474–1566). These abolished formal Indian slavery while affirming the encomienda system in practice. This rough compromise between Christian conscience and Spanish conquest served to encourage colonial settlement by providing a guaranteed Indian labor force to the settlers. A formal ban on the encomienda system was declared by the Spanish crown in 1559, but was mostly ignored by the settlers in practice.

Since the crown refused to make Indian forced labor legally hereditary, the encomienda system could not evolve into permanent or outright slavery and thus slowly died out in most of New Spain and Peru by c.1600. It survived throughout most of the colonial period in Paraguay and Chile, in the latter partly because of successful Indian resistance to conquest in the southern half of the province. The system was supplanted in practice by a near-feudal en-serfment of Indian peasants in a new type of compulsory wage labor called "repartimiento" in New Spain and "mita" in Peru. This was accompanied by forced purchase of goods at fixed prices for the "corregidores" (provincial governors), which ensured pitiable wages led to perpetual indebtedness, and hence effectively hereditary servitude. Even this did not suffice to meet Spanish colonial labor needs, given the rate at which Indians died of exposure to virulently communicable European and African diseases in the 16th century. The complex system of Indian labor was therefore augmented from the 1570s with debt peonage among "free" Indians and importation of African slaves, who were not subject to the "New Laws." For ideological and racist reasons, black slaves never engaged the same sympathy from the Iberian clergy that Indians did. See also *requerimiento*.

Suggested Reading: Leslie Simpson, *The Encomienda In New Spain* (1966).

enfilade. Establishing a position to bring sweeping crossfire to bear on the enemy's flanks or at an oblique angle to his front. See also *solid shot*.

engagements. A Royalist *contribution* system, especially in support of supplying *warhorses*, in use during the *English Civil Wars* (1639–1651). In 1644 such "donations" were made compulsory.

engineers. Troops specializing as engineers developed primarily out of *siege warfare*, in which mining, earthworks, siege engines, and general field fortification were paramount. *Muhammad II* had engineers (*köprücu*) build bridges to move his guns and level roads. Engineer specialties also grew from the increasing importance of artillery in both offense and defense. The first modern corps of military engineers, specializing in field fortifications and building pontoon bridges as well as town walls, was organized by the United Provinces. It had 25 members by 1598. *Gustavus Adolphus* borrowed and adapted this idea, along with many others he took from the Dutch, deploying field engineers who were critical to the success of the Swedish army. See also *Bureau, John and Gaspard*; *lağimci*.

England. The limit of Roman military control of the island of Great Britain was marked by a series of defensive walls crossing the island at a series of narrow waists. The most famous of these frontiers was Emperor Hadrian's wall, which protected Roman towns and settlements from "barbarian" tribes to the north, while also channeling trade with these tribes (and tolls and taxes) through choke-point fortified gates. After the departure of the Romans, who progressively recalled the legions to fight in the protracted civil wars of the later Roman Empire, a progression of fragmented Anglo-Saxon kingdoms succeeded in England. Of these, the most important was Wessex. Next came the Vikings, first as coastal and estuary raiders but later as invaders and settlers. They overran most of the independent kingdoms, leaving only Wessex, which paid tribute to Danish kings resident in the north, in the Danegeld. The rump of Anglo-Saxon England was conquered by the *Normans* under Duke William from 1066 to 1070. Some historians argue that the Normans then replaced a strong, unitary Anglo-Saxon monarchy with a weak *feudal* state and "Norman ascendancy," and that this importantly divided rather than unified the peoples of Great Britain. Norman and Angevin kings of England held vast swaths of territory in France. They also sought to conquer and control Scotland and Ireland, the "Celtic fringe" (and also, strategic flanks) of their holdings in England that might serve as forward bases for invasion by a powerful continental enemy. During this period the main threat to England was local rebellion and the chronic low-level feuding and rural warfare that characterized feudal life in the 12th–14th centuries. Thus, the Barons' War (1260s) saw just two significant battles, at Lewes (1264) and Evesham (1265). The next decade opened a new phase in consolidation of English power in Britain. For 200 years following the Norman conquest, would-be invaders of Wales were stymied by the terrain and by Welsh defenses, notably Offa's Dyke. However, coastal Wales lay open to warships and landings. Edward I "Longshanks" (1239–1307) seized upon this fact and used the sea route to invade Wales in 1277, also resupplying his army from ships. In his second major Welsh campaign (1282–1283) the superiority of English logistics overwhelmed Welsh defenses. Edward then consolidated his hold over southern Wales by building (some historians think, overbuilding) expensive castles, some on nonstrategic sites. The Welsh rebelled in the north in 1294, forcing Edward to end a campaign in Gascony and shift his naval and land assets to Wales, where desultory fighting continued through 1295.

Norman, then Angevin, England had struggled constantly with France over possession of the rich Atlantic provinces of Normandy and Gascony. This dispute intensified at the end of the 13th century as the regional wine trade grew extraordinarily rich (over 1,000 ships per year left the Gironde) and both monarchies grew more potent. In 1293, France occupied English Gascony to force concessions on other disputes. This interrupted the wine trade, as well as English food exports to Bayonne. Hard-pressed to fight the French in Gascony, the English looked to Flanders and Normandy instead. In 1294 an English fleet landed an army that retook Bayonne. Contemptuously defying the English claim to *"sovereignty of the sea,"* in 1295 the French Mediterranean galley squadron came up the Channel, burned Dover and attacked several other coastal towns. Edward organized an alliance with the Flemings, but France invaded Flanders in 1297. A truce was arranged, then a peace in 1299. England's fortunes in France were saved by the stunning Flemish defeat of French chivalry at *Courtrai* (1302). A legacy of hostility remained to erupt again in the 1330s. Meanwhile, the three Edwards were distracted by chronic wars in Ireland and Scotland. Edward I's attempt to conquer Scotland was initially repulsed by *William Wallace*, his son, Edward II was repeatedly bested by the Bruce dynasty, and his grandson, *Edward III* inherited the bitter *"Scottish Wars"* that still wracked the British Isles at the end of his reign. In 1337, Edward III plunged England into a much greater fight on the continent: the *Hundred Years' War* (1337–1453). Edward developed a new tactical system that some think amounted to a *revolution in military affairs* in its use of massed infantry archers and dismounted men-at-arms. This innovation won repeated battles in Scotland and France. Nevertheless, England fell behind continental developments in land warfare by the end of the 14th century, and was greatly retarded also as a naval power: in the 14th century, England was attacked by fleets it could not match from Scotland, France, Genoa, Castile, and even Morocco.

Why? Because military advantages gained from Edward III's military reforms were squandered by moral and military complacency in the nation, and by lesser kings. England then descended into a brief civil war, from the deposition of Richard II (1399) to the victory of Henry IV at Shrewsbury (1403). England was a resurgent power, and a highly aggressive one, under *Henry V*. But after his premature death it again suffered from military smugness born of overly easy victories. It lost the Hundred Years' War in the end, along with all of its once formidable continental empire save for the treaty port of Calais. From 1327 to 1485, England also experienced the violent overthrow of three dynasties: the Plantagenets were usurped by the House of Lancaster in 1399; Lancaster was deposed by the House of York (1461–1485). The so-called *Wars of the Roses* ended with a third dynasty, the Tudors, mounting the throne. The civil wars decimated the landed nobility but freed minor gentry and the merchant classes to fill political and economic spaces. Military niches were also opened by the death or exile of nobles, leading to a new type of professional officer in England in the 16th–17th centuries.

The *Protestant Reformation* gripped England next, but took a peculiar form dictated at first by the marital, monetary, and martial interests of *Henry VIII*, rather than being shaped by the divisive issues of doctrine then shaking Germany and continental Europe. The confiscations of lands and wealth integral to Henry's "reformation" were used to pay for repeated, and ruinous, wars with France and Scotland, notably in 1528 and 1544. For half a century thereafter, the debts created by Henry left successors in penury. The instability and religious turmoil of the reign of Edward VI kept England out of foreign adventures, but this changed when *Mary Tudor* married *Philip II* and

England briefly joined Spain's war against France. That led to loss of the last Angevin territories on the continent: Calais in 1558 and New Haven (Le Havre) in 1562, as well as defeat at *Gravelines* (1558). As France stumbled through 30 years of civil war, *Elizabeth I* cautiously countered Spanish ascendancy and the *Counter-Reformation* in northwest Europe. She allied with Dutch rebels on land and sea, where she also challenged Spain with commissioned *privateers*. This led to a protracted but undeclared naval war. The crisis came a year after Elizabeth executed *Mary Stuart*. In 1588 Philip dispatched the *Invincible Armada* to escort the *Army of Flanders* to England's shores. Twice more before the 16th century ended England was threatened by Spanish fleets and invasions. Yet, during Elizabeth's last decade merchant companies and *sea dogs* planted the first settlements in the West Indies and North America. These were used as bases from which to attack Spanish shipping and ports, to promote English trade inside the Spanish monopoly zone and as a new source of royal revenue.

This colonial effort increasingly became "British" rather than English in the first half of the 17th century, following the union of crowns under *James I*, who also ruled as James VI of Scotland. With the union came peace along the border with Scotland and the proclamation that England and Scotland should henceforth be jointly called "Great Britain." Under the Stuarts the first toeholds of overseas empire were gripped in Virginia (1606), Bermuda (1609), Newfoundland (1610), New England (Plymouth, 1620, Massachusetts Bay, 1628), St. Kitts and Nevis (1924), Barbados (1627), Antigua (1632), and Maryland (1634). Nationalist propagandists and Protestant zealots saw this as fulfilling a providential English mission to uphold the "true Christian faith" and spread it to "heathens" in the Americas. But they also clung overlong to fear of Spain as an imperial and Catholic enemy—long after that threat subsided in fact. After 1600 England had greatly reduced reasons to fear Spain, which was itself much reduced. In any case, religious zealots did not (yet) speak for England: the government and merchant alliance that backed and oversaw early colonization schemes were moved far more by the promise of profits than by Protestantism, and not yet by the runaway Puritan convictions that would mark English policy at mid-century.

England was only briefly engaged in the *Thirty Years' War*. In the 1620s, James I intervened half-heartedly in behalf of the lost cause of his son-in-law, *Friedrich V*. A few years later *Charles I* sent ill-organized and badly commanded fleets that failed to prevent the Huguenots of *La Rochelle* from surrendering to France. Overall, England stayed out of the war upon making separate peaces with France (1629) and Spain (1630). Nevertheless, it was affected by the German war when thousands of English, Scots, and Irish returned to join in the convulsions and rebellions of the *English Civil Wars* (1639–1651). The outcome of the "Wars of the Three Kingdoms" of the 1640s–1650s was social revolution, judicial regicide, *Oliver Cromwell*'s theocratic republic, and the crushing of Catholic Ireland. The Civil Wars formalized the split between the Church of England and dissenters while leaving English, Scottish, and Irish Catholics outside a permanently fractured faith and newly established

Protestant Church. The Civil Wars also established the navy as the principal military arm of an island nation which over the next 200 years would acquire the greatest seaborne empire the world has ever seen. See also *Cromwell, Thomas*.

Suggested Reading: Cyril Falls, *Elizabeth's Irish Wars* (1950); Mark Fissel, *English Warfare, 1511–1642* (2001); Bruce Lenman, *England's Colonial Wars, 1550–1688* (2001); Michael Prestwich, *The Three Edwards* (1980) and *Armies and Warfare in the Middle Ages* (1996); James Wheeler, *Irish and British Wars, 1637–1654* (2002).

English armies. Anglo-Saxon England relied on the *fryd* to raise men for armies and navies alike. The *Normans* replaced this system with enfeoffed feudal military obligations, although the idea of fryd-style "national" service and collective obligation survived beneath the Norman surface to influence later attitudes and ease the transition to pay-for-service and large infantry formations. Still, the medieval English army was principally comprised of heavy cavalry recruited on a feudal basis, supplemented with mercenary infantry from as early as the 11th century. Most often, armies were led personally by the king, whatever his military competence. The cavalry was organized into *bannerets*, with larger knightly armies wrapped around a core of *housecarls*. England made the earliest and most successful transition to paid military service, in part because it had a strong monarchy sooner than most other European countries. In 1181, Henry II passed the *Assize of Arms* requiring "national" service of all knights ("free and honourable men"). In 1230 "unfree" English were added. By 1264 each village was assigned a quota of foot soldiers it had to raise and equip. Units of 100 village infantry were organized, led by mounted *constables*. These troops supplemented the royal housecarls and noble horse of the *servitium debitum*. More noble cavalry and men-at-arms were raised through the feudal levy, last called in 1327. More often, they were paid for with *scutage*.

> *Most often, armies were led personally by the king, whatever his military competence.*

Early in the *Scottish Wars*, Edward I demanded service even from lower propertied orders not bound by vassalage, but who had a specified and substantial annual income. These "distrained" men rode to battle as men-at-arms. All told, England could put about 5 percent of its male population under arms by 1300, at least in theory. The use of scutage and the rise of "bastard feudalism," in which the switch to a system of land tenure made it necessary to create new ties of quasi-vassalage to replace lost real ones, along with massive reliance on the nonfeudal levies with skill in the longbow, meant that England was first to abandon the old idea of reliance on unpaid military service by the landed nobility. The infantry that fought for Edward II at *Bannockburn* (1314) was mostly recruited by "commissions of array," in which the sheriffs and clerks of two counties were paired in order to muster a quota of adult freemen. After the *Shameful Peace* of 1328 even most nobles served for pay. By 1334 all of *Edward III's* men were paid. Scutage slowly faded from use, and was not demanded to raise troops after 1385. Instead, a system of *indentures*, or fee contracts paid to recruiting officers, was employed that lasted into the 15th century. Scholars estimate that as many as 10–12 percent of English armies at this time were outlaws, recruited to fight in the king's wars in return for a royal pardon in lieu of wages. With defeat in the *Hundred Years' War* (1337–1453), English armies ceased to be a factor in land warfare in Europe. England also lost its lead at sea, lagging badly behind several continental navies.

Michael Roberts excluded English armies from his consideration of the *revolution in military affairs*, suggesting that there was virtually no progress made toward military modernization during the *Wars of the Roses*, which saw little to no adoption of continental weapons or tactical advances. More recently, Mark Fissel argued that the English military system actually showed high levels of flexibility and absorbed numerous foreign military ideas, though giving them a unique English character in practice. A major difference from the continent was that military development in England relied far more on private interests than the state, and was more closely tied to naval warfare. From 1588 to the start of the *English Civil Wars* (1639–1651) most English soldiers were raised through conscription. For the first years of the Civil Wars men joined up to fight for pay, or for reasons of religious or constitutional conviction, personal honor, or class or ethnic hatred. While the Civil Wars saw major advances, notably in the *New Model Army*, men had to be conscripted by levy to fight in Ireland. After 1660, the smaller army England retained relied on volunteers. It was not until 1689 that England formally established a standing army. See also *Black Prince*; *Cavaliers*; *chevauchée*; *Cromwell, Oliver*; *Eighty Years' War*; *Essex, 2nd Earl of*; *Fairfax, Thomas*; *Henry V, of England*; *Henry VIII, of England*; *Ireton, Henry*; *Manchester, Earl of*; *Nine Years' War*; *Roundheads*; *trained bands*.

English Civil Wars (1639–1651). "The Great Rebellion." From 1629, *Charles I* governed without Parliament, even raising new taxes such as the infamous *ship money* by decree. He was supported by most of the Anglican episcopacy and segments of the nobility. He looked to *Arminianism* and ascendant royal authority to overcome competing confessional cultures that had divided the "Three Kingdoms" of England, Ireland, and Scotland since the reign of *Henry VIII*. In trying to impose a unitary monarchy and conformist religion on the diverse peoples of the British Isles, Charles provoked three discrete oppositions to himself and the monarchy, each defending a distinct confessional-patriotic identity. Nascent Irish patriotism was linked to international Catholicism but divided by ethnic and religious differences among *Old Irish*, *Old English*, and *New English*. Scotland was steered by a radical assembly of the Scottish Kirk, the *Covenanters*, who sought to outmaneuver rather than overthrow the king. Outlying areas such as Cornwall and Wales, and parts of northern England, were staunchly loyal to the crown. But the English south was very different. English patriots were restrained, at first, by a conservative Parliament that emphasized tradition and public order over aspiration to utopian godliness. But in the end, king and Parliament alike would be set aside by zealots who set up an English theocracy, enforced by military dictatorship, in place of what they saw as the twin evils of a corrupt and heretic monarchy under Charles and moral timidity and an overly compromising spirit in Parliament.

1640–1641

Dissent was everywhere evident in the "Three Kingdoms" in 1640. The Covenanters controlled Scotland, except where Highland clans attacked their outposts in the old style of private raids and warfare, while Ireland was plunging toward a confessional insurrection and murderous violence in 1641. English troops had sacked churches on their way to the *Bishops' Wars*, apprentices rioted in London, and payment of taxes was refused. The Long Parliament, which first met on November 3, focused its discontent on Charles' key ministers, the Earl of Strafford and Bishop Laud, impeaching them for recruiting Catholic troops in Ireland and for promoting Arminianism in the English Church. In December the Commons declared ship money illegal and accepted the *Root and Branch petition*. When Charles refused to disband his 9,000-man Royalist army in Ireland, Parliament sharply curtailed his legal authority (February 15, 1641), then executed Strafford for treason (May 12). Peace talks with the Covenanters nearly foundered over religious conformity, with the Scotts offering Presbyterianism and the English arguing for episcopacy, each deeply distasteful to the other camp. Still, a truce was agreed (Treaty of London, August 1641). Then the long-simmering revolt of Catholics against the advance of Protestantism in Ireland erupted in serial massacres of some 4,000 "Plantation" Protestants. Local Irish armies were quickly reinforced by tough mercenary captains and soldiers home from the German and Dutch wars. Soon, Catholics controlled most of the countryside while Protestant militia and a Royalist army under *Ormonde* held the major towns of the Pale and Ulster. More than any other factor, the Irish rebellion influenced English and Scottish politics until 1651: neither Parliament nor the Covenanters, both virulently anti-Catholic, could accept a Catholic ascendancy in Ireland, but neither would they pay for or entrust any army to the king for fear he would turn it against them. After his death, they could not trust armies raised by Irishmen or by each other.

1642–1643

The Scots sent a Covenanter army to Ulster to assist the Protestant settler militia. No sizeable English army was sent to Ireland until 1647, however, because civil war now broke out in England. The trigger was Parliament's effort to take control of the Army by introducing *impressment*, which in turn brought confrontation between Commons and king over exclusion of bishops from the Lords, where they could block Acts passed in the Commons. Brash young nobles egged the king to confrontation. He gave in, sending the Sergeant-at-Arms to arrest five members of the Commons on January 4, 1642, then going there himself surrounded by *reformadoes*, only to find the sparrows had flown. The members retired to London under protection of the *trained bands*. Charles moved to Hampton Court and then to Oxford, to raise an army to impose his will on Parliament and the Kingdom. The queen crossed to

France to raise money and allies, while Charles tried but failed to seize the armories at Portsmouth and Hull: this was important, as England had been so long at peace, 1603–1642, it was barely armed. By October each side had scrounged or imported enough arms to field large, if rather poorly equipped and trained armies: the king had 19 regiments of foot and 10 of horse, close to 24,000 men; Parliament had a larger force of mostly trained bands, London apprentices, and most of the navy.

When fighting started the Royalists (Cavaliers) were strong in Wales, the West counties and the Midlands, while Parliamentary forces (Roundheads) controlled London and the south, including most naval assets, officers, and men. The first Royalist attempt to take London led to a skirmish at Powick Bridge, near Worcester, on October 23, 1642, where *Prince Rupert* saw his first action. The larger battle of *Edgehill* was also fought that day. A renewed Royalist advance led to a scuffle at Brentford, 10 miles north of London, on November 12, 1642, after which the victorious Royalists sacked the town. However, an uninspired Cavalier pursuit of the beaten Roundheads allowed *Essex* to join with 12,000 men of the trained bands of London. There followed a standoff "battle" at Turnham Green (November 13–14, 1642), where Essex barred the Royalists with a display of superior numbers. The two sides exchanged desultory cannon fire, but neither attacked and no blood was shed. The first year of the war ended ingloriously, with Charles withdrawing to winter quarters in Oxford. The Royalists had displayed a highly aggressive spirit, compared to much lethargy and tactical caution on the part of Essex and other Parliamentary generals. Frustration with the Army built among harder men of zealous views in Parliament's ranks.

Meanwhile, rebellion broke out in Ireland in 1641. It drew thousands of Irish veterans of the continental wars home, including 1,300 from the Army of Flanders and 1,000 from French or Swedish service. These formed the core of the *Confederate Army* that gathered to support the principles of the *Confederation of Kilkenny*. The Irish rebels never controlled a major harbor in Ulster, and thus had great difficulty supplying their troops with modern artillery and shot or preventing Royalist amphibious operations and resupply. In the south the Confederates held onto Waterford, Wexford, and Limerick. While protecting these ports was a drain on limited resources, they supported naval actions and kept contact open with the Catholic powers of Europe. At sea, about a dozen Confederate 18- or 24-gun "Dunkirk frigates" and other light warships were quite successful in coastal raiding, harassment of English supply lines, and protection of southern Irish ports. In addition, *letters of marque* were issued to over 30 foreign frigates to operate in Irish waters against Protestant shipping, of which they took hundreds of prizes. The Confederate navy peaked at close to 50 warships in the late 1640s. From the outset all sides built *artillery fortresses*, most extensively around Limerick, Dublin, and Belfast. In the country, older castles served as forts, compelling the Royalists to spread overly thin as they occupied too many small garrisons. In turn, that meant field armies in Ireland remained small and battles were mostly indecisive.

During the winter of 1642–1643, Parliament created four "Association" armies. The Western Association army was quickly defeated, by *Ralph Hopton* at Braddock Down (January 19, 1643). Then Rupert sacked Birmingham (April 3) and took Lichfield (April 21). The Roundheads struck back as *William Waller* captured Hereford (April 25) and Essex forced surrender of the garrison at Reading (April 26). *Oliver Cromwell* spent a winter training the *Eastern Association Army*, then fought a sharp action at Grantham (May 13) where his *Ironsides* beat a Cavalier force twice their strength: the Royalists no longer enjoyed the advantage of superior cavalry, but not all Parliamentary horse was up to Cromwell's standard. Returning to Oxford from a raid, Rupert met Roundhead cavalry at Chalgrove Field (June 18). He charged, as always, scattering the enemy and killing their commander, John Hampden. Pym ushered the *National Covenant* through Parliament and impeached the queen for raising foreign monies and troops, while Essex only sat while Parliament's army deteriorated from disease and desertion. In Yorkshire, *Thomas Fairfax* was beaten at Adwalton Moor (June 30), but secured Hull for Parliament as he fell back. In the West, Hopton defeated *"Lobsters"* from London at Stratton (May 16) and again at Lansdowne (July 5), where he captured their artillery and baggage train. Hopton lost so many troopers at Lansdowne, however, he had to retreat to Wiltshire. He won again at Roundway Down (July 13), killing nearly 1,000 and capturing or scattering Waller's whole army of 4,500. That opened the way for Rupert to take Bristol for the Royalists, which he did on July 26 after hard fighting and the loss of over 500 Cavaliers. A hard fight, but Bristol was a real prize: it gave the Royalists access to commercial wealth, trade, and foreign aid. The next day a cavalry fight at Gainsborough saw Cromwell and 1,800 Ironsides scatter some 2,000 Cavaliers. Still, the king was enjoying real military success. Cavalier armies moved into Dorsetshire and Devonshire in August, took Exeter, and laid siege to Plymouth and Gloucester. It was the apex of Royalist fortunes: Charles was winning in the regions and planned a final assault on the stronghold of London. In near panic, Parliament approved new excise taxes and ordered conscription of 6,500 horse and 10,000 foot for the Eastern Association Army. Reinforced, Essex relieved Gloucester (September 8) while the navy resupplied Plymouth. Essex's route back to London was blocked by Charles and Rupert, so that Essex had to fight at *First Newbury*. There, Charles deployed poorly and lost badly and Essex fought well and won. In October, Parliament agreed to the "Solemn Oath and Covenant," a military alliance with the Scots against "papists . . . in arms under pretext of serving the king." Meanwhile, the Irish Confederates allied with Charles. It was becoming a whole other war.

1644–1645

In early 1644 the *Earl of Leven* led 21,000 Scots, the largest army in Britain, south to fight the king. As they moved, Rupert took Newark, giving the garrison generous terms. Waller won for Parliament at Cheriton (March 29), forcing Hopton to withdraw to Cornwall. There, he was hemmed in until forced to surrender in 1646. On May 28, Rupert sacked Bolton, massacring

1,600 defenders and civilians. On June 11 he took Liverpool and two weeks later Charles won at Cropedy Bridge (June 29), near Banbury. That rout allowed him to release Rupert to relieve the siege of York, where Fairfax, Manchester, and Cromwell had linked forces with Leven, gathering 27,000 men. Charles gave Rupert just 18,000 men and orders to seek battle. The great clash came at *Marston Moor* on July 2, a disaster for the king that lost him the north and much of the center of England. York fell on July 16, and other garrisons followed as Manchester and Cromwell marched south. Meanwhile, Charles caught Essex at Lostwithiel (September 2), in the far west. Over two days Charles surrounded and crushed Essex, who deserted his men and fled, leaving 6,000 prisoners to Charles. The king magnanimously allowed them to leave, stripped only of muskets and cannon. That was foolhardy considering Parliamentary armies now outnumbered the king's, though it is hard to see what else he might have done short of atrocity. He was aided by Roundhead generals falling into bitter quarrels over strategy and the prestige of command. An indecisive clash at Second Newbury (October 27) did nothing to staunch jealousies, or fears, among higher officers about social radicalism brewing in the Parliamentary Army. The core dispute was that Cromwell and the Puritans were determined on victory over Charles, while Manchester, Essex, and the Lords doubted the war could be won if the king, the rightful sovereign whatever his faults, refused to surrender his will.

> *Over two days Charles surrounded and crushed Essex, . . . leaving 6,000 prisoners to Charles.*

Over the winter Parliament funded, and Fairfax and Cromwell officered and trained, the *New Model Army*. The older, *Northern Army* took Shrewsbury by surprise on February 22, 1646. That forced Charles to send Rupert north and delayed operations to clear the southwest, where Waller's unpaid men were near mutiny and Waller himself resigned. But Cromwell scoured the Oxford countryside, scooping up small parties of Royalists and denying Charles the horses he needed to move his armies while the New Model Army completed training. The war in Ireland continued to no real end other than to tie down potential Royalist reinforcements and 10,000 Covenanters in Ulster. In Scotland, the Royalist cause fared better under the inspired leadership of the *Marquis of Montrose*. He led Highlanders to victory over the Covenanters at *Tippermuir* (September 1, 1644), and three more times in 1645, at *Auldearn* (May 9), *Alford* (July 2), and *Kilsyth* (August 15). However, when Montrose moved south at the behest of the king, who was desperate to retake the north of England and for relief from Roundhead pressure, Montrose's highlanders were wiped out by *David Leslie* at *Philiphaugh* (September 13, 1645). Montrose barely escaped with his life, and later went into exile.

All that was peripheral: the decisive battle was fought in England on June 14, when the New Model Army caught up with the Royalists at *Naseby*. That brilliant and decisive victory for Fairfax and Parliament broke Charles' ability to lay siege or wage aggressive war. Among the spoils were the king's papers, proving he was conspiring to bring 10,000 Irish Catholics to fight in England.

That did in the Royalist cause politically, as well. Fairfax and Cromwell moved directly to the southwest, to reduce that core Royalist stronghold. Cavaliers tried to stop them at Langport (July 10, 1645), but were no match for the New Model Army. That fight cleared the way for a siege of Bristol, starting on August 23. Rupert surrendered the town on September 11, to the lasting disgust of the king, who disgraced and banished the talented if impetuous Bavarian.

1646–1651

The last Royalist field army in England, just 1,500 men, was trapped and crushed at Stow-on-the-Wold (March 21, 1646). Charles I was forced to abandon Oxford, and on May 5 he surrendered to David Leslie's Scottish army. His hopes to bring the Scots to his side foundered on his known mendacity and his lack of understanding of the depth of religious feeling loose in the Three Kingdoms. In any case, Montrose was on the run in Scotland. The Royalists in Ireland were ascendant after *Owen Roe O'Neill* crushed the Covenanters at Benburb in 1646, but that was not enough. Royalist rats deserted the king's sinking ship by the hundreds, going abroad or to London to submit to Parliament. With Charles in semi-exile on the Isle of Wight, the Army and Parliament controlled England. Disputes immediately broke out with the Scots over pay-in-arrears for Scottish troops in England, and over gentler *Erastianism* versus rigid Presbyterianism in the Church of England. The king's continuous plotting with the Irish, French, and Spanish, his duplicitous negotiating and easy lies, raised Cromwell's suspicions that the "peace party" in Parliament might surrender in negotiations with the king all fruits of victory won by the Army. As fighting continued in Ireland, Parliament struggled with paying off its war debts and argued with Fairfax and Cromwell about quartering and arrears, as well as Presbyterianism versus Puritanism and who really controlled policy and the government. Inside the Army grumbling increased as *Levellers* agitated for radical social change. Matters came to a head on August 6, 1647, when Fairfax and Cromwell occupied London over objections of Parliament. For the next eight months they were the effective government. In 1648, Fairfax split with Cromwell over the matter of the king. Cromwell then moved to settle for once and all with a stubborn man who refused to recognize in law what had been decided in fact on the field of battle. In December 1648, Charles was charged with treason and tried before Parliament. He was beheaded on January 30, 1649.

While events were moving toward the king's execution, Royalist and Confederate fortunes also deteriorated in Ireland. The papal nuncio, Rinuccini, failed to unite Irish Catholics politically even as the Confederates lost their Leinster army to defeat at Dungan's Hill (August 8, 1647) and their Munster army at Knocknanuss (November 13, 1647). Anti-Parliament riots by London apprentices, a major Army mutiny, a naval mutiny, rebellion in Wales, and Royalist risings in Essex and Kent consumed the first half of 1648. Cromwell marched to Wales in May and put down the rebellion by July, more by offering generous terms than by fighting. Fairfax smashed the uprising in Kent at

Penenden Heath (June 2) and in Essex at Colchester (June 13), the latter one of his harder fights. A Scots-Royalist army of just 10,000 men invaded England on July 8, reopening hostilities ("Third Anglo-Scots War") over the matter of establishing Presbyterianism in England and demands that religious dissenters be ruthlessly suppressed. The Scots-Royalists were destroyed by Cromwell at *Preston* (August 17–20, 1648). In Ireland, *George Monk* seized Belfast, Colerane, and Carrickfergus for Parliament. In August 1649, Ormonde was surprised and routed at *Rathmines* (August 2, 1649). A month later, Cromwell sacked *Drogheda*, butchering all Catholic clergy still alive when the walls fell; he repeated the deed at *Wexford*. Montrose landed in Scotland a year later with 1,500 men, vainly hoping to spark a Royalist uprising. He was surprised, routed, and captured at *Carbiesdale* (April 27, 1650), and executed by Argyll the next month.

Fighting in the island kingdoms continued for several years, but the major issues were decided by 1649. Parliament was established as supreme in law, though the Army was superior to the Commons in fact and deed. England henceforth was overwhelmingly dominant among the Three Kingdoms, with Scotland warily independent but increasingly subservient, and Ireland pressed under the iron heal of foreign garrisons and government. Catholicism would not be established in Ireland; it would be barely tolerated on the margin in England, and repressed in Scotland. Militarily, guerrilla fighting in Ireland and mopping up operations in Scotland were all that remained, and were mostly completed by 1653. From an amateur start, England had developed one of best land forces in Europe and possessed a superior navy. It was prepared to use both against whatever dash of Gaelic romanticism or fatalistic resistance remained within the Three Kingdoms, and to support a burgeoning overseas territorial and commercial empire. See also *Blake, Robert*; *club men*; *Committee of Both Kingdoms*; *Fifth Monarchists*; *Levellers*; *Nantwich, Battle of*; *Puritans*; *redshanks*; *Winceby, Battle of*.

Suggested Reading: John Barratt, *Cavaliers* (2000); Charles Carlton, *Going to the Wars* (1992); R. Cust and Ann Hughes, eds., *The English Civil War* (1997); James Wheeler, *Irish and British Wars, 1637–1654* (2002).

English Fury (April 1580). English troops sent to the Netherlands by *Elizabeth I* to assist *William the Silent* and the Dutch rebels against Spain, ran amok and sacked the predominantly Catholic town of Mechelen. The appellation recalled what had been suffered in Antwerp during the "*Spanish Fury*" in 1574.

Enrique the Navigator (1394–1460). Prince of Portugal. *Mestre* of the *Knights of Christ*. This Portuguese prince was a navigational and maritime pioneer, a key early explorer of Africa and the Atlantic. A devout Catholic, he wore a hair shirt and performed extreme devotions. He was also dedicated to the expansion of Christendom. To this end, he founded an observatory and school of navigation from which later explorers, aided by Jewish cartographers and Muslim pilots, sailed to map the coasts of Africa, India, and South America. Like Enrique, his captains went in search of gold as well as knowledge, and looked for pagan souls to harvest for "The Christ." Enrique was present at the capture of *Ceuta* in 1415. His explorers discovered Madeira in 1418, en route to the gold fields of *Guinea*. In 1433 his ships reached Cape Bojador and in 1440, Cape Blanco. Enrique settled permanently at Sagres, on Cape Vincent in 1443, and thereafter all his vision and energy was devoted to exploration. In 1427 one of his ships reached the Azores, where Portuguese colonization began in 1439. In 1444 another of Enrique's ships touched shore on uninhabited Cape Verde, and by 1460 other ships made landfall in Sierra Leone, 600 miles farther south along the West African coast. His life's work challenged the scientific—and thus, also certain religious—assumptions of his day and launched Europe into the *Age of Exploration*. His efforts also forced changes in the international law of the sea, and led to the later promulgation of the *line of demarcation* which had such an impact on the fortunes of far-off peoples of whom Enrique and his Brethren as yet knew nothing. Along with Columbus, Enrique is therefore widely considered a key progenitor of the modern age.

Suggested Reading: Peter Russell, *Prince Henry "the Navigator"* (2000).

enseigne. "Band." A small tactical unit in French armies (Huguenot and Royalist). Several enseignes made up a *company*.

ensign. In an early *Landsknechte* company, this was a large man chosen for his strength and bravery to carry the *Fähnlein*, or banner. Later, once firearms came to dominate the field of battle, young boys of little martial value, who could be easily replaced, were assigned the task. From this practice, a junior rank of "ensign" was instituted.

"Enterprise of England" (1588). See *Invincible Armada*.

epaulière. See *pauldrons*.

equine armor. See *armor*.

equitatores. See *lance* (2).

equites. Mounted infantry. See *dragoons*.

Erasmus (1466–1536). See *Luther, Martin*; *Protestant Reformation*.

Erastianism. The argument for state control of the Church (benefices, bishoprics) made by Thomas Erastus (1524–1583), a devout German Catholic who opposed what he thought were Lutheran and Calvinist ambitions and tendencies to local theocracy. Erastus argued for a return to the original condition of the Church, as he imagined it, before the Cluniac and Gregorian reforms of the 11th and 12th centuries expanded papal independence from secular power. Erastian arguments were especially influential in the Protestant Reformation in England. See also *English Civil Wars*; *Gallican Church*.

Ermes, Battle of (1560). An early battle in the *First Northern War* (1558–1583) and last stand of the *Livonian Order*. Several hundred Brethren and 500 auxiliaries foolhardily attacked several thousand Muscovite troops. Half the knights were killed. Most of the were rest captured, taken in chains to Moscow, and executed by *Ivan IV*. The next year, the Order disbanded.

esame. The pay ticket of a *Janissary*. It was the most prized privilege of the Corps. See also *dead-pays*.

escarp. In fortification, the inner face of a ditch that formed a steep bank before and below the *rampart*.

escutcheon. The great shield of a *knight* of the European Middle Ages.

esmeril. By the late 16th century this term described the smallest class of artillery piece, about 200 pounds deadweight and 2.5 feet long. An "esmeril" fired shot weighing less than a third of a pound to an effective range of 200 yards. At sea, it was used principally as a man-killer.

espaliers. Armor protection for the shoulders.

esplanade (1). The sloping part, or *glacis*, of the *parapet* that led away from the main fortification toward the countryside and the enemy's forward position.

esplanade (2). An open space between the *citadel* and a town's buildings and walls.

espringarda. Originally, a type of Iberian crossbow, but by the 15th century it referred to a "hand cannon" that was closely related to the later *arquebus*.

esquire. Originally, one of the lowborn attendants of a *knight*. From the 13th century, esquires (or squires) accompanied aristocratic masters into battle bearing arms themselves. Over time, martial endeavor earned some of them the right to elevation to knighthood, as commoners who had nonetheless displayed the attributes and skill, and thus earned the social status, of a true gentleman. Alternately, a squire was the second stage of apprenticeship and ascendancy to knighthood for a young noble. It followed years as a *page* and preceded the dubbing ceremony and oath-taking of full knighthood. The terms were not written in stone: Philippe Contamine notes that comparable classes of auxiliary knights were called "valets" or just "boys," with corresponding terms in Latin, German, Italian, French, and so on.

Essex, 2nd Earl of (1566–1601). Né Robert Devereux. A court favorite of *Elizabeth I*, and son-in-law to *Leicester*, he fought in the Netherlands, 1585–1586. In 1591 he commanded English forces sent to France to aid *Henri IV* against the Catholic League. In 1596 he captured Cadiz, but the next year led a disastrous expedition to the West Indies. In 1598 he literally turned his back on Elizabeth and fell out of her favor. He served as Lord Lieutenant of Ireland for half a year, concluding a peace with the Earl of Tyrone during the *Nine Years' War* (1594–1603). He was imprisoned and disgraced by the queen. In answer, he formed a quarter-baked plot to do her in, trying to raise London against her (February 8, 1601). Condemned for high treason, he was beheaded.

Essex, 3rd Earl of (1591–1646). Né Robert Devereux. Elder son of the executed 2nd Earl, he took command of the Parliamentary Army in 1642 at the start of the *English Civil Wars*. He was personally brave, but a mediocre strategist and overly cautious field general. He demonstrated both qualities at *Edgehill*. He joined with and led the *trained bands* of London in the stand-off "fight" at Turnham Green (November 13–14, 1642). In 1643 he took Reading, relieved Gloucester, and showed some real tactical skill at *First Newbury*. He was crushed at Lostwithiel (September 2, 1644) by Charles, losing 6,000 men who were taken prisoner, along with most of his guns. His expedition to Cornwall was a major disaster from which he was forced to flee by ship. He resigned his command in April 1646. He died in September.

Estates. Medieval Europe was traditionally divided into three estates, or orders or classes: the clergy, the warrior class of *knights*, and laborers of town or country. In the early modern period most European monarchies had some "representative" institutions for the Estates of their societies, but nowhere was the distinction between l'état and les l'états ("state" and "estates") as sharp as it would become in the 18th century. The Swedish *Rigksdag* may have come closest to representing the "nation," and as such played a key role in sustaining Sweden's conscription and war tax system and military effort in Germany after 1630. An advanced representative institution was the English Parliament at Westminster. During the *English Civil Wars* it defeated the king in arms, tried and executed him, then raised taxes and governed for a time without him— until the Army decided to govern without Parliament. The *Reichstag* of the *Holy Roman Empire* waxed and waned in importance. Although fatally divided by confessionalism during the *Thirty Years' War*, the German

> *The Cortes in Castile was limited to the merchant class and hardly influenced the Spanish monarchy . . .*

Estates still managed to frustrate the attempt by *Ferdinand II* to monopolize the right to wage war. The Dutch Estates, too, exercised sovereignty on matters of war and peace, and gained full legal status in 1648. Elsewhere, the relative power of Estates and monarchs varied widely. In Poland, the *Sejm* was dominated by the barony and persistently hamstrung the monarchy's ability to wage war. The Danish Estates refused to pay for *Christian IV*'s German war, forcing him to wage it in his capacity as the Duke of Holstein. The Russian "zemsky sobor" had only dim influence on governance, and even then only during the reign of *Boris Godunov* and the *"Time of Troubles."* Its single most important act was to elect Michael Romanov tsar in 1613. The Cortes in Castile was limited to the merchant class and hardly influenced the Spanish monarchy on any issue. In France, the Estates General (États-généreaux) had little power and did not even meet from 1484 to 1560. During the *French Civil Wars* (1562–1629) the impecunity of the monarchy forced calling of the Estates in 1560–1561, 1576–1577, 1588–1589, and 1593. After that they did not meet again until 1789. See also *contributions*; "*Defenestration of Prague*" *(May 23, 1618)*; *Edict of Union*; *Imperial Diet*; *Louis XIII*; *Osnabrück, Treaty of.*

étapes. A logistical system developed along the *Spanish Road* in which towns were required to store food and fodder at preset rest stations for purchase by arriving Habsburg troops. This was not quite a *magazine* system, but something close to it. During the *Thirty Years' War* local villagers were replaced by *sutlers* under contract to the crown. The French tried to replicate this system for troops moving to the Rhineland or into Flanders. They were not as efficient as the Spanish due to sabotage of the system by French officers who profited from the older method of regimental supply, corruption among sutlers, and lack of central royal funds.

Eternal Peace (1533). A treaty signed by Poland-Lithuania and the Ottoman Empire wherein Poland accepted the loss of Hungary to the Ottomans. In an exaggeration typical of the age, and of peaces in general, it declared that peace between these powers would be "eternal." It actually lasted longer than most such agreements: the Poles and Ottomans remained mostly at peace to 1620, when Poland was held responsible by the Ottomans for *Cossack* raids into the Crimea.

Ethiopia (Abyssinia). An ancient Christian and feudal empire, Ethiopia maintained pilgrimage ties to Jerusalem even after the expansion of Islam in the 7th–10th centuries cut it off from direct links with the Mediterranean world. Also, it sent to the Coptic community of Egypt for Monophysite bishops to head the Ethiopian church. In 1270, when the Solomonid dynasty was founded, Ethiopian power reached its zenith. The Solomonids abandoned ancient capitals in favor of peripatetic military encampments which furthered their ambition for westward expansion at the expense of smaller, pagan kingdoms. Under Emperor Amda Syon (r.1314–1344) Ethiopia also expanded southward, overrunning several Islamic "Sidama," small Muslim slave-trading states, and exacting tribute from others (Ifat). Solomonid Ethiopia enjoyed mostly peace and prosperity in the 15th century. The first Portuguese visited in 1490 when the explore Pero de Covilhã arrived at court, only to be held prisoner for the final 30 years of his life. A Portuguese mission which arrived in 1510 was similarly detained. A third came in 1520, and was finally allowed to leave in 1526. The Portuguese were astonished to discover a large Christian state deep within Africa, and offered military support. In this, they were matched bid for bid by the Ottomans, who sent firearms in

1527 to coastal Muslims battling Ethiopia's Christian rulers. Portuguese aid was important because Ethiopia's position had collapsed suddenly as a result of a radical shift in the balance of power resulting from an invasion of firearms-bearing coastal Arabs, who were supported by the Ottomans who were themselves then expanding into the Red Sea. In 1529 a technologically overmatched Ethiopian army was crushed in a plunder raid by musketeers from the Muslim coastal state of Adal, which had access to Ottoman firearms. Much of the country was ravaged until 400 Portuguese musketeers, under Vasco da Gama's son, responded to an appeal in 1541, marched with the Ethiopian army and defeated the army of Adal (1542). The Portuguese musketeers remained to train Ethiopians on guns they sold them. The *Jesuits* arrived in 1557 along with artillery and more muskets, and enjoyed a brief success by converting King Susenyos to Catholicism in 1612. However, upon his abdication in 1632 the Monophysite (Coptic) Ethiopian Church reasserted its ascendancy and by 1648 all Jesuits were expelled as Ethiopia entered a period of 200 years of radical isolationism.

Suggested Reading: Roland Oliver, ed., *Cambridge History of Africa*, Vol. 3 (1977); Sergew Sellassie, *Ancient and Medieval Ethiopia* (1972).

eunuchs. In 14th–17th-century China, court eunuchs were often placed in command of the *Ming Army* to prevent an untrustworthy general from challenging the dynasty. Production of military equipment was also largely in the hands of eunuchs, and concentrated around the capital. Different groups of eunuchs controlled the Palace Armory, the Saddlery Service, the Armor Service, and the Sewing Service. In addition, eunuchs indirectly controlled the Gunpowder Office and a Wagon Depot, which manufactured cannon and small firearms. Eunuchs were also powerful in the courts of various Muslim caliphs and sultans. See also *banner system (China/Manchuria)*; *Hongwu emperor*; *Janissary Corps*; *Tumu, Battle of*; *Wanli Emperor*; *Zheng He*.

Everlasting League. See *Swiss Confederation*.

Evesham, Battle of (1265). See *England*.

exact militia. An attempt by *James I* and then *Charles I* to modernize English defenses on the cheap, by commanding the *trained bands* and other militia to purchase on their own, and practice with, the most modern weapons available.

expeditio ultra Alpes. See *Holy Roman Empire*.

Exploration, Age of. Arabs, Indians, Vikings, and Polynesians all made impressive voyages of discovery at the height of their civilizations. In 1400, Ming China was the world's greatest naval power. It sent out seven spectacular and enormous expeditions under *Zheng He*, a Muslim eunuch and admiral. These were vast fleets set on expeditions of trade and exploration which far exceeded anything Europe then mounted, both in size of individual ships and the expeditions as a whole. Yet, having touched the shores of Sri Lanka, Iran, the east coast of Africa, and even distant Australia, the Ming suddenly ceased oceanic travel: Zheng He's expedition of 1433 to the Middle East and East Africa was the last Chinese fleet to sail west. In 1436 a new Ming emperor banned further journeys, dismantled the fleet, and forbade building of blue water ships. It fell to Europe's *carracks* and *frigates*, not to Chinese *Fujian ships*, to map the oceans and force open whole continents to intellectual and cultural intercourse along with economic exploitation and colonization. The "Age of Exploration" by Europeans was different from all others, therefore, in having the lasting effect of linking the world's oceans into unified navigational and trading systems. In turn, this permitted a transformation of world affairs in which the center of gravity of world history shifted to Europe over a 400-year period, based largely on command of the sea.

The "Age of Exploration" was also the second half of a two-part response to the geopolitical reality and power of Islam. Europe's initial military attempt to reverse the Muslim conquest of the Middle East and North Africa, the *Crusades*, had failed after 200 years of effort and much expenditure of lives and treasure. Now, with an even great Muslim power rising in the east—the Ottoman Empire—Europeans sought a way by sea around the immoveable Islamic world to the markets of India and China. The new approach to an old problem was made possible by key navigational innovations, including the magnetic *compass*, *astrolabe*, and *portolan chart*, stern-mounted rudders, and triangular *lateen sails*. Those technological breakthroughs combined with new astronomical knowledge acquired from Muslims via the Norman conquest of Sicily and Iberian contact with the great scholars of the Emirate of *Granada* to make maps more accurate and ocean-going navigation somewhat less perilous to crews and investors. The effort was also partly inspired by the famous journals of Marco Polo and visions of Asia as a land of vast wealth, by dreams of mythical empires like Atlantis or the lost "Kingdom of Prester John," and by desire to reach the sources of African gold suspected to exist somewhere along the Guinea coast. It is important to understand the extraordinary lure of gold (and spices), the core motive behind European voyages of exploration for which religious mission provided a pretext and justifying propaganda. But it is also worth recalling that some monarchs granted clergy extraordinary powers of administration, which suggests a sincere if secondary religious motive was in play as well.

By 1375 the Portuguese reached Cape Bojador, 1,500 miles south of Ceuta. Concerted voyages of discovery were then made in the African Atlantic by *Enrique the Navigator*, whose ships reached the Azores in 1427 and rounded Cape Bojador in 1434. Ten years later Portuguese *caravels* reached Cape Verde, and by the time of Enrique's death in 1460 they had made landfall 600 miles farther south in what is today Sierra Leone. Meanwhile, *Constantinople* fell to the Ottomans in 1453, cutting off the prosperous city-states of the *Italian Renaissance* from their historic commerce with Asia—except for Venice, which continued to trade in the eastern Mediterranean under a monopoly agreement negotiated with the Ottoman sultans. The Genoese explorer Christopher Columbus was one of many who sailed in search of an alternate route to the east, but the first to do so by sailing west, where he encountered the New World in 1492. The next year, the pope drew a *line of demarcation* dividing the globe between the Catholic crowns of Spain and Portugal. Meanwhile, in 1488, Bartolomeu Dias had rounded the Cape of Good Hope. Six years later Portuguese ships reached Ethiopia—was this the fabled lost land of "Prester John"? Vasco da Gama (1469–1524), who explored parts of India's coast, 1497–1498, actually took with him a letter for Prester John which offered an alliance against Islam. In fact, east African shores were reached earlier by Pero de Covilhã, in 1488–1489. As he ended a prisoner of the Ethiopian court, where he spent the last 30 years of his life, his name was lost to fame and almost to history as well. Across the Atlantic another Genoese captain, John Cabot, discovered Newfoundland and Nova Scotia.

In 1500, Pedro Cabral first touched the shores of Brazil, paused to found the town of Veracruz, then continued with his primary mission to bring a Portuguese war fleet to the Indian Ocean to make good on the discoveries of Vasco da Gama. The next year Amerigo Vespucci mapped the east coast of South America, to the La Plata estuary. On the East African coast, Zanzibar was attacked and occupied. Mombasa was sacked in 1505 and once again in 1528, and permanent Portuguese trading forts were set up at Kilwa, Sofala, and in Mozambique, plying trade in east African gold and slaves with the Arabian Gulf states and India. By 1510 small Portuguese war fleets arrived in the Indian Ocean. Employing knowledge of the monsoon winds acquired from local Arab and Indian traders, and with broadside cannon perched on the deck of their ships, they swept much larger Arab and Indian galleys from the East African and Indian coasts and took control of ancient trade routes and markets. On the other side of the Pacific, Vasco Nunez de Balboa traversed the isthmus of Panama in 1513 and became the first European to gaze westward on the Pacific Ocean. In 1514 the pope granted Lisbon the right to any newly discovered lands to the east. The Spanish therefore hurried to cross the Pacific from the west, looking for a route to the Spice Islands from the west coast of Central and South America. Ferñao de Magalhães (Ferdinand Magellan) sailed from Seville in 1519 in search of the Moluccas. He skirted South America and survived mutiny, hurricanes, ship's fever, and scurvy, only to be killed by natives in the archipelago later called the Philippines (1521), which his landfall ensured would become a Spanish conquest and colony. The Pacific was fully crossed, and the world circumnavigated, by his second-in-command, Sebastian del Cano, who returned to Portugal with a single ship and just 18 men from an original complement of 265.

Pacific exploration remained difficult until the 1560s, when the Spanish mapped seasonal circular winds and currents which permitted reliable passage between Asia and the west coast of the Americas, comparable to the seasonal "trade winds" which by then were familiar to all ships plying the vibrant and expanding Atlantic trade in slaves, sugar, fish, and furs. A measure of the difficulty may be seen in the calculation scholars have made of ship losses: of 912 ships Portugal sent to the "Indies" from 1500 to 1635, fully 144 sank before arrival and another 298 never finished the journey home, lost to weather or to pirates. Still, by 1600 Europe's naval powers had charted most of the globe, set up forts and trading posts on—and claimed segments of—the coasts of nearly all inhabited continents, and began to penetrate and colonize the Americas. Portugal had 40 forts and factories (entrepôt) strung out between East Africa and Japan, serving the trade in spices, slaves and gold—and it was already a declining power. Other naval powers soon surpassed those numbers. Lesser voyages of exploration included John Davis in the Arctic in 1586 and 1587, and Henry Hudson's ill-fated Arctic voyage from 1610 to 1611. What

> *He skirted South America and survived mutiny, hurricanes, ship's fever, and scurvy, only to be killed by natives ...*

followed in the 17th century was a raw era of mercantile exploration and exploitation by divers *East India Companies* and other monopoly trading companies in other regions. Accompanying exploration were mercantilist wars over the lucrative spice and slave trades, but little cultural or military penetration of continental interiors other than in the Americas, and only tentative settlement.

Suggested Reading: C. Boxer, ed., *Portuguese Commerce and Conquest in Southern Asia, 1500–1750* (1985); John R. Hale, *The Age of Exploration* (1974); G. V. Scammel, *The World Encompassed* (1981); L. Withey, *Voyages of Discovery* (1989).

expulsion of the Jews (from Iberia). In the mid-14th century civil war in Castile encouraged fanatic persecution of Jews, largely as scapegoats for the nation's troubles and to placate popular sentiment. In June 1391, a Christian mob stirred by a fanatic anti-Semite preacher carried out a pogrom in Seville, killing hundreds of Jews and forcing others to submit to baptism. The violence spread: pogroms were launched in Valencia, Barcelona, and other cities, with many hundreds more deaths (400 in Barcelona alone). Authorities in Aragon and Castile tried to protect Jews from a populace that lusted for blood, led by clerics mouthing the usual blood libels about supposed ritual murders by Jews of Christian children, or opportunistic nobles wanting to be free of debts owed to Jewish moneylenders. These pogroms so changed circumstances for Jews in Spain from 1391 that the majority became *conversos—* real or feigned converts to Christianity. This greatly reduced identified Jews in Iberia. For instance, in Aragon, openly observant Jews dropped to one-quarter the number registered in 1391. However, there was a reversal of misfortune from 1416 when the crown of Aragon protected Jews against popular animosity, mainly because Jews paid special taxes directly to the king, bypassing the Cortes. Aragon also guaranteed autonomy of the Jewish enclave in Saragossa. In the second half of the 15th century, however, the military balance on the peninsula swung decisively in favor of Christians, and *Ferdinand and Isabella* won the civil war over the succession in Castile. Thereafter, they redirected the martial energies of their noble classes into a final crusade against Muslim Granada.

Jews began leaving Spain semi-voluntarily in large numbers in the 1480s, an exodus spurred by social unrest and violent religious excitement occasioned by the war with Granada, and because of the founding of Castilian and Aragonese *Inquisitions* (as distinct from the Medieval Inquisition, based in Rome) to deal with the "converso problem." In theory, Jews (and Muslims) were legally excluded from the Inquisition into "error" because they were theologically excluded from Catholic doctrine. That was moot in practice, however, since Jews were so hounded for their Judaism that most who stayed had to feign conversion, and that exposed them to inquisition into the soundness and sincerity of their newly declared Christian faith. In fact, Jews became the principal target of Inquisitors, who focused on conversos above all others. This led, as severe repression and terror always does, to communal divisions and self-preserving denunciations by frightened conversos of other conversos for supposed backsliding into "heresy" or "secret Judaising." In 1487 the Inquisition overturned Ferdinand's protection order for Saragossa and expelled the city's Jews; it could not have done so without his consent. Other cities soon followed suit, pandering to the worst instincts of Christian populations by expelling Jews and, sometimes, also Moors. The crown did nothing to prevent or reverse these deportations, which were paralleled by expulsion of Italian Jews from Parma (1488) and Milan (1491), and a few years later, by expulsions of French Jews from Provence. The Hebrew communities of Spain were by far the largest, wealthiest, and best educated in Europe, and their destruction arose from more vicious inspiration and had greater and wider consequences than the smaller affairs in Italy and France.

In 1490, Grand Inquisitor Torquemada convinced Ferdinand and Isabella that a radical separation of Christians and Jews was essential, as too many conversos were sliding into heresy or, even worse, "re-Judaizing." In January 1492, Granada surrendered to Ferdinand and Isabella and the "Catholic Crowns" moved to consolidate and celebrate God's great gift of martial victory. They hesitated over an order for total expulsion of Jews as they were advised that such an order would have deleterious consequences for the economy, and that they would lose a unique source of royal revenue since Jews (and Muslims) were taxed directly by the crown, unlike Christians. Also, several officers in the Royal Treasury were Jews, as were the royal physicians. In the end, their bigotry trumped their banking interests: Ferdinand and Isabella issued an expulsion order giving all Jews a choice of immediate conversion to Christianity or permanent exile from July 1492. Many Jews left for Portugal, raising the Jewish portion of the population there to about one-fifth the national total. Others departed for Navarre. More crossed to North Africa. Smaller numbers of highly skilled and affluent Jewish families moved to France, the Netherlands, and England. The Portuguese profited handsomely from Jewish discomfiture: they charged a ducat per head for the right to reside for six months. In 1497 a Spanish princess married the Portuguese king, an alliance that meant Spanish Jews in Portugal were again faced with a choice of conversion or deportation. In 1498, Navarre, too, demanded conversion or exile. Poorer Jews left right away. Many headed to North Africa, where they were met with robbery and murder. Tens of thousands of Iberian Jews left for the Ottoman Empire where *Bayezid II* welcomed them. Many settled around Salonika, others in Athens and Constantinople.

Richer Jews purchased extended toleration in Iberia: the Portuguese court granted a 20-year amnesty in exchange for large financial favors and "loans." In 1507, however, Lisbon's Christians conducted their first great pogrom, rampaging and massacring Jews. Officialdom was more tolerant, at least until 1532, when King João III sought to introduce a discrete Portuguese Inquisition modeled on Spain's. This effort was frustrated for a few years by bribes paid by "New Christians" to the curia in Rome. However, in 1542, Cardinal Carafa (later, Pope Paul IV), a vicious anti-Semite and fanatic reactionary, established a "Holy Office" of the Inquisition in Rome, and the weight of papal influence tipped toward even greater persecution. In July 1547, a papal bull authorized a separate Portuguese Inquisition. The Portuguese and Spanish Inquisitions remained discrete religious courts even after the "union of the crowns" of Portugal and Spain effected by *Philip II* in 1580. By 1600 the Grand Inquisitor in Lisbon had overseen some 50 *autos de fe*, hounding fresh waves of religious refugees out of Portugal.

The severity of the Portuguese Inquisition led Spanish inquisitors to express alarm over what they saw as a new cultural and religious threat to Spain: the return of Spanish conversos and Jews driven out of Portugal. On the other hand, Madrid was facing bankruptcy and this exodus presented a chance to squeeze funds from frightened Jews. Jewish refugees, bounced from one Inquisition to the other, were subjected to intense persecution but offered the chance to save themselves from the flames by paying heavy fines and accepting public baptism. At the turn of the 17th century *Philip III* was so desperate for money to finish his father's wars and pay his father's debts that he sought another way. In 1602 the wealthiest of the exiles heavily bribed Spanish officials, offering Philip personally 1,860,000 ducats, to issue a general pardon to "Judaizers" that would allow them to return to Spain. Over the objections of his own Inquisitors Philip asked permission of the pope to accept the bribe. On August 23, 1604, the pope issued a pardon that came into effect on January 16, 1605, granted in exchange for "gifts" of several million ducats to the king and to the pope raised from Iberian Jewish communities and bankers. The bribe and pardon bought a generation of moderated treatment by the Inquisition, nothing more.

In 1628 an appeal was made by Portuguese "New Christians" to be allowed to leave for Spain, or for the Netherlands, Germany, or England, upon payment to *Philip IV* of 80,000 ducats. When Philip declared the first state bankruptcy of his reign in 1626, older Italian banking houses had suffered such losses that Spanish access to the banking operations and lending capital of leading Iberian Jews proved irresistible to the crown, and Philip permitted some Portuguese Jews to resettle in Spain. At last, but too late, the economic loss to Spain of this skilled exile community was noticed. *Olivares* tried to convince other exiled Iberian Jews, in North Africa and the Levant, to return so that Spain could gain access to their unique skills and their capital. This initiative met with popular hostility, however, and he was compelled to retreat from it. The economic damage done to Spain by the expulsions was considerable. It at least contributed to repeated royal bankruptcy that degraded Spanish credit and wiped out the older Italian (Genoese) banking houses on which the monarchy relied for loans to pay for its old *Eighty Years' War* (1568–1648) and its new *Thirty Years' War* (1618–1648), and additional wars with the Ottomans and France. While the crown eventually sought to place penury before religious principle, if that term may be applied to institutional bigotry, the Holy Office continued fevered work of murderous anti-Semitism throughout the 17th century, continuing its baleful work against the wider national interest.

Some revisionist historians have tried to paint the Iberian expulsions as national policy rather than the result of religious bigotry or clerical fanaticism. Yet, the persecutions were carried out in the face of economic self-interest and for only short-term economic benefit to the crown from confiscation of forcibly abandoned property. Religious prejudice thus seems the better core explanation. Royal anti-Semitism was reinforced by a renewed confidence in Spain's divine mission, which in turn reinforced an ancient but widespread mystic belief—most prominent in Ferdinand's home of Catalan, and a view he is known to have shared—that the defeat of Islam had been identified in prophesy with simultaneous destruction of the Jews. The official justification given in the order was that "New Christians" would be re-Judaized ("seduced...from our Holy Catholic Faith") by contact with unconverted Jews. But money was in play, too: all synagogues and Jewish cemeteries were seized by the crown and families going into exile had to sell everything they could not carry at desperation prices. Those too poor or too frail to leave were forced to choose between baptism and death. The overall numbers involved remain a matter of controversy. Some Jewish historians assert that as many as 200,000 (from a total Jewish population of 220,000) chose exile. Henry Kanem, a sharp revisionist generally sympathetic to the Crown and the Inquisition, claims 80,000 Jews resided in Spain, that fewer than half that number left, and that many returned voluntarily "to the Christian fold" [*sic*]. Most historians believe instead that the forced diaspora was large, that it was devastating culturally and economically to Jews and to Spain, and that it caused considerable suffering and not a few deaths. See also *Bayezid II*; *expulsion of the Moors*; *Fifth Monarchists*; *war finance*.

Suggested Reading: J. H. Elliot, *Imperial Spain, 1469–1716* (1964; 1970); Henry Kamen, *The Spanish Inquisition* (1998).

expulsion of the Moors (from Iberia). In negotiations leading to the surrender of Granada in 1492, *Ferdinand and Isabella* agreed to protections for the city's Muslims, Over the next decade, however, agitation by the Holy Office of the *Inquisition* led to a reversal of policy: in 1499 Grenadine Muslims were told to accept baptism or go into permanent exile, following in the footsteps of Iberian Jews. In 1502 a similar order, "convert or leave," was issued to all Muslims remaining in Castile. The Inquisition was then directed by the monarchs to investigate "Moriscos," former Muslims accused of insincerely converting to Christianity to avoid the expulsion order, heavy fines, or the fires of an *auto de fe*. Even those who had sincerely converted attracted suspicion and investigation by the Inquisition; many more suffered accusations of inconstancy rooted in the confiscatory greed of Inquisitors, or the spite of jealous or vicious neighbors. In addition, there likely was a racist component to Spanish policy toward the Moors. Developing Spanish nationalism did not accept that even converted Muslims, people generally of darker complexion and different ethnicity than Spanish Christians, should or could be assimilated into society. On the other hand, the Moors presented a more complex problem for the Crown than did Spanish Jews. First, there were many more of them. Second, they were concentrated in the Aragon and the south. Their numbers and location suggested a potential for revolt and fed into widespread fear that they might serve as a "fifth column" for Ottoman or Berber raids or even more fantastically, a Muslim invasion of Spain. Iberian Jews posed no comparable security problem, not even in the imagination. Anti-Muslim laws proceeded more slowly, therefore, with bans on traditional dress followed after a few years by bans on Arabic education and writing. Only much later were more forceful policies of "ethnic cleansing" and physical relocation introduced. In all this the Inquisition operated as a principal weapon of political repression and intelligence gathering for the state concerning the Moors. The final, physical expulsion of the Moors from Spain and Portugal was carried out 1609–1614, by order of *Phillip III*. It was overseen by the *Duke of Lerma* and the Inquisition. Expulsions moved perhaps 350,000 Morisco refugees to North Africa. By then the Inquisition was moved as much or more by racialist motives as it was by religious intolerance in its dealings with the last, lingering Moriscos. See also *expulsion of the Jews*.

Suggested Reading: J. H. Elliot, *Imperial Spain, 1469–1716* (1964; 1970); Henry Kamen, *The Spanish Inquisition* (1998).

Eyâlet Askerleri. The "Provincial Army" of the Ottoman Empire, consisting of all troops not in the Sultan's household service (*Kapikulu Askerleri*). It included both cavalry and infantry divisions. Its infantry were local levies, in no way comparable in quality, weapons, or political loyalty to the *Janissaries*.

eyâlet-i Budin. The most strategically important of the four occupied provinces of Ottoman Hungary. It was garrisoned by about 8,000 *Janissaries*.

F

facings. See *drill*.

factory. A fortified overseas base or entrepôt used to carry out trade. See also *East India Company*; *Eighty Years' War*; *Portugal*; *Vereenigde Oostindische Compaagnie*.

Fähnlein. "Small flag." In the *Swiss Army*, below the *Banner*s (great cantonal standards), soldiers were grouped under smaller flags of discrete guilds to which they belonged, or of the towns or rural districts from which they hailed. These "Fähnlein," or companies grouped around a flag, numbered from 50 to 150 men depending on the size of the canton they served. They acted as a large tactical subunit within the *Swiss square*. The majority of Fähnlein were comprised of halberdiers and pikemen, but some developed as specialized units of crossbowmen, arquebusiers, or musketeers. The *Landsknechte* also used this system, though German Fähnlein were larger, from 250 to 300 men. By the mid-16th century regiments of up to 3,000 men were commanded by a *colonel* and organized in 8 to 10 Fähnlein. A key difference from later armies was that Swiss and Landsknechte Fähnlein carried flags in the center of their battle squares, not to the front. These banners were objects of murderous devotion, were therefore highly valued as prizes to be seized from an enemy, and were used to taunt a foe by mistreatment if captured. For example, at *Marignano* one Landsknechte unit cut up and ate a captured Swiss Fähnlein to show contempt for their traditional enemy; more often, they were taken home and displayed as trophies. See also *ensign*; *martial music*.

Fairfax, Thomas (1612–1671). Parliamentary general. He first experienced war in the Netherlands and Germany. He next led a regiment of dragoons for *Charles I* in the bloodless *First Bishops' War* (1639). He raised a Yorkshire army for Parliament when the *English Civil Wars* broke out.

Although a solid cavalry commander, he lost two small skirmishes in 1643 to more skilled Cavaliers, at Seacroft Moor (April 13) and Adwalton Moor (June 30). Fairfax was joined by *Oliver Cromwell* and defeated the Royalists in a sharp cavalry action at *Winceby* (October 11, 1643). He relieved the siege of Nantwich on January 24, 1644, taking 1,500 prisoners. He commanded on the right at *Marston Moor* (July 2, 1644). Fairfax pushed hard for professionalization in the military and was key to setting up the *New Model Army*, which he led to a brilliant victory at *Naseby* (June 14, 1645). To his shame, after the battle he lost control of his men, who murdered hundreds of women taken with the baggage. He later took the lead in pressuring Parliament to meet pay arrears, quartering, and other obligations to the troops. From 1648 to 1649, Fairfax fought in the southeast against Royalist holdouts. United with Cromwell over dealing with Parliament on issues of quartering and payment of arrears to the Army, Fairfax ordered troops to occupy London on August 6, 1647. They marched through the city with swords drawn and matches lighted. Fairfax broke with Cromwell over the great matter of whether to execute the king and on the matter of repressing the Scots. In 1650 he left the military and politics. See also *Levellers*.

falchion. A short, broad-bladed sword with a convex edge introduced in the later Middle Ages. Primarily used by infantry, it caused deep slashing wounds.

falcon. French: "faucon," Spanish "media falconeta." A relatively standardized class of 16th-century cannon weighing about 800 pounds and capable of firing 3-pound *solid shot* or other ordnance to an effective range of 400 yards and a maximum range of 2,500 yards.

falconete. French: "fauconneaux." A "falconete" was a smaller version of the 16th-century *falcon*. It fired a one-pound shot to an effective range of just under 300 yards and a maximum throwing range of 1,500 yards.

Falkirk, Battle of (July 22, 1298). Fought early in the *Scottish Wars*, a year after the Scots crushed an English army at *Stirling Bridge*. The Scots were again led by *William Wallace*, the English by *Edward I*. The Scots formed four *schiltrons* of pikemen and repelled several charges by Edward's *heavy cavalry*, which included some *Templars*. However, the king brought forward Welsh longbowmen who cut bloody gaps in the schiltrons until they ran out of arrows. Into the holes English knights charged with lance and sword, winning decisively. It is thought by specialists that the English army at Falkirk was the largest ever raised to that time. This fact reflected the new realities of an emerging money economy and wage-based system of *war finance*, as well as high population levels that preceded the *Black Death*.

"False Dimitri." See *Godunov, Boris Fyodorovich*; *"Time of Troubles."*

Famagusta, Siege of (1570–1571). See *Cyprus*.

familia. See *housecarls*.

familiares ad arma. See *palace guards*.

famine, as a weapon of war. See *fortification*; *logistics*; *siege warfare*; *Thirty Years' War*.

Farangi. Mughal term for European artillerymen in the service of Muslim emperors in India. See also *folangji*; *renegades*; *Rumis*.

Farnesse, Alexander. See *Parma, duque di*.

fascine. A faggot of brush or cordwood, usually collected and carried to the siege site by the cavalry or in carts by civilian laborers. They were used to fill in ditches or dry moats around besieged fortifications.

Fastolf, John (d.1459). English soldier, and part-basis for Shakespeare's caricature, Sir John Falstaff. The real Fastolf fought in Ireland, Gascony, and France, under *Henry V*. Most famously, he led a supply column to Orléans, fighting off a French and Scots army at *Rouvray* (February 12, 1429) along the way.

Fatamids. See *Algiers*; *caliph*; *Crusades*; *Egypt*.

fathom. A naval measure of water depth equivalent to six feet.

fauld. A skirt of hinged and crenelated *plate* protecting the waist. It was constructed of three or four "lames" of overlapping metal. It might be attached to "tassets" that protected the upper thighs. Also called a "tonlet."

Feldarzt. "Field surgeon." A rough doctor in a *Landsknechte* or other company or regiment, responsible for amputations of wounded limbs, sewing up gaping wounds, and other crude medical treatments. The Feldarzt supervised those doing the actual cutting and sewing.

Feldobrist. "Field colonel." A much higher rank than *Obrist*, an officer of this stature would command a whole army, one comprised of cavalry and artillery as well as *Landsknechte* infantry. Modern German usage is "Oberst."

Feldweibel. "Field sergeant." The lowest rank of *Landsknechte* officer selected by the company or regiment colonel. He was put in charge of all *drill*, including the precise order of battle. This was a crucial assignment, especially when Landsknechte met a *Swiss square* in battle. For this reason the Feldweibel was usually an older, experienced mercenary.

Ferdinand I, Holy Roman Emperor (1503–1564). Archduke of Austria, 1521–1564; King of Bohemia and Hungary, 1526–1564; emperor, 1558–1564. The younger brother of *Charles V*. Ferdinand spent many years in intermittent war with the Ottomans in the *Militargrenze*, but kept the conflict local by also paying tribute to the sultans for lands in Hungary. He put down the peasant uprising known as the *German Peasant War* in 1525, and 10 years later dealt with several rebellious German princes leading into the war with the *Schmalkaldic League*. Ferdinand was an advocate of the *Counter-Reformation*, notably recatholicization of Inner Austria by the *Jesuits*. But he was capable of major compromise on religious issues in the interest of social peace and good order, more so than his more fanatical brother, as was demonstrated at *Passau* (1552) and *Augsburg* (1555). Ferdinand succeeded to the Imperial throne when Charles abdicated because Charles feared softness toward Protestantism of another brother, *Maximilian II*, and to compensate for Ferdinand's being passed over in favor of Charles in 1519. He supported the *Council of Trent*, but hoped for more moderation from the Church than that conclave in fact delivered.

Ferdinand II, Holy Roman Emperor (1578–1637). Archduke of Austria and Styria, 1596–1619; King of Bohemia, 1617–1637; King of Hungary, 1619–1637; Holy Roman Emperor, 1620–1637. He was educated by the *Jesuits* and all his life was a fanatic, as well as devout, Catholic and ardent proponent of the *Counter-Reformation*. He ruthlessly suppressed the *Estates* and Protestants in his hereditary lands, promoting an early "confessional absolutism." He shut out Protestants from his stage-managed coronation as king-designate of Bohemia in 1617, which promised him the Imperial crown upon the death of Emperor Matthias. Bohemian Protestants retorted with the *"Defenestration of Prague"* (1618). Ferdinand then dismissed the dying Matthias' chief minister and began to rule the Empire in fact. When Matthias at last died in March 1619, the Bohemian Estates took the final step into rebellion: they deposed Ferdinand from the crown of St. Wenceslaus (August 19, 1619). Nevertheless, he was unanimously elected Holy Roman Emperor nine days later. With that, each side raised armies and what became the *Thirty Years' War* got underway. Ferdinand crushed the Bohemian revolt inside a year, but there was a key moment when he thought he might lose. Besieged in Vienna by a Bohemian army in 1619, he had, or at least claimed he had, a vision in which the Christ figurine on a chapel crucifix said to him: "Ferdinande, non te deseram!" ("Ferdinand, I will not desert you!"). He considered that divine promise fulfilled with arrival of a Bavarian army to lift the siege. This deliverance confirmed every Habsburg legend Ferdinand already believed about his own, and the Habsburg, providential mission to restore and defend universal Catholicism. It was thereafter celebrated in Habsburg masses and proclaimed in Jesuit-led *Corpus Christi* processions, in imitation of Constantine if not of Christ.

After Ferdinand's armies won at the *White Mountain* in 1620 he forcibly reconverted Bohemia, expelling or executing nobles who would not switch to

Catholicism and making its kingship hereditary rather than elective. His success in reconversion of the nobility of Austria and Bohemia was not just by coercion: he also used shrewd bribery with lands, offices, and benefices. Stubborn and self-righteous at least, and a political tyrant and religious bigot at worst (as were many, it must be said, on all sides of the confessional wars), Ferdinand had no capacity for empathy toward genuine grievances of his Protestant subjects. He turned instead, hard and often, to the sword and the Inquisition as the solutions to problems of Imperial governance. That was a deeply and inherently flawed policy: Ferdinand could field no army that the Estates refused to pay, and they were confessionally divided. That left his only resort to contract the mercenary captain *Albrecht von Wallenstein*. But the armies he raised, financed, and commanded were loyal to their commander, not to Ferdinand. Schooled as a duke in tiny Inner Austria, Ferdinand never displayed a capacity to rule a vast and complex empire. He tried to impose the Counter-Reformation policies that succeeded in the Habsburg hereditary lands everywhere in Germany, but they could not be instituted in the Empire given opposition in the Estates, the military capabilities of Protestant princes, and the internationalization of the war as Protestants called on outsiders to counterbalance the Emperor. And Ferdinand had a habit of making this situation worse with arbitrary and spiteful gestures that gained him no material advantage but united his enemies. For instance, in 1621 he declared outlaw *Friedrich V*, the foolhardy prince who tried to seize the Bohemian

> *And Ferdinand had a habit of making this situation worse with arbitrary and spiteful gestures . . .*

crown in 1618. Friedrich was stripped of all titles and inheritances in the Palatinate without consultation with the Imperial Diet or due process of law. That act of imperial fiat may have been emotionally gratifying for Ferdinand, but, as Tallyrand said of a comparably foolish act by Napoleon, worse than a crime it was a mistake. It clarified that the fulcrum of the balance of power had shifted to the Emperor and away from the Estates, which worried even Catholic princes. And it threatened every Protestant prince with like arbitrary treatment outside imperial tradition and law. It could not stand.

Ferdinand displayed imperial hubris on a grander scale when, again by mere fiat, in 1628 he stripped the Dukes of *Mecklenburg* of all their lands and titles and gave both to Wallenstein, in lieu of cash-for-services rendered. His arrogant confessional intolerance was then codified and announced the next year in the *Edict of Restitution*. This twin assault, on the religious settlement established in the *Peace of Augsburg* in 1555 and against the rights of princes, guaranteed that the war would continue and expand but also that he would face paralyzing opposition within Germany from Catholics as well as Protestants. His power peaked, then began to fade: the princes refused to pay for his proposal to send 50,000 troops to intervene in the *War of the Mantuan Succession* and enticed him to sack Wallenstein. Overconfident as usual, Ferdinand listened to whispering courtiers who hated the upstart Bohemian, and to his own jealousy, and dismissed Wallenstein from command (August 13,

1630). His grand strategy thereafter was blocked by Sweden's king and warlord, *Gustavus Adolphus*, who was supported by Cardinal *Armand Richelieu* of France. Ferdinand did not understand what he had done or what had occurred. He foolishly remarked on Sweden's entry into the war in 1630: "So, we have another little enemy." Sycophants stroked this delusion, telling him that "the snow king will melt" as he moved south under the hot German sun (the sun was a cult symbol of the Habsburgs as it would later be for the Bourbons).

Two years later, frantic over the unopposed advance toward Vienna of Gustavus at the head of a Swedish-Saxon army following *First Breitenfeld*, Ferdinand groveled to recall Wallenstein. Then, after Gustavus died in battle at *Lützen* and the tides of war seemed to turn in his favor, Ferdinand had Wallenstein tried in secret then pursued and murdered (1634). Again acting outside the law to kill a powerful vassal, even if a despised upstart Bohemian, was a grave error that frightened his most powerful subjects, the German princes. Ferdinand did it because he was distraught over lack of military success by Wallenstein the prior year; fearful that quartering the Imperial Army in Habsburg provinces might provoke peasant rebellions; believed he could replace Wallenstein's mercenaries with *tercio* veterans on loan from Spain; and was angered by Wallenstein's secret peace negotiations with Saxony, Brandenburg, and Sweden. Ferdinand later pretended the murder was Providential, not political (a view encouraged by Jesuits who put on a political theater in 1635 where Wallenstein was played as an apostate whose death was ordered by the Virgin Mary). As Ferdinand's fortunes declined his fanaticism increased: starting in 1633 he issued edicts ordering all subjects to inform on any person not leading "a godly life" or just absent from church services. He ordered religious police to enforce attendance at Easter Mass, and violently suppressed common folk belief in witches and magic, substituting for these sanctioned Catholic belief in saints and miracles. His great dream was of a unified Catholic empire, though perhaps not an absolute monarchy. In any case, the dream failed before his death, and he knew it. To gain the Imperial throne for his son, *Ferdinand III*, he abandoned pretensions to confessional crusade and agreed to the *Peace of Prague* in 1635. See also *Congregatio de Propaganda Fidei*; *Corpus Christi*; *Regensburg, Treaty of*.

Ferdinand II, of Aragon (1452–1516) and Isabella I, of Castile (1451–1504). "Reyes Católicos" ("The Catholic Monarchs"). Ferdinand was also King of Naples and Sicily (1502). He reigned as Ferdinand V in Castile. As an 18-year-old prince he married 19-year-old princess Isabella of Castile, a match that united their crowns and kingdoms instead of a union of Isabella with *Alfonso V* of Portugal. But that also meant several years of war to secure the succession, which was challenged by Alfonso and by Isabella's half-sister. The conflict ended with Ferdinand's victory over the Portuguese at Toro (March 1, 1476). The young couple then became joint rulers of a new power formed by their "Union of Crowns," commonly called Imperial Spain. The significance of Ferdinand's legal subordination to Isabella, the senior monarch in the marriage, may be measured by the fact that of 37 years spent as King of Aragon, Ferdinand resided there for only seven. Religious warfare and persecution of Jews and Muslims marked their joint reign, as it did that of contemporary monarchs who also sought tight religious unity as a means to social and political cohesion of a "national" monarchy. Their rough, *conquistadore* armies completed the *Reconquista* on January 2, 1492. The Monarchs then marched in grand procession into Granada, conquerors of the last Moorish state in Iberia. To celebrate, they ordered all Spanish Jews to convert to Christianity by mid-year, then exiled the majority who refused. Nor did they stop with *expulsion of the Jews*. They betrayed their word to the Moors, within seven years breaking the surrender promise of toleration and forcing most Moors to convert (to become "Moriscos") or accept impoverished exile in North Africa. Their successors later completed this process of *expulsion of the Moors*.

One revisionist historian, Henry Kanem, argues that neither monarch was anti-Semitic or anti-Muslim, that their policy was general centralization and conformity of everyone within their domain regardless of faith, that it applied as well to nobles, cities, peasants, merchants, Christians, Muslims, and Jews. He also argues that they did not seek religious conformity per se while admitting that the practical effects of royal policy were disproportionately harsh for non-Christians. Nor does this conclusion accord with his curious admission that the expulsion decision was taken by the crowns alone yet "exclusively for religious reasons." While it is likely true that popular animosity toward Muslims and Jews exceeded that of the monarchs personally, they moved faster toward radical intolerance the closer victory over the Moors of Granada approached. Most important, the expulsions were a colossal strategic error which damaged Span's commercial, social, and intellectual life for many decades.

Also in celebration of the victory over Granada, Isabella sponsored the first cross-Atlantic voyage by Christopher Columbus. Her interest (which was greater than Ferdinand's) was to give thanks to God for victory over the Moors, but also to find a strategic back door through Asia by which Christian armies might attack the Ottoman Empire and again "liberate" the Holy Lands as they did during the First Crusade. Instead, the trip led to discovery of the New World and to an empire many times the size of Spain, in accord with a papal grant of half the Western Hemisphere along the *Line of Demarcation*. Isabella was more fervent in her Catholicism and strove always to continue the crusade against Islam. After her death, Ferdinand turned Spain's enormous energies northward, into Italy and Germany. He expelled the French from Italy at the start of the *Italian Wars*. Castile and Aragon were formally united under Ferdinand, as King of Spain, in July 1512. That same month he conquered Navarre. Yet, when he died four years later he left no Spanish heir. Instead, *Charles V* of Austria and Burgundy, his grandson but also a distant German prince, succeeded to command of the great empire that Ferdinand spent a lifetime constructing. See also *Cerignola, Battle of*; *Oñate, Treaty of*.

Suggested Reading: J. H. Elliott, *Imperial Spain: 1469–1716* (1963); F. Fernandez-Armesto, *Ferdinand and Isabella* (1975).

Ferdinand III, Holy Roman Emperor (1608–1657). His father, *Ferdinand II*, ordered *Albrecht von Wallenstein* killed and replaced by the young Ferdinand III as supreme commander of all Catholic troops in the Empire. He joined his 18,000 men with 15,000 Spaniards under the Cardinal Infante (also called Ferdinand), just in time to crush 25,000 Swedes at *First Nördlingen* (September 5–6, 1634). After the *Peace of Prague* (1635), he was elected "King of the Romans" in 1636 and elevated to emperor in 1637, upon his father's death. By 1640 it was clear to him that desolation and despair in Germany, and the raw fact that the Habsburgs were losing the *Thirty Years' War* militarily, meant it was past time to make peace. He recalled the *Imperial Diet* for the first time since 1613, readmitted banished Protestant princes, abandoned the *Edict of Restitution*, and in general reversed his father's confessional policy. That did not mean he abjured all war: Ferdinand supported Denmark against Sweden in *Torstensson's War* (1643–1645), sending 20,000 troops north. The intervention ended in total failure: the Imperial Army lost two-thirds of its men and Denmark was still forced to accept humiliating terms. After another disastrous loss at *Jankov* (1645) Ferdinand III had no choice but to accept Franco-Swedish proposals for a comprehensive settlement as confirmed in the *Peace of Westphalia* three years later.

Ferdinand V, of Castile. See *Ferdinand II, of Aragon and Isabella I, of Castile*.

Ferrybridge, Battle of (1461). See *Wars of the Roses*.

feudalism. This term remains highly controversial among social historians, with some rejecting it outright. However, it retains validity in military history as a description of a complex organization of social and economic life to support a martial class in Western Europe in the Middle Ages, and in that sense is also roughly applicable to other societies with land-for-military-service systems. Its central characteristic was the semi-sovereignty of hundreds, even thousands, of principalities with independent military capabilities including, as Philippe Contamine put it, "specific means of attack and defense, the right and power to declare, pursue and terminate war." The collapse of the "Pax Romana" and fall of the western Roman Empire left land as the principal source of wealth in the politically, economically, and demographically shrunken successor states of Western Europe. This situation was exacerbated by the "explosion of Islam" out of Arabia in the 7th century, which broke apart the ancient Mediterranean trading economy and further isolated the West. The small Christian kingdoms of Europe next faced six centuries of barbarian invasions, by Goths, Vandals, Vikings, Magyars, and Arab and Berber Muslims. "Feudalism" was a response to this prolonged security threat: it represented a profound militarization on a land-for-military-service system ("tenere in servitio"), as vulnerable populations retreated from cities and seacoasts to hunker down within or near castellan strongholds maintained by a new, knightly class. There has been much debate among historians as to whether adoption of the stirrup in the 9th century drove enfeoffment in France and then Europe, as well as debate over the special role of mounted shock combat in general, and knighthood and *chivalry* in particular. Whatever the connections, military mastery in the early Middle Ages was the province of *heavy cavalry*.

In the "classical" form spread by the Carolingian monarchs, feudalism emerged as a way for kings lacking cash revenues to raise armies, principally of heavy cavalry. It was marked by large-scale demesne land-holding (that is, possession of land rather than ownership, or "tenere in dominico"). In this manorial system, which later became hereditary, peasants owed specified numbers of days of farm labor to the lord of the manor lands. Otherwise, most cropped their own strips and shared access to a "commons," usually a pastureland to graze animals. This proved a fairly stable system, resting on loan of lands and jurisdiction to vassals who owed military service in return. "Feudalism" also denoted radical political and military decentralization: the whole social and economic system sustained a martial order wherein nobles (military specialists sustained by rural labor) pledged military service that was determined by a complex hierarchy of vassalage in return for title to landed wealth (the "fief"), which later rigidified into land claims literally fortified by private *castles*. A notable exception to this system was southern Italy, where urban centers and a town militia tradition survived amidst the ruins of fallen empire and declining commercial economy. Another such area was Muslim Spain, where great centers of commerce and learning such as *Granada* survived the more general economic and cultural decline of the Mediterranean world after the fall of Rome.

> *"Feudalism" also denoted radical political and military decentralization: . . .*

As military technology advanced, when the stirrup and *couched lance* made heavy cavalry shock combat possible, the landed aristocracy adopted equipment, martial techniques, and tactics that further elevated them, literally as well as socially when they mounted great *destriers* to sit above men of town or country. Feudal economic and military structures were overlain by conservative religious sanction under the universal authority of the Catholic Church. Thus, even though the term "feudalism"—especially if used or defined overly rigidly—is viewed with disdain by some scholars, it remains true that throughout the Middle Ages the military structure in Europe was based on land grants to highly privileged lords, the *belatores*. These men held in bonded military service other men of lesser, but still highly prized, social status and specialized martial skill, with the military class as a whole reserving unto itself the right to use force, including a seigneurial right to raise small armies to wage local war over private grievances.

From the 11th century the highly aggressive military aristocracy of Western Europe began to expand, moving from defense against successive waves of invasion to offense against Muslims in Spain and the eastern Mediterranean, as well as into pagan and Slav lands in eastern and northeastern Europe. Among the most successful feudal empire-builders were the *Normans*, who conquered the British Isles, Sicily, and southern Italy. To the north there were bloody campaigns by the *Teutonic Knights* against the Wends and other pagans in Prussia, Poland, and along the Baltic coast. The *Black Death* accelerated breakdown of the land-tenure system by making labor scarce and forcing a shift to wages from service. In turn, that led to economic expansion and diversification in Western Europe. New commercial and trading classes and growing urbanization furthered the change, as did a cultural shift from seeking overlordship to attempts at outright conquest and economic development via plantation of agricultural settlers in annexed regions. The English pursued this policy in Ireland; the Teutonic Knights did it in Prussia; and the Saxons did the same in Wagria. In each case the native population was forced off the most fertile land or exterminated. In easternmost Europe and the Russias, the plague years had a different effect than in Western Europe: peasants were pushed back into a harsh system of serfdom in which their freedom of movement and sale of labor was sharply restricted by the regional nobility. Instead of an agricultural labor market, peasants were more tightly bound to the land they worked and the lords who ruled them. In Medieval Poland weak kings continued to struggle against a powerful barony that insisted upon continuation of their landed privileges and military monopoly.

Warfare in Europe in the Middle Ages was messy. There were few set borders; the idea of territorial "sovereignty" lay centuries in the future; political allegiances were unclear; and along the numerous frontiers or *marches* that marked off clusters of vague loyalty wars, raids, and rebellions were endemic. This was also true between, across, and within societies. Emperors fought popes and kings; kings fought other kings and each others' powerful barons; nobles fought each other over some slight, real or imagined; and lesser knights fought in ubiquitous private wars that ranged from clashes of hundreds of *men-at-arms* per side to smaller cavalry raids, from skirmishes and burning villages and fields, to feuding knightly families entangled in combat for obscure reasons of honor or revenge. Feudal lords fought rebellious peasants while towns and cities raised militia and formed defensive leagues to hold off attacks or assert traditional rights against the barony. Ordinary folk were swept into forced service as expendable auxiliaries in seasonal armies, or they were swept away by tides of war, famine, disease, and death that coursed over the land. Christian fought Christian; Catholic fought Orthodox and Muslim, who fought with and against each other. Armies of all religions repressed and exterminated "heretics" in their midst. Yet, weaknesses of finance, organization, and logistics meant that no one could raise or sustain an army large enough to impose order on a large area, or for long. That forced everyone to seek short-term alliances, pacts among robber-barons and kings who bonded only briefly and by mere convenience for the prospect of shared plunder. Some dynasts sustained longer-term alliances via political marriages, a practice at which the Habsburgs were especially adept. The pace of technological change was slow before the *gunpowder revolution*. The result was a feudal miasma of overlapping historic, dynastic, and familial claims, ever-shifting local political and military alliances, and chronic betrayal, assassination, rebellion, and small wars.

On the other hand, during the 12th century the literacy rate began to climb, contributing to a breakthrough in the bureaucratic administration of war in Europe. With better record-keeping came political centralization and a marked increase in the ability of monarchs to marshal economic resources—in short, to tax and borrow—in order to make war on an expanded scale. During the *Hundred Years' War* (1337–1453), kings in France and England used this capability to lessen reliance on feudal military vassals and the clergy. They slowly but certainly displaced servitor classes and peasant levies with military professionals recruited from an expanded population base, and forced taxes on the nobility and towns that allowed them to hire whole armies of domestic professionals or foreign mercenaries. All this military change rested on prior and more fundamental changes in society at large brought about by demographic expansion, a commercial revolution, more efficient and literate public administration, and new sources of royal revenue and capabilities that allowed monarchs to tap into a growing money economy. The rulers of Spain, too, began to establish large-scale standing forces during the 14th–15th centuries, though from a different economic base. By 1500 rudimentary *standing armies* were forming in several of the larger kingdoms, which used their armed forces to devour neighboring duchies, baronies, free cities, and sometimes entire would-be kingdoms such as Burgundy.

Several military systems in the Islamic world were also feudal or semi-feudal at base. The ancient trade with China enjoyed by Rome and Byzantium which was inherited by the Arab empire declined because of internal chaos in China that sharply limited its external trade, and in part because of a steep economic decline of Western Europe that shrank the end-market for Chinese goods. Also contributing to the decline of the Mediterranean economy from c.500 to 1000 C.E. was culturally based hoarding of precious metals throughout the Middle East. That led, as it had in the ancient world before Alexander the Great broke open the treasure rooms of Persia, to a chronic shortage of monetary metals that stifled new capital investment and trade. As the money economy declined land-for-military-service was substituted for pay through plunder or royal revenue. In Egypt and the Levant, however, Turkish and Circassian slave soldiers, *mamlūks*, displaced the Arab tribal levies that sustained the original Muslim caliphate. In Iran and Anatolia another Turkic people, the Seljuks, established a social order based on military service in return for land granted to officers. Some African and Asian societies had extended feudal periods. The *Hausa* of West Africa developed a system of agricultural enserfment that lasted into the 19th century, sustaining in power a Muslim overlord and military class.

Indian and Chinese agriculture and military systems were so different in comparison to Western Europe, and varied so greatly internally, that most historians reject the term "feudal" with regard to those civilizations. The most notable difference from Europe was that China was highly centralized politically and did not support a servitor martial class, but hired armies paid out of cental tax revenues. Conversely, India had no single religious tradition corresponding to Islam or Christianity, or even Confucianism, and no central political authority to impose uniform military or social conditions. Japanese "feudalism," if the term is to be used at all, had the closest parallels to Europe. In Japan as in late medieval Europe, a parasitic warrior class—the *samurai*—dominated because of its skill in making war from horseback (in the case of the samurai, as mounted archers). They wore armor and were organized around castles and fortified towns or on great baronial estates worked by a bonded and servile peasantry. This system survived until the *Unification Wars* of the late 16th–early 17th centuries, and in emasculated form into the second half of the 19th century. It formally ended with the Meiji Restoration in 1868. See also *bannum*; *demurrage*; *Estates*; *Franks*; *Holy Roman Empire*; *itqa*; *knight*; *Ottoman Empire*; *Salic Law*; *servitium debitum*; *war finance*.

Suggested Reading: Kelly DeVries, *Medieval Military Technology* (1992); D. Herlihy, ed., *The History of Feudalism* (1970); F. L. Ganshof, *Feudalism* (1952); Maurice Keen, ed., *Medieval Warfare* (1999); J. W. Thompson, *Feudal Germany*, 2 vols. (1927; 1962); J. R. Strayer, *Feudalism* (1979).

fief. A grant of land to a *knight* or magnate, held in return for military service and political allegiance to a liege lord. This was a form of military service distinct from that of the *bannum*. See also *feudalism*.

fief de chambre. Military wages disguised as feudal obligations. See also *war finance: France*.

field artillery. See *artillery*.

field fortifications and obstacles. See *abattis*; *caltrop*; *chevaux de fries*; *gabions*; *Grünhag*; *Letzinen*; *redan*; *retirata*; *Spanish riders*; *swine feathers*; *tabor*; *trou de loup*; *Wagenburg*.

Field Marshal. A general officer in the Imperial Army, third in rank below Lieutenant General and Generallissimus.

"Field of the Cloth of Gold" (1520). See *Henry VIII, of England*.

Fifteen Years' War (1591–1606). See *Thirteen Years' War*.

Fifth Monarchists. A millenarian intellectual movement, with some popular following, identifying one state or another as the "Fifth Monarchy," or universal empire, identified in the Book of Daniel (2:44) as the last of five prophesied godly kingdoms on Earth and the one immediately preceding the "Second Coming of the Christ." The prophesy was read as promising the conversion of Jews to Christianity and the collapse of the Ottoman Empire and all other Muslim powers. The movement was mostly intellectual and dynastic in Portugal, where it was employed to glorify the expansion of the whole "Catholic nation" overseas, notably the Iberian empires. Habsburg writers identified Spain rather than Portugal as the chosen nation. To purify the country and ready it for divine mission the other chosen people, the Jews, were forcibly converted or expelled, as later were the Moors. In England, "Fifth Monarchy Men" were most active during the later *English Civil Wars*, from 1649. Their program pointed to the execution of *Charles I* as a sign the prophesy was about to be fulfilled, with godly England the chosen nation. Many served in the *New Model Army* and supported *Oliver Cromwell* and *Thomas Fairfax*, until they crushed the *Levellers*. Fifth Monarchy Men felt betrayed by Cromwell after he became Lord Protector in 1653, and several tried to assassinate him. A Fifth Monarchist coup against the restored monarchy failed in 1660. See also *Third Rome*.

fire. Fire was, as it still is, a principal weapon of war. At sea the use of fire dated to antiquity, to the extraordinary naval flamethrower of the ancient Greeks and the Byzantine Empire that spewed *Greek fire*. Medieval ship artillery included dangerous *pots de fer*. More spectacularly, entire ships—even small fleets—were deliberately set afire and steered toward the enemy, such as the famous English *fireships* that scattered the *Invincible Armada* in 1588. On land, fire was the main tool of destruction during a *chevauchée* and in comparable practices of "scorched earth." This often provided recruits to armies or marauding bands of *Free Companies*. "Whose house doth burn, must soldier turn" was a widely spoken, and true, proverb of the *Hundred Years' War* (1337–1453). *Henry V* put it as only an aristocrat could: "War without fire is as worthless as sausages without mustard." In offense, fire destroyed the enemy's economy and resupply, weakened the wooden palisades of his *motte-and-bailey* forts, or cracked the stone foundation of a resisting town or castle wall. To repel attacking soldiers burning oil was pumped through pipes or poured over the wall, or down a *machicolation*. Fire arrows were used by attackers against town roofs and by defenders against counter castles and siege engines. In Europe, fire was seen as ideologically cleansing, as when used to burn "heretics" by the *Inquisition* or to rid Protestant society of witches on the order of some local civil authority or preacher. In Japan fire was key to a strategy of reducing regional defenses and dealing with over 40,000 forts (*honjō* and *shijō*) during the century of warfare known as *Sengoku jidai*. See also *aftercastle*; *appatis*; *ashigaru*; *blockade*; *divine fire-arrow*; *fire-lance*; *Jeanne d'Arc*; *Hus, Jan*; *naphtha*; *Ōnin War*; *raiding*; *siege warfare*; *trebuchet*; *witchcraft*.

Suggested Reading: J. F. Finó, "Le Feu et ses Usages Militaires," *Gladius*, 9 (1970).

firearms. See *artillery*; *cavalry*; *gunpowder weapons*; *infantry*; *revolution in military affairs*.

fire-lance. "bomba." An early incendiary weapon documented in China in 1132 but almost certainly much older than that in fact. It was a primitive flamethrower formed by slow burning black powder which emitted sparks and flames from a tube made of paper or bamboo. This was attached to a spear or javelin and either thrust toward or thrown at an enemy. The fire-lance may have been the direct forerunner of the first firearm, as sometimes small projectiles were placed in the tube that flew a short distance upon ignition. Fire-lances approached true firearms more closely when the tubes were formed of metal, c.1100. The fire-lance reached the Middle East by 1294. Evidence of its use in Europe dates only to 1396, though it may have been used before that. Fire-lances were employed in close fighting at sea by Spain into the early 17th century: a two-foot incendiary was mounted on a longer stick, to be ignited and thrust into the faces of enemy crew during boarding actions.

firepots. See *alcancia*; *pots de fer*.

fireships. In the age of wooden walls at sea fire was the deadliest of weapons. Fireships took account of this vulnerability to attack the enemy in the confines of a harbor, where lack of maneuverability promised to cause great damage. Small, broken, or obsolete ships were chosen for the suicide run. Their holds were filled with pitch, tinder, and faggots of dry wood. Cannon left aboard might be double or triple-shotted. Skeleton crews steered toward the enemy harbor, lighted the tinder and oils, and made their escape in the ship's boats, rowing at speed. It was important to abandon ship at the last possible moment and to use the tide to carry the fireship deep into the harbor, as once adrift all control was lost. On April 5, 1585, the *Sea Beggars* launched uniquely dangerous fireships, known as "Hellburners," toward a bridge across the Scheldt held by the Spanish. The "Hellburners" were not just packed with the usual combustibles, but with kegs of black powder. Several blew up short of the target but one detonated against the heavily defended bridge, killing over 800 of *Parma*'s men. Unable to stop the *Invincible Armada* at sea even with their superior gunnery, English captains sent eight Hellburners into the densely packed Spanish fleet at Calais, seeding panic and scattering its ships. Then they closed to fight it out in the morning, blasting through the fog and spraying blood and splinters. See also *Lake Boyang, Battle of*; *Rhodes, Siege of (1479–1480)*.

firing on the roll. Firing a ship's guns accurately was highly problematic in any ship-to-ship action. In the absence of scientific aids or mechanical aiming devices strict line-of-sight was all that was available. The best that most ship's gunners could do was to fire at close range while timing ignition to the roll of the ship on the sea's swells. Firing on the down-roll of one's own ship was preferred, as it lessened the chance that the shot would overfly the target. Firing on the up-roll of the enemy's ship, if achievable, improved the chance of holing it below its waterline.

fitna. "rebellion." A Muslim term for the tendency of medieval Islamic military alliances to break down, as loose allegiances shifted when a captain was bought off by an enemy to pre-arrange a battlefield desertion or to attack his former master. Under the *Mughals*, defectors were seldom harmed but were instead brought into the *mansabdari* system. On occasion, military superiority had to be demonstrated by actually fighting, after which it was normal to revert to military accommodation and assimilation.

flagellants. Self-flagellants annually performed displays of corporal "piety" as a key part of the *shi'ia* tradition within Islam, in pilgrimages to the holy cities of Iraq, site of Caliph Ali's murder in the first century A.H. In Europe, mass processions of flagellants appeared in the late Middle Ages mainly in response to war and plague. Their displays of corporal penitence were intended to expiate widespread sin, including—even especially—that of the clergy, believed to have brought such calamities of divine wrath down on the heads of men. The Catholic Church eventually came to see flagellants as heretics, though in some periods it encouraged and benefitted from their displays (as during the *War of the Eight Saints*). Many clergy participated, often leading processions holding up icons and large crosses. Most monkish orders had long practiced self-flagellation within cloister, officially or not. Mendicant penitential and flagellant processions of the 12th century were wildly popular, until repressed by less excitable elements of the clergy.

The *Black Death* revived flagellation as a devotional and penitential practice. It spread from Italy and Iberia to Germany, France, and hence to northern Europe, though it found little favor in England. In Germany, flagellants organized a sado-masochistic sect, the "Brotherhood of the Cross." They proceeded from town to town in ecstatic, bloody processions that greatly excited a population terrified and decimated by the plague, easily riled by apocalyptic visions, despairing over the war-torn woes of the Age, and shaken by schism and corruption in the Church. Sometimes the frenzy of the flagellants led to murders of Jews. When the flagellants began to develop a crude doctrine higher clergy grew alarmed at their challenge to the Church's monopoly on prescribed corporal punishment for moral transgressions. The doctors of theology of the University of Paris asked Pope Clement VI to condemn flagellants, which he did in 1349. They were thereafter hunted down as heretics. There was a brief flagellant revival in Germany in the 1360s, but it was suppressed by the rigors and tortures of the Medieval *Inquisition*. Over the next century smaller instances of flagellant fervor broke out in isolated areas, in response to later waves of plague or war. The Church also dealt with flagellants by incorporating some of their self-abusive methods into accepted penitential orders. For instance, in France, Black, Blue, Grey, and White brotherhoods of flagellants were set up during the dislocations of the *French Civil Wars*, supported and approved by the Church, the *Catholic League*, and sometimes by the monarchy.

> *They proceeded from town to town in ecstatic, bloody processions . . .*

Suggested Reading: G. Dickson, "The Flagellants of 1260 and the Crusades," *Journal of Modern History*, 15 (1989); Malcolm Lambert, *Medieval Heresy* (2002).

flags. In Medieval European warfare flags bearing a family coat of arms of noble commanders were common. On battlefields such as *Agincourt* or *Marignano*, brightly colored fork-tailed *pennants* were attached to the lances of individual knights, while larger square *banners* displayed the coat-of-arms of some great magnate designating his command as a *banneret* in a larger fighting unit of at least 10 knights called a *constabulary*. Royal standards were also displayed. "National" flags were a very late development of the early modern period, and did not appear in medieval warfare, although the radical *Hussites*, or *Taborites*, fought under a goose flag ("hus") befitting their peasant origins. As warfare emerged from the age of *chivalry*, generic flags and pennants served to identify distant bodies of troops (or warships) to their commanders and to each other. This helped avoid casualties by friendly archery or artillery fire, but did not yet represent truly national ensignia. Signal flags were also used, but were of diminishing utility once gunpowder cannon sent up great volumes of smoke to obscure the view.

The Swiss may have been the first to adopt a national symbol, the white cross, which Swiss troops wore or carried from the Battle of Laupen (1339) onward to identify them to foe or friend alike. Yet even the Swiss remained most devoted to their cantonal standards, or *Banners*. They also deployed "small flags" (*Fähnlein*) representing towns or guilds within each Canton. *Charles the Rash* organized the Burgundian army under distinctive tactical pennants, banners, and standards according to whether a unit (*lance*) was made up of men-at-arms, archers, or mixed troops. Polish cavalry carried large, multi-tailed medieval-style banners longer than in the West, where smaller more convenient flags found favor sooner. Polish flags were judged to be important according to sheer size and the number of tails they sported. Many Polish-Lithuanian flags bore heraldic or religious imagery well into the 17th–18th centuries. During the *Thirty Years' War* (1618–1648) more tactically useful flags appeared. The mercenary entrepreneur *Graf von Mansfeld* pioneered battlefield unit flags, but this reform did not keep his poor-quality armies together or prevent their frequent defeats. *Gustavus Adolphus* identified his regiments by the color of their cloth standards ("The Red" or "The Blue"). Like other regimental banners of that war, these were six square feet, in pennant form for cavalry and swallow-tail for infantry.

Outside Europe the use of battle flags was more complex and important. The reorganization of the Manchu (Qing) armies by *Nurgaci* in 1601 was based on four-colored flags (blue, red, yellow, and white), with four bordered flags added later for Han and Mongol regiments. The Qing *banner system* survived to the end of the dynasty in 1911. In Japan, the *horo* signified arrival of a courier, while the colored streamers of the *hata jirushi*, *nobori*, and *sashimono* played an important role in unit designation and deployment. They also painted the battlefield with extraordinary shapes, motions, and colors not seen elsewhere in the history of war. The spectacle they made was vividly recreated in Akira Kurosawa's fictional masterpiece *Ran* (1985). Other interesting variations on flags include the Seljuk Turks habit of tying horsetails ("tugh") to their battle standards. The Ottomans used crescent-shaped finials instead. Muslim troops appear to have put a crescent moon on their green battle flags as a representation of Islam only after encountering Christian armies bearing the cross on shields and battle standards during the *Crusades*. Aztec banners were flown attached to baskets strapped to the backs of notable warriors. On the march, they usually took a center position in a long strung-out formation (most Mesoamerican roads accommodated no more than two walking abreast, as the wheel and cart were unknown in the Americas). See also *ancient*; *cornet (1)*; *knight*; *siege warfare*; *uma jirushi*; *uniforms*.

flagship. The ship in a fleet that bore the commanding admiral or the king, and flew his pennant.

flails. See *mace*; *military flail*.

flanchard(s). Plate armor for *warhorses* that covered the flanks, fitting around the saddle and into the *crupper* to the rear. It was developed in Europe around the mid-15th century.

Flanders. Flanders was among the first areas in Europe to emerge from *feudalism*, during the latter 13th century. By the 14th century the city-states of Flanders, notably Bruges, Ghent, and Ypres, fielded militia organized by guild. They were highly disciplined, wore distinctive uniforms, and fought wearing gauntlets, helmets, shields, and some plate. They were armed with bows, crossbows, and *goedendags*, a specialized Flanders short-pike. Flemish infantry impressed all of Europe with their victory at *Courtrai* (1302), won by shrewd use of terrain that exploited gross overconfidence on the part of charging French *heavy horse*. However, the Flemings were beaten by the French two years later, at *Mons-en-Pévèle* (1304). A treaty was negotiated the next year that surrendered most French-speaking towns to Philip IV ("The Fair"), but left the rest of Flanders autonomous of its erstwhile overlord. However, France was not beaten as easily as its knights. When *Philip VI* ascended the throne in 1328 he raised an army to suppress the Flemings and scored a signal victory at *Cassel* (1328). In the 1380s the Flemish towns allied with England, with which they had close commercial ties and which was then at war with a common enemy, France. A major clash came at *Roosebeke* (1382), where the Flemish infantry were slaughtered by French horse. The next year, Flanders was ceded to Burgundy. By 1385 the dukes brutally crushed the last vestiges of Flemish independence.

Flanders prospered from the Baltic trade in herring, forest, and mining products. It also enjoyed a rich trade with England that underlay its 14th-century military alliances. Blessed with excellent harbors, Flanders led Europe in shipping in the 14th–15th centuries: great merchant fleets (the "Flanders

Fleets") formed annual convoys from Venice and Genoa and smaller Italian cities and sailed to Bruges, carrying an expanding trade between older states of the Mediterranean and rising Atlantic economies. The last "Flanders Fleet" sailed in 1532. Flanders was on the front line in the long war between the great dynastic houses of Valois and Habsburg, and again between the Dutch and the Spanish during the *Eighty Years' War* (1568–1648), when it suffered lengthy blockades by the *Sea Beggars*. With independence of the United Provinces recognized by all in 1648, the Catholic half of Flanders that remained tied to Spain became known as the "Spanish Netherlands."

Fleurus, Battle of (August 29, 1622). Following the Catholic-Habsburg invasion of the Palatinate and the near disaster for Protestants at *Höchst* in June, an Imperial army invaded the Netherlands to aid the Spanish against Dutch rebels. *Graf von Mansfeld* and his mercenaries, and *Christian of Brunswick* and a second Protestant army, moved against the Imperials. The armies met at Fleurus. Christian charged headlong with his cavalry and was initially repulsed. Repeated charges broke the Spanish lines, though at a high cost in Brunswick infantry (nearly 50 percent casualties). Fleurus was one of the first battles to link the *Thirty Years' War* with the *Eighty Years' War*, which had resumed following expiration of the *Twelve-Years' Truce* in 1621.

flintlock. The first flintlock mechanism for firing guns was introduced in Germany in the mid-15th century, but it did not catch on for another hundred years. Around 1547 primitive flintlocks appeared in Florence and Sweden. More advanced models were made in France, but not outside it until the 1640s. By the 1660s knowledge of the flintlock had diffused throughout Europe. Still, this new lock device did not displace the *matchlock* as the preferred firing mechanism for the infantry musket until the 1680s in most advanced armies, and later still among marginal peoples engaged in border and frontier warfare. "Flintlock" was first used about any gun in which the lock mechanism deployed a spring that snapped a piece of flint against steel, creating sparks that fired the fine powder in the pan, which in turn ignited the main charge. "True" flintlocks had the steel striker and pan cover made in one piece, and could be both "half-cocked" and "full-cocked." This mechanism made pistols far more dependable and popular.

Flodden Field, Battle of (September 9, 1513). "Battle of Branxton." The young *Henry VIII* sent an army of 25,000 under the Yorkist Earl of Surrey to secure his northern border against a Scottish army of 50,000 that had invaded Northumberland, an act urged on the equally young and reckless Scottish king, James IV (1488–1513), by Louis XII of France. James took the French lure against the advice of his council. Henry was preoccupied trying to reclaim territories in France lost during the *Hundred Years' War* (1337–1453). The clash in the north opened with an artillery exchange. Then the English charged poorly armed and ill-led Scottish foot dug in atop a small hill, but otherwise badly deployed. The Scots made a fatal error of leaving their trenches to engage hand-to-hand with outmoded weapons. In bloody close-quarter fighting the Scots were dislodged, encircled, and slaughtered. Through all this their reserve inexplicably held back from any fighting. The young king, many Scottish lairds (at least 8 earls and 20 lords), and thousands of clansmen were put to the sword.

Florence. See *condottieri*; *Francis I*; *Giornico, Battle of*; *Italian Renaissance*; *Italian Wars*; *Italy*; *Lodi, Peace of*; *Marignano, Battle of*; *Sforza, Maximilian*; *Swabian War*; *Venice*.

Flores, Battle of (1591). A fleet of seven English warships looking for Spanish treasure ships in the Azores was met by 15 Spanish warships. The action is most famous for the fight of the "Revenge," in which Captain Richard Grenville fought a suicidal rearguard action alone against the whole Spanish fleet for over half a day, sinking two of his tormentors before surrendering the burning wreck of his ship.

flota. "fleet." The primary reference was to the Spanish treasure fleet which sailed yearly from Seville. Once it arrived in the Caribbean it split into smaller flotas that sailed off to collect the treasure brought to the coast from the great Potosi silver mine in Peru, and from smaller mines throughout New Spain to the ports of Nombre de Dios, San Juan de Ulúa, Santo Domingo, Cartagena, and Vera Cruz. The small fleets reassembled into a single flota at Havana to make the journey back to Seville under armed escort. Additional protective measures included fortification of the major Caribbean ports and attacks against hostile settlements, such as the massacres of *Huguenots* in Florida (1565). See also *convoy*; *Fort Caroline*; *"galeones."*

flower wars. See *Xochiyaoyotl*.

fodder. Food supply for horses, cavalry mounts, and draught animals, was a major constraint on military operations throughout this period. Steppe ponies were grass fed, but for settled peoples from China to Europe grave problems with provision and cartage of fodder usually determined the ability of an army to remain in the field. On average, even a small packhorse consumed 14 pounds of hay and 7 more of straw per day, along with $1\frac{1}{2}$ pecks of peas, oats, or other grains. This meant that a good portion of a pack animal's burthen was taken up by its own food requirements. See the main discussion under *logistics*. On related matters see *baggage train*; *chevauchée*; *contributions*; *coureurs*; *étapes*; *gun carriages*; *Le Tellier, Michel*; *magazines*; *requisition*; *warhorse*.

Foix, Gaston de, duc de Nemours (1489–1512). French general. His father was killed at *Cerignola* (1503). In January 1512, at age 22, he carried out skilled maneuvers that positioned him to lift the Spanish-Papal siege of Bologna. Then he stormed and sacked Brescia. His only set-piece battle came at *Ravenna* (April 11, 1512), where he won the field but threw away his life in a reckless pursuit.

folangji. A small breech-loading *swivel gun* manufactured in China starting in 1524. The design was copied directly from more than 20 Portuguese cannon captured in a firefight in 1521. The name appears to derive from the Ottoman *"praṅgi"* and/or the Mughal "farangi," both breech-loading swivel guns of European origin but non-European manufacture with which the Chinese may have been already familiar.

Fontainebleau, Treaty of (May 1631). A defensive alliance signed between *Maximilian I* of Bavaria, and France. It aimed to counterbalance Habsburg power in Germany following the *Edict of Restitution* and France's escape from the *War of the Mantuan Succession* in Italy. In that respect, it was a Catholic counterpart to the *Leipziger Bund*.

Fontaine-Francaise, Battle of (June 5, 1595). See *Franco-Spanish War*.

food. The crucial facts about food and war in this period are discussed under *logistics*. On strategy, tactics and other considerations related to food, see: *Ayn Jālut, Battle of*; *baggage train*; *Barbados*; *Black Death*; *chevauchée*; *civilians*; *contributions*; *coureurs*; *cruising*; *desertion*; *disease*; *étapes*; *fodder*; *galleon*; *galley*; *gun carriages*; *Indian Wars*; *Invincible Armada*; *Le Tellier, Michel*; *logistics*; *magazines*; *ordu bazar*; *prise*; *purveyance*; *quartermaster*; *rations*; *requisition*; *siege warfare*; *Spanish Road*; *sutlers*; *Swiss Army*; *Tatars*; *Treuga Dei*; *victualer*; *warhorses*; *Werben, Battle of*.

foot ropes. See *rigging*.

forecastle. See *castles, on ships*.

Foreign Contingent. See *Polish Army*.

Forest Cantons. Schwyz, Unterwalden, and Uri. They were known collectively as the "Waldstätte." See also *Kappel, Battle of*; *Laupen, Battle of*; *Morgarten, Battle of*; *Swiss Confederation*; *Zwingli, Huldrych*.

forged guns. See *hoop-and-stave method*.

Forlorn Hope. The wings of a *Swiss square*, often comprised of crossbowmen or arquebusiers without protective cover of the pikemen in the strong center of the formation. At *Grandson* (1476), the Forlorn Hope was comprised mostly of crossbowmen and arquebusiers deployed as a skirmish line in front of a massive (10,000-man) pike square. At *Nancy* (1477) a larger Forlorn Hope decoyed the Burgundians out of defensive positions, setting them up for an attack by the *Vorhut* in the flank.

Formigny, Battle of (April 15, 1450). One of the closing battles in the *Hundred Years' War* (1337–1453). An English army of 2,500 men landed at Cherbourg in mid-March 1450, and advanced down the Cotentin peninsula. The landing was made in reaction to a sweeping, three-pronged French assault on remaining English holdings in Normandy. With reinforcements from English garrisons that already had been abandoned this force increased to 4,000. Two smaller French armies, one of 2,000 the other of 3,000 men, maneuvered against the English. After marches and several small skirmishes the English met the first body of French, led by le compte de Clermont, at Formigny, west of Bayeux. Some 75 percent of the English troops were longbowmen. They took positions behind a crop of *Spanish riders*, backed by a small creek. The French probed but were repulsed by the usual English arrow storms. Clermont then brought forward two long-range *coulverines* on wheeled carriages, enfilading the English line. These guns fired into the dense pack of archers, out of range of return longbow fire but with a rate of fire and accuracy of their own rapid enough to tell heavily against limbs and lives. In desperation, the longbowmen charged and overran the coulverines. But terrible casualties had been inflicted and the French had other cannon with which to pound the English position. The second French army now arrived: 1,200 horse trailed by 800 crossbowmen. These reinforcements forced English survivors into a defensive arc so dense that it inhibited firing by many longbowmen, while the French assaulted from two directions at once. The English line collapsed under intense crossbow and gun fire; the whole English army was killed, captured, or fled the field (the latter ran all the way to Caen) in utter panic. The defeat left England without a field army to support its few remaining holdings in Normandy, almost all of which soon fell to the French, including Falaise and Cherbourg. Formigny also ended forever the continental reputation for superiority of the longbow. Henceforth, while the longbow was used in England through the *Wars of the Roses*, elsewhere infantry with handguns predominated along with long-range artillery.

> ...*the whole English army was killed, captured, or fled the field (the latter ran all the way to Caen) in utter panic.*

Formula of Concord (1577–1578). An anti-Calvinist declaration drawn up by Lutheran theologians. It was so rigid in its doctrine that it made forever impossible any reconciliation of the two main branches of reformed religion. This reflected a view among some Lutheran clerics and princes that the Calvinists were worse confessional enemies than Catholics.

Fornovo, Battle of (July 6, 1495). Early in the *Italian Wars* (1494–1559), Charles VIII was forced to retreat from Naples. South of Milan the path of his army of just 10,000 French and Swiss was blocked by 20,000 Venetians and Mantuans led by the *condottieri* captain Giovanni Gonzaga. Instead of the usual feckless and nearly bloodless affair then common in Italian condottieri warfare, the French opened with an artillery bombardment, intending to kill as many of their enemy as possible. Then they charged with *heavy cavalry*, destroying and scattering the disordered Italian ranks in just minutes. The fight was perhaps most memorable for the ineffectiveness of artillery on either side, other than the psychological effect achieved by the French guns: of the 100 French and 3,500 Italian dead, one eyewitness estimated that fewer than 10 men were killed by cannon fire.

Fort Caroline. A Huguenot *privateer* colony was established at Fort Caroline, Florida, in early 1564. The following September the settlement was attacked by a Spanish military expedition led by Admiral Pedro de Menendez, who was determined to protect the annual *flota* and end Huguenot desecrations of Catholic colonies and churches. The Spanish overwhelmed the defenders inside an hour and killed every man in the Fort, though the few women and children were repatriated to France. The fort was renamed "San Mateo." In 1568 a Huguenot fleet returned and hanged every Spaniard in the garrison.

fortification.

Asia

Fortified *citadels* and walled cities were part of warfare in thickly settled areas of China from ancient times. The most spectacular fortification system was the *Great Wall*, dating in some areas to the Han dynasty though importantly upgraded and extended by 700 miles of new walls built by the *Ming* dynasty starting in 1474, to fortify the frontier against *Mongol* raiders. The Ming wall system involved hundreds of watchtowers, signal-beacon platforms, and self-sufficient garrisons organized as military colonies. China's large cities were also walled, but private castles akin to those of feudal Europe or the *daimyo* of Japan were uncommon. Smaller forts beyond border posts or to guard mountain passes in the south did not matter much when China faced great cavalry armies of steppe invaders such as the Mongols or Manchus. Nor was Chinese fortification technology pressed hard by such invaders, since they lacked siege engines or effective artillery. In Chinese civil wars control of the cities was usually key, and siege operations more common. In the later Ming period rebel Chinese armies acquired gunpowder cannon capable of smashing older city walls, and during the first half of the 17th century Manchu invaders captured or bought a siege train they then manned with Chinese gun crews and engineers. Once the Ming field armies were beaten, cities rapidly fell to rebel and Manchu assault.

Japan underwent a period of extensive, even frantic, fortification in its anarchic 16th century (*Sengoku jidai*). Some elaborate *yamajiro*, and perhaps 40,000 lesser forts of the *honjō* and *shijō* type, were erected. Arson was a widespread tool in countering these weaker structures. The Sengoku period also saw proliferation of *jōkaku* (mountaintop forts). In the second half of the 16th century substantial stone castles and full *jōkamachi* (castle towns) were built. *Oda Nobunaga* was a notable castle builder, but from 1580 forward most of Japan's older fortifications were destroyed by decree of *Toyotomi Hideyoshi*. His intent was to facilitate central political and military control and effect national unification under the shogunate, and daimyo forts stood in the way of this just as baronial castles did of centralization in Europe. Late Japanese castles were more elaborate in construction and far more decorative, paralleling a late shift among English gentry and in certain Rhine castles in Germany away from military structures to merely boastful homes.

Korean cities and towns had high, thin walls. Just as in medieval Europe, this impeded scaling but did not stand up against modern siege artillery, which was first brought to Korea by Hideyoshi in the 1590s. Older Korean forts and walled cites fell quickly and easily to Hideyoshi, who used his artillery effectively to breach the defenses of Pusan, Seoul, and Pyongyang. Even where bombardment failed, Korean forts lacked bastions and most had no dry ditches or moats. As a result, Japanese infantry were able to reach the walls with relative ease to overwhelm defenders by storming through even small breaches made by siege cannon.

The Ottomans did not fortify overmuch during the early centuries of their expansion. When they did, they were mostly content with simple *çit palankasi*, or reed palisades. Once their frontiers reached the outer limits of logistical support in the second half of the 16th century they paid more attention to fixed defenses and built more *kale*, or moated stone fortresses. Ottoman builders were especially adept in the "Horasani" ("rose colored") brick technique, which used lime and brick dust instead of sand for mixing mortar. This lent enhanced strength to thick brick or stone walls that were impregnable by most artillery of the day, partly because terracing of kale forts trapped solid shot. The Ottomans adopted the "trace italienne" shortly after it spread into Europe from Italy. Due to their great expense, the Ottomans only built the new bastioned forts in strategic locations such as Baghdad and Mosul in the east, and in key sites in the Balkans. That was military and fiscal prudence, not the product of any putative military "backwardness" of the Ottoman Empire. Ottoman and other Muslim fortification methods had some influence on *Mughal* practices in northern India, arriving along with gunpowder artillery. In Hindu India gunpowder weapons led not to the downfall of fixed fortifications but a revival of forts built by new military elites, the *Marathas, Rajputs*, and *Nayakas*.

Europe

Castles appeared in large numbers in Europe during the early Middle Ages, with a shift in the 11th century in Britain, France, and Spain to more expensive and lasting stone fortifications where earlier *mottes* and simple *donjons* had sufficed, or were all that could be afforded. A variation on this change occurred in Flanders, the Netherlands, and lands controlled by the *Teutonic Knights* in Poland and along the Baltic coastline. There, brick was used in the absence of good building stone, supported by more extensive water barriers.

The move to stone (and brick) fortification reflected a vast increase in expenditure on war by societies growing in wealth and population. Stone walls were also more militarily effective when opposed by ancient or medieval siege weapons comprised of *catapults*, battering-rams, and related torsion weapons. Infantry attack and scaling of the walls became the main threat, with the obvious solution of building walls and towers ever higher, until scaling became impracticable. This trend accelerated in the 12th century after introduction of the counterpoise or torsion *trebuchet*. Facing a stone castle attackers usually concluded that assault or bombardment were too dangerous or likely to be ineffective. Instead, they relied on starvation. That too was difficult: the trick was to avoid starvation oneself, a difficult task in an age of primitive *logistics* where armies needed to move and forage just to eat. Still, sieges often lasted weeks or months; from the late 16th century, some lasted years. This core fact, that a fortified position was a tremendous strongpoint out of which defenders could foray or sit and wait for relief, colored the nature of war in the West until the advent of *gunpowder artillery*.

Early gunpowder artillery was relatively easily deflected: the first cannon were too inaccurate for shots to hit the same target twice, which was critical to cracking stone, and fascines of wood and wool wadding hung over walls absorbed much of the impact of stone cannon balls. As guns grew more powerful and cast iron cannonballs increased impact power, the old high thin walls began to tumble. Cannon did not make castles wholly obsolete, but they forced major changes. High walls and towers fell too easily, so lower walls ("countersinking") were built and insulated with earthworks to absorb iron shot. Cutaway gun ports were added to the *curtain wall* and the base of towers to allow cannon to shoot back at enemy batteries or siege engines or spray sappers and miners with *grapeshot* at point-blank range. To prevent scaling of the lower walls and squat gun platforms by attacking infantry, defenders built bastions that supported each other with enfilading fire from arquebusiers, musketeers, and archers shooting through slits or *merlons*. This forced attackers to counter with siege trenches and armored engines like *cats*, and so on.

By the second half of the 14th century many older castles had gun embrasures cut into their walls, and new ones were designed to accept cannon. However, big defensive guns weakened stone walls through their recoil vibrations. This, too, recommended a move to lower and thicker walls. A major breakthrough in design, which most historians agree caused nothing short of a military revolution, was the *alla moderna* or *trace italienne*: low polygonal forts and bastions fitted with gun emplacements for heavy defensive artillery. The defenders could now shoot down kill zones created by the bastions and further prepared by clearing obstructions and sloping the perimeter to allow unobstructed defensive fire by canon and small arms. Ditches were widened to obstruct and slow defenders, and bastions were further protected by adding a *counterscarp*. Dirt removed from the ditch was thrown against the counterscarp to make a sloped *glacis*, which further slowed infantry trying to fight their way up, keeping them exposed longer to defensive fire. Dutch innovators, notably Adriaen Anthonisz (1541–1620), worked in this basic style while adding features from their special expertise in field works that incorporated dikes and canals and other watery perimeters. The United Provinces established a permanent corps of military engineers, numbering 25 in 1598, that exerted wide international influence in both the new style in fortification and the siegecraft needed to overcome it.

Bridges and Towns

In addition to castles, bridges might be fortified. Large forts protected major bridges across the Seine and the Elbe, for instance. Within riverine towns bridges connecting the halves of a city were usually fortified and garrisoned. The fight led by *Jeanne d'Arc* in Orléans in 1429 was over a heavily fortified bridge spanning the Loire, protected by a *bastille* hosting 500 English troops. Urban fortification in Europe kept pace with castellan developments in wall height and girth, use of towers, *donjons*, citadels, and the like. The key difference was that town fortification took place on a much larger scale and was financed as a form of public defense, unlike castles built for a private purpose with baronial or knightly funds and feudal labor. As towns grew in size and population much longer walls were needed to enclose new suburbs. Even small cities had extensive walls: provincial York's walls stretched for 4,800 yards and some very small towns in France or Germany had walls thousands of meters in circumference. City walls might be 11–12 meters high. They supported defensive artillery, watchtowers, archer and arquebus walkways, and armored and heavily defended gates. An aesthetic yearning for height and civic competition comparable to that seen in cathedral building, especially of towers, has been suggested as reinforcing the general skyward trend in medieval military architecture in Europe. Fortification of towns also produced counter tactics of scorched earth and *chevauchée*, which sought to lure defenders out by destroying all of value outside the walls. To stop Magyar raiders, whole fortress towns in Germany were built from scratch, radiating outward from a citadel position at the center (for example, Brandenburg and Magdeburg). Similarly, the *Hausa* city-states of West Africa were surrounded by high, thick, baked-mud walls. Cities in India, too, were fortified. Some were defended by walls of colossal girth, so strong and wide they withstood bombardment

> *The fight led by* Jeanne d'Arc *in Orleans in 1429 was over a heavily fortified bridge spanning the Loire . . .*

hundreds of years later by 19th-century artillery firing high-explosive shells. Constantinople had three concentric rings of walls, some sections over 1,000 years old. Baghdad had 211 defensive towers and 52 crenels fixed in 25-meter-high walls that were 15 meters thick at the base and 7 meters at the top, built of hard brick in the Horasani mode favored by the Ottomans.

Some medieval and early modern sieges were so spectacular they changed the world, in fact and in psychological and political perception and historical legacy. That was especially true of the Muslim *Siege of Constantinople* in 1453 by *Muhammad II*. His innovative use of heavy bombardment to reduce triple walls that had withstood twenty prior sieges over a thousand-year period demonstrated the new power of gunpowder artillery. Yet, the majority of town defenses built to withstand sieges in Europe or the Middle East or India or China did their intended job of deterrence; they were never attacked at all. Instead, fortifications guarding strategic points or routes or mountain or river passes took the brunt of warfare, suffering assaults or sieges year after year, one campaign following another, decade upon decade, even century after century. See also *abatis*; *artillery towers*; *barbican*; *bastion*; *boulevard*; *cavalier (2)*; *chemin de ronde*; *counter-guard (1)*; *covered way*; *crownwork*; *defilade*; *demi-bastion*; *demi-lune*; *escarp*; *esplanade*; *front*; *gabions*; *hornwork*; *Indian Wars*; *lines of circumvallation*; *lines of contravallation*; *lodgement*; *outworks*; *parapet*; *rampart*; *ravelin*; *redan*; *redoubt*; *retrenchment*; *sap*; *tabor*; *technology and war*; *tenaille*; *terre-plein*; *torre alberrano*; *torre del homenaje*; *trou de loup*.

Suggested Reading: A. Chatelain, *Architecture militaire mèdiévale* (1970); Maurice Keen, ed., *Medieval Warfare* (1999); B. H. O'Neil, *Castles and Cannon* (1960); R. Ritter, *L'architecture militaire mèdiévale* (1974).

foundries. See *casting*.

Fra. Abbreviation of the Latin "Frater" ("Brother"), used in reference to a fully professed *knight* of one of the *Military Orders*. The equivalent Spanish address was "Frey." Among Brethren the abbreviation "Fr." was used. In modern times "Fra" became the more common usage to avoid confusion with the English abbreviation of "Father," meaning Catholic priest.

franc-archers. Regiments of archers armed at first with ordinary bows, not *longbows* or *crossbows*, set up by Charles VII in 1448 in an effort to counter the English advantage in archery. A reserve of some 8,000 men was established utilizing an amended *arrière-ban*. Over time the units came to include pikemen, crossbowmen, and handgunners as well as ordinary archers. *Louis XI* doubled the size of the reserve. However, he subsequently completely disbanded the franc-archers when he became convinced that Swiss infantry victories over *Charles the Rash* had exposed comparable and dangerous weaknesses in his own army. Louis replaced them with Swiss mercenaries who emphasized the pike and halberd as the principal infantry weapons, in preference to archery. His successors reinstated some franc-archers units in the 1490s, rather than pay wages to the Swiss.

France. In 987 Hugh Capet succeeded the last Carolingian king and began the long process of Capetian construction of the state that eventually became France: Capetian monarchs ruled France, descending through several branches, from 987 to 1792 and 1815 to 1848. From Charlemagne's old capital at Aachen, the early Capetians expanded against fierce opposition from feudal barons and rival powers based in Normandy, Aquitaine, and Burgundy. With the *Norman* conquest of England in 1066 the land-owning and martial classes in France and England were entangled in a mailed web of overlapping vassalage, a fact that importantly contributed to entanglement in each other's wars over several centuries. These two emerging polities, each slowly centralizing under royal authority, were at war more often than not for four centuries. That fact compelled France to become a sea power: during the first half of the 13th century the Capetians acquired ports in Normandy (1204) and Poitou (1224) on the Atlantic, and a Mediterranean port at Aigues-Mortes (1240). Capetian France reached the peak of its power and prestige under Louis IX (1226–1270), and so dominated the armies of the *Crusades* that Muslims called all Latin knights in the east "Franks" regardless of their actual origin. French knights also fought bloody, even genocidal, crusades against "heresy" within France—most notably the *Albigensian Crusade* in the Midi. During the 13th century roving bands of mercenaries (*routiers*) were thrown up by incessant internal conflict and protracted fighting with England. To deal with the anarchy they threatened, the merchant classes agreed to levels of taxation that permitted French kings to raise royal armies and later, also the best gunpowder artillery train and park in the world. They used these forces to smash the armed nobility and begin to forge a "French" identity and nation.

The long conflict with England climaxed in the *Hundred Years' War* (1337–1453). The 14th century in France was marked by baleful military defeats and decline, political fragmentation, and nearly endless war fought almost exclusively on French soil with a succession of aggressive English kings. The dynastic and territorial disputes that gave rise to the Hundred Years' War triggered succession crises and civil wars in both kingdoms. For most of the Hundred Years' War victory by England and Burgundy looked to be the most likely outcome. Then France rallied behind *Jeanne d'Arc* in 1429, and later around the king she crowned, Charles VII. Royalists armies used artillery to expell English garrisons from Guyenne, Gascony, and Normandy, indeed all of France except *Calais*. France thus emerged victorious from the long war and under a powerful king, Louis XII (1423–1483). It was one of the first states in Europe to move out of the Middle Ages and assume an early modern form: its great feudatories were beaten into submission politically and militarily, and their interests, titles, and fortunes tied to service to the crown. This resulted in good measure from military reforms implemented by French kings. They replaced old feudal levies raised by barons and comprised principally of mounted knights, with a new army built around the best artillery train in the world and professional infantry, much of it foreign mercenary. The royal army retained nobles as officers but professional gunners and infantry, and even some mercenary heavy cavalry alongside its noble horse. Paid formations dealt with England's archers and dismounted men-at-arms more effectively, and finally expelled English power from the Continent. The monarchy then used its newfound military power to launch the *Italian Wars* (1494–1559). France enjoyed some early success, as in 1515 when *Francis I* defeated the famed pike squares of the Swiss at *Marignano*. Francis did not do so well, however, at *Pavia* (February 23–24, 1525). On the whole, the Italian Wars were a financial drain and distraction for France that lasted seven decades.

In the 16th century, beginning with the Italian Wars, France faced a powerful continental enemy who replaced England in French military imagination and attention until 1660: the *Habsburgs*. The long struggle between the Houses of Valois and Habsburg pitted military giants against each other for 160 years, though with an important interregnum: for over 40 years after 1562, France was torn apart by serial "wars of religion," or the *French Civil Wars*. The *Guise* and *Catholic League*, sometimes in alliance with the crown, sometimes not, warred with the *Huguenots* for four decades. The civil wars ended with the coronation of *Henri IV*, who abjured his Protestantism to ascend the throne and unite a nation. France thereafter reemerged as principal rival to Spain to the middle of the 17th century, supplanting Elizabethan England in that role. France benefitted enormously from the inspired statecraft of *Cardinal Armand Richelieu*, who bribed, cajoled, and maneuvered other powers and other kings' armies to fight the Habsburgs in place of France. Meanwhile, Richelieu and *Louis XIII* finished with France's "Huguenot problem" and girded for the final showdown with the Habsburgs. By the time France overtly entered the *Thirty Years' War* in 1635 it could call upon a rich resource base, a growing and modernizing urban economy, and a swelling population: 16 million in 1600, or four times that of England. By 1635, French finances were in order, the Huguenots had been eliminated as a military factor and threat to internal peace and stability, and the Spanish and Austrians were near military and fiscal exhaustion from over-extension in wars in Germany, the Netherlands, and with the Ottomans. Although the first battles went badly for France, in 1643 a French army crushed the Spanish at *Rocroi*. That victory, and several others, set the stage for peace talks that culminated in the *Peace of Westphalia* (1648). There, French diplomats ensured the continuing division of Germany and the preeminence of France as the dominant military power in Europe. See also *Agincourt, Battle of*; *Cassel, Battle of*; *chevauchée*; *chivalry*; *Courtrai, Battle of*; *Crécy, Battle of*; *feudalism*; *Francis II*; *Free Companies*; *Henri II, of France*; *Medici, Catherine de*; *Poitiers, Battle of*; *Roosebeke, Battle of*.

Suggested Reading: P. S. Lewis, ed., *The Recovery of France in the 15th Century* (1972); Victor-Louis Tapié, *France in the Age of Louis XIII and Richelieu*, D. Lockie, trans. (1975).

Franche-Comté. An Imperial territory for most of this period, it was acquired by Spain under the terms of *Cateau-Cambrésis* in 1559. It was a contested region with France during the *Thirty Years' War* (1618–1648).

Francis I (1494–1547). King of France, 1515–1547. He inherited an army fundamentally reshaped after defeating England in the *Hundred Years' War*. It no longer relied on feudal levies commanded by barons. It was still strong in *heavy cavalry* but it also led the way in gunpowder artillery and expanded infantry. In 1515, Francis took this army back into Italy, where it performed well in a new round of the *Italian Wars* (1494–1559), defeating the pike squares of the *Swiss Confederation* over two days at *Marignano* (September 13–14, 1515) and taking Milan. But the next foe Francis faced was the most powerful monarch in Europe since Charlemagne: *Charles V*. Altogether, his Habsburg territories encircled France on three sides. It was a strategic dilemma that dogged Francis his entire reign. Francis won at *La Bicocca* (April 27, 1522), but then the war in Italy turned against him. There followed an invasion of southern France by *Charles de Bourbon*. The climax came at *Pavia* (February 23–24, 1525), where Francis was defeated, captured, taken to Madrid, and held until he surrendered all claims in Italy and Burgundy, a false promise he renounced immediately upon his release in 1526. Francis spent the next 20 years conspiring against the Habsburgs, but achieved few successes in the continuing Italian Wars despite signing a formal alliance with the Ottoman Empire in 1536. In 1534 he ordered formation of seven "legions" of 6,000 men, each raised within France, to reduce his dependence on the Swiss for infantry and in mimicry of the Spanish *tercio*. These were to be all pike, halberd, and arquebus units. They never challenged the tercio effectively, however, since they were badly officered and ill-trained. In religious matters Francis was a supporter of Christian humanism and scholarship, notably that of Erasmus. He embraced Catholic orthodoxy as defined for the *Gallican Church* by faculty of the Sorbonne. He was among the first major Catholic monarchs to denounce *Lutheranism* and *Calvinism* as heresy. His response to conversion of French nobles to Calvinism was active repression, starting with the *Affair of the Placards* (1534). See also *Corpus Christi*; *Henry VIII, of England*.

Suggested Reading: Robert Knecht, *Francis I* (1982); Desmond Seward, *Prince of the Renaissance* (1973).

Francis II (1544–1560). King of France, 1559–1560. A sickly child, he was married as a youth to *Mary Stuart*. He reigned briefly but never ruled after his father, *Henri II*, was mortally wounded in a jousting accident. His wife's uncles, the militant Catholics *François, duc de Guise* and *Charles, Cardinal de Lorraine*, seized effective power from his mother, *Catherine de Medici*. The Guise brothers arrested and executed many Protestants for heresy, aggravating confessional tensions so that in March 1560, the *"conspiracy of Amboise"* took form around a plot to kidnap Francis and depose the Guise. In the middle of the crisis he died suddenly, from an ear infection. His early death so soon after his powerful father's passing unsettled the affairs of France and its ally, Scotland, and thereby also of England and Spain. In 1562, during the opening skirmishes of the *French Civil Wars* (1562–1629), Huguenot rioters sacked his tomb in Orléans, fed his entrails to dogs, and mutilated his heart.

François I. See *Francis I*.

François II. See *Francis II*.

Franco–Spanish War (1595–1598). Even as the eighth of the *French Civil Wars* was drawing to a close, *Henri IV* declared war on Spain. He had discovered yet another in a long line of plots by *Philip II* to invade France, or at least occupy several of its strategic Atlantic ports. More importantly, the Spanish were supporting *Mayenne*, then in Burgundy with a dwindling but defiant army of the *Catholic League*. Henri intended to push over the tottering League by exposing its alliance with foreign powers against France's legitimate king, while assuring newly suspicious Huguenots that his reconversion to Catholicism had not bound him too closely to a purely Catholic policy. With another of his political master strokes Henri thus converted the League into an association of traitors while uniting and redirecting most of France's martial energy outward, against a hated foreign foe. In May 1595, a Spanish army 10,000 strong moved to Dijon and joined Mayenne. Henri met the enemy at nearby Fontaine-Française on June 5. The fighting was desperate, with Henri leading several cavalry charges, the last French king to personally lead cavalry into battle. His reckless but effective tactics bested the numerically superior Catholic force. General Velasco, the Constable of Castile, then fell out with Mayenne with the result that Henri's enemies divided their forces. Mayenne retreated to Chalon while Henri secured Burgundy with short, sharp sieges, and by bribing the master of the citadel in Dijon to submit. In 1596 the new Spanish governor of Flanders, General Fuentes, invaded from the north and seized Le Catelet, Doullens, and Cambrai (the latter after a fierce bombardment). Henri looked to Italy for Catholic allies but found none willing or able to rise up, while Protestant powers trusted him no more. Another Spanish army took Calais in early 1597 while Spanish troops disguised as French peasants entered and seized Amiens. When Henri moved to retake the city even his old Huguenot comrades-in-arms refused

> *His reckless but effective tactics bested the numerically superior Catholic force.*

to help him. Still, the king managed to raise an army with which he invested Amiens from April to September 1597. On September 25, mounted and holding his scepter and looking every inch the warrior king, Henri reviewed withdrawal of the Spanish garrison to which he had granted terms. Several thousand enemy troops filed past, pulling hundreds of carts loaded with dead and wounded Spaniards while their officers saluted a conqueror. Henri garrisoned Amiens with a citadel and loyal troops then moved on and subdued Brittany, where the last great Catholic rebel, the duc de Mercoeur, submitted in early 1598. Henri made peace with Spain at *Vervins* and settled with the Huguenots in the *Edict of Nantes*. France was at peace for the first time since 1562.

Franco–Spanish Wars (1494–1559). See *Italian Wars*.

Frankenhausen, Battle of (1525). See *German Peasant War*.

Frankfurt-an-der-Oder, Storming of (1631). See *Thirty Years' War*.

Franks. Originally, the Germanic conquerors of Gaul (6th century). They later fended off the Muslim invasion of Gaul, established the empire of Charlemagne, and gave their name to the early medieval kingdom of France. From the late 11th century "Franks" was the Muslim name for all Latin Crusaders, regardless of their actual origin in the divers states of Western and Central Europe. The Byzantines also called Westerners "Franks," though sometimes the Greeks used the still older Roman term, "Celts." See also *Crusades*; *lance (3)*; *Normans*.

Frastenz, Battle of (April 20, 1499). The first battle of the *Swabian War* (1499), in which the Swiss defended their frontier against encroachment by *Maximilian I*, Holy Roman Emperor. His mixed Swabian and German mercenary army took up position hear Frastenz. The Swiss split their force of 10,000 men into two groups. When the *Vorhut* (or van) arrived it attacked the German center. Meanwhile, the second square scaled a small cliff that was left undefended, which allowed it to attack into the German flank. The Swiss "push of pike" was unstoppable: the Germans broke and ran, leaving their wounded to be slaughtered by the merciless Swiss.

free cities. "Reichsstädte." See *Holy Roman Empire*; *Prague, Peace of*; *Schmalkaldic League*; *Westphalia, Peace of*.

Free Companies. The earliest bands of 12th-century "free companions" were small (seldom more than 1,000 men), mostly infantry, and fought under regionally identifiable names such as "Aragonais" or "Navarais." That reflected the tendency of recruits to come from poorer rural areas of southern France, or the fringes of Flemish society. Close bonds formed among these men of violence, many of whom were highly skilled with bows and crossbows. Their independence and knight-killing weaponry competed with the feudal bonds of older, Church-sanctioned social and military relations. Other Free Companies emerged out of mixed bands of mercenaries formed to survive through extortion during lulls in the fighting (and pay) during the 13th–14th centuries. When in royal employ, Free Companies might be as loyal or disloyal on the field of battle as other professional troops. But no duke or baron or even king could pay them year-round, so they resorted to living off the land in winter, and they reverted to existence as military locust whenever peace broke out.

Recruitment into Free Companies broadened during the *Hundred Years' War* (1337–1453), when the fully mercenary character of the companies became clear. More than 100 "Free Companies" appeared after the *Peace of Brétigny* (1360), which let them loose on the people and the land while temporarily ending fighting between the monarchs of France and England. Several of these companies were mixed formations: French and English joined together, out of pay and out of service. They seized strongholds as bases from which to ravage towns and the countryside, extorting *appatis* and terrorizing peasants and good burghers. They were far rougher than the *routiers*, who at least enjoyed the legal (and to a degree, also moral) cover of fighting in the name of kings of England. That the Free Companies recognized and celebrated their rogue status was made apparent in the personal motto of one captain: "Everyone's Enemy." Clifford Rogers makes a key point differentiating routiers from Free Companies: whereas routiers did the dirty work of economic attrition commissioned by *Edward III*, the Free Companies "must be considered as a result of the Hundred Years' War rather than an element of its prosecution." Once they had "eaten out" France some drifted to Iberia; others left for the warm climate and rich vineyards and olive groves of Italy. From 1340 to 1380 the majority of members of Free Companies in Italy were foreigners: mostly English, French, and German *condottieri*. By the end of the 14th century Italians regained majority membership in the condottieri and even foreigners in Free Companies became more settled and semi-permanently attached to one city-state or another. This was the case, most notably, with the English mercenary captain *John Hawkwood*. See also *Armagnacs*; *ashigaru*; *Catalan Great Company*; *Celâli Revolts*; *Ecorcheurs*; *ronin*; *routiers*; *Saracen*; *White Company*.

Suggested Reading: N.A.R. Wright, *Knights and Peasants: the Hundred Years' War in the French Countryside* (1998).

freedom of the seas. A fundamental principle of international law holding that the principle of national sovereignty ends at the edge of the delimited "territorial sea," and therefore that all shipping may by right sail the "high seas" without interference in peacetime and with only limited interference in wartime. Its acceptance and codification was much advanced by the great work *Mare Liberum* by *Hugo Grotius*. Although often associated with England, the eventual rise of British naval mastery actually involved abandonment of older notions of free seas and *sovereignty of the sea* in favor of an incipient policy of continental blockade and commerce raiding, evident as early as the Elizabethan war with Spain.

free quarter. A variation on forced *contributions* used during the *English Civil Wars* (1639–1651), in which a promissory ticket was given in exchange for boarding and feeding soldiers. See also *club men*.

Freiburg, Battle of (August 3–10, 1644). A Bavarian force of 15,000 under *Franz von Mercy* besieged Freiburg, in Baden, from June 17, 1644. A French relief army 16,000 strong, led by the *Great Condé*, with *Turenne* in command of the cavalry, arrived on August 3. The first French attempt to take the city failed, at a cost of 5,000 infantry casualties during a blunt, bloody frontal assault on the German trenches. These were overrun, but too late in the day to exploit fully. That allowed Mercy to fall back on a second line of fortification. Taking advantage of shorter and superior lines of supply and reinforcement the French pressed the attack for a week, finally compelling Mercy to withdraw to Rothenburg.

French armies. Traditional feudal military obligations, and a large population, permitted France to raise armies comprised almost exclusively of knights and men-at-arms, supplemented by occasional peasant and town levies. However, after the crushing defeat and slaughter of the French nobility at *Courtrai* (1302), Philip IV ("The Fair") and the monarchy claimed a right to summon all and sundry physically fit to bear arms under the *arrière-ban* (until 1356), without making the old and legally and socially accepted distinctions as to whether such men were subjects of the crown, other liege lords, or the Church. Also, a tax was offered to those who wished to substitute cash payment to the crown for personal military service. This allowed the crown to hire more professional soldiers, mainly infantry, and the wealthy to avoid risks in battle. During the first half of the *Hundred Years' War* (1337–1453) France developed a recruitment scheme known as "lettres de retenue" that paralleled English "indentures for war." This allowed French kings to engage military contractors for set sums in exchange for provision of agreed numbers and types of troops. Overseeing the national muster were two Maréchals of France, assisted by eight lieutenants, who were charged with ensuring that the terms of contracts were met, appointment of captains, inspection of arms and equipment, and payment of the king's coin to the contracted soldiery. In France to a greater extent and later date than in England, feudal recruitment under the *servitium debitum* was still enforced. For instance, in garrisoning frontier posts or when serving as auxiliaries town militia were paid only from the forty-first day of enlistment, affirming the traditional obligation to provide 40 days of free military service to the crown.

A national French army emerged from the great trials of the Hundred Years' War as one of the most powerful in Europe. For most of the war the French defended fortified positions well, but suffered bloody and humbling battlefield defeats. In the field, the French Army remained a medieval force overly dependent on heavy cavalry. For this it paid a huge price in blood at *Crécy* (1346), *Poitiers* (1356), and remarkably, as late as *Agincourt* (1415). From 1444 to 1448, Charles VII brought roving mercenary bands under control by organizing *"compagnies de l'ordonnance du roi"* (1439). These gave the best soldiers royal pay, and swore all officers to personal service to the crown. Charles paid for these troops with the "taille," a central tax that became the basis of royal military control over what became under his successors one of the great armies of Europe. What was most remarkable was that the French added a corps of permanent infantry ("camp du roi") in form of the *franc-archers* to the previously established permanent *heavy cavalry* and artillery corps. By 1500 the royal army totaled about 25,000 men. French reforms were paralleled in Burgundy under *Charles the Rash*, who organized his army around *lances* with accompanying reforms in drill, officering and equipment. However, Charles rolled the "iron dice of war" far too often, and eventually lost everything—including his army—on the field of battle against the French and Swiss.

The French army that invaded Italy to begin the *Italian Wars* (1494–1559) has been appropriately described as the first modern army, since it sought to use advanced artillery, cavalry, and infantry in a "combined arms" manner and had specialized units of engineers and other troops in its companies and lances. In peacetime the king maintained 64–70 companies in 2,500 lances, or just over 7,000 men. In 1558, *Henri II* inspected the army in Picardy, where it mustered 11,000 cavalry and 29,000 infantry, a vast force for the day. However, over 70 percent were foreign mercenaries. This exposed the great military weakness of France, as of all early modern states: its system of *war finance*. On the eve of the *French Civil Wars* (1562–1629) the core of the Royalist army was still the "gendarmerie," comprised of noble heavy cavalry. These troops were scattered across France, though with the greater concentration in the northeast. The wide geographical dispersal of more than 90 companies of gendarmerie, each comprised of 200 gendarmes, militated against effective mobilization, while the preeminence of cavalry and lack of native infantry made Royalist armies ineffective against Huguenot fortified towns. The crown thus continued to import specialist mercenaries (up to one-third of the army). During the Civil Wars the national component of armies on both sides grew, to over 60 percent for the Royalists in 1562, due to the fiscal strains involved as the ability of either side to raise mercenaries was reduced as fighting dragged on. Nevertheless, many *Landsknechte* and Swiss saw service in France.

The *Thirty Years' War* (1618–1648) stretched the French Army to maximum limits, progressively shrinking it over 10 years through death, disease, desertion, and a fundamental failure of foraging and logistics. Recent research suggests that a maximum of 125,000 men served in French armies in 1639 (including garrison troops) but just 80,000 in 1643, with average annual attrition rates from all causes about 30 percent. One estimate of French military casualties from 1635 to 1659 claims one-half million, not including deserters. Most other historians are sharply critical of that figure as highly exaggerated. See also *arquebusiers à cheval*; *chevaux-légers*; *Francis I*; *Freiburg, Battle of*; *Henri III, of France*; *Henri IV, of France*; *Louis XI*; *Louis XIII*; *pioneers*; *Richelieu, Cardinal Armand Jean du Plessis de*; *Rocroi, Battle of.*

Suggested Reading: James Wood, *The Army of the King* (1996).

French Civil Wars (1562–1629). "French Wars of Religion." Older histories dealing with the French Civil Wars pointed to core material interests as their primary cause, depicting professions of faith by participants (especially nobles) as mostly cynical cover for more mundane concerns. It is clear that underlying this protracted conflict were complex class, economic, and regional fissures within French society, not least between restlessly expanding urban classes and older and more conservative powers in the countryside. Also clearly, the coals of civil conflict were fanned by general discontent among the old "nobility of the sword" and competitive ambitions of specific noble families, especially the *Valois* and *Bourbon, Guise,* and *Châtillon*. All that was intensified by serial succession crises and the always strained politics of long regencies. A drawn-out contest for royal power aggravated the much deeper confessional divide due to the uniquely intimate relationship of Church and crown in France, which was reflected in the oath proclaimed during the coronation ceremony (*sacre*) and venerable royal title (*Rex christianissimus*). Notwithstanding material causes, recent scholarship has persuasively demonstrated that the central issue in the civil wars was, as contemporaries said it was, confessional antagonism. The French "wars of religion" engaged distinct communities of faith, each of which saw the other body of believers (rather than body of doctrines) as a vile pollutant within the national body politic, so that each set out to purge the other by inquisition, burnings, persecution, and force of arms. This clash between opposing "godly cultures" was not resolvable by secular compromise: Catholics saw Huguenots as irredeemable heretics and rebels, while Protestants viewed Catholics as priest-ridden, corrupt, and superstitious idolators beyond hope of spiritual recovery. Each side

> *This clash between opposing "godly cultures" was not resolvable by secular compromise . . .*

believed with matching fervor that the poison of heresy, or of rank superstition, had to be bled from the community of faithful if civic and religious peace were to be restored. Mack Holt summarized the problem thus: "There was a religious foundation to 16th century French society that was shared by elites and popular classes alike, and it was the contestation of this essential religious fabric of both the body social and the body politic that led to the French civil wars taking the shape they did."

The key facts in prolonging the fighting, once it began, were: decentralization of the Royalist army; political impotence of the French monarchy due to serial regencies and ducal and *Catholic League* interference; the inability of 16th-century battle to produce decisive outcomes even though many noble officers were killed (twinned facts which led to smaller fights as the "wars of religion" progressed); the defensive strength of Huguenot-fortified towns capable of withstanding the cavalry-heavy "gendarmerie" that comprised the core of Royalist armies; the sheer size of France, which made decisive defeat and occupation costly and difficult given the scale of forces involved; direct and indirect intervention by external powers that kept the embers of civil and religious strife stoked with new fuel over several decades; and a perennial lack of funds available to the crown, a frailty worsened by a royal debt of 60 million livres held over from the *Italian Wars* with Spain that ended in 1559. Weakness at the center, especially chronic royal debt, led to repetition of the military dilemma experienced by Spain in the Netherlands: final victory was forestalled because royal companies mutinied or deserted in large numbers on numerous occasions, for want of supplies and pay. Moreover, after each "peace" and before the onset of renewed civil war, debt and ongoing military expense compelled the monarchy to demobilize the army, only to have to remobilize it a few months or a few years later. In contrast, the Huguenots were able to stay in the fight despite their smaller resource base because, after 1572, they mostly stayed inside their fortified towns and thus were better able to concentrate available forces to defend selected sites along a limited frontier. And they drew recruits from a highly motivated population, right out of the pews of their churches and from special militia formed all over France before the civil wars began to guard open-air Protestant services from Catholic interference. Pastors and churches were also used to mobilize revenue collection from the faithful, which ensured regular pay for troops foreign or domestic. More often than not, Huguenot generals were also superior strategists and tacticians to their Catholic counterparts.

First Civil War

In 1559 the *Treaties of Cateau-Cambrésis* finally ended the Italian Wars between Valois and Habsburg. That same year, *Henri II* was killed in a jousting accident. Real power now passed to two brothers, the duc and the Cardinal of Lorraine, masters of the House of Guise and uncles to a suggestible 15-year old heir, *Francis II*. The young king was also tied to the Guise as husband of *Mary Stuart*, daughter of Mary of Guise and herself niece to the duc and the cardinal. The known extreme intolerance of the Guise, along with their sudden rise to power at Court, immediately raised confessional tensions. The Huguenots then appeared to confirm the worst fears of Catholics by mounting the ill-advised *conspiracy of Amboise*. When Francis II died suddenly, his mother, *Catherine de Medici*, seized the moment and power at Court by proclaiming herself regent for another minor son, Charles IX. Dismissing the Guise, she moved to end persecution of the Huguenots and restore internal peace by uniting all Frenchmen within the *Gallican Church*. She also released religious prisoners and ended heresy trials and executions. This effort failed, however, as her toleration agitated more radical Catholics who feared that she would concede overmuch to Protestants, even as French Calvinists moved into the open and embarked on campaigns of violent *iconoclasm*, breaking into Catholic churches to smash statues, crucifixes, and altars. Catholics were whipped into hysterical frenzy and counter-violence by accusations and agitations that Huguenot conventicles were really daemonic orgies. Massacres of Protestants ensued in several towns. Catherine's overarching royalism and dynastic interest were thus undermined by her pose of tolerance, which left her holding a weakened center that was unsupported by either side in the brewing confessional confrontation. In this climate, in 1561 the Guise joined *Anne de Montmorency* in an armed Catholic alliance ("Triumvirate") that also sought outside aid from *Philip II* of Spain for a campaign to "extirpate all those of the new religion," including the hated Bourbons. Meanwhile, the Queen Mother called the "Colloquy of Poissy" which wrung fiscal concessions from the clergy but failed to provide a national alternative to the hard terms of the *Council of Trent* for which she had hoped. In January 1562, she tried once more to grant limited legal toleration of the Huguenots in the *Edict of Saint-Germain*. Again, the intemperate Guise but also nearly all Catholics rejected her initiatives.

In July 1562, some 2,000 Protestants were expelled from Dijon, not least because of rank superstition that their heresy had caused withering of the rich vineyards of the region. The first major act of violence came at *Vassy* (March 1, 1562), where the duc de Guise had his men fire on and hack to death dozens of Protestant worshipers. The massacre pushed Protestants into armed defense, while thrilling most Catholics with its cleansing ruthlessness. The confessions were now fully politicized, with local noble interests displacing clerics in the leadership on either side and the ancient rivalry of Bourbon and Valois newly linked to Protestant or Catholic martial fortune, respectively. The Guise marshaled a Catholic army at Paris, which remained a center of radical Catholicism throughout the civil wars. *Condé* quickly raised a small Protestant army and took Orléans (April 2), then called upon the militia of the colloquies of the Midi to assemble. This raised his numbers to 2,000 horse, the core of which was four former *compagnies de l'ordonnance*. He also had 6,000 foot. Money and mercenaries poured in from Germany, some at Jean Calvin's behest: 3,000 *Reiters* and 4,000 *Landsknechte* joined Condé, paid for with private resources, confiscated Catholic property, and royal taxes expropriated in the Midi and Huguenot towns. The Royalists took longer to assemble: the gendarme cavalry were scattered across the north, while bands of *aventuriers* had to be mustered and equipped and teamsters secured to cart the royal artillery train from Paris to the southern theater. A further 6,000 Swiss were hired to stiffen the Royalist infantry. Meanwhile, Condé carried out an urban strategy, taking major towns astride key inland waterways and roads in the Loire valley, then occupying Guyenne, Dauphiné, and Normandy. A dozen large cities went over to him within three months, some by siege or taken from within by Protestant fifth columns, but most by persuasion or from confessional conviction. The Mass was abolished in all captured towns while orgies of iconoclasm and desecration followed, with chalices and bells melted down to make Protestant coins and cannons. Catholic refugees streamed out of the fallen towns, further widening the confessional chasm dividing the French.

After meeting with Condé and other Huguenot leaders, the Queen Mother moved reluctantly to put down what was now a large-scale revolt, threateningly led by a prince of the blood with a legitimate claim to her son's throne. Each side also looked for aid outside France, setting a pattern that would prolong and internationalize the French Civil Wars. Huguenots sought aid from Protestant German princes and imported German and Swiss mercenaries, and they looked to *Elizabeth I* and England for relief. Elizabeth sent some early aid in exchange for a right of occupation of Le Havre and Dieppe (Treaty of Hampton Court), which she planned to hold pending a permanent return of *Calais* to England. Despite Calvin's earlier meddling in French affairs, Geneva remained neutral; it even forbade Huguenot captains from raising troops there or buying arms or horses (though in the usual Swiss style, many arms sales were made anyway). French Catholics turned to the pope, who sent

2,500 men, and the Duke of Savoy. But mostly they looked to *Philip II* for men and money, and they hired religiously indifferent Reiters and Landsknechte.

The fighting that ensued was mainly over control of France's towns, with each side enjoying successes and both engaging in reprisal atrocities. Towns were sacked after surrendering; whole populations had their throats cut or were drowned en masse. Refugees were indiscriminately attacked outside several towns by peasants, animated by much older grievances than the new confessional divisions. From May 28 to October 26, Rouen was besieged by the main Catholic force of 30,000 men. A few hundred Scots and English mercenaries tried to reach the city but failed to bring much relief. In the end, the city was sacked for three days at a cost of 1,000 lives. As part of the Royal army disbanded for the winter, Condé moved on Paris. That forced Guise to force march to reach the city first. On December 10, Condé broke camp outside the capital and marched on Chartres. This move led to the only set-piece battle of the First Civil War (April 1562–March 1563), at *Dreux* on December 19. The Catholics won a close but short-lived victory: each army overran the other at one point in the fight; each thus captured the other side's top commander, Condé and Montmorency, respectively. The Huguenot army withdrew to Orléans. The duc de Guise was assassinated outside Orléans a few months later, while besieging the city. That left three of the top four Catholic generals dead or captured while Protestant towns rested secure. The Queen Mother arranged for Condé and Montmorency to be released once they agreed to the terms she set out in the *Edict of Amboise* (March 19, 1563).

This inconclusive outcome to the First Civil War set the mold for a protracted conflict. Neither side could defeat the other decisively on the battlefield, which forced a search for foreign allies to tip the military balance. Meanwhile, a weak monarchy wished to put down rebellion without succumbing to a total Catholic victory, but could not enforce periodic pauses in the fighting that it arranged. Each lull thus masqueraded as a peace settlement but was in fact a mere truce that allowed all to rearm, rebuild defenses, and ready for the next round of fighting. Not even a joint expedition to expel the hated English from La Havre, a feat accomplished on July 30, 1563, could bridge the deeper national divide.

Second Civil War

The Edict of Amboise proved unenforceable: the Parlement of Paris and several provincial parlements refused to register it, many towns would not enforce it, and murders and atrocities were carried out by both sides. All that compelled Catherine to take extraordinary constitutional measures and embark on a two-year royal tour with her son, Charles IX, to enforce the edict. This helped keep the peace for a few years, but despite her efforts the letter and spirit of the Edict of Amboise were ignored. The growing power of *Charles Guise, Cardinal de Lorraine*, and the radical Catholic faction within France frightened Protestants and drove them back into arms. Their fear was matched by Catholic anger over iconoclastic riots and desecration of Catholic places of worship by radical Dutch Calvinists, spiritual and political allies of the Huguenots. Hard winters and grain shortages aggravated urban unrest. When *Alba* marched up the *Spanish Road* in 1567 with a Catholic-Habsburg army intent on exterminating Calvinism in the Netherlands, unfounded—but reasonable—Huguenot fears of a Spanish–Guise alliance and invasion of France provoked a second Protestant plot to kidnap a Catholic king. Charles IX unwittingly contributed to Protestant fears by contracting 6,000 Swiss guards to protect his person and palaces, also against the chance that Alba might invade France in alliance with the Guise. The Second Civil War (September 1567–March 1568) broke out when a Huguenot army, striking preemptively, failed to capture Charles but went on to seize numerous fortified towns. Coligny and Condé—reinforced by Landsknechte companies—pursued the king to Paris, where he took refuge and which they besieged. The only significant battle took place at *Saint-Denis* (November 10, 1567), where Montmorency beat Condé and Coligny, but later succumbed to his wounds. His death deprived the Queen Mother of any major field commander not loyal to the Guise, leading to a period of unsuccessful collective command

This helped keep the peace for a few years, but despite her efforts the letter and spirit of the Edict of Amboise were ignored.

of Royalist forces. Meanwhile, the defeated Protestants only withdrew to Lorraine in hopes of joining with mercenary reinforcements from Germany. The Royalists pursued with the largest army fielded during the civil wars: 38,000 men with another 12,000 camp followers, swelling to over 60,000 within a few weeks. The Protestants linked with the Germans on January 11, 1568. Despite their much superior numbers, the Royalists balked at another bloody battle that might kill hundreds of nobles. Instead of attacking, they ravished the land. The more nimble Huguenot army marched on to Orléans, then besieged Chartres. Both sides soon ran out of funds: the Germans in the Protestant army went home, as did the Swiss on the Royalist side. The Second Civil War thus ended in stalemate like the first, producing another false peace in the *Edict of Longjumeau* (March 1568).

Third Civil War

The Third Civil War (September 1568–August 1670) started six months later, arising from a conspiracy headed by the Cardinal de Lorraine and Philip II to overturn the terms of Longjumeau. The plan was to capture key Huguenot towns while also murdering Coligny and Condé. But the generals escaped on August 23, 1568. They galloped for La Rochelle in an epic flight that gathered Huguenots to their banner as they rode, until they arrived at the head of an army of thousands. Tens of thousands more Protestants mobilized in the weeks that followed. International events also impinged, as news arrived that Alba's "Council of Blood" had executed hundreds of Calvinist nobles in the Netherlands, including Coligny's cousin. This pushed the Dutch rebels against Spain into alliance with France's Huguenots, a key factor in the wars and politics of both countries over the next 16 years. In addition, England moved more clearly into the Protestant camp, as did Scotland following

Mary Stuart's flight into English exile in May 1568. There was extensive fighting from 1568 to 1570, in which the Huguenots were joined by the usual German mercenaries, but also by Dutch "Beggars" led by *William of Orange* and *Louis of Nassau*. Even so, the Protestants fared badly at first. At *Jarnac* (March 13, 1569) a Catholic army nominally led by the future Henri III defeated the Huguenots. Condé was one of many Protestants murdered as they lay wounded on the field. That left Coligny the preeminent Protestant general. He led the army back to Cognac, where it resisted a Royalist siege. Meanwhile, an army of Dutch Protestants briefly crossed into northern France. Unpaid and unruly, its men soon forced it home. An army of German mercenaries, hired with a loan secured by the crown jewels of Navarre, crossed into France from the east and joined the main Huguenot force. Emboldened, Coligny broke camp and crushed a small Royalist army at La Roche-l'Abeille. Blood revenge for Jarnac was taken when Coligny ordered Catholic prisoners, along with hundreds of peasants, slaughtered. Coligny briefly besieged Poitiers before moving to engage another Royalist army at *Moncontour* (October 3, 1569), where he suffered a stiff defeat.

The remnant of the Huguenot army retreated from Moncontour to Languedoc, where it was reinforced by local troops and soon regained a strength of about 12,000 men. Coligny, believing like Robert E. Lee that he had to invade to bring the war home to his larger northern enemy, marched the Huguenot army into Burgundy in the spring. Accompanied by *Henri de Navarre*, he threatened Paris. Coligny easily defeated a hastily raised Catholic army at Arnay-le-Duc (June 26, 1570), near Dijon, then resumed his march on Paris. However, he lacked the strength or siege guns to take the city. All this maneuvering gave the Third Civil War a different character from the first two: rather than a contest of sieges and relief battles, more men were mobilized and fought actively over a much wider area, killing more civilians and destroying more of the countryside in the process. This brought peasants into the fight in larger numbers, as murder and massacre flowed from religious zeal, pent up rural grievances, or simple opportunity. The *Edict of St. Germain-en-Laye* ended the Third Civil War by confirming the military facts on the ground with a generous settlement of Protestant grievances: the Huguenots won conditional religious freedom commensurate with their battlefield success. Thereafter the question was: Could the terms of St. Germain be enforced on a resistant Catholic majority dedicated to purging heretic-rebels from the New Jerusalem called France?

Fourth Civil War

The rising magma of pietism and bloody-minded zeal of the French masses in the early 1570s confirmed the fundamentally religious nature of the conflict, while also distinguishing the Fourth Civil War (August 1572–July 1573) with an eruption of popular violence unknown to the earlier clashes of confessional armies. Popular and spontaneous religious violence became commonplace, provoked by mocking words or a procession by one side that was seen as sacrilegious by the other. Catholic confraternities carried out violent purges of Protestants. Meanwhile, Huguenot pamphleteers proclaimed new theories of popular sovereignty and a right of rebellion against tyrants. This was important, as Huguenot rejection of the sacral traditions of the French monarchy were seen by even moderate Catholics as undermining the bedrock of social order and peace. The Queen Mother tried to settle the issue at the highest level by marrying Charles IX to a Habsburg princess, daughter of Philip II, and his sister to a Habsburg prince. She also sought a grand reconciliation of Valois and Bourbon via the marriage of her daughter, Margaret de Valois, sister to Charles IX, to Henri de Navarre. Instead, this intrigue at the top brought to a boil popular animosities. Adding fuel to the confessional fires, the *Sea Beggars* took Brill and William of Orange and Louis of Nassau, cousins of the French king, declared war on Spain. In support, excited Huguenots mustered to join the Dutch Calvinist army and others seized Mons and Valenciennes. Coligny urged an alliance with Orange and raised an army of 14,000 men while a second Huguenot army moved to relieve Mons, which was under Spanish siege. It is still disputed among historians whether this moved the Queen Mother to plot against his life. In any case, a failed attempt to assassinate Coligny during the royal wedding celebrations in Paris—most likely by the Guise for reasons of family vendetta—set off the *St. Bartholomew's Day Massacres* in the early hours of August 24, 1572. The capital, where hatred for the Huguenots had built for years, exploded into three days of communal, even ritual, violence. More butchery of Huguenots in provincial towns took place over the following six weeks. Whether planned or spontaneous, the massacres were highly effective: they immediately and severely crippled the Huguenot movement by eliminating much of its noble leadership and reducing its military power and territorial grip. Longer-term, the slaughter undercut via terror the attractiveness of Protestantism to prospective converts and led many more to undertake prudential reconversion to Catholicism. The massacres thus marked the beginning of the end of the Huguenots in France and the key turning point in the French Civil Wars.

The weakness of the monarchy permitted Huguenot armies and fortified "surety towns" (*place de sûreté*) to survive for several decades more, but merely as heretical enclaves not as an alternative godly community. Huguenots also became more clearly political rebels and enemies of the crown, in their own eyes and the king's. To this point the Huguenots had, in Jean Delumeau's felicitous phrase, retained an "underlying conservative royalism." Now, as the Fourth Civil War got underway, Protestant towns for the first time openly rejected the authority of the king, spurned his governors, refused to pay his taxes, and acted in relations with foreign Protestant powers as if they were themselves sovereign. In strictly military terms, after the massacres fewer battles were fought as most Huguenots took refuge in fortified towns in the Midi. Also, as fighting shifted south of the Loire, Royalist capabilities were strained by the great distance from recruiting bases across the north and the royal artillery depot in Paris. The main military event of the Fourth Civil War was the siege of La Rochelle from February to June 1573. Carried out by over 25,000 men, it was the single largest military effort of all the French Civil

Wars. It began after much delay caused by the usual ineptitude of Royalists commanders and the hard realities of 16th-century logistics. With an ill-led and expensive army that Charles could not afford floundering outside La Rochelle's walls, he called off the siege. He had lost 20,000 men to death, disease, and desertion, to no great end. Still, the Peace of La Rochelle (July 2, 1573) reflected deeper post-massacre realities: Huguenot freedom to worship was restricted to noble homes and just three towns—La Rochelle, Montauban, and Nîmes. Everywhere else the reformed religion was outlawed. This ban was ignored in practice wherever Protestants were dominant, a continuing defiance that undermined the young king's authority with his Catholic subjects. In addition, the disaster at La Rochelle prolonged the civil wars by stripping the Royalists of irreplaceable officers and leaving the monarchy once more on the edge of bankruptcy. It also demonstrated the defensive power of large Huguenot towns and the inability of the crown to overcome them. All that set the table for 15 more years of siege warfare, feckless maneuvers, and small battles. Charles was spared further military and political humiliations by his death, at age 24, on May 30, 1574.

Fifth Civil War

Charles' younger brother, Henri Valois, duc d'Anjou, had been elected King of Poland a few months earlier. Upon receiving the news of his brother's death Henri abdicated his Polish title (after just 118 days in Cracow) to mount the French throne as *Henri III*. He returned, very slowly through Italy, to a nation deeply cloven by intense confessional hatreds, threatened by foreign powers, and girding for another round of civil war. As for the Huguenots, after the catastrophe of the massacres they were nearly leaderless on the national stage for several years: Coligny was dead and Henri de Navarre a captive, while Henri and the young *Condé* (Henri I, de Bourbon) had been forced to publicly abjure Calvinism. Local leaders of Huguenot fortress towns therefore filled the leadership vacuum with an urban league, a radical republican alliance that rejected the royal system and elected the young Condé commander of the Protestant army. The Huguenots had moved emphatically and self-consciously toward a new political status and claim: they were now avowedly a state-within-a-state, separate and distinct from old, Catholic France. It was a fundamental challenge that Catholics and the monarchy were fiercely determined to meet and crush. The rebellion posed an even greater threat when Henri III proved unable to keep his greatest enemies prisoners at Court. In September 1575, his brother François, the new *duc d'Anjou*, escaped and fled south to join the rebels. Five months later Henri de Navarre escaped and also joined the rebellion. Meanwhile, Condé signed an alliance with Frederick III of the Palatinate that brought 20,000 German mercenaries into France. Henri III, in contrast, was broke and could not raise a countervailing Catholic army. As a result, during the usual maneuvering of opposing forces only small skirmishes between small armies took place in the near-bloodless Fifth Civil War (November 1574–May 1576). Little serious fighting occurred beyond raids and ambushes and a handful of sieges. Even these were restricted as hungry, unpaid troops deserted Henri's armies by the thousands, scourging the peasants as they fanned over the countryside. In September 1575, some 1,000 noble *Malcontents* rallied against the war in Paris. In October, 20,000 Reiters invaded the Champagne district from Germany. Humiliated and desperate, the king disguised another truce as peace. He sent the Queen Mother in secret to appease the Malcontents and bought off the Germans with all that was left in his treasury, and more. Then he issued the *Edict of Beaulieu* ("Peace of Monsieur") on May 6, 1576, granting nearly all demands made by French Protestants since the onset of the religious wars. Lastly, he brought his renegade brother François back into the Valois fold.

Sixth Civil War

Beaulieu was the apex of paper political advances made by the Protestant movement and the nadir of Catholic legal concessions forced by military weakness. Yet, the underlying fact remained that the massacres of Huguenots four years prior had so severely weakened them that such gains could not be held. Catholic opinion refused to sanction the terms. The Parlement of Paris, the Guise, and militant clergy led ferocious opposition to the edict and now also to the king. Membership in confraternities and Catholic "defense leagues" surged. More moderate Catholics, the so-called *politiques* who favored at least a temporary peace, were shouted down by demands that the king make war on all rebel-heretics, even as the deputies of the Third Estate meeting at Blois refused to vote him the taxes needed to prosecute a successful campaign: bourgeois mouths yelled for war but bourgeois purses stayed clamped shut. This ensured that the Sixth Civil War (December 1576–September 1577) was short and indecisive. An ill-equipped and badly led Royalist army gathered in March, then moved south. It took and sacked two fortified towns after brief sieges, La Charité on April 25, 1577, and Issoire on June 12, 1577. Both were attacked in violation of their security grant to the Huguenots in the Edict of Beaulieu, with Issoire razed to the ground on the personal order of the king. Henri de Navarre—recognized by this time as the Huguenot leader—along with Condé kept a Protestant army in the field. With aid from Elizabeth I they took Brouage on the coast. Once more, royal impecunity forced Henri III to end a war he could not afford in search of a peace he could not sustain. The Peace of Bergerac (September 17, 1577) outlawed all confessional leagues while whittling down toleration of Protestant freedoms to one town in each gouvernement (administrative district). The princes had again agreed on peace despite the fact most Catholics still opposed even limited concessions, while most Huguenots no longer trusted a king who signed serial pacification edicts only to break their terms when the spring rains stopped and the next campaign season arrived. France continued to dwell in a purgatory of confessional conflict half-way between peace and war. In the Midi, local warlordism and regional anarchy were the order of the day. The king was no longer master in Paris, the Catholic League controlled most of the north, and bored courtiers and mignons engaged in stupid duels involving hundreds of restless nobles playing at war.

Seventh Civil War

From 1575 to 1580 further suffering flowed from peasant revolts in Province, Dauphiné, and Vivarais. These were occasioned by the economic dislocations and privation caused by the civil wars, but had nothing to do with the confessional divide in France. Thus, peasants in Provence formed cross-confessional armed bands (*Razats*) that murdered hundreds of nobles and raised the usual grievances of the "Jacques." The response of the Catholic nobility and urban bourgeoisie was to demand the same harsh treatment of the peasants—using comparable methods and displaying similar fervor and savagery—that they demanded against Protestants. No one was permitted to disrupt the sacral social order. Even as the peasant revolts wound down or ended in bloody massacres, the Seventh Civil War (May 1580–November 1580) broke out, provoked by the personal ambitions for office of the young Condé. The shortest and least important of the French wars of religion, the seventh saw fighting that lasted only a few months during the campaign season of 1580. This time it was the Protestants who broke the peace, when Henri de Navarre besieged and took the Catholic stronghold of Cahors, ostensibly in payment of the dowry owed him by virtue of his marriage to Margaret of Valois. Otherwise, neither side had the strength nor money to defeat the other, so that most soldiers remained in barracks or were dismissed from the ranks. This near-farcical conflict was ended by the Peace of Fleix (November 26, 1580), which simply reiterated the terms set at Bergerac.

Eighth Civil War

Such political and military indecision did not guarantee peace so much as set the table for the Eighth Civil War (1585–1589), the most destructive of them all. The spark was the death of the duc d'Anjou. With the monarchy seen to be weakened, the *dévots* increasingly supported the Catholic League, which the Guise formally allied with Philip II in the *Treaty of Joinville* (December 1584). Eight months later the League forced the radically intolerant *Treaty of Nemours* on Henri III, effectively banning Protestantism and stripping Huguenots of legal and military protections. Confused fighting, attempted town coups, and general disruption coursed over the south and the Atlantic coast of France. In January 1585, Pope Sixtus V excommunicated Henri de Navarre and Condé to remove them from the line of succession. Even Catholics were shocked at this foreign intervention in the Gallican Church, but the king was too weak to retaliate. All these events provoked the so-called "War of the Three Henries" (1587–1589). The young *Henri Guise*, the new duc de Lorraine, took the lead military role on the Catholic side, taking control of much of the north out of the hands of the king, Henri III. Supported by Spanish gold, Guise and the League prepared to meet the third Henri, Henri de Navarre, and the Huguenot army. In mid-1587 the Huguenots were reinforced by Palatine

All these events provoked the so-called "War of the Three Henries" (1587–1589).

mercenaries bought with 50,000 English gold crowns sent by Elizabeth I, herself girding for war with Spain (see *Invincible Armada*) and in great need of distraction of potential Catholic enemies in France. Henri de Navarre failed to link with German Reiters hurrying to France under John Casimir, regent of the Palatinate. These mercenaries were instead defeated in two sharp engagements with Guise's army. Surviving Germans were simply bought off by the king and went home. Meanwhile, Navarre aligned with two Catholic Bourbon princes and moved into Maine and Normandy before falling back to winter in Guyenne. He won handily against a small Royalist army at *Coutras* (October 20, 1587).

In the wake of the *Day of the Barricades* (May 12, 1588), a coup d'état in Paris carried out by *The Sixteen* (a radical bourgeois council), and Henri III's murder of Guise in December, the League moved to make war on the king. Most fighting shifted north of the Loire once a truce and alliance was agreed between Henri de Navarre and Henri III, signed on April 3, 1589. A joint campaign to retake Paris from the League followed in the summer, but was interrupted by assassination of the king on August 1, 1589. After that, Royalist troops refused to serve Navarre, reducing his force within days from 40,000 to just 18,000. Henry turned to mercenaries instead, selling off his patrimonial lands in Béarn and Navarre to pay them. Huguenots looked to his coming coronation as their salvation, but despite the *Salic Law* that made Henri the rightful heir, the Catholic League rejected the idea that a heretic and excommunicate could ascend the sacral throne of France. League cells seized control of the cities across the north, bringing to them a fresh League terror and ensuring that the civil war would continue.

Finally, significant battles were fought. On September 21, 1589, the League lost 10,000 men to Henri at *Arques*, despite outnumbering his army 4:1. Reinforced by 5,200 Scots and English, making his army 18,000 strong, Henri marched on Paris and attacked into its suburbs on November 1. Lacking siege guns he could not breach the city's inner walls, and lacking money to pay his troops neither could he starve Paris into submission. He met Mayenne in battle and crushed him, and the last large-scale Leaguer military opposition, at *Ivry-la-Bataille*. The League still backed his uncle, a Bourbon Catholic cardinal (whom they called Charles X) for Henri's throne, but he died in 1590 while in Henri's custody. That gutted the League's confessional hopes and its political program. Meanwhile, supported by 5,000 English troops, Henri leisurely besieged Paris (April 7–August 30, 1590). The city held out, but 13,000 starved to death. Only the intervention of the Duke of Parma with an army of 20,000 Spanish foot and 7,000 horse from the Netherlands saved the French capital from its king. Even after the siege, inside Paris fear and terror governed as The Sixteen purged and murdered "politiques" and "traitors." Mayenne occupied the city (November 28, 1591) and executed several of The Sixteen in their turn.

Pope Gregory XIV now interfered in French affairs, excommunicating Henri IV for a second time in March 1591. A Spanish force landed in Brittany that same month, a fact that frightened Elizabeth I into sending Henri still more men, money, and warships. Her clear interest was to prevent a Leaguer victory that could mean a Franco–Spanish alliance against England. From November 1591 to April 1592, Henri conducted the *Siege of Rouen*. He was forced away only when Parma intervened again from the Netherlands. Papal usurpation of Gallican privileges and Spanish troops on French soil rallied the country's tired nobles for one last hurrah. Henri gathered 24,000 men and moved to trap and destroy Parma. But the irascible old Spaniard crossed the Seine and burned his barges behind him, leaving Henri stranded on the far bank but satisfied to see a foreign army depart in haste. Only a small Spanish garrison in Paris remained and some scattered League resistance in Brittany, Provence, and Dauphiné. In any case, foreign intervention had come too late. By 1592 most Royalist Catholics accepted Henri as their legitimate king. Without an alternate French candidate after the death of Charles X, some Leaguers looked to foreign Catholic princes to displace Henri, but the majority of French balked at renunciation of the traditions and rights of the Gallican Church and the primacy of the Salic Law even over Catholicity. A majority of Catholic delegates in the Estates General reaffirmed this position on June 28, 1593. A month later, on July 25, Henri formally abjured Calvinism and submitted to formal instruction in Catholicism. With a single brilliant stroke he removed the last obstacle to his acceptance by most Catholics. With the country exhausted by war and the majority on both sides reconciled to the monarchy, over the next two years League bitter-enders were run down or driven into exile. On February 27, 1594, Henri was crowned at Chartres (Leaguers still held Reims). Paris submitted on March 22. Its Spanish garrison was given safe passage out of the city and left with arms shouldered and colors intact. Most, though not all, League towns submitted in due course as Henri shrewdly and amply rewarded those which surrendered without violence: he spent over 30 million livres forgiving taxes or bribing nobles and councils to accept him.

During 1594, *Tard-Avisés* peasant revolts broke out in Agenais, Burgundy, Limousin, and Périgord, in part in reaction against economic deprivations of protracted civil war in whose largely urban quarrels and arcane doctrinal disputes peasants in France's 30,000 villages never had much stake or interest. Henri wisely appeased the peasants, as he had Spanish troops and Leaguer garrisons. The next year he declared war on Spain (January 17, 1595), upon discovery of another plot by Philip II to invade France, and to undermine Mayenne and the League bitter-enders by exposing their alliance with a foreign power. That brought about the *Franco-Spanish War* of 1595–1598. Meanwhile, Huguenots became uneasy as Henri became evermore overtly Catholic in his royal persona and public displays of religiosity. Mayenne ritually submitted before his king in 1595, with Henri paying the duc's war debts and restoring him to a provincial governorship. All other great nobles submitted soon thereafter, except the duc de Mercoeur. He did not submit until Henri invaded Brittany in early 1598, gave him a bribe of four million livres, and married Mercoeur's daughter to his own illegitimate son. The Treaty of Ponts de Cé formally ended the eighth war of religion. Henri settled the outstanding Huguenot issue, at least temporarily, with issuance of the *Edict of Nantes* (April 13, 1598). He then made peace with Spain at *Vervins*. Peace in France was born of weariness with protracted war, weaned on famine and massacres, reared on economic hardship and decline, and finally seduced into bed with the king by baubles and bribery. Still, it was peace, at last.

Ninth Civil War

France enjoyed peace under Henri IV for another 12 years, until his assassination by a mad Dominican monk unsettled the realm, plunged it into another divisive regency, and thus raised the specter of renewed civil war. The Huguenots prepared by holding an assembly at Saumur (1611) at which they appointed a young militant, Henri, duc de Rohan, as their commander. In 1614 there was a court revolt against the regency's marriage plans for young *Louis XIII*, with the rebels led in name by the new Prince de *Condé* (Henri II, de Bourbon). As Catholics divided between factions supporting Condé and the Regent, *Marie de Medici*, each side looked to the Huguenots for military aid should it come to a fight. In the midst of this crisis the clerical estate called for an end to the settlement of Nantes and suppression of all Huguenots. In April 1617, the revolt of the princes climaxed in Louis XIII seizing power from his mother and declaring an intention to ruin and reduce the Huguenots. The 16-year-old king issued an Edict of Restitution for Béarn in June, and launched his first military campaign to restore Catholic rights in Béarn and Navarre. His march south and assault on Béarn was bloodless, as the governor capitulated, restored Catholic churches, and allowed Catholics to worship. In November, Huguenots met in assembly in La Rochelle to plan a response. Louis declared the assembly illegal and all participants guilty of high treason. The Huguenots now revived their "republic" in the south, based on their eight place de sûreté, with Henri de Rohan as commander. Events were swirling out of control abroad, as well. In Bohemia the *Battle of the White Mountain* shook the Holy Roman Empire, and soon thereafter all of Europe. With France not yet drawn into the great war looming over Germany, Louis launched a campaign against the Huguenots in 1621 that led to two extended sieges, at La Rochelle and Montauban, along with a handful of skirmishes. Louis was forced to abandon the sieges when a quarter of his army fell ill with "camp disease," and his treasury ran out. Still, more Huguenot notables abjured as La Rochelle was isolated. A second campaign was conducted in 1622, with Louis under intense pressure from dévots and clergy at Court to crush the last Protestant resistance. After the Huguenots lost badly at *Poitou* (April 15, 1622), dozens of smaller fortified towns surrendered as soon as the king reached the outer walls, without a shot fired in anger. The next year a third southern campaign culminated in a great siege of Montpellier and devastating defeat for the Protestant cause. In the Peace of Montpellier (October 19, 1622) over 100 fortified Huguenot towns surrendered to Louis, who then announced that the military brevet of the Edict of Nantes would expire in 1625. Not all Huguenot walls came down as agreed, but the end was in sight.

There followed a slow reduction of the last Huguenot stronghold at La Rochelle. In 1625 much of the coast around La Rochelle and several key islands were captured by the Royalists, despite pledges of English military aid from *James I*, then *Charles I*. Louis allowed a respite in the internal war as he marshaled forces to fight Spain in northern Italy. Even so, in 1626 he landed a royal garrison on *Ile de Ré*. In 1627 the *War of the Mantuan Succession* broke out in Italy, draining money and men from the fight over La Rochelle. The Huguenots were nearly spent in any case. Louis and *Richelieu* began the final siege in August 1627. After 14 months of bombardment and the grinding effects of slow starvation, after a humiliating English failure to raise the siege, the Rochelais capitulated on October 28, 1628. The king and Richelieu led the army into the city, and the rest of the Midi surrendered in short order. The walls of Huguenot towns were demolished, a number under direct supervision by Richelieu. The victory in the civil wars was more Royalist than Catholic, though

> *This pragmatic settlement contrasted starkly with the arrogant, reactionary Catholicism . . .*

such distinctions were less than clear at the time. This fact was personified by Armand Richelieu, the "éminence rouge" who was cardinal and general all at once. The conclusion is also supported by extension of limited religious toleration to the surviving Huguenots in the *Edict of Alès* (1629), even as all their military rights and capabilities—which most threatened the monarchy—were demolished. This pragmatic settlement contrasted starkly with the arrogant, reactionary Catholicism of the *Edict of Restitution* proclaimed by *Ferdinand II* in Germany that same year. Nor were Huguenot commanders executed or exiled. They were instead pardoned and many entered royal service, just in time to partake in the "Great War" of the 17th century in Germany. See also *flagellants*.

Suggested Reading: Denis Crouzet, *Les guerriers de Dieu* (1990); H. Heller, *Iron and Blood* (1991); Mack Holt, *French Wars of Religion, 1562–1629* (1995); Robert Knecht, *The French Civil Wars* (2000); James Thompson, *Wars of Religion in France* (1958).

Frey. See *Fra*.

Friedrich I (c.1125–1190). "Barbarossa." See *Crusades*; *Knights Templar*; *Teutonic Knights, Order of*.

Friedrich V (1596–1632). Elector Palatine; King of Bohemia, 1619–1620. Son-in-law of *James I* and brother-in-law of *Charles I*; nephew of *Maurits of Nassau*; head of the *Protestant Union*. A pleasure-seeking mediocrity, he rashly accepted the Bohemian crown offered by rebels to any Protestant prince in Europe who would defend it, an offer made after the "*Defenestration of Prague*" (1618) and intended to deny Bohemia to *Ferdinand II*. Friedrich's decision ultimately cost him the Palatinate as well as Bohemia. More importantly, it helped bring on the *Thirty Years' War* (1618–1648). Where James I feared a general war and warned Friedrich not to accept, Maurits urged him on in the faux-Machiavellian hope of deflecting Spain's martial energy into the German war, since Maurits was planning to resume the Dutch war with Spain upon expiration of the *Twelve Years' Truce* in 1621. Friedrich hesitated until Maurits sweetened the offer with a large loan and 5,000 Dutch troops. Friedrich moved south and was elected "King of Bohemia" on August 16, 1619. He was glorified by a neo-Platonic Protestant cult, the "Brotherhood of the Rosy Cross" (Rosicrucians), who, appealing to his vanity, acclaimed him as the fulfilment of Biblical prophesy. The glory did not last long: his army and allies were crushed at the *White Mountain* (November 8, 1620) and Friedrich was driven from Bohemia, to be remembered derisively for his brief sojourn there as the "Winter King." He was also soon hounded from the Palatinate, as Habsburg armies brought the war up the Rhine. He was officially declared "outlaw" by the Empire in 1621. He took refuge in the Netherlands, temporarily in 1622 and permanently the next year. Until his death, his court-in-exile in The Hague was a center for Protestant dissenters from across Europe. In the *Peace of Prague* (1635) his heirs were banished from the Palatinate in perpetuity: their lands, rights, titles, and Palatine Electorship were ceded to Bavaria.

frigate (1). A small Mediterranean *galley* of the 16th century.

frigate (2). A fast 17th-century ship of fighting sail, with rows of cannon on a single deck numbering between 20 and 40 guns, with the most common type sporting 24 cannon. It was smaller and faster than a *man-of-war* but larger and better armed than a *sloop-of-war*. It proved ideal for *privateering*, *piracy*, and for long-distance patrols and *cruising*.

Frobisher, Martin (1539–1594). English *privateer* and Arctic explorer. Born in Yorkshire, he grew up in London under the tutelage of an uncle engaged in "discriminating piracy" in the English Channel. He accompanied *Francis Drake* on his 1585–1586 extended raid against Spanish holdings from Cape Verde to Cartagena, and fought as one of four English commanders in the *Invincible Armada* campaign of 1588. He died from wounds delivered by the Spanish during a raid on Brest.

front (1). In fortification, a section of *curtain wall* located between a pair of *bastions*.

front (2). In a line of battle, the first rank of soldiers. In this period, "front" had not yet acquired its modern meaning of a theater of war or long boundary between two or more engaged armies.

fryd. An early, Anglo-Saxon general mobilization of freemen. A "select fryd" was a more limited levy for small campaigns, normally calling up just one freeman in five. The Saxon kingdoms also used the fryd to construct and crew warships by laying a levy on the coastal population. Along with Anglo-Saxon knighthood, the fryd was defeated at Hastings (1066) at the onset of the *Norman* conquest of England. The select fryd survived under the Normans for several decades, as infantry support to Norman heavy cavalry. It was called on a few occasions to fight in Norman wars on the continent. The first English settlers in Virginia revived a version of the fryd in the early *Indian Wars*. See also *English armies*.

Fugger, House of. A Catholic merchant and banking house from Augsburg, Germany, which along with the Welsers and Hochstetters financed most *Habsburg* wars in the 16th–17th centuries. Johannes Fugger (1348–1409) was a master-weaver whose three sons married well and helped build the family business, which profited especially from investment in mining at the dawn of the gunpowder age. The Fuggers made a great deal of money from trade in raw copper and bronze guns manufactured at their family foundry in Fuggerau, near Willbach. The Fuggers dominated international finance in southern Europe by the 16th century, underwriting most wars of the popes, Holy Roman Emperors, and of Habsburg monarchs, notably *Charles V* and *Philip II*. In 1527, Charles V pledged revenues confiscated from all the Iberian *Military Orders* as collateral for Fugger loans. The Fuggers eventually controlled the finances of much of eastern Europe as well. And they made fortunes from the *spice trade* and the wider misfortunes of war which stoked international trade in copper, tin, saltpeter, and cannon. The Fuggers were fiercely opposed to the *Protestant Reformation*, not least because it threatened sales of indulgences and benefices, which were the effective collateral for loans to the popes and emperors. Fugger influence peaked under Charles V then waned along with the fortunes of his heirs in Austria and Spain. See also *Knights of Alcántara*.

Fujian ships. Large, two-masted Chinese *junks* capable of blue water voyages. They carried a crew of about 100. While they sported numerous *swivel guns*, *muskets*, *bows*, *fire lances*, and other anti-personnel weapons, their weak planking could neither support nor withstand large-caliber broadside artillery.

Fulbe (Fulani). Hausa: Fulani; French: Peul. The nomadic pastoralist Fulbe were pagans (Animist) allowed to move with their cattle among settled Muslim towns and empires of West Africa for several centuries after most of the region converted to Islam (c.11th century). By the 16th century they were concentrated around Futa Jalon and the Niger Valley west of Timbuktu, with some found in the *Hausa* lands and as far east as *Bornu*. For the most part they remained distinct from the peoples among whom they moved. Some Fulbe settled in the western towns of Futa Toro (Takrur) and Futa Jalon, and became known as Tukolor; they would found a new Muslim empire in the mid-19th century. Others settled as "town Fulbe" in lands farther east and south, reaching to Lake Chad. The majority remained nomadic. Town Fulbe converted to Islam while most of the nomads stayed Animist, though more were converted to Islam by *marabouts* in the 16th–17th centuries. This late conversion endowed the nomadic Fulbe with a religious fervor which had long since subsided among most urban West African Muslims. The wide dispersal of Fulbe permitted a vast network of contact which played a key role in diffusion of fevered political and religious ideas once these began to grip the Fulbe at the end of the 17th century.

Funj Sultanate. See *Sudan*.

Fürstenberg, Count. See *First Breitenfeld*.

Fürstenverschwörung. "Conspiracy of princes." See *Passau, Convention of*; *Schmalkaldic League*.

Fürth, Battle of (1632). See *Alte Feste, Siege of*.

fuses. See *shells*.

fusiliers de taille. Irregular French mounted soldiers who accompanied war tax collectors ("intendants").

fusta. An oared warship smaller than a *galliot* and much smaller than a war *galley*. It had just 15 banks of oars in bireme formation, and 60 crew at two men per oar. Fustas carried 40 infantry sharpshooters and boarders. See also *Lepanto, Battle of (October 7, 1571)*.

G

gabions. Wicker cylinders, usually four or five feet high, filled with earth and stones to make field fortifications for musketeers or artillery or to reinforce permanent walls. Wicker was easily portable and the shot-absorbing barrier it made had real strength. A major problem was getting overly proud mercenaries to do the spade work needed to fill the gabions. Until the reforms of *Gustavus Adolphus* made entrenchment an accepted part of a soldier's job most spade work in European armies was done by women and children camp followers.

gadlings. Iron spikes attached to the knuckles of a *gauntlet*.

gaff. See *spar*.

Gainsborough, Battle of (1643). See *English Civil Wars*.

"*galeones.*" The Spanish fleet that sailed yearly for Panama from Seville. See also *convoy*; *flota*.

galets. Cast iron cannonballs.

galleass. A hybrid warship with oars and sails and a high forward *castle*. See also *Constantinople, Siege of*; *Great Galley*; *Invincible Armada*; *Lepanto, Battle of (October 7, 1571)*.

galleon. From the late 15th century, but especially preeminent in the 16th century, a revolutionary new sailing ship of war appeared that made oceanic trade a reality and far-flung commerce raiding possible. It had a narrow waist ("fine lines"), two or more gun decks housing *ship-smasher* cannon, and batteries of *chase guns* fore and aft. The galleon essentially added the forepart of a *galley* to the afterpart and fighting castle of a *carrack*, with the additional strength of a *clinker-built* hull. This gave the galleon its trademark crescent shape. It was a fast, powerful warship quickly favored by *pirates* and *privateers*. Its preeminence flowed from several key advantages. First, it combined greater hull capacity and a small crew that consumed less food and water than a galley crew, allowing more goods to be carried farther than ever before. Next, its clinker-built hull was strong enough to mount broadside cannon for defense against pirates and enemy warships. This, too, displaced crew as cannon, not men, became the main fighting instrument in war at sea. Third, the galleon sported full rigging; that is, a combination of square sails for power and lateen sails to aid maneuvering. Along with the new sternpost rudder, this rig gave the galleon unmatched maneuverability. Finally, the long, narrow hull of race-built versions made the galleon sleeker and faster than any warship of comparable size. A galleon was not as powerful as the late-17th-century, full-fledged *man-of-war*, but it was bigger than a *sloop-of-war* and could serve as a *ship-of-the-line*. It excelled in long-range *cruising* and prize-taking and drove galleys and dhows from all but closed, shallow seas. *Francis Drake*'s ship, the "Golden Hind," was a typical race-built galleon. That reflected the fact that it was the English and Dutch who perfected and best exploited this ship type. See also *Arsenal of Venice*; *Gibraltar, Battle of (April 25, 1607)*; *Great Ships*; *Invincible Armada*.

galley. The galley, or oared warship, was an extraordinarily successful ancient ship design that lasted millennia rather than centuries. In one form or another oared warships dominated all coastal waters up to the 15th century, and into the early 17th century in the Mediterranean and other shallow or enclosed seas. Galleys were used far less in the rough waters of the North Atlantic. An important exception was the Viking *longship*. Most longships were used as coastal and riverine raiders but larger models were capable of ocean crossings. In the Middle Ages many areas had native oared ships to which the term "galley" was later, somewhat indiscriminately, applied. Most northern oared ships were descendants of the Viking longship, not copies or derivatives of Mediterranean-style galleys. English kings built dozens of oared warships in the 13th–14th centuries, but these were small *balingers* and *barges*, not true galleys. The Scots and Irish built a few large "Highland galleys" (longships), but far more *birlins* and *lymphad*s, some of which still operated in the western isles in the late 17th century. Other than Viking or Highland longships, war galleys in northern waters were confined to a *Great Galley* commissioned by *Henry V* (which was actually a *galleass*); armed Venetian and Florentine ships that made annual voyages north through the English Channel to the Dutch and Baltic ports; some Italian galleys hired by France for its wars with England; other French galleys built in the "Clos des Gallées" at Rouen, with Genoese assistance, active in the 14th century; and a handful of 15th-century Burgundian galleys. The French used coastal galleys into the 18th century but these were local transports or prison ships rowed by criminals sentenced to hard time at the oars, not warships. The Spanish deployed fleets of true war galleys in the Caribbean to protect their settlements and patrol among the islands. The Portuguese used galleys to service factories and forts along the coasts of East Africa, India, and in Southeast Asia. Malays substituted copies of Portuguese galleys for Chinese *junks* starting in the 16th century. All such galleys preferred calm waters and hugged the coastline. In those conditions they were unmatched as fighting ships and more reliable on patrol than ships of sail.

Most galleys were single, double ("bireme"), or triple ("trireme") oared. A few had four or five racks of oars but size and additional weight of ship and crew set sharp upper limits to galley size and speed. Three men to an oar was normal. Later hybrid oar-and-sail ships such as the *xebec* used as many as eight men per oar because they had a high freeboard requiring longer oars; this caused great energy loss for each oarsman. These were mongrel, dead-end ship designs representing a transition from the true galley to the true ship of sail.

The basic features of a war galley were these: they lay low in the water so that shorter oars could be used, saving crew energy; they were long and narrow to seat the maximum number of oarsmen and reduce drag; they had collapsible masts and lateen sails. Wind power was their primary mode, with human muscle saved for short bursts of battle speed or in becalmed waters. Galleys could be built quickly, as the Ottomans showed by replacing their massive losses at *Lepanto* (1571) in just a few years. By the same token, their hulls rotted easily if left in water and more rapidly if beached and exposed on a tidal flat. This meant building expensive dry docks to preserve a galley fleet. They were also fragile and prone to sink in storm-tossed seas: several entire Roman fleets were lost to storms during the Punic Wars with Carthage. Such frailty meant that safe havens had strategic importance. To make long-range expeditions one needed to control ports and islands along the way. This was hard to do, which helped set the outer limits to seaborne empires. In addition, galleys could not stay at sea for long periods for logistical reasons: they were heavy in crew but severely limited in storage space for food and water. They operated by hugging a coastline, stopping frequently to reload food and potable water. To defeat a galley fleet one thus had to capture and hold its multiple island or coastal bases, so that the deeper one proceeded into the enemy's seas the fewer ships and troops remained to penetrate farther. That was why Malta, Rhodes, Sicily, and Cyprus had strategic importance during the *Crusades*, continuing through the 14th–17th-century trade wars of Western powers with the Ottoman Empire.

A typical war galley had 24 banks of oars served by 144 oarsmen and carried 40 more soldiers, sailors, and officers. A galley with close to 200 crew, marines and officers, consumed about 90 gallons of water per day; food was less important. The oarsmen were sometimes slaves or convicts, but more often in the early modern period they were professional troops who would join boarding parties or fight as missile troops when their ship entered combat. In either case, limited storage space for food and water kept galleys to a maximum of 10–14 days voyaging before they had to put ashore to resupply. That was a sharp limitation which made them useless as ocean-crossing vessels (with the remarkable exception of Viking longships). From c.1500 new types of sailing warships armed with broadside cannon—*carracks*, *galleons*, and *frigates*—repeatedly defeated galleys, even when swarmed by vastly greater numbers. Portuguese, Dutch, French, and English "Fighting Sail," not galleys, explored the coasts of Africa and traded with India and in the Far East. During the first half of the 16th century they also blew the galley navies of Iran, India, and later the Malay kings, out of the water. Only in the Mediterranean and Caribbean did fleets of war galleys survive for another century.

Galley warfare in the ancient world had involved ramming, burning, or boarding. Burning was done with *Greek Fire* or other incendiaries. Since the sides of galley hulls had to accommodate tiers of oars but keep weight down, they were lightly timbered and vulnerable to ramming, a basic tactic in sea fights in the ancient world. But ramming all but disappeared by the early modern period, as did the ancients' use of fire at sea. The ram was abandoned for economic reasons: successor states to ancient Rome were too poor to sustain navies of specialized warships. And once the galley had to double as an armed transport the front half of the ship where the bulky base and bracings of a ram once sat was instead filled with cargo. The surviving spur on the Renaissance galley was a boarding bridge rather than a ram, and just before Lepanto even this was cut off Spanish galleys. The recipe for Greek Fire was lost upon the sack of Constantinople in 1453, and other incendiaries were too dangerous to use from a wooden warship. As a result, all Mediterranean navies abandoned rams and fire. Boarding became the sole method of attack for another reason: it offered opportunities for rich rewards. In this regard pirates and navies had the same objective: capture the enemy ship by killing its crew or taking them prisoner. Boarding required direct contact to enable grappling with hooks and spiked planks, so that an assault could be made over the prow: about 95 percent of the deck of a galley was devoted to oars and benches, which left only the prow (beak) for assaults. This made Renaissance galley fights essentially infantry battles at sea, carried out by shipboard marines. As ships grappled archers and gunmen fired into the enemy ship while other attackers hurled *caltrops* onto the deck to hobble defenders; if the wind was right, lime was thrown, blinding men so they could be more easily killed. Then the assault was made by leaping from the spur or running across a plank bridge.

A running fight between unequal fleets—as so often happened with ships of sail—was nearly impossible for galleys because galley fleets in the early modern period nearly always fought prow-to-prow. Galleys arrayed for battle in *line abreast* (with the flagship in the middle) but with no intention of turning *line ahead* or *line astern* upon contact. A battle line of 60 galleys abreast became the standard formation. Beyond that number the line proved too hard to maintain, as turns at the center or on one flank led to a "crack-the-whip" effect for ships on the other end of the line; that only exhausted crews who were forced to pull hard at the oars to maintain relative position. And exhaustion was fatal in a galley fight. Besides, line abreast was a powerful defensive formation: it was impossible to attack other than with an opposing battle line, since any smaller attack by just a few galleys would be encircled by the defenders. Usually, as at Lepanto, reserve lines stayed close, ready to row into any gap left by a burning or badly bloodied ship. Also, from the rear they could be lashed to a friendly galley already engaging the enemy to feed in marines to replace the first ship's casualties, whose dead bodies were tossed overboard to make way.

Most galley actions were head-to-head jousts, with some ships firing and veering while raising oars at the last second to sheer off an enemy's oars. Most often, a prow-to-prow collision was effected by both sides that resulted in vicious hand-to-hand fighting. Flank attacks were rare, except during a mêlée. If a galley was taken in flank it was game over for ship and crew. Why fight prow-to-prow? Because in the 15th century, Venetian shipwrights put *culverins* in the prows of galleys (the sides could not support artillery), later adding *demi-cannon*, *sakers*, and *swivel guns*. That was a dramatic change in offensive firepower that was quickly copied by every competing navy. Prow guns made the galley a totally offensive weapon: like a mid-20th-century fighter, the gunpowder galley always faced its enemy. Naval artillery was still too inaccurate in the 16th century for long-range stand-off duels between ships or fleets. Galleys had to close range for their guns to be effective. Head-to-head, each galley line rowing at battle speed covered about 200 yards per minute. That meant only a single volley could be fired before the fleets collided. Reloading was impossible under fire, even of breech-loaders, as galleys had almost no shelter from marine marksmen on enemy ships. The result was that captains held fire to maximize effect until point blank range; even until the prow crashed into the enemy ship (hopefully, riding over his prow to give one's own sharpshooters, marines, and boarders the advantage of height). Nor was there much advantage to firing first as big guns were seldom knocked out by ammunition intended to kill men rather than sink ships. It was better to wait to be sure to kill large numbers of the enemy, whatever damage his guns might do first.

As with a flank attack, offering the stern in a galley fight was an invitation to destruction: if a galley turned to run it was naked before the big guns of its pursuer, who would fire from just feet away. Chase guns would devastate a running crew with *grapeshot* and *canister* (Ottoman gunners loaded such anti-personnel ammunition almost exclusively). One galley taken from the rear this way recorded 40 men killed or laid low from a single enemy discharge. If retreat was required the best method was for a ship or the whole battle line to row backwards, always showing iron teeth to the enemy. One could not outrun a pursuer this way, but once ashore (galleys were easily beached) prow guns could be reloaded and fired from a far more stable position than the enemy's guns, as he still roiled on the water. Or survivors could just run away, leaving easily replaceable ships to be taken or burned. Of course, not all could get away: some men in every fight between galley fleets were slaves chained to the oars. For them the romantic exhortation "victory or death!" had a hard, literal meaning. See also *Calicut, Battle of*; *chaiky*; *cruising*; *dromon*; *galley slaves*; *galliot*.

Suggested Reading: John Guilmartin, *Gunpowder and Galleys* (2003); J. Morrison, ed., *Age of the Galley* (2003).

galley slaves. Slaves were used as oarsmen by all the main galley powers of the Mediterranean. The Ottomans preferred free oarsmen because they doubled as marines once a boarding action began. Often, these were Christian mercenaries from Greece and the Balkans who dropped oars and took up weapons in a fight. Most Ottoman ships also had a minority of Christian slaves chained to the oars. Venice also preferred freemen at the oars of its galleys for tactical reasons: it was rich but had a tiny population relative to its enemies, which forced it to hire mercenaries as oarsmen who could double as marines. Venice used a few slaves, usually criminals or prisoners of war. The Barbary Corsairs used all freemen in galliot raids, in which on-deck combat power was the primary concern. In fleet actions they used Christian slaves at the oars. They captured most of these poor fellows in raids on Sicily, Italy, and Spain, but sometimes as far afield as England, Wales, and Ireland. Most captured Christians preferred the hard life of a pirate to the harder life of a slave. Some were skilled seamen and were allowed to leave the oars if they converted to Islam. Some of the most dangerous Muslim captains were therefore Englishmen. Among the Mediterranean powers Spain was the most reliant

> *Most captured Christians preferred the hard life of a pirate to the harder life of a slave.*

on slave oarsmen. This held down costs, a concern for a country over-committed on many fronts against too many enemies in the 16th–17th centuries. Slaves on Spanish galleys were a mix of North African and Ottoman prisoners of war, and religious convicts (*conversos* and *moriscos*) sentenced to the oars after falling afoul of the *Inquisition*. Other Italian powers, including the warrior popes of the Papal States, kept small fleets of galleys rowed by a mix of slaves and mercenaries. The Scots and Irish used galleys that descended from Viking longships. These were rowed by all-warrior crews who took part in raids, not by slaves. The French used coerced oarsmen in coastal galleys into the 18th century, but these were convicts condemned to prison galleys, not slaves per se.

Gallican Church. The Catholic Church in France, which fiercely defended its traditions and liberties from Ultramontane interference by Rome. It rooted its position in the "Pragmatic Sanction of Bourges" (1438), which deprived popes of rights of appointment and taxation (*annates*) and affirmed the supremacy of general councils over the papacy. During the 15th century this became a self-conscious doctrine affirming traditional practice. See also *French Civil Wars*.

Gallican crisis. See *Henri II, of France*.

galliot. A small *galley*.

galloglass. Gaelic: "gallóglaigh" or "foreign warrior." Armed retainers of Celtic chieftains normally depicted wearing armor and armed with a battleaxe. "Foreign" usually meant Scots warriors from another chieftaincy or one of the smaller isles which supplied these mercenaries. During the 14th century hereditary galloglass kinship and retainer groups became more attached to given Irish lords, and probably more Irish in composition. Their reputation improved accordingly. In the Scottish Highlands, "galloglass" could also mean "henchman" or "armored bodyguard." See also *kerne*; *redshanks*.

galloper gun. A small caliber brass field gun mounted on a two-wheeled *gun carriage* and towed by a single horse. They were probably modeled on field artillery pioneered by *Gustavus Adolphus*. The *Cavaliers* deployed them during the *English Civil Wars*.

gambeson. A coat of *mail armor* that was cheaper and less prestigious than a *hauberk*. It was mostly worn by infantry, among whom it replaced cumbersome shields.

Gambia. The mouth of the Gambia River was reached by Portuguese explorers in 1455. The interior of this riparian territory was thereafter penetrated by a variety of European traders, explorers, and slavers, all eroding the traditional tributary relationship to the distant power of *Mali*. From 1618 the British sought a monopoly on Gambia trade. They secured this with a fort on James Island, built in the river's estuary in 1664. The French fortified nearby, at Albreda.

ganimet. The Ottoman pay system for irregulars and auxiliaries (*Voynuks* and *Tatars*) which offered a share in the spoils of the campaign. It was little more than the usual approved plunder, a feature of *war finance* common to all early modern armies.

gardebraces. Add-on armor plates attached to the backside of *pauldrons* from c.1430.

Gardetal. The Swedish system of raising peasant levies by homestead. See also *Swedish Army*.

Garigliano River, Battle of (December 28, 1503). *Gonzalo di Córdoba* led a Spanish army across the Garigliano River and caught a Franco-Swiss army still in its camp. In sharp, close fighting, the Spanish killed several thousand of their enemies and captured the French artillery train. The victory convinced Louis XII to surrender Naples to Spain in return for recognition of his control of Milan, and to sue for peace. This brought a brief respite in the *Italian Wars* (1494–1559).

garrisons. During the *Hundred Years' War* (1337–1453), each side used garrisons not merely to hold territory but to carry out a prolonged war of economic attrition against the enemy. *Edward III*'s garrisons included not just regular troops but also freely operating formations of *routiers*, who savaged the French economy and significantly depopulated whole provinces. The French played this game as well. Their garrisons along the border with English Guienne carried out 100 years of raids and extortions. In Japan during the *Unification Wars* (1550–1615) the loyalty of garrisons was seldom assumed and never guaranteed: garrisons switched sides, sometime more than once, as a result of bribery or threat far more often than as an outcome of siege or battle. The *Janissaries* began by rotating troops into garrisons for nine months, after which they returned to Constantinople. As the Ottoman Empire expanded, permanent garrisons of Janissaries and other troops were established that played a large role in local government as well as regional defense. These troops sometimes took on such a local perspective that they opposed control from the center; that was especially true in Iraq and Syria, and to a lesser degree in Egypt after defeat of the *Mamlūks*. The North African provinces of the empire were virtually independent of Constantinople and raised their own garrisons of local Janissaries and other troops. See also *Akbar*; *Alba, Don Fernando Álvarez de Toledo, duque de*; *amsār*; *appatis*; *Army of Flanders*; *arquebusiers à cheval*; *Baghdad, Siege of*; *banner system (Japan)*; *besonios*; *castles, on land*; *Cebicis*; *citadel*; *çit palankasi*; *contributions*; *desertion*; *Ecorcheurs*; *Eighty Years' War*; *English Civil Wars*; *fortification*; *French Civil Wars*; *guerre mortelle*; *Hongwu emperor*; *Hundred Years' War*; *Indian Wars*; *kerne*; *logistics*; *magazines*; *mercenaries*; *Militargrenze*; *military discipline*; *Ming Army*; *New English*; *Normans*; *place de sûreté*; *Razats*; *ribat*; *schiopettari*; *servitium debitum*; *Spanish Army*; *Spanish Road*; *sutlers*; *Thirty Years' War*; *waardgelders*; *war finance*; *Yongle Emperor*.

garrots. Any of several types of early gunpowder weapons that hurled quarrels rather than stone or iron balls. A synonym was "carreaux." From this primary usage, a secondary usage was large quarrels or bolts that were fired from *pots de fer* or other primitive gunpowder cannon.

gauntlets. Armored gloves made of leather and articulated plate. They replaced mail mittens during the 13th century. Some had iron spikes (gadlings) attached to the knuckles.

Gazi. See *ghazi*.

gekokujō. "The lower overthrowing the higher." A standard reference in Japanese military and political history to the century of *Sengoku jidai* that followed the *Ōnin War* (1467–1477). Peasants and townsfolk (*ashigaru*) took up arms and directly challenged the *samurai*, and abnormal careerism and greed is said to have motivated warriors to betray their honor code along with their *daimyos*.

Gembloux, Battle of (January 31, 1578). *Don Juan* and his cousin, the *Duke of Parma*, routed a Dutch army at Gembloux. The Spanish killed or captured several thousand rebels for a loss of fewer than 100 of their own men. The outcome rendered Brussels unsafe for *William the Silent* and signaled the revival of Spanish military power in the southern Netherlands.

gendarmerie. See *chevaux-légers*; *French Army*; *men-at-arms*.

gen d'armes. Mounted *men-at-arms*. See also *French Army*.

general. A military rank superior to colonel but below field marshal.

General at Sea. See *Blake, Robert*.

Generalfeldobrist. A senior commander of the main Imperial Army. The title was usually reserved to major princes who took personal command in the field, such as Emperor *Maximilian I*.

Generality. The government of the United Provinces formed by its seven constituent member provinces. See *States General*.

Generallissimus. The highest ranking commander in the Imperial Army, above both lieutenant general and field marshal.

Generalobrist. A commander of a German army comprised of several companies or regiments.

general officer. Any military rank or command above colonel.

genitors. Spanish *light cavalry* of the late 15th–16th centuries.

Genoa. This Italian city-state founded a seaborne empire on the ruins of Pisa's sea empire, after the Genoese naval victory at *Meloria* (1284). The Genoese empire nearly equaled that of Venice, its great rival for the lucrative trade of the eastern Mediterranean. From the 13th century the Aegean Sea was divided between the Genoese and Venetians who controlled alternate routes to Constantinople, with the Genoese running via Chios. Genoese trading interests extended as far as outposts on the Black Sea. Genoa controlled Sardinia until 1353 when it lost that large but poor island to Aragon. Genoa's internal politics were violent and forced into exile several noble families, notably the Grimaldis, who set up a powerful private galley fleet at Monaco that allied with France. Genoa taught the French how to build galleys at the "Clos des Gallées" at Rouen. The Genoese were granted a merchants' quarter in the Byzantine capital, a favor they repaid with only minor aid when *Constantinople* fell to the Ottomans in 1453. To the west, Genoa competed with the Iberian states, particularly Catalonia and Aragon, while to the south it fought against the *Barbary corsairs*. See also *Italian Renaissance*.

genouillières. Articulated armored knee-caps.

Gentili, Alberico (1552–1608). Italian jurist. A Protestant, he fled Catholic Italy for England (1580), where he was welcomed and made regius professor of law at the University of Oxford. He specialized in the rapidly developing field of international maritime law, on occasion acting as advocate for Spain and other powers in English *prize courts*. His two greatest works, *De legationibus* (1585) and *De jure belli* (1598), helped shape the diplomatic and legal practices of states in peace and war at a critical historical moment—just as they were moving into the climactic phase of "wars of religion" from which they would emerge with a newly secular understanding of sovereignty and international law in 1648. The themes he broached greatly influenced the writings of *Hugo Grotius*, and through him the legal structure of the emergent state system was shaped.

Georg, Johann (1611–1656). Elector of Saxony. Although a Lutheran prince he maintained an unusually close relationship with *Ferdinand II* and refused to back the bid of *Friedrich V* to take power in Bohemia. In the aftermath of the Protestant defeat at the *White Mountain* (1620), Georg imposed a relatively tolerant settlement on Lusatia and Silesia, at least as compared to what *Maximilian I* did in Bohemia and Moravia. He formed the *Leipziger Bund* to represent a third way, a neutral force in Germany between the Habsburgs and Sweden. He was pulled back into the war by *Gustavus Adolphus*, the impact of the sack of *Magdeburg*, and the move by *Johann Tilly*'s army into Saxony (September 4, 1631) to eat out that country as he moved north to meet the Swedish invasion. Within a week, he allied the Bund with Sweden. However, he fled the field of battle at *First Breitenfeld* (1631). He was always deeply suspicious of Sweden: he saw himself, not Gustavus, as the natural leader of Germany's Protestants. He was also convinced that the best way to remove foreign armies from his lands was to make peace with the Emperor. And he was deeply influenced by the pro-Imperial Count Schwarzenberg. After *Nördlingen* (1634) he abandoned the Swedish alliance and reconciled with Ferdinand. Some of Georg's early commitments to preserve the traditional liberties of the Silesian *Estates* were incorporated in the *Peace of Westphalia* (1648). See also *Arnim, Hans Georg von*; *Prague, Peace of*.

Georg Wilhelm, of Brandenburg (1619–1640). See *Altmark, Peace of*; *Gustavus II Adolphus*; *Thirty Years' War*.

German brigade. See *Bernhard von Sachsen-Weimar*.

German Peasant War (1525). A revolt of German peasants—the latest in a long line of uprisings—began in mid-1524 in Stühlingen and Thuringia, spreading from there to the Black Forest. What began as unconnected local revolts in aid of petitions against serfdom, market prices, and other grievances quickly spread over large parts of southern Germany and into Austria, Tyrol, and Styria. Underlying economic grievances included demands for abolition of serfdom, the uncertain legal status of peasant land holdings, compression of the forests and reduction of the commons, rising local and imperial taxes related to the expanding costs of war, and a price revolution in daily staples brought on by increased population and the influx of monetary metals from the Americas that was aggravated by bad harvests in 1523 and 1524. Political grievances included noble and town demands for institutional reform of the Holy Roman Empire. Religious grievances flowed from ferment over the new ideas of *Martin Luther* and older anger over corruption and clerical abuses in the Catholic Church. Several priests, peasants themselves or only recently removed, joined and led peasant bands. Others looked to the dramatic rhetoric of social leveling of the radical preacher, Thomas Müntzer. Miners and guildsmen also joined in, as the "common man" in town and village rose in general revolt.

The "peasant army" was a polyglot affair. It started with bands of peasants organized regionally, notably around Lake Constance and in the Black Forest, armed with farm implements, long knives, or boar spears which they used to hunt and kill landlords and local nobles. These bands were soon joined by artisans, town militia, some nobles, robber and poor knights, radical preachers inspired by Luther, and *Landsknechte* and *Reisläufer* mercenaries. Some large towns were coerced into the uprising, others joined willingly. Several of the largest German cities barred their gates and denied arms to the peasants. The peasant army swelled to over 40,000 by mid-summer, almost all infantry. While it always lacked sufficient cavalry it acquired some artillery by hiring or capturing guns from smaller cities: Rothenburg hired out two bombards, complete with carts and gunners, while the towns of Marktdorf and Meersdorf were overrun, whereupon they surrendered 13 guns of various calibers along with tons of black powder and shot. In July a peasant band captured intact the entire artillery train of Habsburg Styria. Other arms and armor were

> *Because the "peasants" had no central command the war was characterized by serial uprisings . . .*

looted from sacked castles, monasteries (also plundered of grain and wine stores), and towns along the line of march. Lastly, the peasants employed primitive *Wagenburgs* made from farm carts and hay wagons, not the sturdy *Hussite* type that was purpose-built for war. As a result, these provided little defense when facing *Rennfahne* cavalry of the *Great Swabian League*. Because the "peasants" had no central command the war was characterized by serial uprisings rather than a planned or coherent campaign. This was typical of peasant revolts nearly everywhere, and a key reason why most ended in defeat and savage reprisals carried out by frightened nobility and priests.

On the other side, many nobles were away serving in the army of Emperor *Charles V* fighting the *Italian Wars* with France. Charles asked his brother, *Ferdinand I*, then Archduke of Austria, to take command of Imperial forces in Germany. Georg of Waldburg commanded the separate army of the Swabian League. Meanwhile, the dispossessed and exiled Ulrich of Württemberg raised a private army of Landsknechte and Swiss to retake his ducal lands and marched on Stuttgart. However, news of the Swiss defeat at *Pavia* caused the Swiss part of his force to depart while releasing thousands of Landsknechte to fight against him for the Swabian League. The main advantage of the Swabian Leaguers was their cavalry, which they repeatedly used to flank, chase down, and butcher the peasants. Also, the disciplined pike formations and gunners of the Landsknechte inflicted terrible damage on peasants armed with shorter polearms or clubbing weapons. Joining the Leaguers were contingents of men-at-arms and infantry supplied by various petty territorial German princes, the real enemies of the peasants.

In December 1524, a peasant band formed at Baltringen. In January 1525, Tyrolean miners and Kempton peasants rebelled. The Swabian League sent in negotiators in order to buy time to organize a countering army. In February a third peasant band formed in Allgäu and the next month a fourth band was set up around Lake Constance. The Allgäu, Baltringen, and Lake Band then joined to form the "Christian Brotherhood," a loose confederacy in arms. The Brotherhood had a radically egalitarian command structure but borrowed ranks and unit organization from the Landsknechte. On March 26, the Baltringen Band rejected compromise and stormed the castle at Schemmerberg; a week later the Allgäu Band stormed the monastery at Kempten. Also in April, the peasants of Würzburg formed a new band; a band was established in the Neckar Valley; several small bands joined to form the Tauber Valley Band; other bands were formed in Alsace and Odenwald, and so on. On April 4 the army of the Swabian League met and defeated the Baltringen peasants at Leipheim, killing over 1,000, of whom 400 drowned in the Danube. On April 15 the Lake Band, numbering some 12,000 peasants, town militia, and a leavening of Landsknechte, faced down the Swabian Leaguers and forced them to withdraw. On April 17 a truce was called in Swabia while a court heard grievances and a settlement took Upper Swabia out of the fight. But the revolt had by then spread like wildfire through late summer pastures: a fresh revolt broke out in Limburg and another band, the Werra, was formed in Thuringia. On April 23 fighting broke out in the Rhineland-Palatinate. The next week, Stuttgart and Erfurt fell to peasant bands and revolt spread to several Swiss cantons. On May 5, despite some sympathy for the cause, Luther denounced the peasants, admonishing them from the comfort of a castellan sanctuary where he lived under the protection of a powerful prince and benefactor. "It is not for a Christian to appeal to law, or to fight, but rather to suffer wrong and endure evil," he told the peasants.

Three days later, a peasant band took Würzburg and rebellion broke out in Tyrol. Then the tide turned. On May 12 the Swabian League defeated a peasant band at Böblingen, after which peasant leaders who had sanctioned the execution of nobles were roasted alive. In a two-day fight a noble army of 2,300 horse and 4,000 foot—with contingents from Brunswick, Hesse, and Saxony—smashed the Frankenhausen Band, butchering 5,000 peasants and militia, including 300 beheaded in the town "pour encourager les autres."

The next day Alsatian bands were defeated at Zabern by an army of Lorrainers; many hundreds of peasants were massacred after they gave up the fight. A week later, 12,000 peasants surrendered at Freiburg (May 24), which they had only just taken. The next day Mühlhausen in Thuringia fell and Müntzer was captured, tortured, and beheaded—much to the satisfaction of Luther, who despised the man. On June 2 the Odenwald Band was beaten by the Leaguer army at Königshofen. Two days later the revolt in Franconia was crushed. A prolonged fight with dug-in peasants took place along the Leubas River during July. When key *Landsknechte* "comrades" left the trenches and defected to the Swabian League, the survivors were starved and blasted into surrender by July 23, whereupon they were slaughtered to a man. Thus ended the "Peasant's War" in Germany.

In Austria, however, the fight lasted into 1526. A rare peasant victory came at Schladming on July 2, 1525, where Salzburg miners and peasants beat back an overconfident Austrian army. This forced concessions from Ferdinand and led to a truce signed in September. The princes reneged on their word, leading to renewed fighting in the spring with bands of peasants who took refuge in inaccessible alpine valleys. The death toll for the war as a whole was 80,000 to 100,000, mostly peasants and townsfolk. Defeat left serfdom in place (though in fact, conditions somewhat improved after 1525), the Empire unreformed, and a bitter residue of confessional and class anger across Germany. See also *Anabaptism*; *Croquants*; *Jacquerie*; *Karsthans*; *Razats*; *Tard-Avisés*.

Suggested Reading: Janos Bak, ed., *The German Peasant War of 1525* (1976); R. Scribner and G. Benecke, *The German Peasant War, 1525* (1979).

Germany. See *Holy Roman Empire*.

Gevierthaufen. A pike square formed by German *Landsknechte*. It consisted of anywhere from 3,000 to 10,000 men, with the front ranks filled by *Doppelsöldner* followed by newer recruits, all surrounding and protecting the company *Fähnlein*. The square moved to the beat of a fife-and-drum band and to shouted and trumpeted signals. More Doppelsöldner took up the rear to ensure tactical discipline and keep raw recruits in line and from running. The flanks were herded by sergeants on the outer corners.

Gewalthut. See *Swiss square*; *tactics*.

ghaz. Jihad for Islam. See also *ghazi*; *"holy war."*

ghazi. "Warrior for the Faith." A religious-military title of Muslim warriors embarked on *"holy war."* Many of the first "Turkish" converts to Islam, before the founding of the Seljuk or Ottoman states, became ghazi in the Arab or Iranian Muslim armies. That lent the term an additional meaning of border or frontier warrior. On the controversial thesis that the later Ottoman Empire remained a "ghazi state" in its expansionist motives, see *Ottoman warfare*.

ghulams. "Slaves" (of the shah). At the start of the 17th century *Abbas I* reformed Iran's military, replacing traditional reliance on tribal recruitment (especially in the cavalry) with professional soldiers drawn from communities of former Christian slaves or prisoners or their descendants. Most came from Armenia, Circassia, or Georgia. Upon conversion to Islam these men could join the ranks of "ghulams." Although ghulam units started as infantry, over time they evolved into *dragoons*. As was the case with the *Janissaries* of the Ottoman Empire, ghulams were more trustworthy soldiers in the shah's eyes because they lacked connection to Iran's tribes or any social standing. Tribal leaders resented being displaced from the cavalry with its attendant loss of status and income. But there was little to be done.

Gibraltar. "The Rock." This strategic ground guarding the entrance (and exit) from the Mediterranean into the Atlantic was known to the ancient Greeks, along with Jebel Musa in North Africa, as one of the "Pillars of Hercules" marking the edge of world beyond which few dared sail. It was fortified by the radical Muslim Almohads of *al-Andalus* in 1260 to secure the link between the African and Iberian halves of their empire. In 1350, Alfonso XI (1312–1350) tried to take Gibraltar but died of the *Black Death* en route. The waters around Gibraltar were extremely dangerous. Pirate-infested, they could be safely traversed only in *convoy* or by paying protection money to the corsairs. Gibraltar was taken for Spain by the Duke of Medina Sidonia in 1462.

Gibraltar, Battle of (April 25, 1607). While peace negotiations to end the *Eighty Years' War* (1568–1648) were underway between *Spínola* and *Oldenbaarneveldt*, a Dutch fleet of 26 small and mid-sized warships sailed into Gibraltar harbor and took by surprise a Spanish fleet of 21 ships, all at anchor, including 10 first-rate *galleons*. Although outgunned, the Dutch blocked egress from the bay then blew the startled and unready Spanish ships out of the water, destroying all 10 galleons and many of the smaller warships in a fight that lasted four or five hours. For the loss of a few hundred Dutchmen and Admiral Jacob van Heemskerk, the "Dutch Nelson," an enemy fleet was destroyed and several thousand Spaniards killed. Many were shot in the water as they swam away from burning hulks. However, the victory proved counter-productive: such a humiliating defeat led Madrid to back away from its offered peace terms and to accept only the more limited *Twelve Years' Truce* (1609–1621).

Giornico, Battle of (December 28, 1478). Following the defeat and death of *Charles the Rash* in the *Burgundian Wars*, the Duchy of Milan tried to invade the *Swiss Confederation*. This was unwise. The Milanese were met by veteran pikemen, arquebusiers, crossbowmen, and halberdiers, hardened in earlier battles and now unmatched experts at "push of pike." Although outnumbered, the Swiss formed their usual lethal pike square and overran and slaughtered the Milanese.

gisarmes. A generic term for hacking *staff weapons* ranging from battleaxes mounted on stout poles to *bills*, *halberds*, and *poleaxes*. See also *glaive*.

Giza, Battle of (April 2, 1517). See *Mamlūks*.

glacis. In fortification, the sloping face of the *parapet* of the *covered way*, reaching to the ground so that the entire face was exposed to defensive fire from the parapet. See also *hornwork*.

glaive. A term used confusingly during the Middle Ages in reference to three distinct weapon types: the *halberd*, *sword*, and *lance* (the latter in English only). Which usage is correct may be determined only by reference to the surrounding context, and even then is not always clear. This probably results from the fact that the glaive was essentially a single-edged sword-blade attached to a long haft, and hence might be called a sword by one writer, a halberd by another, or even a lance (as in England). See also *gisarmes*.

Glyndŵr's Rebellion (1401–1406). A Welsh rebellion against English rule. It drew in the French, who landed several small armies in Wales and signed a formal alliance in 1404. Led by Owain Glyndŵr, the Welsh obtained naval support from the Scots, then from France and the Bretons. In 1404 some 120 allied ships landed French troops at Milford Haven from where they walked near to Worcester (all their horses had died of thirst during transport) while the fleet advanced up the Bristol Channel. This and later fleets were attacked by royal ships in alliance with English pirates, who were commissioned as privateers. In 1406 the French army was beaten and withdrew. It took 10 more years of campaigning and hard repression of guerillas led by Glyndŵr, who was never captured, before Wales was subdued.

Goa, Seizure of (1510). See *Portuguese India*.

goat's foot lever. A cloven lever fitted under the bowstring of an early *crossbow* to aid in drawing it.

Godunov, Boris Fyodorovich (c.1552–1605). Tsar of Russia, 1598–1605. A Tartar and *boyar* by ethnic and class origins, after the death of *Ivan IV* he served as regent (1584–1598) for Feodor I, Ivan's imbecilic older son and Boris's brother-in-law. Boris Godunov continued many of Ivan's policies, expanding farther into Siberia and the Crimea and seeking to implement administrative and other reforms to keep the boyars from regaining high office or power over the provinces. This done, an assembly of tamed boyars chose Boris to succeed as tsar in 1598. With the old patriarchate of Constantinople ensconced within the Ottoman Empire, Boris elevated the Russian Orthodox Church to an independent patriarchate (1589), thereby advancing its emergence as the major national church in the Orthodox world even as he rendered it subservient to the Russian state. A great famine from 1602 to 1604 underwrote superstitious suspicions that Godunov had murdered his way to the throne and raised popular mistrust that led ultimately to widespread rebellion. Military opposition to Boris Godunov gathered behind the "False Dimitri," a pretender claiming to be the lost son of Ivan IV whom Boris Godunov had banished to the upper Volga and probably also murdered in 1591. The armies of the "False Dimitri" invaded Russia, to wide popular acclaim, in 1604. Tsar Boris died just before the rebellion reached Moscow, where it would surely have both deposed him and disposed of him. Until 1613, there followed a deepening of this "*Time of Troubles*" ("Smutnoe Vremia"), marked by a continuation of the dynastic struggle, widespread unrest, famine, uprisings, ever more harsh repression, and Polish and Swedish military intervention.

> *...Gudunov had murdered his way to the throne and raised popular mistrust that led ultimately to ...rebellion.*

goedendag. "Good day" weapon. A specialized short pike used by the town militia of Flanders. It was made of a thick staff some four or five feet long, ending in a lethal steel spike and sometimes also an attached mace. It was used to hook a knight off his horses then punch through his armor with the long spike or smash in his helm and skull with the mace. It was used to enormously bloody effect this way by the Flemings against French *heavy cavalry* at *Courtrai* (1302). Its use did not spread far from Flanders since the longer *pike* was preferred elsewhere. Even in Flanders, the goedendag was abandoned at the start of the 15th century.

Golden Bull (1356). See *Holy Roman Empire*.

Golden Bull of Rimini (1223). See *Teutonic Knights*.

Golden Horde. See *Ivan III*; *Mongols*; *Timur*.

gomeres. Black warriors allied with, though more often slave soldiers of, *Berber* and Granadine armies fighting Christians during the *Reconquista*. Their preferred weapon was a long knife, whose use required that they charge rapidly and engage in close-quarter fighting.

Gonzaga, Giovanni (1466–1519). See *condottieri*; *Fornovo, Battle of*.

gorget. A small piece of *plate* positioned to protect the throat.

Grace of Alais (1629). See *Edict of Alès*.

graffle. A claw device used to draw the string on an early model *crossbow*. See also *windlass*.

Granada. Long home to advanced cultural and intellectual life, including a great madrassa where Latin and Greek texts were kept alive in Arabic translations, Granada was the last *taifa* state to fall to the centuries-long Christian *"Reconquista."* By 1264, Granada was already alone facing the Christian onslaught. It adapted by moving from light to heavier, European-style cavalry and armor, and attacking in dense formation rather than the traditional *Berber* style of envelopment. The Granadine heavy horse units were supported by *jinetes*. The last effective emir was Muley Hacen (d.1484), who expanded Granada's frontiers in the 1470s. But the building power of the Christian north was too much to hold back. The final offensive began when a Granadine civil war between Muley Hacen, his brother (Abdullah al-Zagel), and his son (Boabadil) split the kingdom and gave *Ferdinand and Isabella* the opportunity to divide and conquer the last Muslim emirate in Iberia. The first Christian offensive culminated in a successful assault in 1482 against the main outer fortress, the Alhama de Granada. In 1486, Ferdinand took the other guard fortress, at Loja, just 21 miles north of the city. That left only Málaga in the path of the Christians, and it fell following a siege in 1587, after which most of its Moorish population was sold into slavery. As Spanish armies closed around Granada, troops on both sides hurled religious insults across the siege lines. These included tying Christian or Muslim relics or scriptures to the tails of donkeys or swine, respectively, and dragging them in the dirt and muck. The Christians also played hymns endlessly on carillons (an early form of excruciating "psychological warfare"). Granada negotiated surrender terms, including a promise of toleration of the Muslim faith, and opened its gates to Ferdinand and Isabella on January 2, 1492. Partly in celebration, Isabella agreed to finance Christopher Columbus on his search for a new route to India and Cathay and, she hoped, a back door through which to smite the Muslims and retake the "Holy Land." Forcible conversions and *expulsion of the Jews* were ordered immediately, followed after a few years by *expulsion of the Moors*. From 1502 there began burnings of books in old Granada, then of people, by the *Inquisition*.

Grand Parti de Lyon. See *war finance: France*.

Grandson, Battle of (March 2, 1476). After defeat of his relief army at *Héricourt*, Burgundy's Duke *Charles the Rash* moved against Berne. The Bernese reinforced their garrison at Grandson but Charles overran it. He allowed his troops to massacre the garrison, which provoked the Swiss Confederation to rage. A confederate army moved to intercept the Burgundians near Concise, a village south of Neuchâtel a few kilometers from Grandson. The Swiss moved in their standard formation of three pike squares: the "Vorhut," "Gewalthut," and "Nachhut." In the early hours of March 2, 1476, an advance column of Swiss foragers unexpectedly stumbled into the Burgundian camp set up in a shallow valley of small copses and vineyards. Charles hastily formed up his men while more Swiss arrived to take command of the sloped high ground above the camp. Some minor skirmishing by Swiss handgunners provoked Charles to order part of his infantry to attack up the valley side. Archers and gunners of both armies began to inflict casualties, but neither side gave ground. Then the Swiss Gewalthut arrived, raising the number of Swiss on the field to some 10,000. At mid-morning, the Swiss decided to move downslope toward the Burgundians. They formed a single massive square at whose center fluttered the great *Banner* of the Swiss Confederation along with cantonal standards and *Fähnlein*. Charles ordered his artillery to open a bombardment and sent his cavalry to attack directly. The Swiss set a *Forlorn Hope* of 300 crossbowmen and arquebusiers in front of the square to act as a light skirmisher screen. At their rear, atop the slope just descended, canon were manhandled into position and opened fire.

At first the Burgundian canon had the better of it, cutting gaping holes—as much as 10 or 12 files deep—in the Swiss ranks. Burgundian cavalry charged the Forlorn Hope, which scrambled for cover under the pikes in front of the square. Charles led a second charge of *lancers* from which he emerged sans horse and barely in possession of his life. Another company of cavalry tried to flank the Swiss, but could not navigate the steep slope. The result was sharp combat with lance, halberd, crossbow, pike, pistol, and arquebus. The fight lasted several hours, until the Swiss ran out of quarrels, shot, and powder. Charles' artillery was still well-supplied and kept up a deadly bombardment while his cavalry rested and reformed. But then he repositioned the artillery and moved his infantry back, hoping to draw the Swiss off the sloping vineyards. This was a grave error, as at that moment two more Swiss squares arrived. Upon blowing of a Harsthörner ("Great War Horn"), all three squares advanced at once. This movement, along with the disorder of the retreat Charles' men were attempting, spread panic in the Burgundian ranks. Particularly unruly were his German mercenaries. The flight of most of his foot left Charles exposed with only artillery and cavalry, and neither arm could hold the field against the Swiss "push of pike." Charles considered the situation then wisely fled with his army, in part to save himself and partly in an effort to regroup his infantry. The Swiss fell upon the Burgundian camp and looted it, foregoing any advantage they might have had by pursuing a defeated enemy. On the other hand, they captured Charles' superb artillery train of nearly 400 cannon along with many more supply carts. Given the duration of the fight, casualties were relatively low on both sides.

Grand Vezier (*Vezir-i Azam*). The direct deputy to an Ottoman sultan. They enjoyed extraordinary powers over other *kuls* and were the main recruiters (and dismissers) of the Ottoman military. They used their power of dismissal or reinstatement to control the *timariots*, but even more the *Janissary Corps* and *sipahis*, especially the elite administrative sipahis regiments barracked in the capital. Some Grand Veziers took personal command of field armies in the absence of the sultan—after 1596, Ottoman sultans seldom accompanied armies on campaign. The office of Grand Vezier was much sought after and therefore held insecurely in face of constant court intrigue, schemes, and betrayal. Deputies to the Grand Vezier were called "kaim mekam." Some actively campaigned to unseat their master, others coveted his position and tried to seize it upon his death. See also *bey*; *Thirteen Years' War*; *Yeniçeri Ağasi*.

Grantham, Battle of (1643). See *Cromwell, Oliver*; *English Civil Wars*.

grapeshot. French: "mitaille." By the 13th century an early form of grapeshot comprised of a cloth sack of 100 or more lead balls fired from a cannon was in use in China. This ammunition arrived much later in Europe. An early advantage of grapeshot was that the powder charge in unreliable *hoop-and-stave* cannon could be increased without increasing the risk of lethal (to the crew) explosion of the gun barrel. When it finally matured, grapeshot was comprised of musket balls spaced around a wooden spindle and covered by a cotton bag. When fired from a cannon the flame and force of exploding powder consumed the bag and scatter-shot the musket balls (weighing from a half-ounce to one ounce each) into the enemy ranks. A 24-pounder cannon fired grapeshot containing about 300 balls. This was devastatingly effective at close ranges against massed infantry or cavalry. See also *canister*.

Graubünden. See *The Grisons*.

Gravelines, Battle of (July 13, 1558). With the marriage of *Philip II* and *Mary Tudor*, England briefly joined Spain's drawn-out war with France. A Spanish *tercio* of 10,000 men, under *Graaf van Egmont*, moved into northwest France. Supported by a bombardment from a squadron of English warships off Gravelines, Spanish cavalry smashed through French shoreline positions. Some 2,000 French were killed, half of whom drowned when they were forced into the sea by the Spanish horse.

Gravelines, Battle of (August 8, 1588). See *Invincible Armada*.

Great Apostasy. See *Teutonic Knights*.

Great Condé. See *Condé, Louis II, de Bourbon*.

Great Enterprise (1521–1522). See *Henry VIII, of England*.

Great Galley. A hybrid warship which may have first appeared in Venice in 1295. It combined *sweeps* of elongated oars with the higher hull construction of *roundships* and could carry from 30 to 50 guns. A specific ship by that name, actually a *galleass*, was launched by *Henry VIII* in 1515. It had 60 oars, 70 brass cannon, and 147 iron guns. It was broken up in 1523.

Great Helm. See *bascinet*; *helm*.

Great Interregnum (1250–1273). See *Holy Roman Empire*.

Great Schism (1378–1417). "Schism of the West." The "Avignon Captivity" of the papacy lasted from 1314 to 1362, after which the possibility of intervention by France was still felt as a constant threat by the city-states of Italy. In 1378 the last "French" Pope, Gregory XI, died at the end of the *War of the Eight Saints*. Romans insisted that he be succeeded by an Italian. Urban VI was elected, but he soon alienated several powerful church factions. A council of cardinals was held at Agnani that vitiated Urban's pontificate and elected in his place a Genoese pope, Clement VII. Urban refused to step down, however, and Clement was compelled to withdraw into exile at Avignon. Each claimant and faction denied the others' legitimacy, asserting that they alone embodied the apostolic succession claimed by the papacy.

> *And so the scandal of the papacy continued to bitterly divide, humiliate, and undermine respect for the Catholic Church.*

As these men died their place in the Great Schism was taken by successor rivals. In Rome, Urban VI (1378–1389) was followed by Boniface IX (1389–1404), Innocent VII (1404–1406), and Gregory XII (1406–1415). At Avignon, the longer-lived Clement VII (1378–1394) was succeeded by Benedict XIII (1394–1417). And so the scandal of the papacy continued to bitterly divide, humiliate, and undermine respect for the Catholic Church. For a time the *Gallican Church* rejected both lines. There was an effort to revive conciliar authority at the Council of Pisa (1409), but this resulted in election of a third line of claimant pontiffs, Alexander V (1409–1410) and his successor, John XXIII (1410–1415). In 1414, John convened the Council of Constance to decide the issue. Having lost most of his support Gregory XII resigned, but John XXIII and Benedict XIII refused to follow suit. The delegates at Constance resolved the dispute by decreeing ("Sacrosancta") that councils were superior to popes, then deposed the contending popes in favor of a new one they elected, Martin V.

Despite this tortuous rivalry and sequence, the Catholic Church maintained that an unbroken line of popes proceeded in uninterrupted "apostolic" succession to Peter, apostle of Jesus of Nazareth. The claim was upheld by the sophistry of a retroactive agreement that the line from Urban to Gregory was the true, canonical, and authoritative succession. Catholic historians have reinforced this argument by insisting that the schism was merely political in character and so never touched on matters central to papal authority or Church doctrine. The Great Schism helped open the door to the political revolution of the *Italian Renaissance* by whittling down the universalist claims of popes during the formative period of Italy's emergent city-state system. Still, during the 15th century doctrinal disquiet was still treated as heresy, as in the two challenges to papal authority and Catholic doctrine and practice that did make headway during the Great Schism: *Lollardism* in England and the *Hussite* movement in Bohemia. More widely and longer term, the schism exposed the sordid political role and decadence of the papacy in its capacity as a temporal power and undermined for many its spiritual claims as well. This stirred unrest among the faithful that would contribute to demands for reform that fed into the *Protestant Reformation* and the Catholic *Counter-Reformation* in the 16th century.

Suggested Reading: M. Gail, *The Three Popes* (1969); J. H. Smith, *The Great Schism* (1970).

Great Ships. Huge 16th-century ships mounting many guns, with gay decoration and ornate *castles*. They were more waterborne fortresses than true ships of war as they were not fast or handy. Their main purpose was to garner prestige to the king and kingdom that built them. Competitive construction of Great Ships was something of an early modern substitute for medieval cathedral building, this time in wood and canvas, rivets, and rigging. (Would-be sea powers all over the world did this again during the steam battleship craze of the 1890s.) Henry VII of England cannibalized the old "Grâce Dieu" in 1486 and used her parts to build the "Royal Sovereign," armed with 31 big guns and over 100 *serpentines*. By the early 16th century even small nations built at least one Great Ship. Scotland built the "Great Michael" in 1511. *Henry VIII* laid down the "Henry Grâce à Dieu" in 1514, an ungainly and massive vessel that sported 384 guns (counting rail and swivel guns) that was later rebuilt to carry 21 brass cannon, 130 iron cannon, and 100 rail-mounted hand guns. The Maltese Knights built a great carrack, the "Santa Anna," in 1523. France built the "Grande François" in 1527. Sweden launched the "Elefant" in 1532, and two years later Portugal sent to sea the gigantic "São João," replete with 366 guns (counting small pieces). Yet, the "Great Ships" were a design dead end. By the mid-16th century they gave way to the *galleon* as the dominant fighting vessel in actual war at sea; a century later more moderate and functionally designed *men-of-war* were built that carried serious broadside armament. Thus, England launched a 100-gun ship also christened "Sovereign of the Seas" in 1637; France commissioned the comparably powerful "Couronne" the next year. See also *Great Galley*; *Henry V, of England*; *Royal Navy*.

Great Swabian League. See *German Peasant War*; *Swabian League*; *Swabian War*.

Great Wall. Construction of defensive walls began during the reign of China's "First Emperor," Qin Shi Huang, in 221 B.C.E. These connected sections of preexisting border fortifications of Qin's defeated and annexed enemies, dating to the Warring States period, from which the Qin empire had emerged as victor. The building technique of this remarkable structure was the ancient method of stamped earth that employed masses of slave laborers as well as military conscripts. Some parts of the wall stood for nearly two millennia and were incorporated into the modern "Great Wall" built by the Ming dynasty following the humiliation of defeat and capture of the Zhengtong Emperor at *Tumu* (1449). After he regained the throne in 1457, the Ming court decided on a purely defensive strategy and began building 700 miles of new defensive walls starting in 1474, fortifying the northern frontier against Mongol raiders. The Ming system involved hundreds of watchtowers, signal-beacon platforms, and self-sufficient garrisons organized as military colonies. Infantry were positioned along the wall to give warning. But the main idea was for cavalry to move quickly to any point of alarm and stop raiders from breaking through. In that, the Ming strategy emulated Mongol practices from the Yuan dynasty. It was also reminiscent, though not influenced by, the Roman defensive system of "limes" which in Germania alone were 500 kilometers long.

The Great Wall was meant to reduce costs to the Ming of garrisoning a thousand-mile frontier by channeling raiders and invaders into known invasion routes to predetermined choke points protected by cavalry armies. This strategy was mostly ineffective. The Great Wall was simply outflanked in 1550 by Mongol raiders who rode around it to the northeast to descend on Beijing and pillage its suburbs (they could not take the city because they had no siege engines or artillery). The wall was also breached by collaboration with the Mongols of Ming frontier military colonies, which over time became increasingly "barbarian" through trade, marriage, and daily contact with the wilder peoples on the other side. Some Han garrisons lived in so much fear of the Mongols they were militarily useless; others lost touch with the distant court and hardly maintained military preparations at all. Finally, the Great Wall could always be breached by treachery or foolhardy invitation. Either or both occurred when a Ming general allowed the *Manchus* to enter China via the Shanhaiguan Pass to aid in the last Ming civil war in 1644, which brought the Ming dynasty to an end and put the Qing in power.

China never built a defensive wall along its Pacific sea frontier, as it felt no threat from that quarter. And yet, the main threat to its long-term stability and independence came across the Pacific in the form of European navies and marines. As with the 20th century Maginot Line in France, building the Great Wall in some ways signaled Ming defeatism rather than advertised Ming strength. The overall historical meaning of the Great Wall is ambiguous. To some, it signifies the worst features of China's exploitative past; to others, it celebrates the longevity of China's advanced, classical civilization.

Suggested Reading: Sechin Jagshid and V. J. Symons, *Peace, War, and Trade Along the Great Wall* (1989); Arthur Waldron, *The Great Wall of China* (1990).

"Great War" (1409–1411). See *Poland*; *Prussia*; *Tannenberg, Battle of*; *Teutonic Knights, Order of*.

Great Zimbabwe. A stone-building, gold-producing, cattle-rearing, and Indian Ocean–trading East African civilization, usually dated to about 1150 C.E. Some 200 distinct ruin sites have been found, of which the most important was "Great Zimbabwe," probably a royal palace or temple complex. Its stone foundations spread over 60 acres. It clearly achieved real prosperity in the early 13th century, mostly from cattle and farming but also from trading gold with Arab merchants along the Sofala coast. The Shona capital at Great

Zimbabwe was abandoned as the kingdom migrated north, probably in the late 15th century. The Portuguese arrived in the region in the 1560s and set up slave trading stations. The Mwene Mutapa governed the area from the north in the face of rising interference from the Portuguese and growing pressure from surrounding tribes.

greaves. Leg armor comprised of *plate*, usually in front and back pieces linked by leather ties. By the 15th century, in a full armor suit, they were hinged.

Greece. See *Byzantine Empire*; *Ottoman Empire*.

Greek fire. The chemical recipe for this weapon, which reputedly ignited on contact with air and was inextinguishable by water, was a technological secret of the ancient Greeks and closely guarded also by the Byzantine Empire. In the final hours of the *Siege of Constantinople*, defenders poured pots of Greek fire on attacking *Janissaries* and *Bashi-Bazouks*, after which the recipe was lost to history. Modern historians think that Greek fire was mainly petroleum, pumped through pipes and ignited as in a modern flamethrower. Its oil base allowed it to burn atop water, the feature so often wondered about in awe by contemporary observers who lacked the recipe.

grenades. Small hand bombs may have been used in China from the 10th century. They were first clearly used in Europe only in 1382, when hollow cast iron balls were filled with black powder to be set off by a lighted wick. They were sometimes used in land battles but were most effective in marine combat. Much improved grenades were available from 1536 and were used at the siege of Arles. Within 60 years, the invention of stubby *wheel lock* grenade-launchers gave hand bombs much greater range. Primitive portable mortars followed. All such weapons were highly dangerous to users due to unreliable fuses that might result in premature detonation. See also *alcancia*.

Grenville, Richard (1542–1591). English sea captain. He fought against the *Invincible Armada* in 1588. At *Flores* (1591) he fought off 15 Spanish warships for half a day, allowing the rest of his fleet to escape before he finally surrendered the wreck of the "Revenge." He died a few days later. He is most famously remembered in a rather strained, even turgid, verse by Lord Tennyson: *The Revenge*. See also *Mountjoy, Baron of*.

Grey, Lady Jane (1537–1554). See *Elizabeth I*; *Mary Tudor*; *Wyatt's Rebellion*.

The Grisons. "Graubünden" was governed as a bishopric from the 9th century but came under Habsburg control in the 12th century. It was repeatedly drawn into the Swiss wars of the 14th and 15th centuries, ending in the *Swabian War* (1499) which cut The Grisons free of the Habsburgs and gained it protection of the Swiss Confederation. The *Protestant Reformation* sharply divided the population along confessional lines, a rift not healed until well after the *Thirty Years' War*. Throughout the late 16th to early 17th centuries the lower end of the *Spanish Road* cut through The Grisons, making it a strategic territory much coveted and fought over by the Great Powers of Austria, France, and Spain. In 1601 the French secured a treaty reserving The Grisons "for her alone" in terms of military transportation. Yet, in 1603, Venice signed a comparable agreement. The Grisons refused passage to Spanish troops in 1603. That led Spanish engineers to build a fortress, The Fuentes, to guard access to the valleys and mountain passes. There was heavy, if intermittent, fighting over control of the passes, the Protestant Grisons, and Catholic *Valtelline* from 1607 to 1617, involving Spain, Savoy, Venice, and France. In 1618, Grisons troops invaded the Valtelline. In 1620, Madrid moved troops into the Valtelline in support of a Catholic uprising against The Grisons. After the locals massacred 600 Protestants, Spain garrisoned The Grisons with 4,000 men. In 1624, France took over The Grisons and surrendered it to papal control two years later. Until 1634 The Grisons remained hotly contested territory. After that, the French occupation of Lorraine and ascendant French military power in the Rhineland prevented further Spanish overland reinforcement of its armies in Flanders.

Grotius, Hugo (1583–1645). Né Huig van Groot. Dutch jurist, humanist, and diplomat in the Swedish service, 1635–1645, at the French court. His early work sought to frame a republican constitution for the United Provinces that, as in classical antiquity, preserved liberty though rule by an oligarchy of regents. He was similarly conservative in religious matters, personally leaning toward *Arminianism*. His ambition for a moderate political compromise was wrecked by the dispute between *Oldenbaarneveldt* and *Maurits of Nassau*. Grotius was arrested along with Oldenbaarneveldt and others during Maurits' coup d'état of August 1618. He was convicted of treason in May 1619, and sentenced to life in prison (Maurits had Oldenbaarneveldt executed). Grotius escaped in March 1621, concealed by his wife in an empty book chest and smuggled past guards used to seeing crates of books coming and going from a scholar's cell. The couple fled to Paris. The next month, all hopes for domestic and international religious peace were dashed when the princely vanity of Maurits of Nassau united with bloody-mindedness in Catholic Spain to cause resumption of the *Eighty Years' War* upon expiration of the *Twelve Years' Truce*.

Grotius' later and greater works dealt with international affairs: *Mare Liberum* ("Freedom of the Seas") published in 1609, and *De jure belli et pacis* ("On the Law of War And Peace"), published in 1625. The latter was written while in political exile in Paris. Grotius' writings are widely regarded as major landmarks in the development of international law as well as the *just war* tradition. They drew deeply from the well of natural law theory, the prior legal work of *Gentili*, and the new idea of "social contract" that was still germinating in his day and would not flower fully until mid-century, in the great work of Thomas Hobbes, *Leviathan*. Most of all, Grotius' work responded to the awful experience of religious warfare which culminated in decades of conflict that dominated his life, thinking, and writings. Grotius devised from varied sources several general and rational principles, which he put forward as the basis for a system of law among nations. His work was an essential rejection of the international anarchy of his times, especially the unlimited form the wars of religion were taking. Yet, he did not propose legal abolition of war as the solution, knowing full well that was a utopian pipedream. Rather, he argued carefully for moderation in accepted methods of fighting, a more limited notion of conquest, more humane behavior by generals and troops when living off an enemy's land, and more law-governed treatment of the civilian population in countries passed through or occupied.

Grotius bequeathed three key ideas to legal and political discourse about war. First, states ought not to seek to impose their national or religious ideologies—in his day and corner of the world, Catholicism and variants of Protestantism—upon each other; they should instead abstain from interference in each others' "internal affairs." Grotius maintained a theoretical but highly circumscribed exception for "armed humanitarian intervention" to this general rule. Second, he posited that a "law of nature" exists separate from and higher than human affairs but that this natural law is knowable by human intellect through the application of reason. He saw general elaboration and acceptance of this natural law by statesmen and nations as the only path to eventual escape from international anarchy. Finally, he called for an "assembly of the nations" to enforce these laws drawn out of nature by human reason and encoded in treaties and the common practices of states. Grotius profoundly influenced thinkers as diverse as Thomas Hobbes, John Locke, and Immanuel Kant. His works became the foundation for all later thinking about the law of nations and about the character of international relations as a society of states bound by practical requirements of social existence and the balance of power rather than allegiance to a putatively superior religious authority. In his own day his writings were widely influential, affecting the worldview even of a warlord king such as *Gustavus Adolphus*.

Grünhag. An earthwork palisade. See also *Morat, Battle of.*

Grunwald, Battle of (1410). See *Tannenberg, Battle of.*

Guangdong. A large Chinese *junk*, built tougher and stronger than the *Fujian* class and used for coastal and oceanic trade. They were well-armed with a variety of anti-personnel weapons, but given their weak hull design they could not support heavy, ship-killer broadside artillery. Some had long oars ("sweeps").

guardas reales. See *Palace Guard.*

guastatores. See *wasters.*

Guelphs and Ghibellines. Terms of art for two German houses with opposing dynastic and territorial claims in Germany and Italy: the Guelphs ("Welf"), originally based in Saxony and Bavaria, and the Ghibellines ("Waiblingen" or "Waibling"), from the town and castle of that name near Stuttgart. The terms took on far wider significance as "Guelph" came to stand for the papal party and "Ghibelline" for supporters of local autonomy for the Hohenstaufen dynasty and the rights of the Holy Roman Emperor. Each represented leagues of rival lords, cities, and feuding families, including the family of Dante Alighieri, who served in the Guelph army. The two parties engaged in a protracted struggle for supremacy within the *Holy Roman Empire*. Long after the great contest between popes and emperors ended the Guelphs and Ghibellines fought over the baser material interests that had always divided them. See also *corpus mysticum*.

> *The two parties engaged in a protracted struggle for supremacy within the* Holy Roman Empire.

Guerra Arciducale (1615). See *Uzkok War*.

guerra dels segadors. See *Catalonia, Revolt in*; *Spain*.

guerre couverte. Private warfare, as distinct from wars waged by the crown or state. This form of warfare was progressively, but never entirely, suffocated by the emergence of the modern state. On land it marked and even defined the *feudal* eras in Europe and Japan. At sea, it took the form of *privateering* and outright *piracy*. An important distinction was that devastation was not permitted in *just war* theory. However, utilizing the same logic as the *chevauchée*, it was often committed in practice in order to force one's enemy to come out of his fortifications and fight. See also *ashigaru*; *castles, on land*; *castles, on ships*; *Free Companies*; *Ireland*; *Militargrenze*; *ronin*; *routiers*; *wakō*.

guerre d'usure. See *attrition*.

guerre guerroyante. A style of war common to frontiers or *marches*, such as the Inner Asia–China frontier; the Steppe frontier between Russia, Poland, and the Cossacks; the Scottish Highlands; the Gaelic lordships outside the Dublin Pale; the mountains of Hungary and the Balkan *Militargrenze*. In such areas, protracted wars of attrition were fought but on a reduced scale of raids, ambushes, counter-sallies, burnings, and small massacres. Occurring over a long period, attritional conflict took on an incoherent and seemingly disconnected character that approached anarchy more than it reflected strategy. See also *kerne*; *Montrose, Marquis of*; *pillage*; *plunder*; *raiding*.

guerre mortelle. In medieval *siege warfare* proclamation of "guerre mortelle" was permissible against a town or garrison which refused to surrender after some lengthy, but indeterminate, time under assault. This declaration allowed the attacking army not merely to lay waste or pillage property, but legally and morally to forfeit most or all defender lives—whether soldier or civilian. It was a status much abused in order to sanction wanton plunder and slaughter by cruel or disreputable commanders. See also *Albigensian Crusade*; *just war tradition*; *quarter*.

guerriers de Dieu. See *Catholic League (France)*.

guerrilla warfare. See *Glyndŵr's Rebellion*; *guerre couverte*; *Indian Wars*; *Ireland*; *Korea*; *Martolos*; *Militargrenze*; *raiding*; *Razats*; *Scottish Wars*; *"skulking way of war"*; *Toyotomi Hideyoshi*; *Wallace, William*; *William I, of Nassau*.

Guinegate, Battle of (1513). "Battle of the Spurs." See *Henry VIII, of England*.

guisarmes. See *gisarmes*.

Guise, Charles, Cardinal de Lorraine (1524–1574). Practical church reform interested him far more than doctrinal disputes. He was, therefore, initially a seeker after dialogue with the *Huguenots* who thought peace might be restored by their abjuration within a *Gallican* framework. Yet, he became a leading figure in the anti-Huguenot movement of radical Catholics during the first four *French Civil Wars*. He represented France at the *Council of Trent*, whose spirit of militant intolerance he is usually, but wrongly, said to have embodied. In fact, he hoped for German and English Protestant attendance and was dispatched to Trent by *Catherine de Medici* with explicit orders to secure Gallican liberties from papal or conciliar interference. Still, at Trent he cemented the ties of the Guise to foreign Catholic power in Rome and Madrid. Known as the "minister of mischief" by his enemies, he succeeded his brother, *François Guise*, as leader of the increasingly radical Catholic faction from 1563 to 1574. In his last years Charles had two great desires: to crush the Huguenots as a class and confession and to destroy Admiral *Coligny*, blood enemy of the Guise family. To those ends, in 1568 he conspired to revoke the *Edict of Longjumeau*, thereby starting the Third Civil War. He also plotted to place *Mary Stuart*, his niece, back on the throne of Scotland and raise her to the English throne as well. He thus joined in plots with *Philip II* and the pope to overthrow *Elizabeth I*.

Guise, Charles de Lorraine (1554–1611). See *Mayenne, duc de*.

Guise, François, duc de Lorraine (1519–1563). A militant Catholic and key opponent of the spread of *Calvinism* among the French nobility and population. A noted soldier, he was badly wounded at the siege of Boulogne (1545), after which he was known to his men as "la Balafré" ("Scarface"). Guise held the fortress of Metz during a two-month siege by *Charles V* in 1552, forcing the German emperor to pull back after losing 30,000 men. Guise took *Calais* from the English after a five-day siege in 1558. He dominated policy during the brief reign of *Francis II*, who was married to his niece, *Mary Stuart*. He was a powerful noble and one of the principal persecutors of the Huguenots. Along with his brother *Charles, Cardinal de Lorraine*, he headed the Guise family and led the most radical Catholics in France. The Guise lost power to *Catherine de Medici* when Francis died suddenly and she proclaimed a regency for *Charles IX*. When she tried to end the religious divide with an act of legal toleration (*Edict of Saint-Germain*), Guise chose war instead, firing the first shots of the *French Civil War*s against Protestant worshipers at *Vassy*. Received as a hero in Paris for this deed, Guise was raised to lieutenant-general in wake of the capture of *Montmorency* at *Dreux*. While besieging the Huguenot citadel at Orléans he was shot in the back by the Protestant nobleman, Poltrot de Méré, who was a paid spy for Coligny. Guise died after several days. Poltrot was tortured and executed and his corpse torn apart by a Catholic mob. The murder of Guise added to the vitriol in France by framing a blood feud between the noble families of Guise and Châtillon that played out in the horrors of the *St. Bartholomew's Day Massacres* (1572), and after.

Guise, Henri, duc de Lorraine (1550–1588). Son of *François, duc de Lorraine*. Head of the Guise family at a precocious age, once he achieved his majority he assumed leadership of the radical Catholic party in France and of the *Catholic League*. He directly and continually challenged *Henri III*'s authority after 1584. His great popularity among the Catholic mobs of Paris on the *Day of the Barricades* (May 12, 1588) forced the king to flee to Blois. The *Edict of Union* then named Guise overall commander of all Catholic and Royalist forces. That December, Henri III lured Guise to Blois and had him murdered.

Guise family. The most powerful, and reactionary, Catholic family in France during the *French Civil Wars* (1562–1629). Among the "foreign princes" of France, the family was founded by Charles de Lorraine who became duc de Guise in 1527. The Guise had their main client power base in Champagne, but branches of the family controlled much of Brittany, Maine, Normandy, and Picardy. See also *dévotes/dévots*; *Francis II*; *Guise, Charles, Cardinal de Lorraine*; *Guise, François, duc de Lorraine*; *Guise, Henri, duc de Lorraine*; *Henri III, of France*; *Henri IV, of France*; *Mary Stuart, Queen of Scots*; *Richelieu, Cardinal Armand Jean du Plessis de*; *St. Bartholomew's Day Massacres*.

Gujarat. An Indian principality on the Malabar coast of India. A bastion of Jainism until the 12th century, it was overrun by the *Delhi Sultanate* in 1298. In 1390, Gujarat broke free of the Delhi sultans and declared itself an independent Muslim sultanate. It was extraordinarily wealthy, largely due to its strategic position in the Indian Ocean trades in spices and slaves with *Mamlūk* Egypt and other states in the Middle East, and more rare but lucrative exchanges with China. It is known to have used guns no later than 1421, and probably had the technology much earlier than that. Into the early 16th century it was the dominant sea power of coastal India. In 1509, at *Diu*, the Gujarat galley navy was utterly destroyed by a small Portuguese fleet using broadside artillery. Gujarat lost Diu to Portuguese marines in 1536, then failed to retake it in the face of Portuguese fortification and defensive cannon. It never recovered Diu, despite military assistance from the Ottomans. Gujarat was also under pressure from the *Mughals* to its north. Although it briefly recovered after the mid-century mark in its long contest with this Muslim rival, the loss of Diu fatally weakened its economy. In 1572, Gujarat was conquered and annexed to the Mughal Empire.

gun carriages. Early cannon were not held in carriages but either fixed to boards or angled on a sloped mound of earth. The French and Burgundians introduced four-wheeled and two-wheeled carriages toward the end of the 15th century. By 1500 many towns had multi-barreled, small bore guns mounted in shielded carts (*ribaudequins*). In the early 17th century *Gustavus Adolphus* finally introduced small two-wheeled carriages pulled by one or two horses that allowed deployment of the first true field artillery. While this improved battlefield firepower, it also increased the logistical challenge, as more horses to pull more carts filled with power and shot increased the demand for fodder for the horses and food for the gun crews. At sea, the difference between English truck-wheeled carriages and the heavy Spanish two-wheeled carriages made a great difference during the *Invincible Armada* campaign of 1588, giving the English a clear advantage. Because English guns could be run closer to the *gun port* they protruded further out and could be *bowed* and traversed over a greater range. That increased the number of aimed shots which could be fired while passing Spanish ships in broadside *line astern*. Also, English guns could be reloaded and wheeled back into firing position much faster than their Spanish counterparts, an advantage increased by use of blocks-and-tackle which halted full recoil and facilitated rapid return of the gun to the port. In contrast, the Spanish lashed their big guns to the hull and needed a huge crew to manhandle each gun back into position after every shot. Finally, the English truck carriages were smaller and lacked the long tail of the Spanish carriages. This allowed easier handling, and reduced weight and the size of each gun crew. In combination, modern estimates are that the English enjoyed a 3:1 rate of fire advantage. See also *"crouching tiger"*; *galloper gun*; *pots des fer*; *trunnion*.

gun-deck. Whichever deck of a warship supported the main battery of the heaviest guns. In a multi-decked *ship-of-the-line*, this was always the lowest deck. See also *gun port*.

gun metal. Bronze or brass or sometimes iron, but of sufficient strength to cast large gun barrels capable of containing the explosive forces produced by *corned gunpowder*. See also *ship-smashers*.

gunner. On land, a skilled artillery man. At sea, an assistant to the *master gunner* on a warship. Alternately, any infantryman sporting a firearm, of any type.

Gunner's Mark. See *gunner's rule*.

gunner's quadrant. A right-angled instrument held in the mouth of a gun as it was raised, until a plumb line showed the correct muzzle elevation for the estimated range to target. It may have been invented by *Niccolò Tartaglia*.

gunner's rule. Invented in England in the early 17th century, this slide rule aided gunners in finding the proper range, weight of shot, and size of charge. The 1146 mark on the rule became generally known as the "Gunner's Mark."

gunnery. See *artillery*; *broadside*; *fortification*; *galley*; *gun carriages*; *gunner's quadrant*; *gunner's rule*; *linstock*; *mattross*; *powder scoop*; *quick match*; *ramming*; *shot*; *siege warfare*; *sling*; *sponge*; *stiletto*; *Tartaglia, Niccolò*; *teamsters*; *trunnion*; *worm*; *wounds*.

gun port. A small door cut in the side of a ship to permit firing of cannon closer to the waterline of an enemy vessel. Initially, guns were mounted in *castles*. As cannon grew heavier they were shifted to the main deck and fired over the bulwarks. At the start of the 16th century (by convention, 1501) cutting gun ports in the hull was introduced to allow a ship to carry many more and bigger guns by better distributing their weight. The heaviest guns always went on the lowest deck in the ship. This made round ships more seaworthy as well as more stable gun platforms. See also *galley*; *junk*; *port piece*.

gunpowder empires. The rise of large Muslim empires in the 14th century (*Mughal*, *Ottoman*, and *Safavid*) was attributed by historians Marshal Hodgson and William H. McNeill to military adaptation to gunpowder. Just as in Europe, they said, new artillery and infantry formations helped rulers expand and control vast domains that hitherto had seen only cavalry armies and *feudal* politics and military systems. Other historians pointed to the *Ming* and *Manchu* empires in China and Inner Asia as further examples; or Japan during the *Unification Wars* and under the *Tokugawa shoguns*; or to *Muscovy*'s expansion into Central Asia and Siberia. At sea, they noted the Portuguese empire and, greatest of all in terms of global girth and influence, the Spanish Empire. Some historians objected that the term was misleading in its identification of technology as the principal determinant of such vast historical outcomes. For one thing, as late as the mid-17th century the effective range of field artillery was only about 300 meters, and it took weeks to prepare trenches and cover and move heavy siege guns into position. Given constraints of transportation and logistics and the shortness of campaign seasons, critics argued, guns did not provide a sufficiently decisive strategic advantage to supply an explanation for all the military and political success of the major 14th–17th century empires. See also *gunpowder weapons*; *technology and war*.

gunpowder revolution. See *artillery*; *cavalry*; *fortification*; *gunpowder weapons*; *infantry*; *revolution in military affairs*; *technology and war*; *war at sea*.

gunpowder weapons. Gunpowder—an admixture of charcoal, saltpeter, and sulphur—was first fabricated by the Chinese, possibly as early as the 9th century C.E. The first known written instructions on how to compose gunpowder date to a Chinese book on war from the mid-11th century, the *Wujing zongyao* (1044), though its recipe would produce only an incendiary, not an explosive. The Chinese used early gunpowder in public festivals but also—and contrary to widespread belief—extensively in warfare. In addition to noisemakers to frighten less civilized and more superstitious invaders from Inner Asia, the Chinese built hand-thrown bombs, mines, rockets, *fire-lances*, and primitive flamethrowers, graphic representations of which survive from the 9th century. The best available evidence confirms that, contrary to what was long thought, the Chinese also invented the first guns (defined as projectile weapons using chemical combustion to produce explosive propellant gases inside metal tubes). By the late 12th to early 13th centuries Chinese engineers were designing small cannon, some sculpted to appear as fire-breathing dragons. The technology spread from China, though the exact routes and time lines are not clear. Perhaps travelers brought gunpowder and

> *The Chinese used early gunpowder in public festivals but also . . . extensively in warfare.*

early firearms along the Silk Road to India, the Middle East, and Europe. Or maybe gunpowder made the journey in saddle pouches of swift Mongol war ponies. In either case, there is linguistic evidence of Chinese origins of the technology: in Damascus, Arabs called the saltpeter used in making gunpowder "Chinese snow," while in Iran it was called "Chinese salt." Whatever the migratory route of the technology, the remarkable fact is that within just 20 years of the first definitive record of gunpowder weapons in Italy they appeared in every major European country. Manufacture of gunpowder soon became a matter of high importance, demanding government attention and regulation. Saltpeter production from animal manure became a major industry in England, where it was also extracted from human feces and urine collected daily from the doorsteps of the residents of London.

Early Gunpowder

Gunpowder made a huge impression on the leading minds of the day in science and religion in Europe. Roger Bacon (1214–1294) learned of "black powder," experimented with it and secretly recorded the results in his notes in 1267. The Catholic Church remained deeply suspicious and far too quickly decided that gunpowder (called "serpentine" in apparent reference to Satan) made daemon fire and thus must be daemons' work. The Church declared its use in war anathema. Although the ban failed the sentiment lingered. Ben Jonson, war veteran turned playwright, expressed a widely held view about the daemonic genesis of artillery when he wrote: "From the Devil's arse did guns beget." The Puritan poet, John Milton, veteran of the *English Civil Wars* (1639–1651), likewise put guns in the hands of Satan's minions in *Paradise Lost* (1667). Such judgments were ignored on the battlefield in part because

365

the influence of the Church and religious restraint on war in the West was waning, but more because gunpowder promised military advantages that could not be neglected by kings or the warrior classes. Thus, while the gun was invented in China it was perfected in Europe. From there the technology migrated in the reverse direction, spreading directly or indirectly from Europe into the Muslim lands to displace older Asian designs. It reached the Turks, Tartars, Iran, and penetrated northern India no later than the 15th century. Improved, European-style guns were imported to China in the early 16th century, others were taken from the Portuguese in 1521 after a sharp firefight. The return of guns to China in improved models, and with more powerful black powder, closed the circle of global technology migration and diffusion. There were two important exceptions to this pattern: Koreans obtained firearms directly from China in the 14th century while Japan acquired guns from European traders only in the mid-16th century. Thereafter, Europe, the Ottoman Empire, China, and Japan (briefly, to 1615) were the principal regions producing guns of all types.

Gunpowder was refined and became more reliable as a result of numerous experimenters adjusting the proportions of its three ingredients to improve its projectile force (modern gunpowder is normally 75 percent saltpeter, 15 percent charcoal, or carbon, and 10 percent sulphur). Then it was married to advances in metallurgy and ballistic science to form weapons capable of hurling heavy stone balls at increasing range and great destructive impact, although accuracy considerably lagged other properties. The first painted record of handguns in Europe dates to Italy in 1340. The first written reference to firearms, "guns with handles" ("gunnis cum telar"), dates to c.1350. The middle of the 14th century, therefore, is a reasonable marker for the advent of handheld personal firearms in Europe. The first documented use of guns in Poland was 1383, but it was another century before Polish troops used gunpowder weapons extensively. Muscovite troops used guns by 1380, but not effectively until 1481. Hereditary warrior classes were slow to take up guns, which caught on more quickly among mercenaries and rebels: the Swiss first used handguns at *Sempach* (1386) and as early as 1419 the *Hussites* of Bohemia poked guns out firing-slits in their heavy war-wagons (*tabor*) and brought leaden death to Austrian and Imperial troops who charged them with pikes and swords. Yet, some aristocrats were more far-sighted than others. Already by 1411, John the Good, Duke of Burgundy, had a store of some 4,000 infantry firearms and within 40 years Royal French armies were using cannon and arquebuses to destroy English garrisons and even field armies in the last battles of the *Hundred Years' War* (1337–1453).

Gunpowder was expensive, dangerous to use, and easily affected by adverse weather. Gusts of wind might carry sparks from a slow match or wick—which needed to remain lighted at all times—into exposed powder pans or worse, sacks or kegs. Alternately, rain and humidity dampened powder, rendering it unusable. On the road to battle coarse grains of early gunpowder separated as a result of hard jogging in pouches or unsprung wagons. Heavy saltpeter settled to the bottom, sulfur sought the middle, while the light carbon rose to the top. This meant gunpowder had to be remixed before use, which reduced its potency if not done right. Unready powder might leave guns and cannon useless just when they were most needed, as when a column stumbled into the enemy on the march or tripped an ambush. Social inertia, superstition, technological unfamiliarity, and the superiority of nonchemical missile weapons also ensured that guns did not instantly dominate battle. Older arms and armaments, from armored knights with lances and swords, to arrays of crossbowmen or longbows, to squares of pikemen—retained real utility and killing power for over 200 years after the first guns appeared. A major battle was not arguably decided by guns until *Cerignola* in 1503. And it was not until *Marignano* in 1515 that *Swiss squares*, dominant for 200 years, were decisively broken by pistol wielding cavalry and still more, by point-blank cannonades into their ranks. It was at Marignano that gunpowder weapon superiority was finally proven, and even then it was a close-run thing with guts as much as guns deciding the issue. After Marignano older weapons systems survived on the battlefield for many decades. This is best explained by cultural rather than technological factors: the old ways were still favored by the conservative warrior nobility whose exceptional status on and off the field of battle was threatened by the leveling power of musketry. A slower, but comparable, pattern of incremental penetration of older military cultures by gunpowder weapons was repeated in the Middle East, Central Asia, India, China, and Africa, but not Japan, where adoption and adaptation was remarkably rapid and the battlefield results were spectacular.

Social Consequences

Guns shook the social dominance of all warrior classes who ruled from armored equine perches supported by land-for-service feudal military systems. Along with killing large numbers of knights in battle, gunpowder weapons knocked down their castellan strongholds. Armed with ever larger artillery pieces, kings and emperors battered down provincial castles of rebellious, or just defiant, vassals. Once internal enemies fell to their knees before the throne, or were sent sprawling into graves, powerful kings enlarged the royal domain. Guns played a crucial role in this process: nearly everywhere, except in the great sand deserts or on the vast Eurasian steppe where cavalry still moved like ships on the sea, guns facilitated and accelerated the demise of older warrior classes from positions of social privilege. Everywhere, power increasingly concentrated at the center. Guns rendered obsolete and anachronistic military horse cultures of lance and sword by eliminating the need to spend a lifetime acquiring equestrian warrior skills. They eroded the *servitium debitum* by throwing up large numbers of militia or professional infantry who were quickly trainable and reasonably lethal. In sum, guns did not require the skills, weapons, or tactics of established warrior classes and thus undermined entrenched privilege. The dehorsed old aristocracies were bound to royal service as officers of the crown, no longer proud and independent warlords. Or they were emasculated entirely, turned into silken fops desperate to join feckless court societies like the Order of the Garter or the Golden Fleece.

The transition to the new era of socially leveling weapons actually took centuries to complete, proceeded at variable rates in different lands, and began not with guns but with the even earlier "infantry revolution" of massed archers and dismounted men-at-arms. And it should be recalled that aristocratic officers, along with their peculiar values and habits, noble-only military units, and elitist military preferences and prejudices, survived on the battlefield throughout the 16th–17th centuries in Europe, and even into the 19th century in some cases. The cluttered pace of this transition is recorded in diaries, letters, and eyewitness accounts, in etchings and battle paintings. A particularly dramatic painting of *Henri IV* at *Arques* (September 21, 1589) captures this well. It shows Henri and veteran Huguenot fighters wearing leather and cloth and wielding pistols and swords. Arrayed against them are Catholic noble cavalry in full armor and armed with lances. In the background wave groves of pikes upheld by the new style of infantry, supported by musketeers. In the distance stands an undefended castle, toward which all combatants appear utterly indifferent. It is worth noting that this extraordinary painting was composed to represent a battle fought at least 200 years into the "Age of Gunpowder" in Europe. And yet, it remains true that in time the new weaponry overthrew the old moral order as surely as it made for drastic social and political change. The early modern worldview displaced the medieval as it became ever more clear to men that God did not decide the outcome of battles, not even those fought in his name. Only raw military power and skilled generalship did that. God was not yet dead for kings and warriors, but *Machiavelli* and the artilleryman stood pointing to his gaping tomb.

Gunpowder and the State

Gunpowder weapons gave all older, settled societies an enhanced ability to fend off invasion by powerful nomad nations still organized mainly to raid and make war. Gunpowder thus contributed to the final victory of Russians, Iranians, and Ottomans—all descendants of earlier invading armies—over the age-old scourge of those countries: invasion by fierce warrior peoples chased out of Central Asia by even fiercer peoples behind them. These long-settled and advanced areas now expanded into previously unreachable lands, subduing or exterminating nomads as opportunity or policy suggested. Only in this sense, rather than from technological determinism, can it be fairly said that "gunpowder empires" emerged, including the French, Russian, Ottoman, and Mughal (and later, American), while other states succumbed because they were unable to make the wrenching social adaptations necessary to incorporate guns into their military culture. The *Mamlūks* of Egypt, for instance, were overly wedded to a centuries-old but too rigid slave-recruitment and cavalry system which led them to disdain firearms. They fell under Ottoman control not just because they were defeated by the firearms corps of the *Janissaries*, but because of the larger resource base of the Ottoman Empire that could sustain a protracted war of attrition they could not. In sub-Saharan Africa firearms shifted the balance from medieval cavalry and slaving empires based in the savannah to rising and expanding states of previously subservient coastal and forest peoples but who had first come into contact with European traders. Thus, *Songhay* relied far too long on armored cavalry while the military balance shifted to coastal infantry bearing muskets bought from Portuguese, Dutch, and English traders. Songhay was itself overrun in 1591 by Moroccan gunmen known from their weapons as the *arma*, or "gunmen." In Japan gunpowder weapons arrived (1543) in the middle of the ongoing chaos of *Sengoku jidai* warfare among dozens of feudal warlords (*daimyo*). Unquestionably, guns helped *Oda Nobunaga*, *Toyotomi Hideyoshi*, and *Tokugawa Ieyasu* conquer the daimyo and centralize power in Japan during the final decades of the *Unification Wars*. The *Battle of Nagashino* (1575), for instance, witnessed radical military change as mounted Takeda samurai were destroyed by *volley fire* from 3,000 of Nobunaga's musketeers.

In Western Europe topography and local history combined to produce a uniquely decentralized state system by the 17th century, as feudalism was progressively replaced by *new monarchies*. In this process, gunpowder artillery was used to smash baronial opposition—because it brought down castle keeps, towers, and walls that in some cases had withstood catapult and trebuchet assaults for centuries. Adjustments were made by defenders, of course, such as building lower walls and earthen breastworks that better absorbed high impact shot. Still, the balance swung irrevocably in favor of kings since only they could afford the powerful new weapons and expensive professionals who operated them. With this literally elemental force the barony was harried from power and position. Instead of a unitary gunpowder empire, gunpowder kingdoms arose in Europe that asserted independence from the old idea of a single *res publica Christiana*. That ideal had been marked by a medieval muddle of overlapping vassalage, and always was nearer in fact to anarchy than to God. The hard reality of the European balance of power replaced it.

The late medieval *revolution in military affairs* stimulated a frantic search by everyone—princes of the blood and the Church, free cities, duchies and baronies, petty kingdoms, great lords from ancient houses, and Holy Roman Emperors—for short-term military advantage against all the other rapacious cities, states, armed popes, and rising kingdoms. This gave European military and political culture a deeply pragmatic, empirical, and competitive impulse and edge over more staid military cultures. An extraordinary military dynamism was revealed in France and England during the final phase of the Hundred Years' War, again and more clearly among the city-states of the *Italian Renaissance*, and in Germany during the wars of the *Protestant Reformation*. The wars of religion masked more basic military and cultural changes that soon spilled out of Europe into naval campaigns conducted thousands of miles away, stimulating and shaping world exploration and commerce. Such martial and commercial vigor was not enjoyed—or perhaps suffered—by more rigid, hierarchical, and intellectually conservative societies in China, India, and the Americas. After 1500, European militaries slowly pulled away from all others, until by 1700 even smaller European powers had sophisticated and advanced military systems and cultures. Europe was armed to the teeth by

1700, and on its way to eventual global military, political, and economic dominion though overseas conquest and colonial settlement.

These processes were most advanced where the "gunpowder revolution" went to sea, where it mated with advances in oceanic navigation to develop rich trade routes that spurred merchants to arm and rulers to pay for permanent national navies. Europe's navies were far more potent than its armies, relative to non-European military systems. They launched massive ships sporting hundreds of cannon that served as mobile artillery platforms the like of which the world had never seen, and wondered at. Navies gave Europe's monarchs (and one republic, the United Provinces) the ability to project military power and national cultures hundreds and even thousands of miles away. Meanwhile, the obsolete navies of Africa, Arabia, Egypt, India, and Southeast Asia were swept out of their home waters and barred from oceanic trade. By 1650 the only threat to a European-built and -crewed *man-of-war* on the high seas was another man-of-war built and crewed by other Europeans.

> *They launched massive ships sporting hundreds of cannon that served as mobile artillery platforms ...*

One sea power after another—Portugal, Spain, the Netherlands, France, and England—rose to global dominance starting in the 15th century, a pattern of naval dominance not broken until the 20th century when two non-European powers, Japan and the United States, challenged Europe's naval supremacy. See also *carreaux*; *Constantinople, Siege of*; *corning/corned gunpowder*; *garrots*; *hoop-and-stave method*; *mining*.

Suggested Reading: Brenda Buchanan, *Gunpowder: The History of an International Technology* (1996); J. Guilmartin, *Gunpowder and Galleys* (1974; 2003); Robert Held, *The Age of Firearms* (1967; 1970); Marshall Hodgson, *The Gunpowder Empires and Modern Times* (1974).

gun tackle. Blocks and tackle used to move or restrain a *gun carriage* aboard ship.

Gur states. Five slave-raiding and heavily militarized West African states of the 14th–15th centuries, located in the "middle belt" between savannah and the forested south of the great bend of the Niger: Dagomba, Fada N'Gurma, Mamprussi, Wagadugu, and Yatenga.

Gustavus I (1496–1560). Also known as Gustav I, Gustav Vasa. King of Sweden. During patriotic disturbances over Sweden's ties to Denmark, Gustavus was taken hostage in 1518. A year later he escaped to Lübeck. He wandered as an outlaw with a price on his head, doing menial work to stay alive while failing to rouse his fellow Swedes to revolt. After the "bloodbath of Stockholm" (1520) many Swedes finally joined him. He led an army that took Stockholm in 1523, broke the *Kalmar Union* with Denmark and Norway, and drove Danish forces out of the country. That same year Gustavus was elected king. Domestically, he allied with the merchants and lesser gentry against the entrenched power of the great nobility and the Catholic Church. He attempted extensive centralizing reforms but met stiff resistance within the ranks even of his noble supporters in the provincial Estates, and among peasants. His most significant reform was establishment of Lutheranism. His main accomplishment was to give Sweden several decades of peace, guaranteed by a full treasury. He also left Sweden a modernized army for when war later broke out with Poland.

Gustavus II Adolphus (1594–1632). "Lion of Midnight" (that is, of the North). Also known as Gustav II and Gustav Adolph. King of Sweden, military reformer, statesman, and greatest general of the *Thirty Years' War* (1618–1648). Gustavus was crowned at age 17 when his father, *Karl IX*, died prematurely in the midst of the bitter *War of Kalmar* with Denmark. Gustavus immediately proved a brilliant organizer, innovator, and diplomat. Later, he would prove an even more able battlefield commander: Napoleon actually compared him to Alexander. For the first 10 years of his reign he was preoccupied with consolidating Sweden's territory against Danish and Polish encroachment. He negotiated a peace with Denmark that permitted Swedish goods and copper, largely carried on Dutch ships, to pass through the *Baltic Sound*, in exchange for payment of a burdensome indemnity. He ended Sweden's wars with Poland and Muscovy temporarily so that he could modernize Sweden internally and militarily, largely on the Dutch model. He compromised with the Swedish nobility, agreeing to a constitutional Charter that promised to uphold Lutheranism as the state religion. He did all this in order to clear the way for Sweden's rise as a Great Power in the north, but also because he was a sincere Lutheran: he led troops in singing hymns as they marched to war, ordered prayers twice daily by the whole army, and assigned pastors to every regiment. This blend of prayer and black powder made the Swedish army feared and respected. It also gave Swedish troops unusual discipline and character on the battlefield.

Key to Gustavus' political success was his thoroughgoing reform of the Swedish military. He professionalized the army, changing it from a semi-feudal levy whose formations consisted of ill-trained peasants recruited locally to a national force of well-trained regulars secured through conscription. He emphasized *drill, military discipline*, and *volley fire* by regiments freed from the old formation of infantry squares and reorganized instead into flexible linear formations. Most of these changes had been advanced already by *Maurits of Nassau*. Gustavus took the best Dutch innovations out of the waterlogged and canalized environment of the Netherlands to maximize their revolutionary battlefield potential on the broad plains of Poland and Russia. This made the Swedish Army one of the first and the finest *standing armies* of the era. This well-drilled and disciplined army, infused with a conjoined spirit of martial patriotism and fervent Protestantism, was uniquely able to shift from offense to defense with a speed and efficiency unmatched by any other army in

Europe, or the world. Gustavus then elevated Sweden to the first rank of powers by taking his new model army, strategic vision, and advanced and well-drilled tactics to Germany, where he decisively intervened in the "Great War" of the 17th century.

Artillery

Gustavus understood the role of *shock* in combat and sought to maximize it by hauling genuine field artillery to the field of battle to support his infantry while it maneuvered, and in firefights, rather than having the big guns follow in a cumbersome siege train to be deployed mainly against fortifications or solely in static position in battle. This achievement of massed, mobile cannon fire was made possible by long experimentation with shortening and thinning the extremely heavy barrels of the cumbersome *Murbräcker* cannon that then dominated Swedish (and German) service. This reduced weight, cut back the number of horses or oxen (and fodder) required to move the guns, and thus greatly improved their mobility. While Gustavus' experiment with "*leather guns*" failed, he produced 4-pounder iron cannon that could be towed from place to place according to the dictates of battle. In 1629 he ordered a series of small caliber, short-range pieces cast. They were pulled by a pair of horses using a two-wheeled *gun carriage* and hence were capable of off-road maneuvers. Some pieces were so small (1½- and 3-pounders, sometimes called "regiment guns" or "regementsstycke"), they could be towed by a single horse or manhandled by a crew of two or three men. Several of these small cannon achieved rates of fire that exceeded the best rates of musketeers.

Swedish light pieces were supported by heavies, which Gustavus standardized at 6-, 12-, and 24-pound calibers. The heavy cannon traveled with the siege train, each piece hauled by large teams of draught animals, or he moved them by barge, marching the army alongside the guns along riverine routes. The light pieces always traveled ahead, along with his infantry and cavalry for quick deployment. Gustavus also refined and standardized gunpowder charges for each caliber of gun. Bagged powder in pre-measured cartridges improved rates of fire and increased accuracy. His main tactical innovation was to reorganize the heavies into batteries to concentrate fire at selected targets. This was a highly effective and then still novel battle tactic. His light pieces were deployed in front of his infantry lines to provide harassing fire. In sum, changes in size and weight and standardization of caliber and ammunition permitted Gustavus to deploy the first true field artillery of the gunpowder era. In the view of some historians, this feat represented nothing short of a *military revolution*. If it did, that was not universally recognized by contemporaries: after his death even the Swedish Army sometimes reverted to using larger guns that were best suited to the siege operations that dominated mid-17th-century war in Europe. It was not until the innovations of Frederick the Great, who studied and appreciated the Swedish example of the previous century, along with more frequent battles of encounter in the mid-18th century, that field artillery became standard in all modern armies.

Infantry and Cavalry

Gustavus reformed the infantry by increasing the proportion of musketeers to pikemen to two-to-one (with variations), so that more men in each formation were able to bring fire to bear on the enemy, giving each brigade—the main Swedish formation—greater punching power. He adopted *wheel lock* muskets that were smaller and lighter than the Spanish *matchlock* and did not require a forked rest, which made his musketeers more mobile. He shortened the pike to just 11 feet, making his pikemen just as light and maneuverable as the musketeers they protected and drilled with. Brigades were divided into three "squadrons" of about 500 men each. More importantly, Gustavus reduced the ranks to six, so that interior and back ranks had clear fields of fire (after firing, the front ranks knelt), while at any given moment a brigade was confident that half its men (three back ranks) stood ready to repel an attack with muskets loaded. Gustavus developed new divisional tactics to overcome the solid and less mobile Spanish *tercios*. He shifted from dense infantry squares to linear formation, wherein three or four brigades formed a flexible, articulated and extended battle line. The thinner ranks of his line infantry gave the Swedish Army a tactical maneuverability denied to heavy squares. Gustavus placed his smaller iron cannon before the infantry, adding to firepower in attack or defense. When flanked, Swedish infantry quickly articulated their line to bring musket volleys and light ($1\frac{1}{2}$-pounder) field artillery to bear on their tormentors. The cavalry was deployed more traditionally on the wings of the infantry, from where they might attack the enemy's cavalry and exploit exposed enemy flanks or rear. But the weight of a Swedish attack came from the infantry. The mobile field guns raked the enemy square or line with *canister*, punching bloody gaps in the ranks. Then the infantry closed to about 40 yards to maximize the effect of their musket volleys. After firing two or three salvoes, at most, the front ranks charged with pikes level and muskets reversed and used as clubs. Through all this, the back three ranks stood ready to exploit a breakthrough or pivot to defend the brigade's flanks, or to counterattack if arrayed in defense.

Gustavus modeled his cavalry on the superb Polish horse that was still dominant in East European warfare but largely unknown in Western Europe. He stripped armor from men and mounts and replaced the wheel lock pistol, used to such little effect in the *caracole*, with the saber. Horses were retrained to trot and gallop rather than cantor toward the enemy. In sum, as Michael Roberts has shown, Gustavus returned to cavalry shock and speed in place of firepower. This took advantage of a widely noted Swedish military ferocity and ability to pursue a defeated enemy, whereas other cavalry deployed in overly dainty and largely ineffectual columns to perform the caracole. In battle, the first obligation of Swedish horse was to block enemy cavalry from taking offensive action, and secondly to exploit gaps or exposed flanks or other opportunities created by the superior firepower of the Swedish infantry and artillery. In strategy and tactics Gustavus stressed preparation, deliberation, and an offensive spirit that sought always to carry war to the enemy. He was among the first to employ recognizably modern techniques of combined arms by coordinating attacks by mutually supporting infantry, artillery, and cavalry units. Similarly, he pioneered fire and movement, and reverted to and restored the ancient principle of concentration of force at a chosen point of local superiority on the field of battle. The changes Gustavus wrought stunned more staid and conservative enemies and set their armies and generals reeling. These reforms took many years to implement, however, even in the Swedish Army: more recent research than Roberts' has shown that Swedish cavalry never entirely abandoned the caracole before the 1680s.

At War

While Gustavus honed the Swedish military and replaced its old guard of senior officers with new professional officers he personally trained and promoted, he relied more on diplomacy than battle to consolidate and protect his northern realm. He thus recovered Sweden's Baltic provinces by appeasing Denmark with a huge indemnity that ended the Kalmar War in 1613. In a sharp war with more backward Muscovy, he added parts of Finland (1617) to the Swedish empire, and he continued to fend off Polish territorial and dynastic claims on Sweden. His power rested solidly on his successful reform of the bureaucracy, the education system, and a national military. Since Sweden was a poor and sparsely populated country he went to war to enrich it with new lands. Like all commanders of his era, he sought to "make war pay for war" by battening and billeting his army on other people's estates and cities. He briefly made peace with Poland in 1620, only to regroup the next year and capture Riga in the first real use of his reformed army. By 1626 he added most of Latvia to the Swedish empire. Next, he campaigned to take Royal Prussia, driving amorphous Polish forces before him. He won in the forest at Wallhof (January 17, 1626) in a surprise dawn attack on an ill-sited camp. At Mewe (September 22–October 1, 1626), Swedish infantry firing volleys with heavy "Dutch muskets" overmatched Polish infantry armed with arquebuses. Shooting from behind field fortifications, they devastated Polish hussars, taking a measure of revenge for the slaughter at *Kirkholm* (September 27, 1605). In 1627, Gustavus attacked *Danzig*. At *Dirshau* (August 17–18, 1627) he was seriously wounded in the neck but won the battle. This was one of many occasions where he led bravely but recklessly from the front, and not the last: he was nearly killed or captured, as well as badly beaten, at *Stuhm* (June 17/27, 1629). As Gustavus withdrew to prepare defenses, Cardinal Richelieu arranged the *Truce of Altmark* with *Sigismund III*, who finally renounced his claim to the Swedish throne. That freed Gustavus to enter the *Thirty Years' War*.

The Imperial defeat and humiliation of *Christian IV* in 1629 ended the Danish phase of the German war and opened to door to Swedish intervention.

> ...*he sought to "make war pay for war" by battening and billeting his army on other people's estates and cities.*

Geopolitics, piety, princely ambition, fear of Habsburg domination of the Baltic, and long-standing Swedish ambition to control the mouths of major Baltic rivers and the Baltic trade combined to shape Gustavus' fateful decision to intervene. Yet, he would not move until assured of rich financing from the deep coffers of France. Despite that alliance with Catholic power, Gustavus was received by ordinary Protestants as the great, indeed prophesied, champion of the Reformed Faith come to rescue the cause at the apex of Catholic-Habsburg triumph. He was widely seen as nothing short of a Protestant Joshua marching at the head of an "Army of God." Singing Lutheran hymns on the march only reinforced this popular image. Protestant princes were not nearly so enthusiastic: Saxony and Brandenburg alike refused his initial entreaties to form an alliance of northern powers. As a result, Gustavus landed at Peenemünde, on Usedom, in July 1630, with just 14,000 men. He brought with him 80 field pieces along with larger siege guns. The ratio of nearly 10 artillery pieces per 1,000 men in the Swedish Army compared to just one cannon per 1,000 men for the Imperials. Bogged down by the need to secure provisions for the Imperial Army, the Habsburg General Conti failed to concentrate against Gustavus at this, his most vulnerable moment. Yet, supply problems—which were endemic to the age—along with Gustavus' great caution about securing a strategic base in north Germany also delayed any decisive move on the Swedish side.

Instead, Gustavus moved slowly and in force from Straslund to Stettin in search of food and fodder. This took the Swedish Army beyond Pomerania which had already been eaten out by prior invasions and other armies. As he moved along the major river routes, Gustavus subjugated and garrisoned the largest towns, securing lines of supply and building a buffer between Sweden and its enemies in Poland and the Habsburg lands. Then he settled down for the winter months, during which he recruited and trained tens of thousands of Germans and other mercenaries in the Swedish way of war. This grew combat strength but exacerbated logistical problems and so forced him onto the road with the spring thaw of 1631. Gustavus marched into Brandenburg to expand his base and force the Elector to join the war. Insofar as he took a strategic direction it was south to capture the fortress at Küstrin, then west to Berlin to take Spandau. This move secured the confluences of the major navigable rivers in north Germany, which Gustavus needed to move his heavy artillery closer to the Habsburg heartland and bring in follow-on supplies. While he was thus engaged *Magdeburg* fell to *Johann Tilly* and was sacked, before the Imperial siege could be relieved by Gustavus, who was unable to move his artillery or army without negotiating with Elector Georg Wilhelm for unimpeded access down the riverine routes of north-central Germany. Gustavus belatedly engaged Tilly at *Werben* (July 22–28, 1631), inflicting a hard and punitive defeat on the Catholic army.

At the peak of his power Gustavus commanded a coalition army that exceeded 100,000 men and was supported by river barge supply lines drawing resources from half of Germany. By 1632 this host was no longer made up of disciplined Swedish conscripts but of largely non-Swedish mercenaries, including 10,000 Scots. It was reinforced by several untrustworthy Saxon regiments supplied by a most reluctant ally he essentially forced into the war. With this polyglot force he won at *First Breitenfeld* (September 17, 1631) over the combined Imperial Army and the army of the *Catholic League*, led by Tilly. The defeat scattered Habsburg and Catholic forces. Once again, logistical problems slowed Gustavus so that he was unable to pursue the Imperials or the advantage won in battle. In the autumn of 1631 he moved farther south, to Erfurt, thence west to winter in Frankfurt. For the 1632 campaign he hoped to raise a force of 200,000 men with which to invade the Habsburg heartland from multiple directions, coordinating attacks by five armies. This strategic ambition was admirable, but also technically and logistically impossible in his day (war on such a scale would not be achieved until Ulysses S. Grant managed multiple invasions of the Confederacy using railways and the telegraph in 1864). Nor was he able to raise the forces envisioned. The lands he traversed could not sustain so large an army, and by 1632 even allies feared what the great Swede might attempt and achieve with such a force. Might not the Empire itself fall to him if he drove *Ferdinand II* from Vienna? Gustavus instead sought a decisive battle of encounter with the Imperial Army. In March 1632, he moved southeast to Nördlingen, then stormed the Bavarian fortress of Donauwörth. He again defeated the Imperials, mortally wounding Tilly, at *Rain* (April 5, 1632). That left the Catholic armies scattered and leaderless. Gustavus was free to eat out Bavaria or move on to Vienna; he chose Bavaria. He received huge *contributions* from Nuremberg and Augsburg. Even so, he was once again impelled by logistical need to keep moving his men, who ate out the country as they meandered through it following the course of the Danube.

With Tilly dead Ferdinand had no choice but to recall *Albrecht von Wallenstein*, who raised a new army of 70,000 mercenaries from his own resources which he hired to the desperate Ferdinand. Meanwhile, some Protestant cities and princes were restless as the Swedish Army moved through Germany for a second season, eating out whole regions like so many locust. They had reason to be suspicious: it was likely the Swedish king's plan to make Germany a forward base to defend his enlarged Swedish empire, to include large parts of northern Germany. Through deliberate depredations, Gustavus tried to compel Wallenstein to move into Bavaria to protect its Catholic population and towns. Instead, Wallenstein marched into Bohemia to drive out the Saxon Army. This might look to modern eyes like an effort to cut off the Swedish *lines of supply*, reinforcement, and communication, but those were minor considerations in 17th-century warfare. Instead, as Basil Liddell Hart argued, Wallenstein was employing a strategy of "indirection." By taking Leipzig and despoiling Saxony he looked to break the fragile Swedish–Saxon alliance and draw Gustavus north, away from Vienna. It worked: Gustavus swung north with 20,000 men, arriving at Nuremberg in May and moving to Naumburg in October, capturing crucial crossings over the River Halle. North of the river, near Leipzig, he caught up with Wallenstein's army of 33,000 men. The two great captains and armies fought a desperate battle at *Lützen* (November 6,

1632). Gustavus was brought low while leading a cavalry charge, shot off his horse by three musket balls: one struck his arm, a second hit him in the back, the fatal third opened his skull. The Swedes won the battle but Gustavus was dead before it ended. The Swedish warlord-king and champion of the Protestant cause was just 38 years old.

What Gustavus proved in his battles was that the old tactic of standing on the defensive behind a wall of pikes no longer assured victory. He showed that superior mobility, combined with rapid rates of musketry and field artillery, could dislodge and defeat even a numerically superior force in prepared defensive positions, such as behind the double ditch line at Lützen. This put another nail in the coffin of late-medieval-style warfare. No more was it sufficient to raise lumbering armies of pikemen protected by a few musketeers. That was the style of Tilly and Imperial tercios. Modified by the contribution system, it was also Wallenstein's before he saw the Swedes in action. After Lützen, Wallenstein and other generals and militaries imitated to the degree they were able the new Swedish way of war, emphasizing drill, professionalism, firepower, and mobility. So influential were Gustavus' reforms and reputation as a field commander that, 70 years later, Peter I of Russia, and 50 years after him, Frederick II of Prussia, emulated the great Swede's reforms in their own armies so that they, too, could ride a military tiger into the upper ranks of the Great Powers. See also *Alte Feste, Siege of*; *baggage train*; *Bärwalde, Treaty of*; *brigade*; *buff coats*; *Chodkiewicz, Jan Karol*; *engineers*; *Haiduks*; *Grotius, Hugo*; *Hague Alliance*; *military discipline*; *New Model Army*; *Oxenstierna*; *Prague, Peace of*; *uniforms*.

Suggested Reading: Nils Ahnlund, *Gustavus Adolphus the Great* (1940); Michael Roberts, *Gustavus Adolphus and the Rise of Sweden* (1973) and *Gustavus Adolphus* (1992).

Haarlem, Siege of (December 11, 1572–July 12, 1573). The *Duke of Alba* sent 30,000 Spanish and Imperial troops to take Haarlem, defended by just 4,000 militia. An initial bombardment and direct assault failed. As the Spanish dug entrenching lines the Hollanders frequently sortied, damaging the works and killing Alba's engineers. There was little mercy on either side: the Dutch hanged Spanish prisoners in full view of the besiegers in retaliation for sacks and massacres carried out at Mechlen, Zutphen, and Naarden. When Haarlem finally surrendered on July 12, 1573, its 1,800 surviving militia were butchered by the Spanish, along with hundreds of burghers. Haarlem's resistance did much damage to Spanish arms and prestige and gave the rebellion time to take root in other towns.

habergeon. A small mail coat. It was lighter, shorter, and less expensive than a full-length *hauberk*.

Habsburgs. The great dynastic house founded by Albert in Swabia in 1153, which expanded as often by marriage as by war to rule large parts of Europe from 1282 to 1918, including most of Germany for four centuries, and for a time also Spain and its vast overseas empire. The original family lands were absorbed by the *Swiss Confederation*, 1386–1474. The dynasty thereafter was centered on its holdings in ducal Austria and its reign over the *Holy Roman Empire*, 1438–1740, and again, 1745–1806. The marriage of *Maximilian I* to Mary of Burgundy connected rich lands in northwest Europe with the Austrian heartland. Their son, *Charles V*, governed all Habsburg territory, including Imperial Spain from 1519 to 1556. The Habsburgs were intricately involved with the great banking house of *Fugger*, which financed their wars over many decades. Charles fought France for much of the *Italian Wars*, the Ottoman sultans intermittently, and against German princes and cities of the *Schmalkaldic League*. He was hampered in pursuit of his Imperial and Catholic causes by the fact little linked the scattered Habsburg lands except a union of crowns and his person: they shared no single army or navy, no common language or economy or currency, no uniform code of law, and after 1517 and the *Protestant Reformation*, no common faith. When he abdicated in the Empire in 1555 and in Spain in 1556, the succession was divided between his brother, *Ferdinand I*, and his son, *Philip II*, into Austrian and Spanish branches, respectively. Even divided, these remained the two great centers of Catholic power in Europe for another century. Governed by discrete branches of the House of Habsburg, they did not always cooperate closely or well as they faced a shifting coalition of German princes, France, the Ottoman Empire, and despite Habsburg championship of Catholicism, sometimes one or other of the popes (a Habsburg army sacked Rome in 1527 and another starved the Papal States into submission in 1556–1557). The compromise *Peace of Augsburg* (1555) brought confessional peace in Germany in reflection of the reality that Habsburg emperors were too weak to reimpose Catholicism on all their Protestant subjects.

Things changed in the last decades of the 16th century as the Habsburgs successfully reimposed Catholicism and imposed the *Counter-Reformation* on Austria, Carinthia, Carniola, Styria, and other core areas. In several cases Habsburg troops backed Catholic bishops in repression of Protestantism, closing parishes, burning books, and exiling reform clergy. As the *Thirty Years' War* (1618–1648) approached, the Austrian Habsburgs had already remade their core territories Catholic. Their policies thus stood as a warning to other Protestants of what might be in store should the Catholic-Habsburg powers win the German war, and the *Eighty Years' War* (1568–1648) with The Netherlands. On the other hand, the Habsburgs came close to collapse from 1606 to 1612. *Rudolf II* was by then gravely mentally unbalanced and his powers were progressively stripped from him by his brother, Matthias, though not without a threat of a Habsburg civil war over Hungary and Bohemia in 1606 and again in 1611. This weakness at the center permitted militant Catholics to gain influence at Court even as Protestant Estates forced concessions on toleration that reached their apogee in 1611. That set the stage for crisis and war once *Ferdinand II* (then Ferdinand of Styria) moved to claim the Imperial throne and fanatically advance the Counter-Reformation everywhere he could reach.

Meanwhile, Spain was led into long, losing wars with the Netherlands and England by Philip II. His reign saw both the launch of the Eighty Years' War and the despair of the *Invincible Armada*. Upon his death his son, *Philip III*, made a humiliating peace with England in 1604 and then agreed to the *Twelve Years' Truce* (1609–1621) with the Dutch. Ferdinand II and *Philip IV* took Austria and Spain, respectively, into the Thirty Years' War, which the Habsburg lost. All these Habsburg rulers were religious zealots convinced that the family had an Imperial as well as a Catholic mission. There were also chronic wars with the *Barbary States* to the south and the Ottomans to the east, including the *Thirteen Years' War* (1593–1606) in the Balkans. For those reasons and others, an anti-Habsburg coalition won the Thirty Years' War while the Dutch won the Eighty Years' War, both outcomes codified at *Westphalia* in 1648. Spain then bowed to a final defeat by France in 1559 from which it never recovered.

The Habsburg drive for dominance was never an effort to achieve *monarchia universalis*, despite that charge leveled by their enemies (and some historians). Habsburg policy was limited to seeking hegemony within an emerging system of independent powers. Even so, it was an ambitious failure. Principally, this was due to the balance of power which arrayed most of Europe and the Ottomans against the Habsburgs. The rise of new Atlantic economies in the Netherlands, France, and England lay beyond Habsburg reach and eventually gave those northern powers a far greater capacity to sustain protracted war than Austria or Spain could achieve. Misunderstanding and mismanagement of Imperial economics was severely damaging—the Spanish Habsburgs declared bankruptcy in 1557, 1575, 1596, 1607, and 1647, while debasement of the currency contributed to the "*price revolution*" of the 17th century which fatally undermined their grand strategic plans. The intervention of Sweden in the German war presented the Habsburgs with a whole new enemy which they seriously underestimated. The situation was made worse by confessional and imperial hubris such as Ferdinand II's stripping princes of lands and titles by fiat and his confessional overreach in the *Edict of Restitution*. The limits to Habsburg power in Central Europe were set by 1630. After that, the Habsburgs fought more to retain what they held than to add to their German estates. Finally, the revival of France after 1600 under the fiercely anti-Habsburg *Henri IV*, and later the brilliant anti-Habsburg diplomacy of *Cardinal Richelieu*, confirmed that not even the combined populations and resources of Austria and Spain could overmatch the new balance of power in Europe. These powerful facts were compounded by Habsburg failure to match any of their major enemies in war at sea, where the Dutch, English, and French all surpassed Habsburg naval power by the mid-17th century. All that occurred as a *revolution in military affairs* dramatically raised the costs and expanded the scale of war, which the new urban and market economies of the north could sustain but the conservative dynasts and rural economies ruled by Madrid and Vienna did not understand and could not emulate. See also *German Peasant War*.

Suggested Reading: R. W. Evans, *The Making of the Habsburg Monarchy* (1979); R. Kann, *The History of the Habsburg Empire, 1526–1918* (1974); V. S. Matmatey, *The Rise of the Habsburg Empire, 1526–1815* (1978); Robin Okey, *The Habsburg Monarchy* (2000); A.J.P. Taylor, *The Habsburg Monarchy* (1948); Andrew Wheatcroft, *The Habsburgs* (1996).

hackbut. "hook gun." Also aquebute, hackbush, hakenbüsche, haquebut, harqbute. A handheld *culverin* usually operated by two men, though smaller versions could be fired by one man. The "hook" was a small metal pin at the base of the front of the barrel that allowed the gunman to rest the barrel on a battlement or atop a *pavise* to prevent recoil. This did not so much improve aim as lend support in place of a bipod or tripod rest.

hackbutters. An English corruption of "harquebusiers" used in reference to mounted gunmen (more dragoons than cavalry) armed with *arquebuses*. It probably did not, as it might otherwise seem, refer to infantry troopers armed with *hackbuts*, though both meanings may have been in use. Sometimes spelled and pronounced in the German manner, as "hagbutters."

hackney. A nag. A cheap horse good for packing goods or carrying a retainer or mounted infantryman. Not a true *warhorse*.

hagbutters. See *hackbutters*.

Hague Alliance (December 9, 1625). In the mid-1620s *Cardinal Richelieu* was moving toward an alliance with Spain (*Treaty of Monzón*) that would permit him to finish off the Huguenot rebellion. England, Denmark, and the Netherlands were thus left without France as their main anti-Habsburg ally. They formed this truncated, all-Protestant alliance instead, opposing *Ferdinand II* and the *Catholic League* in the war in Germany. Sweden declined membership once *Gustavus Adolphus* learned of the paucity of the military contribution actually made by *Charles I* of England. Joining the allies more as a supplicant than partner was *Friedrich V*, who had already lost Bohemia and the Palatinate to Ferdinand. See also *Thirty Years' War*.

Haiduks. "Marauders." A style of infantry that originated in Hungary, but became famous in Poland where they were the core infantry from 1569 to 1633. They were nearly exclusively musketeers, although their *dziesietniks* ("tenth-men") carried staffs as well, possibly as a device to signal and time *volley fire*. They fought in standard square formations of 10×10 ranks and files (or more likely, 8×10 if one discounts the usual *dead-pays*). Unusually, these squares were not protected by pikemen. Instead, the vast Polish cavalry detached troopers to guard the infantry. That proved successful against some Western pike formations in the 16th century, but whenever the cavalry screen failed in the east Haiduks were left utterly exposed to Cossack or Tartar horsemen. In several battles with Sweden the combined arms approach taken by *Gustavus Adolphus* demonstrated the need to add pikemen to the front ranks of Haiduk infantry. Westernizing reforms that followed the clash with Sweden signaled terminal decline for the all-firearms Haiduks. They lingered as ceremonial troops into the 18th century, with the last serving as mere decorations in the palace guards of wealthy Polish nobles.

hail shot. A type of *small shot* comprised of many small pellets, akin to shot fired from a modern shotgun. So-called because it was said to fall like hail on the enemy.

Haiti. See *Hispaniola*.

Hakata (Hakozaki) Bay, Battle of (1274). In 1268 the Mongol lord Kublai Khan (1214–1294) was refused tribute by Japan. Each side marshaled forces for a coming invasion. In Japan the *samurai* made ready while commoners were inspired by the charismatic but doctrinaire prophet and reformer, *Nichiren Shonin* (1222–1282) and his *Buddhist* followers. In 1274 some 50,000 Mongols, along with forced Chinese and Korean auxiliaries, embarked on 900 *junks* and barges and crossed the Sea of Japan. After capturing Tsushima Island the invasion fleet moved to Hakata Bay on the northwestern shore of Kyushu. They seized Hakata after a fierce fight with local samurai. Mongol horse archers were highly effective against the Japanese infantry along the shore. The Mongols also employed a catapult, almost certainly captured from the more technologically advanced Chinese, that shot a primitive, exploding gunpowder shell. The combined effect of these blows drove the Japanese into prepared earthworks as night fell. To escape exposure to a great storm rising on the horizon many Mongols reboarded the invasion junks. During the night they were blown to sea by the storm, where as many as one-third of the Mongol army drowned. Korean pilots then led surviving ships back to the Asian mainland.

Hakata (Hakozaki) Bay, Battle of (1281). Kublai Khan (1214–1294) finished repressing the Southern Song in China in 1279 and began planning a second invasion of Japan. He correctly concluded that his first attempt in 1274 was not repulsed by the Japanese so much as blown away by forces of nature. He planned to return with a *Mongol* army three times the size of the one lost in 1274. In the meantime, the Hojo dynasts in Japan fortified the shoreline and harbor at Hakata Bay and built up a small, coastal navy with which the *bakufu* hoped to hinder the Mongol's impressed Korean and Chinese junks. Kublai Khan assembled two invasion fleets, the first utilizing Korean junks and pilots ("Eastern Route Army"), the other using captured Song junks ("Southern Route Army"). Over 3,000 junks and barges may have been assembled to transport 100,000 Mongols and their horses, along with tens of thousands of Korean and Chinese auxiliaries. The smaller Eastern Route Army arrived at Hakata on June 21, landing to the north of the town on a small peninsula where the Japanese had not finished the defensive wall. Local *samurai* and some peasants threw themselves into the

At night stealthy Japanese boats carried samurai into the harbor to slip aboard invasion junks …

gap, trapping the Mongols along the shore. At night stealthy Japanese boats carried samurai into the harbor to slip aboard invasion junks and kill the Mongols and Korean crews. This tactic drove the ships of the Eastern Route Army back to Tsushima. The far larger Southern Route Army arrived in mid-July. By early August the full invasion force was assembled and readied to move inland. But on August 15 a cyclone struck the coast of Japan. Over several days it battered the exposed fleet at Tsushima Island and in Hakata harbor, severely damaging or destroying most of the junks. The majority of Kublai Khan's vast army drowned. Those stranded ashore were butchered by the Japanese, who alternately slaughtered or enslaved thousands of prisoners. The Japanese later called the storm "kamikaze" ("divine wind") out of belief that the Deity had intervened to save them from the Mongol scourge.

Suggested Reading: Theodore Cook, "Mongol Invasion," *Military History Quarterly*, 11/2 (1998); Stephen Turnbull, *The Samurai: A Military History* (1977).

hakenbüsche. See *arquebus*; *hackbut*.

haketon. A hardened leather jacket reinforced with, or worn over, a mail surcoat.

halberd. An elongated axe in which an ash handle five to six feet long was tipped with a cutting blade that ended in a forward-aiming spike, with the metal head attached by metal straps to the wooden shaft or by a two-eyed socket. Later halberds added a bill, or hook, which protruded horizontally just below the forward spike. This was used to great effect in pulling armored riders off their mounts. Still later versions, made famous by the Swiss at *Sempach* (1386), trimmed or even eliminated the cutting blade, substituting two horizontal iron spikes faced in opposing directions at right angles from the shaft. This gave the weapon three lethal spikes, two of which also served as hooks. Late-14th-century halberds were also much stronger by virtue of rivets that replaced the older eye/socket attachment of blades and spikes to the shaft. In whatever form, the halberd was the favorite weapon of nearly all late medieval infantry. In China a trident-halberd was in wide use during the Ming dynasty. It had a half-yard steel blade-head fitted with a crescent-shaped crossbar attached to a haft seven to eight feet long. Variations went by such names as "gilded halberd," "dragon-beard," "ox-head," "swallow-wing," and so forth. All could be used to club an enemy or to thrust at and penetrate his armor. Defensively, the head and heavy staff were used to deflect blows. See also *Ahlspiess*; *brown bill*; *chauve-souris*; *couseque*; *gisarmes*; *glaive*; *lochaber axe*; *Mordax*; *partisan*; *rawcon*; *Swiss square*.

halberdiers. See *Appenzell Wars*; *Arbedo, Battle of*; *brown bill*; *Fähnlein*; *Giornico, Battle of*; *Grandson, Battle of*; *halberd*; *Laupen, Battle of*; *La Bicocca, Battle of*; *Marignano, Battle of*; *mercenaries*; *Morat, Battle of*; *Morgarten, Battle of*; *Näfels, Battle of*; *Nancy, Battle of*; *pike*; *Sempach, Battle of*; *St. Jacob-en-Birs, Battle of*; *Swiss square*; *uniforms*.

half-pike. A short pike, eight to nine feet in length. It was used mainly in ship-to-ship actions, especially by the Spanish.

Halidon Hill, Battle of (July 19, 1333). A late battle in the *Scottish Wars* prompted by *Edward III*'s siege of Berwick. Having adapted English tactics from lessons learned from prior defeats at Scottish hands, Edward dismounted his *men-at-arms* and split the army into three formations: heavy infantry at the center with the flanks protected by longbowmen deployed slightly forward. The Scots charged headlong and were cut down at long range by Edward's archers, then finished off by the men-at-arms who remounted to pursue when the Scots turned to flee. This tripartite deployment was Edward III's signature tactic. The *Black Prince* also used it to win several battles in the *Hundred Years' War* (1337–1453) and in Portugal. See also *Agincourt, Battle of*; *Aljubarrota, Battle of*; *Crécy, Battle of*; *Poitiers, Battle of*.

Hamburg, Treaty of (March 15, 1638). Signed reluctantly by *Oxenstierna* for Sweden and more eagerly by *Cardinal Richelieu* of France, it provided a French subsidy to the Swedish army in Germany for three years but gave France control of alliance policy. Most importantly, both parties foreswore any separate peace with the Holy Roman Empire. The treaty also called for a general settlement based on a *Normaljahr* of 1618, with "satisfaction" for France and Sweden in territory and indemnities. The treaty was extended in 1641 and lasted the duration of the war.

han. The ruler/commander of the *Tatars*.

hand cannon. See *arquebus*.

hanger. A short sword originally used in hunting that was taken to sea in the 14th–16th centuries for use in boarding actions. It was later replaced by the cutlass.

Hansa. See *Hanse*.

Hanse. "Hanseatic League." A medieval association of Baltic coastal cities from the late 12th century that dominated the Baltic end of trade with the rich Mediterranean cities and economies. They had limited defense arrangements but were capable of raising war fleets when necessary. They were more likely to employ bribes, punitive tariffs, and embargoes than arms in a conflict. Only if pushed too hard did the Hanse resort to naval blockade. Although active from the 12th century the Hanse was not formally organized until 1367, in response to a threat from Denmark to curtail the independence and privileges of Baltic merchants and towns. It eventually grew to include over 200 large towns and cities, most prominently Bremen, Brunswick, Breslau, Cologne, Cracow, Danzig, Hamburg, Lübeck, Magdeburg, Memel, Straslund, and Riga. It backed England, where it was granted special diplomatic and trade privileges, during the *Hundred Years' War* (1337–1453). By 1400 the Hanse was in decline as a result of a sharp drop in trade related to the *Black Death*, as well as military decline of the *Teutonic Knights* and *Ordensstaat*. In 1425 the Scanian herring fisheries failed, further undercutting the Hanse. Its dominance was challenged in the Baltic by the rise of Danish, Dutch, and English traders and pirates, and later also the expansion of Muscovy toward the Baltic coast, as its very success in developing the Baltic trade attracted competitors. The Hanse towns were outmatched in war with the Dutch, 1438–1441. In 1467 cities in Livonia and Prussia abandoned the Hanse, and in 1493, *Ivan III* expelled Hanse traders from Novgorod. Dutch naval and merchant fleets accelerated Hanse loss of control of the key herring trade, and it was expelled from the London Steelyard by *Elizabeth I* as she moved to consolidate English naval and commercial power. As the Hanse declined, Antwerp, then Amsterdam and London, replaced Baltic seaports as the great entrepôts and banking centers of northern Europe. See also *Drake, Francis*; *Olivares, conde-duque de*; *Straslund, Siege of*.

   Suggested Reading: P. Dollinger, *The German Hansa* (1964; 1970).

Hanseatic League. See *Hanse*.

Hara Castle, massacre of Christians at (1638). See *Japan*.

haramaki. See *armor*.

Harfleur, Battle of (1416). See *Henry V*; *Hundred Years' War*.

harness. An archaic term for *armor*, as in Shakespeare's "Blow, wind! come wrack! At least we'll die with harness on our back." *Macbeth*, act 5, verse 51.

harquebus. See *arquebus*; *hackbutters*.

Harsthörner. "Great War Horn." The Swiss used these large and resounding alpine horns for military signaling. Their low reverberations, similar to an elephant's trumpeting, carried much greater distances than high-pitched notes of brass trumpets. Harsthörner were borne into battle by the Swiss, often at the cantonal level and almost always by large Confederate formations. In a mature *Swiss square* Harsthörner players stayed close to the senior commanders, usually beside the well-guarded cantonal *Banners*. The Great Horns served two main purposes: they were used to rally troops and to signal—well beyond the normal range for shouted commands—the general advance of squares toward the enemy. A valuable side effect was that they inspired fear, and on occasion induced panic, among enemy troops. See also *Grandson, Battle of*; *Swiss Army*.

Hashemites. A line of Arabian emirs claiming direct descent from Muhammad. They served for generations as sharifs in Mecca under the Ottomans.

Hastings, Battle of (1066). See *England*; *fryd*; *Normans*.

hata jirushi. Colored streamers used in early Japanese warfare to signify positions of units of *samurai*. They were later supplemented by *nobori* and *sashimono*.

hatamoto. See *banner system (Japan)*.

hauberk. A knee-length *mail* shirt dating to the 11th century. It was slit in front and back to facilitate mounting a *destrier* or other charger, and slit at the hip to take the knight's sword. It weighed 25 or more pounds, and was made in one piece from between 25,000 and 40,000 individual rings. The hauberk was worn over a quilted undercoat such as a *gambeson* or *aketon*. So labor intensive was the production of such ring mail, a single hauberk might cost the equivalent of the annual wealth of a fair-sized village. The term was sometimes also used for later "suits" of lamellar-style plate armor. See also *habergeon*; *surcoat*.

Haudenosaunee. "Great League of Peace and Power." Called by the French the "Five Nations," this Iroquois confederacy was formed by the Cayuga, Mohawk, Oneida, Onondagas, and Senecas. They were joined by the Tuscaroras in 1714, to form the "Six Nations" that played such a key role in the wars of North America in the 18th century. See also *Indian Wars*.

Haufen. "Heap" or "company." See *Swiss square*.

haul close. On a warship or other sailing vessel, to steer as near the direction of the prevailing wind as the sails would allow and the ship would go. See also *weatherly*.

haul wind. On a warship or other sailing vessel, to change course into the prevailing wind.

Hauptmann. "Headman." A late medieval rank in a German mercenary company, equivalent to captain.

Hauptstuke. A class of *bombard* cast for the Habsburgs in their Austrian foundries.

Hausa. An agricultural people long-settled between the southern Sahara and the great rainforest of the coast of West Africa. They developed advanced manufacturing centuries prior to most of their neighbors and were renowned as early as the 13th century for leather production, dyed cloths, and vibrant markets. They were organized in a complex city-state system (comprised of Kano, Katsina, Kaduna, Gobir, Daura, and Zaria) which pre-dated the arrival of Islam. The governing class was converted to Islam during the 15th century, likely by Dyula traders and teachers from Mali. The Hausa also adopted cavalry and armor in the 15th century, on the Turkish model, and began to expand. They conducted slave raiding among tribes farther south, settling captives in slave villages which supported with forced farm labor the growing sophistication of Hausa urban life. They fended off invasion by *Songhay* in c.1515 and absorbed a mass migration from Kanem which began in the late 14th century. They were great indirect beneficiaries of the defeat of Songhay by the Moors, seeing a real expansion in their trade and power.

havoc radius. See *chevauchée*.

Hawkwood, John (d.1394). Commander of the *White Company* and *condottieri* captain of the first order. He entered Italy to sell his services as a mercenary officer in 1362. He fought against Florence initially, then against the Papal States and Holy Roman Emperor Charles IV. In 1372 he left the White Company and raised another to fight for the pope against the Visconti of Milan. When the Papal States and Milan made peace he turned his men—who were always most deeply loyal to his purse—against Florence, savaging its lands and outer villages. He returned to papal service in 1375, invading Tuscany in behalf of the pope. Florence bought him off and he entered its employ with a salary guaranteed for life, and titles and lands that made him one of the wealthiest men in Italy. Despite taking Florentine gold he fought again for the popes against Florence in the *War of the Eight Saints*. In 1377 he ordered a massacre of some 5,000 innocents at Cesena. In 1387 he made the first undisputed use of gunpowder field artillery in European warfare. He returned to Florentine service as "Captain-General." Florence's lifetime guarantee of a large salary and awards of lands and titles was designed as much to tame and control him as to reward service. Hawkwood was for two decades the most powerful and feared military man in Italy. See also *ribaudequin*.

Hawkyns, John (1532–1595). Elizabethan *sea dog*. Born into a Plymouth merchant and shipping family, Hawkyns made his fortune running cargos of slaves to the Spanish Main in 1563. This breached the Spanish trade monopoly but met the interests and enjoyed the connivance of local slave dealers and planters. Queen *Elizabeth I* joined other investors in financing his 1565 slave run to the port of Borburata. On his third voyage in 1567 he was accompanied by *Francis Drake*, whom he mentored in the ways of piracy and the sea. The voyage was dogged by trouble from the start. Hawkyns took a raiding party onshore to join a local war in Sierra Leone and to capture enough slaves to fill his holds. He later met armed resistance when he tried to dock in the Caribbean port of Rio Hatcha, but took the town and managed to sell some of his human cargo at Santa Maria. When he reached Cartagena the governor refused to deal with him, so Hawkyns bombarded the town. On September 16, 1569, he seized the port of San Juan de Ulúa, near Veracruz, Mexico. The next day a 12-ship *flota* arrived and docked alongside Hawkyns' small fleet.

> *Hawkyns made his fortune running cargoes of slaves to the Spanish Main in 1563.*

On September 23 fighting broke out and Hawkyns was chased away, losing many men and suffering great damage to his ships. Hawkyns struggled back to England with few men left alive, and no profit. This ended his active sea career: he was instead made navy treasurer in 1573. In 1595, Drake and Hawkyns sailed to plunder the Caribbean with 26 ships and 2,500 men. The two "sea dog" captains had a falling out over strategy which was only resolved by Hawkyns' death from fever on November 22, 1595.

Suggested Reading: Harry Kelsey, *Sir John Hawkins: Queen Elizabeth's Slave Trader* (2002).

heave to. On a warship or other sailing vessel, to stop moving forward by backing the sails ("drop the wind").

heavy cavalry. Cavalry wearing heavy or full armor and mounted for battle on a *destrier*. Heavy cavalry began a rise to preeminence under the Carolingian kings of France in the 8th and 9th centuries with adoption of nailed horseshoes, the stirrup, and a saddle with pommel and cantel that kept a horseman mounted and upright as he collided with an enemy. The era of heavy cavalry dominance of warfare in Europe is said by some to have dawned at Civitate (June 17, 1053) in southern Italy, where *Norman* heavy horse rode down German and Italian infantry in the service of Pope Leo IX, who was captured as a result. Some historians dispute that conclusion, arguing that Lombard infantry ran away before the fight began, leaving just 700 Germans to fight several thousand mounted Normans, a superiority in sheer numbers that renders meaningless any judgment as to which was the superior arm that day. In any case, heavy cavalry thereafter rose in importance throughout Western Europe to culminate as a full horse-and-warrior culture of *chivalry* and *knights*. By the 11th century heavy cavalry was clearly the dominant battlefield arm, though that did not mean it was always and everywhere victorious. Its primary role was *shock* using the *couched lance*. The roles of escorting land convoys, ambush, and scouting were left to *light cavalry* that supplemented heavy cavalry during the 14th century. In response to the imposing defense of a pike square, archers (and later, arquebusiers) were sent forward to harry enemy infantry and open gaps in the front ranks through which the heavy horse could charge. Heavy cavalry in the old style was made obsolete by the steel crossbow and heavy, armor-piercing *musket*, the latter from 1570 onward. Once knights discarded their armor and shifted to lighter horses the principal difference from light cavalry was that heavy cavalry still made occasional *close order* charges, whereas light horse were used nearly exclusively to scout, forage, ambush, and skirmish. Unlike European cavalry, most Chinese, Mongol, Central Asian, and Indian cavalry throughout this period was light to medium in its mounts, armor, and weapons. See also *Agincourt, Battle of*; *armor*; *arrière-ban*; *Bannockburn*; *Boroughbridge, Battle of*; *Cassel, Battle of*; *Courtrai, Battle of*; *Crécy, Battle of*; *Crusades*; *cuirassier*; *demi-lancers*; *drill*; *Falkirk, Battle of*; *Fornovo, Battle of*; *fryd*; *hussars*; *Laupen, Battle of*; *Mohács, Battle of*; *Mons-en-Pévèle, Battle of*; *Morgarten, Battle of*; *Mughal Army*; *Poitiers, Battle of*; *Roosebeke, Battle of*; *Spanish Army*; *Stirling Bridge, Battle of*; *warhorses*.

Hedgely Moor, Battle of (1464). See *Wars of the Roses*.

Heemskerk, Jacob van. See *Gibraltar, Battle of*.

Heerschild. The body of armed retainers of a German prince or abbot, comprised mainly of mounted *men-at-arms* of one or another class, of which there were at least seven.

Heerschildordnung. The "Knightly order," or ranking system, of feudal classes of German knights. At the top was the Kaiser. The lowliest rank were known as "einschildig Ritter" ("single-shielded knight") and were not permitted to sub-infeud other knights.

Heilbronn, League of. An alliance formed by *Oxenstierna* in April 1633, to secure Sweden's interests in Germany after the death of *Gustavus Adolphus*. It sought to secure Sweden to its main allies among the German princes. The tug of Imperial ties and possibilities for a separate peace with the emperor rendered the League a hollow vessel. Saxony soon pulled out and other princes followed suit, leaving the Swedes exposed and overly reliant on their main alliance with France. Its nominal field commander was *Bernhard von Sachsen-Weimar*.

Heiligerlee, Battle of (1568). See *Eighty Years' War*; *Louis of Nassau*.

Hejaz. The religiously and historically important region within Arabia which hosts the holy cities (for Muslims) of Mecca and Medina and was the scene of most of the Prophet Muhammad's life. See also *Islam*.

Hellburners. See *fireships*; *Invincible Armada*.

helm. The early helm in Europe (11th–12th centuries) was flat-topped and had a fixed visor, posing the ancient problem of the trade-off between vision and protection. The visor was mainly a defense against missiles and was probably lifted during close combat. For the same reason, *knights* often fought back-to-back, protecting each others' blind spots. Even so, the obliteration of clear vision by the visored helm made identification of friend and foe difficult, a fact which encouraged wearing of heraldic devices. The "Great Helm" was a heavy, full-cover helmet (in various styles) adopted by European knights in the early 13th century, and was most often complemented with gaudy decorations and worn in *tournaments*. In battle, plainer versions of the Great Helm were worn over a skull plate, or *arming cap*, with a mail coif that protected the neck. Little more than a cylinder in its earliest form, it deflected glancing sword blows and missile strikes but did not protect well against a crushing blow on its flat top. Later models tapered the top and added deflecting surfaces. See also *bascinet*; *chapel-de-fer*.

helmets. See *armet*; *arming cap*; *barbuta*; *bascinet*; *cabasset*; *celata*; *chapel-de-fer*; *helm*; *ichcahuipilli*; *kabuto*; *kettle-hat*; *kulah*; *mail-tippet*; *morion*; *salade*; *sallet*; *secret*.

Helvetian Confederation. See *Switzerland*; *Westphalia, Peace of*.

Hemmingstedt, Battle of (1500). See *Landsknechte*.

Hendrik, Frederik (1584–1647). "Frederick Henry." Prince of Orange; Stadholder and Captain-General of the United Provinces. His father, *William* *the Silent*, was assassinated the year Frederik was born. He was a *politique* by instinct and experience who evinced little interest in religion or spirituality and none in confessionalism. He succeeded as head of the army when his half-brother, *Maurits of Nassau*, died in April 1625. Hendrik's initial command went badly: he failed to relieve Breda and lost most of Brabant to *Spínola*. From 1628 to 1629 he took full advantage of Spanish distraction with the *War of the Mantuan Succession*, and of the growing strength of the Dutch army, to launch a grand offensive that broke the ring of Spanish fortresses that encircled the United Provinces. He retook so many towns, starting with 's-Hertogenbosch and Wesel, he was soon called "stedendwinger" ("city-taker") by admirers. After that, for two decades he dominated Dutch politics and warfare. Still, things did not always go his way. In 1631 he invaded Flanders with 30,000 men and an artillery train of 80 big guns, all moved and supplied via 3,000 riverboats and barges. However, arguments with civilian authorities over whether to risk the army forced him to turn back without making any strategic gains. The next year he promised toleration of southern Catholics who surrendered to the *Generality*, and again invaded Flanders with a large army. He took Venlo, Roermond, Sittard, and Staelen in quick order, securing the Maas valley. He then besieged *Maastricht* while calling on all Catholics to rebel against Spain. Some did, but most did not. Still, when Maastricht fell the whole strategic situation changed in favor of the Dutch, never again to reverse. From 1633 he was in constant conflict with the regents of Holland, over the invasion and occupation of coastal Brazil and the governance of the United Provinces. Against his will, Holland forced drastic cuts in army size (to 35,000) and finance in the 1640s. In this and other ways, Holland whittled away at princely power and regained control of the United Provinces. Although his son, William, married a daughter of *Charles I* of England, Frederick Hendrik made no effort to intercede in the *English Civil Wars* (1639–1651). Long ill, he died on March 14, 1647.

Henri de Navarre. See *Henri IV, of France*.

Henri II, of France (1519–1559). King of France, 1547–1559. Son of *Francis I*, from whom he inherited a war with Spain and growing confessional division at home. A ferocious fanatic for Catholicism, he severely persecuted French Protestants from the beginning of his reign, when he introduced the infamous *chambre ardente*. Yet, he also opposed the popes, against whom he defended the traditional liberties of the *Gallican Church*. French–Papal relations reached their nadir in the "Gallican crisis" when Henri ordered French bishops not to attend the *Council of Trent*. He was nearly excommunicated by Pope Julius III, who threatened to replace him with Prince Philip of Spain. That was at most a hollow threat—the popes had long since lost power to effect such changes in Europe's governing classes—but it could have caused Henri still more diplomatic and military difficulties. The definitive split of England from Rome under *Henry VIII*, and the succession of Edward VI in 1547, brought Henri II and the pope together again in the interest of avoiding a further weakening of the Catholic Church. In June 1551, Henri issued the "Edict of Châteaubiant" comprehensively banning Protestantism in France, and with it the danger he saw of fissures in the body politic that might lead to rebellion. The Edict proscribed publication or dissemination of Protestant ideas, banned Protestant gatherings, set up a system of paid informers, and prohibited Protestants from holding public offices or teaching posts. He followed this with the Edict of Compiègne (1557), sharply increasing the penalties for persistent heresy.

Henri oversaw some important military reforms, notably standardization of French artillery into six calibers. In 1555 he tried to reform France's system of *war finance*, but within a few years was deeper in debt and then went officially bankrupt. On the field of battle he was even less successful in the continuing *Italian Wars* (1494–1559). While Henri was fighting in Italy, an army under *Montmorency* lost badly to an invading Spanish force at *Saint-Quentin*. Henri was forced to concede formal surrender to Spain of all French claims to northern Italy in the *Peace of Cateau-Cambrésis* (April 2–3, 1559). On June 30 he was severely wounded in a jousting accident, taking a lance though the eye during a tournament celebrating the Peace. He died 10 days later, struck down by God for his great sins and repression of the Huguenots, said his Protestant subjects. He was succeeded by his minor son, *Francis II*.

Suggested Reading: Frederic Baumgartner, *Henri II* (1988); I. Cloulas, *Henri II* (1985).

Henri III, of France (1551–1589). Duc d'Anjou; King of Poland (1574); King of France (1575–1589). Refined to the point of effeminacy and prone to extravagant penitent gestures that even devout Catholics thought oddly out of place in their king, Henri III was also an intelligent reformer who tried to unite and serve France during its civil wars but who lacked the political, financial, or military means to do so. As a young prince he fought at *Jarnac* and *Moncontour*, earning an early military reputation that he failed to match in later years. With his older brother ensconced as Charles IX of France, and in the midst of a siege of *La Rochelle*, in May 1573, Henri accepted election to the Polish throne. He swore the oath in Notre Dame Cathedral and left for Cracow. He abdicated after just 118 days when Charles died unexpectedly, at age 24. Henri returned to France at leisure, through Italy. He was crowned at Reims on February 13, 1575. His younger brother François, the new *duc d'Anjou*, escaped from Court on September 15, 1575, after three years of captivity following the *St. Bartholomew's Day Massacres*. François embraced the rebellion in the south, where he was joined by *Henri de Navarre* after he, too, escaped from a Court prison in February 1576. Facing bankruptcy as well as a powerful alliance of Protestant princes and foreign mercenaries, Henri III tried to end the *French Civil Wars* by granting unprecedented legal rights to the Huguenots with the *Edict of Beaulieu* (May 6, 1576). As had been the case with his mother, *Catherine de Medici*, the effort to extend toleration to Protestants provoked deep suspicion and active hostility among the Catholic majority and brought Henri III into protracted—and ultimately, mortal—conflict with the *Guise* and the *Catholic League*. Unable to wage the war of suppression that Catholics demanded, Henri was also too weak to sustain the peace that Protestants sought. As a result, he dwelled throughout his reign in a shadow-land of confessional conflict, rising violence, and weakening authority. Thus, in 1585 Henri was forced by the League to agree to the *Treaty of Nemours* which banned Protestantism in France and precipitated the Eighth Civil War.

A pious Catholic, Henri's very piety and genuine religious humility undercut his following among Catholics of the militant Leaguer persuasion, who objected to the king's personal fasting and participation in rituals that abdicated royal symbols of the sacral nature of the French monarchy. Henri was forced to flee Paris in haste and humiliation on the *Day of the Barricades* (May 12, 1588), after which *Henri, duc de Guise* entered the city to wild acclamation. *The Sixteen* and Guise forced the king to issue the *Edict of Union* (July 1588), reaffirming the harsh terms of Nemours and abjuring from ever again making peace with Huguenots. When the clergy and the Catholic bourgeoisie split in December over the issue of new taxes to pay for a final crusade against the Huguenots, Henri finally acted: he called the duc to Blois on December 23, and had him murdered by the "Forty-Five," the king's hand-picked royal guards who also killed the *Cardinal de Guise* the next day. The bodies of the Guise brothers were hacked apart and burned to deny them status as holy relics. The king also had the mother and son of the murdered duc arrested, as well as many leaders of the Catholic League. Then he went to Christmas Mass, exuding a rare royal contentment. But Henri's belated boldness came much too late: *Charles, duc de Mayenne* took over command of the army of the League, enraged Catholics in Paris went back to the barricades, and the League made a radical call for Henri's deposition as a tyrant, something that all Leaguers had found repugnant and treasonous when earlier preached by Protestants. The Sorbonne declared Henri excommunicate, Parisians whispered he was the Antichrist, and all good Catholics were exhorted to rise in rebellion. A Leaguer army was raised against Henri and entered Paris on February 12, 1589, led into the city by Mayenne.

Isolated from his people, absent from his capital, and opposed by the Gallican Church to which he was personally devoted, Henri III agreed to an alliance with Henri de Navarre (April 26, 1589). They joined forces and besieged Paris, but their assault plans were interrupted by an assassin. On the morning of August 1, 1589, Henri III was stabbed in the stomach by a zealous Dominican monk, Jacques Clément, acting out the call of the Catholic League to bring down the tyrant. Before Henri collapsed he drew his knife and slashed open the young monk's face; his retainers did the rest, cutting Clément to pieces and throwing the corpse out the palace window (it was later drawn and quartered). Before expiring, Henri III recognized Henri de Navarre as his legitimate heir. Rather than stopping Henri de Navarre from mounting the throne as the League hoped, assassination of the last and childless Valois king instead cleared the way for a blood enemy of the Leaguers to ascend as Henri IV. Henri III's heart was interred at St. Cloud with his other bodily remains stored in an abbey at Compiègne; the parts were reunited upon a final entombment in St. Denis in 1610.

Suggested Reading: Jacqueline Boucher, *La cour de Henri III* (1986); K. Cameron, *Henry III* (1978); Robert Sauzet, ed., *Henri III et sons temps* (1992).

Henri IV, of France (1553–1610). King of Navarre; King of France (1589–1610). Henri was born to a zealous Calvinist mother who raised him in the *Huguenot* religious and political faith. In 1569 she took him to the Protestant fortress port of *La Rochelle*. He first stood at the head of a Huguenot army at age 16. He was a born fighter rather than thinker and, while a good tactician, no strategist at all, political or military. He acquitted himself well at Arnay-le-Duc (June 26, 1570), leading a cavalry charge into the Royalist ranks. Following the Third of the *French Civil Wars* the Queen Mother, *Catherine de Medici*, tried to effect a religious and dynastic compromise by arranging the marriage of Henri de Navarre, a Bourbon prince, to her daughter, Margaret of Valois. The marriage took place on August 18, 1572, but was quickly followed by an assassination attempt against *Coligny* and then the *St. Bartholomew's Day Massacres* (August 24, 1572). Henri barely survived and was forced to abjure his Calvinist faith. He was held prisoner at Court for over three years, until he escaped in February 1576. Henri then renounced his conversion to Catholicism and resumed command of the Huguenot army in the south of France, leading it throughout the Fifth, Sixth, and Seventh Civil Wars. By 1584 a sequence of royal deaths ending with the death of the *duc d'Anjou* left Henri presumptive heir to the throne. To forestall his claim the *Guise* and *Catholic League* forced the *Treaty of Nemours* on Henri III while Pope Sixtus V excommunicated Henri de Navarre to remove him from the line of succession.

> *Henri III had the Guise brothers murdered just before Christmas and the League declared war on the king.*

Henri won his first real battle convincingly at *Coutras* (October 28, 1587), then he squandered the result by tending to his mistress rather than his army. Fortunately, his Catholic enemies fell out in the wake of the *Day of the Barricades* (May 12, 1588) and a coup d'état in Paris by the Catholic League and Guise. Henri III had the Guise brothers murdered just before Christmas and the League declared war on the king. This led to a remarkable alliance between Henri de Navarre and Henri III signed on April 26, 1589. A joint campaign to retake Paris from the League followed in the summer, but was interrupted by the assassination of Henri III by a Catholic monk on August 1, 1589. Henri de Navarre's blood claim to the throne was clear but his path remained blocked by his Protestant faith, which offended too many of his countrymen. He quickly assured the country that he would protect its dominant Catholic faith, but still faced the conundrum of swearing a pending coronation oath to repress heresy that would put him at odds with his old companions, the Huguenots. The League rejected Henri's claim regardless, which delayed his decision by ensuring that the civil wars would continue. At the head of the Royalist army, Henri pushed aside the last Catholic military opposition at *Arques* in 1589 and *Ivry-la-Bataille* in 1590. Political considerations still barred him from the throne, even though Pope Sixtus V—to whom he was reconciled—invalidated his 1572 forced conversion so that he could not be charged by fanatic Catholics with being a "lapsed heretic." On May 16, 1593, Henri announced his intention to abjure Calvinism. After submitting to several weeks of Catholic instruction, on July 25, 1593, Henri abjured, made a public profession of Catholic faith, and was formally absolved by the French bishops.

Henri did these things to end the civil wars and restore the luster and authority of the crown, but also as a sincere—if sometimes indifferent and sinful—believer. He probably never said "Paris is worth a mass" ("Paris vaut bien une messe"), a charge of coarse cynicism that was hurled against him by embittered propagandists from the Catholic League. He was in fact broadly accepted and embraced by the nation as a unifying, sacral king. An exhausted, bleeding, and demoralized France turned to Henri to restore social peace because his conversion met the condition of preservation of the Catholicity of the throne, and he was trusted by the Calvinist minority which he had led for so many years in war and peace. Besides, neither party had much choice. The military and political power of the League was spent while the Huguenots knew that they had been sharply reduced by war, abjurations and emigration, and that while they had not been defeated in the civil wars neither could they ever win them. On February 27, 1594, Henri was consecrated with holy oil and crowned at Chartres (the League still held Reims). Paris submitted peacefully on March 22; Henri let the Spanish leave with full military honors, then attended mass at Notre Dame. Other League cities followed, as Henri offered conciliation to Catholic moderates rather than threats, and hurled at them bribes instead of bullets. In September 1595, he received absolution from Pope Clement VIII, as much to serve the papacy's interest in lessening its dependency on Spain as for sincere religious purposes. In return, Henri helped the pope secured Ferrara for the Papal States in 1598 and agreed to publish the articles of the *Council of Trent*.

Henri was not wholly devoted to the arts of peace. During his reign he made much love but also war. On January 17, 1595, he declared war on Spain, inaugurating the *Franco-Spanish War*. He did so mainly to undercut *Mayenne*, who was still holding out in Burgundy, and other League bitter-enders allied with the ideologue in Madrid, Philip II. Henry made peace within France in April 1598, by extending legal toleration to the Huguenots in the *Edict of Nantes*. The next month he made peace with Spain at *Vervins*. He married *Marie de Medici*, princess of Savoy, securing all territory west of the Rhône for France in the Treaty of Lyon (1601). But why did he oversee a wholesale reconfiguration of French artillery, ordering castings which totaled 400 field pieces for the royal artillery park before his death in 1610? It is likely that he was preparing to resume the old wars between France and Spain, not for religious reasons this time but in favor of the new idea of the balance of power: he needed to break what many French perceived as Habsburg strategic encirclement. To that end, Henri built a system of alliances across confessional lines that he hoped would counter-balance and contain Spanish influence in Germany, Italy, the Rhineland and Flanders. That is also why he supported the *Protestant Union* as it intervened in the crisis in *Jülich-Kleve*. Just before his death he was poised to attack Spain on three fronts: at Milan, along the Meuse, and in the Rhineland. He also looked to cut the *Spanish Road*. But while prepared to fight Spain over specific interests, Henri did not want unlimited war: his effort to gain influence over the Protestant Union aimed at preventing an all-out international religious war, the outcome he feared most.

In just a dozen years, assisted by superb administrators such as Maximilien de Béthune, duc de Sully, Henri set France on the road to recovery and even to greatness. That was not recognized by many in his lifetime. The country still seethed with religious fears and hatreds and Henri was not fully accepted by all: no fewer than 20 assassination attempts were made against him during his reign. The work of this tolerant king was cut short when one assassin finally got through. Henri was stabbed to death through the window of his coach by a pious, deranged Catholic, François Ravaillac. The murderer heard voices telling him to kill the king because he had failed to convert the Huguenots and was secretly planning to slaughter Catholics. Ravaillac was terribly tortured, drawn and quartered, but confessed no wider plot. It was a testament to Henri's success at national reconciliation that, despite the fact he was succeeded by an 8-year-old, *Louis XIII*, under the regency of Marie de Medici, the French Civil Wars did not immediately resume. On the other hand, the assassination showed that no French king could pursue a purely secular foreign policy when Europe had not yet burned out all the fires of Reformation and Counter-Reformation. The best that could be done was to retreat into isolation from the religious war that was about to break out in Germany, which is just what the regent Marie de Medici did. And although *Cardinal Richelieu* de facto, and Louis XIV de jure, undid Henri's legal toleration of the Huguenots by revoking the Edict of Nantes, it was still thanks to Henri that France emerged from the French Civil Wars intact and a powerful rival to Spain as the dominant power in the European states system.

Suggested Reading: Henry Baird, *The Huguenots and Henry of Navarre* (1886; 1970); David Buisseret, *Henry IV* (1984); Mark Greengrass, *France in the Age of Henry IV* (1995); Michael Wolfe, *The Conversion of Henri IV* (1993).

Henry the Navigator. See *Enrique the Navigator*.

Henry V, of England (1387–1422). King of England, 1413–1422. While still Prince of Wales he began to collect warships. He was the only English king to own a true Mediterranean galley. He also spent royal revenues to build a fleet that included the usual English oared vessels, *balingers*, and *barges*, but also *Great Ships* that modified and advanced the design of *carracks*. Henry tried to enforce the idea of England as *safeguard of the sea* with only limited effectiveness. He was more successful in his larger effort to exploit the strategic advantages of mobility provided by sea power to wage the *Hundred*

Years' War (1337–1453) in a way that prior English kings had not. Where *Edward III* and his successors struck overland from distant but friendly bases, rarely achieving sustainable successes, Henry used sea power to invade and occupy nearby Normandy. This was the start of the great quest of his reign: the attempt to conquer France, to which end he reasserted England's old claim to the French crown in 1414 and revived major fighting in France after a period of dormancy. He used his fleet not just to escort armies across the Channel or to Gascony, but to destroy French seapower in the Atlantic as a prelude to stripping France of its Atlantic ports and establishing permanent English naval dominance in the Channel. He invaded in August 1415, taking Harfleur on September 22 after battering its walls with his artillery. A month later he won a spectacular victory at *Agincourt*. His fleet won at Harfleur (August 15, 1416), and again at the Bay of Seine (July 25, 1417). In 1417 he invaded France again, conquering Normandy by the end of 1418. In the Treaty of Troyes (1420) he appeared to achieve complete victory: he was recognized as "heir of France" and secured the title by dynastic marriage to a daughter of the House of Valois, even though his claim was rejected in fact by many Frenchmen. Henry died at age 35, leaving an expanded but unconsolidated empire to an infant son. The long war with France thus intensified after his death as the French rejected the inheritance provision of the "perpetual peace" of Troyes. The regents and Henry's successor lost most of his conquests during the 1430s and 1440s. English seapower also dissipated upon his death as most of his royal ships were sold off by the regency. See also *fire*; *piracy*; *uniforms*.

Suggested Reading: Christopher Allmand, *Henry V* (1992); M. Labarge, *Henry V: The Cautious Conqueror* (1975).

Henry VIII, of England (1491–1547). King of England. The young, virile Henry ascended the throne in 1509 but took little interest in government, much preferring hunts for wild game or women. Politics he left to his chief minister, Cardinal Thomas Wolsey (1471–1530), Archbishop of York, the most powerful English cleric since Thomas à Becket. In matters religious Henry was a loyal Catholic who wrote a scholarly treatise arguing against *Martin Luther*'s ideas. For this the pope granted him the honorific: "Defender of the Faith." Along with the hunt Henry enjoyed a good war. In 1513 he invaded France in a vain attempt to recapture territories long since lost by his forebears, winning a meaningless skirmish against a handful of French knights at Guinegate, or the "Battle of the Spurs" (August 13, 1513). He also sent armies north to secure his border against a Scottish invasion. At *Flodden Field* the Scottish king, James IV (1488–1513), was killed, after which the frontier was pacified for a generation. Henry used the time for self-absorbed splendor and indulging his lusts, while Wolsey governed the realm with an extraordinary free hand. In 1521–1522, Henry launched the foolhardy and ill-fated "Great Enterprise," an invasion of France for which he was preposterously ill-prepared. His ally was *Charles V*, Holy Roman Emperor and King of Spain. With the aid of Pope Leo X, Charles took Milan from France in 1521. When

Charles won his great victory over *Francis I* at *Pavia* (1525) without Henry's aid, England was denied any spoils of war. Henry proposed that the captive French king be executed, portending his later solution to all thorny issues of legitimacy. Charles refused and also declined Henry's proposal to partition and annex large parts of France. Henry never forgave the slight or what he thought was a lost opportunity. He became a lifelong enemy of the German emperor.

Though always concerned with affairs of the heart, or at least the bedroom, Henry now took a closer interest in affairs of the realm. Wolsey was dismissed from all civil offices and had his property seized by the king (1529), dying in disfavor and disgrace in 1530. The Cardinal was treated with such rank ingratitude for failing to secure an annulment of Henry's marriage to Catherine of Aragon from Pope Clement VII. Henry claimed the marriage was illegitimate, unlawful, and immoral, since he had bedded his brother's widow. The real reasons for seeking annulment were Catherine's failure to produce a male heir and the king's rising lust for Anne Boleyn. But a princess of Aragon was not lightly discarded in a world where the Habsburgs ruled much of Europe. Charles V was Catherine's nephew, and he intervened with the pope to deny Henry's annulment request. Henry's blood was up—Anne held him at sexual bay until he delivered on his courtship promise to make her Queen. Breaking with the pope and the wider Catholic world, Henry divorced Catherine by fiat. He married Anne on January 25, 1533, thereby conceiving the *Protestant Reformation* in England. In 1635, to his lasting disgrace, Henry carried out the execution of his erstwhile chancellor, Sir Thomas More. The legally and morally murky circumstances by which Henry married Anne left a cloud of illegitimacy over their daughter, *Elizabeth I*, which would plague her entire reign. Easily bored once his lusts were satisfied and still without a male heir, Henry had Elizabeth's mother executed on May 19, 1536, on trumped-up charges of treason.

> *Henry claimed the marriage was illegitimate, unlawful, and immoral, since he had bedded his brother's widow.*

While this domestic drama played out Henry was busy at serious governmental reform. He called the famous "Reformation Parliament" in 1529, instructing it to pass a series of extraordinary statutes that reshaped the governmental and religious face of England over the next several years, not least because Parliament declared the sovereign supreme in all matters ecclesiastical (May 15, 1532). By asserting royal supremacy in religion through these Acts, Henry gave the unfolding English Reformation a legal basis and confirmed its moderate character (most changes affected ritual rather than dogma). He also ensured that the coming struggle over a divided faith in the Three Kingdoms centered on succession to the English throne and the crown's relation to the English Church. The English Reformation retained its moderate character until the question of which sovereign in England was supreme—Parliament or the king—led to the enormous religious and constitutional upheaval of the *English Civil Wars* of the mid-17th century. Henry cemented the Reformed Religion in place by dissolving the great monasteries of England to seize their wealth, which he took mostly for himself but shrewdly also distributed among the higher nobility to buy loyalty. Most of this treasure was wasted in serial small wars, for which bronze bells ripped from the monasteries were literally recast as cannon. In his final years Henry descended into ever more sordid personal and dynastic acts, just as he grew more corpulent and corrupt in his person. Jane Seymour followed Anne Boleyn to Henry's bed and in time gave birth to *Edward VI*, a male heir but a sickly youth. Three more wives followed: Anne of Cleves (divorced), Catherine Howard (beheaded), and Katherine Parr (who outlived him). *Thomas Cromwell* also went to the block for having recommended Anne of Cleves to Henry and otherwise serving his king, and himself, too well.

In his early years Henry had sought to catch up with continental rivals militarily. His enemies and allies alike were far ahead of England in the growing professionalization of their militaries, and in use of *gunpowder weapons*, especially artillery. Henry's most significant military move came not in battle but in setting up royal armories and gun foundries and promoting cast iron cannon manufacture. In this he was aided by England's exceptional iron ore deposits and rich forests (for making charcoal). To these resources he added imported and highly skilled foreign gunsmiths. He had *sakers* and other smaller cannon cast in England but imported large *bombards* and siege *mortars* from Germany and Flanders. He built expensive but ineffective artillery forts along England's southeastern coast to ward off an invasion that was not really threatened during his reign. In 1543 he again waged wasteful war in France, to no lasting gain beyond a mere technical feat of arms at *Thérouanne*. In 1544 his army besieged and took *Boulogne*, but it was sold back to France after his death. And in 1545 he had Edinburgh burned in a failed effort to reduce Scotland. In naval affairs, Henry added several *"Great Ships"* to the Navy Royal. In general, he lacked the strategic sense of his predecessor, Henry VII, and the diplomatic skill of his daughter and ultimate successor, Elizabeth I. They both understood in ways that escaped Henry VIII's ken that England was a minor power and best served by a policy of cautious isolation from the struggle underway between the titans of Valois and Habsburg. A light touch of nuisance-making in increasingly Protestant northern Europe might be all that was needed to deflect those Catholic giants away from England into entangling wars with each other. Instead, Henry pursued rash but spectacular interventions for which he lacked proper military means and which worked against England's strategic interests. See also *artillery*; *Henri II, of France*; *Kildare Rebellion*; *"King's Two Bodies"*; *Mary Tudor*.

Suggested Reading: H. M. Smith, *Henry VIII and the Reformation* (1948); D. Starkey, *The Reign of Henry VIII* (1986).

herald. In ancient and medieval diplomacy a herald was a minor official who announced the arrival of peace envoys and invoked religious sanction and the protections of diplomatic immunity. In war, heralds formally notified a castle or town that a siege had begun, arranged truces and parlays, and negotiated ransoms for prisoners. In Medieval Europe heralds were also responsible for interpreting and upholding aspects of the chivalric code. Heralds were displaced by the creation of permanent diplomatic missions during and after the *Italian Renaissance*. However, as late as the *Thirty Years' War*, on May 19, 1635, a French herald was sent to the marketplace in Brussels to read out a formal declaration of war against Spain.

Herat, Battle of (1221). See *Mongols*.

Herat, Battle of (1598). See *Abbas I*; *Uzbeks*.

heresy. See *Affair of the Placards*; *Albigensian Crusade*; *Anabaptism*; *Arianism*; *Arminianism*; *Assassins*; *Buddhism*; *caliphate*; *Calvinism*; *Catholic Church*; *chambre ardente*; *Ecumenical Councils*; *Eighty Years' War*; *English Civil Wars*; *expulsion of the Jews*; *expulsion of the Moors*; *Ferdinand II, Holy Roman Emperor*; *flagellants*; *Francis I*; *French Civil Wars*; *Henri II, of France*; *Hussite Wars*; *Index Liborum Prohibitorum*; *Inquisition*; *Islam*; *Ismaili*; *Knights Templar*; *Lollards*; *Luther, Martin*; *Nichiren Shoni*; *Orthodox Churches*; *Philip II, of Spain*; *Philip III, of Spain*; *Philip IV, of Spain*; *Protestant Reformation*; *Richelieu, Cardinal Armand Jean du Plessis de*; *sacre (2)*; *Safavid Empire*; *Savonarola, Girolamo*; *Seljuk Turks*; *shi'ia Islam*; *Thirty Years' War*; *sunni Islam*; *witchcraft*; *Zwingli, Huldrych*.

Héricourt, Battle of (November 13, 1474). This first field battle of the *Burgundian Wars* resulted when a Swiss army, supported by minor allied contingents from Austria and Alsace, besieged the Burgundian garrison town of Héricourt. A column of some 12,000 mercenaries was sent to relieve Héricourt by *Charles the Rash*, who was engaged besieging the Lower Rhine town of Neuss. The Burgundians built a large *Wagenburg* outside the Swiss lines, then forayed cavalry toward Héricourt to draw out the Swiss. But the Swiss had heard of the Burgundian Wagenburg and were already on their way to attack it. The Burgundian horse turned back toward their field fortification but were caught between two bodies of Swiss. The highly effective tactics of the mature *Swiss square* combined with the usual ruthlessness and aggressiveness of Swiss infantry to overwhelm the Burgundians. The Swiss suffered few casualties but nearly annihilated the entire relief column. Charles did not learn much from this encounter, however: he would again overestimate his strength, blunder, and lose even more severely to the Swiss at *Grandson*.

Hermandad(es). "Civic Brotherhood(s)." Town-based militia in medieval Iberia. The Hermandades were the backbone of military organization of the Christian armies of the late *Reconquista*. They organized as militias in imitation of the successful Muslim *rabitos*. They supplemented Castilian and Aragonese men-at-arms and the knights of the Iberian *Military Orders*. The martial skills of these town brethren did not suffice during the *Italian Wars* (1494–1559), where they soon were replaced by the tougher, better armed and armored men of the *tercios*. See also *Spanish Army*.

hermangildas. Small groups of Iberian farmers banded together for self-defense against raids (*razzia*). These served as a model for later town militia, the *Hermandades*. In addition, two frontier hermangildas evolved into full *Military Orders*: *Alcántara* and *Calatrava*.

Herrings, Battle of the (1429). See *Rouvray, Battle of*.

hetman (*otaman*). The armies of Poland-Lithuania were commanded by hetmans, a military office held for life and enjoying wide powers. Given reliance on *contributions*, the office of hetman was also highly lucrative to its holder. Hetmans participated in Commonwealth politics, though usually only as a potential rival to a weak monarch or a rally point for the political opposition. Poland and Lithuania each had a Grand Hetman nominally in charge of all their military operations. In fact, these officers usually were resigned to giving out loose strategic directions. On the march or during a siege a Field Hetman made the key maneuver, tactical, and other operational decisions.

Hexham, Battle of (1464). See *Wars of the Roses*.

Highland galley. See *birlin*; *galley*; *lymphad*.

hijra. See *Islam*.

Hinduism. An umbrella term for the varied beliefs of 80–85 percent of medieval India's population, as well as significant historic populations in Java, Nepal, Burma, and Indochina. Ancient India was conquered by the "Aryans," Indo-European, Sanskrit-speaking tribes which spilled out of the Caucasus and Central Asia around 2000 B.C.E. Their migration was multifaceted, fracturing into Greek, Germanic, Italic, Celtic, Iranian, Sanskritic, and Hindi peoples who moved in nearly every direction and remade the history of Europe and the Mediterranean as well as India. The Aryan migration-cum-conquest of India is conventionally dated to c.1500 B.C.E., when their cavalry armies overran less militarily proficient Indian city-states. The Aryan conquerors subsequently intermingled with the indigenous population to form a new ruling elite, while also absorbing much from the peoples they had mastered. It was long thought that the Aryan conquest destroyed India's ancient urban civilizations, but that thesis is now widely disputed; catastrophic ecological and economic changes have been offered as competing explanations. Aryan contribution to the rise of classical Indian civilization is also moot. Some evidence suggests that—contrary to the conclusions of earlier historians who saw the Aryans as having civilized a more primitive India—they were in fact semi-barbarians, the Mongols of an distant age, organized for war but inferior in cultural terms to the more advanced city-dwellers and cultures of Gangetic India which they overran. On the other hand, the Aryans were singularly responsible for writing the *Vedas* (magical incantations and hymns with assumed scriptural form, reverence, and veneration) and they thus contributed importantly to the development of Brahman Hinduism. That syncretic religion combined pre-Aryan indigenous cults of worship with the institution of Aryan priesthood and Aryan traditions of sacrifice and elaborate ritual ("Brahmanas," or "manuals of ritual"). And Aryans composed the *Upanishads*, key texts of secret knowledge of the path to salvation. These deeply influenced Indian systems of belief and contributed to the reformation of Hindu society, along with a new rigidification of the caste system. Also, the Aryans introduced Sanskrit, giving license to an efflorescence of much wider Indian literature, poetry, and spiritual speculation.

Recognizable Hinduism emerged many centuries after the Aryan conquest but before the rise of the Gupta kingdoms. It, too, was a highly syncretic belief system drawing from Buddhism, Jainism, and even early Christianity, with strong influences from the *Vedas* and Brahmanism of Aryans. Hinduism's main books of scripture were settled as the *Vedas*, the *Upanishad*, and the *Bhagavad-Gita*. These works and the intellectual tradition they recorded established formal law and taught broad tolerance and respect for all life. Also finding expression in Hinduism were pre-Aryan Indian myths, devotional cults, and many local folk beliefs. Yoga, one of six "schools" ("darshana") of classical Hindu philosophy, probably antedated the Aryan conquest of the subcontinent in some form. The other schools of Hindu thought were Samkhya, Nyāya, Vassesika, Pūrva-mīmānsa, and Vedānta. All of these traditions emerged more fully developed during and after the 6th century C.E. Hinduism is only quasi-polytheistic: at the elite, if not at the local folk level, it always had a strong monotheistic principle at its core, as reflected in the view that all sub-deities were really different aspects of the trinity of Brahma, Vishnu, and Shiva. It suggested that spiritual learning through reincarnation was a pathway to perfection of the spirit and eventual unity with the deity (godhead).

Hindu scripture and practice also supported and underwrote an elaborate caste system. This originated in an idealized Vedic class division of Hindus by Aryans according to skin color ("varna") and social status. The four broadest varnas (color categories or castes) were brahman, kshatriya, vaishya, and shudra, each ranked morally and socially by the degree of "pollution" which attached to its members at birth. The class of "untouchables" ("harijan") developed later, as a lower-ranking "fifth caste" or "out caste" ("panchamas") for those shudra (or "dasas") in the most menial occupations, which were considered wholly "unclean" by all the higher castes. The caste system thus arose not just from socio-economic forms and conquest, though both played a role, but also from Hindu-Aryan ritual and ideas of religious and racial taboo. Thus, an even older, pre-Aryan "jati (birth group) system," which determined one's occupation, worked to subdivide each varna class into many hundreds of sub-castes. This complex socio-economic and political arrangement, sustained in religious guise and with ritual sanction, varied even further in India's diverse regions. Although there was some social mobility among castes, overall the caste system hobbled economic development by decreasing incentive and erecting barriers to upward mobility based upon occupation and merit. This kept a large portion of India's population restricted to subsistence agriculture and other forms of menial, unproductive labor. In turn, that limited their purchasing power as consumers and retarded development of a merchant/middle class and service sector. Those problems were only compounded by a deeply rooted misogyny in Indian society, whether Hindu or Muslim.

Hinduism developed complex theories of "karma" (action) and samsāra (metaphyschosis), in which every good or evil action has repercussions at some point: the sum of past karma determined the course and stature of one's present lifetime. This evolved into a profoundly negative view of material life, in which cyclical suffering predominated and accidents of birth and caste position were instead seen as incarnations of moral judgment on one's past deeds. On the other hand, much of Hinduism in practice—as was also the case with medieval Christianity—derived not from points of scripture or elaborate theology but from local folk traditions and cults of worship. Bhakti Hinduism, for example, involved deep devotion to Shiva and Vishnu and their various incarnations (Avatars). In its early form in southern India, it was greatly intolerant and led to widespread violence against Buddhists and Jains. Members of both those older, rival confessions were slaughtered or driven from large areas of India they had historically occupied.

> ...*the sum of past karma determined the course and stature of one's present lifetime.*

Suggested Reading: A. L. Basham, *The Origins and Development of Classical Hinduism* (1989); Jeaneane Fowler, *Hinduism: Beliefs and Practices* (1997); Burton Stein, *A History of India* (1998).

Hispaniola. This large Caribbean island was inhabited by Arawak Indians when discovered by Columbus in 1492. As the Arawak died off from disease and mistreatment African slaves were imported in large numbers to work a growing plantation economy located mainly on the eastern part of the island. From this base *conquistadores* fanned out to conquer the other islands of the Caribbean, and then the *Aztec* and *Inca* empires. In the 16th century French "boucaniers" (*buccaneers*) so harried Spanish trade and shipping that in 1603 all Spanish settlers on the north coast of Hispaniola were resettled elsewhere. The buccaneers then moved in, transposing their language onto the slave population during the course of the 17th century in a French colony known as St. Domingue (Haiti), which was only formally ceded to France by Spain in 1697.

hobelars. A class of lightly armed and armored horse archers and lancers peculiar to medieval England, though actually Irish in origin. They were named for their ponies, or "hobelins." Their first recorded appearance was in the early *Scottish Wars*, under *Edward I*. They did not fight from horseback but rode to battle as early *dragoons*. This required that they own a cheap nag or hackney, but not a *warhorse* out of their financial and social reach such as a *rouncey* or *destrier*. Hobelars were deployed as inexpensive auxiliaries to English *heavy cavalry* and in marcher wars in Ireland and Scotland where terrain made longbowmen and heavy horse ineffective. See also *stradiots*; *turcopoles*.

Hochmeister. The commanding officer of the *Teutonic Knights*.

Höchst, Battle of (June 20, 1622). The army of the *Catholic League* under *Johann Tilly* and an allied Spanish army moved north from the Palatinate to Main to block *Christian of Brunswick* from linking forces with *Graf von Mansfeld*'s mercenaries. Christian was caught at the bridgehead at Höchst with about 12,000 men and little artillery, trapped by a much larger force under Tilly. Under heavy fire, Christian held a tight defensive perimeter with a blocking force while his main body crossed. He lost most of his baggage train and nearly 2,000 men, but managed to escape with the rest and join Mansfield. Two months later their conjoined armies beat the Catholics at *Fleurus*.

Hofkriegsrat. The Imperial War Council of the *Holy Roman Empire*. It controlled, at the maximum, about 25,000 Imperial troops. These were mostly called up from the "armed provinces" of the Empire and were in fact controlled by the electoral princes. These were impossibly divided during the *Thirty Years' War* (1618–1648), rendering the Hofkriegsrat ineffectual.

Hohenzollern. A north European dynasty with roots traceable to 9th-century Swabia. In 1165 the house split into two lines. The Franconian line received the electorate of Brandenburg from Holy Roman Emperor *Sigismund* in 1415, and later founded the rising state of Brandenburg-Prussia. It acquired East Prussia in 1618.

Holk, Heinrich (1599–1633). Mercenary field marshal. He fought for Denmark in the 1620s and withstood the siege of *Straslund* (1628) by *Albrecht von Wallenstein*. In 1630 he went over to the Imperial side, taking a cavalry command ("Holk's Horse") under Wallenstein. He was an enthusiastic collector of *contributions*, ravaging Protestant Saxony especially hard. He was chased from the field at *Lützen* (1632) by the Swedish horse under *Gustavus Adolphus*. Holk died ingloriously, of the plague.

Holy Lands. See *Crusades*; *Hejaz*; *Holy Places*; *Jerusalem*; *Military Orders*.

Holy League (France). See *Catholic League (France)*.

Holy League (Italy). "Sacra Ligua." An anti-French coalition formed in 1495 in response to the French invasion of Italy. It was comprised of Spain, the

Holy Roman Emperor, the pope (as ruler of the *Papal States*), Milan, and Venice. Later, Venice was excluded out of papal enmity and territorial jealousy. See also *Italian Wars*; *Cambrai, League of*; *Novara, Battle of*; *Preveza, Battle of*.

Holy Office. See *Inquisition*.

Holy Places. Sites of spiritual importance to one or other of the three main faiths that originated in the Middle East: Christianity (Catholic, Orthodox and Protestant), Islam (sunni and shi'ia), and Judaism. They included the Dome of the Rock mosque, the Church of the Holy Sepulcher, the "Wailing Wall" (the surviving remnant of the Temple of Solomon), the Tomb of David, and other tombs of divers prophets.

Holy Roman Empire (of the German Nation). A mostly Germanic empire, but at times including also parts of northern Italy, Bohemia, Flanders, the duchies of Schleswig-Holstein, and some Swiss cantons. It was established in 962 C.E. by Otto I, "the Great" (912–973). It was self-consciously modeled on the empire of Charlemagne, which also maintained the fiction that it was the linear successor to the Roman Empire in the West. Otto succeeded in uniting most of Germany, Italy, and Burgundy into a medieval empire of overlapping vassalge. From the beginning the Empire was at odds with France: Otto invaded France, then ruled by Louis IV, in 942 and again in 948. For centuries emperors competed with the popes for primacy within Latin Christendom while also cooperating with the papacy to prevent the rise of challengers to either from among the barony and minor kings of Germany. Emperors were crowned by popes and claimed supreme temporal authority over all Christians in greater Germany. During this period the defenses of the Empire, which was still a frontier state facing multiple barbarian threats, were organized into eight military districts known as *Marches*. These were, north to south: Billungs, Nordmark, Lusatia, Misnia, Ostmark (Austria), Styria, Carinthia, and Carniola. The main military activity was fending off Slavic raiders, along with larger campaigns over the Alps into Italy called the "expeditio ultra Alpes."

In the 11th century, papal–imperial relations were rent by the "Investiture Controversy" over whether popes or secular rulers should appoint local bishops. This was crucial since several sees hosted Imperial electors who chose the emperors. Investiture itself was a feudal ceremony that granted a fief or clerical office to a vassal, and few fiefs in Europe were as valuable as bishoprics and abbeys which were held by lords both temporal and religious. The emperors had long asserted a right of "lay investiture," and as the Church entered one of its cyclical convulsions of reform enthusiasm, those seeking to eliminate corrupt practices focused on lay investiture. In 1075, Pope Gregory VII forbade the practice, but Emperor Henry IV (r.1084–1105) refused to accept papal appointees. For this "disobedience" he was excommunicated in 1076. In theory, that dissolved all bonds of vassalage binding barons, dukes, and princes of the Empire to the emperor. This was a radical papal challenge to Imperial power and it launched the "Wars of Investiture" (1077–1122). The excommunication initially proved a near fatal blow to the emperor's perceived legitimacy, forcing Henry IV to "go to Canossa" in 1077 to perform public penance before Gregory. He groveled and gained absolution and lifting of the interdict on Church services and sacraments that accompanied the excommunication. War came anyway, during which Henry—who did not regain Gregory's favor but did recover enough legitimacy in the eyes of his subjects that he saved his crown—organized a conclave to elect a more friendly pope, Clement III. In 1084, Henry took Rome and installed Clement. However, Clement was chased from Rome by Norman knights from southern Italy, rough allies of Pope Gregory who reinstated him after sacking his city. The sack of Rome left the populace so opposed to Gregory that it quickly became prudent for him to withdraw. Henry was then forced to abdicate (1105) by relatives and other members of the Imperial party who feared a long-term breach with the papacy would undermine the dynasty's claim to the throne. Thus began a battle between popes and emperors that would last several centuries. Ultimately, the Investiture controversy severely undermined the temporal and spiritual authority of popes and emperors, in time helping to clear the way for the rise of local monarchs across Europe.

In 1156 the dukes of Austria were granted the "Privilegium minus," which excused them from long-distance military expeditions. In 1212, Bohemia was dispensed from its military obligations by payment of a lump sum of silver. These territories remained part of the Empire in name, but grew more distant and independent in fact. An imperial succession crisis from 1250 to 1273, "The Great Interregnum," reduced parts of the Empire to military anarchy after 1250. At its close Count Rudolf of Habsburg was elected "King of the Romans." Thereafter, secure control of the Holy Roman Empire was the central preoccupation of the Habsburgs, who brought mystical imagery and belief in a Catholic mission to their reign in Germany. The affairs of central Europe and the Balkans were another Habsburg concern, as myriad German-speakers migrated into once Slavic lands as far east as the Vistula, led by a powerful but fractious nobility and warrior monks such as the *Sword Brothers* and *Teutonic Knights*. The murder of Albert I in 1308 led to ascension of a Luxemburg dynasty to the Imperial throne, causing high tension between Habsburg designs in Germany and Luxemburg dependence on Bohemia for electoral support. In 1356 the "Golden Bull" was forced on Emperor Charles IV. This recognized local rights and established election procedures by which seven *"Kurfürsten"* ("Elector Princes"), three bishops, and four territorial princes chose the emperor. These electors were autonomous rulers acting through representatives who met in the *Reichstag* (Imperial Diet) at Ratisbon, with representation also for hundreds of large and petty dukedoms, bishoprics, baronies, fiefdoms, and free cities. To many, the Empire seemed to be in terminal decline at the start of the 15th century. However, in 1438 the Habsburgs united the Austrian, Hungarian, Bohemian, and German crowns through a series of dynastic marriages. From 1504 to 1508, Emperor

Maximilian I instituted modernizing military reforms, including setting up a royal foundry in Innsbruck and lesser foundries elsewhere. These cast iron and bronze cannon of various quality and caliber, from great *bombards* known as "Hauptstuke" to small "falconettes" and other early field artillery which could be pulled by just one horse.

With the ascension to the throne of *Charles V* in 1519 it seemed to many that a great military and imperial revival might be underway centered on events in the Holy Roman Empire. At that moment, Europe was sundered by the first soundings of the *Protestant Reformation*. In Germany this led to confessional division and then warfare between the emperor and some territorial princes, culminating in war with the *Schmalkaldic League* from 1546 to 1547. A general truce was achieved on the religious issue in the *Peace of Augsburg* (1555), which instituted partial religious toleration for Lutherans. Charles left the Imperial stage that year, dividing his vast inheritances between Austrian and Spanish branches of the Habsburg dynasty. In Germany, Augsburg helped avoid war over the religious question for 60 years. Under *Maximilian II* and even the erratic and actively anti-Protestant *Rudolf II*, Germany was relatively peaceful into the early 17th century. This was the case even though France descended into religious civil war and Habsburg cousins in Spain, *Philip II* and *Philip III*, conducted a protracted Catholic crusade against Protestantism in northern Europe. However, beneath the surface peace debate over the emperor's constitutional position was unresolved and had become fixed to permanent religious conflict. Protestant princes were deeply loyal to the Empire, but felt the tug of reform subjects who demanded defense of their religious and legal rights against emperors and courts increasingly devoted to the *Counter-Reformation*. The stage was thus set for a great struggle, and eventually a great war, to reinterpret constitutional meanings in an ancient empire newly split by tri-confessionalism. Perhaps only war could resolve the attendant question of whether Germany's territorial princes, Catholic and Protestant alike, were merely *Estates* of a larger and far more powerful monarchy, or themselves sovereign, joined in a voluntary confederation of over 1,000 polities, which in 1600 contained 20 million souls. Of the Empire's component polities, eight large and populous principalities were key: Bavaria, Bohemia, Brandenburg, Hesse, the Palatinate, Saxony, Trier, and Württemberg. None could dominate the Empire, but neither could the Habsburgs of Austria. And all efforts to establish a joint *standing army* were frustrated by refusal of the Imperial Diet to vote the necessary funds.

The great crisis of 1618–1648 had roots in the paralysis of Imperial institutions (the *Imperial Diet, Hofkriegsrat, Reichskreis*, Chancery, Aulic Council, and Imperial Tribunal). Erosion of the great religious and constitutional compromise of the Peace of Augsburg accelerated as all Europe headed toward war. Institutions and principles alike fell into disuse and disdain without being fundamentally challenged on grounds of legitimacy. Instead, they unraveled from the 1580s as Rudolf II supported the Counter-Reformation and the Chamber Court of the Empire repeatedly ruled to restore secularized estates and benefices to the Catholic Church. In 1588, Catholic bishops in the

Court refused to sit the Protestant bishop of Magdeburg. In 1600, Protestant princes paralyzed the "Deputationstag," a subunit of the Diet, by abstaining from its deliberations. The first overt military move was Imperial occupation of the free city of Donauwörth in 1607, in behalf of a Catholic minority at war with the Protestant majority and town council. This violated the traditional right of each of the Reichskreis to maintain internal peace, and that provoked the founding of the *Protestant Union* in 1608. Bavaria and southern Catholics responded by founding of the *Catholic League* in 1609. Both steps further divided the Empire on confessional lines and moved it closer to war.

From 1609 to 1614 inability to resolve a succession crisis in *Jülich-Kleve* demonstrated the Empire's precipitous fall from real authority on the ground, and dangerous connections between German princes and external allies and interests. Within four more years these would propel Germany into the *Thirty Years' War* (1618–1648). That great conflict began with a crisis over who would succeed as king of Bohemia, and thus exercise the deciding vote for the new emperor as an Imperial elector. An awful war was extended and widened by the fanatic Catholicism of *Ferdinand II*, whose overreach united the princes against him, prolonged the war, and ensured that outside powers intervened in German affairs. The primary beneficiary of the effective demise of the Holy Roman Empire by 1648 was France, which emerged as first among equals among the Great Powers of the European state system as ratified by the *Peace of Westphalia*. Lacking any standing army, permanent corps of state officials, or central organs of government—at a time when other monarchies in Europe were beginning to build centralized nation-states—the Holy Roman Empire was thereafter a mere constitutional shell. It was kept in place by component members because this appeared to protect their freedoms from the larger powers which surrounded Germany, but it also allowed external powers to control parts of Germany, keeping it divided and weak as they added bits of its latent strength to theirs. See also *German Peasant War*; *Imperial Army*; *Livonian Order*; *Reichsgrafen*; *Reichsstädte*.

Suggested Reading: James Bryce, *The Holy Roman Empire* (1892; 1978); John R. Hale et al., *Europe in the Late Middle Ages* (1965); Friedrich Heer, *The Holy Roman Empire* (1968); R. E. Herzstein, ed., *The Holy Roman Empire in the Middle Ages* (1966).

Holy Union. See *Catholic League (France)*.

"holy war." The notion that war is imbued with religious purpose was a persistent approach to armed conflict in many eras and societies. For a "holy warrior" (soi-dissant), one's own cause was seen as perfectly just and oneself as entirely moral, while the enemy was perceived as the personification of evil and battle as an all-out contest between forces of light and forces of darkness. Many faiths have engaged in "holy war," though under various names. The most prominent historically were the warrior faiths of Islam and Christianity. For Muslims the doctrine of "jihad" dates from the founding of the Faith, to the teaching and leadership of the Prophet Muhammad. Jihad is translated as "striving [in the path of God]," by some modern Islamic scholars, who interpret it as a moral command to individual self-improvement rather than a collective obligation to armed defense of the Faith. Historically, however, the majority of Islamic jurists considered jihad—identified as one of the five fundamental duties or "pillars" of Islam—as armed struggle against pagans, infidels, and apostates and "heretics." As a core obligation, this more militant understanding was codified in the sharia (Islamic law), which explicitly delineated when force could be used, against whom, and under what circumstances, as well as detailing when mercy in war should be offered. If a jihad was offensive in character (intended to spread the Faith), it was deemed the responsibility of the whole community of the Faithful. In practice, that meant military volunteers who expected, and enjoyed, broad public support. If the jihad was one of defense of Islamic lands or people against external enemies, which was its main meaning, it became the obligation of all able-bodied Muslim males (women were strictly forbidden to participate in military jihad).

The original jihad of the 7th century, led by the Prophet Muhammad himself, was waged against the pagans of the Arabian peninsula. Launched from Medina, it gained control of the traditional holy places in Mecca, uniting them in the territory called the Hejaz. It was underwritten by sincere spirituality as well as material greed and took place within a context of historic unification of the Bedouin tribes into an Arab nation. For Allah and booty, desert warriors riding under the green banners of Islam swarmed out of Arabia into Syria and Anatolia, through Egypt, across North Africa, and into Iberia. Only at the *March* of the Franks was the high tide of the first Islamic jihad stopped, in 732 C.E., by a cobbled-together Frankish army under Charles Martel ("The Hammer," c.688–741), whose heirs headed the Carolingian dynasty. Eastward, the Arab jihad washed over Iran, converting that ancient civilization to Islam with the sword and with word of its success elsewhere. The Muslims later expelled the Crusaders from the Holy Land and pushed the failing *Byzantine Empire* out of Anatolia. As Bedouin power declined *Seljuk Turks* converted to Islam and renewed its *ghazi* expansion with the enthusiasm of fresh converts. Successive "Turkish" or slave (*Mamlūk*) dynasties adopted Islam and dominated the Middle East for the next 1,000 years.

> *If a jihad was offensive in character, it was deemed the responsibility of the whole community of the Faithful.*

After converting to Islam the Ottomans defeated the last serious *shī'a* challenge to orthodoxy, confining the shī'a to Iran and isolated mountain valleys scattered across the Middle East. The Ottoman tide then washed into the Balkans and against the walls of Constantinople. That great fortress was finally overwhelmed by *Muhammad I* in 1453. The Ottoman surge carried to Vienna in 1529 before subsiding. Was this grand advance of the Ottoman Empire motivated primarily by jihad transmuted into rank imperial aggrandizement? For the most part, no. From the 16th century, the Ottoman Empire was a sophisticated and complex state in many ways more materialist and secular in its functioning than most states in Europe prior to the 18th century. The sultans routinely employed Christian troops, notably in the *Militargrenze* along the frontier with the Habsburgs. While they used violent religious rhetoric concerning Christian enemies, this was more exhortation and propaganda than base motive that was (and is) common to most wars. And although they fought heterodox shī'a Muslims in Iran they did so mostly reluctantly and without railing about crushing "heresy," lest they open religious fissures within their own Empire. Lastly, they tolerated a wide range of Islamic beliefs and practices as well as large communities of Christians and Jews. Rhoads Murphey is therefore right to conclude that "Ottoman sultans, unlike the contemporary rulers of Reformation Europe, studiously avoided embroilment in what is often termed 'wars of religion.'"

Second only to Islam historically in its penchant for "holy war" was Christianity. In the Christian world the tradition dates to the time of the Roman Emperor Constantine the Great (c.274–337 C.E.). He claimed a vision in which the Christian cross appeared in the heavens before a great battle in a Roman civil war, accompanied by the message "In hoc signo vinces" ("In this sign you shall conquer"). That remained the motto of repression of heretics in early Medieval Europe, the Crusades against Islam and for *Outremer*, the *Reconquista* in Iberia, and all 16th- to 17th-century wars between Catholic and Protestant. Latin Crusaders invaded the Muslim Middle East in the late 11th century, retaking Jerusalem during the First Crusade (1099). Christian invaders established several Crusader states in Palestine and Syria, some of which survived for nearly two centuries. They faced constant Muslim counterattacks organized by the main Islamic power in Egypt, and by the fanatic *Ismaili* sect of *Assassins*. Savage wars of Christian conquest were also waged by the *Teutonic Knights* against the pagan tribes of the Baltic region, to exterminate Wends and native Prussians, and to wipe out or convert pagan Lithuanians and Poles. The crusade in Iberia (the Reconquista) was a "holy war" as protracted migration-cum-invasion of Muslim *taifa* states. Drawn out over centuries, it concluded when the walls of the last emirate, the magnificent scholarly and trading city-state of *Granada*, fell before a Spanish gunpowder siege in 1492. The campaign provoked several jihads out of North Africa—Muslim counterattacks against the Christian counterattack. Granadine troops were assisted, but also swept aside, by powerful dynasties like the Almohads and Almoravids, Berber radicals from North Africa intent on retaking the fabled gardens of "al-Andalus" for Islam. In the end, Iberian Christians triumphed when *Ferdinand and Isabella* besieged Granada and accepted its negotiated surrender on January 2, 1492.

All that notwithstanding, one should not exaggerate the motive power of "holy war" for most ordinary soldiers, whether Muslim ghazis or Christian Crusaders. With rare exceptions, foot soldiers or sailors fought not for God but for money, or advancement, or their families and comrades, after their homes and farms were burned, or because they were forced to fight by more powerful men. In this era, as in most others, soldiers displayed a mix of motives ranging from vulgar and venial to the most ideal and romanticized. In short, the motives of warriors in the era of "wars, of religion" resembled those of most soldiers in most countries in most other wars, including those of secular ages and civilizations. See also *Chaldiran, Battle of*; *Dar al-Harb*; *Dar al-Islam*; *just war tradition*; *Ottoman warfare*.

Suggested Reading: James T. Johnson and John Kelsey, *Cross, Crescent and Sword* (1990); P. Murphy, ed., *The Holy War* (1976).

Holy Water Sprinkler. A *staff weapon* of the late medieval period combining the main features of a multi-headed *mace*, or spiked flail, with the longer reach of a *lance*.

Homildon Hill, Battle of (1402). See *Scottish Wars*.

homosexuality. See *Henri III, of France*; *Knights Templar*; *Mary Stuart, Queen of Scots*; *military discipline*.

Homs, Battle of (1281). See *Mongols*.

Honganji fortress, Siege of (1570–1580). *Oda Nobunaga* had already occupied Kyoto and was well on his way to winning the first phase of the *Unification Wars* in Japan. To take the fortress headquarters of the *True Pure Land* Buddhist sect in Osaka he sent 20,000 troops, including 3,000 musketeers as well as *sōhei* from the *Negora Temple*. Honganji was protected by its position at the end of the Inland Sea. The defenders resisted Nobunaga for 10 years, holding out against his bombardments and assaults behind moats and dry ditches filled with straw fascines. The sectarians had guns, but far fewer than Nobunaga's men. In the end, Nobunaga forced Honganji to surrender via a sea blockade supporting his envelopment.

Hongwu emperor (r.1368–1398). "Vast Military emperor," né Zhu Yuanzhang. Zhu was a peasant who rose to power through rebellion and sheer military exploits to become the founder of the Ming dynasty. His path to power was leveled by two decades of social, political, and military chaos in China following the ravages of the *Black Death* from c.1331 and a sudden change of course in the Yellow River in 1344, a colossal tragedy for China that also killed Zhu's whole family and left him a destitute beggar. He began his astonishing climb to the throne as a minor bandit, then a warlord fighting the Mongol (Yuan) dynasty as part of a radical "White Lotus" Buddhist sect know as the "*Red Turbans*." Squat and famously ugly, he governed from his capital at Nanjing, which he captured in 1368 after breaking with the Red Turbans. In 1372 he sent several armies across the Gobi Desert to cut out the heart of Mongol power. In 1373, Hongwu sent 150,000 men into Mongolia some 600 miles north of Beijing. The Ming caught the Mongol horde encumbered with its women, children, and herds, defeated the fighters, and took nearly 80,000 Mongols prisoner as well as 50,000 horses. The Mongols were beaten by the Ming at the Tula River, but two months later a Mongol horde caught a Ming army strung out and exposed in the desert and savaged it. It was another 15 years before the Ming again tried to quell the Mongols on the northern frontier and then they struck at Mongols in Manchuria, not Mongolia proper. Once again, as the campaign closed and the Ming withdrew, a pursuing Mongol force ambushed and destroyed a Ming detachment.

To hold the north Hongwu copied from the Yuan dynasty a system of frontier garrisons comprised of resident troops and their families, military colonies located at eight strategic choke points. He planned, and to some degree he succeeded in creating, a self-sufficient system of military-agricultural colonies that transferred the expense of border defense to the frontier itself. Meanwhile, he used a powerful *standing army* to prosecute the Ming conquest of southern China, though fighting continued throughout his reign: Ming armies pacified Sichuan province by 1371 but did not control all of Yunnan until two years after Hongwu's death. Hongwu was ferocious and intense by nature. He may have had good governing intentions to begin, but as his long reign passed he grew ever more cruel, suspicious, despairing, and bitter. In his later years swelling suspicion led to frequent bloody purges reminiscent of Josef Stalin in motivation, even if carried out on a 14th-century, nonindustrial scale: not only his enemies but their entire extended families, even whole communities, were wiped out. The usual method was beheading. In 1380 alone Hongwu butchered 40,000 people, most of whom were only nominally and distantly associated with a conspiracy against him led by a former prime minister. In his deepening isolation and paranoia Hongwu deliberately hamstrung the Chinese bureaucracy in order to concentrate all power in the Imperial Court (again, reminiscent of Stalin). Over time, that Imperial precedent and governing legacy meant that successive Ming courts became profoundly corrupt, detached from the people, and eunuch-dominated. Hongwu was succeeded, but only after four years of Ming civil war, by the *Yongle* emperor. See also *elephants*; *Great Wall*; *Tumu, Battle of*.

Honigfelde, Battle of (1629). See *Stuhm, Battle of*.

honjō. Japanese forts, mainly wooden and often supported by branch forts called *shijō*. They were prevalent in the *Sengoku* era. During the *Unification Wars* and under *Toyotomi Hideyoshi* most were razed by fire.

hook gun. See *hackbut*.

hoop-and-stave method. In the early days of gunpowder weapons in Europe small artillery pieces such as *"pots de fer"* were directly cast from iron, or more rarely, from expensive bronze (brass was not available until the early 16th century). Longer-barreled guns were beyond medieval casting ability. If their size and weight did not surpass the skills of gunsmiths they exceeded the technical capabilities and temperatures of existing forges. An alternative method was required to make larger cannon. It was found by adapting the practice of coopers, who made wooden barrels by fastening staves together with hoops. Cannon were assembled in a similar fashion: billets of heated iron were welded together by placing them around a central wooden form ("mandrel"), then hammering hot hoops around the billets to fix long iron bars in place. When two dozen or more rings of iron were assembled around lengths of iron in this way they created a type of simple tube, termed a "barrel" from its manufacturing origin in cooping. This type of "forged gun" manufacture permitted breech-loaders to be built, although by the start of the 15th century most cannon were made as muzzle-loaders. There is strong evidence that this early method of assembling large cannon was used in China as well as Europe by the 13th century, but none to say which area was first, if one learned from the other, or if the inventions were wholly independent. A major problem with hoop-and-stave guns was that the smallest imperfection in a hammered weld or billet permitted violently expanding gasses to escape the barrel when the gun was fired, which meant it was liable to explode with deadly results for the crew. Even if a gun worked at first, repeated firings would in time open hairline fractures and imperfections in the metal or welds. Therefore, as casting methods and capabilities improved for larger pieces, the hoop-and-stave method was slowly abandoned. See also *bombard*; *corning/corned gunpowder*; *strategic metals*.

> *...the smallest imperfection ... permitted violently expanding gasses to escape the barrel ...*

Hopton, Ralph (1598–1652). Cavalier general. He was mainly active in the southwest of England, especially in Cornwall, from 1642 to 1646. He won four small actions in 1643, at Bradock Down (January 19) and Stratton (May 16); he won again at Landsdown Hill (July 5), and beat *William Waller* a week later at Roundway Down (July 13). Hopton was beaten by Waller at Cheriton (May 29, 1644), where his 6,000 Royalists were pushed off the high ground by 10,000 Roundheads. He managed to keep his little army together and in the field for another two years, until he was defeated by *Thomas Fairfax* at Torrington. He went into exile in Flanders, where he died.

Horasani **technique.** See *fortification*.

Hormuz. This island sited in the Strait of Hormuz was for centuries a key port in the rich Indian Ocean trade in spices, slaves, gold, and other goods. It was attacked by armed Portuguese led by *Alfonso de d'Albuquerque* in 1507. The assault was repulsed, but Hormuz fell to a second Portuguese attack in 1514. The Ottomans failed to retake it in several expeditions launched from 1551 to 1554. For over a century it served as a gateway to the Portuguese empire in India and East Asia. In 1622 it was captured by Emperor *Abbas I* of Iran in alliance with the *East India Company* (EIC). Abbas granted monopoly trade privileges to "John Company" but moved the main trading station to the mainland, sending Hormuz into terminal decline.

hornwork. In fortification, an outwork made of two *demi-bastions* joined by their own curtain wall, in turn connected to the main fortification by two connecting walls. It took advantage of ground left outside the main *enceinte*. See also *crownwork*.

horo. A cloth stretched over a wicker frame and bearing the insignia of a *daimyo*. It inflated as the horse and rider moved. It was the signature flag of a courier in Japanese warfare.

hors de combat. "Beyond battle." In *just war* doctrine this referred to a wounded enemy incapable of further fighting, who therefore reverted to the moral status of a civilian and was protected from further harm. This status also applied in theory to the clergy, unarmed lay folk, and any nonresisting townsfolk during a siege. It could even apply to religious edifices, mills, or other places of gainful but nonmilitary employment. In practice, the status was observed as much in the breach as the observance.

horse. Military idiom for *cavalry*, as in "a thousand French horse advanced toward the English line."

horse armor. See *armor*.

horseman's axe. See *axes*.

horses. See *barded horse*; *cavalry*; *destrier*; *dragoons*; *hackney*; *hobelars*; *logistics*; *palfrey*; *rouncey*; *sumpter*; *warhorses*.

Hospitallers. "Order of the Hospital of St. John in Jerusalem." An international *Military Order* originally comprised of male nurses devoted to providing succor to Christian pilgrims in the "Holy Land." It was founded in 1070 by Italian merchants from Amalfi. Following the capture of Jerusalem by the *First Crusade* the nursing brothers hired a number of *knights* with crusading experience in Iberia to protect pilgrims journeying to nearby holy sites and shrines, a service already offered by the *Knights Templar*. The Order of the Hospital was recognized by the papacy in 1113 and was much pampered by successive popes. Its first military action was in 1136, when the Order was given land to fortify and defend at Beit Jibrin, between Gaza and Hebron. In the 1140s the Brethren fended off Muslim raids into the Crusader states, after which more Hospitallers took up arms and accepted contracts to protect Latin castles and pilgrims. Soon this military function overshadowed the original nursing purpose of the Order: by 1187 it held over 20 key strongholds in the Holy Land, including the spectacular Krak des Chevaliers. However, the Brethren always took their hospital duties seriously. Perhaps that was because, unlike the rival Templars, Hospitallers permitted women in the Order. Like other military orders, they had four classes of Brethren: knights, sergeants, serving brothers, and chaplains. They also allowed *confrère knights*. Any knight catching leprosy was required to leave the main Order to join the Knights Hospitaller of St. Lazarus. Although few in number, the "Lazars" founded many leper asylums in Europe (200 in England alone), supported by *commanderies* in the Holy Land. In 1134 defense of Aragon itself was left to the Hospitallers and Templars. As Iberian Hospitallers were drawn more into the *Reconquista* fewer left as Crusader reinforcements for the Middle East. Still, the main concern of the Order remained *Outremer*.

When Jerusalem was recaptured for Islam in 1187 by the great warrior-prince *Salāh al-Dīn*, the Knights Hospitaller retreated to Acre. In the Muslim storming and sack of Acre in 1291 every Knight Hospitaller, Lazar, Knight of St. Thomas, and Teutonic Knight (except the Hochmeister) died fighting. Upon the loss of that last Crusader state in 1291, the Hospitallers withdrew to island strongpoints from which their long-established navy continued to fight ascendant Muslim power in the eastern Mediterranean. Along with other defeated Latins, surviving Hospitallers settled on Cyprus (1291) then Rhodes (1306). Although they benefitted hugely from persecution of the Templars, fear of similar treatment confirmed the Hospitallers in their decisions to make Rhodes their headquarters (1310) and to reorganize as a federation of national associations. From Rhodes they remained active as pirates ("Sea Brothers") against Muslim and Christian ships alike. In 1344, in alliance with *Venice*, they captured Smyrna. In 1365 they captured Alexandria. In neither case could they hold what they took, and Muslim counterattacks soon retook both cities. In 1440 and 1480 the Hospitallers repelled two Muslim sieges of *Rhodes*. In 1522 they were finally defeated by the Ottomans; survivors were allowed to depart Rhodes (January 1, 1523). Already well-established and respected in Austria and Germany, in 1530 *Charles V* granted the Order sovereignty over Malta. It held that island as a Christian outpost in the Muslim eastern Mediterranean for several centuries. A much different and distant outpost was on St. Croix in the Virgin Islands. The *Protestant Reformation* led to suppression of Hospitaller branches in most Protestant countries, and confiscation of their great estates, although the Lazars continued a quiet, almost underground, existence in France and Italy. Attenuated in all ways, the Hospitallers remained in control of Malta until Napoleon dispensed with them in 1798. See also *battle cries*; *Johannitterorden*; *wounds*.

Suggested Reading: E. Bradford, *The Shield and the Sword* (1973); Helen Nicholson, *The Knights Hospitaller* (2001); Desmond Seward, *The Monks of War* (1972; 1995); Jonathon Riley-Smith, *The Hospitallers* (1999).

hostage-taking. Taking hostages as a means of enforcing peace terms or of deterrence against rebellion was an ancient practice, still common in medieval warfare, and not unknown in early modern warfare in Asia and Europe. The term "a king's ransom" meant literally the price of recovery of a king, whether taken by treachery or dehorsed in battle. In the late 16th century *Tokugawa Ieyasu* was given to a rival *daimyo* by his father at age 4 and served as a hostage until age 18. To ensure compliance with their overlordship the *Inca* took hostage the sons and families of rulers of conquered cities. In Europe hostage-taking and killing was upheld as legal and proper by leading jurists, including Johann Moser and Emerich de Vattel, well into the early modern period. See also *Gustavus I*; *Toyotomi Hideyoshi*; *Poitiers, Battle of*; *siege warfare*.

Hotin, Battle of (1621). See *Khotyn, Battle of*.

hot shot. Heated shot, made of stone early on but of cast iron later. It was used in *siege warfare* to set fire to towns or fortifications. Less common and more dangerous in war at sea, it was nevertheless used to set fire to enemy rigging and decks, or in hope of exploding exposed powder beside the guns. A tripod holding a pan of hot coals heated the shot; these coals could also be used to light the slow match or heat a wire primer used to set off the cannon.

housecarls. The king of England's personal, household troops. Before the *Norman* conquest they were known as "gesiths" and later as "thegns." The Norman term was "familia." The housecarls formed a near-standing army that was tied to the king by blood or intimate family, or by oaths of loyalty, or tenancy on the king's lands. Some were foreign *knights*. Others were children of defeated rebels who sought to earn back the king's favor. Their numbers varied from a peacetime low of perhaps 40 to a wartime peak of several hundred or more. They formed the core of English royal armies in the medieval period.

Howard, Charles (1536–1624). Admiral Lord Howard of Effingham. Son of a Catholic, though displaying no sign of that faith himself, he was raised to Lord High Admiral by *Elizabeth I* in 1585. He was the overall commander of the English fleet that sailed to meet the *Invincible Armada* in 1588. He commanded the 1596 raid-in-force on Cadiz, accompanied by the *2nd Earl of Essex* and *Walter Raleigh*. For that successful undermining of Spanish naval power and prestige he was elevated to Earl of Nottingham. In 1601 he quashed Essex's abortive rising against Elizabeth.

howdah. A high platform perched on the back of a war *elephant*, carrying archers or javelin throwers.

Hsiang-Yang, Siege of (1268–1273). See *China*; *Mongols*.

Huguenots. French Calvinists. They formed a separate body of believers in an age and country where orthodoxy was associated with loyalty and "heresy" with sedition and rebellion. *Henri II* and his contemporaries, and numerous historians, believed that most Huguenots came from the lower social orders. This has been disputed in more recent studies. On the eve of the "Wars of Religion" in France they numbered about 1.8 million, or 10 percent of the population. Some communities were scattered over the north, particularly in Normandy where they enjoyed noble protection, but the majority were south of the Loire. There, traditional regional autonomy and animosity to northern rulers became linked to Protestantism and resistance to rising royal taxation in several provinces. Almost no Huguenots lived in Brittany, Burgundy, Champagne, or Picardy. Significantly, in recently annexed Burgundy the question of local autonomy was associated with royal protection of Catholicism, not Protestantism, in large measure because the rich vineyards of the region were mostly owned by cathedral towns and monasteries and peasants were closely tied to the vines. Early on, Protestantism was most successful in the towns among literate classes of artisans and the professions. These communities were protected by local nobility, among whom Protestantism made early and disproportionate numbers of converts. Huguenots were predominant among French *boucaniers* in the Caribbean, with some based locally and others sailing from as far away as *La Rochelle*. In the 1540s Huguenot pirates attacked Havana and Santiago, Cuba. The Canary Islands were raided in 1552, as were many ports along the Spanish Main over the following decade. In 1555, Havana was taken by the Huguenot captain Jacques de Sores, who looted and burned the town and tortured and murdered all priests he found. Sores made smaller but similar raids against coastal towns of the Spanish Main for another 15 years. Most Huguenot corsairs took special pleasure in attacking the shipping and settlements of Catholic Spain, whatever the state of war or peace between Spain and France. They did not just plunder, rape, and kill; they desecrated Catholic churches in orgies of violent *iconoclasm*, killed priests and nuns, and burned out whole towns. The Spanish responded with two massacres of Huguenots, at *Fort Caroline* and *St. Augustine*.

The real test of Huguenot arms came inside France. Calvinist piety and independence presented a threat to the French crown and patronage interests, as the king controlled all Church appointments. Even more dangerous, Huguenots represented a threat of social and political heterogeneity which neither the crown nor the bulk of the French population was prepared to accept. *Jean Calvin* launched a mission to France in 1555 that aimed at recruiting nobles, and this made much headway in the Midi. Several Bourbons from Navarre converted, led by Queen Jeanne, daughter of *Francis I*. She raised her son, Henri de Navarre, the future *Henri IV*, in the reformed faith. Also converting were such key military men as Louis de Bourbon, Prince of *Condé* (killed at *Jarnac*), and *Coligny*, Admiral of France. Conversion of militarily skilled nobles—up to one-third of all French provincial nobility converted—was crucial to Huguenot hopes once fighting broke out in 1562, when the "massacre" at *Vassy* led Condé to issue a call to arms that began the protracted *French Civil Wars* (1562–1629). In 1574, in the wake of the *St. Bartholomew's Day Massacres* of 1572, a Huguenot federation was established in the Midi ("United Provinces of the Midi"). After the massacres, sharply reduced Huguenot numbers (many more abjured from fear than were killed or exiled) led to a change in tactics: Huguenot armies tended to use forests for cover and to set ambushes; they lived directly off the land and set up forts from which they sallied to eat out the countryside in Catholic areas.

A second low point in Huguenot fortunes came with the *Treaty of Nemours* in 1585. Huguenot fortunes improved once Henri de Navarre became king in

1589, even though he was not initially accepted by Catholics and ultimately was compelled to abjure five years later in order to actually mount the throne. Henri delivered peace of a sort to the Huguenots in the *Edict of Nantes*, but fighting resumed after his assassination in 1610. The end of Huguenot claims to be a distinct godly community and their ability to sustain a state-within-a-state came under *Louis XIII* and *Cardinal Richelieu*. They took the Huguenot capital of La Rochelle in 1628 and crushed all military resistance to royal authority, ending forever Huguenot military power and political independence within France. Survivors subsequently were driven out by Louis XIV, who finally and fully revoked the religious and civic toleration clauses of the Edict of Nantes in 1685. Some Huguenot refugees joined the militaries of adopted countries to fight France. Others migrated to the Americas or South Africa, where they blended with other refugee and Protestant populations.

> *They took the Huguenot capital of La Rochelle in 1628 and crushed all military resistance to royal authority . . .*

Suggested Reading: Henry Baird, *The Huguenots and Henry of Navarre* (1886; 1970); Janine Garrison, *Protestants du Midi, 1559–1598* (1980); N. M. Sutherland, *The Huguenot Struggle for Recognition* (1980).

hulk. "*Urca.*" In the 15th–17th centuries, a class of three-masted, *clinker-built* merchant ship as big as 650 tons. A hulk or urca was usually armed and could serve as a warship. It was a later development from the original *cog*. It was widely used in the Baltic in the 16th century. The Spanish took a number of urcas along as supply ships with the *Invincible Armada*. Several wrecked off the west coast of Ireland.

Hunderpanzer. "Dog armor." Armor for dogs of war was developed and used in Germany, Italy, Spain, and the Netherlands. In some places, armored war dogs wore "Hunderpanzer" into the 17th century. It usually consisted of heavily padded linen or hardened leather plates, often with a spiked collar. Some fully articulated suits of steel dog armor were produced in Germany, but probably for court display rather than battlefield use.

Hundred Years' War (1337–1453). In 1328 the young French king, Charles IV, "The Fair" (1294–1328) died. Two claimants to the throne stepped forward: England's *Edward III*, whose mother was sister to the deceased king; and *Philip VI*, "The Fortunate," representing a competing dynastic line, the House of *Valois*. Under the *Salic Law*, which barred succession to women and to descendants in the female line, Edward's claim was denied in favor of Philip. In the long-running conflict between England and France that ensued the main issue was a contest for control of Normandy. The war was also stoked by discontent of Flemish cities with their French overlords and English attempts to monopolize the Flanders trade, and French aid to Scotland aimed at tying down English armies there. Still, the main casus belli was a raw territorial quarrel over Normandy and other provinces of France. The political and dynastic conflict broke into open warfare in 1337 when Edward agreed to pay simple homage but not liege homage to Philip of France, as required of Edward as a feudal vassal of Philip with regard to holdings in Guyenne. Philip seized on this breach of formal obligation to proclaim all English territories in France forfeit, and moved to occupy them militarily. The war that followed greatly aggravated the suffering and dislocation of population caused by epidemics that raged wildly in the second half of the 14th century in nearly every country in Europe.

In 1339, Edward III crossed the English Channel with a largely mercenary army (partly paid for by the *Hanse*) to prosecute his claim to the French crown in the first of many great *chevauchées* that desolated large parts of France in a deliberate war of scorched earth and economic attrition. After losing a series of skirmishes the French wisely avoided further battle, retreating instead into fortified "surety towns" (*place de sûreté*). Edward brought with him some 15 cannon and about 40 kilograms of gunpowder, but this early artillery was not powerful enough to break stone defenses and was too clumsy and unreliable to use to any real effect on the battlefield. Repeated attempts to invade northern France failed due to the usual causes of poor logistics, insufficient finances, and unreliable weather, weapons, and troops. Indeed, English forays are best thought of not as efforts at conquest but as futile, indeed reckless, military parades by outnumbered English armies through the French countryside. On some occasions the French moved a field army to intercept and block English withdrawal. But these moves did not lead to what many anticipated would be catastrophic English defeat. Instead, spectacular English victories were won over a far more numerous enemy, partly due to the *longbow* deployed in support of new infantry tactics devised by Edward and earlier tested in his Scottish Wars. The longbow far outranged the crossbows wielded by mercenary Genoese serving the French. More importantly, English commanders took advantage of their enemy's inferior frontal assault tactics and obsolete weapons to draw French knights down upon longbowmen protected by terrain and *Spanish riders*. Thus, Edward's archers devastated great numbers of heavily armored French knights and men-at-arms at *Crécy* (1346). The year after that victory Edward besieged and took *Calais*. Then the war settled into a pattern of intermittent raids and sieges, as each side was ravaged by the arrival of a far greater foe, known in France as "le morte bleue" and in England as the *Black Death*.

In 1352 the quaintly chivalric "Battle of the Thirty" was fought, in which 30 French knights challenged and defeated 30 English knights in a lethal exhibition of mostly archaic tournament skills. That demonstrated knightly courage, but even more the rooted backwardness of the military culture of Europe's aristocratic warrior caste. In fact, knights were becoming irrelevant on the battlefield as combat was increasingly decided by armor-piercing missiles from longbows and crossbows deployed in ever larger numbers, joined later in the war by the arquebus, musket, and cannon. Facing these powerful projectile weapons an armored noble mounted on an armored warhorse became as militarily obsolete as he was overly expensive, socially privileged, and politically reactionary. Even so, several crushing defeats of French chivalry would be needed to drive that point home, and drive *heavy cavalry* from the battlefield. A second great victory of English longbowmen over French heavy horse and mercenary Italian crossbowmen came at *Poitiers* (1356). There, King Jean II ("The Good," 1319–1364) was taken prisoner, held for a "king's ransom," and compelled to sign a draconian peace with England (*Treaty of Brétigny*, 1360). There followed a decade of English dominance in which *routiers* accepted English silver to hold down hundreds of strongpoints and continued Edward's war of economic attrition against France even more brutally and successfully than in the great chevauchées of 1339–1360. English rule and taxes sat poorly with most French, however, and large-scale fighting resumed in 1369, once Charles V (r.1364–1380) reconstructed much of the government of France and its army. By the mid-1370s he won back much that had been lost at Poitiers, forcing numerous English garrisons and castles to capitulate.

By 1380 the burden of a protracted war fought mainly on French soil meant that financial and social strain reached crisis point. Bertrand the Guesclin, the "Eagle of Brittany," led a sustained guerrilla resistance and forced the garrison at Châteauneuf-de-Randon to surrender (1380), but this did not drive the English from the country. France was only saved by England's distraction during the minority of Richard II (1367–1400), and the attendant succession struggle leading to Richard's dethronement and probable murder by Henry IV (1367–1413). In addition, a peasant revolt rocked England in 1381 while complications related to the *Great Schism* unsettled much of Europe from 1378. The 1380s saw a short period of French ascendancy in alliance with Castile against England. In 1387, however, an English fleet destroyed over 100 French and Castilian warships in the Channel, ending a French threat to land an army in England. Thereafter, both monarchies hovered near bankruptcy and fought only limited campaigns in France. It was not until the ascent of a vigorous and aggressive new king, *Henry V*, that England reasserted with strong force its old claim to the throne of France. Henry resumed chevauchées, leading one in 1415 that resulted in the fight at *Agincourt* where he won an extraordinarily lopsided victory over a superior force of French knights and Genoese crossbowmen. That fight on St. Crispian's Day, 1415, devastated the French aristocracy. Before the battle the flower of France's chivalry (and its *Armagnac* allies) expected an easy victory over a boxed-in, tired, hungry and smaller English army. At the end of the day 5,000 Frenchmen lay dead or dying on Agincourt's rain- and blood-soaked field. Adding injury upon injury, an English fleet won at Harfleur (August 15, 1416), and again at the Bay of Seine (July 25, 1417). These multiple defeats on land and water were far worse than the French losses at Sluys, Crécy, and Poitiers in their combined demoralizing and strategic effects. Henry was free to conquer Normandy in a two-year campaign from 1417 to 1419 (Rouen fell in January 1419). Shaken and defeatist, France agreed to the "perpetual peace" of Troyes (1420) in which Henry was recognized as "heir of France" and large territories were ceded to England and smaller lands granted to

Henry's Burgundian ally. France looked to be decisively defeated. And yet, Troyes actually guaranteed that the war continued since it disinherited the Dauphin, the future Charles VII, left the Armagnacs wholly outside the peace settlement, and pushed all of France south of Gascony into opposition to a shameful peace with the English aggressor.

The great war thus lasted for 40 more years. When it finally ended England was expelled from lands in France it had held since the heyday of the Angevin Empire. How did this extraordinary reversal happen? It came about because the French reshaped a feudal muddle of knights and retainers into a semi-professional and disciplined army that effectively combined cavalry with infantry, with both supported by mobile artillery. It happened because France overcame the longbow with more advanced military technology: cannon and effective hand guns. It helped greatly that the English rested cocksure on old laurels won with the longbow by fathers and grandfathers in battles past, and thus failed to adapt to the rising black powder face of war. First, the French used cannon to bash down English castles and fortified towns, consolidating and extending central control of the countryside. Next, arquebusiers protected by ranks of pikemen appeared in large numbers in French ranks, where they proved the equal and then the better of longbowmen. An early indication of the shift in military fortunes to come was seen at *Beaugé* (March 21, 1421). The French cause was also helped by accidents of death and birth, notably as the early expiration of Henry V in 1422, the same year Charles VI died. Henry VI (1421–1471) was anointed at less than a year old and although the English crushed the French (and the *Scots Archers*) at *Verneuil* (August 17, 1424), during his long minority most English holdings in France were lost.

For decades the war had been marked by one indecisive siege leading to the next. But in the late 1420s the French asserted a new forcefulness and offensive spirit and capability. There is no doubt they were inspired by *Jeanne d'Arc*, "The Maid." On May 8, 1429, she raised the English siege of Orléans; on June 12 she led the storming of the fortress at Jargeau; on June 18 her army slaughtered a fleeing English column at Patay before it could deploy archers. This precipitated a strategic collapse of the English military position north of the Loire. In the last two weeks of June, garrisons at Meung and Beaugency surrendered. *John Talbot* gathered in most remaining garrisons and retreated to the Seine, where he was taken prisoner by Jeanne d'Arc. She then persuaded a reluctant Dauphin to lead the army to Reims. On July 17 she watched in religious ecstasy and adoration as he was elevated to the throne as Charles VII. French military and political fortunes subsequently improved dramatically. As for Jeanne d'Arc, she was repaid with martyrdom by fire at English Catholic hands without any succor from the French Catholic army she led to victory and without an offer of ransom from Charles.

The Maid burned but after her death French armies remained on the permanent offensive. Final French victory had nothing to do with divine intervention, though faith in that idea was a great spur to morale and there can be no doubt that France's fortunes were turned decisively by The Maid and her "Voices." Victory came primarily from feats of French arms made possible by gunpowder troops organized by a centralized bureaucracy: France won the war because it undertook essential military reforms that led to basic reorganization away from a feudal military culture and social order in favor of a modernizing, bureaucratic, centralized monarchy and state. This shift to a gunpowder/fiscal-state entailed more than accepting new technologies into the order of battle. It meant core reform of the king's finances and tax collection; royal determination to elevate his forces above all baronial rivals; reducing resistance of provincial castellans to the royal will; and taming of the rough warriors of the *"Free Companies"* who were running amok, occupying French towns, ravaging the countryside, and forcing peasants into desperate rebellions reminiscent of the infamous *"Jacquerie"* of 1358. In carrying out this great reform French kings were aided by an early, pre-modern form of "nationalism," an emerging sense of "Frenchness" separate from the old *res publica Christiana*. That was what Jeanne d'Arc had tapped into, furthered, and deeply inspired. Her martial successors then rode this proto-nationalism to final victory over the English and Burgundians.

By 1435 it was clear that the tide had turned irreversibly. And so, England's ally Burgundy switched sides (Treaty of Arras) and its duc restored long-occupied Paris to France (1436). Other than Bordeaux and Bayonne, Gascony fell to the French by 1442. During these advances and contributing to them, *Jean and Gaspard Bureau* made major strides in casting field cannon. With these guns, Charles VII retook Normandy from the English in 1449. Rouen surrendered on October 19, 1449, Harfleur in December 1449, and Honfleur in January 1450. Two months later the French took Caen. In 1450 came another major blow to English fortunes as a field army of some 4,000 men—three-quarters of them still armed with longbows—was trapped and decimated at *Formigny*. Winning the field that day were French cannon, arquebusiers, musketeers, but only a few bowmen, who together broke up the ranks of English archers with a bloody barrage of shell and shot. Once the English ran, the job was finished with lance, sword, and dirk. The French went on to reconquer all Normandy and Guyenne, often without firing a shot as English garrisons capitulated out of fear of the new French artillery. Bordeaux fell on June 30, 1451. The final battle was fought at *Castillon* on July 17, 1453, marking the failure of an English counter-invasion of Guyenne, where Gascons had risen to preserve a long-standing trade relationship with cross-Channel English overlords as against new lords closer at hand. French cannon great in number, power, and accuracy pounded the last English and Gascon resistance into agony, death, and surrender. Once Bordeaux submitted the war was over. In the end, France overmatched an overly confident but less prepared enemy with greater firepower and a more efficient marshaling of superior economic and military resources. When fighting subsequently broke out in England over yet another succession crisis, starting the bloody torment romantically disguised by the name *Wars of the Roses*, the English at last abdicated their long cross-Channel war and agreed to reduce their hold on the continent to the single port of Calais, which they controlled until 1558.

The Hundred Years' War was also fought importantly at sea. Each of the English chevauchées required an extraordinary naval effort, especially to transport the horses. The French replied with raids into England and efforts to intercept invasion fleets. In 1338 they chartered 20 Genoese galleys and 17 more from the Grimaldi family fleet in Monaco. They also built a fleet of their own, with Genoese technical advice, at the "Clos des Gallées" at Rouen. England had no effective naval reply to French galleys in the Channel, which burned Portsmouth and raided Jersey while the Genoese took Guernsey. These ships arrived too late to intercept Edward III's crossing of the Channel but they burned Southampton, sending southern England into a state of panic. In 1339 the Genoese entered the North Sea and attacked Harwich. On the return journey the Genoese entered the Bristol Channel, destroyed Hastings, and captured a number of ships at Plymouth. The English finally responded by organizing a *convoy* system for their armies and merchants trading with Gascony. Henceforth, each side preyed on the other's merchants, with escorts fighting a few sharp though indecisive actions. Eventually, the Genoese mutinied over lack of pay and rowed back to Italy.

At sea, the English were always less disciplined: their *privateers* constantly raided neutral shipping, costing England much financially and diplomatically. In 1340 the *Cinque* Ports sent a fleet to Boulogne harbor that burned 18 galleys and 24 merchantmen, as well as a large part of the town. Other English raids hit Dieppe and Le Tréport. The climax of the opening phase of the naval war came at *Sluys* (1340), the major sea battle of the 14th century and a devastating—but still not decisive—defeat for France. Within a month of Sluys the French navy—which was always more professional and better administered in this period than the ad hoc English navy—cut 30 ships out of a wool convoy. Three months later the French raided Portland and attacked Plymouth. The next year a French fleet cut off Gascony from England, and in 1342 another fleet burned Portsmouth. In 1345 a French galley fleet took Guernsey again. In 1346 a fleet of 32 large galleys from Genoa, Monaco, and Nice moved north, but failed to intercept Edward's crossing and chevauchée through Normandy. Moving overland, Edward took Caen, where he burned over 100 ships built to replace the French fleet lost at Sluys.

> *Edward took Caen, where he burned over 100 ships built to replace the French fleet lost at Sluys.*

A Castilian fleet allied to France ran the English Channel but was intercepted by Edward and the Black Prince, leading to a fight at Winchelsea called "Les Espagnols sur Mer" (August 29, 1350), a modest English victory. A civil war in Castile prevented further naval battles for another 20 years. The next major raid on England was in 1360, when a French fleet burned Winchelsea. Throughout this period, England's armies were unmatched on land, but it had no fleet to compare or contend with the professional forces of Castile, France, or Genoa—a rare moment in England's military history where its army surpassed its navy in value and effectiveness.

In 1364 civil war in Castile drew in England and France, leading by 1369 to most Castilian galleys pulling oars for France (this distraction delayed resumption of the *Reconquista*). That same year Denmark and Scotland allied, posing a major new naval threat to England in the north. The English response was to mandate archer practice for all freemen and to ban all other Sunday sports (including football), a deeply unpopular effort to reinforce homeland defense. Undeterred, French raiders burned Portsmouth in 1369 and the next year sent a small galley fleet into the Channel to take prizes. Two years later 12 Castilian galleys intercepted a fleet at La Rochelle, took on board a huge amount of English gold, and burned all ships in the harbor. In response, England at last set out to build a "Navy Royal." By 1375 this new force led to an uneasy naval truce with Castile and France (though mere legalities did not prevent a Castilian fleet later capturing 37 merchants, the largest loss of English shipping in the century). On June 24, 1377, just days after the death of Edward III, a massive galley fleet attacked and destroyed seven English coastal towns, including Folkestone, Portsmouth, and Plymouth. More amphibious raids followed, in both directions. Coastal towns were deserted and English prestige plummeted, only to be saved by a new French king, Charles VI, who did not appreciate France's naval advantage. Also tipping the balance was Portugal, already an important naval power that now allied with England in opposition to Castile. Portuguese raids on Castile forced its galleys home in 1381. Domestic and dynastic unrest in England and France quieted the war for a decade, though France made a Scottish alliance, briefly invaded Kent (1383), and planned but did not carry out a massive amphibious invasion in 1384. Three years later an English fleet was beaten off Dieppe, but another French invasion plan failed. In 1389 a truce was agreed, and the war at sea declined to little more than chronic piracy until 1406. An exception was a Welsh-Bretagne-French naval threat to England, and several French troop landings, related to *"Glyndŵr's Rebellion"* in Wales (1401–1406). Piracy and privateering—at which the English were more adept than any other sea nation—thereafter became the main form of naval conflict. French pirates also fared well, operating under Scottish protection while English pirates acted independently or under licence from the crown. Hundreds of prizes were taken and dozens of coastal towns were raided and burned. Still, the English monarchy failed to see the strategic advantage of seapower or develop the ability to finance it, so that by the time Henry V prepared to invade France the state of English shipping had sunk so low that the majority of ships carrying his horses, cannon, and troops were Dutch or Flemish hires.

France's ultimate victory in the "Great War" of the Middle Ages ended England's military importance for many decades. It also set the stage for a new round of dynastic conflict, this time between the houses of Valois and Habsburg, centering initially on control of northern Italy as in the *Italian Wars* (1494–1559), and continuing with the complex 17th-century struggle over Germany and northwest Europe generally known as the *Thirty Years' War* (1618–1648). A major effect of the long war over Normandy and Gascony was to propel both France and England far down the road toward powerful centralized monarchies, decades ahead of most other powers in

Europe. Finally, and most importantly, the war clearly demonstrated that lower-class folk protected by nothing more than plain cloth, but quickly trained to deploy lethal projectile weapons, could unhorse the chivalric order of Europe. By defeating the old warrior nobility in battle, the only sphere of activity which justified the social and economic privileges enjoyed by Europe's landed aristocracies and upheld by law and the Church, the way was cleared for radically egalitarian ideas about reordering society. Most of all, the way was freed by war for political reforms that looked to represent the interests of rising classes of urban professions who made up the new infantry. No place was this change more evident than in Italy, where the wars and ideas of the *Renaissance* continued some and adapted other changes that began during the Hundred Years' War. See also *Black Prince*; *drill*; *flagellants*; *Rouvray, Battle of*; *safeguard the sea*; *War of the Breton Succession*.

Suggested Reading: Christopher Allmand, *The Hundred Years' War* (1988); Alfred H. Burne, *The Crécy War* (1955; 1999); and *The Agincourt War* (1999); Anne Curry, *The Hundred Years' War, 1337–1453* (2003); J. Favier, *La Guerre de Cent Ans* (1980); Frances Gies, *Joan of Arc: The Legend and the Reality* (1981); Robin Neillands, *The Hundred Years' War* (1990; 2001); Édouard Perroy, *The Hundred Years' War* (1951); N.A.M. Rodger, *Safeguard of the Sea* (1997); Jonathon Sumption, *The Hundred Years' War* (1990; 1999); Malcolm Vale, *English Gascony, 1399–1453* (1970).

Hungarian Army. The protracted threat to Hungary from the advancing Ottoman Empire led King Mathias (1458–1490) to set up the first *hussars* as a permanent, mobile force to protect the frontier. He supplemented these with mercenaries of the *Black Company* and levies of wilder troops from Wallachia and Moldova. But Hungary was not as wealthy as Austria, France, or the Ottomans, and could hardly afford all the mercenaries it actually needed to defend its frontiers. Its forces thus were not so much a standing army as an ad hoc frontier defense screen in front of a still medieval land-for-service army.

Hungary. This former Roman province was settled in the 9th century C.E. by Magyar nomads from out of Central Asia. Others arrived after being driven south from Germany by the *Teutonic Knights* and hemmed into Hungary by Otto I, founder of the *Holy Roman Empire*. Hungary became a Christian kingdom during the 11th century. In 1222 its nobility forced the "Golden Bull" on its kings, establishing effective government by the aristocracy. In 1241 the *Mongols* invaded, defeating the Hungarians decisively at Mohi. That defeat opened Hungary to repeated Mongol depredations and to social chaos. In the 14th century it slowly recovered, expanding to the Dalmatian coast and into Poland. János Hunyadi led Hungarian resistance to the Ottomans, but also suffered major losses at *Varna* (1444) and *Kosovo Polje* (1448). The core of Hungarian armies was still mailed cavalry, supplemented by lighter horse archers in the form of auxiliaries drawn from fierce but minor Steppe peoples such as the Cumans, Pechenegs, and Szeklers. From this system the first *hussars* originated under King Mathias (1458–1490), who deployed them as a mobile force to protect his endangered frontier with the Ottoman Empire.

Mathias also assembled a permanent artillery park and hired Serbian and Bohemian mercenaries (the "Black Company") to supplement his feudal heavy cavalry. The Hungarians were greatly aided by inhospitable terrain: northeast Hungary was almost impenetrable by Ottoman armies, with other regions of the country crisscrossed by rivers or hosting large areas of marsh and bog that impeded cavalry.

Nevertheless, the Ottomans brought large armies into Hungary, notably under *Muhammad II*, who was repelled by Hunyadi, and *Suleiman I*, who crushed the Hungarians at *Mohács* (1526). *Charles V* sent Habsburg forces to Hungary's aid. Still, after the capture of Buda and annexation of central Hungary in 1541, the Ottomans were well-ensconced. They garrisoned their new province with a peak force of 22,000 men paid with revenue from Egypt. In 1552 the Ottomans unsuccessfully besieged the fortress of Eger (Eğri), but added territory in northern Hungary to their empire. From 1593 to 1606 much of the "Long War," or *Thirteen Years' War*, was fought in and over Hungary. Eger fell to Muhammad III in 1596. For most of the 17th century Hungary was divided between its erstwhile ally and its great enemy, as Austrian emperors paid tribute to the Ottomans in return for a share of Hungarian territory and peace along the *Militargrenze*. Hungary avoided total conquest less due to its own military efforts than because the two contending empires preferred that it remain a buffer between them. Religious differences began to impinge on Hungarian affairs as they did everywhere in Europe in the 17th century, though in odd ways: from 1604 to 1606 Stephen Bocskay led a Hungarian revolt in alliance with the Ottomans against an effort by *Rudolf II* to reimpose Catholicism. Hungary thereafter was a *marcher* state, with the dominant player the Ottoman governor in Buda. The main pattern of warfare was small scale border raiding carried out by local forces. Hungary remained militarily quiet as the Ottomans completed their long wars with Safavid Iran, and the Austrian Empire was sucked deep into the *Thirty Years' War* in Germany. Thus, from 1606 to 1660 there was no large-scale war on the Hungarian frontier.

Suggested Reading: J. M. Bak and R. Király, eds., *From Hunyadi to Rakocki* (1982); Géza Perjés, *The Fall of the Medieval Kingdom of Hungary*, Mario Fenyó, trans. (1977; 1989); K. Péter et al., eds., *A History of Hungary* (1990).

Hung Taiji (d.1643). See *China*; *Manchus*; *Nurgaci*.

Hunyadi, János (c.1407–1456). Hungarian patriot; Transylvanian knight; Habsburg general. Governor of Hungary, 1446–1452. He led the Hungarians in many battles against the Ottomans, including sharp losses at *Varna* (1444) and *Kosovo Polje* (1448). In his last year he organized resistance to the invasion of the Balkans by *Muhammad II*, routed the Muslim army before Belgrade, and lifted the Muslim siege of the city. It remained in Christian hands until 1521.

Hurenweibel. "Whore sergeant." In a *Landsknechte* company or regiment this officer was responsible for overseeing the *baggage train*. The train included women, many of whom were prostitutes, which gave the position its unusual name. He was charged with making sure fights among the men did not get out of hand, but his most important duty was to maneuver the train out of danger when contact was made with the enemy. It was important not only to prevent the train from interfering with field maneuvers but to reduce the likelihood that an enemy threat to the women of the baggage train would entice fighting men to abandon their positions in order to save their wives and children, and other valuables.

Hus, Jan (1369–1415). Bohemian reformer. He was born into a peasant family in Husinetz, the village for which he was named. In his study at the University of Prague he was deeply influenced by the reformist teachings of *John Wycliffe*. Hus was named rector of the University in 1402. In 1409 the Archbishop of Prague began an inquisition into his writings and preaching, even as Pope Alexander V consigned all books by Wycliffe to be burned as heretical texts. In July, Hus was excommunicated. Riots ensued throughout Bohemia. This popular support among the common people and nobility kept Hus in place at the University. In 1411, Prague was placed under papal interdict for protecting Hus. By 1413 his thinking was more radical: he published scathing critiques of scandalous and immoral practices among the clergy, high and low, from concubinage to preying on the superstitions of the ignorant and simple. In addition to protesting abuses by the clergy Hus parted company on doctrine by upholding the *Utraquist* position that lay folk be allowed to take the sacrament of the Mass *sub utraque specie* ("in both kinds"). This undermined his support at the University. He was advised by King Wencislaus to leave Prague and took refuge in a castle of one of his noble supporters. Hus was ordered to appear before the *Council of Constance* (1414–1418), to which he was given a "safe conduct" pass by Emperor *Sigismund* (r.1411–1437). Within three weeks the safe conduct was broken and he was arrested and imprisoned, in violation of the Imperial promise. At his trial he was not permitted to speak in his own defense, not given a defense counsel, and was ordered to recant in full on pain of torture and death. He refused. He was burned at the stake for "heresy" on July 6, 1415. This enraged his followers and launched the *Hussite Wars*. A century later, *Martin Luther* remarked: "We are all Hussites without realizing it."

hussars. The term originates either from the Hungarian "husz," meaning "twenty," or more likely from Slavonic "gussar," meaning "bandit." In either case, hussars were light cavalry that originated in the Balkans and took formal shape in Hungary's hybrid system of mailed feudal cavalry supplemented by mounted archers on faster, smaller mounts. Hussars were recruited by King Mathias (1458–1490), who saw that Hungary needed a frontier force to face the Ottoman threat. These wild horsemen were deployed as fast reinforcements for a barrier of permanent fortresses and watch posts that guarded Hungary's southern frontier. On the offense, they conducted harassing and punitive raids into Muslim lands and participated in rare battles fought in the mountains. They held the Hungarian flanks at the losing fight with the Ottomans at *Kosovo Polje* (1448). As the battlefield dominance of purely *heavy cavalry* faded everywhere other armies adopted the Hungarian hussar model. That included their famously elaborate dress: hussars were distinguished by brilliant colors and ornate embellishments, notably the long, Turkish-style dolman with loose-hanging sleeves and a tall fur cap with attached cloth bag or busby.

Polish hussars were originally modeled on Hungarian hussars, except for the important difference that most Polish horsemen ultimately hailed from the upper reaches of the *szlachta*. Polish hussar units were comprised of one "comrade" ("*towarzysz*") and four retainers ("pacholeks"). This was reduced to two "pacholeks" in the late 17th century. Early Polish hussars were mainly foreign mercenaries known as "Racowie" (or "Serbs," from their locale of origin, Ras). Over time, Poland's hussars grew heavier in horses and weapons to become medium cavalry, whereas Hungarian hussars remained true light cavalry, and Polish nobles replaced foreign mercenaries. Polish hussars were primarily lancers, but also carried two swords: a short saber ("szabla") worn on the belt, and a long, rapier-like sword ("koncerz") carried astride the saddle and wielded almost like a lance. Many also carried bows, and from 1576 all were required to carry two pistols holstered to the saddle. Hussars were the mainstay of Polish cavalry by the time of *Stefan Báthory*, but fell to just 20 percent of the cavalry force by 1648. Famously, they attached great "wings"

> *Many also carried bows, and from 1576 all were required to carry two pistols holstered to the saddle.*

to the back of their armor in the Serbian and Turkish manner. These were in evidence from the mid-16th century. Tremendously elaborate versions appeared early in the 17th century. They were made from a wooden frame covered in velvet and brass. Each brace held a row of large feathers that might rise two or three feet above the rider's head. No one knows why this was done. Theories range from a rear defense against swords (unlikely), to a display of trophy tokens from prior battles (but why so unwieldy?), to psychological intimidation of infantry (the most likely reason). Any psychological benefit— and wings made hussars appear as angels of death to superstitious, foot bound enemies—was reinforced by every cavalryman's normal vanity, accentuated in Poland by his haughty noble origins. See also *Pancerna cavalry*; *Polish Army*.

Hussite Wars (1419–1478). This prolonged conflict was provoked by the trial and burning at the stake of *Jan Hus* by the *Council of Constance* in 1415, in violation of an Imperial "safe conduct" issued to coax him to travel to Constance. His followers rebelled against the Catholic Church and Emperor *Sigismund* (r.1411–1437). Their reasons were doctrinal as well as "nationalistic" and constitutional: they were *Utraquists* in doctrine who opposed the episcopalian structure of the Church as well as the German constitution of the *Holy Roman Empire*. The Hussite revolt was the largest religious rebellion in Europe since the rising of the Cathars of France and the *Albigensian Crusade* of the 13th century. The conflict began when the Hussites carried out the first *"defenestration of Prague"* (1419). Fighting began after King Wenceslaus died, shortly after the defenestration. The main aim of the Hussites was to prevent the hated Sigismund mounting the throne of Bohemia, but fighting between Bohemian Hussites and Catholics spread into Moravia. Hussite armies would later carry the war beyond these core areas to terrorize the nobility of much of Central Europe. Masses of peasants organized into Hussite bands and joined with militia from Hussite towns. The Hussite army was officered by nobles and knights who embraced the teaching of Jan Hus, though not always with the same passion as the burghers and peasants. Still, this cross-class support gave the Hussite Wars a tripartite and even "national" character unusual for the age, and a religious and social unity of purpose, faith, and hate.

The experienced mercenary *Jan Žižka* quickly emerged as the top Hussite commander, winning an initial victory at Sudomer (March 25, 1420). He then organized the defense of Prague in which the Hussites bolted the city's gates and fortified and defended the nearby Hill of Vítkov with 9,000 men. On July 14, 1420, a large Imperial and Catholic army attacked the Hussite hill fort, only to be repulsed with heavy casualties by the unmatched firepower brought to bear by the military genius of Žižka and the fanatic ferocity of the Hussites. Žižka subsequently cleared all remaining Imperial forces out of Bohemia. At the Diet of Nuremberg (1422), Sigismund and the German territorial princes agreed to raise two armies to put down the Hussites. The first was sent to raise a Hussite siege of Karlstein; the second was commissioned to pursue the Hussite field army until it was utterly destroyed. Instead, Žižka led the Hussite army flying a goose flag ("hus") to a major victory over the Imperials at *Kutná Hora*, and beat them again just four days later at *Nêmecký Brod*. In each rout Žižka and the Hussites employed their soon-to-be-famous *Wagenburg* (mobile fort) from behind which they fired hand culverins, early arquebuses, and several small cannon. This devastated the surprised Imperial cavalry at close range. Two unexpected victories for the Hussites ended the first Imperial and Catholic attempt to crush the Bohemian "heretic rebellion."

However, civil war broke out among the Hussites that split them into a radical Taborite sect named for their mobile war camps (*tabor*) and drawn mostly from the lower social orders, and a more moderate and predominantly noble Utraquist faction. The Tabor were not merely religious dissenters. Their actions and demands spoke to a radical social and even proto-socialist agenda that alienated and frightened the Utraquists, who had doctrinal differences with the Catholic Church but were propertied, social conservatives. Žižka was killed (October, 11, 1424) in fraternal fighting that ensued between the factions. Pope Martin V preached a crusade against the Hussites in 1427, calling especially on England to provide knights to put down, as Martin put it, the "awful heresy" for which he held the English heretic Wycliffe responsible. Most English nobles were too busy besieging Orléans and fighting Frenchmen to participate, but German Catholic knights and princes formed another army to crush what they regarded as an army of upstart peasants. The

Germans engaged the Hussites at *Ustí nad Labem* (1426). Once more, Taborite peasants prevailed over the armored knights and men-at-arms of the Holy Roman Empire. After their third defensive victory over the best that German chivalry offered, the Hussites went on the offensive. They attacked into Austria, Hungary, and Germany, everywhere enjoying success and everywhere pillaging and killing the ungodly. What stopped them was not German arms but another outbreak of doctrinal argument and Hussite civil war.

A Hussite army invaded Germany again in 1429–1430, reaching deep into Franconia. As before, the late-medieval tactics of their militarily conservative enemies failed to beat the mobile fortification and firepower of the Wagenburgs. The *Council of Basel* then offered an olive branch that was accepted by moderate Hussite nobles but was rejected by the Taborites. This renewed the civil war between Taborite and Utraquist factions, leading to fratricidal carnage at *Český-Brod* (1434). The blood of confessional brothers left on that field so weakened the Taborites they were forced to accept Sigismund as King of Bohemia in 1436. A desultory peace ensued until the *War of the Cities* in the 1450s, when Hussite Wagenburgs raided deep into the *Ordensstaat* in mercenary service. There followed another uneasy peace to 1462, until the pope revoked the "Compactata" agreed at Basel 30 years earlier. The Hussite Wars thus broke out again in 1466. This time they took on the character of an Utraquist revolt against papal and Imperial authority, not a war of radical Taborite "heresy" against Catholic orthodoxy. They thus lacked the bitter hatred and uncompromising positions of the first war. A peace was agreed in 1478, after which Hussite bands again hired out as mercenaries well beyond Bohemia. The Hussite motto, "Truth Prevails," became a powerful nationalist slogan for all later generations of Czechs, including Catholics after 1620.

Suggested Reading: F. Bartos, *The Hussite Revolution* (1986); F. Heyman, *John Zizka and the Hussite Revolution* (1955); H. Kaminsky, *A History of the Hussite Revolution* (1967).

ichcahuipilli. Aztec cotton *armor* formed of a knee-length padded jacket, with a cotton helmet. It was useful against Mezoamerican obsidian-blade weapons, but did not protect against Tuledo steel blades or arquebus-fire by the *conquistadores.*

iconoclasm. Smashing of holy images and statuary thought to be conducive to idolatry, heresy, or rank superstition. Iconoclasm had an ancient pedigree within the Byzantine Empire and under Islam. In the 8th century, for instance, fanatic Muslim invaders of India smashed Buddhist and Hindu statuary and images. In Latin Christendom it was more a phenomenon of the *Protestant Reformation*, usually carried out by fresh converts to Protestantism against Catholic imagery and statuary, crucifixes, and altars. Protestant mockery of Catholic icons extended to roasting crucifixes over bonfires, feeding the eucharist to dogs or pigs, fouling altars with excrement, and scattering bones from the reliquaries of Catholic saints. Clergy who resisted were beaten; some were killed. *Martin Luther* opposed these practices but many Calvinists and all followers of *Zwingli* were fanatic iconoclasts. Waves of violent iconoclasm ("beeldenstorm") across the Netherlands were part of the essential prelude to the *Eighty Years' War* (1568–1648), as what began as spontaneous violence became organized repression of Catholic worship in the northern Netherlands in 1566, 1576–1579, and 1580–1581. In Holland, the Mass was no longer allowed anywhere after 1581, partly for iconoclastic reasons. See also *Anabaptism*; *French Civil Wars.*

Ifriqiya. A North African kingdom comprising much of *Tripoli* and *Tunis.* In 827, Muslims from Ifriqiya began the conquest of Sicily, which they completed in 969. Sicily was divided into emirates sustained by an imported *itqa* system of military recruitment. Its ruling Hafsid dynasty broke away from the Almohads of Morocco from the 13th century onward. Centered on Tunis at one terminus of the trans-Saharan trade, Ifriqiya conducted maritime trade with *Mamlūk* Egypt and overland trade with *Kanem*. It reached its peak in the 15th century as a major naval power in the western Mediterranean, employing Christian galley-slaves captured from Italy and the Dalmatian coast. It expanded during the 15th century at the expense of neighboring Tlemcen, which it made a tributary. From 1504, Muslim "pirates" infested the Ifriqiya coast, leading to Spanish occupation of Tripoli in 1511. The Ottomans tried to impose their writ over Tlemcen and Ifriqiya, causing a turn by those smaller Muslim powers to Spain for protection. The Hafsids were briefly chased from Tunis in 1534 by *Algiers* corsairs working for the Ottomans, but returned with Spanish help to rule for 40 more years. Expelled again in 1569, and again restored by Spain after 1571, the Hafsids were ousted for good by the Ottomans in 1574. Ifriqiya thereafter remained an Ottoman province.

Ikkō-ikki. See *Odo Nobunaga*; *True Pure Land.*

Île de Ré, **Siege of** (July–October, 1627). An ill-fated English naval expedition, badly organized and commanded by the *Duke of Buckingham*, was sent by *Charles I* to support the Huguenots at *La Rochelle*. When the French Protestants refused Buckingham permission to bring his ships and 8,000 soldiers into the harbor, he disembarked the troops on nearby Île de Ré. In desultory fighting, the English failed to take the citadel held by Royalist forces since their defeat of the Rochelais in February 1626. The English suffered many casualties in an incompetent military misadventure that brought Buckingham to disgrace, Charles into disfavor, and lasting embarrassment to English arms.

Il-Khans. The Mongol rulers of Iran; they converted to Islam in 1295.

imam. In the majority *sunni* tradition of *Islam*, the head of a mosque and a prayer leader. In the minority *shī'a* tradition of Islam, a Muslim leader said to descend from Muhammad's family (Alid candidate) and, therefore, a divinely appointed guide and the sole rightful ruler of the Faithful, to be upheld above all secular authority. A quasi-messianic variant of this tradition, called "Twelfth-imam shī'a," or just "Twelvers," recognized eleven anointed imams but asserted that the rightful succession stopped in 765 C.E. with the death of the sixth *caliph*, Ja'far al-Sādiq, the last true caliph visible to earthly eyes. Ultimately, they held that the succession rightly fell to his son, Musa, and awaited his return as the 12th or "Hidden Imam." *Ismailis* (Fatamids) are sometimes called "Seveners" because they believed the succession fell immediately to Ja'far al-Sādiq's other son, Ismail. Similarly, the Nizari sect followed the rightful succession only to the fourth caliph.

Imperial Army (of the Holy Roman Empire). "Landesabwehr." The emperor traditionally had the right, as a German king, to issue a *"bannum"* in times of extreme need. In theory, this and other edicts applied to all subjects of military age, excepting only women, shepherds, and clergy. In fact, the bannum mostly called on the feudal service obligations of German knighthood (the *"Ritter-stand"*). In some cases, peasant militia were called up as foot soldiers while townsmen served as auxiliaries, usually, as archers or crossbowmen. The old feudal military order, dating to Charlemagne, required enfeoffed nobles and retainers to serve free for three months, which was significantly longer than the *servitium debitum* in France and England. This rule was invoked as late as the mid-13th century, but otherwise was eroded by the rise of service-for-pay arrangements even among German nobility. Still, as late as the early 15th century the idea of mandatory feudal service survived in the Empire: in 1401 German towns and nobles were summoned to an Imperial campaign in Italy by region ("Landesaufgebot") and by individual fief ("Lehnsaufgebot"). While noble "officers" were paid a set fee, town militia received nothing. In the late 1480s, Emperor *Maximilian I* organized *Landsknechte* companies to mimic, and hopefully to best, the *Swiss squares*. In 1500 he gave responsibility for regional defense and recruitment to the *Reichskreis*.

In the 16th century the *Hofkriegsrat*, or Imperial War Council, controlled 25,000 Imperial troops, but only on paper. Real control rested with the Imperial princes, and with commanders responsible for regional military order appointed by discrete Reichskreis. The Landsknechte were strictly mercenary troops. That meant in a shooting war the emperors relied principally on military contractors to raise mercenary armies to supplement noble heavy cavalry. There was no serious attempt to raise a conscript Imperial force because the emperors had no funds to pay for it outside revenues from their hereditary lands. Once the *Protestant Reformation* took hold in Germany it was next to impossible for emperors to obtain necessary funds and authorization from divided princes to raise and maintain Imperial troops, a problem made evident during *Charles V*'s desultory war with the princes of the *Schmalkaldic League*. Just before the outbreak of the *Thirty Years' War* (1618–1648) the Imperial princes divided openly into confessional associations that briefly fielded their own armies: the *Catholic League* and *Protestant Union*. As a result, most Imperial troops from 1618 to 1648 were mercenaries raised by military entrepreneurs and sustained not by taxes but by forced *contributions*. On Imperial commanders, battles, wars, and related matters see: *Alte Feste, Siege of*; *armories*; *Breitenfeld, First*; *Breitenfeld, Second*; *Dessau Bridge, Battle of*; *Ferdinand II, Holy Roman Emperor*; *Ferdinand III, Holy Roman Emperor*; *Fleurus, Battle of*; *Freiburg, Battle of*; *The Grisons*; *Gustavus II Adolphus*; *Höchst, Battle of*; *Holy Roman Empire*; *Italian Wars*; *Jankov, Battle of*; *Kutná Hora, Battle of*; *Lützen, Battle of*; *Maximilian I*; *Mercy, Franz von*; *Německý Brod, Battle of*; *Nördlingen, First Battle of*; *Nördlingen, Second Battle of*; *Pappenheim, Graf zu*; *partisan* (2); *Tilly, Count Johann Tserclaes*; *Wallenstein, Albrecht von*; *war finance*; *White Mountain, Battle of*; *Zusmarshausen, Battle of*.

Imperial Diet. The assembly of all territorial rulers of the *Holy Roman Empire*, divided into three colleges: Electors, Princes, and Towns. It met at Regensburg. The Diet called for 1541 by *Charles V* to heal the breach between Catholics and Protestants failed miserably. The Diet met just six times from 1555 to 1603. It was paralyzed by *confessionalism* in 1608, when Protestant princes refused to attend. It was suspended in 1613 in the run-up to the *Thirty Years' War*, and was never convened during the long reign of *Ferdinand II*. However, *Ferdinand III* recalled the Diet from 1640 to 1641 to raise taxes for the final phase of the war and strengthen the negotiating position of the Empire in coming peace talks. In return, he was forced to agree that all territorial princes should be separately represented at the peace conference. This principle was extended in 1645 to allow all *Estates* to participate in the talks leading to the *Peace of Westphalia* (1648). See also *contributions*; *Imperial Army*; *Prague, Peace of.*

impressment. In England, county authorities and the central government encouraged impressment of local vagrants, masterless men, the lame or diseased, and local criminals. Since the attrition rate from disease or combat was extremely high and most men sent overseas never saw England again, this was seen as a useful way to rid the country of "undesirables" while sparing its favored sons. For war at sea, most impressment was of whole ships and crews. Carpenters and shipwrights were also impressed to build or repair the king's ships with little or no recompense, but at least they served in major ports where most already lived. The king's prerogatives did not just concern war: impressment was a traditional right that extended to his household services, fishing and gaming for the king's table, and construction of his palaces. As the Middle Ages waned, so too impressment of skilled craftsmen was slowly replaced by paid labor. However, impressment was revived by *Charles I* to replace politically unreliable *trained bands* during the *Second Bishop's War.* When Parliament turned to impressment in 1642 as a means of whittling away the king's control of the Army, the move provoked a national division and the first skirmishes of the *English Civil Wars* (1639–1651). See also *Cinque Ports*; *club men*; *"coat-and-conduct" money*; *demurrage.*

Inca Empire. "Tahuantinsuyu" or "Land of the Four Quarters." In c.1200 C.E., the central Andes was politically fragmented with one concentrated but declining power, Tiahuanacu, presiding over the region south of Lake Titicaca. As Tiahuanacu decayed each mountain valley hosted an irrigation-based microstate, usually involved in violent competition for arable land and potable water with neighboring valley-states. Around 1440 a hitherto little-known mountain tribe, the Inca of the Cuzco valley, took advantage of this situation in the Andes highlands to expand along the west coast of South America. From this process emerged the Inca Empire, the largest Indian state created in the Americas. It was managed by forced resettlement to break up resistance after conquest, and political assimilation of neighboring tribes. The Inca Empire boasted populous cities sustained by high-calorie crops of potatoes and maize. It governed most of the 20–25 million who lived in the Andes region, making it one of the larger states in the world at that time. The

Inca domain was assembled and ruled by a powerful military headed by a warlord called the "Sapa" ("Sole") Inca. It was sustained by a sophisticated bureaucracy which included an elaborate system of runners ("chasquis") and imperial roads, the latter providing for communication, political and military intelligence, and rapid military reinforcement throughout an empire thousands of miles long. The main founder was Pachacutec (né Cusi Yuanqui), who as Sapa Inca from 1438 to 1471 expanded the state 1,000 miles from Cuzco. His successor, Túpac Yupanqui (r.1471–1493), overcame a rival empire, Chimor. He thereby added the most territory of any Sapa Inca, though he sometimes did this by negotiation and treaty rather than military conquest. Under Huayna Capac (r.1493–1525) the Inca pushed out of northern Peru into modern Ecuador, to Quito. At its greatest extent the Inca tribute empire stretched 4,500 miles along the Pacific coast of South America, nearly the full length of the Andes range. Yet, it was rapidly conquered by a small group of brutal Spanish *conquistadores* led by a reckless adventurer, *Francisco Pizarro*. How?

Politics in the Inca Empire were marked by frequent violent rebellions and by "caesarism" and palace revolt in Cuzco. This gave the Spanish an opportunity to divide and conquer. Afro-European diseases had already reached the northern Inca lands, traveling overland from Mexico through Central America, by the time the Spanish arrived. The demographic collapse these virgin diseases caused aggravated an Inca civil war already underway over the succession. The Spanish entered the Inca domain just as it was consumed by demographic devastation and divided by a major civil war. They were thus able to form alliances with oppressed or recently conquered tribes before moving against the center of Inca power at Cuzco. Also, the advancing wave of disease appeared to the Inca to be a divine scourge. The Spanish agreed with this thesis, seeing outbreaks of plague, smallpox, and other epidemic diseases as God's just punishment of non-Christian Indians: natural phenomena caused one society to lose religious confidence while giving the other an ideological swagger and renewed enthusiasm for martial

> *Politics in the Inca Empire were marked by frequent violent rebellions and by "caesarism" and palace revolt in Cuzco.*

adventure. Atahualpa, the last Sapa Inca to rule, gravely underestimated the technological advantages of Spanish horses, firearms, and cannon, none of which his legions possessed. He was captured by surprise and murdered by Pizarro in July 1533, possibly in deliberate imitation of how the Spanish thought *Hernán Cortés* toppled the Aztecs. A climactic battle between warring factions of conquistadores took place after Pizarro's death, at Ayacucho (Huramanga), on September 18, 1542. The losers were beheaded. Surviving conquistadores in Peru refused to submit to the authority of the royal viceroy who was trying to limit the excesses of the *encomienda* system they had introduced, and to impose Imperial rule from Spain. Pizarro's half-brother Gonzalo led an attack on Lima in 1546 and won a victory over the viceroy, whom he beheaded. Some rebels urged Gonzalo to proclaim a Peruvian kingdom with himself as monarch. However, a replacement viceroy suspended the "New Laws" protecting Indians and offered pardons to most rebels. This caused the rebellion to collapse and led to the beheading of its leaders, including Gonzalo (April 1548).

Upon direct contact with the Spanish, the Indians of the Andes suffered a catastrophic population decline from a witches' cauldron of epidemic diseases of European or African origin: typhus, tuberculosis, bubonic plague, but especially smallpox, and killer "childhood" diseases such as measles, whooping cough, mumps, dysentery, meningitis, influenza, and jaundice, which also wiped out Amerindian adults who lacked the slightest natural resistance. Within 50 years of the conquest the native population of the Andes had been reduced by 90 percent. This had more than a physical impact: it fundamentally demoralized Amerindian civilization, reducing the will to rebel against Iberian overlordship imposed during the 16th century and conducing to mass conversions to Christianity by populations made docile and compliant by too much death and despair, and perhaps by priest-obeying habits learned under the Inca. Further south, small tribes of nautical migrants known as "sea nomads" and Araucanian Indians remained independent into the 19th century. From 1541 to 1664 fighting was heavy and bloody, with the Araucanians forcing the Spanish to remain north of the Bío Bío.

Suggested Reading: Geoffrey Conrad and Arthur Demarest, *Religion and Empire* (1984); Richard Keatinge, ed., *Peruvian Prehistory* (1988); Thomas C. Patterson, *The Inca Empire* (1991).

incastellamento. See *castles, on land*.

incendiaries. See *fire*; *fire-lance*; *Greek fire*; *gunpowder weapons*; *naphtha*.

indentures for war. A type of military contract. With England waging the *Scottish Wars*, then involved in the *Hundred Years' War* (1337–1453), the old system of *feudal* levies no longer sufficed. *Scutage* also failed to raise funds to recruit enough of the new types of specialized infantry and archery *dragoons* needed by warlord monarchs like *Edward III*. Instead, contracts for military service farmed out recruitment to a contractor ("conductor") who brought groups of "retainers" to camp in return for a fee drawn from land tenures or other royal revenues. Such "indentures for war" were used starting in the 14th century and survived into the 15th century. Indentures also served naval recruitment. During the *Wars of the Roses* indentures were used by both sides, though when loyal troops were needed personal recruitment among "clients" and tenants of the great magnates was the mainstay.

Index Librorum Prohibitorium. Cardinal Carafa (later, Pope Paul IV) established the "Holy Office" of the *Inquisition* in Rome during the Catholic *Counter-Reformation*. As pope, in 1559 he revived a little used medieval practice of listing on an "Index" books prohibited to the faithful. Since most Catholics still could not read, this measure aimed mostly at clergy and the lay upper classes.

India. In the early 8th century plundering Muslim invaders swept into India from the northwest. Fanatic iconoclasts, they smashed *Hindu* and *Buddhist* temples. The Ghaznavids (originally based in the Afghan town of Ghazi, southwest of Kabul) were the first of several Turkic-Afghan Muslim peoples to raid north India, riding on an Indian military revolution all its own—the *warhorse*. The Ghaznavids overran the Punjab, to which they brought *Islam* in its early and highly militarized form. They caused much bitterness with a policy of forced conversions of Hindus, but succeeded in planting the new religion deep in the soil of northern India. Islam also attracted many voluntary converts, especially among the lower Hindu castes and "untouchables" who were drawn to its doctrine of moral and spiritual equality among all believers. Others were attracted to the ability of Muslim emirs to protect local areas militarily and provide law and public order. As so often in world history, religious change followed migration and conquest, then took deeper root with peacetime trade, assimilation, and state support. The Ghaznavids were followed by the Ghurids, who captured and plundered Delhi in 1193. In 1202, Ghurid persecutions scattered most of India's remaining Buddhists to Nepal, Tibet, and beyond, so that already by the 12th century north India was divided among Muslim kingdoms. The most important of these was established by Turkic invaders in 1206 in Delhi, employing *mamlūk* slave soldiers to ensure elite and military loyalty. The *"Delhi Sultanate"* lasted from 1200 to 1526 under various dynasties. Afghan in origin, it sought an ethnic identification of elite troops as the path to dynastic security, which left it exposed to rebellion by the excluded majority. A third wave of Central Asian invaders, the Khaljis, took over in Delhi in 1290. All these invasions were opposed by Hindus, notably the warrior *Rajputs*, themselves probably descended from earlier Central Asian invaders. The Muslim states were in turn subjected to assault by pagan *Mongols*. A Mongol horde moved into India from Afghanistan in the first decade of the 14th century. The earlier Turkic-Muslim invaders of India thus probably preserved it from still worse depredations by the Mongols, deflecting that appalling scourge instead into Ukraine, southern Russia, and Anatolia and Iraq.

Sultan Ala-ud-din (r.1296–1316) turned Muslim military attention south, overrunning the Rajputs and invading the ancient Tamil states for the first time. The Tughluqs, a Muslim dynasty founded by a slave soldier, followed Ala-ud-din to the throne of Delhi, ruling much of the north from 1320. However, a terrible famine from 1335 to 1342 spawned rebellions by Muslim and Hindu chieftains alike, in Madura, 1335; Vijayanagar, 1336; Bengal, 1338, which remained independent to 1576; and the Deccan Sultanate in 1347, where the vaguely Turkic Bahmāni dynasty ruled independently of Delhi until 1528. The "Lords of the Horse" in Vijayanagar fought the Bahmāni Deccan Sultanate in 10 indecisive wars over the following 150 years, with Vijayanagar progressively adopting imported Arabian horses and Ottoman cavalry tactics along with Muslim advisers and mercenaries. It thus survived as the major non-Muslim state on the subcontinent. The chronic nature of Indian wars reflected the *March* character of the "inner frontiers" of India's states, with most fighting occurring in the frontier zones. Campaigns were launched to coincide with the end of the monsoon season in October, once the mud dried and rivers receded from their crest and became fordable. They ended before the high heat of March or April.

Adding new torments to already great suffering born of India's internal conflicts, *Timur* took advantage of the lack of a single center of power to invade. He sacked Delhi in 1398 but was drawn away by his own restless nature and rebellion elsewhere in his sprawling, incoherent, and not-fully subjugated empire. For another hundred years, into the early 16th century, India remained badly fragmented, at war internally, and laid open to Central Asian raiders. Into this vacuum of power stepped the Timurids (descendants of Timur), out of Afghanistan. They brought with them imported firearms from 1400 and European and Ottoman *renegade* gunsmiths. Only much later did they import the technology needed to produce guns and cannon locally. *Mughal* rule over most of northern India was established in 1526–1527 by *Babur*. He beat the army of the Delhi Sultanate at *Panipat* (1526), and defeated the Rajputs at *Khanwa* (1527). Thereafter, the Mughals shrewdly used marriage ties to forge alliances with leading Rajputs and consolidate their hold on northern India. See also *Akbar*; *artillery*; *corning/corned gunpowder*; *fitna*; *fortification*; *Marathas*; *mansabdari*; *mulkgiri*; *Portuguese India*; *Sher Khan*.

Suggested Reading: John Keay, *India: A History* (2000); Dirk Kolff, *Naukar, Rajput, and Sepoy* (1990); J. Sarkar, *A Military History of India* (1970); Stanley Wolpert, *A New History of India*, 6th ed. (2000).

Indian (subcontinental) armies. See *Akbar*; *artillery*; *Babur*; *elephants*; *infantry*; *Khanwa, Battle of*; *Marathas*; *Mamlūks*; *Mughal Empire*; *Panipat, Battle of (April 21, 1526)*; *Rajputs*; *Timur*.

Indian Wars (Mexico, Central and South America). See *Alvarado, Pedro de*; *Aztec Empire*; *Brazil*; *Charles V, Holy Roman Emperor*; *conquistadors*; *Cortés, Hernán*; *disease*; *encomienda*; *Inca Empire*; *Jesuits*; *Moctezuma II*; *Otumba, Battle of*; *Pax Hispanica*; *Peru, Viceroyalty of*; *Philip II, of Spain*; *Pizarro, Francisco*; *real patronato*; *requerimiento*; *Spain*; *Tenochtitlán, First Siege of*; *Tenochtitlán, Second Siege of*.

Indian Wars (North America). In 1492 the Indian population of North America probably numbered several million (estimates range wildly, from one to twelve million). But European and African *diseases* ravaged all Indian nations which came into contact with settler populations. Half or more of most tribes died; up to 90 percent of Great Lakes Indians perished. More than any other factor, mass death from disease assured the eventual military defeat of the Indians of eastern North America. As the European and African populations significantly increased in the late 17th and early 18th centuries, demographics multiplied settler military resources while disease divided those of the Indians. Thus, New England Indians decreased from over 100,000 in 1600 to 8,600 seventy years later, while immigration and natural increase raised the settler population to 50,000. Comparable shifts occurred in other regions of European–Indian conflict. On first contact, the Iroquois *Haudenosaunee*, the "Five Nations," had about 25,000 members divided among the Cayuga, Mohawk, Oneida, Onondagas, and Senecas (they were joined by the Tuscaroras in 1714). Despite the Iroquois practice of assimilating captives into their own nations, disease and casualties from chronic warfare with settlers over land, and even more with neighboring tribes over control of the fur trade, ensured that Haudenosaunee numbers did not rise significantly over the next 200 years. The Huron of Upper Canada were similarly devastated, losing half their numbers to epidemic diseases and still more to death or capture at the hands of Iroquois war parties. These reductions were compounded by cultural factors, notably internal contention over the conversion of some Indians to Christianity. Many Huron were converted to Catholicism by *Jesuits* who astutely controlled access to European trade goods as an inducement. In New England, Puritan preachers converted "praying Indians" among some tribes, while others refused all entreaties and most converts retained many traditional beliefs. Besides, conversion was no guide to Indian loyalty or participation in settler wars: Christian Indians fought for and against Europeans, just as those who retained native faiths allied, or not, with the English or French. Indians, in short, looked to their immediate interests in deciding when to make war and whom to make it alongside or against.

In an older historiography marked off by the works of Francis Parkman, the technological, organizational, moral, and cultural superiority of European settlers was assumed; the "frontier" was portrayed as the cutting edge of civilization shearing through barbaric and pagan regions; and the level and effectiveness of Indian military resistance was underrated and portrayed as primitive and savage. Some later writing moved to the other extreme, wrongly portraying Europeans as uniquely murderous and rapacious and engaged in a deliberate genocide of all Indians. Setting aside the important fact that much peaceful trade and other interaction occurred between settlers and Indians, more recent military histories have placed the Indian Wars of eastern North America in a proper global context. In so doing, historians have uncovered a remarkable martial adaptability of settlers, but especially of natives, as compared to European regulars, and told a far more complex tale than either earlier version of events.

The long conflict began with arrival of English settlers in Virginia in 1607 and the French in Québec in 1608. Thus was initiated what amounted to a series of invasions of Indian lands and nations that mixed cooperation with hostility and crossed trade with religion and war. The actors were many and the play complex: American settlers, English regulars, French regulars,

French-Canadians, and some Spanish fought other white troops or allied with multiple Indian nations, including the Algonquian, Huron, Iroquois, Mohawk, Mohican, Narragansett, Pequot, Powhatan, and Wampanoag. Also, the military balance of power was far more even than the later history of the continent suggests. Indeed, in this era Indians showed great ability to adapt and adopt imported technology, while Europeans and settlers were slow to appreciate that native irregular tactics were far better suited to a land of thick forests and strange topography than the set-piece formations and tactics then in vogue in Europe. It was, in fact, only those settlers and imported European regulars who adapted to the Indian *"skulking way of war,"* and who appreciated and used the special military virtues of Indian allies (notably their extraordinary woodcraft and high skill as scouts and skirmishers), who succeeded and survived when fighting Indians or even other Europeans in eastern North America. So what did Europeans bring that was new to North American warfare? Horses, steel weapons, gunpowder, muskets and cannon, and stronger fortifications. Yet, these new technologies did not assure settler military dominance prior to the late 18th century. Before then, it was Indians who remained masters of the "skulking way of war," and who were more than the equal in battle of regular troops or settler militias.

Samuel de Champlain (1567–1635), French explorer and soldier, is usually identified as the first to provide matchlock firearms to Indian allies (Mohawks). Forming an alliance with the Huron, from 1608 to 1609 Champlain led several French-Indian expeditions against the Iroquois. In 1615 he led another mixed French-and-Indian war party against the Iroquois. Later, as governor of Québec, he cemented the French alliance with the Huron nation based on the fur trade that set the stage for a century of French-Indian wars with the English and their key Indian allies in the Iroquois Confederacy, a native military alliance formed in response to the new pressures of 17th-century eastern warfare. Regulars were scarce before the 1660s, so that settlers formed and relied on local militia for defense or aggression, including black slaves and white indentured servants (many former rebel soldiers deported from Ireland) at first, but not later. Militia played a role from the founding of Jamestown, Virginia, when fighting with the Powhatan nation began there in 1609. The settlers were led from 1610 by regular officers with experience in anti-guerilla tactics learned in the Elizabethan conquest of Ireland. They built out-garrisons and scorched the Powhatan food supply to force pitched battles where superior firepower and steel armor told the tale against braves armed as yet only with bows and arrows (this would not be repeated in later decades, once Indians adopted and became expert in firearms). In addition, the English secured the waterways of the Chesapeake with armed boats, progressively squeezing the Powhatan into defeat and surrender by 1614.

> Samuel de Champlain . . . *is usually identified as the first to provide matchlock firearms to Indian allies.*

Although natives soon outmatched even frontier settlers as expert rifle marksmen, Europeans maintained a monopoly on artillery before 1660. This meant that Indian pre-artillery fortifications were useless, or worse, became death traps for entire settlements. Thus, Pequot villages were assaulted and massacred in New England in the *Pequot War* (1636–1637). This led to a new defense: native women and children scattered into the forest when a European army approached while braves set ambushes, picked off stragglers, and sent war parties to counter-burn white farms and kill white families. As for the reputed greater savagery of Indian warfare, in fact both sides indulged. Some Indian tribes *scalped* to collect battlefield trophies; others did not. Some indulged cannibalism; others did not. Or they gave up the practice, as did the Huron after 1550. Some Europeans accepted the full humanity of Indians, others did not (this was also true in reverse). Some settlers murdered Indians on sight and massacred whole villages, others sought peaceful trade and comity. Whites and Indians fought each other, but also as allies against other whites and Indians. War and politics, in short, pretty much ran their normal course in North America as elsewhere in the 16th–17th centuries. See also *armor*; *beaver wars*; *mourning war*.

Suggested Reading: W. J. Eccles, *The French in North America, 1500–1783* (1998); J. Ferling, *A Wilderness of Miseries* (1980); N. Salisbury, *Manitou and Providence* (1982); A. Starkey, *European and Native American Warfare* (1998); Ian Steele, *Warpaths: Invasions of North America* (1994); B. Trigger, *Children of Aataentsic* (1976); A. Vaughan, *The New England Frontier* (1965).

indulgences. See *Council of Trent*; *Fugger, House of*; *Luther, Martin*; *Protestant Reformation*.

inermis. "unarmed." See *civilians*; *just war tradition*.

infantry. The first organized and drilled, offensive infantry formation of note was the Macedonian phalanx, which devastated much larger armies of the ancient world with its extraordinary discipline. Similarly, the core of all Roman armies was highly organized infantry armed with stabbing weapons and shields for close fighting, intensely drilled and disciplined and capable of highly sophisticated battlefield tactics and maneuvers. The basic formations of the cohort and legion remained intact and dominant for over a millennium, to the end of the Roman Empire. In India, in contrast, massive infantry armies were usually deployed yet they appear to have been ineffective when facing cavalry, which remained the principal Indian arm into the 18th century. As Jos Gommans frames it, given its "almost limitless supply of superior cavalry, India lacked the inducement to develop disciplined and drilled infantry." A huge peasant population enabled Chinese armies to field large formations of infantry, but these did not fare well against peoples born to war and to horses, such as the *Mongols* or other nomadic invaders who made *light cavalry* their principal arm.

It is events in Europe that most military historians identify with the "infantry revolution" that had such a lasting impact on world history. Throughout the Middle Ages *heavy cavalry* still predominated in Europe. As army sizes increased after 1200, infantry began to specialize into "light infantry" (missile troops such as crossbowmen, longbowmen, or *arceri* and *pavesari*) and "heavy infantry" (wearing armor and wielding pikes, halberds, and other staff weapons). Most infantry units were organized by county or town. Town militia tended to be much better trained and disciplined, especially in Flanders. The Swiss cantons produced superb rural units as well as town *Banners*, and proved the most effective offensive infantry for over 200 years. Infantry broke the dominance of heavy cavalry progressively, starting with defeats of England's mounted chivalry by Scots infantry at *Stirling Bridge* (1297) and *Bannockburn* (1314), which bracketed the stunning Flemish militia defeat of the French heavy cavalry at *Courtrai* (1302). That was a special feat of arms widely admired, studied, and imitated. Yet, the Flemings lost badly to the French just two years later at *Mons-en-Pévèle* (1304), where they did not have the advantage of terrain they had exploited so well at Courtrai. It was instead the Swiss who emerged as the dominant force in the "infantry revolution" of the 14th century, beginning with a series of progressively greater victories over Austria's mounted nobility at *Morgarten* (1315), *Laupen* (1339), *Sempach* (1386), and *Näfels* (1388). The rule (though not the role) of the armored knight on a heavy horse, armed with lance and sword, drew to an end during the *Hundred Years' War* (1337–1453). *Edward III* dismounted his *men-at-arms* against the Scots at *Halidon Hill* (1333), to great success. He took his new tactical ideas and thousands of Welch and English archers armed with longbows to France, where he deployed them to unhorse and slaughter the flower of French chivalry at *Crécy* (1346). The *Black Prince* repeated his father's feat at *Poitiers* (1356), where French knights dismounted as well. On the grand *chevauchées* Edward III and the Black Prince conducted, their archers traveled on horseback as mounted infantry rather than true foot. To the end of the period most infantry were best deployed behind natural or prepared obstacles such as ditches, sunken roads, or artificial forests of *caltrops*, *Spanish riders*, or *chevaux de frise*.

The shift to mass infantry led to changes not just in battle but in wider society, as new classes of men fought in wars that had previously passed them by. Commoners could be made into soldiers cheaply and quickly because they were armed and trained with inexpensive and simple weapons such as the *pike* or *halberd*. Even the skills needed to use the *crossbow* or *arquebus* could be taught in weeks or months, rather than years. Thus, large numbers of lightly armored and inexpensive commoners slowly replaced the hugely expensive warrior aristocrats, armed with weapons that took years to learn, clad in costly armor and mounted on great *destriers* that required a small fortune to purchase and maintain and also took years to train. Now, man and mount were vulnerable to impalement or slashing by a cheaply raised, lightly armed and unarmored peasant or townsman. Infantry, not cavalry, was fast becoming the principal source of military power in Europe. This new infantry went about the business of war with less concern for the life or limb of nobles than had been the case earlier, when aristocratic warriors expected the price of defeat to be paid in gold rather than blood. The Swiss rarely took prisoners, and *Henry V*'s lowborn infantry disabused the highborn of France of the old conceit when they massacred over a thousand prisoner knights at *Agincourt* (1415) after English men-at-arms refused to carry out the deed. In return, when aristocratic warriors gained the advantage they did not spare common soldiers who could not pay a ransom and were not worth feeding or keeping alive. In short, rage trumped ransom and class conquered chivalry on the sanguinary battlefields of the 15th–17th centuries. It was also harder to take prisoners when most men were packed into disciplined formations wherein any break in the line either to take or guard prisoners—whether prompted by motives of pity or greed—threatened all one's comrades in the ranks with wounds or death.

From the 14th century it was common for veteran mercenary infantry to be recruited from areas of endemic frontier warfare such as the Pyrenees, Flanders, Scotland and northern England, Ireland, or the Balkans. Also in the 14th century the Cantons developed a deadly new formation, the *Swiss square*, comprised of pikemen protecting halberdiers, and later *arquebusiers*. The Swiss became the most deadly and feared infantry in Europe by the end of the 15th century, a reputation secured by decisive victories over the Burgundians at *Grandson* (1476), *Morat* (1476), and *Nancy* (1477). Swiss pike infantry were the most admired and feared until they met defeat in 1515 at *Marignano*, where they were beaten not by cavalry but German *Landsknechte* infantry and especially *Francis I*'s artillery and gunmen. Similarly, the French finally won the Hundred Years' War when their superb artillery, rather than noble cavalry, tore apart English archers on the field of battle and breached the stone walls of English and Burgundian castles and fortified garrisons. A pattern was developing of artillery as the answer to infantry, as infantry had earlier proved the answer to cavalry. As infantry took more and more arquebuses and *muskets* into battle they further displaced cavalry to supporting roles—scouting, foraging, and pursuit. Also contributing to the rise in the importance of infantry were improvements in fortification and a general drift into *siege warfare* in which cavalry was virtually useless (except in Poland, where tactics were developed by which cavalry effectively blockaded besieged sites). This shift had an enormous impact on society and politics over time. It helped break down the old monopoly on force of the feudal knighthood—a narrow aristocracy based on exclusive and lengthy weapons training and skill and tied to monopoly control of land and enserfed rural labor. Reliance on knights was eased by a move to cheaper and far more numerous town militia. This also promoted a decline in social standing for aristocrats and a concomitant elevation of townsfolk who served as militiaman. As J.F.C. Fuller famously put the argument in its most extreme form: "The musket made the infantryman and the infantryman made the democrat." A nice phrase, but the "infantry revolution" actually predated the use of firearms. Besides, since the adoption of muskets foot soldiers have raised up and sustained terrible tyrants far more often than they ever midwifed democracy.

Whether armed with an early arquebus or with later *smooth-bore* muskets, the accuracy of infantry gunpowder weapons was so poor that European armies in this period usually closed to within 50–90 yards of each other before firing. Weapons utilizing unreliable matchlock firing mechanisms also had slow rates of fire. This led infantry to organize ranked formations many men deep. As lock technology improved the rate of fire of muskets by 1600 the number of ranks declined: *Maurits of Nassau* deployed just 10 and *Gustavus Adolphus* reduced the number to six. This trend would continue in the next era, that of the fusil or *flintlock*, dropping to four ranks in the mid-18th-century system of Frederik the Great and just two or three during the Napoleonic Wars of the early 19th century. The new power of commoner infantry at first made it easier for small nations to assert themselves in arms, as did the Flemings, Portuguese, Scots, and Swiss. It also made it possible for regions of large nations to rebel more successfully and more often. There was a further impact of infantry on warfare: as its role expanded, so too did the size of armies and the corresponding destructive scale of the wars they fought. During the *French Civil Wars* (1562–1629) armies rarely exceeded 25,000; a few decades later *Cardinal Richelieu* raised nearly 100,000 to intervene in the *Thirty Years' War*, with the additional levies mostly made up by infantry; by the 19th century infantry armies counted millions of men and by the mid-20th century, tens of millions. See also *arceri*; *ashigaru*; *Azaps*; *Aztec Empire*; *balestrieri*; *Charles the Rash*; *compagnies de l'ordonnance*; *conquistadores*; *countermarch*; *drill*; *franc-archers*; *fusiliers de taille*; *galloglass*; *Inca Empire*; *Janissary Corps*; *kerne*; *Kur'aci*; *lanceri*; *levend/levendat*; *Martolos*; *peones*; *picchieri*; *rotularii*; *schiopettari*; *Sekban*; *targhieri*; *Tüfeçis*; *Voynuqs*; *Yaya infantry*.

Inner Asia. A wide, sweeping plateau region outside classical China from Manchuria, Mongolia, and Turkestan to Tibet, forming a grand crescent embracing the historic Han lands and bordering also on India and eastern Russia. From the time of the Aryans through to the *Mongols* and *Manchus*, Inner Asian nomads played crucially important roles as raiders and conquerors of settled peoples, deeply affecting the history of India, Iran, Russia, the Middle East, the Western Roman Empire, the Byzantine Empire, North Africa, and Europe. Inner Asia's history was especially linked to that of the Han (Chinese) and northern India. Inner Asian peoples organized for war repeatedly raided China and India, and for several centuries ruled both regions through imposed dynasties. They did this despite China and India being settled civilizations that were technologically far more advanced. Ultimately, nomadic and semi-nomadic invaders were assimilated into the larger and far more deeply civilized agrarian societies they overran. The *Ming* tried to reverse the process by incorporating parts of Inner Asia into their empire and subordinating its minority ethnic groups. However, the *Qing* eventually overran China from Manchuria, forcing the final collapse of the Ming. The *Mughals* enjoyed slightly more success in counter-invading Afghanistan.

Suggested Reading: *Cambridge History of Early Inner Asia*, Denis Sinor, ed. (1990); Sechin Jagchid and Luc Kwanten, *Imperial Nomads: A History of Central Asia, 500–1500* (1979); Morris Rossabi, *China and Inner Asia from 1368* (1975); Svat Souchek, *A History of Inner Asia* (2000).

Innocent III (1198–1216). See *Albigensian Crusade*; *Knights of Calatrava*; *Knights of Santiago*.

Inquisition (1478–1834). The "Medieval Inquisition" into dissent ("heresy") from Catholic orthodoxy dates to Pope Gregory IX (r.1227–1241), who instituted it as a special court of inquiry in 1231. Its initial purpose was to aid in suppression of heresy, specifically the bloody campaign in southern France to extirpate the *Albigensian* and Waldensian heresies. Inquisitors used interrogation into faith and morals, including torture and threats of excruciating execution, to ferret out and purge heretical belief among Catholics. The court also spread its inquiries to include charges of witchcraft, divination, demon-worship, blasphemy, and other religious crimes, and acquired extraordinary powers to summon accused. A distinct Inquisition was established in Castile by *Isabella* in 1478 with the approval of the corrupt Pope Sixtus IV (1414–1484, r.1471–1484). It had a high degree of involvement and control by the monarchy. In 1483, *Ferdinand* revived the Medieval Inquisition in Aragon after a long dormancy. With the union of the crowns of

> *The court also spread its inquiries to include charges of witchcraft, divination, demon-worship, blasphemy . . .*

Aragon and Castile the Iberian variant became known, infamously, as the "Spanish Inquisition." A separate Inquisition was set up in the Netherlands by *Charles V* in 1522. The Inquisition was formally established by *Philip II* throughout the vast overseas Spanish empire, which included Portugal and its empire from 1580. It expanded to the New World in 1565 and was in place by 1570 in Lima and Mexico City. It drew many an unfortunate colonial Spaniard or Creole into dark and bewildering chambers of canonical law and torture. Indians were exempt: their faith (or faithlessness) was left to inquiry by the local bishops of the *real patronato*. In accordance with the ban issued by the *Council of Trent* on vernacular translations of scripture, in 1576 the Inquisition seized and burned texts translated into native languages. The main focus of the assault was on Franciscans, the leading translators of the day.

All non-Christians were theoretically exempt from jurisdiction of the various Inquisitions. However, in Spain that amounted to a distinction without a difference as the Court applied itself principally and ruthlessly against Jews and, to a lesser extent, Muslims. Persecution accelerated after the fall of *Granada* in 1492. Isabella celebrated the victory by dispatching Christopher Columbus on his first voyage to the New World but also by coerced conversion and the *expulsion of the Jews* from her kingdom. Forcible conversions of Granadine Moors from 1502 were accompanied by a similar *expulsion of the Moors* and violent persecution of all refusing to convert. This included a public ban on "non-Christian" (that is, Moorish) dress. For many "Moriscos" (converted Moors) this persecution forced a retreat across the water to join co-religionists in North Africa. For the Jews, Isabella's edict led to yet another diaspora which scattered hundreds of thousands across Europe and the

Mediterranean. Some ultimately settled in faraway Russia, Poland, and Ukraine; others went north, where in later decades they played a role in bankrolling Dutch resistance to Spain; many settled in Ottoman Greece, welcomed by Sultan *Bayezid II*. Subsequently, the Spanish Inquisition investigated former Jews and Muslims thought to have insincerely converted to Catholicism to avoid the expulsion orders. Such converts, known as "New Christians," swelled the ranks of older "converso" communities of Jews and Muslims who had been baptized, often forcibly, during the *Reconquista*. Some inquisitors doubted the sincerity of mass conversions, others were moved by anti-Semitism, while a great many were more basely interested mainly in confiscated Jewish or Moorish property or imposing large money fines. Those New Christians who admitted to "secret judaizing" (practicing their real faith in private, as a matter of conscience) were heavily fined and faced a second choice of conversion or exile. Under such pressure Jewish life was driven underground and largely out of the country as New Christian communities were severely eroded over time by a combination of fear, death, and exile. By the 1530s conscientious Jews who remained in-country lived completely hidden religious lives in constant danger of betrayal to the avaricious savagery of the Inquisition by some other of its frightened victims, or by a covetous neighbor or business competitor. Ultimately, even those who honestly converted did not escape suspicion and accusations of inconstancy. And despite conversion, early in the 17th century many New Christians were expelled anyway by *Philip III*. This was not merely religious or racial prejudice, though it was that in good measure, too. It had much to do with consolidating royal control of Spain as one of the *"new monarchies"* in an Age that believed only religiously homogenous societies were sustainable.

The Inquisition and monarchical absolutism together ended centuries of vibrant and civilized life for the Jews and Moors of Iberia. This had two major consequences for the long-term future of Spain as a Great Power. First, forcing abroad many of Spain's most skilled and entrepreneurial subjects left the economy in the hands of a rude country gentry, and over-reliant on the heavily protected and traditional wool industry they controlled. Moreover, this happened just as the *"Age of Exploration"* introduced competitive fabrics such as calico to the European marketplace. Over the next 150 years not even American gold and silver would make up for Spain's lack of a modernizing economy, without developed banking and commercial sectors, the very areas where Jews and Moors had predominated and excelled before 1492. Second, Spain's enemies in the Netherlands, north Germany, Denmark, and England welcomed exiled Jewish scholars, and more important, embraced the secular and classical knowledge which had been kept alive for centuries in Arabic translation in Spain. Meanwhile, the Inquisition denied these same works to Catholic scholars.

As the once vibrant intellectual and commercial life which Muslim and Jewish scholars and communities had provided in Spanish cities was lost, a long night of repressive religious orthodoxy descended. A deep cultural and intellectual isolation from the mainstream of Europe set in from which Spain arguably did not truly emerge until the last decades of the 20th century. Lest this vision be overdone, however, it is important to recall—as the latest scholarship does—that the Spanish Inquisition was never a large or pervasive affair and was almost wholly confined to the cities where most conversos and Moriscos lived. That meant it left largely untouched the majority of the Christian population, which was predominantly rural. Which is to say, the Inquisition in Spain was a fairly typical instrument of early modern repression: it was limited in its reach and capability, though not its intent, to produce conformity through pervasive fear. That said, some of the worst inquisitors—notably the Dominican Torquemada (1420–1498)—would have done far worse than they did if they only had the means. True mass terror was simply beyond the capability of a 15th- or 16th-century state or Church. It awaited the mass industrial technologies and exterminationist ideologies and hatreds of a later age.

Outside Spain, after 1500 the Inquisition had twin purposes: to oppose heresy and to bring the weight and authority of the Catholic Church down upon all political and military enemies of the popes, who were secular rulers in their own right (of the *Papal States*). It also acted in behalf of key papal allies, notably the *Habsburgs*. In 1542, Cardinal Carafa (later, Pope Paul IV) established a "Holy Office" in Rome. This "Roman Inquisition" was to advance an inquiry into the new heresies of *Lutheranism*, *Calvinism*, *Anabaptism*, and others. More intellectual and tightly controlled than either the Medieval or Spanish Inquisitions, the Holy Office in Rome served principally as an instrument of the Catholic *Counter-Reformation* against the burgeoning *Protestant Reformation*, as did the militant new order of the *Jesuits*. To a lesser extent, it was also a weapon in the Habsburg effort for hegemony under Charles V and Philip II, whose armies were heavily engaged in war with Protestant princes in Europe through most of the 16th century. In 1559, Carafa, a true fanatic and one of the original cardinal Inquisitors, instituted the infamous *Index* of books prohibited to literate Catholics. It was the Roman Inquisition which in 1616 first censored the work on Copernican motions of the planets by Galileo Galilei (1564–1642), then condemned it as heretical after a trial in 1632. "And yet, it does move" ("Eppur si muove"). In 1992, 360 years later, the Catholic Church formally acknowledged that it, not Galileo, had erred.

As the wars of religion faded in intensity and from living memory, as the secular settlement of the *Peace of Westphalia* took hold, as Spain fell precipitously from the ranks of the Great Powers and the Habsburgs of Austria were beaten back from Germany in the *Thirty Years' War* (1618–1648), the influence of the Spanish and Roman Inquisitions also waned and their activity abated. Heavy restrictions were placed upon Inquisitors in Spain in the 1760s and the Jesuits were expelled from Iberia and France. The Spanish Inquisition was formally ended by decree on July 15, 1834. As an instrument of internal Church governance on issues of "error," the Roman Inquisition survived to be replaced (or rather, renamed) by a new doctrinal body, the "Congregation for the Doctrine of the Faith," in the early 1960s. It was long headed by Cardinal Joseph Ratzinger, who was elected Pope Benedict XVI in 2005. See also *casting*; *chambre ardente*; *Henri II, of France*; *Henri IV, of France*; *Hus, Jan*; *Hussite Wars*; *Jeanne d'Arc*; *Knights Templar*; *Kakure Kirishitan*; *Kirishitan Shumon Aratame Yaku*; *Lollards*; *Savonarola, Girolamo*; *witchcraft*.

Suggested Reading: J. H. Elliot, *Imperial Spain, 1469–1716* (1964; 1970); B. Hamilton, *The Medieval Inquisition* (1981); Henry Kamen, *The Spanish Inquisition* (rev. ed., 1998); Albert C. Shannon, *The Medieval Inquisition* (1991).

intelligence. Ancient and extensive empires such as China or the Ottoman and Byzantine Empires were practiced in the art of spying, and incorporated political and military intelligence into their planning of major military campaigns. More primitive governments gathered intelligence on an ad hoc basis, buying information—good and bad—from foreign merchants and other travelers where and when they could. Medieval Europe had only peripatetic ambassadors who rarely were able to gather operational intelligence and did not even see that as a legitimate function of their office. The city-states of Italy set up more substantial intelligence operations during the wars and intrigues of the *Italian Renaissance*, attaching these to the staffs of the first resident ambassadors and permanent diplomatic missions. Otherwise, armies on the march sent out a screen of scouts and foragers before them. Some, like the Austrians and Ottomans, had specialized troops for this function. Most just made do. *Philip II* and *Elizabeth I* had spies at the highest levels of each others' courts and diplomatic service, but it was *Cardinal Richelieu* who established and maintained the first large and permanent espionage bureau, an innovation other European states copied during the latter part of the *Thirty Years' War* (1618–1648), and after. Poor military intelligence was bad enough in land warfare, but it was the major reason that sea battles were few and far between in this period: navies, such as they were, seldom knew the whereabouts of enemy fleets. Most major clashes, such as *Sluys* (1340), happened because enemy fleets accidentally collided at sea or moved deliberately just outside known and likely target ports. See also *Akbar*; *Cecil, William*; *Cortés, Hernán*; *Deshima*; *Inca Empire*; *Inquisition*; *maps*; *military discipline*; *Mary Stuart, Queen of Scots*; *Moctezuma II*; *Mongols*; *Nagasaki*; *ninja*; *Twelve Years' Truce*; *Walsingham, Sir Francis*.

interior lines (of operations). See *lines of operations*.

Inverlochy, Battle of (February 2, 1645). See *Montrose, Marquis of*.

Invincible Armada (1588). "Spanish Armada." Dispatch of a large fleet by *Philip II* of Spain to escort an invasion army against England was a decision long in the making. In 1585, Pope Sixtus V called on Philip to launch a crusade in behalf of the *Counter-Reformation* to restore England to the Catholicism it enjoyed when Philip was wed to *Mary Tudor*. Philip demurred, as he was preoccupied with the *Eighty Years' War* in the Netherlands and protracted conflicts with the Ottomans and Barbary corsairs. When *Elizabeth I* finally executed *Mary Stuart* in 1587, a 20-year cold war between Protestant England

and Catholic Spain finally went hot. At age 53, the shrewd and cautious "Virgin Queen" would never have provoked so powerful an enemy as Philip if she thought peace could be preserved. But she knew the dice were down the moment Mary's head landed in the executioner's basket. Therefore, striking with bold preemption, she ordered *Francis Drake* to the Galicia coast to burn Philip's ships and dockyards to reduce any fleet he might send against her. This was escalation, but not the first shot of the war. For decades English and Dutch pirates had raided Spanish colonies and taken Spanish prizes in the Caribbean. Elizabeth had personally financed and profited from several *privateer* expeditions. However, the judicial murder of a Catholic queen by a heretic strumpet tipped the balance for Philip (who neglected to recall his own plotting with Mary Stuart to assassinate Elizabeth). He dusted off invasion plans tinkered with for over a decade, took money offered by the pope, and ordered an invasion. His weak private code for the project of conquest and reconversion of the island kingdom was "Enterprise of England."

Methodical as always, years earlier he had commissioned a study of previous invasions and learned that since the Norman conquest of 1066 England had seen nine governments fall or be seriously weakened by invasion from the sea, seven more landings of armies in Britain, and dozens of successful large-scale coastal raids. After his usual vacillation, Philip settled on a plan of attack that involved bringing together all his ships into a grand armada. This would be sent to collect the *Army of Flanders* and escort it to England. An armed host of 40,000 tough *tercio* veterans led by *Parma* would then march on London, topple the harlot usurper, and restore the "one true faith" (in place of the other one). Knowing what was coming from well-placed spies, from 1685 Elizabeth had intrigued with the sultan of the Ottoman Empire (though to little avail), supported the Dutch rebellion to keep Philip tied down in the Netherlands, commissioned new royal warships, and embargoed all merchant vessels which might be converted into warships from leaving English ports. It was only then that she sent Drake to Spain with a squadron to destroy all ship-

> *For decades English and Dutch pirates has raided Spanish colonies and taken Spanish prizes in the Caribbean.*

ping he found there that might be used in Philip's invasion. On April 29, 1587, Drake entered the harbor at Cadiz and destroyed or captured 24 Spanish ships and burned the docks and warehouses. He then cruised the coastlines of Spain and Portugal, burning whole towns, taking hostages, and desecrating every Catholic church he found. The religious hatred was real and cannot be subtracted from explanation of the Armada campaign: men of the 16th century did not fight merely for economic or rational causes; they sincerely believed in religious war. Even a cut-throat like Drake wrote in his notes as he left for Cadiz that Philip was the Antichrist. Among all the major players, perhaps only Elizabeth was a mild skeptic at heart. In any case, the Cadiz raid steeled Philip's determination to deal once and for all with England. The cost of his grandiose invasion plan was so fearsome he had to sell his wife's jewels to finance it; his righteousness caused him to do so.

Elizabeth, too, was feeling stretched: she had one army guarding the Scottish frontier and another she could ill-afford in Flanders. Unbeknownst, her ambassador in Paris, Sir Edward Stafford, was actually a spy for Philip and fed him much accurate information. Her spies were similarly well-placed—one delivered an exact copy of Philip's plans. But the sheer disparity of forces was truly intimidating. Elizabeth knew she could not stop Parma's veterans on land with her ill-equipped and outnumbered *trained bands*. She and her captains therefore decided to stop the Spanish at sea. That is why, as she laid the keels of new fighting *galleons* and converted armed merchants to full-fledged warships, she sent Drake to reduce the size of the coming Armada even before it assembled. Upon his return Drake told her: "I have singed the beard of the King of Spain." He had done much more: Philip could stand the loss of a few ships, but neither he nor Drake yet knew that the real damage had been done when Drake's crews burned thousands of barrels and barrel staves stacked in warehouses waiting to be filled with potable water for the Spanish fleet. These had to be replaced with fresh-cut, green staves which would slowly poison their contents and later, Spanish crews.

Philip's plan called for a fleet of 50 royal galleons and 100 more "great ships," plus 40 *hulks* to carry supplies. Parma's men would cross on 200 flat-bottomed barges being built in Flanders. By the spring of 1588, Philip had gathered only 13 galleons, 6 galleasses, 40 galleys, and a dozen small cargo ships. To these he added a motley crew of 70 hired or commandeered merchants, many of them rotten and slowed by cracks, bilge water, and barnacles. Worse, Spain did not have the skilled sailors to man even these ships. Men were hurriedly pressed from all over Iberia, and not just the sea towns. This produced seamen but not seamanship. When his top admiral, the *Marques de Santa Cruz*, died before the Armada was ready to sail Philip gave the task to Medina Sidonia on short notice. Sidonia hailed from a respected Castilian family but had no experience of either the sea or war, told Philip this, and begged to be relieved. He was denied. Sidonia arrived in Lisbon, where the Armada was assembling, to find utter chaos. Guns and powder, barrels of fresh water, casks of ship's biscuit, had all been loaded in haste. And Philip kept some ships at the ready all winter: crews and marines had eaten the stores and many were already sick with "ship's fever." There were no reliable records as to what was stored on any given ship. Some had cannons but no shot or the wrong shot (the Spanish failure to standardize calibers would cost many lives); some had shot but no guns; other ships had guns and shot buried so deep in their holds they were effectively lost. Sidonia set about redistributing guns and stores and buying new supplies to replace those rotten or eaten: bacon, fish, hard cheese, rice, beans, vinegar, olive oil, and water by the hundredweight stored in new, green barrels. He doubled the powder order and raised the rounds of shot to 50 for each gun, for a total of 123,790 cannonballs (Sidonia and Philip kept excellent records, which have survived). Everyone in command thought that was plenty of powder and shot. In fact, the supply would prove woefully short. Smartly for a man with no sea experience, Sidonia ordered rotten timbers replaced and had ships careened, scraped, and tallowed. Still, in the nature of a convoy, the Armada would sail at the speed of its slowest ships.

As these preparations were underway Philip agreed to lend the Armada great ships from his India fleet, eight huge galleons from Portugal, which he had annexed in 1580, and more from the Caribbean. Other ships straggled in from Naples or Sicily. On May 25, 1588, Sidonia attended mass in Lisbon Cathedral. Every man on every ship was confessed and took communion; each captain read warnings of severe punishment for blasphemy and cursing; each ship was searched to ensure no women were aboard; and 180 priests boarded the fleet, to tend to its crews but more, expecting to land in England to do God's work of reconversion of a heretic land, where they expected to be received by English Catholics as liberators. Each ship was freshly painted, though in too many the new paint merely hid rotten decks and creaky, unsound hulls. In the Cathedral the Archbishop gave Sidonia a great banner with the Arms of Spain and Christ crucified on one side and the Virgin Mary on the other. In Latin, it read: "Arise, O Lord, And Vindicate Thy Cause." It was not just Philip who thought God fought on Spain's side: most everyone in Lisbon and Madrid believed the Armada was Invincible. Later, the name "Invincible Armada" stuck, not as a boast but as tragic irony remembering a terrible national disaster.

In contrast, the English fleet stayed at the half-ready over the winter with most crew ashore and thus with ship's stores intact. Its sailors were men and boys who had grown up to the sea and knew their home waters. Also, where the Spanish fleet took 20,000 marines onboard, expecting an infantry battle at sea, English ships had only a few dozen sharpshooters each. The English plan was to stand off and use long-range *ship smashers*, not grapple and fight in galley-fashion as the Spanish, with a long history of Mediterranean naval warfare, intended. Yet, even the English would be surprised at what actually happened when the battle fleets met in the Channel. Never before, and never again until the great carrier battles of World War II, had so many warships put to sea with so little knowledge of their own or their enemy's real capabilities. It was, after all, the first fleet-to-fleet battle of the "Age of Fighting Sail."

The Armada sailed by national contingent: 10 galleons of Castile paralleled by 10 more from Portugal; next came 4 galleasses from Naples; then 40 armed merchants in squadrons of 10; plus 34 small and fast ships to serve as couriers, scouts, and dispatch carriers. Bringing up the rear were 23 hulks and 4 galleys. Flitting and darting among the larger ships were a squadron of *zabras* and *pataches*. All together 143 ships, 8,000 sailors, and 20,000 soldiers, among them 12,000 raw recruits, moved out of the harbor that fine May day. Sidonia had salted renegade English and Dutch pilots into each squadron to guide his captains through unknown Channel waters, but his crews were mostly green and lacked seamanship. It thus took 13 days for the Armada to move just 150 miles up the Portuguese coast. Then the crews were sorely tested by a great storm. When it was over it took Sidonia four days just to find and gather his ships and another month to repair them. The Armada did not set out again until July 21.

The English commander waiting to meet it was Admiral Lord *Howard of Effingham*. His top captains were all once and future privateers: *John Hawkyns*, *Francis Drake*, and *Martin Frobisher*. They set sail with Elizabeth's fleet on July 29. The next night, Saturday, having weathered a second storm in which four galleys were lost along with another ship, the Armada moved into the Channel. It was spotted from shore and beacon fires lighted. Quickly, a line of fires hopscotched from hilltop to hilltop until the entire south coast of England was awake and warned from Plymouth to Dover. A second string of signal fires raced inland faster than man or horse or ship, to London, York, and as far north as Durham. The queen and militia were alerted and England readied to repel invasion.

From the moment the Spanish entered the Channel they lost the *weather gauge*, as English ships pulled in behind them out of Bristol and Portsmouth. Because winds held steady westerly for the next nine days, the English kept the wind advantage throughout. Moreover, the best English galleons were race-built and had skilled crews while too many Spanish ships were ponderous, leaky hulks or crewed by inexperienced sailors. Unable to outrun his more agile pursuers, Sidonia formed a great crescent with his strongest fighting ships at the tips to ward off the English and protect his weakest and slowest ships at the center. Howard and his captains followed at a distance while much of England gather at the coast to watch the fleets slowly pass. If the English were astonished at the size of the Armada the Spanish wondered at the speed and handling of the English race-built galleons, and at their number. No one had seen fleets like these before. This was something entirely new in the world: great battle fleets of Fighting Sail. Although no one knew it then, these ships and their descendants would dominate war at sea for the next 300 years, until the advent of steam and armor plate.

The first battle in modern naval history, fought by broadside navies, began on July 31, 1588, with an old chivalric gesture: an exchange of defiant notes delivered by each admiral's pinnace (ship's boat). Howard then formed a *line astern* and moved to attack the north tip of the Spanish crescent while Drake and Hawkyns attacked the southern wing. Each side's tactics failed. Sidonia wanted to force a mêlée in which his ships would close and grapple and his marines overmatch the English. But even his best ships were not fast or handy as the enemy, so he was forced instead to hold formation and crawl northeast at one or two knots per hour. Howard wanted to stand off and hammer away with his long-range ship-smashers, a tactic never before used in a fleet-to-fleet action at sea, to avoid tangling with Spanish boarders and thousands of shipboard marines. English long-range gunnery was accurate, scoring many hits, but to Howard's surprise his great *culverins* did not fire or sink any enemy ships. He moved his line in to 300 yards range to pound away some more. English gunners were again faster and more accurate than the Spanish, partly due to a difference in *gun carriages*. Hundreds of Spaniards died and Spanish sails flapped uselessly in the wind as rigging and spars were shot away at close range. Still without sinking one of Sidonia's ships, Howard finally turned away at 1:00 P.M. Sidonia immediately broke the tips off his defensive crescent and sent his best warships in columns after the fast-fading English. Howard simply outran them, refusing to close for boarding actions with ships that over-matched his in upper deck small arms firepower and the number of their ma-rines. After three hours the Spanish gave up, turning back north to rejoin the crescent that became their signature formation. That ended the first day.

The Spanish had been bloodied and were frustrated, but not seriously hurt. If this was all Howard and "El Draque" could do, they would soon join Parma's army and escort it to English shores, and the invasion would succeed. The English ships were hardly hurt at all, but the English captains were deeply alarmed. They had scored hundred of hits with their big guns, yet the Armada still moved in unbroken order toward its rendezvous with Parma, and Eng-land's bane. The first real losses came not from English gunning but when two Spanish capital ships fell to accident: one lost to a collision that forced her into a French port, the other blown up by ignition of its magazine. With the English closing, the burning wreck was left behind. So close were the English, in fact, that Howard was startled to discover on the second night that he was following the poop lantern of Sidonia's flagship, not one of his own galleons in *line ahead* as he thought. Finding himself deep inside the curve of Sidonia's crescent, Howard silently tacked away. The English pursuit lines broke up overnight in the foggy dew and had to reform in the morning. On the third day Drake, ever the pirate, broke away to take a 46-gun Spanish straggler and prize into port, for his personal profit. And so it went for a week, the Spanish crawling north hugging their vulnerable hulks; English ships following to pick off the wounded and stragglers, but not slowing the herd. There was also one skirmish in which a Spanish galleon dropped its topsails in the classic invi-tation to a boarding action, only to have English galleons race in to fire point-blank broadsides as they passed her in a tight battle line.

A second big fight took place off Portland Bill, 170 miles south of Calais. It went much the same as the fight on the first day: men died and ships were damaged, but somehow struggled on. The English were learning that only close-in broadsides did real harm to the thick beams of Spanish galleons. And there was something else: both fleets were out of shot, or nearly so. Howard restocked with cannonballs brought out to the fleet by fishing boats from nearby English ports. More ammunition was rushed to the coast from all over England. Soon, even this supply would run low. The Spanish were in worse shape: many ships were almost out of shot; others discovered they still had the wrong sizes, rendering their guns useless. Deep into hostile waters against a fleet that showed itself equal or better than their own in seamanship and fire power, all Spanish thoughts turned to Calais. For all the dash and daring of experienced English captains, however, nothing they did stopped the slow progress of the Armada. When it hove to at the safe harbor of Calais on August 6 it looked like the "Enterprise of England" might well succeed de-spite English skill. Fortunately for England, Sidonia was still 30 miles from

Dunkirk where the invasion army and its 200 barges were blockaded by small but deadly warships of the *Sea Beggars*, then allied to England. Parma refused to load men on the barges without Sidonia dealing with the Dutch ships. He might have walked his men to Calais but he could not get the barges there, unescorted through the Dutch blockade. This was a major flaw in Philip's grand design all along. As so often, Philip had trusted to God to find a way that he could not see yet. Now it was God's favor the Spanish could not find.

As matters turned out Parma's dilemma did not matter: Howard sent eight *fireships* two-by-two into Calais harbor that night, riding brilliantly toward more than 100 tightly packed Spanish vessels. These were not the usual ship's boats or burning rafts: they were "Hellburners," copies of explosive fireships the Dutch used to blow up 800 of Parma's men on a fortified bridge over the Scheldt three years earlier. Tall ships culled from the weaklings of the fleet, soaked in tar, loaded down with faggots of oil-soaked wood, with barrels of black powder on their decks and in holds, they floated in with the wind and on a rising tide. Their iron cannon were loaded with double or triple shot, each a time bomb waiting for flames to lick its barrel and explode the gun into deadly shrapnel. These were fireships that might blow up the harbor. Beyond them, waiting in line along the horizon, curved the English battle fleet readying to blast away at all who sought escape. To his credit, when the little lights appeared over the distant water Sidonia did not panic. He sent out pinnaces with grapples to tow the fireships ashore shy of the harbor. Brave Spaniards got the first two, but then white-hot cannons on the second pair went off and all hell broke loose. Panic swept through the suddenly vulnerable ships of the Armada. Captains slipped or even cut their cables and scattered in utter disorder as the four remaining Hellburners floated into the harbor, double-shotted guns exploding at random, burning rigging and spars falling onto the wooden decks and rolled canvas of trapped ships and men desperate to live another day.

When dawn came, the Spanish were completely disordered. Some captains ran before the wind and the English battle line; others had floundered onto rocks in the night. Regardless, they were set upon by English sail and guns. This was the "Battle of Gravelines." Through collisions at sea, shot off rudders and random groundings in night fog and unknown waters, the Spanish lost several capital ships. The fighting was ship-to-ship rather than fleet-to-fleet as all order was lost in a tangled, swirling fight in which all were carried by heavy winds farther up the Channel toward the North Sea. The Spanish fought bravely, desperately trying to close and board—the only fight left in their ships. The English fought ferociously, standing off and blasting men and ships into surrender or the sea. The English ships came in close, to 50 yards or less, not to board but to make every shot and broadside count. English crews and captains were proving fast learners of this new way of war at sea. At Gravelines they sank one Spanish ship-of-the-line and forced two Portuguese galleons to run aground, losing no ships themselves in any engagement beyond the eight small suicides they had expended the night before. The key was superior gunnery: the Spanish lacked heavy naval artillery and had much inferior gun carriages, which made even their smaller guns cumbersome to reload and fire. And they carried a motley crew of calibers. That may well have befitted the convoy escort assignment for which Philip intended the Armada, but it ill-served a battle fleet engaged with the well-trained and better-armed Elizabethan navy, commanding large caliber weapons and enjoying possibly a 3:1 greater rate of fire. Nor did any of the 20,000 soldiers the Spanish ships carried in order to close and board the enemy actually manage to do so: not a single English ship was boarded, and while Spanish marines killed English sailors with volley musket fire the English killed far more with grapeshot and snipers.

Sidonia gave no more thought to the invasion. All his thinking was of getting home with as many ships and men as he could. He shepherded survivors back into a ragged defensive crescent and looked to escape. He had few choices: prevailing winds and the English fleet blocked the Armada from the direct route back to Spain. It would have to go the long way around the British Isles, with English guns barking at its heels. The two fleets thus resumed their northward passage and sedate chase. When the Armada was off the shores of Scotland Howard at last turned away, confident Sidonia could not now meet with and escort Parma. It was now that Spanish suffering really began. The fleet spent many days rounding Scotland and the Orkneys, through frigid and unfamiliar seas without even portolan charts for guidance. Then it was south past the west coast of Ireland: more days of struggling through vicious Atlantic storms, shipwrecking on unseen Irish rocks or promontories, tending to 3,000 horribly wounded and burned sailors and marines, sick with hunger or from spoiled fish and bad water, days upon nights of despair and death. On the voyage home though Gaelic waters dark to Spanish ken or experience, the Armada lost fully one-third of its complement: 50 ships and 15,000 men. In all this misery military discipline at last broke down. Sidonia removed and condemned 20 captains and actually hanged one, a neighbor of his from Castile. The corpse dangled from the yardarm of a pinnace which Sidonia paraded through the fleet "pour encourager les autres."

> *...while Spanish marines killed English sailors with volley musket fire the English killed far more with grapeshot and snipers.*

There was no fresh food and the salt fish and pork were rotten in the casks. Far worse, there was almost no unspoiled water. It was only now that the full import of Drake's raid on Cadiz was understood and felt. To save potable water for the men Sidonia had all horses and mules thrown overboard. The strange sight of thousands of poor beasts swimming in open ocean with no land or ship to be seen was later reported by English and Danish fishing boats. Besides those men dying of battle wounds, burns, and impalements by huge wooden slivers blasted out of the wooden walls of the Spanish ships, hundreds more fell deathly ill daily from disease. When the tattered fleet rounded the bitter coast of Galway it must have seemed that God had abandoned Spain: two weeks of storms ensued and thousands of Spaniards drowned in cold Irish waters as ships wreaked almost daily. Hundreds more had their brains caved in by Irish bounty hunters or English troops as they lay exhausted on rocky beaches. A few made it inland and were given shelter, but most died or were murdered. What is remarkable is that Sidonia got as many ships home as he did: 44 straggled into Spanish harbors, though some of these never sailed again. Nor did the suffering stop even then. For weeks men kept dying, victims of fevers or wounds and of neglect. They died in droves in England, too, from the same causes: medical ignorance and military backwardness that made no provision for plain folk, victor or defeated.

What was won and lost? England remained Protestant and independent. The Eighty Years' War burned on for another 60 years, leading ultimately to independence also for the Calvinist Netherlands. Yet Spain remained so militarily dominant that it sent two more armadas north against England in the coming decades, and still fought several wars at once against mightier enemies than Elizabeth. But Spain's reputation for invincibility was lost forever and its confidence was deeply shaken. Imperial Spain was not yet the decrepit and delusional old man it was portrayed to be by one of Philip's own soldiers, not yet the Don Quixote of Miguel Cervantes' gentle and affectionate mocking. But it was a wounded and shaken power. The evidence of that change was not long in coming: the very next year Elizabeth sent Drake and a fleet of 126 English warships to Santander, to destroy at anchor what was left of the Spanish Armada.

Suggested Reading: J.F.C. Fuller, *A Military History of the Western World*, Vol. 2 (1954; 1955); David Howarth, *Voyage of the Armada* (1981); Colin Martin and Geoffrey Parker, *The Spanish Armada* (1988); Geoffrey Parker, *The Grand Strategy of Philip II* (1998).

invincible generalissimo. A Chinese-designed, muzzle-loading cannon of the mid-15th century. It was essentially a *bombard*, massive in size and served by a crew of several dozen men who were needed to reposition it after each firing and to cart its ammunition and shot. By the mid-16th century the term was applied to a smaller breech-loader that came with a towable cart and a crew of just three or four gunners.

Iran. In the 8th century Zoroastrian Iran was forcibly converted to *Islam* by Arab conquerors. This was a key period for the Iranian nation and for Islam. Within a generation of the Prophet Muhammad's death a succession crisis had divided Islam into *sunni* and *shī'a* branches. Most Iranians cleaved to the minority shī'a faction. This split deepened over the centuries, adding to the ethnic differences which divided Iran from the dominant Arab, and later Turkic, nations of the Muslim world. In the 12th century the *Mongols* overran Iran, an interregnum which actually gave the country some internal stability and even prosperity without much influencing or changing its unique Islamic culture or people. The Mongol ruling class was slowly assimilated to the majority culture, with the Il-khans converting to Islam in 1295. The main contest of these years was with *Mamlūk*-governed Egypt, though a peace was agreed in 1323. Islamicized Mongols divided Iran into small states upon the death of their Il-Khan in 1336. This weakening opened the door to later conquest by *Timur* and his Turkish-Mongol followers. After Timur's death in 1405 his "Timurid" successors ruled eastern Iran from militarized capitals at Herat, Samarqand, and Bukhara. They were followed by Turkic overlords until 1502, when the *Safavid* dynasty was founded by Shah Ismail I (1486–1524, r.1502–1524) in partnership with the *Qizilbash*. Shī'a Iran thus regained its political independence from foreign (and sunni) rule. Under Ismail, shī'ism was established as the state religion. This aggravated tensions with the Uzbeks and Ottomans, both sunni peoples. In 1510, Ismail pushed the Uzbeks back but chronic warfare along the frontier continued throughout the 16th century. In 1514, Safavid Iran was attacked by Ottoman Emperor *Selim I*. Conservative Safavid military elites had not yet adapted to the gunpowder revolution, viewing firearms—as did the Mamlūks of Egypt—with distaste and as dishonorable and disruptive of their preferred social order and feudal levies. The Iranian Army was still comprised mostly of mounted archers. These were overwhelmed by musket-bearing *Janissaries* and some 200 cannon which the Ottomans mustered for battle at *Chaldiran* (1514). Only a mutiny in the Ottoman ranks afterward prevented Selim from occupying and destroying the Safavid regime in Iran.

Chaldiran initiated a century of violence along the Iranian border arising from a potent mixture of religious, ethnic, and imperial divisions and ambitions. The shahs learned from Chaldiran and began to adopt gunpowder weapons along with imported military advice from Venetian, Portuguese, and English *renegades* and some Ottoman deserters. Within a year of Chaldiran 2,000 muskets were manufactured in Iran along with 40 cannon copied from a broken and abandoned Ottoman gun found in a river bed. Still, this was merely ad hoc and supplementary, not a true reform of the Safavid reliance on mounted archers. The Safavids were additionally handicapped by numbers: in the mid-16th century they could field only about 20,000 troops, far fewer than the Ottomans. Fighting continued along the frontier despite the *Peace of Amasya* (1555), which ended the Ottoman–Safavid war by recognizing Ottoman rule over Iraq and eastern Anatolia and Iranian suzerainty over Azerbaijan and parts of the Caucuses. Iran used the respite to rearm. By the 1570s the Iranians were manufacturing larger numbers of handguns with imported machinery. Nevertheless, Iran was so weakened by internal dissent under Muhammad Khudabanda (1578–1587) the Ottomans launched an offensive into the Caucasus in 1578. The threat from the Ottomans caused the Safavid capital to be moved from Tabrīz to Qazwin in 1555, then to Isfahan in 1597.

During most of this period the Iranian Army was still an almost exclusively tribal cavalry force armed with bows, swords, and some firearms. It was not until truly radical military reforms were instituted by *Abbas I* that the Iranian Army became an infantry-heavy and predominantly firearms-using force. When it did, it emerged as an even match for the Ottomans as war resumed in 1603, while the latter were distracted by the *Thirteen Years' War* (1593–1606) with the Habsburgs in the *Militargrenze*. The shift in the military balance was made clear at *Sis* (1606), where Iranian guns left 20,000 Ottoman dead on the field. Safavid capture of the key fortresses of Tabrīs (1603) and Erivan (1604) quieted the Caucasus frontier for several decades. But from 1623 to 1638 the rival Muslim empires struggled over Iraq, after the Ottoman garrison in Baghdad went over to the Safavids in 1623. Iranian offensives were launched into Iraq in 1624, 1629–1630, and 1638. After the death of Abbas the Ottomans made gains as the division of Europe by the *Protestant Reformation* freed troops and resources to retake Iraq from Iran. The Safavids lost Kandahar, then Baghdad to the Ottomans. Iraq returned to the Ottomans and the balance of power was restored in 1639, as codified in the *Treaty of Zuhab*, or Qasr-i Shirin. The settlement left each empire intact and reasonably secure. The Iranians held their own against other regional enemies during the 17th century even as the Safavid regime itself went into terminal decline. Iran had avoided being absorbed into the powerful Ottoman Empire. That meant creating a key and lasting historical distinction to add to the cultural and religious differences from the Arab and Turkic areas of the greater Middle East, and the wider Muslim world.

Suggested Reading: Charles Melville, ed., *Safavid Persia* (1996); David Morgan, *Medieval Persia, 1040–1797* (1988); A. T. Olmstead, *A History of the Persian Empire*, 2nd ed. (1969); Said Arjomand, *The Shadow of God and the Hidden Imam* (1984); Roger Savory, *Iran Under the Safavids* (1980).

Iraq. Iraq was overrun by the Arab conquest of the 7th century, which brought with it a new language, military elite, and religion (*Islam*). During the first centuries of the Islamic era Baghdad was home to the Abbasid *caliphs*, to great universities (madrasa), and a florescence of ancient science and learning. Baghdad fell to the *Mongols* in 1258. It was sacked and burned and the caliph and his family slaughtered in a gory public spectacle. As the regime collapsed so too did the great irrigation works that sustained high civilization along the Tigris and Euphrates. The Mongols chose to rule from distant Azerbaijan (Tabrīz), leaving Iraq so weakened that the desert Bedouin were emboldened to raid its southern reaches. Unlike in Iran, therefore, Mongol rule had a devastating impact on Iraq. In the early 17th century the Ottomans and Safavids fought several times over possession of Baghdad and greater Iraq. In 1623 the Ottoman garrison in Baghdad defected to the Safavids, provoking a sustained Ottoman campaign to recover Iraq. After three *sieges of Baghdad* the city was recovered by the Ottomans in 1638. Iraq was then secured permanently to the Ottoman Empire by the *Treaty of Zuhab* (1639).

Ireland. Ireland was formally annexed by Henry II (1133–1189) of England. Between 1169 and 1175 it was invaded by the *Normans* under "Strongbow" (Earl Richard de Clare). This was part of the larger Norman attempt to conquer the "Celtic fringe" of the British Isles. Norman castles and garrisons soon controlled Irish towns but the bog country and forests remained Irish, home to guerillas and ambushes. The Normans stayed inside their castles or retreated into *"The Pale"* around Dublin, while small war became a way of life. This period of Irish history was not marked by national differences from England, Scotland, and Wales so much as by the shared "Norman Monarchy" that was rooted in England but had branches in the Gaelic areas of the British Isles (except for Scotland). An attempted invasion of Ulster from Scotland, 1315–1318, was beaten back. Thereafter, war in Ireland was marked by skirmishes and raids typical of frontier zones, or *Marches*. This was not fundamentally changed until the mid-17th century when the main currents of European military advances in artillery, fortification, infantry firepower, and naval armaments finally reached Ireland's shores. Until then the *Old English* remained in control of most Irish towns, outside of which there were few roads, many impassible bogs, and a "bandit-ridden" countryside dominated by *Old Irish* Gaelic warlords and clan wars. In fighting the English these lords usually avoided pitched battle but were expert at ambush and ruse and other elements of *guerre couverte*. It was thus topography more than technology, along with appropriate tactics, that kept the Irish and English military worlds separate and in rough balance.

Although Irish labor migrated across the Atlantic as an integral part of the Anglo-Scottish colonization of the New World, and some Irish prospered as landlords and plantation owners in the West Indies, in general Ireland was more a target of colonization than a source of colonists prior to the 18th century. Successive waves of Anglo-Scottish colonization, the so-called "plantations" of the 16th–17th centuries, aimed at securing England's strategic rear from foreign invasion and to enforce a Protestant ascendancy over Ireland's stubbornly Catholic population. The key event was the *Kildare Rebellion*, a violent response by Catholic Ireland to Protestant reforms in England. Over the next 70 years the Tudor conquest was completed, but it would be misleading to say that Ireland was constantly at war. Prior to the 1590s most conflicts were local and sporadic and not always against the government in the Pale. The masters of the Lordship had only 1,200 men available to them in 1560, rising to 3,000 in 1570 but falling thereafter to 1,500 in 1593. Fortunately for the Tudors, Shane O'Neill's battles of the 1560s were mainly against Scots and other Irish, not the "English garrison." A revolt in Munster from 1569 to 1573 was but a sporadic guerilla affair. Besides, many lords, notably those of Ulster, actively supported the Crown until the great revolt of the 1590s. The major English military effort was thus made from 1598 to 1603 to put down the one truly national revolt that threatened Tudor governance: the *Nine Years' War* (1594–1603). The victory of 1603 established English rule unchallengeably over the whole island for four decades, broke the old Gaelic aristocracy, and opened the door to a further and deeper "Plantation of Ulster."

Ireland remained nearly as religiously divided as contemporary Poland or Germany. Catholics were split between a Gaelic peasant underclass and a ruling class of Catholic Old English and Old Irish, both divided from the Protestant *New English*. Constitutionally, too, Ireland was a confused domain falling part way between colony and kingdom. In October 1641, a religious rebellion broke out in Ireland led by Old English and Old Irish landowners who feared the success of the *Covenanters* in England and Scotland would lead to massive plantation of radical Protestants. Starting in Ulster in December, some 4,000 Protestants across Ireland were massacred. That was far fewer than alleged in Protestant propaganda at the time, but about as many as died in the *St. Bartholomew's Day Massacres* in France in 1572. The massacres and repeated efforts of *Charles I* to raise Catholic Irish armies to put down Parliamentary and Protestant rebellion in Scotland and England meant that Ireland was swept into the *English Civil Wars* (1639–1651) that engulfed the Three Kingdoms in the 1640s.

Throughout these wars Gaelic Irish were seen by plantation Protestants, and by the merchant-monarchical alliance in England that dispatched them, as barbarous and backward, on a social and moral par with New World "savages." They would surely benefit from enforced subservience to the "true religion" and superior culture and law of the Anglo-Scots, it was thought. As Gaels were progressively dispossessed of lands and legal rights, like New World Indians they rose in rebellion in the mid-17th century. Their rising was met with ferocious military, legal, and political retaliation by the Anglo-Scots, leading to additional dispossession and efforts at furthering Protestantization through plantation. The military-settlement technique used in the plantations of Ireland resembled the Roman and Norman models of expansion by colonization, and the Iberian *Reconquista*. Irish plantations later became a model for methods used by Anglo-Scots colonizers overseas: stark military assertion of authority over the native population, expropriation of land, and marginalization of the native elites. *Oliver Cromwell* later dragooned thousands of Irish as forced laborers sent to the Bahamas. Other Irish dispossessed "voluntarily" joined the flow of conquered Celtic peoples to England's overseas colonies. This migration of cheap indentured Irish labor "was the largest single flow of white immigrants to the 17th century West Indies." The loss of population was not made up by Protestant inflows as from the 1660s Ireland proved less attractive to potential settlers than the brave new worlds opening in America. Even some former planters uprooted to seek greater fortune across the Atlantic. See also *Confederation of Kilkenny*; *Confederate Army*; *galloglass*; *hobelars*; *kerne*; *March*; *Ormonde, 1st Duke of*; *redshanks*; *Wars of the Roses*.

> *...cheap indentured Irish labor "was the largest single flow of white immigrants to the 17th century West Indies."*

Suggested Reading: T. Bartlett and Keith Jeffrey, eds., *A Military History of Ireland* (1996); Nicholas Canny, *Making Ireland British: 1580–1650* (2001); Pádraig Lenihan, ed., *Conquest and Resistance* (2001).

Ireton, Henry (1611–1651). Roundhead general. His first military experience came after he raised a troop of cavalry for Parliament. He fought at *Edgehill* (1642), Gainsborough (1643), *Marston Moor* (1644), and Second Newbury (1644). When the *New Model Army* was organized by *Thomas Fairfax*, Ireton was appointed Commissary General of Horse under *Oliver Cromwell*. He was bested by *Rupert*, wounded, and taken prisoner at *Naseby* (1645). In 1646 he married Cromwell's daughter. A close ally of his father-in-law, he was among those who signed the king's death warrant. He served with Cromwell in Ireland, 1649–1650, and took command when Cromwell departed for England. He was especially cruel to civilians during the siege of Limerick (October 1651), but merciful upon the town's surrender. He died of fever in Ireland. In 1660 his corpse was exhumed and displayed by the king's men, marked as that of a traitor and regicide. See also *Levellers*.

Ironsides. Originally, a Royalist appellation for *Oliver Cromwell*. Later, it was used for all *Roundhead* troopers but especially Puritan devouts. Ironside cavalry abandoned most armor, which offered little protection against heavy *muskets* and *calivers*. Instead, they wore *buff coats* and buff leather thigh-high boots to protect against slashing swords and bills. They had a rough merit system in which troopers who proved mettle in battle, whatever their social origin, might rise to command. They were well-trained, well-armed, highly disciplined, and devout "soldiers of the Lord." Cromwell said of his Ironside cavalry: "I raised such men as had the fear of God before them, and made some conscience of what they did; and from that day forward...they were never beaten." See also *English Civil Wars*.

Iroquois Confederacy. See *Haudenosaunee*; *Indian Wars (North America)*.

Isabella I (1451–1504). See *Ferdinand II, of Aragon, and Isabella I, of Castile*.

ishan. Cash bonuses given to *Janissaries* and other Ottoman troops by the sultan or his *serdar*. They were usually distributed ritually, to mark important political milestones or reward service in battle.

Islam. "Submission" (to the will of Allah). The prophetic revelation to Muhammad (570–632 C.E.) is traditionally dated to 609 C.E. Persecuted in Mecca by its polytheistic community, in 622 Muhammad and a handful of monotheistic followers moved 220 miles north to the oasis town of Yathrib (later called Al-Madīna, or "The City"), which promised them the protection of a political and military alliance. This "Hijra" (migration) of the first Muslims was key to Muhammad's apostolate and to Muslim military success. In recognition of this, it marks the first year of the Muslim calendar (A.H.). Muhammad soon wielded supreme military and political power as well as religious authority within the "Umma" (community of the faithful). Proclaimed as the "Seal" (last) of the Prophets, he suppressed idolatry and polytheism, proclaimed Allah's final revelation, and waged *holy war* against surrounding pagan communities. Conversions came through persuasion but also by way of the sword, as pagan *Bedouin* were defeated and absorbed into the Umma and their desert power made subservient to Muhammad's urban leadership. At Medina the first Muslims thus gained valuable experience in desert warfare. They not only fought and subdued nearby pagan tribes, they campaigned as well against the rich caravans and more substantial armies of the pagan rulers of Mecca. After eight years of *razzia* and some set-piece battles, Muhammad led his Muslim followers in the conquest of Mecca. He expelled from that great crossroads city all idol-worshipers who would not convert, and enacted Muslim law and rule. This made the Umma the most powerful religious and political community in Arabia. The faith was then spread throughout the desert peninsula by the sword of "jihad" and by devout preachers and prosperous Muslim traders. Within a few generations of Muhammad's death on June 8, 632, the Umma had expanded far beyond his Arabian homeland to become one of history's great empires, shaped and sustained by a major world religion.

The "explosion of Islam" out of Arabia in the 7th century C.E., was one of the seminal and spectacular events of world history. Along with prospects of plunder the new faith inspired, or at least justified, conquest of non-Muslim areas by Arab armies. Islam spread with Allah's promise to desert armies of sure conquest of fertile, irrigated lands beyond Arabia. And what a conquest it was: Arab armies overran the Middle East, North Africa, Spain, Iran, Anatolia, Central Asia, northern India, and reached into parts of what is today western China. A new world power had arisen that was Arab in its military organization and rulership and Muslim by faith. Its emergence cut off the Byzantine Empire and Western Europe from their ancient and rich trade with the Far East. As it spread, Islam attracted the genuine loyalty of conquered populations, and especially of opportunistic elites. Many traders were drawn to Islam as a means of gaining access to the markets of the new Arab *amsār* (garrison) towns, which soon became the foci of political and economic power in a transformed region. Some converted out of sincere piety, others to avoid special taxes on non-Muslims or to improve social standing: Arab military-governing elites kept themselves separate and upheld sharp social distinctions concerning even non-Arab Muslims. This situation lasted until a set of great social reforms were implemented during the second century A.H. (ninth century C.E.). Thereafter, Arabs played an ever-decreasing role in leadership of the Muslim world, assimilated into or displaced by converted local elites and later by Islamicized dynasties and empires founded by various Turkic peoples.

The location and power of this new empire, and direct military pressure from Muslim armies, helped push Byzantium on the path toward terminal decline and, though less directly, helped move Western Europe down the road to impoverished, castellan *feudalism*. Within the conquered areas of the Mediterranean world older communities of Christians and Jews were tolerated as "dhimmîs" ("peoples of the Book [of God]"), who earlier had received partial prophesies from Abraham, Moses, and Jesus, among others. Some peoples were classified as pagans ("infidels," or "*kaffirs*") and might be put to the sword if they refused conversion, though this practice proved impracticable on a large-scale in densely populated Zoroastrian Iran and Hindu India. Those who persisted in faiths that were acceptable but inferior (because prior) to Islam, Christians and Jews, were subjected to the *jizya*, a tax imposed on non-Muslims. Taxes were lower for any who converted while broad religious tolerance of those who did not preserved civic peace. In the ancient world Alexander had overrun the Persian Empire and unintentionally freed enormous stockpiles of gold and silver hoarded for centuries, which thereafter stimulated an economic renaissance. So, too, the Arab conquest freed vast amounts of wealth that had been underutilized in pre-Islamic economies by nonproductive and highly privileged aristocracies, or locked up as bequests to monasteries and churches. The economic boom which followed additionally facilitated acceptance of foreign Arab military aristocracies and their new religion, laws, and language.

As Islam expanded into areas of large non-Muslim populations exceptions to persecution of adamant nonbelievers were allowed. Persia's Zoroastrians and India's Hindus, who each proved too numerous to wholly convert or annihilate, in time achieved de facto status as dhimmîs. Indeed, Iranian influences importantly reshaped Islamic culture and government, as that nation's highly talented ruling classes worked from within to hold onto what they could. By the 10th century, in many lands Islam had discarded its original Arabian character through absorption of local influences from older, much more established and literate civilizations in Egypt, Iran, India, and across North Africa (for example, "sufi" mysticism was deeply rooted in pre-Islamic Iranian practices). Relations with the Christian world were permanently damaged by centuries of warfare with the Byzantine Empire, and several centuries more war with Latin Christians who joined the *Crusades* or fought the *Reconquista* in Iberia. Islam's political capital moved several times after the 8th century: from Medina to Damascus, and thence to Baghdad, with important outposts in Egypt, North Africa (*Ifriqiya*), and Iberia (Córdoba and *Granada*). Much of the eastern and central Mediterranean became a Muslim lake with the conquest of Malta, Sicily, Corsica, and Sardinia. However, Muslims had to fight constantly to retain those islands from assaults by Pisans, Genoese, Venetians, Byzantines, and the *Normans*. The loss of these island outposts, mainly during the 11th century, ruined the Muslim sea empire.

By about 1000 C.E., the dominance of the original Arab-Bedouin conquerors drew to a close. From the 11th through the 20th centuries, almost without exception, every major Muslim dynasty and empire from India through Central Asia to the Middle East was established by converted *Turks* or *Mongols* or intermingled groups of both. The first major Turkic conquerors were Islamicized Ghaznavids, who ruled Afghanistan and the Punjab until displaced by the *Seljuk Turks* in 1040. Starting in the early 13th century Mongol hordes invaded and overran successive Muslim lands. By mid-century all of Central Asia and Iran succumbed. In 1258 the Mongols captured Baghdad and murdered the last Abbasid caliph (though a branch captive to the *Mamlūks* reigned, without ruling, for some time still in Egypt). This precipitated a succession crisis within Islamic civilization that marked a major turning point in Muslim history: long moribund, the caliphate was finally buried by a non-Muslim military power. Sultanates now replaced it in distinct power centers of a fractured Islamic world: Egypt, Iran, and what is today Turkey. This new political fact—the Umma was permanently fractured and broken—was accommodated to religious tradition by most Muslim jurists and holy men, though fundamentalist purists still looked to a restored, unitary caliphate at some future date. From this point onward the dominant Muslims were not Arabs but converted Slavic or Turkic tribes: the Mamlūks of Egypt and the Ottomans. The latter claimed the caliphate only much later (a claim not universally accepted), and governed Arab Muslims (and many non-Muslims) in a vast empire run from Constantinople after that city was captured from the Christian Orthodox in 1453. In sum, Islam controlled the eastern Mediterranean and was firmly established in the northern third of Africa by c.1400, controlled the northern half of India (under the *Mughals*) by c.1500, and was still expanding into West Africa, Central Asia, Southeast Asia, and western China during the 16th–17th centuries. In short, it had become a principal world religion and power.

Historically and doctrinally Islam is closely related to *Judaism* and *Christianity*. All three religions are apocalyptic in their eschatology, all originated in the Middle East, and they share variations of certain core beliefs. For Muslims, these are: monotheism; a succession of revelatory prophets with Muhammad the last and greatest of these; social justice based upon the radical equality of (male) persons in a single brotherhood of the faithful ("umma"), which is open to all who accept Allah; and for some, a recessed messianism in the form of latent expectation of arrival of the *mahdi*. All Muslims are enjoined to embrace the great monotheistic credo: "There is no god but Allah and Muhammad is his Prophet." They are expected to give alms to support the poor; to pray five times per day while facing Mecca; to fast during the daytime in the ninth lunar month (Ramadan); and, if feasible, to make the pilgrimage (*haj*) to Mecca. Islam's scripture is *al Qur'an* (the *Koran*) revealed to Muhammad from the true book of law written by Allah and resting in Heaven, declaimed on Earth by Muhammad and copied in earthly form, for the edification of men. Islam's jurisprudence (fiqh) is enshrined in a legal code (sharia) drawn from the Koran and the Sunna, or accepted interpretations by leading religious scholars (ulema) of the meaning of the model life and practices of Muhammad. No new interpretation was permitted after the first two centuries of debate on the meaning of the Sunna. Still, until the 14th century, Islam was among the most progressive cultures and civilizations in the world. Prohibition on fresh interpretation subsequently produced a rigidity in Islamic customs and public institutions, notably banking, that gravely handicapped Islamic civilization when faced with competition from early modern Europe. In its most fundamentalist guises Islam offered a distinctly lesser place to women in public and even in family life. Purist, or reactionary, Islam was thus propelled into direct conflict with cosmopolitan conceptions of

> *...until the 14th century, Islam was among the most progressive cultures and civilizations in the world.*

social and political organization as well as the practical needs of early modern market efficiency. Yet, much the same could be said of contemporary Christian societies, several of which were less modern in other ways in comparison to Islamic countries. In addition, because Islam offered equality to all believers it was and is still a greatly attractive faith to the socially disadvantaged and anyone trapped in rigid hierarchical cultures. And so it continued to make converts in sub-Saharan Africa and southeast Asia, especially in the 16th–17th centuries. Moreover, while in theory Islamic societies did not accept the separation of religion and state, the standard for international order established in the *Peace of Westphalia*, in practice Ottoman rulers subsequently adapted with their usual pragmatic realism to newly secular principles of international law and state conduct. See also *Assassins*; *ayatollah*; *caliph*; *Druse*; *Fulbe*; *imam*; *Ismaili*; *mullah*; *zakat*.

Suggested Reading: F. Gabrielli, *Muhammad and the Conquests of Islam* (1968); Marshall Hodgson, *The Venture of Islam*, 3 vols. (1958–1961); Hugh Kennedy, *The Prophet and the Age of the Caliphates* (1986).

Ismaili. A sect of radical *shī'a* Muslims who split with other shī'a over the succession of the 7th caliph (Ismail). They emphasized the sufi (mystic) tradition. They tended to be extremists not just doctrinally, but also politically, seeking to erect a radical theocracy over the whole Islamic world. They established an early base in Yemen from which they attacked North Africa, where they set up the Fatamid *caliphate*. From there they conquered Egypt in 969, building a new capital at Cairo. Thereafter they assumed some characteristics and pretensions of the ancient Pharonic power. Out of Egypt they conquered Palestine, Syria, and parts of Arabia; to the west they invaded Sicily but traded peacefully with the rising city-states of Medieval Italy. From the 11th century the Fatamids were governed in fact by generals though still in name by local caliphs. Sub-sects or offshoots of the Ismaili movement included the original *Druse* and the infamous *Assassins*. Ismailis eventually concentrated in the Indian subcontinent and Central Asia, with smaller communities scattered across the Middle East and Africa. See also *imam*.

Italian armies. In the urban north of Italy feudal military service never took a deep hold, and paid military were more often recruited to wage the endless small wars of the peninsula. For instance, by the end of the 13th century Milan could raise a militia of 25,000 from its population of about 200,000. Florence, which had a population of 400,000, could raise 17,000 troops, including 2,000 *heavy cavalry*. Of these, only 1,500 were mercenaries. In the 14th–15th centuries, *Free Companies* and *condottieri* dominated Italian recruitment and warfare. Cities always kept some militia on hand for core defense and to man the walls, but Italy's rich urban elites generally preferred to hire expensive mercenaries rather than perform military service themselves or arm the general populace. On other matters relating to Italian armies and warfare see *Italian Renaissance*; *Italian Wars*; *Machiavelli, Niccolò di Bernardo*; *Papal States*; *trace italienne*; *Venice*.

Italian Renaissance. A profound intellectual and cultural efflorescence, as well as a political and diplomatic revolution away from the *res publica Christiana* toward the modern secular state, which began in Italy but influenced all Europe and even all the world. It can be traced as far back as the life work of Francesco Petrarch (1304–1374), among others in the high Middle Ages, but reached its vital and brilliant peak in the late 15th century. Some consider it to have spread beyond Italy, lasting through the life of René Descartes (1596–1650). The Italian Renaissance is closely identified with events in Venice and Florence and other northern Italian polities, but affected most of the peninsula before spreading over the Alps to influence all Europe and shape the character of the emerging modern age. Culturally, it was distinguished by a revival of classical learning—in particular in the natural sciences, but also in theological criticism and moral philosophy—inspired in part by recovered or newly translated Greek and Roman texts acquired from Muslim middlemen in such great centers of Islamic scholarship as Sicily, Granada, and Seville. Its profound impact on cultural life arose from an empirical ideal and spirit of celebration of humanism and rationalism, if not yet full secularism. The Italian Renaissance is justly famous, though historically less important, for its extraordinary advances in the fine arts and literature. Commercially, it marked a dramatic expansion of commerce by credit in which the Medici political and banking family of Florence played a central role as the single most important financial center in Europe from the late 14th century until 1494, the year of the French invasion of Italy by the brash young king, Charles VIII (1470–1498). That brought on a Habsburg counter-intervention and the protracted woes for Italy of the *Italian Wars* (1494–1559).

The most world-changing influences of the Renaissance concerned war and diplomacy. Italian thinkers changed perceptions of the political realm forever, away from the ideals of *chivalry* and the *just war* toward more realistic assessments of base material motivations and the requirements of *raison d'état*. Italian diplomats and contract soldiers (*condottieri*) fanned out into Europe after the French invasion of 1494, selling their martial services to powerful foreign monarchs along with new ideas about resident diplomacy, Machiavellian state ethics, and close coordination of espionage with sovereign representation. Europeans flocked to Italy to study the "Italian school" of war, fortification (the *alla moderna*), and diplomacy, as much or more than to study the new Italian styles in painting, poetry, and sculpture. The Renaissance witnessed the "golden age" of the Italian system of city-states, whose unique political patterns later were copied and helped supplant more general feudal relations in Western Europe, and helped overturn the old sense of universal community in Christendom in favor of more narrow definitions of political loyalty to individual secular states. Italy gave Europe a more lusty exercise of power by new "princes" who governed through exciting, and often also illicit, new political relations. It was these city states which first explicitly formulated and practiced as a mutual policy the concept of the balance of power, following agreement on the *Peace of Lodi* (1454). Beginning as an empirical description of the actual state of affairs in Italy, it evolved into a theoretical justification for sustaining an interstate equilibrium among the five largest Italian powers: Venice, Florence, Milan, Naples, and the Papal States. The machinations and wolf-like relations of this insulated sub-system, isolated by Alpine borders and the distant preoccupations of the Great Powers with other wars during most of the 15th century, gave rise to the central ideas of early modern ethical and political theory. That included a revival of interest in constitutional republics and civic militias.

The new diplomacy of the Italian Renaissance took form roughly between 1420 and 1530. It would become the model for all subsequent diplomacy. When the movement passed north of the Alps it reinforced a shift in the European balance of power already underway from the Mediterranean to the Atlantic states, from Byzantium and the Holy Roman Empire to England, France, and the Netherlands. In sum, the Renaissance marked the transition from the ancient and feudal eras to modern times, not just in culture but also in war and diplomacy, and not just for Europe but through the subsequent expansion and global dominance of Europe in the age of imperialism, for the entire world. Its rational curiosity, core empiricism, and impulse toward creative change in economics, politics, religion, philosophy, and technology, echoes familiarly to modern hearing. See also *Art of War*; *Machiavelli, Niccolò di Bernardo*; *Muhammad II*; *Savonarola, Girolamo*; *spice trade*.

Suggested Reading: Thomas F. Arnold, *The Renaissance at War* (2001); Jerry Brotton, *The Renaissance Bazaar* (2002); G. Gash, *Renaissance Armies* (1975; 1982); John R. Hale, *War and Society in Renaissance Europe, 1450–1620* (1986) and *Machiavelli and Renaissance Italy* (1960); Niccolò Machiavelli, *The Prince* (1532); M. E. Mallett, *Mercenaries and Their Masters* (1974); Garrett Mattingly, *Renaissance Diplomacy* (1955).

Italian traces. See *alla moderna*; *trace italienne*.

Italian Wars (1494–1559). A series of sharp but also intermittent conflicts broke out over control of Italy at the close of the *Italian Renaissance*, shattering the peninsular balance of power system achieved in the *Peace of Lodi* (1454). The main antagonists were no longer Italy's city-states, but two rival dynasties: the *Valois* of France and the *Habsburgs* of Austria and Spain. Northern Italy— occupied by small and fractious states—was vital to Habsburg security, and secondarily to their control of Burgundy and the Netherlands: it was both a base for the strategic *Spanish Road* and a recruitment area for reinforcements for the Army of Flanders. Open warfare began when France's young king, Charles VIII (1470–1498), invaded Italy in 1494 with an army of 25,000, including a cohort of Swiss mercenaries. With a siege train of 40 smaller and mid-sized mobile cannon he blasted through and captured, in just days, fortified towns that had stood against prior sieges for months or in some cases for years. His powerful artillery astonished Italian observers, including *Machiavelli*. The French penetrated as far south as Naples, entering the city in February 1495. That provoked formation of an anti-French coalition ("Holy League") comprised of Spain, the Holy Roman Emperor, the pope,

Milan, and Venice. But Charles won at *Seminara* in June and still held Naples. Under Louis XII, in 1499 the French took Genoa and seized Milan, where they deposed the *Sforzas* (1499). A brief respite from fighting resulted from the Peace of Trent (1501) between Louis XII and *Ferdinand II* of Spain, who agreed to partition Naples but leave the French in occupation of northern Italy. A quarrel soon broke out over details of the Milanese partition and the war resumed in 1502. The Battle of Barletta (1502) was indecisive, but the Spanish won definitively at the *Garigliano River* (1503), where French and Swiss troops suffered sharp reverses at the hands of the new Spanish *tercios*, even though French artillery sometimes ripped bloody lanes in the Spanish ranks. France accepted the permanent loss of Naples to Ferdinand of Aragon in the *Treaties of Blois* (1504–1505), in return for confirmation of French control of Milan. In 1508, Pope Julius II (1443–1513) arranged an aggressive alliance, the *League of Cambrai*, nominally aimed at the Ottomans but in fact intended to reduce or at least contain Venice. That city-state had taken advantage of the chaos in the peninsula engendered by the Italian Wars to expand its holdings within Italy, not least at papal expense. The Venetians were bested by a French army at *Agnadello* (May 14, 1509). Meanwhile, armies and populations alike were decimated by epidemics of syphilis and typhus directly related to the spread of fighting, and therefore of infected soldiers, flowing from the Italian Wars. Syphilis notably infected the ruling House of Valois in France, and spread as well into the harems and blood streams of the rulers of the Ottoman Empire, weakening both royal families.

French success broke up the League of Cambrai, as Venice appeased the pope and emperor with fresh concessions. The renowned army of the Swiss Confederation then intervened, taking Milan from the French in 1512. At *Ravenna* (April 11, 1512), the French destroyed a sizeable Spanish army, but at *Novara* (1513) the Swiss routed the French to take control of Lombardy. The young French king, *Francis I*, crushed the Swiss at *Marignano* (1515), regaining Milan and most of Lombardy for France. The Peace of Noyon (1516) essentially partitioned Italy between France and Spain until a vigorous young Emperor, *Charles V*, united all Habsburg power in a single pair of hands in 1519. Fighting recommenced in 1521. Francis was defeated at *La Bicocca* (April 22, 1522), and trounced and taken captive at *Pavia* (February 23–24, 1525). That forced him to sign the Treaty of Madrid renouncing French claims in Italy. Francis denounced this coerced concession once he was ransomed and set free. He assembled an anti-Habsburg alliance, the "League of Cognac," that included England, Florence, Venice, and the Papal States. Charles responded to the pope's perfidy by sending an army to take Rome, which it did with real ferocity, running amok there in May 1527. Francis besieged Naples but could not take the city. In September 1529, Charles and the Austrians were briefly distracted by the first Ottoman *siege of Vienna*. This may have been coordinated in secret with Francis to draw the Emperor east. If so, the plan failed: Charles stayed in the west and forced France to terms in the Treaty of Cambrai (1529), which reconfirmed renunciation of French claims to territory in northern Italy.

War between the Valois and Habsburgs over control of Italy resumed from 1542 to 1544. Battles, such as the French victory at Ceresole (April 14, 1544), were indecisive: neither victory nor defeat led to permanent political change. In any case, France was militarily incapable of matching its Habsburg enemies or displacing them by force from north Italy. A final try to push back the French frontier in the south came in 1556–1557. At *St. Quentin* (August 10, 1557) the French lost 14,000 men out of a 26,000-man army and *Coligny* and *Montmorency* were both captured. This time the defeat was complete: the supremacy of *Philip II* and the Habsburgs in Italy was codified in the *Peace of Cateau-Cambrésis* (1559). It was then sanctified by royal marriages between and among the various warring houses. The end of the Italian Wars and the start of the *French Civil Wars* (1562–1629) then together opened the door to the Spanish effort to crush rebellion in the Netherlands during the *Eighty Years' War* (1568–1648). See also *Alba, Don Fernando Álvarez de Toledo, duque de*; *Carafa War*; *disease*; *Fornovo, Battle of*; *Savonarola, Girolamo*; *Swabian War*.

Suggested Reading: J. R. Hale, *Renaissance War Studies* (1983); Bert Hall, *Weapons and Warfare in Renaissance Europe* (1997); F. L. Taylor, *The Art of War in Italy, 1494 to 1529* (1921).

Italic League (1454–1494). See *Lodi, Peace of*.

Italy. After the fall of the Western Roman Empire the Catholic Church remained fixed in Rome, radiating doctrinal authority and cultural and legal influence across the Latin world. This state of affairs lasted until doctrinal and other disputes shattered agreement with the Orthodox of the Byzantine Empire, most notably over the authority of *Ecumenical Councils*. An irreparable schism with the Orthodox Church cut the Latin Church off from the Christian communities in the old Eastern Roman Empire. The explosion of *Islam* out of Arabia in the 8th century then cut Italy and the Catholic Church off from the historical birthplace of Christianity in Middle East, as well as from formerly Christian areas in North Africa and Iberia.

The *feudal* military system of the Carolingians was not adopted in Italy, as it was elsewhere in the *res publica Christiana* that succeeded Rome in the West. Instead, economic and military life remained centered on towns and cities, which survived post-Roman economic and demographic contraction in Italy to a greater degree than elsewhere in the Christian West. As a centuries-long contest was waged between popes and the Holy Roman Emperors, between *Guelphs and Ghibellines*, each camp drew external military forces into Italy. The Wars of Investiture continued even as new barbarian tribes attacked from the east. By the 12th century Magyars and Muslims alike had been repulsed, although coastal raiding by *Barbary corsairs* remained a common affliction. The *Norman* conquests of Sicily and southern Italy were slowly assimilated into a monarchical system. Elsewhere, Italian politics and wars remained communal, as hundreds of towns and cities fought for control of trade routes, for access to agricultural regions and hinterlands, and to control and tax markets. In 1200 there were nearly 200 warring city-states in Italy. The

Italian countryside became the most heavily encastellated region of Europe, and in the 13th and 14th centuries also the most war-ridden. The basic cause of conflict was the richness of the land and the large towns, which justified the cost of stone defenses as well as town militias and intercity wars for control of the sources of wealth. The richest families built castles in the countryside to protect their private agricultural holdings, and also built stone towers inside the towns. Historian John Gillinham noted: "city governments tried to set legal limits to the height of towers. Aggrieved neighbors took more direct action, bringing up their own siege artillery." In Medieval Italy, good cannon made better neighbors.

Within the Italian communes (the early form of the central and northern city-states) the military was highly organized and specialized. Each "sesto" ("sixth") of an Italian commune provided both infantry and cavalry, with the latter coming from the "consorterie" (aristocratic clans). As each growing city tried to enforce control of the surrounding grain-producing areas and markets, areas from which it also drew manpower for its civic militia and taxes to pay for it, conflict grew apace. Outside powers, notably the Holy Roman Empire in the 12th and 13th centuries, tried to gain control of Italy. However, heavy fortification and the ability of cities to form coalitions and to contract *condottieri* kept Italy mostly free of external interference. Italians used this liberty to fight each other all through the 14th and 15th centuries. Italy's relative isolation was reinforced by Iberian preoccupation with the *Reconquista*, and France's and England's long and distracting *Hundred Years' War* (1337–1453). On the other hand, republicanism declined as the "Signorie," or urban magnates, rose to power in several key cities in the latter 13th century. In the last third of the 14th century the larger cities consolidated surrounding territories under powerful military leaders: the Visconti controlled Milan and much of Lombardy; the Medici dominated Florentine politics and war in Tuscany; Venice used its sea-bought wealth to extend its influence into eastern Lombardy; and the Avignon popes began to plot a return from French captivity. That provoked the *War of the Eight Saints* (1375–1378), sparked by disagreement over the conditions of the papal return to Rome. This dispute also contributed to the *Great Schism* that so scandalized the devout of the Christian commonwealth. In the south an Angevin-Aragonese conflict for control of Naples ended in 1442 with the triumph of Alphonso V of Aragon. Meanwhile, war broke out between Florence and Milan from 1423 to 1445. It was fought by the condottieri captains Niccolò Piccinino in behalf of Milan and Francesco Sforza for Florence (except for the three occasions when he switched over to fight for Milan). Venice allied with Florence until 1427, with the Papal States and Naples drawn into the war during the 1440s. The conflict ended with the *Peace of Lodi* (1454).

Much of Italy remained fragmented and either at war or preparing for it through most of the period known as the *Italian Renaissance*. That

> *In Medieval Italy, good cannon made better neighbors.*

extraordinary outburst of economic, intellectual, and martial energy gave Europe its modern diplomacy, including the idea of the "balance of power," and its first generation of resident ambassadors. Italy in the 15th–16th centuries incubated the remarkable political thought of *Machiavelli*, and many new ideas arising from unbound scientific inquiry. And of course, Renaissance Italy produced much of lasting cultural and artistic value in the visual and musical arts. Not all of this was interrupted when the French invasion of 1494, the *Habsburg* counter-invasion, and the onset of the *Italian Wars* (1494–1559) ended the independence of most of the Italian city-states. Continual internecine warfare (the last all-Italian conflict was the Castro War, 1642–1644) and serial foreign invasions left Italy fatally weak vis-à-vis the Great Powers of Europe, especially France and Austria, over the next three centuries.

Suggested Reading: Jacob Burkhardt, *The Civilization of the Renaissance in Italy* (1995); J. R. Hale, *Machiavelli and Renaissance Italy* (1960); Bert Hall, *Weapons and Warfare in Renaissance Europe* (1997); M. E. Mallett, *Mercenaries and Their Masters: Warfare in Renaissance Italy* (1974).

itqa. A form of *feudal* military recruitment common among the Muslim states of North Africa, who also extended it to Sicily and parts of Iberia. It blended feudal features of the European *fief* with aspects of contract akin to the Italian *condottieri*, though it predated both. Essentially, emirs contracted out land grants known as "itqa" to tribal chiefs, who in turn recruited mercenaries for the emir. The caliphs in Córdoba employed this system to supplement their central reliance on imported *mamlūks*, their lesser supply of *jihadis* from North Africa, and the weak militla of *al-Andalus*. See also *Ifriqiya*; *taifa states*.

Ivan III (1440–1505). "The Great." Ivan III was the Grand Duke of Moscow when he threw off the "yoke of the *Tatars*" from Muscovy and united the Orthodox peoples of the surrounding steppes into a powerful and aggressively expansionist Slavic dukedom. He launched Muscovy on a historic trajectory of imperial expansion, tripling its size in his lifetime and setting it on the path to creation of a vast continental empire. As a young man he led an expedition against the Tatars in 1458. Upon becoming Grand Duke in 1462 he set about the defeat of the "Golden Horde," the vestige of the Mongol empire which held Muscovy and other Rus states in vassalage for 200 years. He struck in 1467–1469, liberating Muscovy from Mongol overlordship in a series of brilliant victories. He next conquered the surrounding Rus city-states which lay within reach, including Tver, Yaroslavl, Rostov, and most importantly, Novgorod. From that long-time military-commercial rival to Moscow he expelled the traders of the *Hanse* and all Germans. There followed a bitter contest with several of his brothers, two of whom allied with *Poland-Lithuania*.

In his wars Ivan made use of large cannon as siege weapons. The biggest was cast from bronze in 1502. It was a gigantic *bombard* over five meters long, which Ivan called "King of Cannon." This monster could fire a huge stone ball some 1,000 kilograms in weight. More importantly, he reformed the

Muscovite military around *"servitor cavalry"* whom he seeded throughout the countryside to control his conquests. These military vassals helped him keep order locally, while owing him several months riding service each year, aiding greatly in his wars of expansion. At his death Ivan had converted Muscovy into a rising empire which would one day dominate much of eastern Europe and expand deep into the Caucasus, Central Asia and Siberia.

Suggested Reading: Ian Grey, *Ivan III and the Unification of Russia* (1964).

Ivan IV (1530–1584). "The Terrible." Grand Duke of Moscow (1533–1584). He ended his regency at age 17, then moved quickly to tame the *boyars*, transferring their traditional powers to a bureaucracy and governing council he controlled. He set up the *strel'sty* palace guard in 1550. Ivan conquered the *Tatar* khanates of Kazan (1552) and Astrakhan (1556), which he held against an invading Ottoman army in 1569. Ivan also beat back Polish and Lithuanian assaults, including by the *Livonian Order*. In 1558 he sent an army into Estonia that slashed and slew, massacring 10,000 at *Dorpat*, sacking 20 other towns, and launching the *First Northern War* (1558–1583). In 1559 he sent 130,000 men to devastate Livonia. These brutal advances opened access to the Baltic trade long closed to Muscovy. Trade contacts were even made with England, from where sailors arrived in strange ship types unknown to Russians, selling and buying goods out of Archangel. Ivan suffered defeats, too: in 1564 the Lithuanians crushed his armies at Czasniki and the Ula River, driving him into mad revenge against the boyars whom he blamed for his setbacks. Evermore paranoid and subject to wild and violent rages, he launched a reign of brutal terror known as the *Oprichnina*. His main targets were boyars and subject cities he suspected of rebellious intent, with or without evidence. From 1564 to 1572 he earned his infamous sobriquet "The Terrible" by stripping boyar families of land holdings, crushing their traditional liberties, then taking their lives with horrible torments and sadistic methods of execution. In one fit of rage he killed his own son, an act that shocked his countrymen and haunted him in his final days. The chaos permitted the Crimean Tatars to sack Moscow in 1571. Then Ivan killed the oprichniki who had carried out his orders to kill the boyars—no wonder or accident that Ivan IV was Joseph Stalin's favorite tsar. In 1583, Ivan lost the First Northern War to Poland and Sweden, returning to those Baltic powers what he had earlier gained in the north. In the interim, he had begun a creeping annexation of Siberia, where he used *Cossack* cavalry and peasant conscripts to overwhelm sparse native resistance.

Suggested Reading: Hugh F. Graham, *Ivan the Terrible* (1981); R. G. Skrynnikov, *Ivan the Terrible* (1981); Henri Troyat, *Ivan the Terrible* (1984).

Ivry-la-Bataille, Battle of (March 14, 1590). Fought six months after *Arques* (1589) about 40 miles west of Paris, this was the last significant battle of the eighth of the *French Civil Wars*. The *duc de Mayenne* raised 20,000 troops for the *Catholic League*, who were joined by some 2,000 Spanish arquebusiers sent by *Philip II*. Most of the Leaguer host were poorly armed pikemen or light horse deploying lances. In opposition, *Henri IV* had 12,000 men, of whom 9,000 were veteran Huguenot infantry, Swiss pikemen, or mercenary musketeers. Fully 3,000 were disciplined and experienced Huguenot cavalry skilled in Henri's patented *pistolade* tactics. Henri formed a line of six cavalry squadrons screened by light infantry, with blocks of heavy infantry interspersed between two squadrons of cavalry. He put his artillery at the center. Right away, both sides opened with their big guns. The Catholic horse then charged the Huguenot infantry, whose natural defenses were reinforced with field fortifications, while the Huguenot cavalry charged the Catholic infantry. Protestant musketeers firing in volley, along with supporting cannon, cut bloody swaths in the Catholic ranks. Some 6,000 Leaguers were killed to just 500 dead Protestants, and thousands more were captured. Determined not to repeat his mistake of failing to pursue after Arques, Henri marched on Paris immediately after the battle. But once more, he had too few men to storm or besiege that great capital. He broke off the siege after learning that *Parma* was approaching with part of the *Army of Flanders* out of the Netherlands. After Ivry-la-Bataille, Mayenne's reputation went into permanent decline even as Henri's soared, both facts conducing to a quicker end to the long civil wars in France.

J

jack. A coat made from canvas or other cloth into which were sewn iron plates. It was worn by Elizabethan soldiers as well as American colonists. Although outdated for war in Europe, the "jack" served well enough against Indian archers in North America.

Jacob's staff. See *cross-staff*.

Jacquerie (1358). A violent peasant uprising named for the French sobriquet "Jacques Bonhomme." It was particularly bloody and ferocious in Champagne, Picardy, and the Beauvaisis. It was underlain by the economic dislocations and privations of the *Hundred Years' War* (1337–1453). Peasant anger aimed at occupants of the chateaux, excessive royal taxation, and hated tax collectors. They resented making payments in labor or kind to a privileged warrior class and a distant king (Jean II, taken prisoner at *Poitiers* and held for ransom by the English) who did not provide them with protection from the appalling *chevauchées* of *Edward III* and the *Black Prince*. A secondary symptom of this fundamental problem was their suffering from excesses and exploitation by freelance mercenary bands, the *Free Companies* who marauded across France as social and military order broke down. These bands of mixed French and English veterans continued depredations and extortions long after the fighting stopped between the main armies. The direct trigger for the rebellion was a demand for forced labor to rebuild chateaux damaged in the war or by Free Companies. The rising was extensive and bloody but initially unorganized. A leader then emerged, Guillaume Cale, who gathered a large peasant army near Clermont, 40 miles from Paris. The peasants were routed there, and nearly 1,000—including Cale—beheaded or otherwise butchered by local nobles. The rising was squashed everywhere within a few weeks. Like most peasant armies, the "Jacques" lacked cohesion, strategic planning, and a precise and articulate agenda of reform. They were, as a result, savagely repressed by the crown and nobility, which set aside all differences when faced with rebellion by armed "Jacques." See also *Croquants*; *German Peasant War*; *Razats*; *Tard-Avisés*.

Jagiello dynasty. A powerful family whose members ruled Bohemia, Hungary, and Poland-Lithuania, and were related by marriage to the Wittelsbach and Habsburg dynasties. It was founded by a grand duke of Lithuania who became Wladyslaw II Jagiello, King of Poland-Lithuania in 1386. The family also sat on the thrones of Hungary (from 1440), and Bohemia (from 1471). The most important of the Jagiellon monarchs was *Casimir IV* of Poland. After Casimir, and in part because of him, the dynasty lost real authority to the untamed and unruly Polish-Lithuanian nobility. The dynasty lost control of Bohemia and Hungary in 1526. The last Jagiellon king was *Sigismund II* of Poland (r.1548–1572). Anna, a Jagiellon princess, was then twice compelled to marry princes chosen for her by the Polish nobility and elected to the kingship: Henri Valois (later, *Henri III* of France) and *Stefan Báthory*, Duke of Transylvania.

jaguar knight. A class of elite soldier of the *Aztec Empire* who dressed in a jaguar-skin-and-fur suit, with the dead cat's head cut and sewn to wear as a headdress. The other class was *eagle knight*.

jamber. Pieces of plate armor protecting the shins. Also called *schynbalds*.

James I and VI (1566–1625). James VI of Scotland, 1567–1625; James I of England, 1603–1625. He was crowned king of Scotland five days after his mother, *Mary Stuart*, abdicated in 1567. He grew to despise the Calvinist teachers of his boyhood for their dour doctrines and because they helped depose his mother. He succeeded *Elizabeth I* in 1603. Raised a Protestant, as monarch he avoided religious conflict fairly well, despite ruling three kingdoms divided by deepening confessional argument. In 1603 he was asked by German princes to head an international Protestant alliance. He declined, and thereafter showed little interest in German affairs. His domestic policies were helped by a quiet international scene prior to 1618. James was initially popular but slowly lost support by excessive partiality to court dandies and favorites, especially *Buckingham*. Puritans looked to James as a righteous king who would act with just force against heresy at home and aid and succor the "True Protestant Faith" abroad to preserve it from pernicious popery and superstition. James gravely disappointed them when he instead pursued policies tolerant at home and mostly peaceful abroad.

Why he did this is crucial to understand. Some historians agree with contemporary critics that his basic policy of appeasement of Spain was foolish and dangerous. Yet, England was in no position to wage war against any Great Power in the early 17th century. And if James appeared to veer the other way, toward a Protestant policy after 1610 in his support of intervention by the *Protestant Union* in the crisis over *Jülich-Kleve*, and by signing a treaty of assistance with the Union in 1612, he likely did so to counterbalance the rising influence of *dévots* in France following the assassination of *Henri IV*. Similarly, his 1620 dispatch of just 2,000 troops to aid his foolhardy, over-reaching son-in-law, *Friedrich V*, Elector Palatine and would-be King of Bohemia, did as little as possible to assuage Protestant demands without leading to all-out war with the Habsburgs. In 1621 James rejected Parliament's demand to declare war on Spain. Just before his death he made a feeble military gesture against Spain to symbolically avenge a marriage slight to his son and heir, *Charles I*, which had no chance of harming Spain or restoring Friedrich. James used his meager funds to finance a meaningless expedition by *Graf von Mansfeld* in Germany, which only backfired by worsening England's relations with France. In matters administrative and fiscal James was neither shrewd nor successful, and this severely undercut his effort to conduct a more military foreign policy late in his reign. He tried to get by on the cheap with *exact militia*; let the *Royal Navy* fall into disrepair and abject corruption; refused to issue *letters of marque* even though other nations still supported *privateering*; and failed to protect merchants from Dunkirk and Barbary pirates who operated with impunity in the Channel. See also *Raleigh, Walter*.

Jamestown. See *Indian Wars (North America)*.

Jand, Battle of (1240). See *Iran*; *Mongols*.

Janissary Corps. Turkish: "jeniçeri" ("new militia" or "new army") "Ocak" ("corps"). They were the heart of the *Kapikulu Askerleri*, the sultan's personal or household troops. Janissary infantry at first included enslaved prisoners of war. They began as infantry archers, though they also used javelins and swords, but they ended as a premier firearms corps. Starting under *Murad I* in 1438 the Ottomans raised an annual levy of boys from the corps from subject Christian populations, through the *Devşirme system*. By the 1470s there were nearly 10,000 Janissaries, far surpassing any palace guard maintained by European rulers (only the tsars came close), and thereafter forming an elite infantry rather than a mere household guard. Greek and Slavic boys inducted into the elite Janissary Corps underwent years of training. The *Bektaşi* dervish sect had considerable influence over their education as Muslims, with Bektaşi often living in barracks with the recruits and enjoying an honored place in parades and other public occasions. Recruits were raised and lived in barracks as strict Muslims, forbidden alcohol and gambling, banned from marrying before reaching pensioner ("Oturak") status, and barred from inducting their children into the Corps. That rule was intended to prevent the rise of a hereditary military caste. After six years of religious indoctrination, another six years of military training followed under instruction by adult eunuchs. While most boys entered the ordinary infantry, the brightest—Janissaries received an excellent education at state expense, and were tested on it—served in the administration as effective "staff officers" for the army and navy. Other promising candidates went to the technical corps: the *"Cebicis"* ("armorers"), *"Topçu"* ("gunners"), or *"Top Arabacs"* ("gun-carriage drivers"). Drawn from the large Bostanci ("Gardener") division were two more elite units: the "Hasekis" (personal bodyguard of the sultan) and "Sandalcis" (personal rowers of the sultan). All Janissary units had a highly sophisticated system of unit flags, emblems, and badges, well beyond anything then extant in European armies. Some cleaved to the strong Muslim preference for geometric or astrological symbols; most, however, had culinary themes.

To avoid concentrating wealth where military power also resided, Janissaries were not allowed to engage in commerce of any sort. Trained from an early age solely for war, and sporting a white felt cap ("Börk") that distinguished them from regular Ottoman troops wearing red headgear, Janissaries were the most professional and tactically disciplined troops of their time. As such, they formed the stable core of one of the first and finest *standing armies* of the early modern age. Given each sultan's primary reliance on this body of elite infantry, the feudal masters of the outer provinces of the widespread Ottoman Empire seldom rose to become regional warlords. The sultans thereby avoided the baronial problem posed by feudatories in Europe. On the other hand, sultans were exposed to danger flowing from Janissary disgruntlement: at Buçuk Tepe in 1446, anger over arrears in military pay delayed the ascent of *Muhammad II* to the throne until 1551. Into the 17th century Ottoman lords made up a solid cavalry force that augmented the Janissary infantry; politically, however, they remained a loose aristocracy that seldom challenged central authority. This military system guaranteed that the sultans could always deploy a crack infantry corps with a cavalry auxiliary always available that could be expanded quickly when needed.

No other army that the Ottomans fought, whether in Iran, North Africa, Central Asia, or Europe, could field units even close to a match for the first-rate Janissaries and the flexible military organization that produced them. The Janissaries were also the first Ottoman troops trained in firearms, and hence formed the paramount military corps during the first decades of adoption of gunpowder weapons by the Ottoman army. In the wake of the Janissaries strike of 1446–1451 Muhammad II increased their pay, improved their weapons, and expanded their numbers. He also disbanded several of the original *Orta*, replacing them with three new divisions drawn in inspiration and original membership from the sultan's Royal Hunt: "Sekban" or "dog-handlers," further subdivided into elite guard units; "Doğanci" or "falconers"; and somewhat later, "Bostanci" or "gardeners." The latter were responsible for defense of Constantinople and dozens of imperial estates scattered over the Empire. By 1475 there were 6,000 Janissaries compared to 40,000 *sipahis* and another 3,000 household cavalry. Fifty years later Suleiman I had nearly 38,000 household troops, including the Janissaries. By that time their principal weapon was a "log-barrel" wheel lock musket made by *renegade* German gunsmiths in Ottoman foundries. Older, "pensioner" Janissaries served as marine archers on the sultan's galleys and as amphibious assault troops in the Black Sea. Over the 16th century the Janissary barracks in

Constantinople usually housed about 14,000 boys and men, but at their peak in the 17th century they contained 40,000 troops organized into 196 companies. Another 14,000 Janissaries served in garrisons in strategic provinces such as *eyâlet-i Budin* in Hungary, bringing peak Corps numbers to about 54,000 by 1650.

The first major Janissary battle was against the Karamanian Turks in 1389, where they fought as archers. They were defeated with the rest of the Ottoman army by *Timur* at *Ankara* (July 20, 1402), even though the Corps fought well. The Janissaries began the switch from bows to *arquebuses* in the 1440s, having felt the sting of these new weapons in frontier fights in Hungary. Thereafter, the Corps became most renowned as an elite firearms unit. Janissary musketeers were unique in that they did not deploy pikemen in square for protection as they reloaded. Instead, in a trick learned fighting the Hungarians, who learned it from fighting *Hussites*, Janissaries made wagon-forts (*Wagenburgs* or *tabor*) by chaining together heavy carts. This was so successful they set up

> *...a common Janissary tactic was to fire all guns at once, form a wedge, and charge into the breach ...*

a specialized "gun wagon corps" that accompanied musketeers to battle. From behind these war wagons Janissaries fired muskets and cannon while larger formations of *timariot* cavalry attacked the enemy's flanks. If a break in the enemy line appeared a common Janissary tactic was to fire all guns at once, form a wedge, and charge into the breach swinging swords and maces. This was the closest the Corps came to *volley fire*: their strength was instead individual marksmanship, which they practiced and emphasized to a degree unknown in Europe, where unaimed fire remained standard.

In 1514 the firearms discipline and superiority of the Janissaries utterly destroyed a *Safavid* army, made up mostly of mounted archers, at *Chaldiran* (August 23, 1514). Over time Janissary political power grew. From 1550, like the Roman Praetorian Guard which once made and unmade emperors, the Corps sometimes elevated or deposed sultans. This led to a shift in 1568 toward allowing sons of older Janissaries into the Corps, and from 1582 to permitting free men to enlist so that by the start of the 16th century the Janissaries were a mostly hereditary outfit. In 1594 the wealth and political power of the corps so attracted Muslim recruits eager for political advancement that the Devşirme system was effectively phased out, disappearing entirely by 1648. The Janissaries remained influential within the empire throughout this period, though near its end their military effectiveness was already fading. After their defeat and humiliation by the Poles and Cossacks at *Khotyn* in 1621, a Janissary revolt deposed and killed Sultan Othman (Osman) II. By mid-century, recruitment was kept low as the expense of the Corps no longer led to commensurate battlefield reward for the sultan. See also *Çorbasi*; *ishan*; *Kazan*; *levend/levendat*; *rations*; *Saka*; *sekban*; *Serdengeçti*; *Thirteen Years' War*; *uniforms*; *Varna, Battle of*; *Yeniçeri Ağasi*.

Suggested Reading: Ahmed Djévad, *Etat Militaire Ottoman*, Vol. 1: *Les Corps des Janissaires* (1882); Geoffrey Goodwin, *The Janissaries* (1995).

Jankov, Battle of (March 6, 1645). "Jankau." Even as talks dragged on at Westphalia, fighting continued where the *Thirty Years' War* first broke out, in Bohemia. *Lennart Torstensson* led a Swedish mercenary army 15,000 strong against Prague. It was met at Jankov by an Imperial-Bavarian force of comparable size. The heavily forested terrain broke up formal battle lines, which disadvantaged the heavier Imperial units. When Torstensson's cavalry chased its Austrian counterpart from the field the Imperial infantry turned and followed. Abandoned, the Bavarians could not stand alone and fell back toward Prague. Torstensson besieged the city but could not sustain the effort due to a failure of logistics. He moved on Vienna but was again too undermanned and ill-equipped to take the city. The major effects of Jankov were to break the military power and will of Bavaria and conduce it to peace, to compel *Ferdinand III* to accept the Franco-Swedish proposal for a comprehensive peace to be negotiated in Westphalia, and to ensure that the settlement would be unfavorable to the Habsburgs, who had no army left with which to fight since the entire Imperial "general staff" (or rather, its cruder 17th-century equivalent) was captured and held for a ransom of 120,000 thalers.

Jansenism. A Catholic mystic movement following the teaching of the Holland theologian Cornelis Jansen (1585–1638), Bishop of Ypres. His major work was the four-volume *Augustinus*, completed just before his death and published in 1640. It caused an immediate firestorm of theological controversy. It was placed on the *Index Librorum Prohibitorium* by the *Inquisition* in 1641 and condemned in a papal bull issued by *Urban VIII* in 1642. Jansen's core and austere contention, which was aimed squarely at the *Jesuits*, was that salvation depended on "divine grace" not good works or predestination, and that the gift of "interior grace" was irresistible but received only if one abandoned selfhood before the majesty of God. Such pessimistic, inwardly directed pietism directly challenged traditional Catholic devotion, and implicitly joined in Protestant criticism of the veneration of images and saints. Politically, Jansen opposed France's leadership of the anti-Habsburg coalition during the final phase of the *Thirty Years' War*. *Cardinal Richelieu* held in contempt all *dévots* who embraced Jansenism. The controversy was most acute in France, where occasional violent clashes between Jansenists and Jesuits occurred over nearly a century, until most French Jansenists migrated to the United Provinces. The *Missio Hollandica* sharply divided over Jansenism, with Jesuits leading the opposition. Yet, Jansenists in Utrecht were in fact such strict Catholics that Dutch Calvinists knew them as "Oude Roomsch" ("Old Roman").

Japan. By the start of the 13th century Japan was already on a descending path from aristocratic-emperor rule to fragmented provincialism under warlord clans, to protracted civil war and anarchy. The *Mongols* twice tried to invade Japan but were repulsed at *Hakata Bay* in 1274 and 1281. The Kamakura *shogunate* ended in violence in 1333. The Ashikaga shogunate

(1333–1603) was born into chaos and bloody strife as rival military houses backed rival imperial lines, and as turmoil in China spilled over into destabilization and civil war in Japan. This "War Between the Courts" lasted from 1336 to 1392. As central power collapsed Japan's coasts and outer islands were preyed upon by *wakō* (pirates). In the mid-15th century more decades of civil war climaxed in a shogunal succession dispute, leading to the *Ōnin War* (1467–1477). Thus began a period known as the *Sengoku jidai* or "Warring States," during which power shifted to the "Sengoku daimyo," or military houses of the regions, and Ashikaga shoguns ruled only on paper. Several emperors despaired and fled ruined Kyoto; others were assassinated. This era of so-called *gekokujō* saw general anarchy, widespread arson (a favorite weapon of the *ashigaru*), a plague of *ronin*, and ubiquitous civil warfare marked by endless small battles. One defense against this anarchy was the growth of *jōkamachi* ("castle towns"). A better defense would have been unification and pacification, but before 1560 no one among the daimyo could provide this.

The arrival of firearms in Japan changed all warfare and politics. Samurai faced gunpowder weapons (small rockets) at Hakata Bay, but not guns. Korea acquired firearms from China around 1300 but kept the technology secret from the Japanese for over 200 years. Some primitive Chinese firing tubes were used during the Ōnin War, but did not catch on. Japan acquired its first true guns not from China but from Europe, when several Portuguese merchants shipwrecked at Tanegashima. Portuguese records set the date as 1542; Japanese histories say 1543. What is important is that they brought with them two matchlock arquebuses. These merchants, the first Europeans to visit Japan, were followed by *Jesuits*, experts in forging guns and peddling Catholicism. Spanish traders arrived in 1581 with more guns and cannon, by which time some Japanese daimyo were manufacturing their own firearms and were already using them to overwhelm more traditional neighbors (in battle, perhaps as early as 1549). This is when large infantry formations first appeared in *daimyo* armies, partly in response to the breakdown of *samurai* loyalty during Sengoku, but also due to the introduction of peasant levies armed with arquebuses.

The last half of the 16th century saw the unification of Japan by three great warlords, each effectively using guns in combination with older arms to wage and win the *Unification Wars*. The first was *Oda Nobunaga*, who put an end to the Ashikaga shogunate and the old daimyo order. He conquered the most advanced and heavily populated third of Japan, crushing daimyo and Buddhist opposition by 1582. The second unifier was *Toyotomi Hideyoshi*, who rose from modest origins to rule much of Japan from behind the imperial throne. Hideyoshi twice sent massive armies into Korea. He planned this as the start of an empire to include Indochina, Siam, the Philippines, and China, but was not able to conquer even Korea. In 1587 he ordered Christian missionaries to leave Japan. Ten years later he oversaw mass executions of Japanese Christians, whom he feared as a fifth column and as adherents of a subversive cult. In 1600, Dutch traders arrived and Western trade interests and influence looked set to make headway. The last of the unifiers, *Tokugawa Ieyasu*, triumphed at

Sekigahara in 1600 and became shogun in 1603. His successors, the Tokugawa shoguns, chose a path of isolation from the West trod by Japan for 250 years. Having overcome endless civil wars and the arrival of strange and perhaps threatening foreigners, the Tokugawa steadfastly resisted externally induced change. This policy was undertaken at a time when China was overrun by the *Manchus* and penetrated by Europeans, India was conquered by the *Mughals*, and Europe itself was wracked by sectarian wars. However, the price of the Tokugawa "great peace" was suppression of creative social forces and a self-imposed technological and military inferiority to the West. The Tokugawa shoguns gave Japan political stability and domestic peace, albeit harshly enforced, along with seclusion from Western and Christian influence. Isolation was not as extreme toward Korea and China, however. Ieyasu restored relations with Korea in 1609 and during the Tokugawa shogunate Korea sent twelve major missions (tsūshinshi) to Japan. Westerners, on the other hand, met harassment and were forbidden to take up permanent residence. Thus English traders who arrived in 1612 left in frustration in 1623, while the French established no trade links with Japan in this period.

After 1613, Buddhism—its martial monks now disarmed and so mostly harmless—was reestablished as the state religion, while "Kirishitan" (Japanese Christians) were sharply persecuted. In 1614 all Catholic clergy were expelled. In 1618 other Christian missionaries were killed or forced to leave. A ferocious persecution of Christianity followed, including a series of "seclusion decrees" passed from 1633 to 1641. These aimed at tightening control over the daimyo, among whom a handful were "Kirishitan," and ending all Christian subversion of Japan's putatively homogenous religious and social order. Under pressure from enforcement of anti-Christian edicts by the Tokugawa inquisition, the Kirishitan Shumon Aratame Yaku, in 1637–1638 the Kirishitan of Shimabara rebelled. Mostly converted peasants supported by a few samurai, and with some aid from Europeans in the area, they were brutally crushed: some 35,000 were butchered in their last stronghold at Hara Castle. With the rebellion ended, survivors went underground as *Kakure Kirishitan* ("Hidden Christians"). Western trade also fell away: England's *East India Company* left in 1623, the Spanish were expelled in 1624, and the Portuguese were thrown out in 1639. That left only the Dutch *Vereenigde Oostindische Compaagnie* (VOC), and it was confined to the single entrepôt of *Deshima*. Chinese merchants were more welcome, but they too were controlled in their movements and trade. Additional "seclusion decrees" by Shogun Tokugawa Iyemitsu forbade any Japanese from leaving the home islands and enforced execution of all who returned from abroad, even shipwreck survivors. Shipbuilders were ordered not to construct vessels capable of ocean travel, trade with Europe was limited to regulated and authorized goods through Deshima, and all Korean and Chinese junks were directed to the confined port of *Nagasaki*. Korea retaliated by limiting Japanese traders to Pusan while China banned official trade with Japan, though an extensive private trade (smuggling) flourished that was permitted by the shoguns as a valued source of intelligence on the wider world.

There has been a fierce argument among military historians as to whether or not the Japanese "gave up the gun" during the long Tokugawa shogunate. At one level, they clearly did not: firearms were still produced in Japan and gun militia were maintained under strict shogunate and bakufu control. Yet, prohibitions on anyone other than samurai owning firearms (but also any other deadly weapon, including bows and swords) were enforced by occasional gun and "sword hunts" in the spirit of Hideyoshi's 1588 decree banning ownership of military weapons by commoners. The main argument in favor of the "Japan gave up the gun" thesis is that after the isolated rebellion of 1637–1638 it saw no more battles for 200 years, not until 1837. But it would be more accurate to say that Japan gave up civil war rather than guns. Once Japanese made war again in the second half of the 19th century they took guns out of storage, bought modern models from the West, and took to battle again with real gusto. See also *jōkaku*; *Nichiren Shoni*; *sōhei*; *True Pure Land*; *yamajiro*.

Suggested Reading: W. G. Beasley, *The Japanese Experience: A Short History of Japan* (2000); J. Hall et al., eds., *Japan before Tokugawa* (1981); George Sansom, *A History of Japan, 1334–1615* (1961); R. Toby, *State and Diplomacy in Early Modern Japan* (1984); Conrad Totman, *Early Modern Japan* (1993).

Jargeau, Battle of (1429). See *Hundred Years' War*; *Jeanne d'Arc*.

Jarnac, Battle of (March 13, 1569). The future *Henri III* nominally led a Catholic army to victory over the Huguenots at the start of the third of the *French Civil Wars*. For several days the armies held fast on opposite banks of the Charente river, then the Royalists crossed over to offer battle. The Huguenot army was divided between *Condé* at Jarnac and *Coligny* several miles off. The Catholics attacked Coligny first. He was quickly reinforced by the main Protestant battle under Condé, who led a foolhardy charge in which he was dehorsed then murdered after he was taken prisoner (other Protestant noble prisoners also had their throats cut at Jarnac). After the loss of Condé the Huguenots withdrew to Cognac, nursing their casualties. The Royalists pursued but failed to take Cognac since their siege artillery was still en route from Paris.

Java. In the 7th century C.E., a mixed Hindu-Buddhist kingdom was founded on Java. The Sailendra dynasty (760–860) then unified Java with Sumatra, governing an archipelagic empire from Java. An invasion attempt by the *Mongols* was repulsed in 1292. There followed several centuries under a Hindu kingdom (Majapahit), which expanded throughout the Indonesian archipelago and part of the Malay Peninsula. Islam made inroads from the 13th century. In the 16th century a Muslim state, Mataram, was established in Java. Portuguese traders arrived toward the close of the 16th century, followed closely by the Dutch *Vereenigde Oostindische Compaagnie* (VOC) and English *East India Company*. The Dutch displaced the Portuguese and slowly took over the Javanese interior, ruling harshly and imposing a forced-labor system that by the mid-17th century amounted to effective slavery.

Jeanne d'Arc (1412–1431). "La Pucelle" ("The Maid"). Jeanne, daughter of the shepherd Jacques d'Arc, was born at Domrémy in Lorraine in 1412. According to her testimony delivered to the *Inquisition* that burned her, at age 13 she began hearing voices which she believed were those of the Saint Queens of France, Margaret and Catherine, and Archangel Michael. At age 17 they told her she was appointed to break the siege of Orléans by the English, and to escort the Dauphin Charles from Poitiers to Rheims (the French did not then hold Paris) to be crowned King of France. She traveled to Vaucouleurs, where her renown and reputation took flight and great merchants outbid each other for the honor of arming and armoring her. It was late in the *Hundred Years' War* (1337–1453), and France had known nothing but defeats for several decades. Word of her mission reached the Dauphin, and fanned over a country emiserated by war, long desolate of hope of victory, and fervently ready to believe that God would send help to punish the cruel English occupiers of their ravished homeland. This was normal for an age that took for granted angelic interposition in everyday affairs, a belief enthusiastically encouraged by the Catholic Church, which also taught that diabolical spirits vied directly for the will and souls of men and women. Thus, everyone—friend and foe—accepted that Jeanne d'Arc was inspired by incorporeal creatures. Where the French, like Jeanne herself, believed these to be saints and angels, the English and Burgundians feared that "The Maid" was in league with daemons who had taught her Satan's enchantments. Even the Dauphin rigorously tested her faith, fearing that she might prove to be a sorceress. When satisfied,

. . . at age 13 she began hearing voices . . .

and noting the patriotic and martial passion she inspired in the army and the common people, he agreed to let her try to relieve Orléans. Henceforth, she normally appeared clad in *white armor* and mounted on a white horse. She was armed with a small battle axe inscribed with small crosses and devotions and a lance, the weapon of choice of the warrior class. Her lance was white and topped by a white pennant embroidered with fleurs-de-lis and the words "Jhesus Maria." She held it aloft as *Crusaders* had, assuring the French that God was on their side and that in his sign they would conquer ("In hoc signo vinces," as in Emperor Constantine I's vision). This was critical, as France was deeply defeatist. Jeanne d'Arc's promise of divine assistance was essential to shake off decades of torpor and make the soldiery believe again in the possibility of victory.

On April 25, 1429, the 17-year-old Jeanne d'Arc rode from camp at Blois, co-commander with the duc d'Alençon. She rode at the head of a supply and relief column, a mere girl untested in war yet welcome in the company of, indeed adored by, most of the veteran soldiers and captains of France. Three days later, under cover of night, this column slipped past lax English guards and entered Orléans. Jeanne d'Arc rode through the city in the morning, inspiring a religious rapture in many who saw her, for she looked the part to fulfill an old prophesy which foretold that a maid from Lorraine would save

France. Preferring a bloodless victory over fellow Christians, Jeanne d'Arc rode out to address the English soldiery at the great armored gate (Tourelles) on the main bridge over the Loire that prevented relief of the city. She was met with coarse sexual mockery and defiant contempt by the English captain, and told to go home and mind her cows.

The next day an assault was launched against English garrison troops barricaded into one of eight fortified siege towers, some connected by earthworks, that blockaded Orléans. "The Maid" was absent at the start of the attack, which was repulsed. She rode to the fight to rally the bloodied and retreating French, who turned to follow her and took the tower. On May 5, Jeanne d'Arc led the French across the Loire in boats to attack two more English positions. In close fighting, during which she was wounded slightly in the heel, they captured two small forts. Word was received in town that English reinforcements were on the way so it was decided to assault the Tourelles—manned by some 500 English archers and men-at-arms—without delay, on May 7. While climbing an assault ladder Jeanne d'Arc was pierced in the shoulder by a crossbow quarrel, helped down, and carried to the rear. Shaking off the wound, which was slight, she returned to battle. This inspired the French to heroic efforts. The victory came with an attack into the rear of the English position by a separate group of French led by a wily, veteran captain. The next day the English lifted the siege and abandoned two military camps across the Loire. After burning their stores, they departed. She forbade pursuit in favor of prayers of thanks, banished prostitutes from the company of camp followers, banned swearing by all soldiers of France, and gave personal thanks to her God for victory. It was barely three months since she had promised the Dauphin to relieve Orléans and already she had changed France forever.

After Orléans volunteers flocked to Jeanne d'Arc's banner. She and the army quickly took back Jargeau, Meung-sur-Loire, Beaugency, and other French towns and fortresses. Troyes and Rheims, held by the Burgundians, surrendered to her without resistance. Her army defeated an English force at Patay (June 18, 1429). Within just three months of the relief of Orléans she fulfilled the rest of her mission by escorting the Dauphin to liberated Rheims, where she watched in rapture as he was invested as Charles VII, heir to St. Louis, on July 17, 1429. Jeanne d'Arc asked leave to go home to Lorraine, but she was far too valuable to the king, the army, and France to permit her departure. Reluctantly she took up arms again and captured Compiègne. She led a failed attack on Paris in September, where she was seriously wounded and found herself bereft of the comfort of her Voices, which fell silent.

With premonitions of defeat and her own death, she campaigned for Charles again in 1430. Jeanne d'Arc was with the army when it captured Laon, Soissons, Beauvais, and other fortress towns. She next rode to relieve a Burgundian siege of Compiègne, where she was captured while making a sally from the town. The Burgundians took her to Arras and then into Flanders. In November she was sold to the English, who took her to Rouen. There she was tortured, recanted, relapsed, and was formally tried before an English Catholic court of Inquisition. During her ordeal Charles made no effort to aid the girl who put him on the throne; he proved more rousable by the tickles of his mistress, Agnes Sorel, than by the torments of The Maid. Abandoned by her king and her Voices, Jeanne was condemned to death for witchcraft and heresy by the English court. On May 30, 1431, age 19, she was burned at the stake. In 1456, three years after the French finally retook Rouen, a court of the *Gallican Church* reheard the witnesses against her and revoked the verdict as fraudulent and malicious. From witch she was elevated to martyr, reclaimed for the Faith. Five centuries removed from the passions of her day the Catholic Church canonized her (1920). In death she became a supreme martyr of France, whose story riveted and helped shape its national imagination. It was no accident or coincidence that Free French forces in World War II wore as the symbol of their patriotism and willingness to sacrifice for France her Cross of Lorraine. See also *chivalry*; *Talbot, John*; *Verneuil, Battle of*.

Suggested Reading: Edward Creasy, *Fifteen Decisive Battles of the World* (1851; 1992); Kelly DeVries, *Joan of Arc: A Military Leader* (2003); J. Glénisson, ed., *Jeanne d'Arc, une èpoque, un rayonnment* (1982); M. Gordon, *Joan of Arc* (2000); H. Guillemin, *Joan, Maid of Orleans* (1973); Bonnie Wheeler and Charles Wood, eds., *Fresh Verdicts on Joan of Arc* (1996).

Jemmingen, Battle of (July 21, 1568). A Spanish army under the *Duke of Alba* smashed a Dutch rebel army of 15,000 led by *Louis of Nassau*, brother of *William the Silent*. The rebels lost over 7,000 men, most of them pursued and slaughtered by Alba on the German side of the River Ems, whose banks and waters literally ran with rebel blood. The victory freed Alba to turn to meet an invasion by William with a mercenary army out of Germany, in Brabant.

jeniçeri Ocak. See *Janissary Corps*.

Jerusalem. Capture of Jerusalem was the main objective of the Latin *Crusades*. The First Crusade captured the city in 1099 and sacked it, butchering thousands of inhabitants, Muslim, Christian, and Jew. Once the blood was washed from the paving stones of the *Holy Places*, the Crusaders erected the "Latin Kingdom of Jerusalem." The city was recovered for Islam in 1187 by *Salāh al-Dīn*. It remained in Muslim hands (Arab, Mamlūk, then Ottoman) into the second half of the 20th century.

Jesuits. "Society of Jesus." A highly disciplined, rigorous, militant Catholic religious order founded in 1540 by the Spaniard Ignatius Loyola (1491–1556), under the authority of Pope Paul III. Loyola had served in the Spanish Army in the *Italian Wars* from 1517 to 1521, and was severely wounded in both legs. Military surgeons badly set the breaks, leaving a bone protruding, and he was later racked to stretch one leg back to its original length. It was during convalescence from this excruciating ordeal that Loyola experienced visions of saints and underwent a spiritual epiphany, that he should become a "soldier of Christ." He made a pilgrimage to Montserrat, reputed resting place of the Holy Grail, where after fasting and acts of self-abnegation he dedicated his crippled body to a lifetime of spiritual knighthood. This formerly proud and lusty youth, infused with romantic visions and histories of chivalry, henceforth would limp though the world of ordinary men, a monastic and saintly presence commanding others to join his "holy army" on a new crusade for Christ. At least, so Loyola convinced himself. Like medieval *Military Orders* the Jesuits ran hospitals, orphanages, missions, and schools, and bound members by oaths of rigid obedience, including the infamous 13th rule of Loyola's *Spiritual Exercises*: "I will believe that the white that I see is black, if the hierarchical church so defines."

Reflecting its origins in Loyola's romanticized missionary militarism, the Society of Jesus was headed by a "General" chosen for life. Its initial goals were to serve the *Counter-Reformation* by combating the *Protestant Reformation* on intellectual grounds, but still more to make Catholicism appealing to laity by inculcating an activist spirituality to match the raw energy that made reformed religion so appealing to so many. The Jesuits conducted missionary work in Old World areas such as Inner Austria where Protestantism had made inroads in Catholic-governed lands. They also went abroad. In 1540 the first Jesuits arrived in Goa to begin centuries of proselytizing work in Asia. Jesuit missionaries worked in India, the Philippines, Japan, and China, all through New France (where they were known as the "Black Robes"), Brazil and Spanish America (c.1570), and wherever else Iberian or other Catholic wood might carry a priest. They showed their Counter-Reformation iron teeth at the intermediate session of the *Council of Trent*, 1551–1552, and remained adept casuists ever after. In 1580 the Jesuits sent a mission to England, stirring the already boiling pot of religious conflict in Great Britain leading to *Philip II*'s dispatch of the *Invincible Armada*. They remained keen supporters of Irish Catholic rebellion for many decades more. They were intensely devoted to the cause of indoctrination through religious education. Jesuits tutored many of Europe's leaders, including *Albrecht von Wallenstein*, though the course did not take at all with him. Close to the popes, whose ear they had and to whom all Jesuits were deeply loyal by conviction and oath, the Order was correspondingly unpopular and distrusted by Catholic opponents of excessive papal power and by all Protestants.

During the 16th century the Jesuits expanded their overseas mission along with the Portuguese empire into east Africa, coastal India, and Southeast Asia, and with the Spanish empire into the Americas and Philippiness. In Europe, however, its area of operations contracted during the 17th century: the Order was expelled from Venice, traditional enemy of the popes, in 1607. They were banned in Bohemia in 1618 when that kingdom's Protestants rebelled and the *Thirty Years' War* began. That same year, they were tossed out of Ethiopia at the urging of Coptic bishops. Jesuits returned to Bohemia to impose the Counter-Reformation after the defeat of the Protestant army at the *White Mountain* (1620); they were not allowed back into Ethiopia. They were a major influence on *Ferdinand II*. In 1634 they agreed to say 1,000 masses calling for divine favor for him and for Habsburg arms. More important and just as profitable, they were successful in recatholicizing Austria and southern Germany: where there were four Jesuit colleges in the Habsburg lands in 1550, by 1650 there were 50, and nearly a thousand priests.

The Jesuits were stern and unbending, rigid, and legalistic. In Asia, on several occasions Jesuit fathers capitalized on the intense interest of local rulers in firearms and cannon to trade knowledge of European military secrets for a monopoly foothold in the Court or better, a right to open Catholic missions. This was especially the case in Ming China, where these "soldiers of Christ" were the chief instrument of the transfer of Western gun technology, including on occasion to enemies of the Ming. During a Dutch attack on the Portuguese at Macau in 1622 an Italian Jesuit commanded the artillery that blew a Dutch ship apart and ended the assault. Nor were some Jesuits loathe to turn guns on fellow Catholics: also at Macau, Jesuit gunners blew up a mission of their rivals, the Dominicans. A German Jesuit built a large cannon foundry near the Imperial Palace in the 1640s. Other Jesuits built cannon for the new Qing court in the 1670s, easily adapting their service to the destroyers of their former Ming patrons. In this way, as a Chinese scholar put it: "While Buddha came to China on white elephants, Christ was borne on cannonballs." See also *Ferdinand I, Holy Roman Emperor*; *Indian Wars (Mexico, Central and South America)*; *Jansenism*.

Suggested Reading: John Aveling, *The Jesuits* (1982); Robert Bireley, *Jesuits and the Thirty Years' War* (2003); Philip Carman, *Lost Paradise* (1976); John O'Malley, ed., *The Jesuits* (1999).

Jews. See *anti-Semitism*; *Bayezid II*; *Black Death*; *civilians*; *Cossacks*; *Crusades*; *Devşirme system*; *expulsion of the Jews*; *flagellants*; *Inquisition*; *Jerusalem*; *Reconquista*; *Seljuk Turks*; *Swiss Confederation*; *Thirty Years' War*.

jihad. The Muslim obligation to armed struggle against pagans, infidels, apostates and "heretics." See also *Assassins*; *ghazi*; *"holy war"*; *Islam*; *mujahadeen*; *Ottoman warfare*.

jinetes. Lightly armed and armored, highly mobile mounted warriors who served as dragoon auxiliaries to the *heavy cavalry* in Christian armies and *Military Orders* during the *Reconquista*. They were meant to match Muslim light cavalry in speed and style of fighting. They were drawn from towns or supplied at the expense of rural magnates in return for land from the crown. They rode in distinctive low saddles upon fleet thoroughbred breeds introduced to Iberia by the Muslims of Sicily and North Africa. Jinetes were clearly distinguished from ordinary infantry, who were called *peones*. See also *Granada*.

jizya. A traditional poll tax on all non-Muslims ("dhimmîs") in strict Muslim societies. It was a source of conflict wherever non-Muslim communities were ruled by strict Muslim regimes, especially within the Christian areas of the Ottoman Empire and among subject Hindus in Mughal India. See also *Akbar*; *zakat*.

Johannitterorden. Protestant *Military Orders* in Germany, known together as the "Alliance Orders of St. John," which descended from the *Hospitallers* of Brandenburg. An amicable settlement with the Catholic Maltese Knights was reached in the *Treaty of Osnabrück* in 1648.

John Company. See *East India Company (EIC).*

Joinville, Treaty of (December 31, 1584). By this treaty *Philip II* supported the *Guise* and the *Catholic League* in opposing the ascension to the French throne of *Henri de Navarre* or any other "heretic" prince, and the Guise and League agreed to collaborate in crushing Protestantism in the Netherlands. France was bound to end its alliance with the Ottoman Empire and stop privateering against Spanish and Portuguese shipping out of Dunkirk. Philip subsidized the Guise thereafter in their war with the Huguenots in return for minor Spanish claims against the territory of Navarre and a promise of enactment as part of the fundamental laws of France of decrees issued by the *Council of Trent*, which until then had been resisted by Gallican Catholics. Joinville kept Spain involved in the *French Civil Wars* for more than 10 years.

jōkaku. Mountaintop forts that proliferated in Japan from the 14th century. Their great remove and use of extreme topographical features enabled defenders to withstand sieges even by large armies.

jōkamachi. "Castle towns." During the anarchic *gekokujō* period in Japan, outer walls were added to enclose buildings that lay outside the perimeter of existing castles, converting the castle into a *citadel.* As merchants and ordinary folk sought refuge inside the new walls, markets, and fortified towns grew up protected by the outer wall and citadel. Several grew into considerable cities. By 1600 many *samurai* had taken up permanent residence in the castle towns of their *daimyo.*

Juan of Austria. See *Don Juan, of Austria.*

Jülich-Kleve, Crisis over (1609–1614). This small Rhineland duchy strategically located on the border of the Spanish Netherlands and the Dutch Republic became a focus of diplomatic intrigue when its last duke, long mentally unfit, died in 1609. The main claimants to the succession were Sigismund of Brandenburg, the Count Palatine, and the Elector of Saxony, but also pressing a claim was Holy Roman Emperor Matthias. The Netherlands, Spain, and France all had interests in the outcome. When *Henri IV* intervened an international crisis ensued. The *Catholic League* and *Protestant Union* also intervened, with the latter opposing an effort to govern the duchy through an imperial commissioner in the name of *Rudolf II.* In July 1609, the Archbishop of Strassburg occupied the Imperial fortress town of Jülich. The Protestant Union, with Dutch and French support, took the fortress in 1610 and attacked the Archbishop's holdings in Alsace. Then

Henri IV was assassinated in France and the Protestant princes of Germany argued over division of the spoils. The two confessional alliances now gave way before the intervention of larger powers, as the Dutch and Spanish made clear that no settlement was acceptable that gave the other side control of the duchy. In 1614 the duchy was partitioned in the Treaty of Xanten, mediated by France and England after Spain and the Netherlands had intervened militarily (the Spanish took Wesel and the Dutch occupied Jülich). This compromise split the duchy between a Catholic, the pro-Spanish Wittelsbach Prince of Pfalz-Neuburg, and a Protestant, the pro-Dutch Johann Sigismund of Brandenburg, who converted to Calvinism in 1613.

Although it took five years to settle the succession and required some force to do so, the dispute was not permitted to break the *Twelve Years' Truce* (1609–1621) between the Spanish and Dutch that temporarily suspended hostilities during the *Eighty Years' War* (1566–1648). This ability of the diplomats to isolate a serious local conflict strongly suggests that neither the outbreak of the *Thirty Years' War* (1618–1648) four years later, nor its swift spread across Europe, was "inevitable." The dispute over Jülich-Kleve revealed that religious differences and confessional alliances were not of themselves sufficient to provoke a general war, not least because neither Catholic nor Protestant solidarity could be assumed. On the other hand, the crisis also showed that the Holy Roman Empire was impotent, no longer master of its internal affairs. And it demonstrated that the various powers and princes of Germany were closely linked to external allies and hence tied to external interests and initiatives. Under these circumstances, any major change in Germany would affect overall international relations and vice versa, which is exactly what happened from 1618 to 1648. Once war broke out the Dutch held the fortress of Jülich only until 1622, when it was taken by storm by the Spanish.

> *...the Dutch and Spanish made clear that no settlement was acceptable that gave the other side control of the duchy.*

Suggested Reading: Alison Anderson, *On the Verge of War* (1999).

Julius III (r.1549–1555). Pope. See *Council of Trent*; *Henri II, of France*.

junk. A variety of highly seaworthy sailing ships of Chinese origin and design, widely employed in war and commerce in Asia. From the 10th century Chinese junks displaced Arab and Indian ship types on the Sino-Islamic trade routes, voyaging as far west as southern India. Junk warships protected against pirates on the Huai and Yangzi Rivers and in the East China Sea, at least from the Song dynasty. The *Mongols* took control of the junk fleets of Korea and south China to launch two invasions of Japan that met defeat at *Hakata Bay*, in 1271 and again in 1284. War junks were designed for ramming and boarding actions. They had high *castles* for archers, but their hulls were too thin to take *gun ports* or heavy cannon. Some Asian nations stopped building them once they encountered Western ships. The Malays, for example, no longer built war junks after the Portuguese arrived. But instead of copying Portuguese *galleons* they built European-style *galleys*, which they as well as the Portuguese used effectively in coastal waters. In 1565 a Portuguese *carrack* was attacked by several dozen Japanese junks but fought them off with its broadside guns. This helped discourage further building of war junks. For other reasons, after the voyages of *Zheng He* the Chinese no longer built junk war fleets (or blue water fleets of any kind). However, they still built ships for trade, including such large types as the *Fujian* and *Guangdong*. See also *tribute*.

Junkers. See *Preussische Bund*; *Prussia*; *Thirteen Years' War*.

jupon. A short, tight-fitting coat of armor peculiar to England. It replaced the *surcoat*.

Jürchen. See *banner system (China/Manchuria)*; *China*; *Manchus*; *Nurgaci*.

jus ad bellum. "Law of going to war," or right to wage war. It incorporated notions of just cause, right intention, right authority, proportionality and the requirement that the decision for war be taken as a last resort. Fundamentally, jus ad bellum said that one could go to war only for just reasons, such as self-defense or last resort resistance to great evil. It was never morally permissible to make war for bad reasons, such as conquest or other collective theft. In practice, this principle was observed more in the breach than the observance. The right to embark on a war was limited to legitimate secular authorities to whom *knights* were bound or, for those embarking on a *Crusade*, to the Church itself. As primitive and self-serving as this system of religious law was, it nonetheless represented a sustained effort within the limits of the day to morally restrain warriors and subject war itself to the rule of law. It is also worth noting that moderns seldom fared better than medievals in later legal efforts to limit or restrain war.

jus armorum. "Law of arms." See *jus ad bellum*; *jus in bello*; *just war tradition*.

jus emigrandi. The legal right within the Holy Roman Empire, established by the *Peace of Augsburg* in 1555, to leave towns and villages where one's religion was persecuted. It extended beyond princes to the humblest subjects of the emperor, which was an extraordinary advance in law for that time. On the other hand, leaving one's home was exceptionally hard for most people so that in practice the jus emigrandi could be as much or more a punishment for religious dissent as it was a legal right.

jus in bello. "Law of making war," or the law of combat. Its cardinal principles were noncombatant immunity (immunity of *civilians*), with only combatants constituting morally permissible targets. Note that causing "collateral damage" to civilians or property was permitted if targets were selected with

491

"right intent" and the violence done respected the principle of "proportionality" wherein retributive violence was proportionate to the original injury suffered. The jus in bello sought to restrain the extent of harm done by combatants even in a just war and further, to limit the violent and destructive means by which even permissible harm was carried out. In practice, jus in bello limitations were even less regarded that those of the *jus ad bellum*. Even most theorists paid it little attention once it became clear it was wholly unenforceable and that most men thought judgment of warriors' actions should only be made by God.

jus pacis et belli. "Law of peace and war." The legal right to declare war or make peace, to build fortifications and maintain garrisons, to raise and field armies, and to levy war taxes or billet troops. Originally a right of all *belatores*, by the mid-17th century it was increasingly limited to recognized sovereigns. See also *Grotius, Hugo*; *Westphalia, Peace of.*

justification by faith. See *Calvinism*; *Counter-Reformation*; *Luther, Martin*; *Protestant Reformation.*

just war tradition. A centuries-old tradition of moral reasoning about war that waxed then waned during the Middle Ages and "wars of religion," to wax again in more secular form in the mid-17th century. It drew on the writings of Augustine of Hippo (354–430 C.E.) and Moses ben Maimun, or Maimonides (1135–1204), but was most importantly extended and elaborately codified by Thomas Aquinas (1225–1274). Aquinas and other medieval theologians were interested in expanding moral and religious restraints on war already found in the *Pax Dei* and *Treuga Dei*. The just war school thus sought to make all private war illegal and to limit violence to acts necessary to the prosecution of a just or good war. The just war doctrine of the Catholic Church was challenged during the *Italian Renaissance* by the new military theories and overtly pagan political ethic of *Machiavelli* and other thinkers. In turn, that intellectual challenge provoked an effort to save the tradition by adapting it to emerging secular international law and the looming reality of the end of the *res publica Christiana*. Despite being rooted in religious thought (not only Christian, but also Jewish and Islamic traditions), the just war gained an international legal, secular, and rationalist pedigree when adapted by secular jurists such as *Hugo Grotius*, who hoped thereby to limit the horrors of the great wars of the first half of the 17th century, the *Thirty Years' War* (1618–1648) and the *Eighty Years' War* (1568–1648).

The just war tradition required moral distinctions to be drawn between aggressor and victim which obliged third parties to aid the victim of an unjust war, unjustly waged. Practitioners of the tradition, clerics and the first international lawyers mostly, asked key questions to arrive at reasonable judgments in specific cases. These were: Was the cause just (did it proceed from self-defense, protection of prior legal rights, reparation of injuries, or punishment of wrong-doers)? Was it declared by "right authority," a legitimate sovereign power, or merely by a raw de facto power? Was it marked by "right intention" on the part of kings and warriors? Were soldiers using force to promote the general good, or was the force used merely self-serving and egoistical? Was the violence used and the physical and moral damage done in close accord with the moral ends sought? That is, was the principle of "proportionality" between cause and consequence, provocation and response, respected? Finally, was care taken to minimize damage and casualties among the innocent ("collateral damage")?

On the other hand, medieval thinkers also saw war as a valid tool of statecraft and even as essential in the resolution of disputes among kings and to preserve the general good of the Christian Commonwealth (res publica Christiana). Destruction of lives, livelihoods, and property in a *bellum hostile*, and just war waged by a just ruler, was even seen as the correct punishment by God of sinful men. War was a scourge brought down on the wicked not by the hand of other men but by sinfulness that moved the "Hand of God" to correct injustice on Earth. In practice, most rulers neither learned about nor cared for such fine moral reasoning about the military instrument of kingship. For them war was the blunt force of their political will. It sustained all power, privilege, and prestige. If some bishop or abbot scribbled an objection to a king's acts of war, well, priests and monks were bribed easily enough. And if that failed, they could be held prisoner until they agreed to grant absolution to the king, or hard men would be found to rid the king of some "scurrilous priest." Even so, the just war was a sophisticated yet practical approach to the problem of war. Even for theologians it was concerned far more with practical application than abstract dogma or doctrine. This was its great strength and real contribution.

In its later secular form, the just war continued to reject pacifism but added rejection of the idea of "*holy war*." A core moral presumption was held against war, but the just war school recognized that secular powers would nonetheless resort to violence to advance their material interests. The tradition did not bemoan this fact. It sought instead to lend guidance as to when war was morally or legally permissible. It asked: "What are the exceptional cases which overcome the core moral presumption against war?" It sought the answer in sophisticated historical casuistry. Rather than railing ineffectually against reality, the just war looked to limit the occasions when war was accepted as a legitimate recourse for civilized men and states. It sought formal agreement on the *jus ad bellum*, or the legal right to make war under specified conditions and within an overarching moral context. It proposed that no war could be just on both sides and allowed that some might be unjust from all points of view. It sought to limit the killing and destruction which accompanied even a just war. That aspect of the doctrine was the *jus in bello*, or the search for mercy and justice in the conduct of warfare, which emphasized restraint in the force used and respect for innocents (civilian immunity). For a war to be just both jus ad bellum and jus in bello requirements had to be met. Hence, it was possible to wage war unjustly, in terms of means, even in a just cause. In this rational form the just war tradition entered the secular realm, infusing its principles and formal reasoning into the laws of war of the modern states system. See also *chivalry*; *Crusades*; *German Peasant War*; *guerre couverte*; *guerre mortelle*; *jihad*; *knights*; *Lipsius, Justus*; *Luther, Martin*; *Magdeburg, Sack of*; *prohibited weapons*; *requerimiento*; *siege warfare*.

Suggested Reading: James Turner Johnson, *Just War Tradition and the Restraint of War* (1981); Maurice Keen, *The Laws of War in the Late Middle Ages* (1965); F. H. Russell, *The Just War in the Middle Ages* (1975).

K

kabuto. A spectacularly ornate and fierce Japanese armored helmet and mask (the "men gu," replete with oversized silk mustache) dating to the 14th–16th centuries. It was worn over a padded skull cap, holed at the top to allow the *samurai*'s queue an exit.

kaffir. In *Islam*, an "infidel" or nonbeliever. This usually meant a pagan, but for extremist Muslims the term also embraced Christians and Jews who were otherwise considered by most Muslims to be "people of the book" of divine revelation by a succession of recognized prophets, of whom Muhammad was the last, or "Seal of the Prophets."

kaim mekam. A deputy *Grand Vezier*.

Kakure Kirishitan. "Hidden Christians." Japanese Christians who went underground to survive anti-Christian edicts, persecution, and the inquisition ("Kirishitan Shumon Aratame Yaku") pursued by the *Tokugawa Shogunate*. There were about 300,000 left after the failed Shimabara rebellion (1637–1638) and attendant massacres. Some survived 250 years of Tokugawa seclusion of Japan from contact with the West by outward conformity with Buddhism and Shinto observance.

kale. Ottoman stone fortresses surrounded by several wide moats. They were built in more strategic locales where simple *çit palankasi*, or reed palisades, proved inadequate.

Kallo, Battle of (1638). See *Eighty Years' War*.

Kalmar, Union of. See *Union of Kalmar*.

Kalmar War (1611–1613). The immediate cause was Sweden's wish to escape payment of the *Sound Tolls* claimed by Denmark by opening a new, northern trade route. Denmark responded by invading Sweden. Fighting commenced along the border with each side enjoying small victories and suffering modest defeats. Denmark prevailed at sea while Sweden—engaged also in Muscovy—fielded contingents of raw conscripts to fight it out in the arctic Finnmark. On August 26, 1612, at Kringen, a force of 500 Norwegians intent on revenge for an earlier Swedish massacre ambushed 300 Scottish mercenaries who were cutting across Norway to reach employment with Sweden. After the fight the Norwegians massacred all their prisoners. With the unexpected death of Sweden's *Karl IX*, the young *Gustavus Adolphus* needed to end the war quickly. He did so in the *Peace of Knäred* (1613), which favored Denmark and forced Sweden to pay a large indemnity.

kamikaze. See *Hakata Bay, Battle of (1281)*.

Kandurcha, Battle of (1391). See *Timur*.

Kanem. A large medieval state in the central sudan, north of Lake Chad on the southern fringe of the Sahara. It was governed by martial nomads whose range straddled one of the trans-Saharan trade routes between Tripoli and Tunisia on the coast and *Hausa* lands to the southwest. It sold slaves to *Ifriqiya* and Egypt and was extant in some form from the 9th century C.E., when references to it first appear in Arab chronicles. The kings and much of the population of Kanem converted to Islam in the 11th century, and thereafter Kanem helped channel Islam into the southern sudan and to *Bornu*. From the 10th to the 19th centuries Kanem was ruled by some faction of the Saifawa dynasty, though with interruptions. These Muslim kings claimed a Yemeni origin. They may actually have had one, but just as likely this was a propaganda device to attain greater legitimacy within the wider Islamic world of which Kanem was an integral part. In the 13th century Kanem extended its control to areas south of Lake Chad, then entered upon three centuries of near-constant internal quarreling among its ruling class and dynasty. In the late 14th century Kanem's military elite (Mais) retreated into eastern Hausaland, and Kanem went into steep decline as its northern provinces were conquered by a rising cavalry power, the Bulala. In the 16th century a new Saifawa kingdom arose in Bornu. It made the Bulala rulers of Kanem its tributary. Still, even in reduced form Kanem remained among the most advanced sudanic states into the 18th century, a time when it still raided for slaves among less advanced areas and stateless peoples to its south and east.

Kapikulu. "Slave of the Porte." *Devşirme* employed in the Ottoman military or in the sultan's palace.

Kapikulu Askerleri. "The Sultan's Army." The permanent, household troops of Ottoman sultans. They were salaried and comprised both infantry and cavalry, as distinct from provincial levies (*Eyâlet Askerleri*) of *timariots*, seasonal cavalry tied to land revenues in exchange for military service. At first, household regiments were merely palace guards, with many recruited among military slaves or prisoners of war. The combination of *Janissaries* and *sipahis*, who otherwise maintained a deep inter-service rivalry, along with *silahdars*, greatly enhanced the power of sultans within the Empire. From the late 16th century the Kapikulu Askerleri formed the core of Ottoman armies fighting on the frontiers even when the sultan was not present, which was most often the case after 1596. Kapikulu Askerleri troops were extremely well-trained and highly specialized, dividing into various technical units (armorers, engineers, gunners, wagoners, training units), while retaining units of regular infantry and cavalry. Kapikulu Askerleri were paid quarterly and well, with active units receiving an additional campaign bonus (*sefer bahşişi*). This meant the sultan's armed *kuls* rarely refused to fight for want of pay, though they were known to refuse long service in the harsh eastern deserts. Six richly paid regiments of sipahis ("alti bölük sipahileri") held noncombat, military administration posts ("divanî hizmet"). It was the ambition of *Serdengeçti* Janissaries to receive, as a permanent reward, elevation to the higher paid ranks of these pampered sipahis regiments. See also *askeri*; *Devşirme system*; *magazines*; *Thirteen Years' War*.

Kappel, Battle of (October 11, 1531). The teachings of *Zwingli* held sway in Zürich but not in the Catholic *Forest Cantons* of Switzerland. The latter formed an alliance in 1528, supported by Ferdinand of Austria. Zürich declared war in 1529 following the burning of a reformed preacher who had been seized on neutral territory. The "war" lasted only 16 days, as fighting was avoided when Zürich marched out and demonstrated its army. Two years later 8,000 men from the Forest Cantons made a surprise assault on Zürich, which could only muster 2,000 men to meet them, at Kappel. Both sides fought with high religious zeal, but raw numbers told the tale. Zwingli was found among the wounded after the battle and was killed. His corpse was burned, his ashes mixed with dung and scattered.

Kapudan-i Derya. The grand commander (admiral) of an Ottoman fleet.

kapu kulu. See *Kapikulu Askerleri*.

karacena. A Polish term for what was otherwise known as *sarmatian* armor.

Karl IX (1550–1611). King of Sweden, 1604–1611. He deposed the Catholic king of Sweden, *Sigismund III*. That provoked a long and costly war with Poland in which Swedish arms, which were still semi-feudal, were closely tested. Sigismund landed at Kalmar with a Polish-Lithuanian army in 1598, but was met by Karl and defeated at Stangebro (Stegeborg), on September 8/18, 1598. In 1600, Karl invaded Livonia, launching an intermittent but six-decade-long struggle with Poland for control of that territory (to the Peace of

Oliwa). He beat Sigismund III at Linköping (1598), south of Stockholm. Fighting with Poland over the succession in Sweden continued to the end of his reign. Despite a private leaning toward elements of Calvinism, at the national level Karl reaffirmed the Lutheran profession of Sweden. From an early age he educated his son, *Gustavus Adolphus*, in the arts of war and governance. His death in the midst of the *Kalmar War* thrust on his young son the full demands of making war and negotiating peace.

Karrenbüchsen. Czech: "houfnice." Medium-caliber, mid-14th-century guns mounted on carts. The *Hussites* used them to defend gaps in their *Wagenburgs*.

karr-wa-farr. A common Muslim and light cavalry tactic (also used by Mongols and *jinetes*). It was based on the ancient ruse of a feigned retreat from the enemy designed to draw overeager pursuers out of position into a trap, whereupon the simulated flight was terminated as erstwhile retreating horsemen turned to envelop and destroy their pursuers, usually with the aid of additional ambushers.

Karsthans. From "Hans Karst," the German caricature of peasant life and manner represented by "Hans," a crude bumpkin and political equivalent to the "Jacques Bonhomme" figure of France. It was a widely used term of contempt for peasant rebels during the *German Peasant War* (1525).

Katzbalger. "Cat's claw." A short sword with a double-edge and a sharp, though rounded tip. It was a favorite close combat weapon of the *Landsknechte*.

Kazan. A large copper cauldron that was the prized possession of every Janissary unit. It was used to prepare the single meal per day promised by the sultan ("The Father Who Feeds Us") to every Janissary. *Ortas* (companies) carried it in military parades and protected it in battle. To tip over the Kazan was the accepted signal to begin a mutiny. An Orta that lost its Kazan in battle was disgraced before all.

Kazan, Conquest of (1552). See *Ivan IV*.

keel-haul. A rare, brutal naval punishment that entailed hauling a man by ropes beneath a ship from one side to the other. If done slowly this could lead to drowning. More often, it led to death from severe loss of blood caused by scraping against the sharp encrustation of marine life that adhered to the hulls of all wooden ships.

keep. The inner *donjon*, tower, or stronghold of a castle. See also *keep-and-bailey*; *shell-keep*; *torre del homenaje*; *tower-keep*.

keep-and-bailey. An early form of stone castle built from the 12th century to replace the *motte-and-bailey* fort. It combined a new stone *keep* built atop the old *motte*, while either retaining the existing wood *bailey* or replacing it with a stone perimeter.

kenshin. The *samurai* belief in total self-sacrifice as a vassal to his lord (*daimyo*).

Kephissos, Battle of (1311). The *Catalan Great Company* learned from the victory of Flemish infantry over French knights at *Courtrai* (1302), and adapted their infantry tactics when fighting against the so-called "Frankish" Duke of Athens at Kephissos. Specifically, the Catalan infantry took position behind a marsh that impeded the cavalry of their enemy, as the Flemings had done at Courtrai.

Keresztes, Battle of (1596). See *Thirteen Years' War*.

kerne. Gaelic: "ceithearnach." An Irish light infantryman, though sometimes also used to refer to Scottish infantry. They had a reputation for ill-discipline and atrocity that earned them hatred from Irish peasants and townsfolk, but not from Irish poets. This reputation probably reflected Church propaganda and distaste for the pagan origin of kernes, as well as their actual deeds. After the *Kildare Rebellion* Irish kerne were employed by English armies in Scotland and France and to garrison the *Pale*. The end of the Tudor conquest of Ireland in 1603 rendered kerne unemployed, since private warfare was banned, and most became outcast or were deported to overseas colonies. See also *galloglass*; *redshanks*.

kettle-hat. A conical infantry helmet with a wide brim in common use in the 14th–15th centuries. In appearance, essentially the same helmet as worn by British and Commonwealth troops in World War I.

Khanua, Battle of (1527). See *Khanwa, Battle of.*

Khanwa, Battle of (March 16–17, 1527). "Khanua." A clash in north India between *Babur*, who founded the *Mughal Empire* in Delhi the year before, and a coalition army of seven *Rajput* rulers. The Rajputs were nominally generaled by one of their greatest warrior heroes, Maharana Sangram Singhi, better known as *Rana Sanga*. His army enjoyed a huge numerical advantage, deploying 80,000 men and some 500 war *elephants*. Moreover, Babur's army of just 20,000 Afghans, Mongols, and Turks was virtually surrounded, in unfamiliar territory, unused to the oppressive Indian heat, and most of its men wanted to go home after more than a year of campaigning in India. Only the promise of more plunder of India's wealth kept the men from returning to cooler homes around Kabul. At Khanwa, as also happened to the army of the *Delhi Sultanate* at *Panipat* (1526), the marked superiority in musketry and artillery of Babur's men told the tale against superior Indian numbers. Babur also displayed exceptional leadership. When the clash came the Rajputs overwhelmed by sheer numbers a Mongol van of just 1,500 men. The advantage gained by Rana Sanga was dissipated, however, by dissent among his confederate generals over how to proceed and who would command. In the interim the Afghans entrenched, forming a strong defensive line and securing their position as they had at Panipat by lashing together wagons to make a field fortification (*tabor*). They left strategic gaps among the wagons through which artillery could fire and their cavalry sally forth. Rajput warriors repeatedly hurled themselves against the center-right of Babur's line, making furious charges and fighting hand-to-hand over several hours. Sanga, who was wounded several times, then sent his elephant corps forward. Babur's cannon killed a number of the beasts and panicked and stampeded the rest. This swung the battle for the Afghans. Seeing this, part of Sanga's army crossed over to join Babur. After his victory Babur decamped for Agra, 60 miles away.

> *Rajput warriors repeatedly hurled themselves against the center-right of Babur's line . . .*

Khotyn, Battle of (September 21–October 9, 1621). The Christians of Moldavia rebelled against Ottoman suzerainty in 1621 and allied with Poland. The Ottomans responded with an invasion of Ukraine with a huge army, led by Othman (Osman) II. *Jan Chodkiewicz* rode to meet the invaders at Khotyn (Chocim), astride the Dniester River. The Poles were badly outnumbered until reinforced by 40,000 Ukrainian Cossacks. Chodkiewicz won the battle but was killed. The fight was notable for the breaking and panicked flight of the *Janissary Corps*. The sultan was forced to return in defeat and disgrace to Constantinople, where the Janissaries revolted and killed him.

kieko. See *armor*; *samurai*.

Kievan Rus. See *Crusades*; *Lithuania, Grand Duchy of*; *Livonian Order*; *Muscovy, Grand Duchy of*; *Sweden*; *Ukraine*.

Kildare Rebellion (1534–1535). A rebellion in the Lordship of Ireland arranged by Gerald Fitzgerald, Ninth Earl of Kildare, but provoked by the evolving religious policies of *Henry VIII*. Most fighting was in or around the *Pale*. The Archbishop of Dublin was murdered (July 27, 1534) and the city besieged by 15,000 men, including reluctant Pale landowners forced to take part in the siege. The rebellion was so dangerous that Henry dispatched the largest expedition to Ireland in 140 years. Once it landed at Dublin most "Englishery" found their courage and deserted Kildare to rally to the Crown. After a 10-day siege of Maynooth the rebel garrison surrendered, only to be summarily executed. Similarly, Kildare was promised mercy but executed in the Tower on February 3, 1537. This rendered the "Pardon of Maynooth" a bitter phrase and memory of English military justice that inspired generations of later Irish rebels. Once the last Irish *kernes* and *galloglass* were suppressed the ascendancy of the *New English* Protestant military class was established. The New English were dedicated to the Tudor project to end medieval disunity in

Ireland and unite it under the Crown. They became major landlords in the process.

Kilsyth, Battle of (August 15, 1645). The Royalist *Marquis of Montrose* continued his successful Scottish campaign which led to victories at *Auldearn* (May 9) and *Alford* (July 2). At Kilsyth he again beat a *Covenanter* army. Several thousand Covenanter infantry were wiped out, perhaps as many as 6,000. That left Montrose militarily supreme in Scotland. See also *English Civil Wars*.

"King's Two Bodies." An English legal doctrine developed under *Henry VIII*. It sought to reconcile England's deeply fractured religious and political communities under the doctrine that the people and Church were alike subsumed in the king's "royal body" (his "body politic" rather than his "body natural"). After Henry's death there was misogynist opposition to allowing his daughters, *Mary Tudor* and *Elizabeth I*, to make the same claim. In the end, Elizabeth settled on the title "governor" rather than "head" of the Church of England. The doctrine was vehemently repudiated by Parliament when *Charles I* tried to uphold it before and during the *English Civil Wars*. See also *corpus mysticum*; *Rex christianissimus*.

Kinsale, Battle of (1601). See *Nine Years' War*.

Kirishitan. Japanese Christians. See *Japan*; *Kakure Kirishitan*; *Kirishitan Shumon Aratame Yaku*; *Tokugawa Ieyasu*; *Toyotomi Hideyoshi*; *Unification Wars*.

Kirishitan Shumon Aratame Yaku. The office of inquisition set up under the *Tokugawa Shogunate* in 1640 to enforce anti-Christian edicts and seclusion decrees. See also *Japan*; *Kakure Kirishitan*.

Kirkholm, Battle of (September 27, 1605). A Swedish army, led, trained, and newly equipped by *Karl IX*, met a smaller Polish-Lithuanian cavalry army under *Jan Chodkiewicz*. The Swedes had 8,500 foot and 2,500 horse against fewer than 4,000 Poles and Lithuanians. The Swedes made a rash, frontal cavalry assault which the Poles met with a fast counterattack that dispersed the Swedish horse on either wing. Then they attacked the abandoned Swedish infantry, breaking through their pike defenses and massacring foot soldiers where they stood. The Swedes lost 75–85 percent casualties, or nearly 9,000 men. The Poles and Lithuanians suffered just 100 dead.

kizilbash. See *Qizilbash*; *Safavid Empire*.

Klozbüchse. A German multi-shot gun dating to the early 16th century. The barrel was loaded with several charges and balls in succession so that as the first charge at the front of the muzzle fired it ignited the second, the second ignited the third, and so on.

Klushino, Battle of (1610). See *"Time of Troubles."*

Knabenschaften. "Band of (young) companions." See *Landsknechte.*

Knäred, Peace of (1613). This treaty put an end to the *Kalmar War* (1611–1613) between Denmark and Sweden allowing the young Swedish king, *Gustavus Adolphus*, time to consolidate his hold on power and complete crucial internal political and military reforms. It permitted Swedish goods and copper to pass through the Baltic Sound without triggering the *Sound Tolls*, in exchange for a burdensome but not crippling indemnity paid to Denmark. The Swedes also withdrew their forces from northern Norway, allowing the Danes to add Lappland to their empire.

Knechte. See *Landsknechte.*

knight. French: "chevalier," German: "Ritter." Knights were mounted, armored, aristocratic warriors who enjoyed a special or even exclusive right to use force, and who constituted the hard core of any *battle* in a Medieval European army. The martial class of Europe was raised within a literary tradition, which matured during the 12th century, that emphasized a code of *chivalry.* They also participated in a cult of honor that emphasized personal courage, strength, skilled horsemanship, mastery of a variety of (mainly edged) weapons, and ferocity in battle. This code was presented and accepted as a Christian vocation, an idea promulgated by the Church and reinforced with social privilege matched to the critical function of a hereditary military *Estate.* Still, as late as the 11th century European knights did not enjoy full mastery over infantry on the battlefield. They gained supremacy during the 12th century when the *couched lance* was more widely adopted. This was not a wholly new weapon or fighting technique, but its spread proved decisive as cavalry tactics were developed to accommodate the lance. These were practiced in tournaments where bodies of knights jousted while infantry was elsewhere engaged, or even sat on the sidelines watching. Knighthood was the principal role and aspiration of the noble fathers and first sons of Europe, and carried great social prestige as a result. In many areas the old rule of inheritance by primogeniture coupled with general population growth in the 11th century to create a class of landless nobles—second, third, or fourth sons of landed nobles. These were knights by class, name, and training but had no title, land, or vassals and thus made up a body of rootless armed warriors. Some sought to shelter in one or other of the *Military Orders.* Others went on *Crusade.* Hence, while some knights were great magnates and the wealthiest men of the age, whose armor, steeds, and retainers boasted wealth, power, and social dominance, others were landless and near-penniless men-at-arms who fought for pay or the chance to get rich through plunder and holding one of the richer knights for ransom.

All knights were distinguished in battle by their *armor, weapons, warhorses,* attendants, and the *pennants* on which they displayed their family's or liege lord's coat-of-arms. Costs of knighthood varied by country and century but a rough guide would be that it took about a year's landed income, or the equivalent in *scutage*, to outfit a knight. Regardless of wealth, knights wore expensive armor. They started out with *mail* protection, usually a *hauberk*, which was supplemented from the 14th century by heavy *plate*, usually worn over the mail as "double armor." Later plate displaced mail, with the full "suit of armor" donned only with great difficulty and assistance, from the feet up. Further protection came from the *escutcheon* that knights carried. The *sword* was the preferred weapon of warrior-aristocrats in all ancient and medieval martial cultures, from Japan to Roman Britain, to India or Medieval Europe. Alternately, the mace or some other clubbing weapon was acceptable. In the 12th century the couched lance was widely adopted as the main weapon, which greatly increased the shock value of *heavy cavalry*. Most knights disdained missile weapons for reasons of cultural and class prejudice, but also from practical concerns: bows and crossbows were difficult to aim and shoot from horseback while rattling and bouncing inside cumbersome armor; and they were impossible to reload without leaving go the reins. Early firearms faced the problem of wind extinguishing a *slow match* or blowing powder out of the firing pan. Again, reloading guns was impossible on horseback while in the midst of combat.

On the way to and during battle knights were accompanied by retainers: *esquires*, *pages*, *valets*, and personal servants. The page or a trusted commoner was assigned the task of holding the reins of the knight's *destrier* and of any additional horses. A valet helped the knight mount (a fully armored knight could not do this unaided), and followed behind to assist him regain the saddle should he fall or be wounded. The esquire carried his weapons and escutcheon (heavy shield), and handed these up to the knight prior to, or even during, combat. A fourth attendant might follow with a packhorse in expectation of collecting armor from the dead or shepherding noble prisoners back to camp to be ransomed another day. Socially important and wealthier knights were escorted and protected in battle by several armed retainers, mounted or on foot as men-at-arms. Such an enfeoffed knight flew his own banner. If he had paid knights and armed retainers serving under him he was known as a "knight banneret." A lowlier knight serving under the enfeoffed knight's banner or alongside him was known as a "knight bachelor."

There was once great debate over whether medieval knights fought as disjointed bodies of individuals or as cavalry. Hans Delbrück, writing during World War I, argued that knights were not cavalry, which replaced them rather than evolved out of medieval equestrian warfare. Later research showed that while most knights did not drill anywhere near the extent that later cavalry did, they fought in sufficiently coordinated ways—as tactical units rather than as individual warriors—to qualify as true cavalry. See also *Agincourt, Battle of*; *Assize of Arms*; *Bannockburn*; *Bornu*; *camino francés*; *Cassel, Battle of*; *cavalry*; *confrère knights*; *Courtrai, Battle of*; *Crécy, Battle of*; *daggers*; *eagle knight*; *einschildig Ritter*; *estates*; *feudalism*; *Grandson, Battle of*; *Héricourt, Battle of*; *housecarls*; *jaguar knight*; *Johannitterorden*; *Knights Templar*; *Laupen, Battle of*; *Livonian Order*; *milites*; *Morat, Battle of*; *Morgarten, Battle of*; *Näfels, Battle of*;

Nancy, Battle of; *Order of the Golden Fleece*; *Poitiers, Battle of*; *Reconquista*; *recruitment*; *Roosebeke, Battle of*; *routiers*; *salute*; *samurai*; *Schlegelerbund*; *Sempach, Battle of*; *servitium debitum*; *Sickingen, Franz von*; *tabard*; *Teutonic Knights, Order of*; *valet*; *wheel lock*.

Suggested Reading: Andrew Ayton, *Knights and Warhorses* (1994); G. Duby, *The Chivalrous Society* (1978); Maurice Keen, ed., *Medieval Warfare* (1999); R. E. Oakeshott, *A Knight and His Armour* (1961) and *A Knight and His Weapons* (1964); Nigel Saul, *Knights and Esquires* (1981); J. F. Verbruggen, *The Art of Warfare in Western Europe during the Middle Ages* (1977).

knighthood. See *chivalry*; *knight*.

knight marshal. The effective commander of the English garrison army in Ireland, though not necessarily the formal commander.

Knights Hospitaller. See *Hospitallers*.

Knights in the Service of God in Prussia. A small crusading order that waged a war of conquest and forcible conversion against the native pagans of Prussia, but failed to make much headway. Their place was taken by the *Teutonic Knights*, who succeeded with "Sturm und Drang" to spread "Gottesfurcht" ("fear of God") where the Brethren of Dobrzyn failed.

Knights of Alcántara. Named for the Roman bridge over the Tagus River, this Iberian *Military Order* originated in 1170 out of a local *hermangilda* on the frontier of Léon. Originally called "Knights of San Julián de Pereiro," it was chartered by the pope in 1176, at first in association with *Calatrava*. It was integral to the *Reconquista* in Portugal. Over time, the Brethren were drawn into secular politics. Then *Pedro the Cruel* murdered the Order's *Mestre* and intimidated some of the Brethren. Thus, at *Najera* (1367), Alcántara knights fought on both sides. In 1394 the Mestre proclaimed a new crusade against the Moors of Granada, but led the Brethren into a mountain valley ambush and massacre. Until the reign of *Ferdinand and Isabella* they were larger and better equipped than royal armies, which they accompanied in the final conquest of *Granada*. Then they gave way to the new *terclo* infantry. In 1523 *Charles V* took over all Iberian Military Orders and in 1527 pledged their resources as collateral for *Fugger* loans. Thereafter, they lost all military function but retained social prestige as a court list.

Knights of Aviz. See *Aviz, Order of*.

Knights of Calatrava. The fortress of Qalat Rawaah ("Castle of War") was a forward base for Muslim *razzia* against Toledo. It was captured by a Christian army in 1147, given to the *Templars* to hold, and renamed Calatrava. In 1157 the Templars quit Calatrava under pressure from new *rabitos* and razzia. From 1158 to 1164 the fort was held by armed monks and volunteer soldiers from a nearby *hermangilda*. This became the foundation of a new *Military Order*, named for the castle. They wore black armor, kept monkish rules of silence, and lived in fortified barracks. In 1179 they expanded to Aragon. In 1195 they were overwhelmed by the Berber invasion, losing Calatrava and most of the Brethren. A counterattack retook Calatrava on July 1, 1212. The knights marched out to fight at Las Navas de Tolosa two weeks later, wining a victory that opened the crucial Guadalquiver Valley to a Christian advance into Córdoba. In 1218, Calatrava transferred its Portuguese holdings to *Aviz*, to reconcentrate in Castile. The Order held a large expanse of land which it worked with *mudéjar* slaves. The Masters of the Order evolved into great landowners who hired secular mercenaries to reinforce the ranks of knights.

After the death of Alfonso XI in 1350 the Brethren were drawn into secular politics and thereafter more often fought rebellious Christian barons than enemy Moors. *Pedro the Cruel* murdered the Order's *Mestre*, which cleft its command and loyalties. In 1366 one of the rival Mestres of Calatrava murdered

> *In 1476 the Mestre was thrown out a window by angry townsfolk, landing on a hedge of pikes upheld to greet him . . .*

the Archbishop of Santiago, then joined the invasion of Spain by the *Black Prince*. As a result, at *Nájera* (1367) the Order saw its members fight on both sides. By the 15th century Calatrava was wholly decadent: Brethren did not keep vows and commanders were viewed as, and were, petty tyrants. In 1476 the Mestre was thrown out a window by angry townsfolk, landing on a hedge of pikes upheld to greet him by a mob of women. On the battlefield, however, during the last phase of the Moorish wars the Brethren remained formidable. Into the reign of *Ferdinand and Isabella* they were larger and better equipped than the royal armies which they accompanied in the conquest of *Granada*. The centralization of state power under the Catholic Crowns replaced them with tough veterans of the new *tercio* infantry. In 1523, *Charles V* took over all Iberian Military Orders and the next year pledged their resources as collateral for a *Fugger* loan. Thereafter, they lost all military function but retained a certain social status.

Knights of Christ. Suppression of the *Templars* led to creation of this new *Military Order* in Portugal in 1318 and its installation in confiscated Templar *commanderies* under a former Brother of *Aviz*. It remained a minor order in Portugal relative to the dominant *Hospitallers* and Aviz. In the early 15th century their *Mestre* was *Enrique "the Navigator."* Under him, the Brethren colonized Madeira (1425) and the Azores (1445). In 1437 they mounted a raid on Tangier, only to suffer defeat and death. But they grew rich off growing overseas trade for which they manned African and Atlantic entrepôts. In 1460 Enrique granted his Order 5 percent of all African revenues. From 1496 the knights were allowed to marry, mainly to mask extant widespread concubinage. In 1523, *Charles V* took over all Iberian Military Orders and in 1527 pledged their resources as collateral for *Fugger* loans. The Brethren were reduced to an honorary society of no military importance.

Knights of Malta. See *Hospitallers*.

Knights of Our Lady of Montesa. An Aragonese *Military Order* created upon the ruination of the *Templars*. It was given control of several confiscated Templar *commanderies* and charged with putting down *mudéjar* piracy and rebellion. It was unusually poor, which meant it upheld less demanding recruiting standards. In 1400 its penury drove it to join with the Order of Alfama.

Knights of Our Lady of Montjoie. A 12th century *Military Order* in *Outremer* named for the location of their castle in the mountains outside Jerusalem where pilgrims reputedly cried out in joy upon first seeing the Holy City. The Brethren swore an oath to fight the Saracens and dedicated special funds to this end. Unlike the *Templars*, the Brethren of Montjoie were permitted to take prisoners for ransom. Founded by a former *Knight of Santiago*, over time they accrued lands in Castile and Aragon. The Order withered when recruiting fell as Iberian knights joined the *Reconquista* Orders instead. In 1187 the last Montjoie knights in the Middle East retired to Aragon under the name Order of Trufac.

Knights of San Julián de Pereiro. See *Alcántara, Knights of*.

Knights of Santa Maria. A Portuguese *Military Order* founded in 1162. In 1169 they were promised one-third of any lands they reconquered from the Moors. This gave them their major fortress at Thomar.

Knights of Santiago. Founded in Léon in 1171 to protect pilgrims headed for Iberian shrines, this *Military Order* quickly spread throughout Aragon, Castile, and Portugal, and later drew recruits from England, France, Hungary, Italy, and Outremer. Each *commandery* housed thirteen Brethren. Unusually among Military Orders, knights of Santiago were allowed to marry. By 1287 the Order separated from the *Knights of Calatrava* with whom it was initially associated. Over time, Santiago knights were drawn into secular politics. With the treachery and murders of *Pedro the Cruel* the Order was so divided that at *Nájera* (1367), Santiago knights fought on both sides. In 1523, *Charles V* took over all Iberian Military Orders. The next year he pledged their collective resources as collateral for a *Fugger* loan. Thereafter, Santiago lost all military function. See also *Alvarado, Pedro de*.

Knights of Santo Stefano. A Tuscan *Military Order* that maintained a small navy on Elba. It was active until 1684, usually in cooperation with one or other "Holy League" arranged by the popes.

Knights of St. George. A late-founded *Military Order* that claimed a Byzantine origin but was actually formed by Greek exiles from Albania. The popes recognized it as the rightful inheritor of the lost Greek empire in Constantinople. Some of its Brethren fought at the siege of Vienna in 1683.

Knights of St. James of the Sword. See *Knights of Santiago*.

Knights of St. John of the Hospital. See *Hospitallers*.

Knights of St. Lazarus. See *Hospitallers*.

Knights of St. Thomas Acon. A *Military Order* with a preceptory in Cyprus through the 14th century, and 30 *commanderies* in England, including Hampton court, with others in Wales and Ireland. Its Grand Commandery was at Kilmainham, Ireland. In the Muslim storming and sack of Acre in 1291 every defending St. Thomas knight died fighting.

Knights of the Sword. See *Livonian Order*.

Knights of Trufac. See *Knights of Our Lady of Montjoie*.

Knights Templar. "Knights of the Temple of Solomon," or "fratres militiae Templi." Also known as the "Poor Knights," "Red Friars," or just as the "Templars." One of the three major *Military Orders* of the Middle Ages, along with the *Knights Hospitaller* and *Teutonic Knights*. The Templars took early form c.1119 under the guidance of their Burgundian founder, Hugues de Payens. In effect military Cistercians, they took vows of poverty, chastity and obedience; lived together in humble barracks; and undertook to aid and protect pilgrims en route to Jerusalem. In 1120, King Baldwin II gave them the captured al-Aqsa mosque, built atop part of Solomon's Temple. From this central locale they derived the popular name "Templars." They were also called "Red Friars" by common folk. In 1128 they received the rule of their Order from the towering intellectual of the Church Militant and 12th-century Latin renaissance, the Cistercian Abbot Bernard of Clairvaux. This made them holy warriors of the *Crusades*. Their rule precisely defined the equipment each warrior monk was expected to maintain, from his armor to shields and weapons (spears, swords, clubs, and daggers), and his three warhorses. This was an expensive kit. Fortunately, the role of Templars in protecting pilgrims in the "Holy Land," along with military service to Crusader states, gained endowments from charitable beneficence, alms, and private wills, and attracted volunteer knights to fill the places of the fallen. The growing wealth of the Templars in Europe enabled them to equip knights in the Middle East, expand their military and economic activities, and led to a large part of the Order's personnel remaining in Western Europe to manage estates and assets. In 1134 the protection of Aragon itself was left to the Hospitallers and Templars, and Iberian Templars were increasingly drawn off into the *Reconquista*.

The Templars in *Outremer* fought hard and often. In their first century five Masters died in combat, and several times the whole order was nearly wiped out in battle. Of 22 Masters in the history of the Brethren, five fell in battle or died in sieges, five more died later of wounds, and one starved to death in a Muslim prison. In battle they did not request or offer quarter, and were not permitted to take prisoners for ransom. They waged a protracted war with the *Assassins*. The Templar objective, in the words of Bernard of Clairvaux, was "killing for Christ." Like their fiercest Muslim opponents, Templars viewed death in battle as the path to martyrdom. In all, 20,000 Templars died in 200 years of fighting, and not always against Muslims: Templars at times allied with Turks to fight the Hospitallers after 1201. After the fall of Jerusalem to *Salāh al-Dīn* ("Saladin") in 1187, the Templars fell back to Acre. In 1242 the Poor Knights captured Nablus and massacred the whole population, including many Arab Christians. In 1243 they retook the Temple but within months they were turned out by Kwarismian Turks fleeing the Mongols. At La Forbie (October 17, 1244), Templars, Hospitallers, and other "Franks" were all crushed. Lax and corrupted far from their rule and vows—they no longer lived in barracks and hardly a knight kept his vows of poverty and chastity—the Templars were also a much reduced military force. When Acre was overrun and sacked by a Muslim army in 1291, the last Templars left the Holy Land for Cyprus.

While the Templars lost their bases in the Middle East other than Cyprus, they retained vast wealth in Europe. This was put to use in money-lending: the Paris Temple was banker to kings and emperors, financing secular wars. The "Poor Knights" became widely unpopular because their Temples were more splendid than their hospitals, which were notably few, and avaricious knights too often enforced claims to benefices left the Temple by dead husbands or fathers with brutal violence against widows and children. Rumors spread that the Templars (and other Military Orders) reached secret treaties with the Muslims to abandon the Holy Land. The fall of Acre thus opened floodgates of suspicion. Philip IV of France coveted Templar wealth for his fight with Rome and the Empire, even though in 1306 he took refuge in the Paris Temple in fear of the pope's wrath. Aided by a Chancellor whose parents had been burned as heretics during the *Albigensian Crusade*, and thus who had little love of the papacy, Philip moved against the Templars. His was mainly a campaign to expropriate Templar wealth for the French monarchy, but also reflected the fact that no one, least of all a king, loves their banker. On October 12, 1307, he struck: within a week 15,000 Templars were arrested. Some were the richest men in France but many were ordinary folk. The Templars were always an association mainly of common folk rather than the nobility or clergy, which is a main reason it was unable to defend itself when the wolves of monarchy and church, already red in tooth and claw, circled for more.

Templars were charged with denying Christ, worshiping cats, idols, and daemons, "indecent kisses" and sodomy, spitting on the crucifix, ritual child murder, and similar tired but useful falsities of the Dominican "Hounds of Heaven" who conducted the Medieval *Inquisition* in France. Thousands were tortured into forced confessions; over 100 were burned for heresy. Sensational "discoveries" of demon-relics and forged "secret documents" followed. Pope Clement V, who initially baulked at arrest of the Templars and how this would enhance the French monarchy, was persuaded to issue a Bull confirming the arrests. This spread the persecution outside France, across the *res publica*

Christiana. Proud Aragonese Templars made last fighting stands in several commanderies while Templars on Cyprus were allowed to negotiate surrender terms. English Templars were sent to the Tower but most Scottish Templars were quietly allowed to escape, though without their property. In Castile, Cyprus, and the Holy Roman Empire, bishops reported urgently to the pope that the Templars were innocent. Clement would not listen. Instead, he ordered lay rulers to use torture to extract confessions from all Templars who denied their dark acts. Before a grand commission of the Church in Paris in 1309 hundreds of Templars, momentarily free of the tongs or rack or wheel, retracted their forced confessions. Of these, 120 were burned as lapsed heretics, and the rest of the retractions were soon retracted. On April 3, 1312, the Templar Order was condemned for harboring heretics, almost certainly unjustly and without canonical evidence, and was formally disbanded by

> *On April 3, 1312, the Templar Order was condemned for harboring heretics . . .*

Clement. A second bull issued on May 2 dispossessed the Templars and gave all their wealth to the Hospitallers. In fact, their ancient rivals only got half, as the rest had already been seized kings or bishops, and by the pope. The last Master of the Temple, Jaques de Molay, was roasted to death slowly over low-burning coals by officers of the Inquisition. See also *Art of War*; *confrère knights*; *Falkirk, Battle of*; *Knights of Calatrava*; *Knights of Christ*; *Knights of Santiago*.

Suggested Reading: M. Barber, *The New Knighthood* (1994); Edward Burman, *The Templars* (1986; 1990); Piers Read, *The Templars* (2000); Desmond Seward, *The Monks of War* (1972; 1995).

Knights' War (1522–1523). See *Sickingen, Franz von*.

knocking. Fitting an arrow or bolt onto the drawstring.

Knocknanuss, Battle of (1647). See *English Civil Wars*.

Knollen. See *corning/corned gunpowder*.

knot. One nautical mile per hour sailing or rowing speed.

Knox, John (c.1513–1572). Scottish reformer. In 1535, at age 22, he was ordained a Catholic priest. He became an enthusiast for *Martin Luther* by the mid-1540s but thereafter was most impressed by *Jean Calvin*. He preached briefly at St. Andrews until taken captive by the French, who held him for 18 months on a prison galley. He rose in prominence under Edward VI and helped shape English Protestantism. Upon the failure of *Wyatt's Rebellion*, which he supported, and the ascension of *Mary Tudor*, he fled to Dieppe. From there he moved to Geneva where he came under the direct influence of Calvin. Knox's singular contribution to Protestantism was to devise justifications for the overthrow of unjust and ungodly rulers, whom he saw as those failing to uphold "true religion," the definition of which he abrogated to people such as himself. In this he parted company with Calvin, who disapproved of any association between religion and rebellion. In 1558, Knox was summoned back to Scotland by the *Covenanters*, to become the key figure in establishing Protestantism in Scotland from August 1559. Thunderous in his misogyny and hatred for Catholicism alike, he vehemently objected to private Masses said for *Mary Stuart* and was instrumental in turning her out of Scotland. *Elizabeth I* never forgave Knox, even as she received his principal victim into prison exile within her realm.

Suggested Reading: Jasper Ridley, *John Knox* (1968).

Komaki-Nagakute, Battle of (1584). See *Tokugawa Ieyasu*; *Toyotomi Hideyoshi*.

Konfessionalisierung. See *confessionalism*.

Kongo, Kingdom of. In 1400, Kongo, a tributary empire spanning the great Congo River, was the largest state in Central Africa. In 1482 the first Portuguese ships reached the mouth of the Congo. Upon their return they carried Kongo emissaries to Lisbon. These Kongolese were baptized in Portugal and in 1491 returned to Kongo along with several Portuguese *Jesuits*. They quickly converted Kongo's king. Portuguese mercenaries and guns then helped Kongo fight border wars from which Portuguese ships carted away enemy captives into slavery. This slaving partnership, along with patronage of Christianity, lasted to 1543 and the death of Afonso I. By then Portugal had shifted its main trading interests southward into *Ngola* (Angola). In 1556 a Kongo army was defeated by Ngola, which was supplied with firearms by Portugal. Kongo thereafter went into decline, passed over by the main currents of the slave trade and itself raided rather than raider. The main slavers were Ngola and *Yaka*, hunting for the São Tomé and Principe slave markets. In 1569 the eastern half of the kingdom was overrun by Yaka and many Kongolese sold into slavery. An appeal to Lisbon secured Portuguese military intervention, 1571–1574, in behalf of Kongo's Christian monarchy. However, the permanent Portuguese military presence in Ngola eventually led to large-scale slaving wars which helped break up Kongo. At Ambuila (1665) a large Kongo army was destroyed by the Portuguese and their African allies and Kongo broke into provincial factions governed by rival dynasts.

Königshofen, Battle of (1525). See *German Peasant War*.

Konitz. See *Chojnice, Battle of*.

köprücu. Ottoman military *engineers* who specialized in bridge and road repair.

Korea. "The Hermit Kingdom." Throughout this period Korea was the most stable of all tributaries of China. The *Mongols* invaded in 1231, conquering

Korea by 1259. Koreans obtained their first firearms from China sometime in the early 14th century. Records also show a request to the Ming in 1373 for a large shipment of guns, powder, and shot. Once Koreans discovered the secret of extracting saltpeter they began manufacturing small arms from 1377, including arrow-firing "hand cannon." They made cannon from 1445, if not earlier. Guns proved useful in warding off raids by *wakō* which continued to the end of the 15th century. In 1392 the Koryo dynasty (918–1392) was displaced by the Choson dynasty (1392–1910), which valued guns even more highly and manufactured them on an expanded scale. The Koreans kept guns secret from Japan for some 200 years. In that they mimicked the Chinese, who kept their most modern designs secret from Koreans and Japanese alike. In 1545 shipwrecked Chinese and their guns fell into Korean hands and were quickly copied. Secrecy about gun technology did not help in the long run because Japan obtained even better guns and cannon from the Portuguese in 1543. When *Toyotomi Hideyoshi* twice sent Japanese armies to invade Korea the Japanese outgunned the Koreans and the Ming. Japanese troops in the 1590s were better armed, better drilled, and more tactically disciplined than the Koreans. As a result, the Korean army had great difficulty holding back the ferocious *samurai* and *ashigaru* in set-piece battles. The Koreas were more effective when they resorted to resilient guerilla resistance outside the fallen cities. At sea it was a different tale. The Korean navy, always the country's main strength, performed exceptionally well. Admiral Yi Sun-Sin's ironclad *turtle ships* destroyed much of Hideyoshi's war fleet and sank many of his resupply junks.

The Ming intervened in Korea to prevent Hideyoshi from conquering one of their tributaries and to protect their own border. An initial Ming force of just 3,000 was quickly crushed, but by the end of 1592 some 40,000 Ming and 10,000 Koreans marched together against the Japanese at Pyongyang. After a three-day siege in which the Chinese and Koreans deployed fire-arrow artillery as well as more modern cannons, the allies took Pyongyang back from the Japanese. The Ming–Korean coalition army moved on Seoul where the Japanese came out to meet them, presenting a battle front outside the city walls. The main Chinese attack was blunted, demoralizing Ming commanders and troops. The Japanese then turned on the Koreans who fought back with fire-arrows and rockets as well as hand guns and more traditional weapons. Their second attack frustrated, the Japanese returned to the safety of the city. The Ming and Koreans could not take it, but neither were the Japanese strong enough to drive them away.

The war was effectively stalemated on land, so it was decided at sea. Admiral Yi Sun-Sin cut off Hideyoshi's army from resupply from Japan by continuous aggressive actions against convoys of supply junks. Running out of food and ammunition, Hideyoshi agreed to a truce early in 1593. The Japanese withdrew to Pusan while the Ming agreed to remove their army from Korea. A formal treaty was not agreed for some years, however, as each side demanded the other perform ritual submission without fully understanding that was what the other was also asking. A diplomatic trick left both persuaded the other had conceded the ritual point and a treaty was finally signed in 1596. But no treaty could decide the main issue of Japan's ultimate position in Korea and the fate of the Japanese garrison in Pusan. Only another war could provide an answer to that question.

In 1597, Hideyoshi realized he had been duped and, in one of his more prolonged rages, re-invaded Korea with a second massive army. This time he brought fewer traditional samurai cavalry and more of the invaluable musketeer infantry. The Ming counter-intervened immediately. Knowing the terrain and the enemy better than in 1592, the Japanese moved across Korea like a tsunami. They washed over by storm or battered down thin-walled Korean fortresses incapable of withstanding bombardment from late 16th century gunpowder cannon. The Japanese overwhelmed several Korean garrisons and cities, annihilating their civil populations. Savagery abounded: mounds of Korean and Chinese ears and noses were collected and sent to Kyoto as symbols of Hideyoshi's victory. As matters turned out, he proclaimed victory prematurely. The Japanese were beaten in a major battle fought at Chiksan, south of Seoul, in late 1597. Their northward advance was halted. With a week the Korean navy won a major naval battle at Myongnyang, and once again Hideyoshi was cut off from his bases of supply and left to face winter in a hostile and scorched land. He had an impossible logistical problem and therefore fell back to a defensive perimeter around Pusan. The Koreans and Ming followed and attacked him there over the winter of 1597–1598. After a failed frontal assault, a siege was instead undertaken for which the Japanese were most ill-prepared. However, the Chinese and Koreas were little better off. As each side settled in both were afflicted by slow starvation and epidemic disease. When Hideyoshi died in 1598 the second invasion of Korean ended. The Japanese army pulled out with the Korean navy harrying them even as they boarded transports and sailed for Japan. The years of Japanese invasion left Korea weakened military, fiscally, and demographically; much of the land and most of its cities were ruined. The war also inflicted huge Chinese casualties, possibly to the point of fatally undermining the Ming military and dynasty. Forty years later, as Japan entered its *Tokugawa* isolation, a new enemy rode out of the north to overrun China and Korea: the *Manchus* conquered Korea in 1637–1638. Once they conquered northern China in 1644 Korea became once again a Chinese tributary, only of the Qing rather than the Ming dynasty.

Kosovo, Battle of (June 20, 1389). Under Sultan *Murad I*, the Ottoman Empire expanded deep into the Balkans. In 1365, Adrianople fell and was made into the second Ottoman capital, the first inside Europe. In 1389, Lazar I of Serbia marshaled a multi-ethnic, Balkan army of perhaps 25,000 to face the advancing Ottomans, led by the sultan. Despite the Serbs deploying cannons, Ottoman horse (*sipahis* and *timariots*) and the *Janissary Corps* decisively defeated the Serbs and their allies, capturing and later executing Lazar I. However, on the night of his victory Murad was assassinated, run through with a sword inside his own tent by a disguised Serb. Kosovo was a turning point in Serb and Balkan history. Along with *Maritza*, it shifted most of the Balkans under Ottoman control for the next 500 years.

Kosovo Polje, Battle of (October 16–17, 1448). Four years earlier the Hungarians were badly defeated by the Ottomans at *Varna*. Their leader, *János Hunyadi*, gathered a new army 25,000 strong, including *knights* from Transylvania, *hussar* cavalry, and *Landsknechte* infantry. Hunyadi inflicted major casualties on a much lager Ottoman army led by Sultan *Murad II*. The key to initial Hungarian success was deployment of arquebusier infantry, which held the field on the first day. However, the next morning Hungarian lightly armed and armored hussars were overmatched by Ottoman *sipahis* (heavy mailed cavalry) on the flanks of Hunyadi's infantry. That allowed the sheer weight of massed Ottoman forces, infantry and cavalry, to overwhelm the Hungarian and German infantry at the center of the line, which bent backward under heavy assault, then broke. Casualties were enormous: half the Hungarian army never rose from the field while over a third of Ottoman troops were dead or wounded by the end of the second day. But the Ottomans could more readily absorb such loss. The battle thus allowed completion of the Ottoman conquest of much of the Balkans and opened the way for Murad's successor, *Muhammad II*, to conduct the *Siege of Constantinople* in 1453.

kote. A Japanese armored sleeve made of *mail* and *plate*.

Kreise. See *Reichskreis*.

Kreisoberst. The commander of a *Reichskreis*. See also *Christian IV*.

Kremlin. "The Citadel." The exceptionally ornate *citadel* of Muscovy surrounded by churches, living quarters, and barracks. It was designed and built for Muscovite princes by Italian engineers. In addition to serving as a palace and seat of central government, it was used as an *armory* and stored the Muscovite artillery train.

Krevo, Union of (1385). See *Union of Krevo*.

Kriegskasse. See *war chest*.

Kringen, Battle of (1612). See *Kalmar War*.

kubi jikken. "Inspection of heads." See *samurai*; *scalping*; *swords*.

Kublai Khan (1214–1294). See *China*; *Hakata Bay, Battle of (1274)*; *Hakata Bay, Battle of (1281)*; *Mongols*.

kul. "Slave of the sultan." Top servants of the Ottoman sultan, including the *Grand Vezier.* Competition for favors and office was intense, and sometimes deadly, among senior kuls.

kulah. A conical-shaped, Persian-Mughal spiked helmet. It had sliding bars that could be positioned over the nose. It fully covered ears and neck, ending on the shoulder. They were often decked out with bird plumage, especially large peacock feathers.

Kulikovo, Battle of (1380). See *Muscovy, Grand Duchy of.*

kumade. "bear claw." A rake-like weapon used by infantry grooms who accompanied *samurai* into battle.

Kur'aci. "Conscripts." Regular troops conscripted for service in the armies of the Ottoman Empire.

Kurds. Ottoman Sultan *Selim I* (r.1512–1520) granted limited autonomy to the "Black Nation" of southeast Turkey, thus uniting an eclectic group of Turkomen, Assyrians, Arabs, and other tribes under the name "Kurd." This new "nation" lacked a common culture or religion (most were sunni Muslims, but some were Christian). The Kurds retained a chieftain system and clan military organization for centuries. Although they often enjoyed de facto independence in their mountain strongholds and valleys, they never attained sovereignty or much affected the larger ebb and flow of military affairs in the region.

Kurfürsten. The seven "Elector Princes" who formally elected and crowned the emperors of the *Holy Roman Empire.* In theory they selected and closely advised the emperor; in practice, they usually thwarted attempts by strong emperors who sought to concentrate power at the center. Just before the onset of the *Thirty Years' War* (1618) three Kurfürsten were "Princes of the Church": the Catholic Archbishops of Cologne, Mainz, and Trier. They were offset by three Protestant territorial princes: the Duke of Saxony, a Lutheran, and two Calvinists, the Count Palatine of the Rhine and the Margrave of Brandenburg. The King of Bohemia thus held the decisive seventh vote, from the confessional point of view, and in 1618 the Bohemian throne was vacant. That is why the Empire was thrown into deep crisis and then war following the *"Defenestration of Prague"* (1618). In 1630 the Kurfürsten played the key role in opposing enforcement of the *Edict of Restitution* in Germany and subsequently forcing *Ferdinand II* to dismiss *Albrecht von Wallenstein.* The Imperial dignity of the Palatinate was ceded to Bavaria during the war, after *Friedrich V* was declared outlaw within the Empire. His heirs sought its return when the war ended but instead, in the *Peace of Westphalia* (1648), an eighth Imperial dignity

> *In theory they selected and closely advised the emperor; in practice, they usually thwarted attempts by strong emperors . . .*

was created and granted to the Palatinate so that Bavaria might retain the seventh.

kurofune. "Black ship." Japanese term for European *carracks*, and later a generic for all European ships of sail.

Kutná Hora, Battle of (January 6, 1422). An early battle in the long *Hussite Wars*. The Hussite army was led by *Jan Žižka* who expelled the Imperial Army from Bohemia in 1420 that was sent to crush the rebellion by Emperor *Sigismund* (r.1411–1437). The next year Sigismund took direct command of the Imperial Army, intending to again invade Bohemia to crush the Hussites. In the interim, Žižka developed the Hussite *tabor*, a system of mobile wagon forts that protected Hussite archers and arquebusiers. The two armies clashed at Kutná Hora, about 45 miles southwest of Prague, in a rare winter battle. Žižka had about 25,000 men to face a much larger, but less tactically disciplined, Imperial Army. Žižka assembled and deployed his tabor as a field fortification and assumed a defensive stance. The cocky Imperials attacked in their usual manner, with cavalry charges and push of pike, and were cut down in droves by heavy fire from arquebuses, crossbows, and small cannon from within the tabors. As the Imperials fell back in bloody confusion Žižka ordered his men out from gaps deliberately left in the circle of wagons. The Hussites, filled with religious zeal and a bitter taste for revenge for the judicial murder of *Jan Hus*, commenced a pursuit and slaughter of the badly beaten Imperials. Four days later Žižka and the Hussite army met and severely defeated Sigismund a second time, at *Německý Brod*.